The Psychology of Health

■ **An introduction**

Second edition

Edited by

Marian Pitts
and Keith Phillips

ROUTLEDGE
Taylor & Francis Group

London and New York

ROUTLEDGE

First edition published 1991
by Routledge
Reprinted 1992, 1993, 1995

Second edition published 1998
by Routledge
11 New Fetter Lane, London
EC4P 4EE

Simultaneously published in the
USA and Canada
by Routledge
29 West 35th Street, New York,
NY 10001

Reprinted 1999

*Routledge is an imprint of the
Taylor & Francis Group*

© 1991, 1998 Selection and
editorial matter, Marian Pitts
and Keith Phillips; individual chapters
© the contributors

Typeset in Century Old Style
by Florencetype Ltd, Stoodleigh,
Devon
Printed and bound in Great
Britain by TJ International Ltd,
Padstow, Cornwall

*British Library Cataloguing in
Publication Data*
A catalogue record for this book
is available from the British
Library.

*Library of Congress Cataloguing in
Publication Data*
The psychology of health: an
introduction / edited by
Marian Pitts and Keith
Phillips. – 2nd ed.
p. cm.
Includes bibliographical
references and indexes.
1. Clinical health psychology.
2. Medicine and psychology.
I. Pitts, Marian, 1948–. II.
Phillips, Keith, 1951–.
R726.7.P794 1998
616'.001'9–dc21   97–40283

ISBN 0–415–15023–X (hbk)
ISBN 0–415–15024–8 (pbk)

The Psychology of Health

Its scope and accessibility make it an ideal introduction to health psychology for undergraduate students. The overall tone is sensible, friendly, and even at times humorous, combining detached, rational appraisal of psychological theory and research with reflective comments and questions. ... Chapters have been updated with reference to recent research and the 'Social Circumstances, Inequalities and Health' chapter reflects the shift towards a greater awareness of the importance of gender, class and ethnicity.

Lucy Yardley, *University College London*

Health psychology is one of the fastest growing areas of the behavioural sciences. As such it occupies an increasingly important place in undergraduate and post-graduate courses. Students in other disciplines, such as nursing, social work, physiotherapy and occupational therapy, also need to learn about the role of psychology in understanding health and the treatment of illness.

The first edition of *The Psychology of Health* was very well received and has become the standard recommended text for many courses. This completely revised and updated second edition contains new material in all chapters and has several additional chapters on such topics as cancer, nutrition and exercise, social drugs, and the impact of social inequalities upon health. This edition also contains annotated further reading, a glossary of key terms, boxes with ideas and questions for seminar topics, helpful revision points in chapter summaries and an extensive bibliography. *The Psychology of Health* will continue to be invaluable for students of health psychology and related behavioural and health sciences, including nursing, community care and health studies.

Marian Pitts is Professor of Psychology at Staffordshire University. Previously she worked in Africa and has taught at the universities of East London, Tennessee and Zimbabwe. She is author of *The Psychology of Preventive Health* (1996).
Keith Phillips is Professor of Psychology and Head of the School of Social and Behavioural Sciences at the University of Westminster. Both have published widely in the area of health psychology.

Comments on the first edition:

'I do not know of a better book in this field.'
Health Education

'This is a very thorough and well-compiled text which should be on student reading lists
a good few years to come.'
Journal of Occupational and Organizational Psycho

'Pitts and Phillips have given introductory-level health psychology teachers a valuable b
tool. . . . The editors and authors who came together to produce this fine volume have sha
their extensive knowledge of health psychology and successfully conveyed their own exc
ment and enthusiasm about its goals and progress.'
Contemporary Psycho

'An interesting and worthwhile contribution to important topics often neglected by ot
books.'
Stress N

'A valuable overview text, pulling together a wide range of material which will aid stude
understanding of the health dimension of social work. Offers a broad range of foundat
knowledge for first year post-graduate social work students.'
Sandra Butler, School of Social Studies, *Nottingham Univer*

'Presents an issue-based approach to health psychology, therefore very useful for pr
tioners working in these specific areas.'
Frank Jacob, Faculty of Health and Community Care, *University of Central Engl*

'A thorough and up-to-date text in a new and growing field of study.'
Yvonne Crome, School of Health and Applied Sciences, *University College Su*

'Ideal for nurses who are updating skills to degree level.'
Martin Johnson, Department of Psychology, *Teeside Univer*

'Excellent overview with substantial reference list.'
John Wilson, Social and Professional Studies, *Humberside Univer*

'Highly accessible to undergraduate students. The range of topics is highly relevant t
wide range of health care professionals.'
Lynette Rentoul, Nursing Studies Department, *Kings College Lon*

'Brings together various strands of psychology into a very useful and readable text.'
Peter Wybrow, Social Sciences Faculty, *Southampton H. E. Insti*

To
Gina, David and Sheila
and
Rosa and Bernard

Contents

CONTENTS

Figures

FIGURES

Tables

Contributors

Jacqueline Barnes Senior Lecturer and Honorary Senior Psychologist, Leopold Muller University Department of Child and Family Mental Health, Royal Free Hospital School of Medicine and the Tavistock Clinic, Hampstead, London.

Mary Boyle Professor of Psychology and Course Director for Clinical Psychology, Department of Psychology, University of East London.

Philip Evans Professor of Psychology and Director of the Psychophysiology and Stress Research Group, Department of Psychology, School of Social and Behavioural Sciences, University of Westminster.

Paula Hixenbaugh Department of Psychology and Member of Health Psychology Research Group, School of Social and Behavioural Sciences, University of Westminster.

Andrew Parrott Reader in Psychology, Department of Psychology, University of East London.

Keith Phillips Professor of Psychology, Member of the Health Psychology Research Group, and Head of School of Social and Behavioural Sciences, University of Westminster.

Marian Pitts Professor of Psychology, Division of Psychology, Staffordshire University.

Hartwin Sadowski Lecturer and Honorary Senior Registrar, Leopold Muller University Department of Child and Family Mental Health, Royal Free Hospital School of Medicine and the Tavistock Clinic.

Tara Symonds Lecturer in Health Psychology, Division of Psychology, Staffordshire University.

Laura Warren Research Associate, Department of Psychology, School of Social and Behavioural Sciences, University of Westminster.

David White Professor of Psychology, Division of Psychology, Staffordshire University.

Preface

The initial stimulus for this book came from the many students whose obvious enthusiasm for health psychology caused us to undertake writing the first edition. At that time we (the editors) could not find a book that was suitable to recommend to our students as a standard text. Those texts that did exist were written by American academics who had different experiences and were writing from knowledge of a different health system. We were encouraged by colleagues and students to compile a book that would be relevant to UK students and teachers. The contribution of those students was great and we hope that they will gain some satisfaction from realising their part in the appearance of the first edition.

This, the second edition, builds upon the first, which we are gratified to say was well received and has become the standard recommended text for many courses in the UK. It has been updated by the addition of new material in all the chapters and by the addition of entirely new chapters, including those on cancer, nutrition and exercise, and the impact of social inequalities upon health.

Since the first edition was published in 1991, learned societies for the study of health psychology have been established and several new journals have begun to publish research in this new and exciting area of psychology. Courses dedicated to the study of health psychology have been developed in our universities and colleges, and many areas of the health and nursing sciences include health psychology as part of their curriculum.

The book is divided into four parts. Part One provides an introduction to health psychology, including its definition and an overview of its scope and ambitions. There is a discussion of the principles and techniques of psychophysiology and consideration of an area that has been central to the understanding of individuals' health, namely stress and coping. This section concludes with an update on the developing area of psychoneuroimmunology. Part Two considers studies that are relevant to the experiences of illness, hospitalisation and the management of disease. Part Three contains topics of significance for health psychologists. These have been chosen to reflect the diversity of health issues studied by health psychologists, including acute and chronic illness, primary prevention of illness, and health promotion. Many of these have been highlighted by the UK government's Health of the Nation programme. Part Four broadens the book's perspective, moving beyond an individualistic approach to consider the importance of family and wider social contexts for health.

In this edition you will find a glossary, boxes with ideas and questions about the contents of each chapter, helpful revision points in the key summaries, suggestions for further reading, indexes, and an extensive bibliography.

The book is aimed at advanced undergraduates in psychology and related disciplines, especially the behavioural and health sciences, including nursing, community care, and health studies. It does not assume that you will have extensive prior knowledge of psychology. However, we hope too that some of the ideas contained in the chapters will provoke thought among those of you who are embarking upon postgraduate study in health psychology.

We hope that you will find the book readable, interesting and challenging, but most of all that it will excite you to read more about health psychology and perhaps become a health psychologist yourself. Whatever your reasons for choosing to read this book we hope that you will find within it something of value to you.

Marian Pitts
Keith Phillips
July 1997

Acknowledgements

The editors would like to thank first the contributors, who adhered to their deadlines and helped us in many ways throughout the preparation of this book. We would like also to acknowledge the support given to us by our colleagues and friends in our respective departments in Staffordshire and Westminster. We have received advice from many friends; all errors remain, unfortunately, our own.

We also thank those students whose enthusiasm for health psychology caused us to compile the first edition and the many groups of students since whose feedback has encouraged us to undertake this second edition.

Again we also owe great thanks to our partners and families for their support during the period of production of the book; their tolerance, good humour and general assistance throughout the project has done much to ensure its final delivery. We owe particular thanks to Carol Austin and Qazi Rahman, who have been very helpful in tracking down elusive references and compiling the index, and to Sheelagh Rowbottom, Social Sciences Librarian at Staffordshire, who was always eager to provide help.

All photographs were supplied by Photofusion:

Part one (page 2)
Marylebone Station, copyright Steve Eason
Dance and exercise class, copyright Bob Watkins

Part two (page 70)
GP and patients, copyright Reen Pilkington
Ambulance, copyright Sam Tanner

Part three (page 130)
Beer belly, copyright David Montford
Active elderly man, copyright Tim Dub

Part four (page 286)
Bengali children playing on Whitechapel Estate, copyright Crispin Hughes
School nurse discussing anti-smoking campaign project with pupils, Surrey Docks,
copyright Brenda Prince

The following organizations have kindly given permission to use figures: Figure
1.1 Lippincott–Raven Publishers; Figure 1.2 Elsevier Scientific Publishers; Figure
1.4 Open University Press; Figure 4.1 Oxford University Press; Figures 7.2 and
9.1 Carfax Publishing Limited, PO Box 25, Abingdon, Oxfordshire OX14 3UE;
Figure 10.1 (adapted from Strasser, 1992), Macmillan Press Limited; Figures 14.1,
14.2 and 14.3 Cancer Research Campaign and its Scientific Yearbook; Figure 15.2
reprinted with permission of the Helen Dwight Reid Educational Foundation.
Published by Heldref Publications, 1319 Eighteenth Street, N.W., Washington,
D.C. 20036–1802. Copyright © 1967; Figure 15.3 W.B. Saunders Company.

The following organizations have kindly given permission to use tables:
Table 8.1 Blackwell Scientific Publications; Tables 15.1 and 15.2 the BMJ
Publishing Group.

Every effort has been made to trace copyright holders and obtain permission
to reproduce figures and tables. Any omissions brought to our attention will be
remedied in future editions.

Finally, we would like to thank Vivien Ward of Routledge for suggesting that we
produce a second edition and Jon Reed for his patience, encouragement and assistance throughout the production process.

Abbreviations

ACTH	Adrenocorticotrophic hormone
AIDS	Acquired Immune Deficiency Syndrome
ANS	Autonomic nervous system
APA	American Psychological Association
ARC	AIDS-related complex
BAC	Blood alcohol concentration
BDA	British Diabetic Association
BDI	Beck Depression Inventory
BPL	Blood pressure level
BPS	British Psychological Society
BRS	Bortner rating scale
BSE	Breast self examination
CHD	Coronary heart disease
CNS	Central nervous system
CO	Carbon monoxide
CRF	Corticotropin releasing factor
DCCT	Diabetes Control and Complications Trial
DFBC	Diabetes family behaviour checklist
DQOL	Diabetes quality of life (scale)
DUKE	Duke health profile
ECG	Electrocardiogram
EEG	Electroencephalogram
EMG	Electromyogram
EORTC	European Organisation for Research on Treatment of Cancer
EPIC	European Prospective Investigation of Cancer
ESRC	Economic and Social Research Council

5-HT	Serotonin (5-hydroxytryptamine)
FAAR	Family adjustment and adaptation response
FAM	Fear avoidance model (of pain)
FTAS	Framingham Type A Scale
GHP	General health perceptions (scale)
GP	General practitioner
HAPA	Health action process approach
HBM	Health belief model
HDL	High density lipoprotein
HIV	Human Immunodeficiency Virus
HPA	Hypothalamic pituitary-adrenocortical (axis)
IBQ	Illness behaviour questionnaire
ICU	Intensive care unit
IDDM	Insulin-dependent diabetes mellitus
ivdu	intravenous drug user
JAS	Jenkins Activity Survey
JHPS	Johns Hopkins Precursors Study
MDMA	Ecstasy
MI	Myocardial infarction
mmHg	Millimetres of mercury
MMPI	Minnesota multiphasic personality inventory
MPI	Multidimensional pain inventory
MPQ	McGill pain questionnaire
MRFIT	Multiple risk factor intervention trial
MSPQ	Modified somatic perception questionnaire
NIDDM	Non-insulin-dependent diabetes mellitus
NK	Natural killer (cell)
PCA	Patient controlled analgesia
PNI	Psychoneuroimmunology
PNS	Peripheral nervous system
PVC	Premature ventricular contraction
QOL	Quality of life
SAM	Sympathetic adrenal medullary (system)
SI	Structured interview
sIgA	Secretory immunoglobulin A
SIP	Sickness impact profile
SLM	Social learning model
THC	Tetrahydrocannabinol
TPB	Theory of planned behaviour
TSE	Testicular self examination
WCGS	Western Collaborative Group Study
WEHS	Western Electric Health Survey
WHO	World Health Organization

Introduction

PART ONE introduces you to the basic elements underpinning the psychology and experience of health. We need explanations of the ways in which psychological variables interact with biological predispositions of disease, and environmental and social factors such as economic status. These explanations give rise to theories of health behaviour. Chapter 1 reviews the evidence which implicates health behaviours and other psychological variables as major determinants of health; it shows how the causes of ill health and death have changed in the western world over the last century from infectious diseases to those linked to behaviours, including cancers, and circulatory diseases. The approach adopted throughout the book is to view health as a function of biological, psychological and social elements – known as the biopsychosocial approach. Several models are reviewed in Chapter 1, and will be used as the basis for understanding a range of health issues that are covered by chapters in Part Three.

Chapter 2 reviews the biological underpinnings of health and health behaviours. It is necessary to understand how the nervous system, the endocrine and immunological systems together regulate physiological reactions and behaviour. Biofeedback is introduced as an example of the importance of physiological regulation in modifying reactions, and hence to reducing risks associated with psychophysiological disorders. Chapter 3 considers the constructs of stress and coping. Stress has come to be regarded (rightly or wrongly) as one of the major problems of our busy lives. In this chapter we consider carefully the nature of the construct and look at how it has been measured. Philip Evans examines closely the physiological basis of the concept. He then considers the other construct: coping. Coping also needs to be 'unpacked' to understand how it is that we can cope with stress and why some people appear to manage to do so better than others. Finally, the exciting new field of psychoneuroimmunology is reviewed to show how psychology and physiology interact in determining health.

Chapter 1

An introduction to health psychology

Marian Pitts

Introduction

This chapter will introduce the area of health psychology. It will outline briefly the historical background to the field, consider the development of our understanding of health behaviours and introduce the major models which have been developed to aid our understanding of people's health-related behaviours. We will look at individual differences and how they impact on health behaviours. Finally, we will consider the methodologies used in health research and the particular ethical problems which accompany research in these areas.

What is health and what is health psychology?

How are you feeling today? As you read these words are your eyes sore? Does your back ache? How's the head? Do you find your concentration wandering (already?!). It is extremely unlikely that anyone reading this book is entirely and absolutely healthy and free of symptoms. It would be difficult to know what that would mean; we all are 'imperfect machines'. The study of health psychology is concerned with the ways in which we, as individuals, behave and interact with others in sickness and in health. Any activity of psychology which relates to aspects of health, illness, the health care system, or health policy may be considered to be within the field of health psychology. Health psychology deals with such questions as: What are the physiological bases of emotion and how do they relate to health and illness? Can certain behaviours predispose to particular illnesses? What is stress? Can educational interventions prevent illness? And many others. The beginnings of the formal interest of psychologists in these areas can be dated to the convening of a conference in the USA in 1978 and to the creation of a section devoted to health psychology in the American Psychological Association in 1979. The British Psychological Society (BPS) set up a Health Psychology Section only in 1986. This year (1997) the section should become a formally recognised division of the BPS and the profession of health psychologist may be established in the UK.

Some time ago the World Health Organization put forward a definition of health which has been widely quoted. Health is 'a state of complete physical, mental and social well-being and not merely the absence of disease or infirmity' (WHO, 1946). Recently this definition has come under scrutiny and some criticism as representing an unrealistic goal, nevertheless it does emphasise the holistic nature of health involving body and spirit, physical and mental states.

Matarazzo in 1980 offered a definition of health psychology which has become widely accepted:

> Health psychology is the aggregate of the specific educational, scientific and professional contributions of the discipline of psychology to the promotion and maintenance of health, the prevention and treatment of illness, the identification of etiologic and diagnostic correlates of health, illness and related dysfunction, and the analysis and improvement of the health care system and health policy formation.

This definition emphasises the diversity of issues encompassed by the emerging discipline. There is also variety in the approaches brought to those issues. Some health psychologists would see themselves primarily as clinicians, others as psychophysiologists, and others still as cognitive psychologists; some will practise health psychology in the health care settings, others will teach and research in academic institutions – what unifies them is their interest in the areas delineated by Matarazzo and their approaches to these issues.

Historical background

The recognition of health psychology as a clearly designated field is very recent, as we have seen; however, many of the ideas and basic concepts have been around psychology for a great deal longer. The relationship between mind and body and the effect of one upon the other has always been a controversial topic amongst philosophers, psychologists and physiologists. Within psychology, the development of the study of psychosomatic disorders owes much to Freud. Psychologists such as Dunbar (1943), Ruesch (1948) and Alexander (1950) attempted to relate distinct personality types to particular diseases with an implicit causation hypothesis. Work of this type has become more sophisticated in its approach and the chapters in the book on coronary heart disease and cancer are illustrative, and critical, of this orientation. This approach has been largely abandoned by health psychologists in favour of more behavioural or biological approaches which seek to employ interventions derived from behavioural medicine (see the chapters concerning pain (Chapter 6) and hypertension (Chapter 10) as examples of this).

Another important aspect in the development of health psychology has been the changing patterns of illness and disease. If we were to compare 1898 with 1998 we would see that contagious and infectious diseases now contribute minimally to illness and death in the Western world, and other illnesses have become more frequent and are of a different nature. Major breakthroughs in science have reduced the prevalence of diseases such as smallpox, rubella, influenza and polio in the Western world; more deaths are caused now by heart disease, cancer and strokes. Recent studies and theories suggest that these diseases are, in part, a by-product of changes in lifestyles in the twentieth century. Psychologists can be instrumental in investigating and influencing lifestyles and behaviours which are conducive or detrimental to good health. The chapters in this book on AIDS (Chapter 8) and coronary heart disease (Chapter 11) illustrate areas where such interventions are being attempted. Increasingly, then, the major causes of death are those in which so-called behavioural pathogens are the single most important factor. Behavioural pathogens are the personal habits and lifestyle behaviours, such as smoking and excessive drinking, which can influence the onset and course of disease. It is not just the diseases of the 'developed' world which can be affected by behaviour and attitude: combating malaria, schistomiasis and other diseases endemic in different parts of the world can also be greatly helped by psychological input into campaigns to change behaviour. As people the world over live longer, the long-term effects of what Matarazzo (1983) calls 'a lifetime of behavioural mismanagement' can begin to express themselves as diseases such as lung cancer, and heart and liver dysfunctions.

Health behaviours

We will now look at behaviours which can be part of maintaining a healthy lifestyle and avoiding ill health. These are known as (protective) health behaviours. Harris and Guten (1979) conducted an exploratory study of 1250 residents in Greater Cleveland, USA. Residents were asked: What are the three most important things that you do to protect your health? Following this free recall, they were presented with statements on cards which described health behaviours and were asked to sort them into those that they did and those that they did not practise. Cluster analyses performed on these data produced categories to account for the various responses obtained by both methods. Categories of health protective behaviours thus found were:

- environmental hazard avoidance – avoiding areas of pollution or crime;
- harmful substance avoidance – not smoking or drinking alcohol;
- health practices – sleeping enough, eating sensibly and so forth;
- preventive health care – dental check-ups, smear tests;
- safety practices – repairing things, keeping first aid kits and emergency telephone numbers handy.

Other studies carried out by Pill and Stott (1986) and Amir (1987) confirm these findings that people can identify behaviours which they carry out to protect health. Amir (1987) developed the General Preventive Health Behaviours (GPHB) Checklist. It consists of twenty-nine items which were selected to represent a range of behaviours thought to be relevant to a British population. Amir carried out the study on elderly (65–75 years) Scottish people and found the following items to be endorsed by more than 90 per cent of respondents:

- Avoid drinking and driving
- Wear a seat-belt when in the car
- Do all things in moderation
- Get enough relaxation
- Check the safety of electrical appliances
- Avoid overworking
- Fix broken equipment around the home
- Eat sensibly

At the other end of the spectrum, only 10 per cent reported taking dietary supplements or vitamins, and only 12 per cent regularly got a dental check-up. It is likely that these percentages would look very different in different age groups (see the discussion topic at the end of this chapter).

There is thus a common-sense notion that a relationship exists between good health and personal habits. Plato said, 'where temperance is, there health is speedily imparted'. Many groups have codified 'good' living habits into their religions and there is strong evidence of the outcome of healthy living and abstinence in such communities: Mormons in Utah have a 30 per cent lower incidence of most cancers than the general population of the USA, and Seventh-day Adventists have 25 per cent fewer hospital admissions for malignancies (Matarazzo, 1983). Such statistics are powerful indicators that personal lifestyles do much to ensure healthy bodies. This idea was first studied systematically by a much cited study carried out in Alameda County, California and reported initially by Belloc and Breslow (1972). They asked 6928 county residents which of the following seven health behaviours they practised regularly:

- not smoking;
- having breakfast each day;
- having no more than one or two alcoholic drinks each day;
- taking regular exercise;
- sleeping seven to eight hours per night;
- not eating between meals;
- being no more than 10 per cent overweight.

They also measured the residents' health status via a number of illness-related questions: for example, how many days they had taken off from work due to sickness in the previous twelve months. They were also interested in physical, mental and social health which they defined as 'the degree to which individuals were functioning members of their community'. Although criticisms have been made of this study, most notably the lack of independence between the questions, some strong and well-replicated relationships were demonstrated. A health *habit* is a health behaviour which is well established and often carried out semi-automatically: do you actually decide each morning and evening to clean your teeth, or do you 'just do it'? Adults in the study who engaged in *most* of the health habits reported themselves to be healthier than those who engaged in *few* or *none*. A follow-up study nine-and-a-half years later showed that mortality rates were significantly lower for both men and women who practised the seven healthy habits. Men who had all seven healthy habits had only 23 per cent of the mortality rate of men who carried out none or fewer than three health habits (Breslow and Enstrom, 1980). There were also clear links between physical, mental and social health. These findings reinforce the holistic notion of health proposed by the WHO as a composite of effective functioning, whether physically, mentally or socially.

This original Californian cohort has been studied for twenty-five years. A survey in 1982, seventeen years after the study first began, considered those individuals who had been at least 60 years old at the time of the first survey. It was found that not smoking, taking physical activity, and regular breakfast eating were strong predictors of their mortality (Schoenborn, 1993). The Alameda Study reinforced the idea of 'moderation in all things' as the basis of good health. It also emphasised the role of social and mental aspects in achieving good physical health.

Although most of us are familiar with the need to engage in preventive health behaviours, few of us actually do so. Berg (1976) has stressed that most people are aware of which health behaviours should be engaged in; however, they frequently do not do so, and furthermore *do* engage in activities which they know to be harmful to their health. It is this cantankerousness which psychologists have spent a great deal of time examining. The dilemma or challenge then is how best to encourage, persuade or coerce people into adopting the healthy habits which it is believed are good for them. This enterprise carries values and expectations which will be examined in the final chapter. The dilemma for health psychologists is to explain why some or many people do not do what they know is in their own best interests to do; and why some people are more amenable to the adoption of healthy habits than others.

A consistent focus has been the role of knowledge in changing behaviours. People need to be informed of the risks to themselves that certain behaviours (or non-behaviours) can engender. Having been apprised of the risks they will then decide, so the argument goes, in a rational manner, to modify their behaviours in the direction of greater health promotion and protection. Studies examining a range of issues relevant to health such as smoking, drug-taking, medical checks and adopting safer sex have fairly consistently shown that knowledge, by itself, does not lead to behaviour change.

Kelley (1979) examined the role of media in improving public health. He pointed out that the use of safety-belts in cars greatly reduces the probability of death and injury following crashes. However, the availability of seat-belts in cars does not guarantee their use. A study conducted in the USA in 1968 recorded only 6.3 per cent of car drivers wearing seat-belts in a city area. Kelley attempted to design and execute a definitive test of mass media effectiveness in increasing seat-belt use. He was able to utilise cable television such that he could have a number of households which would receive advertisements concerning seat-belt use, and another, equivalent number of households which would not. He used six different advertisements, produced professionally, and shown at specific times designed to target specific audiences. The advertisements were shown regularly over a period of nine months. He estimated that the average television viewer in the experimental group saw one or another of the messages two or three times a week over the test period. Observers positioned at designated sites within the area under study recorded seat-belt use and the car licence plate which enabled a trace to be made to indicate which of the two cable television companies was available to that person's house. Kelley's conclusion was depressing: 'The results were clear-cut. The campaign had no effect whatsoever on seat belt use.' There were no significant differences between drivers from households which had received the messages and drivers from the control households. Nor did the drivers from the test group change their seat-belt wearing at all across the test period. Kelley argues very forcefully from this study that mass media campaigns are ineffective and an inefficient means of changing health behaviours. So what else is required, other than knowledge, to persuade people to look after their health? We will now examine suggestions for other factors which could influence health behaviour.

Models of health behaviour

Early studies of protective health focused upon demographic variables such as age, race and socioeconomic class as determinants of the adoption and practice of health behaviours. This research resulted in descriptions of population groups which did or did not engage in health behaviours. These findings were sometimes contradictory and often did not serve any great purpose – one cannot change one's age, sex or race and there is only limited opportunity to change occupation or alter income. Consequently research has shifted to structural variables such as the cost or complexity of the behaviour, with a view to improving the adoption and practice of preventive health behaviours. There are several theories or models which have evolved in this context. All the models share a common framework in that they exemplify a biopsychosocial approach to health. Such an approach recognises the biological and genetic bases of many illnesses, acknowledges the role of psychological elements such as beliefs, behaviours and cognitions in the development of all illnesses, and recognises that the social, economic and cultural setting will have great impact on health. This approach, first developed by Engel (1977), underpins much of health psychology and will be apparent throughout this book. We will now consider in detail some of the more important models and note their shared characteristics.

The health belief model (HBM)

This is probably the 'oldest' and best known of the models of health behaviour. It is the one against which more recent models have been developed. This model was specified initially by Rosenstock (1966) and was modified by Becker and Maiman (1975). It attempts to explain both health behaviour and compliance. It should be useful in predicting both health behaviour before illness, such as screening for cancer, and compliance with medical regimens once ill. Thus, both sick role behaviour and preventive behaviours should be capable of being predicted. The model proposes that a person's likelihood of engaging in health-related behaviours is a function of several dimensions. An outline of the model is presented in Figure 1.1. It proposes that for a person to take preventive action against a disease, that person must:

- feel personally susceptible to the disease (perceived susceptibility);
- feel that the disease would have at least moderately serious consequences (perceived severity);
- feel that preventive behaviour would be beneficial either by preventing the disease, or by lessening its severity (perceived benefits);
- that barriers, such as pain, embarrassment or expense (costs) should not outweigh the perceived benefits of the proposed health action in order for the preventive health behaviour to occur;
- that cues to action may trigger a consideration of the proposed health action.

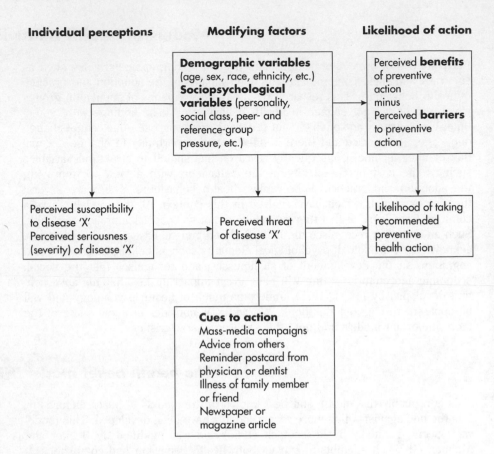

Individual perceptions   **Modifying factors**   **Likelihood of action**

Figure 1.1 Health belief model

Source: Becker and Maiman (1975). Copyright Lippincott–Raven Publishers.

The model has been used with some success to predict the adoption of several different health behaviours, including vaccinations, screening for cancer and contraceptive behaviour (Harrison *et al.*, 1992; Herold, 1983; Janz and Becker, 1984). For some behaviours, perceived severity may be less important for preventive behaviours than either perceived vulnerability or cost–benefit considerations (Cleary, 1987). There can be problems of response bias when questionnaires which have operationalised the HBM construct are used. This is discussed by Sheeran and Orbell (1996), who recommend several ways of avoiding this problem. Harrison *et al.*'s meta-analytic review of HBM in 1992 originally identified 234 published studies. Of this large number, however, only sixteen had examined all the major components of the model and had included reliability checks. Harrison *et al.* then converted effect sizes of the sixteen studies into correlation coefficients and calculated correlations for susceptibility, severity, benefits and barriers. Whilst all the correlations were statistically significant they were also rather small, accounting for less than 4 per cent of the variances across the studies. Despite the fact that the model has been around for more than two decades, it is rarely used carefully and with sufficient reliability to be confident of its results. The major problems with it as an account of health behaviours are that it assumes rationality as the basis for an individual's decision making, and downplays the role of emotions, for example, fear and anxiety. It also tends to assume that beliefs are static and, once formed, fairly fixed. Other models which have been developed from the HBM have attempted to incorporate some of these additional elements.

Protection motivation theory

Rogers (1984) examined health behaviours from the point of view of motivational factors; thus it built on HBM by incorporating motivational elements into its basic structure. The protection motivation model suggests that motivation to protect oneself from a health threat is based on four beliefs:

- that the threat is severe (magnitude);
- that one is vulnerable to the threat (likelihood);
- that one can perform the behaviour required to protect against the threat (self-efficacy);
- that the response made will be effective (response-efficacy).

Early research emphasised fear as a motivational factor but Rogers now suggests instead that attempts need to be directed at all four of the elements described above to achieve effective change. It is not clear which of the four elements is more important than the others, nor how to develop a campaign which can adequately address all elements simultaneously.

Leventhal's self-regulatory model

A rather different approach is that of Leventhal and co-workers who have developed a model of illness behaviour and cognitions. This could be characterised as a problem-solving model since it conceptualises the individual as an active problem solver whose behaviour reflects an attempt to close a perceived gap between current status and a goal, or ideal state. Behaviour depends on the individual's cognitive representations of his or her current health status and the goal state, plans for changing the current state, and techniques or rules for assessing progress.

Leventhal's self-regulatory model of illness (Leventhal and Cameron, 1987) defines three stages which regulate behaviour. These stages are:

- Interpretation of the health threat – this concerns the cognitive representation of the threat, which includes dimensions such as symptom perceptions, and social messages such as potential causes or possible consequences.

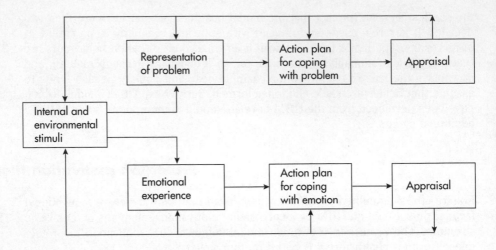

Figure 1.2 Leventhal's self-regulatory model of illness behaviour

Source: Leventhal and Cameron (1987). Copyright Elsevier Science Ireland Ltd.

- An action plan or coping strategy – this may take a variety of forms; the major ones are an *approach* coping strategy which would include seeking medical attention, self-prescribing, discussing the symptoms with others; or an *avoidance* strategy, i.e. denial that there might be a problem and wishing it away.
- The last stage is the appraisal stage, in which the individual utilises specific criteria to gauge the success of coping actions, with perceptions of insufficient progress leading to modifications.

The model is presented in diagrammatic form in Figure 1.2. The self-regulation comes from the individual's attempts to maintain the status quo and return to the 'normal' state of health. Emotional reactions can be evoked at any stage; cultural or social differences, for instance in symptom perception or illness expectations, can lead to differing representations and different coping structures. An attractive feature of this type of model is that it is active: it stresses the individual and how that person can operate and reflect on his or her actions. This, though, is also its potential weakness; it has not been as amenable to testing, particularly through questionnaire construction, as has the health belief model.

The theory of planned behaviour (TPB)

The theory of planned behaviour derives from social psychology and is a development of an earlier theory of reasoned action. Both models emphasise the role of decision making and seek to explain the suggested relationships between attitudes and behaviours. The theory of planned behaviour has become a major model for health promotion. The models have as their central premise the notion

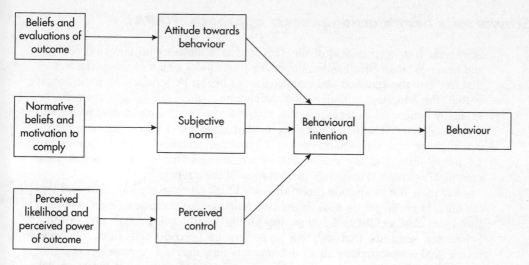

Figure 1.3 Theory of planned behaviour

that people make decisions about their behaviour on the basis of a reasonable consideration of the available evidence. TPB stresses that behaviour is planned and that the planning is, in part, a function of an individual's intentions. The model identifies intention as the most immediate determinant of behaviour (Ajzen and Madden, 1986; Fishbein and Ajzen, 1975). Intentions are themselves a function of three separate elements – privately held attitudes towards the particular behaviour, a perception of socially determined norms that represent a person's belief that others think he or she should behave in a certain way, and perceived behavioural control, which is a person's belief that they can carry out the planned behaviour, that they have the necessary skills and abilities and that they can overcome potential external barriers (Figure 1.3). The model attaches values to each of these factors. The particular values attached to each factor will depend upon the individual's beliefs and thus in many ways this model is similar to the health belief model.

One difficulty with this model is that it identifies a direct link between intentions and behaviours, but intentions are not always translated into actions. Even when an individual holds an intention towards some behaviour, action does not necessarily result. There may be one or more reasons for not carrying out an intention to act in a particular way that is perceived as beneficial. The action may not be possible in a particular situation or at a particular time, it may be difficult or time consuming or it may simply be suppressed. From the point of view of the promotion of health behaviours, much greater consideration needs to be given to the impact of situational influences of this kind upon adherence to an intention to act in accordance with prevention (see Abraham and Sheeran (1993) for a fuller discussion of this point).

Schwarzer's health action process approach (HAPA)

Schwarzer has been critical of the TPB in that it includes no temporal element and hence is 'static'. He has developed his own model which explores the factors that facilitate the adoption and maintenance of health behaviours. Its basic notion is that 'the adoption, initiation, and maintenance of health behaviours must be explicitly conceived as a process that consists of at least a motivation phase and a volition phase. The latter might be further subdivided into a planning phase, action phase and maintenance phase' (Schwarzer and Fuchs, 1996). See Figure 1.4 for an outline of the model. Schwarzer stresses that perceived self-efficacy (see p. 17) plays a crucial role at all stages of the model.

During the motivation phase the individual develops an intention, and this intention is predicted by self-efficacy and outcome expectancies ('I am confident that I can lose weight and I know that losing weight will improve my health'). Schwarzer suggests that outcome expectancies precede self-efficacy because people make assumptions about outcomes before they ask themselves whether they can perform the action. They then carry out an appraisal of threat or risk – a little like the perceived severity element of HBM. Schwarzer suggests that this element may be minimal in many cases and specifically that fear appeals may have only limited value.

'It is common knowledge that good intentions do not necessarily guarantee corresponding actions' (Schwarzer and Fuchs, 1996): thus the right-hand section of Figure 1.4 consists of three levels: cognitive, behavioural and situational. Here again, self-efficacy plays a role in determining the amount of effort invested in the action and the perseverance with the action phase.

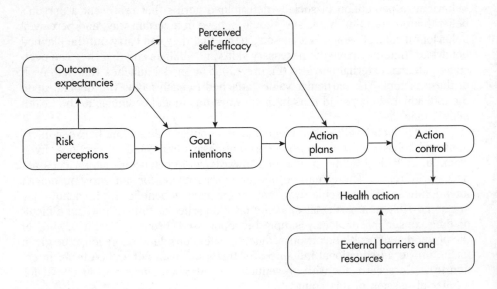

Figure 1.4 Schwarzer's health action process approach

Source: Schwarzer and Fuchs (1996)

It should be noted that all these models tend to rely on a model of a person as a rational decision maker, subject to motivational forces but essentially making decisions and following them through. Once again, the roles of emotions and of situational variables (for example chocolate in the cupboard, wine in the fridge) are relatively underplayed.

The transtheoretical model

Finally, a rather different approach to health behaviours is that of the trans-theoretical model developed by Prochaska and DiClemente (1983, 1992) as an integrative and comprehensive model of *behaviour change*. They suggest that people move through a series of stages in changing their behaviour. They label them *precontemplation, contemplation, preparation, action* and *maintenance*. Using studies on how people begin and maintain an exercise programme as an example, the stages would be like this:

- *Precontemplation:* a period during which a person is not seriously considering the need for regular exercise: 'No problems, I'm fine as I am.'
- *Contemplation*: a period during which a person is seriously considering exercise: 'I can't do what I used to; I need to get fitter.'
- *Preparation*: a period during which a person seriously thinks about beginning an exercise programme, say, during the next month: 'That new gym has opened up nearby; I'll buy myself a track suit.'
- *Action:* a period ranging from nought to six months during which the person is actually exercising 'three times a week in the gym – I'm feeling good.'
- *Maintenance:* a period beginning six months after the start of the exercise programme: 'I'm attending regularly, and rarely miss a session.'

Thus the model is temporal and describes the process of change rather than only identifying the precursors to that behavioural change. The decision-making element associated with the model derives from Janis and Mann's conflict model (1977), which involves a consideration of benefits and costs (pros and cons) associated with a behavioural change.

Prochaska *et al.* (1994b) applied the stages of change to a number of problem behaviours which included: smoking cessation, weight control, quitting cocaine, using condoms, applying sunscreens, and others. Twelve separate samples were drawn on for each of the problem behaviours, yielding a total sample size of 3858. Looking at costs and benefits of behavioural change, the study showed that for all problem behaviours, the cons of changing were higher than the pros for those respondents in the precontemplation stage. The opposite was true for those respondents in the action stage. For seven of the twelve behaviours the cross-over in the balance between pros and cons occurred during the contemplation stage; for the other five behaviours it occurred during the action stage. This suggests that a costs–benefits analysis fits well within this approach.

Prochaska *et al.* (1994a) review studies on the transtheoretical model of change and HIV prevention and conclude that the model is also generalisable to

HIV prevention. They highlight the importance of distinguishing between main sexual partners and casual sexual partners and suggest different factors are operating in decisions to use condoms with these two groups (see Chapters 8 and 9 for a discussion of the issues of contraception and HIV prevention).

Comparing the models

There is a clear need for further empirical studies that test these and other models for the adoption of preventive health behaviours, since interventions based upon them have implicitly accepted their assumptions. If the determinants of precautionary behaviours could be identified this would be a significant step forward in campaigns against behavioural diseases such as AIDS, or smoking-related illnesses. There is little doubt that the principal variables identified by these models – perceived risk, perceived severity of the disease, perceived effectiveness of precautions, social norms, self-efficacy and cost–benefit payoff – are important predictors of preventive health behaviours of many kinds. However, the value attached to each element remains uncertain.

Individual differences

People vary in how they respond to a health threat or prevention measure. Some of this variation can be accounted for by considering person variables. These variables should begin to account for the differences between people in how they respond to similar health threats.

Health locus of control

In the mid-1960s the concept of 'locus of control' was introduced by Rotter and others (Rotter, 1966). This grew out of a social learning tradition which considered the expectations of individuals and how they related to reinforcements. Individuals with an internal locus of control were more likely to believe that reinforcements were contingent upon their own efforts, whereas those with an external locus of control were likely to regard their life as determined largely by external forces such as fate or 'powerful others'.

A development of this broad construct of locus of control was the health locus of control scale constructed by Wallston *et al.* (1978). Questions reflected the three factors mentioned above – an internal focus for health: 'I am in control of my health'; the powerful others factor: 'Whenever I do not feel well I should consult a health professional', and the role of fate: 'Luck plays a big part in determining how soon I will recover from an illness.' There is some evidence (reviewed by Wallston and Wallston in 1984) that high 'internal scorers' carried out a greater range and number of health behaviours; but differences between internals and externals are not diverse, and the amount of variance accounted for by this measure is frequently small (Pitts *et al.* 1991). Furnham and Steele (1993) reviewed the outcomes of locus of control questionnaires, including those for health, and also found that they accounted for only a low amount of variance. A number of disease-specific questionnaires has been developed; Bradley and colleagues, for example, have considered locus of control in relation to diabetes (Bradley *et al.* 1984, 1990); others have applied the approach to cancer (Pruyn *et al.*, 1988), and to hypertension (Stanton, 1987). Furnham and Steele point out that the critical practical issue for further research is whether locus of control beliefs can be altered by interventions or whether they are more or less 'fixed' traits. Many researchers make the point that the aim of devising a scale is to identify those people who hold maladaptive beliefs. Very little, however, has developed from these identifications. We have already encountered the next variable to be considered in models of health behaviour.

Self-efficacy

Bandura, again from a social learning perspective, has suggested that self-efficacy is a major factor to be considered in accounting for differences in health behaviours (Bandura, 1977, 1986). It has been applied to helping people to quit smoking and to persuading people to indulge in physical exercise. It examines people's beliefs in their own abilities with questions such as: 'I am confident I could deal efficiently with unexpected events', or 'I can always manage to solve difficult problems if I try hard enough'. It has been studied both as a behaviour specific to a narrow situation and as a more general trait construct.

The model has recently been applied to condom use by Wulfert and Wan (1993). They developed an outline of a model which uses self-efficacy as a common pathway to integrate the effects of several cognitive variables that might predict condom use. The first of these variables is sexual attitudes, the second is outcome expectancies, i.e. what would be the effect of using a condom. Comparison and influences from a peer group were seen as important, as were knowledge and perceived vulnerability about AIDS.

The results from this study support the role of self-efficacy as a mediating variable between factors such as peer influence, knowledge and perceived vulnerability and an actual behaviour. Such studies have prompted attempts to enhance self-efficacy beliefs, especially among young adults. Schwarzer has developed a general self-efficacy scale which aims to measure a broad and stable sense of personal competence to deal effectively with challenges in one's life from a variety of sources. Schwarzer contrasts self-efficacy with the concept of optimism described below. Self-efficacy is restricted to one's beliefs about personal resources, focusing particularly on competence; in contrast, optimism is a broader construct which may incorporate a number of other elements, for example luck. That said, clearly the relationship between the two constructs is very close. Schwarzer has translated the self-efficacy scale into several languages. Cross-cultural comparisons can be very tricky; but there is an interesting finding which emerges from a comparison of the studies in different countries. Sometimes gender differences are found, and sometimes not; but in no country yet studied have women been found to score higher than men (Schwarzer *et al.*, 1997). As

Schwarzer *et al.* suggest, research is now needed to establish whether the scale itself is gender-biased or whether the construct of self-efficacy favours men.

Optimism

A relatively reliable finding in health psychology is that when asked to compare one's own risk of something negative against the risk of others like me, I will tend to underestimate my own risk against others'. Judgements are required for statements such as 'Compared with others of my age, my chances of developing ... are greater than / the same as / less than them.' The usual response is to judge oneself at less risk of almost any health threat than one's contemporaries. It appears that most people engage in this social comparison bias with regard to many health issues such as risks of lung cancer, AIDS, traffic accident or heart disease. There is also evidence that this kind of optimism is particularly characteristic of adolescence, where it is known as 'adolescent invulnerability' (Quadrel *et al.*, 1993).

These biases are dysfunctional in terms of health behaviours and health promotion. They are likely to act as defence strategies against behavioural change: 'Others need to change their behaviour, not me.' Other kinds of optimism are, however, more adaptive because they imply coping strategies and behavioural change. Researchers such as Sheier and Carver (1992) have shown that optimists have better health and practise more health behaviours than pessimists; this is possibly linked to the fact that optimists expect good outcomes and hence cope better with short-term distress or discomfort. The links between optimism and self-efficacy are close; each construct is measured by questionnaires which are rarely unidimensional. Dispositional optimism is measured by the life orientation test (Sheier and Carver, 1985). This is a short, twelve-item test, which taps people's approach to life with statements like 'I always look on the bright side' or 'I hardly ever expect things to go my way.'

Wallston (1994) has offered an interesting distinction between 'cautious' and 'cockeyed' optimism. The cautious optimist is 'pretty much in touch with reality'; being fairly confident that things will turn out right, the person nevertheless does everything in his or her power to ensure that it does. Confident of success in my driving test I nevertheless revise the Highway Code the night before. The 'cockeyed optimist' – in the words of Rogers and Hammerstein – is 'Stuck like a dope with this thing called hope', who lives in a world of illusion and hardly raises a finger to help bring about his or her desired outcomes. In the context of health care this results in little change towards healthy habits and avoiding unhealthy ones. Given this, one would predict a curvilinear relationship between optimism and health behaviours with only the cautious optimism items predicting uptake and maintenance of health behaviour. Optimism has generated a great deal of research and is likely to remain a key variable in future work.

Doing health psychology research

Next we need to consider the ways in which data and evidence are gathered in health psychology. Many of the methods are similar to other areas of psychology – experimental tests undertaken in a carefully controlled setting, psychophysiological measures which are related to behaviour, observational studies, are all examples of standard techniques. However, there are a few methods which are used in health research and are less commonly encountered by those with a background in psychology. Some of these will be introduced briefly here.

Research in health psychology shares many characteristics with all psychological research. These are: that the research usually originates with a question; that it demands clear articulation of a goal, and that it requires a specific plan or procedure. Often a large problem, for example 'How can we best help patients recover from surgery?', becomes divided into smaller problems: 'Which kind of information provision before surgery aids recovery?'

Health psychology research is also guided by hypotheses and endeavours to use objective measures. A method frequently used in health research is that of a *clinical trial*, in which one approach (usually treatment) is compared with another to see which is better. It is imperative that such comparisons are fair and one of the basic ways in which this is achieved is by random allocation of people to one treatment or another. Such random allocation should ensure that any differences found between treatments are genuinely just that, i.e. treatment differences, and are not the outcome of a particular kind of person choosing one treatment over another. Randomised clinical trials are often regarded as 'the gold standard' for health research against which other studies may be assessed.

Cohort trials are used when a group of people is followed through an experience (treatment) to see how they may change or improve over time. This is a particularly interesting way of examining a chronic condition, or the outcome of a particular intervention or treatment, say, chemotherapy. It is still important, though, that there should be a comparison group against which changes in the cohort may be compared. This is the only way in which we can be sure that the changes observed in the cohort are not simply the result of time passing.

The survey is probably the most widely used, and abused, method in psychological research. Surveys seek to examine people's attitudes, opinions or beliefs about a health issue. Frequently people are asked to report on their own behaviour. It is important that those surveyed can, in some sense, be compared with a wider group of people. We need to know how people were selected for the survey, what the response rate was and whether the findings can be generalised. Finally, the relationship between self-report and behaviour needs to be carefully examined.

Focus groups, favoured by political parties and market researchers, are being used increasingly frequently in health research. Focus groups should allow us to gain a greater psychological understanding of human experience by gathering together the opinions, beliefs and attitudes of between six and twelve individuals who are similar in some way. They are brought together to discuss a specific set of issues. Focus groups rely on the dynamics of group interaction to stimulate the thinking and contributions of group members. This explicit use of group dynamics is what distinguishes the technique from more general 'group interviews'. Focus groups have been used to investigate a wide range of issues such as people's views on contraception (Barker and Rich, 1992), drink driving (Basch *et al.*, 1989), and media coverage of AIDS (Kitzinger, 1994). The focus must be clearly set – for example via a short video. The group must 'gel' – often achieved via introductions and sharing of common experiences/goals – and contributions must be encouraged, and opposing views as well as consensus examined. There is more than one way to cook a goose, and focus groups are frequently used in conjunction with other methods. Sometimes they are a first method and used as a preliminary tool, for example, before designing a questionnaire. This enables the use of appropriate terms and words in the questionnaire, which otherwise might be imposed by the researcher. Focus groups are usually used when issues are poorly defined, when the *quality* of information to be elicited is vital and participants for the groups can be recruited relatively easily.

Epidemiology is the study of how often diseases occur in different groups of people and how disease outcomes can be measured in relation to a population at risk. This population is defined as those people, sick or well, who would be counted as cases if they contracted the disease. A study population might be defined by a shared characteristic such as geographical location, as in the Alameda County study (Belloc and Breslow, 1972), by occupation, as we shall see in the Whitehall studies (Chapter 16), or by diagnosis, i.e. people in a given location who were first diagnosed with a disease in a given period of time.

It is important to remember that, unlike clinical observations which relate to individuals, epidemiological observations determine decisions about *groups*. Its conclusions are frequently based on comparisons between groups of people. It may also estimate the relative risk of a person contracting a disorder by comparing incidences. However, this cannot and does not predict with any degree of certainty that an individual will develop a disease or disorder. You will encounter the results of epidemiological surveys throughout this book.

Finally, there are some general questions which should be asked of any research: these (adapted from Crombie, 1996) can be characterised as follows:

- Was the research worth doing?
- Are the findings substantial or trivial?
- Do they have theoretical and/or practical import?
- Are we the better for them having been done?

Ethics in health psychology research

Ethical issues must inform all research, but there are particular responsibilities within the area of health psychology. There is nearly always some conflict between the needs of research and the needs of individuals who are 'being researched'. The following quotation makes this tension explicit:

> Social scientists . . . have a genuine obligation to devise protections for the right of privacy and to avoid mere psychic voyeurism. At the same time

they have a compelling obligation to collect data: there is an obvious conflict between the need of society to know and the right of the individual to dignity and privacy.

(Stagner, 1967)

Many of the participants in health research are especially 'vulnerable': they may have just received bad news, they may be anxious about impending treatment, they may be children. As such, we have special responsibilities to ensure that we respect their rights when carrying out research; there is a basic edict which is: do no harm. All health research should require that participants give informed consent; in other words, that participants in the research understand what it is that is being asked of them and formally agree to participate. Issues of understanding become central to this process. Participants in research must also understand that the research is separate from their treatment and that a refusal to participate will not jeopardise their chances of the best treatment available. Research that is carried out in medical settings can be particularly problematic in establishing this. Anonymlty and/or confidentiality are critical in settings where information can be passed to a fairly wide range of people, and where it can be potentially damaging or embarrassing for the participants.

Finally, issues of creating a comparison group can be extremely difficult to justify to oneself and to participants. If we believe that a particular intervention may be beneficial to patients, how can we withhold it from randomly selected patients allocated to the control condition, to establish its efficacy? This dilemma is usually resolved either by comparing different possible treatments – not really a resolution of the difficulty, but at least countering the 'no treatment' issue; or by offering the treatment to the 'control' or comparison group following completion of the study – again hardly a resolution of the dilemma. Would you withhold treatment from participants to achieve a comparison group?

As researchers in the area of health psychology, we must be aware of these problems and ensure that the research we carry out follows the highest possible ethical standards.

Other chapters in this book will enlarge on much of what has been covered here. Specific problems and issues will be examined in detail in the light of the theories and models described above. We need, though, having examined some of the areas of interest to health psychologists, to consider further its future as a discipline. Marteau and Johnston (1987) have sounded a warning note about the development of the field. They caution that 'the relative neglect of psychological models and paradigms in work considered under the rubric of health psychology, results in approaches to problems in clinical and research contexts that owe more to a medical than a psychological perspective.' Johnston (1988) also suggests that at least five separate kinds of literature on health psychology appear to be developing, according to the problem studied and the journal in which the research is published. It is becoming increasingly difficult for any one person to keep abreast of the literature on the diverse areas of interest that are encompassed by health psychology. It must be hoped that increasingly research and theory building for one particular health issue will more clearly inform and guide research in other related topics, and that psychological models of health behaviour will give rise to effective interventions for promoting health.

HEALTH AND BEHAVIOUR

- Make a list of five things you do to protect your health.
- Now list five things you do which are injurious to your health.
- What do the two lists tell you about health protective behaviours and behavioural pathogens?
- How would you change two of the behaviours on the 'dangerous list'?
- Are there barriers to making that change? What could you do to overcome these?
- How does your analysis compare with any one model of health behaviour outlined in this chapter?
- You may like to compare your lists with that of another person who is different in age or gender from you. Why are your lists similar or different?

Key point summary

- Any activity which is related to health, illness, the health care system or health policy is within the domain of health psychology.
- Certain health behaviours or habits are related to good health and others can be predictors of mortality. There are wide differences between people in the extent to which they practise such health behaviours.
- Theoretical models incorporate concepts such as risk perception, severity, barriers and motivational aspects which come together with any particular model as an explanation of the process of adopting healthy behaviours, or avoiding unhealthy ones.
- Individual differences are important in predicting health behaviour. Constructs such as self-efficacy, locus of control and optimism have been found to be useful in explaining people's behaviour.
- Health psychologists have a duty to ensure that participants in their studies are protected from harm and able to make informed decisions about their participation.

Further reading

Conner, M. and Norman, P. (1996) *Predicting Health Behaviour*. Buckingham, Open University Press. This book provides a review of the major models of health behaviour outlined in this chapter and gives good coverage of relevant studies and criticisms of the models.

Karoly, P. (1991) *Measurement Strategies in Health Psychology*. London, Wiley. This is the standard textbook outlining the variety of measures used in health psychology.

Nicolson, P. (1993) A day in the life of a Health Psychologist. *The Psychologist*, 6 (11), 505–509. This article gives an idea of what it is like to work as a health psychologist and the kinds of problems encountered.

Chapter 2

Psychophysiology, health and illness

Keith Phillips

Introduction

This chapter briefly describes the structure and organisation of the nervous, endocrine and immunological systems and their roles in the regulation of physiological responses and behaviour. Techniques for recording and measuring responses of these systems are considered, and their roles in the determination of health and illness are discussed. Finally, the use of biofeedback as a clinical treatment for psychophysiological disorders is reviewed.

Organisation of the nervous system

The mammalian nervous system is made up of millions of individual nerve cells that are arranged in complex networks. Individual cells and groups of cells communicate with each other via special chemicals called neurotransmitters which trigger electrical events within these networks. These electrical events, called *action potentials*, are the code or language by which information is communicated within the system. In total, the nervous system can be regarded as a highly sophisticated communication system that enables interaction between an organism and the physical world in which it lives. The individual elements of this system are arranged within a highly structured organisation as one would expect of any communication network.

When describing the organisation of the mammalian nervous system it is usual to identify its central and peripheral components. The central nervous system (CNS) comprises the brain and spinal cord; the peripheral nervous system (PNS) is the collection of nerves from the CNS to the periphery and from the periphery to the CNS. These nerves may be further subdivided into somatic and autonomic components. Before we consider each of these components it is important to appreciate that though they are described separately they are not separate systems in terms of their functions. The component structures are fully integrated with each other; changes that occur in the activity of the central nervous system will be accompanied by changes in the peripheral system and vice versa. The nervous system has evolved as a whole to allow behaving organisms to make successful adaptations to their environment. Ill health and disease may be regarded as indicators that successful adaptation has not been achieved.

Central nervous system

The central nervous system is made up of the brain and the spinal cord. These are developed from the same embryonic nerve tissues, are entirely interactive, and share an internal circulation of cerebrospinal fluid which protects against physical damage and provides a stable chemical environment to allow nerve cells to function. The CNS is enclosed by the bony coverings of the skull and vertebral column. In general terms, the CNS can be thought of as having an executive role in the control and regulation of behaviour. It receives information from the outside world, integrates current information with past experiences and instructs the responses of agents or effectors that have effects upon behaviour. The obvious effector agents are the muscles of the skeletal system which cause our actions, but other effectors are the hormones secreted by the endocrine system and responses of the automatic nervous system (ANS), such as changes in cardiac activity or electrical signals from the skin. Though the CNS prepares the instructions for changes in the activities of these effectors it does not deliver them; that is the job of the peripheral nervous system (PNS). Similarly, the PNS delivers to the CNS information from the outside world. Though the CNS may be considered to have an executive role, the regulation of behaviour is not entirely feudal since the operations of the CNS are influenced to a very large degree by feedback from the PNS.

Peripheral nervous system

The nerves of the PNS are divided into the somatic or autonomic nervous systems. The somatic system includes nerves from the sense organs (eyes, ears, skin, tongue and nose) which carry information from the outside world to the CNS. However the CNS is not simply a passive recipient of sensory information; it has nerves connected to the sense organs which actively and selectively filter out information. As well as sensory nerves, the somatic system also includes motor nerves that travel from the CNS to the muscles whose contractions result in actions (behaviour). Again this is not a unilateral operation, as there are also sensory nerves from the muscles that relay the consequences of those actions back to the CNS. The interaction between the sensory and motor nerves of the somatic system and the CNS can be organised within the spinal cord alone, for example for simple reflexes such as the knee-jerk reflex, but more usually it involves both the spinal cord and the various component structures of the brain.

The ANS is divided into two divisions – the sympathetic and the parasympathetic divisions whose actions are opposite though complementary. Usually, though erroneously, these two divisions are described solely in terms of their effector nerves which travel from the CNS to the organs and glands within the body. These innervations provide regulation of those visceral structures and hence regulation of the internal responses of the body. However, there are also sensory autonomic nerves carrying feedback from the viscera to the CNS. This of course is how we become aware of sensations such as emotional states, hunger pangs, or visceral pains. Thus the somatic and autonomic systems are similarly organised (see Figure 2.1).

The sympathetic and parasympathetic systems have antagonistic actions yet play a combined role in regulating the internal environment of the body. Typically, each organ of the body receives inputs from both the sympathetic and parasympathetic divisions. However, the sympathetic system is diffuse and sympathetic nerves innervate several organs and glands. Thus when activated, a generalised sympathetic reaction is observed in many of the body's internal organs. By contrast, the parasympathetic innervation is more discrete and individual organs have their own particular innervation, which allows more fractionated regulation

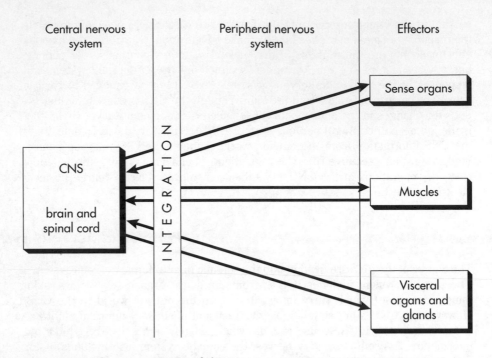

Figure 2.1 The organisation of the nervous system

of their responses. The sympathetic action causes mobilisation of the body's energy resources preparing the body for action. It is accompanied by multiple response changes including increased cardiac output, sweating, inhibition of digestion, increased blood flow to the muscles and dilation of the pupils. These responses prepare the body for action. This pattern of sympathetic activation is often referred to as the 'fight or flight reaction' and is considered to represent a reaction to stress (for further discussion see Evans, Chapter 3). The parasympathetic division exerts an opposite effect. It acts to conserve the body's energy resources and its action is characterised by slowing of the heart, stimulation of saliva, digestive activities such as gastric secretions and intestinal peristalsis, and pupil constriction (see Table 2.1).

Response regulation via these two divisions is highly sensitive, as they do not operate in an on-off fashion. Each division maintains some input to each of the various internal organs and the momentary response of any one organ is determined by the relative balance that exists between the two divisions at any given moment. To take a specific example, the control of heart rate depends upon the relative inputs of sympathetic and parasympathetic innervations. When the heart rate alters, it is caused by a shift in the overall balance between the systems; for example, a slowing of the heart rate could be caused by increasing the parasympathetic stimulation or equally well by maintaining the parasympathetic input at its current level but reducing the level of sympathetic input. The alterations of internal responding are sensed by internal sensory receptors which

TABLE 2.1 Antagonistic actions of the divisions of ANS

Organ	Sympathetic stimulation	Parasympathetic stimulation
Eye	Pupil dilation	Pupil constriction
Salivary glands	Mucus-rich saliva	Copious watery saliva
Blood vessels	Dilation	Constriction
Skin	Constriction	Dilation
Heart	Increased blood pressure	Decreased blood pressure
	Increased rate	Decreased rate
Digestive system	Decreased motility	Increased motility
Liver	Glycogenolysis	Glycogenesis

provide feedback to the CNS and may result in the initiation of behaviours by the CNS. For example, changes in gastric motility may be recognised as 'hunger', which may lead to initiation of actions to gather food whose consumption may eliminate the gastric contractions of the stomach: food-related behaviours will then cease. Within this closed loop there is no executive operator; merely mutual interdependence between the various components (see Brener, 1981).

Despite its name it is also quite wrong to suppose that the ANS is an automatic system showing simply reflexive changes in activity. As the studies on biofeedback (see p. 36) have clearly demonstrated, the ANS is an adaptive system that is capable of learning to respond to the demands imposed by different environments.

Neuroendocrine and neuroimmunological systems

Neural systems are not the only means for regulating behaviour. The endocrine and immune systems also have prominent roles to play in maintaining health. These systems are well described by Rasmussen (1974) and Ader (1981) and are only briefly outlined here.

The endocrine system further extends the functions of the nervous system and their actions are fully integrated with reciprocal influences upon each other. The system controls several glands within the body that secrete into the bloodstream chemical messengers called hormones which activate specific receptors in target organs which may show specific responses or may themselves be stimulated to produce other hormones and which in turn act upon other organs including the brain.

Secretion of many of these hormones is regulated by trophic hormones released from the pituitary gland which has a significant function in integrating the release of dozens of other hormones within the body. This highly complex chemical regulation system is itself regulated by the CNS and in particular the hypothalamus and limbic system which are structures involved in the regulation of emotional and motivational states. The endocrine system is itself critically involved in basic biological functions including sexual differentiation and reproduction, metabolism and growth, emotional activation and reactions to stressors. It would be impossible to review all the different neuroendocrine actions that exist within the body, but one example of its actions is the reaction to stress (this is discussed further in Chapter 3).

In humans there exists next to each kidney the adrenal gland which is made up of an outer cortex and an inner core, the adrenal medulla. Both of these are involved in the body's reaction to stressors. The adrenal medulla is innervated by the ANS and releases adrenalin and noradrenalin into the bloodstream. These circulating hormones prepare the body for action by increasing cardiac output and stimulating respiration. It has been found in both laboratory studies and real-life situations that psychosocial stressors such as facing danger, working under time pressure or admission to hospital cause increased output of adrenalin and noradrenalin. It may be that the extent of this response varies between individuals according to how they react to environmental demands, and it has been suggested that this differential response or reactivity may be associated with the development of certain diseases such as coronary heart disease (Manuck, 1994).

The neuroendocrine system has long-acting influences upon the body. Once they have been released, hormones can circulate and have effects over substantial periods of time. Some act on receptors in the brain and influence behaviour directly; others have indirect influences via feedback from internal organs. The amounts of hormones circulating change in response to psychological influences, and at the same time it has been established that dysfunction of neuroendocrine systems such as the hypothalamic pituitary adrenocorticoid axis is associated with the incidence of a variety of diseases and illnesses (Chrousos and Gold, 1996). For example, the opportunity to control an aversive stressor in rats influences the extent and duration of release of stress hormones by the pituitary-adrenal system (Dantzer, 1989). Experimental studies with animals have shown that stress-induced increases of corticosteroid release are associated with the suppression of immune system activity (Cox and Mackay, 1982). In human beings, these same psychoendocrine mechanisms are implicated in the growth of some tumours such as breast cancer (Stoll, 1988). It may be speculated therefore that between prolonged exposure to psychosocial stressors and development of cancer there exist links which may depend upon neural and neuroendocrine mechanisms and their influence upon immunocompetence (Ben Nation *et al.*, 1991; Cella and Holland, 1988).

The human immune system exists to protect the body against infection and diseases. Protection against harmful bacteria and viruses is provided by barriers including, for example, the skin and various mucous membranes of the mouth and nose as well as by active immunological processes including secretion of chemicals that can detect and inactivate pathogens, and activation of antibodies to give specific resistance to particular diseases. The immune system is continuously active but its effectiveness is sensitive to psychological influences including, for example, the effects of psychosocial stressors (Koolhaas and Bohus, 1989). The relationship between psychological factors and the function of the immune system has been brought into prominence recently by the research upon Acquired Immune Deficiency Syndrome (AIDS), which shows that the immunosuppressive effect of the Human Immunodeficiency Virus (HIV) is influenced by co-factors including experienced or perceived stress (see Chapter 10). Similarly, there is strong evidence that psychoimmunological influences are involved in the development and progression of cancers such as breast cancer (Cox, 1988; Stoll, 1988). There are indications too that recurrent infections with the genital herpes virus are related to changes in immune system function and those changes are themselves associated with experienced life stresses (Kemeny *et al.*, 1989). Though much more research is needed into the precise mechanisms involved, it is plausible that the competence of the immune system for resisting infection and disease is influenced by psychological processes and states such as stress, depression, major life events such as bereavement and even minor daily hassles such as your car breaking down (Evans, Chapter 3, discusses further the significance of psychoneuroimmunology and health).

Recording psychophysiological responses

Psychophysiology is concerned with the influence of psychological processes or changes in behaviour upon physiological responses. It has played a significant role in the development of health psychology. Its methods depend upon measuring responses during ongoing behaviours in the performance of challenging tasks such as solving problems, learning, and so on. The techniques used to collect physiological data during these and other behaviours are often, though not always, non-invasive. Psychophysiological data are correlates of behaviour and can be used to index psychological processes such as attention, fear or stress. However, the data can be used more productively to identify the processes linking physiology and behaviour (Obrist, 1981; Phillips, 1987). Only if the data are used in this way does psychophysiology as a discipline have significance for health psychology. The psychobiological approach demands that investigators move beyond simple assertions of the type, for example, that 'psychosocial stress causes hypertension' to true explanations that identify the processes involved in translating the impact of exposure to psychosocial stressors to disease states such as hypertension. This is more demanding, since it involves much more than simply identifying psychophysiological correlates of hypertension but is all the more rewarding when successful, as the elegant studies of Obrist (1981) have clearly demonstrated.

Psychophysiological recording techniques have been developed that allow quantification of physiological responses of many different kinds including central nervous system activity (individual nerve responses, the electroencephalogram, or EEG), autonomic system activity (for example, heart rate), endocrine responses such as the blood levels of circulating stress hormones, and indices of immune system function such as level of immunoglobulin in saliva. Each of these clearly requires specialised recording techniques whose description is beyond the scope of this discussion. Fortunately there are many good introductory texts that give an outline of the techniques involved in the measurement of these and other psychophysiological responses (Andreassi, 1980; Hassett, 1978) as well as comprehensive volumes that should be consulted by anyone wishing to make use of these techniques (Coles *et al.*, 1986; Martin and Venables, 1980). Some basic principles of recording are outlined below.

Recording bioelectric responses

Though the particular techniques used vary for different response systems, certain general features are common to all. These are illustrated in Figure 2.2 below. The measurement of bioelectric signals can depend upon direct recording, indirect recording, or the recording of transduced bioelectric signals. The differences concern the origins of the signals to be measured. Direct bioelectric signals originate in living tissues as a result of metabolic activity, and suitable electrodes placed on or near to those tissues detect those signals as electrical potentials. Good examples of this type of signal include the electroencephalogram which arises from cortical tissues, the electrocardiogram recorded from the heart, and the electromyogram recorded from skeletal muscle fibres. Indirect signals are recorded indirectly from tissues by, for example, measuring the resistance offered by the skin to passage of a mild electric current presented via attached electrodes (skin resistance). Other signals are physical and non-electrical in origin, for example, pressure or temperature, and special devices called transducers must be used to convert the physical signal into an electrical equivalent before they are recorded.

Once detected via electrodes or transducers the electrical signals must generally be amplified, since their magnitudes are small, many in the range of millivolts but some such as EEG measures in the microvolt range. In addition to simple amplification there may be further processing of the signals using electronic devices such as filters, integrators and rectifiers to isolate further the signal and to eliminate artefacts that can arise from the recording techniques. Once

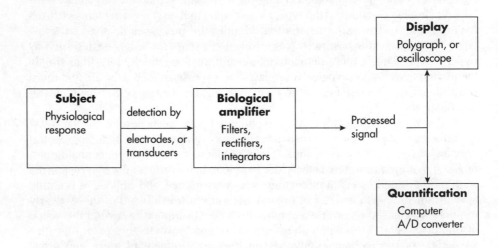

Figure 2.2 Generalised features of a psychophysiological recording and measurement system

processed, the signal is then available for display which may be in real time using an instrument called the oscilloscope, or as a permanent written record on a paper chart by use of the device called the polygraph (literally 'multiple writer') which allows several response recordings to be displayed simultaneously on a single chart. For most applications it is usually necessary to quantify the changes occurring in the recorded signal. This may involve further processing such as the transformation of an analogue signal into a digital measure or sampling the response at fixed time intervals. Most quantification systems these days are based upon microcomputers with purpose-written software packages. The basic assumption underlying the psychophysiological approach is that changes observed in the recorded signals correspond to psychological processes or behaviour that have significance for the subject or patient.

Ambulatory recordings

The system for recording bioelectrical responses from living tissues described briefly above is employed in laboratory- and clinic-based investigations. Unfortunately it may be the case that subjects' or patients' responses in the laboratory or clinic do not compare to their reactions in other settings such as their work or home environments. This limitation has prompted the development of portable recording devices based upon instruments, using either radio-telemetry or portable data storage by cassette tapes or small microprocessors, that can be worn by individuals during their everyday lives. Considerable progress has been made with these devices in recent years and there are now several ambulatory monitoring systems available. They have been used with some success to record responses over long periods of time during patients' everyday lives including their home and work environments (Turpin, 1985). The techniques have been used with some success, for example, to monitor changes in heart rates of patients who experience a sudden onset of uncontrollable and unaccountable attacks of panic (panic disorder). In this context the technique has shown that the attacks are accompanied and perhaps preceded by sudden acceleration of heart rate above normal levels suggesting that panic may arise from internal autonomic sensations which the person interprets in a catastrophic manner (Taylor *et al.*, 1986).

Biochemical recordings

As pointed out in the first section of this chapter, psychophysiology is not only concerned with nervous system responses. Equally important are the responses of the endocrine and immune systems and special biochemical techniques have been developed to measure the responses of these systems (Ader, 1981; Christie and Woodman, 1980). In some cases the biochemical measures provide data that are additional or complementary to those from electrophysiological recordings. In others such as diabetes, the biochemical methods used to monitor the blood glucose response are essential for understanding the nature of the disorder and the opportunities for treatment.

Biochemical methods depend upon the analysis of one or more of the body fluids – saliva, blood, urine or sweat. These contain a variety of chemicals including salts such as sodium or potassium, metabolites including glucose, hormones such as adrenalin or noradrenalin, and indicators of the competence of the immune system such as immunoglobulin.

The choice of fluid for analysis depends upon which chemical is to be screened. Analysis of chemicals from blood is a popular method since blood levels show the current status of metabolic function, unlike urine analysis which shows only the products of previous metabolic function. However, for psychophysiological studies blood analysis is not always appropriate since the techniques of collection – involving syringe and needle or pinprick – may themselves act as a stressor causing changes in biochemical reactions for at least some subjects. Collection of urine is a less stressful alternative but again there are problems. The constituents of urine vary considerably during the day and analyses may require collection of total urine output over twenty-four hours rather than analysis of a single sample. Clearly this can be problematic for subject and experimenter alike. Recently, saliva has become a popular fluid for analysis. Salts, some hormones and immune system indicators (see Chapter 3) can all be readily measured from saliva though again there are procedural difficulties associated with its collection that can influence the analyses of content and confound interpretation of the data. The fluid secreted by sweat glands offers a further source of biochemical data, though to date it has been less investigated than other body fluids.

Psychophysiology and health psychology

The definition of health psychology given in Chapter 1 emphasises the opportunities of psychology for promoting health, preventing and treating illness, identifying the aetiology of diseases, as well as informing health care policies. Psychophysiology makes direct contributions to understanding the aetiologies of diseases and suggests interventions that may be used to prevent and treat illnesses. The knowledge it brings about the links between psychosocial factors and disease indirectly assists strategies for health promotion and the planning of health care policies. Its contributions, however, must be integrated with those from other types of psychological enquiry including social and cognitive approaches. The challenge facing health psychologists is to develop models that can take account of these different perspectives upon health and accommodate data derived from these different disciplines.

Epidemiological studies have established that illnesses are not randomly distributed. Psychosocial factors such as socioeconomic status, social mobility and unemployment have been shown to be reliably associated with the incidence of several diseases such as coronary heart disease (Marmot *et al.*, 1978). Similarly, psychosocial factors encountered in individuals' workplaces such as their authority over decisions and the opportunity to use and develop skills, which contribute to their decision latitude and sense of personal control, are associated with physiological responses such as changes in blood pressure and may contribute to ill health. Broadly speaking, it has been found that the more decision latitude at work the better the workers' health (Theorell, 1989). Clinical studies have concentrated upon the relationships between adverse or significant life events and illness and found associations between life events and psychiatric disorders such as depression (Brown and Harris, 1986). Other studies indicate that even the relatively minor life events referred to as 'uplifts' or 'hassles' predict measures of immune system function and susceptibility to minor infections such as the common cold (Evans *et al.*, 1993). At an individual level research into the links between the Type A behaviour pattern and coronary heart disease (see Chapter 11) finds increased risk for those individuals displaying the behavioural characteristics that describe the Type A pattern. The demonstrations of these associations between psychosocial variables and illness or risk of disease pose fundamental questions for health psychology. How is it that psychosocial factors influence patterns of illness and disease within a population? Why is one individual but not another vulnerable to the effect of a particular psychosocial factor? These questions are discussed further in Chapter 16. Ultimately, however, the links between psychosocial factors and disease must depend upon changes in neurological and biochemical responses. The challenge for psychophysiology is to identify the mechanisms involved in maintaining good health and to identify the processes that give rise to illness.

Biopsychosocial models of disease

Within health psychology one model that has enjoyed considerable popularity is the 'stress-diathesis' model (Steptoe, 1989) which may be called a 'biopsychosocial model' since it emphasises the interactive effect of environmental and individual vulnerability (genetic and psychological characteristics) factors upon health.

According to this model, psychological and physical threats present demands upon an individual's resources and capacity for coping which give rise to physiological reactions involving the ANS, endocrine and immune systems of the body. The effects include both short-term and long-term components and these may have consequences for health depending upon the individual's predisposition or vulnerability to adverse effects. The physiological responses observed themselves may be entirely appropriate reactions to the demands faced and yet still pose threats to health. Sterling and Eyer (1988) have proposed the term 'allostasis' to describe the matching to demand of physiological resources that is provoked by the environment–individual interaction. Whether or not some or all of these responses have an effect on health depends upon the individual's biological predisposition or diathesis. Vulnerable individuals develop chronic allostatic reactions such as reduced immunocompetence, or exaggerated sympathetic activation of the ANS, or increased secretion of adrenal hormones. Physiological reactions of these types have been implicated in the development of many disease states, including cancers, cardiovascular diseases, and susceptibility to infections. According to the stress-diathesis model there are several stages which lead finally to the development of a disease state. It is the interaction between the individual and the environment that is significant in giving rise to the necessary physiological reactions but it is the individual's biological vulnerability that finally allows those reactions to become translated into illness or disease.

Psychophysiological treatment of illness

In addition to providing the methods for unravelling the mechanisms involved in the aetiology of disease states, psychophysiology can also contribute to their treatment. The knowledge gained from psychophysiological studies of illnesses can be used to develop clinical interventions to prevent or treat those disorders. Steptoe (1989) has described how behavioural medicine has adopted interventions based upon the stress-diathesis model of disease. The interventions may act at different stages of the disease process. Thus, cognitive interventions may be used to modify an individual's psychosocial resources. If it were confirmed that hypertension develops as a result of exaggerated cardiovascular reactivity (see Chapter 12), then interventions designed to reduce reactivity in vulnerable individuals, for example through relaxation training or biofeedback (see below), might well be effective. Alternatively, interventions may be adopted that alter an individual's biological vulnerability, for example exercise training. At the moment the effectiveness of these interventions is still being evaluated. Initial indications provide cause for optimism and, as Steptoe (1989) has pointed out, 'The treatment of medical disorders is an important aspect of contemporary clinical psychophysiology and the methods that have been developed are likely to have a major impact on health care in the future' (p. 233). Within behavioural medicine, biofeedback is one clinical technique among many others which have been introduced as interventions for health disorders (see Steptoe, 1989).

Biofeedback

Biofeedback refers to training procedures used to modify physiological responses or patterns of physiological responses and has become widely used as a clinical intervention that aims to achieve self-regulation of maladaptive responses and disordered states. It has been defined as 'a set of procedures that enable the individual to control some specified physiological process by providing an external cue or monitor to indicate the activity of that process' (Phillips, 1979).

Biofeedback developed from experimental learning studies that involved training animals to modify physiological responses for negative or positive reinforcement. These studies implied that, contrary to previous belief, *all* responses, including those governed by the autonomic nervous system, could be brought under voluntary control (Miller, 1969).

Principles of biofeedback training

Studies of biofeedback began in the late 1960s when it was shown that certain physiological responses which are regulated by the autonomic nervous system and

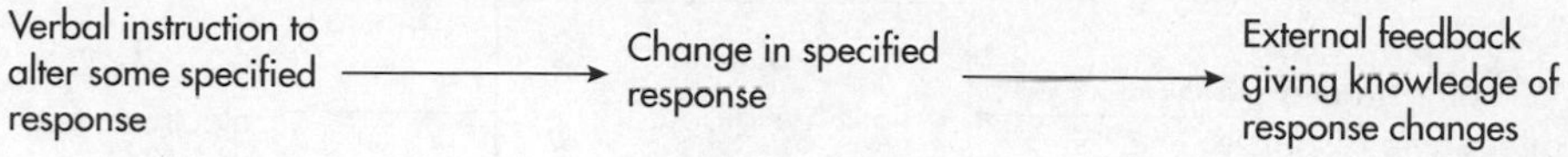

Verbal instruction to alter some specified response   ⟶   Change in specified response   ⟶   External feedback giving knowledge of response changes

Figure 2.3 Biofeedback – the voluntary control paradigm

which previously had been assumed to be outside voluntary control could be modified and brought under instructed control in human subjects, i.e. learned as a result of training that provided information or knowledge of results about the response. Such training became known as the voluntary control paradigm (Figure 2.3).

There are four essential elements of biofeedback training

1   *Instruction.* An appropriate verbal instruction is given that identifies a particular response to be altered, for example 'try to lower your blood pressure' or 'slow the rate at which your heart is beating'. This instruction indicates to the subject both the physiological system to be regulated and a directional requirement (raise/lower, speed/slow, increase/decrease) for the response that is to be modified.

2   *Patient/subject motivation.* For biofeedback to be successful it is necessary that the subject should be motivated to try to achieve the changes in response indicated by the instructions given. Assuming that the patient, or subject in an experimental study, is motivated, attempts will be made to alter the response.

3   Some means of *recording and monitoring* the physiological response specified by the instructions to the subject. This is fairly straightforward, since many of the changes in bodily responses are electrical in nature, for example, involving changes in electrical potential or resistance, and these can be recorded via electrodes attached to the surface of the skin. Other responses may involve physical and non-electrical changes. Blood pressure, for example, involves variations in pressure within a closed circulatory system. In instances of this type, however, other devices called transducers are used to convert the physical changes into electrical signals. The techniques for measuring a wide range of physiological responses including responses measured from the skin (electrodermal activity), cardiovascular system such as blood pressure and heart rate, patterns of brainwave activity, gastro-intestinal responses, and patterns of muscular activity (electromyographic responses) are well established (Martin and Venables, 1980). There are available commercially many devices for measuring these responses and using the responses to generate external feedback signals.

4   *Feedback signal.* The electrical signals recorded via electrodes or transducers are used to generate an external signal such as a sound that varies in loudness or pitch, or clicks whose rate fluctuates, or a display of several lights where the number lit alters. Patients or subjects are told to attend to the external signal and informed that the changes indicated by the signal will provide them with the knowledge of whether or not they are successfully controlling the response specified by the initial instructions.

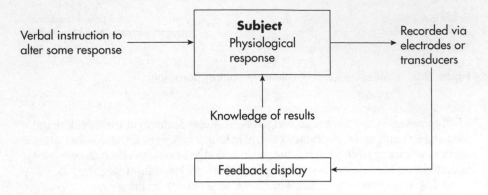

Figure 2.4 The elements of biofeedback training

The elements of biofeedback training are summarised in Figure 2.4

Clinical applications of biofeedback training are based upon the voluntary control paradigm by which an individual is able to self-regulate some physiological response or state without needing further to rely upon the external feedback signal. In some way the individual has to learn to recognise and achieve the desired goal through his or her own internalised control processes. The mechanisms by which such control becomes realised are still poorly understood and, though several theoretical models have been suggested, there is no agreement about how control becomes established. Whatever the mechanisms are, the finding that biofeedback training can be used to train self-regulation is a well-replicated and consistent finding for many different physiological responses. As a consequence biofeedback has been adopted as a clinical intervention for disorders that involve dis-regulation of physiological activity.

Clinical applications of biofeedback

Biofeedback has been used in the treatment of a huge number of clinical disorders (McManus, 1996). In some instances the rationale is clear, but in others reasons for its use appear, at best, speculative. Further problems exist when examining the literature on the clinical efficacy of biofeedback, including the fact that the training techniques themselves differ considerably between studies on a number of dimensions, for example, number and duration of training sessions, type and amount of feedback given, support by additional exercises, and so on. Moreover, the methods used to assess the effect of training also differ considerably from uncontrolled single case study designs, single treatment group studies with before and after designs, to larger scale controlled group outcome studies (Blanchard and Young, 1974). It is the latter that are desirable for making a true assessment of biofeedback's clinical effectiveness. Unfortunately these designs have been rarely used and much of the clinical literature reports studies that have employed weak methodological designs, which limits the conclusions that can be drawn.

Two quite distinct methods of applying biofeedback as a clinical intervention can be identified. The first of these may be called 'direct symptom control'. In this case some clearly identifiable target symptom or response is identified as requiring modification and the biofeedback training is based exclusively upon that single feature. A good example of the direct symptom control approach is the treatment of elevated blood pressure in the patient with hypertension by training, based on a feedback signal generated from monitoring the patient's blood pressure. In this case the response selected for training may be regarded as the pre-eminent symptom of the disorder. Other examples of the direct control approach include feedback of patterns of brainwave activity (EEG) for treatment of epileptic seizures, feedback of muscle activity (EMG) for various neuromuscular disorders including muscle spasticity or paralysis (Jahanshahi and Marsden, 1989), feedback of heart rate for cardiac arrhythmias (Pickering and Miller, 1977) and feedback of temperature for treatment of Raynaud's Disease, a distressing disorder characterised by vasoconstriction of peripheral blood vessels in fingers or toes precipitated by emotional stress (Freedman and Ianni, 1985).

The second type of application involves the use of biofeedback for training relaxation to achieve a generalised change in physiological state rather than direct control of a single response. During the last 15 years it is this approach that has become most widespread and it has been used for the treatment of a bewilderingly diverse range of disorders. For these applications the choice of which physiological response is adopted to provide the external feedback signal is essentially arbitrary. All that is needed is a source of feedback that indicates an individual's state of general arousal or relaxation. Any response that varies according to these states would be appropriate. In practice, particular responses have been adopted at particular times including, in early studies, one type of brainwave activity known as the alpha rhythm, and more recently electrodermal activity and EMG activity.

Relaxation training has become one of the central interventions of behavioural medicine (Blumenthal, 1985). Its use is predicated upon the assumption that the disorder being treated is stress-related and that it is accompanied by a generalised state of sympathetic nervous system activation which maintains the disorder. Relaxation training is used to restore normal regulation by eliminating the maladaptive state and replacing it by an antagonistic condition described as 'cultivated low arousal' (Stoyva and Budzynski, 1974) in which parasympathetic nervous responses are dominant.

Various relaxation methods including progressive muscle relaxation, yoga, meditation, autogenic training as well as biofeedback have been used to produce changes in autonomic and skeletal responses in the direction of parasympathetic control and reduced muscle tension. It is often assumed that the mechanisms by which they have their effect are the same. Yet this may not be so; it is not clear that meditation, for example, produces reductions of autonomic and endocrine responses although muscular relaxation training does (see Steptoe, 1989). Biofeedback may be used in isolation to train relaxation responses or in combination with other relaxation techniques as part of a treatment package (Phillips, 1979).

Biofeedback may be used to train relaxation by self-regulation of physiological responses. The rationale for this approach is based on the assumption that learned changes in one response system will be accompanied by parallel changes of other response systems. Thus lowering of heart rate, for example, will be accompanied by similar reductions in other autonomic responses. If this assumption of generalisation is appropriate, then in principle it does not matter which response system is employed to generate the feedback signal given to the patient. Early clinical studies frequently used feedback derived from a particular frequency of brainwave activity measured as the electroencephalogram (EEG), called EEG alpha activity. EEG alpha activity is frequently seen during meditational states (Elson *et al.*, 1977) and it was assumed that alpha enhancement would promote the relaxation state. However, while biofeedback can be used effectively to modify EEG activity there is no evidence that alpha activity is associated with any specific therapeutic benefits nor that, in itself, it produces generalised relaxation. In recent years most studies of biofeedback training for relaxation have adopted EMG feedback as the preferred technique.

Many stress-related disorders are accompanied by tension in specific muscles or throughout the skeletal musculature and at first sight it would seem appropriate to provide EMG biofeedback training to reduce that activity. However, there exists again an implicit assumption that generalisation will occur, and that may be unwarranted. Most EMG biofeedback treatments generate the feedback signal from electrodes recording the activity of a single muscle, the frontalis muscle of the forehead. Patients are encouraged to learn to decrease tension within this muscle in the belief that the effect will generalise to other muscle groups in the body. Empirical studies have found that this is not so. For example, Alexander (1975) found no evidence of generalisation from reduction in frontalis EMG to levels either in the forearm or leg. A further problem is that even where successful reductions of EMG activity are trained, these are not inevitably accompanied by subjective sensations of relaxation (Shedivy and Kleinman, 1977). Clearly, unless the patient 'feels' relaxed, whatever changes in EMG activity have actually occurred, the treatment has little hope of success. Finally, there is no guarantee that relaxation training based on EMG biofeedback will generalise from the clinic to real-life situations where real or potential stressors are encountered. Even after prolonged training such transfer may not occur, and there is little evidence to support the notion that generalisation of effects will occur following EMG training based on recordings from one specific muscle site such as the frontalis muscle (Carlson *et al.*, 1983).

Despite these serious reservations there is evidence that EMG biofeedback training can be beneficial for some disorders and particularly in the treatment of various forms of pain (see Chapter 6). The success of biofeedback in these instances, however, may not be related to changes in physiological state *per se*, but rather to changes in the cognitive activity of patients. For example, biofeedback training may alter patients' perceptions of pain and their beliefs in their own efficacy in controlling the pain (Andrasik and Holroyd, 1983; Flor *et al.*, 1983). These cognitions may be quite independent of measured changes in the response being recorded and monitored during training.

Other forms of biofeedback, including thermal and electrodermal biofeedback, are also employed for relaxation training. Again the rationale underlying their use is suspect and their effectiveness is doubtful. In general, the use of biofeedback to train generalised relaxation does not offer any specific advantage over the more traditional techniques such as cognitive therapy or muscle relaxation. What it does do is to focus attention upon the patients 'doing something for themselves'. This non-specific characteristic of biofeedback training is highly self-motivating and may be helpful for achieving the cognitive changes that are associated with its effectiveness in treating headaches and other types of pain (Arena *et al.*, 1995).

The existence of these two very different types of application presents something of a puzzle, or what Yates (1980) has referred to as the 'paradox of biofeedback training', as it raises a question about what type of influence the training is having upon the physiological systems involved and the accompanying learning processes. Is biofeedback a means of training specific control where the specificity of the trained response improves with practice? Or is it simply a means of signalling to an individual their general state of activation? If it is the former, then applications for relaxation seem inappropriate, but if the latter, applications for specific control of individual responses would be excluded. Insufficient consideration of the nature of the mechanisms involved in biofeedback has undoubtedly hindered the development of successful clinical applications for biofeedback training.

Biofeedback and reactions to stressors

Though biofeedback training has been used as a clinical treatment primarily to teach individuals to control and regulate the symptoms evident on an enduring basis within some existing disorder, it may also be used in anticipation of reactions to stressors. All individuals facing potentially painful experiences and other aversive events show psychophysiological reactions that include autonomic activation. However, some individuals show greater reactivity than others and exaggerated autonomic reactivity has been implicated in the aetiology of certain disorders including hypertension (see Chapter 10). It is possible that biofeedback training could be used to reduce an individual's reactivity to aversive events or situations, in which case it might be a valuable intervention that offers protection against future disease.

Feedback training is often offered to individuals in a relatively stress-free environment, for example, while resting in a quiet clinic. This is entirely appropriate if the patient's condition involves tonic maladjustment of some response that endures and represents a sustained dis-regulation. Some individuals however may only experience their maladaptive response as a reaction to or anticipation of particular events or situations. For example, fear of pain or anxiety about public speaking might provoke an exaggerated reaction that is so severe that the individual finds it disabling. In these circumstances biofeedback training could be given to allow patients to reduce their symptoms on those specific occasions when they encounter their particular environmental stressor. Used in this way, biofeedback is analogous to the use of a beta-blocker such as propranolol to control cardiac reactivity during anxiety, but of course, being a behavioural treatment it does not suffer from the adverse side-effects that so often accompany use of these medications.

A number of studies have been reported which indicate that biofeedback may be useful in such circumstances. Studies by Sirota *et al.* (1976) showed that volunteer subjects who were given heart rate feedback were able to acquire control over heart rate reactions in anticipation of electric shocks applied to the forearm. Significantly, self-ratings of the painfulness of the experienced shocks corresponded to changes in heart rate, i.e. where reductions of heart rate were trained during anticipation of the shock these were accompanied by lower ratings of the subsequently experienced pain. A further study by Victor *et al.* (1978) examined the effects of biofeedback training upon subjects' ability to regulate heart rate whilst experiencing a painful aversive experience in the form of the cold pressor test. This involves immersing the hand up to the wrist in a freezing mixture of ice and water for thirty seconds. This experience reliably provokes cardiac acceleration and subjective reports of pain. Subjects were given appropriate feedback and asked to control their heart rate during immersion of the hand in the freezing mixture. It was found that even during the painful task, subjects could regulate both increases or decreases of heart rate that were greater than changes shown by subjects who were not given feedback. In addition, self-reports of pain corresponded to heart rate changes: those subjects increasing their heart rate reported the highest levels of pain and those regulating decreases in heart rate reported the lowest levels of pain.

Biofeedback training is not unique in allowing individuals to reduce reactivity to experimental challenges. Other techniques, including relaxation training and muscle relaxation, are also effective in decreasing reactions to environmental stressors (Connor, 1974; Puente and Beiman, 1980). However, the effects achieved through biofeedback training do not seem to be produced by some non-specific relaxation-type effect since the reductions in reactivity observed are specific to the feedback used. For example, Gatchel *et al.* (1978) trained subjects to use EMG feedback recorded from the frontalis muscle to reduce EMG activity in anticipation of mild electric shock. However, though EMG activity was successfully reduced there were neither similar reductions for heart rate nor electrodermal responses. This of course is consistent with the view that biofeedback is most effective for training direct symptom control and that it may be less effective for producing generalised relaxation effects.

Is biofeedback effective clinically?

When first introduced, biofeedback training was hailed as a panacea and was adopted enthusiastically by clinicians with little regard for its underlying mechanisms and applied to what in retrospect seems to be a bewildering variety of behavioural, psychological and psychiatric disorders as varied as alcoholism, sexual dysfunction, or obsessive-compulsive behaviours (see Yates (1980) for comprehensive coverage of these and other applications). The rationales for many of these applications were often unclear and the clinical designs used were poorly controlled. Not surprisingly, reports began to emerge of the 'failures' of biofeedback and the question posed was whether biofeedback represents 'a promise unfulfilled' (Blanchard and Young, 1974). Two decades later, we can take a more measured view of its clinical effectiveness.

Methodological issues

The point of biofeedback training is that the provision of feedback, an external signal that has meaning and gives knowledge of results, should influence the patient's ability to self-regulate some specified response or state. In addition to this aspect, however, biofeedback training also inevitably involves non-specific effects upon the patient. Merely the fact that the patient is involved in a clinical programme may in itself lead both the patient and the clinician to expect beneficial changes to follow. Those expectancies are not specific to biofeedback and may accompany other quite different types of treatment. Yet they alone could account for any change in the patient's condition quite independently of the specific effects offered by the feedback. It has been suggested that non-specific or 'placebo' effects could account entirely for any beneficial clinical gains that result from biofeedback training (Stroebel and Glueck, 1973). The power of placebos in clinical settings is well documented and biofeedback training fulfils many of the criteria that characterise placebos. It is innovative, impressive in its technology, and involves investment of time and effort on the part of both patient and clinician (Miller and Dworkin, 1977).

In terms of the outcome for the patient, it may not matter whether any clinical improvement results from specific or non-specific effects, but from the point of view of understanding the mechanisms that underlie clinical success it is important to distinguish between them. This can be done by adopting appropriate clinical designs when evaluating biofeedback training. This issue has been well aired by Blanchard and Young (1974). They identify five types of design ranging from, at the weakest level, anecdotal case reports to the most powerful design of controlled group outcome studies. These compare the effects of biofeedback training given to a homogeneous group of patients with the effects of a control condition that gives equal attention but no feedback training to an equivalent group of patients suffering from the same disorder. The non-specific effects should be the same for both groups but the experimental group has the additional benefit of the specific influences of feedback training. Unfortunately, few biofeedback studies have used this powerful design and studies with less adequate designs are often difficult to assess, since the specific and non-specific effects of training are confounded.

In addition to design factors, Blanchard (1979) has identified other dimensions which he argues can be used to evaluate clinical applications of biofeedback. Taken together, they can be viewed as indicators of the extent to which the outcome of biofeedback training has clinical relevance and applicability for the patient's life. Blanchard makes the simple but often overlooked point that the changes in response or symptom can be statistically significant and yet still lack clinical significance. For example, if biofeedback training reliably reduced blood pressure by one or two millimetres of mercury the effect might be statistically significant, though it could hardly be claimed to have altered the patient's condition to any significant degree. Another way of measuring success is in terms of the number of patients treated who show clinical improvement. It may be that biofeedback is effective for some individuals but not for others. When assessing its effect overall, it is important to know what proportion of patients with a particular disorder might be expected to benefit from this form of treatment.

A further problem concerns the transfer of training. The outcome of biofeedback training is often measured immediately following treatment in a clinic. Beneficial effects of biofeedback training may be reliably found in the clinic but the outcome cannot be considered successful unless the effect transfers to the patient's home and work environments and endures over a substantial period of time. Evaluation of these factors requires testing in real-life settings, with follow-up studies to assess the long-term effects of training. Again these procedures have been frequently neglected in clinical biofeedback studies.

When judging its clinical effectiveness it should not be forgotten that biofeedback training is often applied to disorders that have proved highly intractable to other forms of treatment. It is unfair to measure the absolute rate of success; a more appropriate measure is its efficacy relative to alternative treatments. In making this comparison, there are several factors apart from the treatment outcome that are relevant, though that is obviously the most important. Other factors which may also be considered include the efficiency, convenience, cost-effectiveness, generality and durability of the treatment. Each of these can be assessed, though all too frequently they have not. In a review of the relative benefits of biofeedback compared with relaxation training, Silver and Blanchard (1978) concluded that for those disorders where comparisons have been made such as hypertension, migraine, tension headaches and pain, 'there is no consistent advantage for one form of treatment over the other'.

Biofeedback in combined therapies

Much consideration has been given to whether or not biofeedback is effective as a treatment for various disorders. It has been suggested that some applications have been successful, though not all. Evaluations of its clinical efficacy have usually considered biofeedback as an *alternative* to other treatments. A more meaningful approach, however, might be to examine the extent to which biofeedback can be used as an adjunct to other treatments within combined treatment programmes. The nature of biofeedback training suits it very well for combining with other types of treatment such as muscle relaxation or autogenic training (Phillips, 1979), or drug treatments to reduce the amount of medication required, for example in the treatment of anxiety (Lavallee *et al.*, 1977), or in more comprehensive treatment packages which contain several different elements such as that developed by Patel and her colleagues (Patel and North, 1975) for treating hypertension (see Chapter 10). As a part of combined treatment approaches, biofeedback is assured an enduring role in the treatment of disorders that have a psychophysiological component. When applied to well-defined psychophysiological maladaptations it can make a valuable contribution within combined treatment packages.

A patient has been complaining of frequent tension headaches for several months and no treatment has altered his symptom reporting. His clinician decides to use biofeedback to treat the patient's experience of headaches.

- What type of biofeedback should the clinician use? Why?

After ten sessions of biofeedback the patient reports that although he still experiences occasional headaches the frequency of occurrence is greatly reduced. His clinician decides that the use of biofeedback has been clinically effective and resolves to employ biofeedback in the treatment of all other patients complaining of tension headaches.

- Why might the clinician's positive evaluation of the effectiveness of biofeedback be overly optimistic?
- What additional evidence might she seek before judging its effectiveness?
- Are there any other treatments that might be used alongside biofeedback in the treatment of tension headaches?

Key point summary

- Nervous, endocrine and immune systems together regulate the physiological functions of the body.
- Dysfunction within and between these systems can result in ill health.
- Psychophysiology provides the techniques for measuring how these systems are working.
- Clinical psychophysiology aims to develop models that explain how and under what circumstances dysfunctions arise and become translated into illness.
- Psychophysiological techniques such as biofeedback can be used for treatment of a wide variety of health disorders, especially those that are stress related and which are characterised by a distinct psychophysiological symptom(s).
- Biofeedback may be used most effectively as part of a combined treatment package.

Further reading

Ader, R. (ed.) (1981) *Psychoneuroimmunology*. New York, Academic Press.

Carroll, D. (1984) *Biofeedback in Practice*. London, Longman. This book provides a readable and critical account of the applications of biofeedback.

Martin, I. and Venables, P. H. (eds) (1980) *Techniques in Psychophysiology*. Chichester, John Wiley & Sons. This book gives a comprehensive account of the methods and applications of psychophysiology.

Thompson, R. F. (1985) *The Brain. An Introduction to Neuroscience*. New York, W. H. Freeman & Co.

Van Toller, C. (1979) *The Nervous Body: An Introduction to the Autonomic Nervous System and Behaviour*. Chichester, Wiley and Sons. These excellent books describe the organisation of body systems.

Stress and coping

Philip Evans

Introduction

Psychological stress is commonly thought of as the great modern disease. Moreover, not only is it labelled by convention a 'bad thing' in its own right, but it is increasingly assumed to make us more vulnerable to other diseases, mental and physical. If even half of the commonly held beliefs about stress were true, it would be enough to give it a prime place among the concepts of interest to health psychologists.

If stress is taken to be so pervasive in modern industrialised societies, it is not surprising that there is also a great deal of interest in understanding how we can limit its impact; in other words, how we may cope with it better. Stress, coping with stress and managing stress are all issues that are addressed almost daily somewhere in the popular media. But, from a scientific perspective, are we able to define stress, and can we scientifically examine the claims that are made about it? These are the key questions to be addressed in this chapter.

Empirical studies touching on stress and coping issues can be found in several chapters in this book. How do people react to the prospect of surgery? Does stress make people more vulnerable to coronary heart disease? How do diabetics and others with chronic disorders cope with the daily burden of extra demands that follow in the wake of the disorder? The focus of this chapter is more theoretical. It proposes structures for considering stress and coping issues; it raises and discusses methodological issues in researching the area; finally, it considers the richness, complexities and health implications of our biological response to stress, involving neural, neuroendocrine and immune systems.

A question of definition

Readers often, I suspect, find introductory sections concerned with definitions a trifle tedious, wanting to get straight into the factual content of a chapter. I have some sympathy, but in the case of stress there really are important definitional issues to be addressed. This is not to say that we need to tie up the construct of stress in a strait-jacket of rigorous usage criteria. We shall in any case find that it defies such attempts and is better left as something of an umbrella term. What is necessary, however, is to be aware of the definitional issues involved. The answers to even seemingly simple questions about the effects of stress are likely to begin with the judicious words: It all depends on what you mean by stress.

When people in an everyday sense use the word 'stress' in a psychological context they will often have one of two things in mind: either events in life that are happening or have happened *to* a person, or processes, mental or physical, which are happening or have happened *within* a person. In other words, people sometimes talk of responding to stress, or they sometimes talk of suffering it. Each is an acceptable usage of the word stress in the English language but each usage has important implications. In the discussions below, we shall colloquially refer to these usages as *stress outside* and *stress inside* respectively.

Stress outside

When people say they are under stress, they will point to various pressures at work, for example difficult deadlines or troubles at home, in order to make their use of the term 'stress' more concrete. In that sense the troubles are taken to be examples of stress. In an analogous way we may talk of structures, such as bridges, being subject to the stress of gale-force winds, extremes of temperature, or abnormal weight of traffic.

This seems at first glance to be a promising way of looking at psychological stress, and indeed it has given rise to much research in the area. In the language of research design it invites us to treat stress as an *independent variable* which we may observe or even manipulate with a view to specifying its effects on an organism. Thus a variety of factors from major disasters to minor hassles, from cognitive overload to sleep deprivation, from overcrowding to isolation, from electric shock to aversive noise, have been examined for their supposed stressful effects on behaviour.

Whether stress, as an independent variable, has been manipulated or merely measured is of course an important factor in interpreting such research, since an unambiguous cause–effect relationship between a supposed stressful experience and subsequent behaviour can only be properly shown in a genuine experiment which does manipulate stress. In the case of major or prolonged exposure to stress, such experiments have been largely confined to animals. However, by measuring several variables simultaneously and by carefully timing events, it has been possible to support causative hypotheses in relation to human beings whose natural exposure to stress has been systematically observed. Sophisticated work in this vein has the benefit of avoiding distressing work with animals, which is increasingly seen as ethically dubious and which, in any event, often presents problems in generalising to the human arena.

However, treating stress solely as an independent variable – something out there – has one rather serious drawback. It ignores the important point that different people may react differently to exactly the same so-called stressful event. Do we say that one person is stressed and the other not stressed? Or do we say that both are stressed but their reactions are different? If one person's behaviour were to indicate a very positive response to the so-called stressful experience, we may feel that it is stretching semantics to say that he or she has nevertheless been under stress. However, if we say that such a person has not been under stress, we are implicitly recognising that the meaning of the word stress resides, partly at least, inside the person. We shall now consider the notion that stress is to be defined as something inside the person.

Stress inside

Put in its strongest form, this view suggests that if we can measure a certain pattern of 'stressful' responses within a person, this is the sole criterion of whether or not that person has been 'stressed', regardless of the nature of the experience undergone. From this perspective, an apparently very positive life event may cause stress, or equally an apparently very negative life event may not do so. In a sense, this way of defining stress should take priority over external criteria, since investigations of stress as an independent external variable focus on just those sorts of variables which we normally may expect but not necessarily know will produce certain types of 'stressful' effect. If no evidence of 'stress inside' were ever to be forthcoming following exposure to a purported external source of stress, we can be fairly sure that such an external state of affairs would very soon not be viewed as stressful. However, the difficulty for the 'stress inside' view becomes one of specifying exactly what constitutes a stressful reaction.

With regard to the physiology of stress, we shall see in a later section of this chapter that to an extent it is possible to specify processes which can be identified as evidence of the occurrence of stress. The first major theory of stress as a physiological process was put forward by Selye (1956). Selye defined stress in terms of a general pattern of 'adaptive' responding, involving a number of neuroendocrine mechanisms, whose chronic activation ultimately led to the 'exhaustion' of the organism and an inability to cope with further challenge. The trouble with this kind of model, as we shall see, is that the assumed processes are not so general as might first be supposed. There are individual differences in the way people react physiologically to stress. Moreover, in the case of some physical sources of stress involving pain, for example, local physical responses can at the very least muddy the waters when it comes to identifying an assumed general pattern of physiological responding associated purely with something called stress.

It is of course theoretically possible to look for evidence of stress in what might conventionally be called a person's mental state: episodes of anxiety or depression, for example, which are more pronounced and long-lasting than the blips which occur on any baseline of ordinary mood states. In this case, however, there is a potential conceptual difficulty which arises: mental symptoms shade inevitably into episodes of what is conventionally labelled psychiatric illness, and such illness episodes have often been used by researchers as distinct dependent variables, in the aetiology of which stress itself is investigated as a factor.

All in all then, there seem to be problems in defining stress solely in terms of a range of specifiable external situations or in terms of internal responses to unspecified external stimuli. The approach of most modern researchers has been to adopt what might be called an interactionist position. Stress is seen as a transaction between the environment and the person and a good deal of emphasis is placed on how the person *perceives* the challenges which the environment presents. The perception of challenge is also taken as crucial to the business of *coping* (or failing to cope) with potentially stressful circumstances.

Coping and controlling

Many recent models of stress implicitly or explicitly see it as the outcome of a cognitive process in which a challenge or threat is first of all perceived, the ability to control the challenge or threat is assessed, and finally a computation

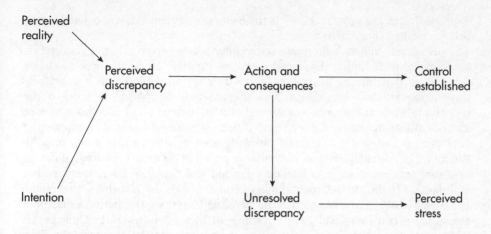

Perceived
reality

Perceived
discrepancy → Action and
consequences → Control
established

Intention → Unresolved
discrepancy → Perceived
stress

Figure 3.1 Cognitive control model of stress

Source: After Fisher (1986)

of discrepancy is made (Fisher, 1986, 1996). Stress is thus seen as a consequence of perceiving a 'deficit' picture: uncontrollability, or helplessness. An example of a simple 'control' model of this type is illustrated in Figure 3.1. Although such models are attractive in that they seem to have a potential for great generality, they do tend to replace one tricky concept (stress) with another (controllability). Of course that is quite legitimate. What it means, however, is that we must now address the issue of controllability in more depth.

Seligman (1975) wrote a book on 'Helplessness' which did much to stimulate interest in the consequences of an organism learning that it lacks control over events. Various stressful and depression-like symptoms were shown to be associated with learned helplessness across a variety of species.

The original work of Seligman and his colleagues had come from the animal laboratory, where it is relatively easy to define control in an exact way. Some overt behavioural response is usually 'instrumental' in avoiding, escaping, or otherwise mitigating the aversive event, usually electric shock. This kind of obvious control we shall term 'instrumental control'. In the case of human beings, however, instrumental control is only one of many kinds of more general control that people have, or at least believe they have. Let us begin with that last qualification: 'or believe they have'. Note that the model in Figure 3.1 refers not simply to *reality* and *discrepancy* but to *perceived reality* and *perceived discrepancy*. In the context of our current discussion, this means that the control a person actually has is unimportant: it is how much control people believe they have which really matters. This allows for all sorts of stress-reducing stratagems on the part of individuals. For example, someone may respond well to a potentially stressful situation if they believe that their prayers have prevented a worse tragedy happening. Superstitious behaviour can be rationalised by the agent as a form of 'magical' control, the main feature of which is the impossibility of falsification. However, we are still dealing here with a form of instrumental control, since the person involved is

51

supposedly making some response in the belief that certain aversive consequences will be avoided or mitigated.

However, human beings are often differentiated from other organisms on the basis of their highly developed cognitive capabilities. In the area of stress, this means that human beings can show diversity in response to a potentially threatening situation according to how they cognitively *appraise* it. Much of the pioneering work in this area was carried out by Lazarus and his colleagues (see Lazarus, 1974). In essence, they showed that physiological arousal prompted by exposure to a stressful film could be moderated by instructions given prior to the film. The instructions were deliberately varied in order to encourage different appraisal processes, such as intellectualisation and denial. If cognitive appraisal is important in the stress process, this of course raises the possibility that cognitive/behavioural interventions may be possible to reduce the harmful effects of stress in certain individuals. One example of this is discussed in Chapter 11, where cognitive/behavioural intervention has been used to try to modify the Type A behaviour pattern, a construct related to issues of stress and controllability which is associated with greater risk of coronary heart disease.

Thus appraisal processes can be seen as ways of controlling and coping with potential sources of stress. This also raises the issue of individual differences. Presumably people learn characteristic ways of appraising threats, which may in turn be fairly general across many areas of their lives, or alternatively may be fairly specific to certain domains. Although instructions, as used by Lazarus and his colleagues, may modify people's appraisals, we may suppose that ordinarily habitual appraisal strategies exist.

Individual differences also exist in the extent to which people appear to seek information about stressful circumstances. The link between information seeking and control seeking is not always simple. Information usually brings a measure of predictability. In regard to something like surgery, for example, the patient may learn when to expect certain types of pain, how long it will be likely to last, and so on. A distinct preference for information about the course of aversive procedures is the general finding, certainly in the large number of studies which come from the animal laboratory, which may lead us to suppose that predictability always entails a degree of controllability which in turn is stress reducing (Evans, 1989). However, in the case of human beings, matters are once again more complex. We shall see below that being informed about a forthcoming aversive event, for some people and in some circumstances, is far from being either a preferred or a stress-reducing state of affairs.

However, in general and certainly in the case of the animal studies, predictability is sought, and there are persuasive theories which can explain why, for example, predictable aversive stimuli are generally preferred to unpredictable stimuli, even though the predictable stimuli may be more intense or more frequent (Evans, 1989). The major theory in this area emphasises the role which predictability plays in signalling periods of safety. Many experiments have shown that preference for information about impending electric shock is clearly demonstrated when warning signals are *necessary* but *not sufficient* conditions of shock (i.e. no shock is ever given without a prior warning signal but some 'false alarms' may be given): they are not however preferred when they are *sufficient* but *not necessary* (i.e. no 'false alarms' are given but some shocks may be delivered without warning). Put more simply, the evidence indicates that the important factor is the safety which is guaranteed by the absence of a signal, rather than the certitude of shock in the event of a signal. It is arguable that being able to separate periods of danger and periods of safety enables an organism to opti-mise, in terms of time allocation, a variety of competing goal-seeking behaviours. Essentially, predictability confers controllability.

With regard to measures of stress, we have tended so far to assume that perceived controllability is linked to low levels of stress. There is of course evidence for such a view. Animal experiments have once again provided the clearest picture, insofar as they have been able to manipulate the principal vari-ables. Weiss's work on stress-induced gastro-intestinal lesions (Weiss, 1977) is among the most compelling. When rodents are paired off ('yoked') so that the aversive experience of one member of a pair is made identical to that of the other member, and when only one member of the pair can exercise control over the aversive stimulus (electric shock), it is the other animal, the passive partner with no control, which develops more severe lesioning. Note that the exposure to the physical 'stress' is identical for both animals: when the controlling animal fails to respond, both receive shock. Thus the two animals vary solely on the psycho-logical dimension of being in control or not.

However, even in the world of animal experimentation, the above findings need some qualification. Controlling responses require effort and Weiss found that effortfulness itself produces stressful reactions if it is too great. This may well explain the results of an earlier study of similar design by Brady (1958) in which monkeys were used as subjects. Here it was the active controlling monkeys – the so-called 'executives' – who suffered more ulceration. However, Brady's executive monkeys could only maintain control through highly effortful responding on a fatiguing time schedule, and this effortfulness was almost certainly a factor in producing Brady's results. Thus controlling may often be a stress-reducing method of coping, but it is necessary to take the cost of the controlling itself into consideration.

A similarity exists here with respect to psychophysiological studies of human subjects coping with mild laboratory stressors. Active coping, which often involves exercising control, is associated with increased cardiovascular arousal. The greatest effects, however, are elicited by tasks of moderate difficulty, neither very easy, nor next to impossible (Light and Obrist, 1983). More broadly, it seems that maximal physiological arousal is obtained when maximal uncertainty exists about outcome (Evans *et al.*, 1984; Phillips, 1989a). Contrarily, both very easy and very difficult task demands can lead to clear expectations of success and failure respectively, and a similar lack of activity in certain physiological systems, which primarily register extra effort and readiness for active responding.

As we shall see later, when we consider in detail the physiological systems involved in stress, the stress response is not a homogeneous 'lump'. Heightened autonomic activity is a primordial response to the recognition of threatening circumstances, but a certain pattern of autonomic responding also characterises in the short term our efforts to cope, our rising to meet a challenge. The active controlling sort of coping which we have so far considered is typically associated with high autonomic arousal. What seems to be true, bringing together all strands of our discussion, is that total stress in such circumstances is best seen as a composite resulting from the magnitude of the external demand and partly from the uncertainty and effort involved in trying to meet the demand.

Individual differences

As we have mentioned earlier, not everyone always seeks or desires information about an impending threat (see Chapter 5 for discussion of this issue in relation to surgery). Some would prefer perhaps to bury their heads in the sand and forget about the matter. Such coping strategies are often referred to as avoidant styles, in contrast to the vigilant style of behaviour which is usually required when obvious controlling responses are needed. In a variety of studies with human subjects, experimenters have tried to measure preference for information about aversive events by giving subjects a choice between monitoring for a warning signal and an alternative strategy: the opportunity to engage in a distracting (avoidant) activity of some kind. In all such studies it has been found that a percentage of individuals favour a distraction strategy and a percentage favour vigilance.

The exact percentage of so-called 'monitors' and 'distractors' varies according to the particular contingencies of the experiment. For example, people are more likely to monitor when effective control is available (Evans *et al.*, 1984). However, even when no control over the aversive event is possible, some subjects prefer to engage in monitoring. Equally, when total monitoring would permit complete avoidance of an aversive event by detection of a warning signal, some subjects will still choose the distracting activity. It is interesting to ask why.

In regard to active coping involving exercising controlling responses, we stated earlier that total stress is likely to be a function not only of the magnitude of the threat but also the effortfulness and uncertainty of exercising effective control. In the kind of experiment described above, it is generally found that monitoring is associated with higher autonomic arousal than is distraction (Evans *et al.*, 1984). If vigilant coping inevitably involves a certain amount of stressful arousal, it is likely that the degree of such arousal differs from subject to subject, depending perhaps on such factors as a native or learned tolerance of ambiguity or uncertainty. For some people therefore, it may well be the case that total stress is reduced by relinquishing control. However, whether we describe such ostrich-like strategies as distraction, denial or as control-relinquishing becomes largely a matter of semantics. By relinquishing uncertain control over a source of stress and avoiding needless worry by distraction, a person may in fact be exercising a kind of superordinate control and be minimising the stress involved in the whole 'package deal' of threat and anticipation of threat. There are of course plenty of everyday examples where we routinely surrender control to experts, who look after our lives in hospitals, on aeroplanes, and in many other places. How much we simply surrender and relax or still wish to be kept informed has also been the subject of investigation in coping research.

Just as the laboratory experiments which we have considered distinguish vigilant and avoidant coping styles, so these are found also in real-life settings, such as facing surgery. We will not go into the vast area of whether greater information in general helps or hinders patients, as this is considered in detail in Chapter 5. We can however emphasise that individual differences and habitual coping styles are likely to be important modulators of stress experience. Surgery is just one of the many life events which we have to experience on occasion. Let us now turn to a consideration of life events in general, their role in creating or relieving stress, and the part that stress itself may play in the causation of physical illness.

Life events research

Since Dohrenwend and Dohrenwend (1974) published a major book on life events and stress, there has been a continuing research impetus in this area. The focus has been on potentially stressful situations to which nearly everyone is exposed to some degree during the course of their lives: major upheavals such as marriage, birth of a child, divorce or bereavement, as well as minor everyday upheavals of all kinds, which are often referred to as 'hassles'. Physical illnesses, major and minor alike, have been linked to such life events, for example heart disease (Theorell, 1996), cancers such as leukaemia (Wold, 1968), colds and influenza (Cohen *et al.*, 1993; Evans *et al.*, 1996). Psychological illnesses such as depression (Brown, 1993) have also been associated with life events. To the fore when we wish to review studies of life events and illness are considerations of methodology. There is now a vast amount of data, but its interpretation is by no means a simple matter.

A question of measurement

Measuring life events presents considerable problems. One of the first approaches to the question of measurement was to draw up lists of events, based on the judgements of researchers themselves. Criticisms of these early attempts could be made on several grounds. They sometimes lacked comprehensiveness, it being by no means certain that the events chosen were fully appropriate to the sampled populations. Non-events were typically ignored even though they may sometimes be very important to individuals, for example not being promoted at work. Some of the events were confounded with consequences which were also the subject of investigation. For example, an individual who loses his job may subsequently suffer from depression: however, it is possible that a detailed investigation of the circumstances of the job loss may reveal it to be tied up with early symptoms of depression. In other words, the job loss may not be so much a cause of depression as an effect. Alternatively some third variable related to both job loss and depression may cause a spurious 'association'. However, the major criticism of early life event 'scales' was that they were unidimensional. They only considered the quantity of life events and not the quality. This point needs expansion.

One of the most widely used early scales was the readjustment rating scale of Holmes and Rahe (1967). A number of subjects were asked to rate items such as 'marriage' in terms of how much adjustment they entailed with reference to other items. Average ratings were then used to come up with general calibrations for future studies. The drawback of such averaging procedures is that there seems to be plenty of evidence of variability in the way that different target groups, not to mention individuals, perceive such events. In view of the models of stress which we detailed earlier in this chapter, it would seem a requirement of more precise research that a subject's own ratings of events are taken into account.

A similar consideration of more recent life events research has been to explore other dimensions of events, such as perceived control and perceived desirability. We may note that undesirability does not necessarily equal stress-fulness, since desirable events may involve adjustments from a routine which may be partly stressful. Other aspects that may be important concern the domain in which the events occur (work, family, etc.). Such refinements may accomplish various goals. It may increase the significance (by which is meant 'importance' rather than just statistical significance) of associations between events and illness measures. It has often been pointed out that most studies of life events and illness, despite their statistical significance, do not explain much of the variance in illness incidence. Second, refinement of life events measurement may discriminate what factors are important in relation to illness, and what are not.

Methodological issues

There is general agreement among researchers that even unrefined life event scales weakly predict a variety of illness episodes, and that illness episodes follow on from 'stressful' periods within a time span not exceeding two years (Chalmers, 1982). Even such a limited conclusion, however, relies on taking a broad view of a number of studies and arguing from consistency of effects, since the problems of clearly interpreting individual studies are manifold due to a variety of method-ological issues. We shall mention just a few.

Many early studies were *retrospective*. Thus researchers would probe people about their life events record after they became ill. This raises problems of recall accuracy, including the general difficulty with retrospective designs that people may well be motivated to 'find' causes for their present illness in preceding events. Even prospective designs have had to face the problem of recall accuracy, since they often involve the same process of trawling a past period (typically the previous six months prior to a follow-up period). Most researchers would nowa-days recommend that designs should be prospective and that measures of life events incidence should obtain ratings from structured interview procedures which allow detailed consideration of the accurate timing of recollections, clearly a vital matter.

Fixing the timing of illness onset with a view to investigating the aetiolog-ical role of stress is another potential methodological problem. Psychiatric illnesses are notoriously nebulous in regard to both clear diagnosis and clear time of onset. We have already commented on the problem that evidence for stress and evidence for the presence of psychiatric illness may actually overlap. Cancers offer clear diagnosis but exact time of onset is not so clear. Several studies have looked at life event stress in relation to episodes of common illnesses such as colds and flu. However, there are often difficulties, or at least a need for caution, in deciding whether life event indices are affecting vulnerability to infection or the degree to which symptoms are expressed (Cohen *et al.*, 1993; Evans *et al.*, 1996).

Moderating variables

It has been emphasised throughout this chapter that individuals and their perceptions of reality intervene between objective events and the experience of stress. It therefore should come as no surprise that some people who have high life event scores sometimes show little or no illness reactions. Moderating variables, lying within the person or in his or her social context, have thus been found to influence the impact of life events. In general, researchers refer to the phenomenon as 'buffering'.

One variable that has received much attention is social support. Brown and Harris (1978), for example, in their study of depression, found that the deleterious effects of life events could be attenuated if the person was, so to speak, socially embedded, and had a good network of social support within a community. Stone *et al.* (1988) and Evans and Edgerton (1991) have found that the desirable life events ('uplifts') predict the onset of colds *by their absence* as much as *hassles* by their presence. Kobasa *et al.* (1982) have described a trait of 'hardiness' centred on the individual's belief in the controllability and normality of challenge, which seems to predict resistance to illness in the face of life event stress.

General versus specific theories

The discussion of life events so far has echoes of Selye's general adaptation theory of stress. Although some researchers have chosen to look at specific illnesses, while others have looked at general illness susceptibility following stress, the implication of both sorts of evidence has been that stress as measured by life events predisposes to illness in general. No doubt such a position would also attach to itself a vague working hypothesis which might be called 'somatic weakness', whereby, in certain individuals, certain somatic systems might be weaker than others and, like a car that is driven too hard, the parts that fail will be those which were weakest to start with.

Suggestions have been made, however, which countenance different routes to different types of disorder depending on a more refined analysis of how a person may characteristically respond to the potential stress of life events. In particular, Fisher (1996) pulls together various strands of evidence in a tentative attempt to identify two possible routes to illness, depending on the coping resources of the individual. It is argued that situations which lead to effort and challenge but that are not obviously distressing result in physiological arousal but operate primarily via the traditional autonomic route, as was mentioned earlier. Activation in this case may put a person at risk of what Fisher calls 'somatisation', whereby *persistent* abuse of the biological systems leads to anatomical changes, which in turn increase the risk of disorders such as coronary heart disease. The second route becomes relevant when coping is less effective, and when effort is accompanied by distress. The mechanism here is thought to depend upon greater involvement of the adreno-cortical system (see below) and involves lowered immune system efficiency and thus heightened susceptibility to infectious and perhaps cancerous illnesses. Discussion of sympathetic arousal in relation to coronary heart disease can be found elsewhere in this book (see Chapter 11). In the final section of this chapter, therefore, we shall examine the evidence that life events and stress can be linked to impaired immunocompetence and increased vulnerability to infectious disease and cancer. Before that, however, we need to say a little more about the general physiology of stress.

The physiology of stress

What Selye did establish in the early years of stress research was the importance of two physiological systems in reactions to a wide variety of potential sources of stress. The first involves the autonomic nervous system (ANS), the 'medulla' or inner core of the adrenal glands situated immediately above the kidneys, and the release of the powerful hormones, adrenalin and noradrenalin, which are known collectively as catecholamines. This system had already been given promi-nence in Walter Cannon's theory of emergency motivation, which was expounded in the early part of this century. Sympathetic arousal, through its effects on a variety of internal organs, mobilises the organism for what has commonly been called 'fight or flight'. The adrenal medulla, itself sympathetically innervated, secretes adrenalin and noradrenalin, which mimic the effects of direct sympa-thetic stimulation and provide a continuing back-up in the mobilisation of the body's resources. The system as a whole is known as the sympathetic adrenal medullary (SAM) system. This should not be thought of as a stress-only system. Periodically elevated levels of catecholamines characterise our everyday efficient coping with the challenges of life: when we are concentrating hard on achieving normal goals, both at work and at play. It is when levels are more chronically high and do not return to normal that we should talk more realistically of stress processes. Indeed in a study by Evans and Moran (1987b) it was found that a failure or slowness to return to 'baseline' values of heart rate, for example, char-acterised individuals who scored high on the so-called Type A behaviour pattern risk factor for coronary heart disease (see Chapter 11).

The second system is known as HPA, which stands for the hypothalamic pituitary-adrenocortical axis. The hypothalamus secretes a hormone called a corti-cotropin releasing factor (CRF) which in turn causes the pituitary gland to produce adrenocorticotrophic hormone (ACTH) which circulates to the adrenal cortex (the outer 'skin' of the adrenal glands). The adrenal cortex in turn produces corti-costeroids of various kinds which help the adaptive process by, for example, providing muscles with long-term access to the body's energy stores. The key corticosteroids in stress responding are known as glucocorticoids, and, in humans, the principal glucocorticoid is cortisol. In normal circumstances this system is

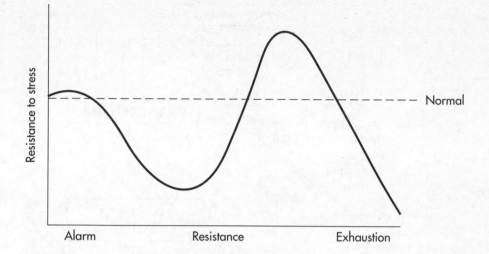

Figure 3.2 Selye's General Adaptation Syndrome

adaptive in responding to limited stress, since cortisol feeds back to the pituitary and hypothalamus to limit further production of CRF and ACTH, thus limiting the activity of the entire HPA.

The total adaptive response in Selye's original theory was seen as triphasic (see Figure 3.2). An original alarm stage gives way to a resistance stage during which the organism's resistance to stress is heightened, unless new sources of stress appear. If, however, the source of stress continues despite the organism's efforts to resist, then the third 'exhaustion' stage ensues. Here, harmful effects of high corticosteroid levels, such as ulceration and immunosuppression, begin to become apparent, and overall resistance is decreased. If the process is allowed to continue, recovery is not possible and death is the final result.

Selye's original view was that the above represented a general response to stress of all kinds as, indeed, is implied by the term 'general adaptation syndrome'. As we suggested above, this is in need of qualification, since not all people respond in the same way to identical stress sources and the same individual may respond differently on different occasions. This has led more recent commentators on stress to emphasise the role that psychological processes play in mediating physiological effects.

We also know that the physiological processes involved in adaptation are even more complex than envisaged in Selye's original model, involving, for example, the release of chemicals known as neuropeptides, with possible analgesic effects, and even neurally mediated effects on the organs of the immune system. We address the latter in more detail in the final section of this chapter, but we may note here that analgesic effects would be in the short term adaptive in any 'fight or flight' situation. The pain of a slight sprain, with its message to rest, would be singularly undesirable when running to escape a deadly predator.

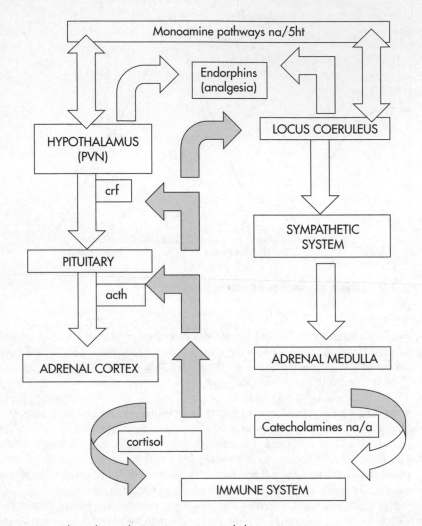

Figure 3.3 Physiological stress systems and their interactions

Notes: White arrows = excitatory influences; grey arrows = inhibitory influences; half-grey/half-white arrows = mixed or uncertain pattern; upper case = structures; lower case = active substances

Abbreviations: a = adrenalin; acth = adrenocorticotropic hormone; crf = corticotropin releasing factor; na = noradrenalin; pvn = paraventricular nucleus; 5ht = 5hydroxytryptamine or serotonin

    The fact that we have described separate systems should not obscure the true reality, which is that all these systems interact. Indeed at the level of the central nervous system, the crucially important SAM and HPA systems can be considered as one complex: they are as it were the lower limbs of one body. The reader may well be aware of those important neurochemical messengers of the central nervous system, collectively known as monoamines: we have already mentioned noradrenalin since it is also produced by the adrenal medulla, but there are also dopamine and serotonin (or 5-hydroxytryptamine). Monoamine pathways in the brain are associated with a number of motivational and emotional behaviours, and are crucially involved in 'driving' both the SAM and HPA systems (Chrousos and Gold, 1996; Clow *et al.*, 1997). A simplified diagram is given in Figure 3.3, which shows the principal links between the different system parts.

You should note the positive and negative feedback loops which normally ensure a richly complex, integrated, adaptive, but, most importantly, self-limiting response to an external challenge or threat. Thus the different parts of the whole can 'kick in' to differing degrees and with subtly different timings depending on the nature of the challenge. Psychophysiologists interested in stress are usually at pains to emphasise that these systems were designed to be adaptive. The question is what happens if they are abused. What happens if we are constantly and chronically activating the SAM system, for example, by responding to everything in life as a minor emergency or challenge? Each challenge may be 'actively coped with', and be insufficient to trigger much in the way of an HPA response, but chronic hyper-reactivity of the SAM system, whether due to individual temperament or circumstance, is likely to impose undue wear and tear on the cardiovascular system (see Chapters 10 and 11). If stress is both intense and chronic and, moreover, control is less certain, and helplessness more apparent, then disturbance of HPA regulation seems more likely. The production of corticosteroids is a key feature of HPA and since corticosteroids have profound effects on immune functioning, it is perhaps a suitable point to move on to a consideration of the new interdisciplinary science of psychoneuroimmunology.

Psychological influences on immunity and disease

The immune system is crucially involved in defending our bodies against infection by dangerous micro-organisms, including bacteria and viruses. It also probably plays an important role in protecting us against certain cancers, by targeting abnormal cells for destruction. Increasing knowledge that the immune system is sensitive to psychological and psychosocial influence, particularly psychological stress, has led many to believe that the interdisciplinary science of psychoneuroimmunology (PNI) may illuminate the mechanisms whereby psychological stress can affect vulnerability to real physical illness.

A potential problem for PNI research is that change and fluctuation of different parameters of functioning is a normal characteristic of the immune system, and seeing the system as a whole as being in a certain state (for example, 'suppressed' or 'enhanced') is at best an over-simplification. Notwithstanding this difficulty, researchers have shown that something approximating the degree of alertness of the system can be measured by certain techniques. Readers with a psychology background may not have much knowledge of immunology, so in discussing these techniques I have endeavoured *en route* to provide a short and simplified introduction to a notoriously complex discipline. Those who wish to know more should consult a specialised introductory text in immunology, such as Davey (1989).

One technique of investigation has been to measure the efficiency of certain key immune-system cells (called lymphocytes) in subjects who have been exposed to some major stressful event. Lymphocytes are of different types and have a range of functions, but one important function is to be able to proliferate and multiply when required. For example, one important class of lymphocytes (B-cells) produces antibodies, proteins which have a characteristic structure known as immunoglobulin. Antibodies can lock on to so-called antigens, which are distinct features of an invading micro-organism, and target the invader for destruction. However, the 'binding' of an antibody to an antigen is usually a very specific business, and precisely the right antibody is required. Thus once a connection is made it is important for the specific B-cell, which has antibodies offering the correct key to the lock, to multiply and produce myriad carbon copies of itself to carry on the business of mopping up the antigen with its antibodies. If an invader (notably a virus) actually gets inside a cell, another arm of the immune system – the so-called cellular arm – is important. Its lymphocytes (T-cells) need to recognise and destroy infected cells. Recognition is again about 'binding' operations, and efficient proliferation of the right lymphocytes.

If we take a blood sample from someone, we can expose the lymphocytes in the sample to particular substances (known as 'mitogens') which are particularly good at triggering proliferation. The degree of proliferation thus triggered *in vitro* is then taken by PNI researchers to be one plausible indicator of the alertness of the immune system, since it has reference to an important functional property of it.

Another way in which the immune system keeps alert for invaders is by so-called 'trafficking' of cells through the circulation. Thus a reduced lymphocyte count can also serve as an indicator of reduced immune system alertness. One type of lymphocyte, far less numerous than T and B cells, is the Natural Killer (NK) cell. Unlike some T-cells, these cells do not need complex instructions in order to kill; they can naturally target and kill suspect cells. They seem to be particularly adept at targeting cancerous cells. Once again, the efficiency of their *cytotoxic* (toxic to cells) functioning can be measured in vitro.

Finally, in terms of common PNI measures, we can look at numbers of antibodies of various types, although here the arguments are a bit more complex. One particular antibody measure which has been used in a number of studies is the level of a certain class of antibody, known as secretory immunoglobulin A (sIgA). As the name implies, this is the major type of antibody found in the mucous secretions of the body, and can therefore be sampled fairly non-invasively in saliva. However, sIgA coats all mucous membrane tissue: the linings of the mouth, nose and respiratory tract, the gastro-intestinal tract, the genito-urinary tract. Of course, total amounts of sIgA include all antibody regardless of specificity to any particular antigen. However, the general form of the sIgA molecule, acting in the mucosal system, is believed to offer a more primitive protection against possible infection by forming a competitive barrier to infectious agents, preventing them from adhering to mucosal surfaces. Those who are naturally deficient in sIgA are reported as having a greater incidence of respiratory infections (Evans *et al.*, 1995).

Another antibody measure which supposedly indicates lowered efficiency of the immune system involves measuring the amount of specific antibodies to certain herpes-type viruses. Herpes infections are extremely widespread, but these viruses are notoriously latent, remaining dormant for long periods. If the immune system is weakened, however, the virus attempts to resurface and this has to be checked by the immune system. It does this by producing more specific antibody to the virus. So paradoxically perhaps, *heightened* antibody counts to the specific virus are taken as revealing an underlying weakness of the immune system as a whole.

Having introduced some of the principal immune system measures used in PNI research, we may note that all of these have shown to be associated with psychological stress (see Herbert and Cohen, 1993): stress is associated with reduced proliferation, reduced numbers of many types of lymphocytes, reduced levels of total sIgA, reduced NK cell activity, and raised antibody levels to herpes viruses.

The most compelling evidence comes from studies where participants are, or have been, most clearly and plausibly under major stress. The experience of bereavement was used in two early studies (Bartrop *et al.*, 1977; Schleifer *et al.*, 1983). Compared with matched controls in the first study, and compared with pre-bereavement scores in the second prospective study, it was found that bereavement produced significantly lower levels of immune response. As Baker (1987) points out in a review article, this lends some substance to an observation recorded in the *British Medical Journal* of 1884 to the effect that bereaved persons are abnormally prone to infection.

In another review of psychoimmunological research, Kiecolt-Glaser and Glaser (1986) report on their own research on marital disruption. Poorer immune function on a set of measures, including lymphocyte responsiveness, was shown by separated and divorced women compared with matched controls. Amongst the sample of married women, poorer immune functioning was associated with poorer state of marriage and greater depression.

Jemmott and Magloire (1988) demonstrated lower concentrations of sIgA in students during an exam period compared to control periods before and after exams. Moreover, sIgA concentrations paralleled reported stress levels. Evans *et al.* (1993) found lower sIgA over a period of several days for subjects reporting relatively more undesirable events and relatively less desirable events over the same period. Given the protective role that sIgA may play in regard to respiratory illness, it is interesting that this study used the same life event instrument as was used in an earlier study by Evans *et al.* (1988), which found an association between life event reporting and episodes of upper respiratory illness. This latter study used a prospective within subjects design, in which subjects filled in life event scales daily for several weeks. Among those subjects who succumbed to colds during the investigative period, there was a quite pronounced dip in desirable event reporting around four days prior to onset of illness episodes.

Turning from a focus on infectious illness to cancer, the time-scale for the development of disease is altogether much less certain. Researchers have certainly consistently found that natural killer (NK) cell activity is impaired by stress (Herbert and Cohen, 1993). NK cell activity, as mentioned above, is thought to be possibly important in our natural defences against cancer. However, definite links between stress and cancer in humans have not yet been fully established, although there is a considerable body of reports from experiments on animals (see Justice (1985) for a review). Although the role of life events is uncertain,

63

what seems to be a feature of human-based research is the association between depression and cancer, and depression can, as we have noted, arguably be linked via helplessness and control theory to an HPA-immune system route (Fisher, 1996). Higher cancer mortality rates for bereaved spouses have been reported (Fox, 1981), although a later longitudinal study (Jones *et al.*, 1984) only found suggestive statistics for breast cancer. Perhaps the most suggestive results as to the link between depression and cancer come from a seventeen-year follow-up study of over two thousand factory workers in Cleveland, Ohio (Shekelle *et al.*, 1981). All subjects were between 40 and 50 years of age and all completed the Minnesota Multiphasic Personality Inventory (MMPI). Among those scoring high on depression, the death rate from cancer during the follow-up period was twice the expected norm. The result was not explicable in terms of confounding variables such as age or smoking. The work of Greer and his colleagues with breast cancer patients has also been illuminating in regard to affective processes. Initially, Greer and Morris (1975) showed that women who proved positive for cancer at biopsy were more likely, prior to biopsy, to report very little tendency to express anger. In a later study, Greer *et al.* (1979) reported on the progress of patients with breast cancer. The greatest mortality was shown by the group which exhibited a hopeless attitude to their illness, and the least mortality was associated with groups which showed either fighting spirit or denial styles of coping.

Chronic stress and individual differences in stress-proneness have been related fairly consistently to lowered alertness of the immune system on the sorts of measures outlined at the beginning of this section. However, recent research is now suggesting that in the case of acute short-term stress, the picture may be very different. There is a pattern of increased rather than decreased alertness for several immune measures. Acute stressors used in these studies included evaluative public speaking tasks, mental arithmetic, challenging computer games, and confrontational role play. On such tasks, we see increases in the number of NK cells and also lymphocytes of certain kinds, notably CD8+ cells, largely T-cells which can recognise and kill virally infected cells (Herbert *et al.*, 1994; Marsland *et al.*, 1995; Naliboff *et al.*, 1995). Similarly, there is an increase in the activity of natural killer cells (Delahanty *et al.*, 1996; Naliboff *et al.*, 1991). Finally, sIgA levels are increased (Bristow *et al.*, 1997; Carroll *et al.*, 1996; Evans *et al.*, 1994; Tamura *et al.*, 1995; Zeier *et al.*, 1996).

How, then, do we interpret these findings? At present much is speculative, but what might well be the case is that the two well-researched physiological stress systems (SAM and HPA) have different effects on immune system parameters. In short-term stress, where coping resources are adequate, the SAM system is temporarily activated. One possibility is that this system may actually in some way stimulate the trafficking of lymphocytes, the secretion of sIgA, and the cytotoxicity of NK cells, although not the proliferative potential of lymphocytes which seems to be depressed by acute stress. Certainly there is evidence that a number of acute challenges which induce short-term immune changes are characterised by sympathetic arousal. Such challenges either involve no consistent HPA response or the immune response precedes any rises in cortisol. Speculatively, from an evolutionary point of view, it might make sense for an organism rapidly to mobilise some aspects of immune function at the time of an emergency which may well involve greater exposure to pathogens, either through cuts and grazes or massive increases in quantity of air taken through the respiratory tract. However, what we have not so far mentioned is that there are great hazards associated with over-activity of the immune system. Immune responses after all involve inflammatory processes, cell destruction, and much else besides. We see this destructive potential very clearly in so-called auto-immune diseases such as rheumatoid arthritis where the immune system attacks its own healthy tissue. The system has to be balanced and regulated. The suggestion then is that one of the functions of the HPA axis which kicks in later than the SAM system may be to limit and regulate the immune system responses to acute challenge. The fact that corticosteroids such as cortisol are very clearly immunosuppressive lends support to this view.

The final picture is likely to be far more complex, but I have probably said enough to get across a main message which I will now endeavour to spell out. The body's physiological responses to stress are likely to have evolved for meeting relatively short-term acute emergencies. Faced with such challenges, the systems are adaptive and almost certainly involve several exquisite negative feedback loops and regulatory controls additional to those few which we currently know about. The corollary of this is that we are probably not well adapted to chronic stress, where the threat or challenge does not go away, and where control seems to be difficult. In such cases dysfunction of the physiological stress systems (including immune system) is a plausible expectation, and there are then equally plausible links with real physical pathology which may be significant. The relevance of PNI research to health psychology should not be overstated. These are early days. But the endeavour, I think, is proving worthwhile.

LIFE EVENTS AND STRESS

Many researchers in the area of stress have looked at the relationship between life events and vulnerability to illness. What sort of events are typically examined? The following is a list of the top ten potentially stressful life events taken from the original Holmes and Rahe (1967) social readjustment scale.

1 Death of spouse
2 Divorce
3 Marital separation
4 Gaol term
5 Death of close family member
6 Personal injury or illness
7 Marriage
8 Fired at work
9 Marital reconciliation
10 Retirement.

Reference to the text of this chapter should make the reader cautious about jumping to the conclusion that stress can be simply quantified by adding up the number of events which an individual has recently experienced. People react differently to nominally the same sort of event. The full impact of many of these major events may be more clearly seen in the consequent changes of routine as evidenced by a record of more minor but regular events. Note also that this scale includes some major events which can also be classified as 'pleasant', for example marriage. This indicates very clearly the need to consider individual reactions to events and not just the event itself.

Key point summary

- Stress is a very broad term involving a transaction between an individual and his or her environment.
- Psychological theories of stress emphasise the way in which individuals both appraise potentially stressful situations and also evaluate their coping resources.
- Coping in turn is seen in terms of controlling. Human beings, however, can exercise control in subtle ways, including defensive forms of appraisal and psychological distraction, and the theoretical issues are far from being simply stated.
- Associations between stress and illness have been suggested by writers of every century. However, recent research on life events has given an empirical justification to such claims. Although life events research in relation to illness has to face considerable methodological problems, there is now a large body of findings which supports the idea of such associations.
- Certain patterns of physiological activity are associated with 'being stressed', but important variation exists in such patterns. However, the physiology of

stress is vital to our increasing understanding of how psychological pressures come to have pathological consequences for our physical selves.

● The new hybrid science of psychoneuroimmunology is beginning to show us more about the mechanisms by which psychological stress may come, partly at least, to influence health outcomes.

Further reading

The reader who wishes to explore the issues raised in this chapter in more detail will find plenty of detailed books on stress. The following are useful examples.

Chrousos, G. P. and Gold, P. W. (1992) The concepts of stress system disorders: overview of behavioral and physical homeostasis. *Journal of the American Medical Association*, 267, 1244–1256. This gives a detailed overview of physiological stress systems in relation to their possible dysfunction.

Cooper, C. L. (1996) *Handbook of Stress, Medicine and Health*. London: CRC Press; Fisher, S. and Reason, J. (1989) *Handbook of Life Stress, Cognition, and Health*. London: John Wiley & Sons. Two edited collections of relevant contributions published as 'Handbooks'.

Evans, P., Hucklebridge, F. and Clow, A. (1997) Stress and the immune system. *The Psychologist*, July, 303–307. This offers a review of stress in relation to the immune system.

Patient behaviour and the management of illness

JUST AS PART ONE guided you through the experience of health, Part Two aims to give an overview of the experiences of illness and medical treatment. In Chapter 4 we chart the course of a potential episode of ill health from the experience of the first symptoms, through a decision to consult a doctor or health professional for an opinion, through the process of diagnosis and on to treatment. We consider why some people consult a doctor fairly frequently whilst others almost never do so, and we show that this is related only indirectly to the severity of the symptoms they experience. It looks at the reasons why a patient may or may not decide to follow the medical advice he or she has been given in a consultation.

Chapter 5 examines the experience of hospitalisation. We show that this can be a potentially anxiety-provoking life event, and that aspects of the hospital setting can exacerbate or alleviate the stress involved. We examine in particular the experience of surgery, showing how interventions such as adequate preparation can not only be effective in reducing anxiety associated with the experience, but can also directly aid the process of recovery, by making a person's stay in hospital shorter and reducing the incidence of post-operative complications and their need for analgesics. The experiences and special needs of children in hospital are also considered. Chapter 6 examines the nature of pain. Pain is shown to be a useful aspect of our lives, offering signals that something is wrong or that we are abusing our bodies. Tara Symonds examines theories of pain, and how this subjective experience can be quantified and recorded. She then considers in some detail how pain, particularly chronic, long-term pain, can be managed. Using the example of low back pain, she describes management strategies which help sufferers to deal with their experience of pain and resume many of the necessary activities of daily living.

Taken together, these chapters guide the reader through the experience of illness, as Part One guided you through the experience of health.

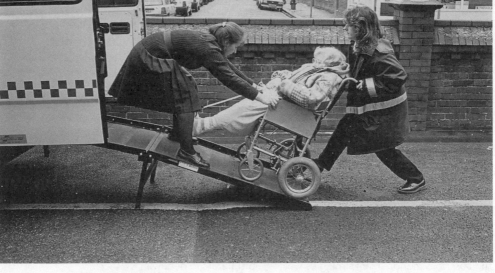

Chapter 4

The medical consultation

Marian Pitts

Introduction

> Nobody goes to a doctor with just a symptom, they go with ideas about the symptom, with concerns about the symptom and with expectations related to the symptom.
>
> (Tate, 1994, p. 6)

This quotation shows that the processes of symptom perception and medical consultation are complex. This chapter will consider the ways in which we decide to use primary health care services and what happens when we do. It will show that doctors and patients may have different expectations of the consultation process and may sometimes not communicate effectively with each other.

Experiencing symptoms

The majority of symptoms of illnesses are not reported to a health professional, and Last (1963) coined the term 'illness iceberg' to describe this phenomenon. We experience minor symptoms much of the time; Morrell and Wale (1976) and Scambler and Scambler (1984) investigated the perception of symptoms in samples of healthy women. Both report about one medical consultation for every eighteen 'symptom episodes'. Hannay (1980) asked a random sample of people registered with a health practice to indicate on a symptom checklist whether or not they were currently experiencing a symptom and to rate its severity and the degree to which it was disabling. He reports that 26 per cent of people who rated themselves as suffering from at least one severe symptom did not refer themselves for medical treatment. Cunningham-Burley and Irvine (1987) interviewed fifty-two women with young children about their treatment of their children's illnesses. They also collected diary data from the mothers. They found that on 49 per cent of the days for which data were collected, mothers reported that their children had at least one symptom. For a large proportion of these symptoms no action was taken by the mothers; most commonly no action was taken for respiratory symptoms (for example, a runny nose), sickness or diarrhoea and changes in behaviour. For the rest – cuts, grazes and coughs – by far the most common action was to purchase an over-the-counter remedy. Analgesics, such as aspirin and cough mixtures, were most frequently used (56 per cent and 52 per cent respectively of all medications administered). Mothers reported contacting a health care professional on only 7 per cent of the days when a symptom had been noticed.

Thus the overwhelming response to noticing a symptom is not to seek professional help immediately but to self-treat or do nothing. Pennebaker (1982) has carried out extensive research on the perception of symptoms and their interpretation. He has found that awareness of symptoms varies greatly between people, and that we are more aware of bodily symptoms when bored and less aware when fully absorbed in a task. He has even used this finding to show that the greater the incidence of coughing during a university lecture, the lower its interest value.

Mechanic (1978) presents a simple model of health decisions which suggests we attend to the *number* and the *persistence* of symptoms; we consider whether the symptoms are recognisable or familiar, the possible disabling aspects of the symptoms and apply our cultural and social definitions of illness. Other factors also play a part: there is considerable evidence that people experiencing psychological distress may use the health services more frequently and for different purposes, such as gaining access to wider social services (Tessler *et al.*, 1976).

Thus the decision to visit the doctor is usually taken after some analysis and discussion of the problem. The opinion of significant others is nearly always sought first. Scambler and Scambler (1984) report a ratio of eleven 'lay' consultations usually involving a spouse or close friend to every medical consultation. These opinions are then taken as indications that it is legitimate to seek medical help. As Stimson and Webb (1975) report, there is an almost universal concern expressed 'not to waste the doctor's valuable time' and the opinion of others is regarded as an endorsement that the problem is not trivial. Another incentive or trigger to consultation may be when a minor problem persists longer than anticipated. This 'wait and see' strategy has been commented upon by Locker (1981, p. 146): 'any symptoms which last for a few days or more are seen to be of a more serious nature.' Locker also describes the 'critical incident' which can trigger a consultation. The incident might be a sudden change in the nature of the symptom, an increase in pain level, or the discovery that a previous interpretation was no longer appropriate: all are possible critical incidents. Finally, the decision to consult is premised by the expectation that the doctor can take some useful action; the recurrence of a symptom which the person has experienced previously and for which he or she has received no useful treatment may well not result in a further consultation – 'I think it's a waste of time because I've been through the pipeline before ... so I don't really feel there's a lot of point going through that lot again' (quoted in Locker, 1981).

These antecedents to the consultation are described by Pendleton *et al.* (1984) as follows: a change in health is noted; our health understandings lead us to decide whether it is a problem for the doctor or one which is best dealt with by either no care, self-care or alternative care (Figure 4.1). Salmon *et al.* (1996) constructed a questionnaire which examined patients' beliefs about the origins of their symptoms. Exploratory interviews with a hundred randomly chosen patients attending general practice surgeries asked: 'What symptoms have brought you here today?' and 'What do you think has caused your symptoms?' From these and other answers, a scale was devised which included seventy-one items. Further analysis and refinement has resulted in a final scale which is designed to measure quantitatively the beliefs of patients attending general practitioners' surgeries. There are key belief dimensions which seem to apply to most common illnesses. These include the major role played by 'stress' in our lives. Symptoms are often attributed to the psychological demands we experience which are the result of work or domestic life – 'nerves' or 'overwork'. The role of the environment is another important dimension which includes beliefs about the role of the weather, dampness, infection and pollution in causing symptoms of ill health; an example of an item reflecting this belief in Salmon *et al.*'s questionnaire would be 'something I caught'. Another important domain is lifestyle

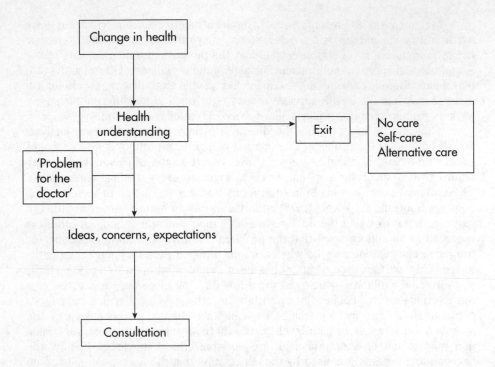

Figure 4.1 Antecedents to the consultation process

Source: Pendleton *et al.* (1993)

management which includes elements that patients feel are, in part, their responsibility: 'something I ate', 'not looking after myself properly'. Vulnerability which covers beliefs about a weak constitution or predisposition located in a specific part of the body is important. The notion of the body 'wearing out' is frequently expressed, particularly with musculoskeletal symptoms; and finally the belief in an internal-external structure where the cause may be hidden but still rectifiable: 'something out of place' or 'something seriously wrong'.

It is clear that patients' beliefs about the causes of their symptoms will directly influence their decisions about care. These beliefs can also indirectly affect how information and treatment suggested by the doctor will be received. To take a concrete example, a patient who believes that a gastrointestinal problem is the result of a serious organic disorder rather than the outcome of certain lifestyle habits is less likely to implement a recommended change in his or her eating behaviour.

Deciding to consult

Public health researchers have established that a number of demographic variables are related to the use of primary health care services. Age is especially relevant; the young and the old consult more frequently than do adolescents and young adults. The young are taken for vaccination or common childhood illnesses. As the child's immune system becomes stronger, consultations decline and remain low until middle age when the onset of chronic conditions may occur.

Another aspect which relates to consultation rate is gender. It is well established that women make greater use of health service facilities than men. There are a number of elements to explain this gender difference, which is not apparent during the childhood years. Contraception, pregnancy and childbirth necessitate use of health care facilities but, even when these elements are removed, the gender difference remains (Verbrugge, 1985). It may simply be that women develop more illnesses requiring medical attention than men, though this is surprisingly difficult to establish; women are also more likely to *report* acute illnesses and symptoms than men (Verbrugge, 1985). Perhaps gender stereotypes inhibit men from reporting symptoms or seeking medical opinion; women, because of the necessity to consult on behalf of their children or themselves during pregnancy, develop a greater familiarity with health care services and a greater willingness to use them. 'Well men clinics' remain a rarity whilst 'well women clinics' are now firmly established. Ingham and Miller (1986) suggest that demographic variables play a minor role in determining consultation rates in comparison with the role of symptoms. They found that the people who are most likely to consult are those who cannot say what is causing their troubles, and those who believe that there is an internal physical cause, rather than an external physical or a psychological cause of their trouble.

Thus there is a complex relationship between the perception of symptoms of ill health, the responses to such symptoms, and the decision to seek the opinion of a health professional. The next section examines the experience of a medical consultation.

The medical consultation

The consultation is the central act of medicine, and as such it deserves to be understood.

(Pendleton *et al.*, 1984)

The unique and defining characteristics of general practice care are contact care, co-ordination of care and comprehensiveness (Starfield, quoted in Buetow, 1995). First, contact care considers the accessibility of the doctor, which is a function of availability, geographical access, accommodation, including the organisation of the practice, the method of making appointments, and the affordability and acceptability of any treatment prescribed.

Any general practitioner may see around 6000 patients in a year; put another way, 'on some days there are more than one million general practice consultations in the United Kingdom alone' (Pendleton *et al.*, 1984). A medical consultation is not like an ordinary social encounter or conversation; Stimson and Webb (1975) describe it as a focused interaction which is geographically and temporally defined and which has a high degree of specificity – peripheral topics are only rarely mentioned – and in which there is a competence gap between doctor and patient. Both patient and doctor bring to the meeting a number of expectations of how the encounter will go and what the outcome might be. How different are the set of expectations of doctors and patients?

The patient has first to describe a symptom or set of symptoms to the doctor who, in turn, is expected to provide an explanation (diagnosis) and possibly advice or medication. The patient necessarily must be selective about what he or she reports and decisions on how to present the problem can influence the doctor's response. As Blaxter (1983, p. 62) describes it, 'a consultation presents incompatible obligations: to be brief and helpful, not waste time which is manifestly in short supply, and yet somehow to tell the story of a life in all its long detail'. Stimson and Webb report a great deal of anticipatory work before the encounter takes place; patients rehearse what they will say either to themselves or to others. This aspect may enable patients to present their concerns in the most appropriate light; rehearsal may also change the emphasis of what is being conveyed. Patients choose an order in which to present their concerns: 'physical' problems are often mentioned first. It is not always (if ever) that the most serious problem is raised first. Patients frequently seem to need some time to work their way into the consultation and tend to 'save' their underlying concerns until they are confident of a sympathetic hearing. The absence of such reassurance could result in a major concern not being mentioned at all. Korsch *et al.* (1968) reported in their study of consultations at a paediatrics outpatients department that 24 per cent of mothers failed to raise their major concerns. Researching patient concerns may even interact with such concerns. For example, Stimson and Webb (1975) comment that questioning prior to the consultation may raise a problem to a level of awareness which affects the later interaction. They describe a woman who, while responding to a checklist of problems presented by the researchers, said: 'Now you've mentioned it I might ask him about that' – and she did!

Patients do more than describe symptoms in neutral fashion; they often hint or suggest possible causative factors; should the doctor fail to respond to these hints then the symptoms may be represented in a somewhat different manner. Scott *et al.* (1995) studied GPs' attitudes to patients who offered a self-diagnosis of myalgic encephalomyelitis (chronic fatigue syndrome). They randomly selected 200 GPs and sent each of them the following case description:

> Mrs M. is a 28 year old personnel officer for a computer firm who has previously been in good health. She attended the surgery complaining of general malaise which had lasted for six months. The malaise had increased in severity and by the time she had presented it was accompanied by intermittent abdominal pains, severe tiredness, insomnia, and crying easily for no good reason. She denied any serious financial, social or marital stressors. Physical examination, full blood count, urea and electrolytes, liver function tests, and thyroid function test showed no abnormalities.

Half the GPs received a description with the woman's occupation changed to office cleaner. The following sentence was included in half the descriptions:

'She had read newspaper articles about chronic fatigue syndrome and believed this was her problem.'

Doctors were asked a series of questions about their case management and their attitudes towards this hypothetical patient. They were more likely to refer the personnel officer than the office cleaner for counselling. This supports previous findings that social class influences referrals for psychological treatments. Self-diagnosis led doctors to consider the patient to be less likely to comply with treatment, more likely to pose difficult management problems and more likely to take up a great deal of time. Doctors were significantly less likely to wish to have such patients on their lists and more likely to refer for a second opinion. Generally then, the attempt at self-diagnosis in this case description resulted in more negative attitudes on the part of the doctors.

Doctors and patients communicating

Talk is the main ingredient in medical care and It Is the fundamental instrument by which the doctor–patient relationship is crafted and by which therapeutic goals are achieved.

(Roter and Hall, 1992, p. 36)

According to Ong *et al.* (1995), there are three different purposes of communication between doctors and patients. These are: to create a good interpersonal relationship; to exchange information; and to make treatment-related decisions. There have been numerous studies which have examined the importance of establishing good interpersonal relationships between doctors and patients (D'Angelo *et al.*, 1994; Dimatteo *et al.*, 1993, 1994). However, it is of course essential that the doctor also engages in the other two functions of the communication: the exchange of information and the decisions associated with treatment.

Exchanging information relies on effective description and discussion and good understanding of what has been said. Effective description can involve the use of booklets, checking understanding, etc. (Barlow *et al.*, 1996; Frederikson and Bull, 1995). Later in this chapter we will consider the effect that these exchanges can have on patients adhering to medical advice.

Blanchard *et al.* (1988) found that 92 per cent of patients suffering with cancer whom they interviewed indicated a strong desire for information. They felt that the kind of information being provided was often inadequate. Chaitchik *et al.* (1992) showed that doctors were concerned to convey information about the cancer condition in an objective way, whilst patients wished it to be defined in terms of themselves: 'How much pain will I have?' 'Will I fully recover?' (quoted from Ong *et al.*, 1995). The oncologist usually initiates most discussion and rarely addresses patients' emotional concerns (Siminoff and Fetting, 1991; Siminoff *et al.*, 1989).

White (1988) argues that there is an imbalance in the attention given to the technical-medical side of the literature rather than the psycho-therapeutic side. 'We should be crystal clear . . . that probably no more than 20 per cent of the therapeutic interventions are supported by objective evidence that they do more good than harm' (cited in Bensing *et al.*, 1996). Some of the good that is done is the result of an effective doctor–patient relationship. Bensing *et al.* (1996) investigated the influence of the affective dimension of GPs' behaviour. They showed that GPs' affective behaviour – as measured by eye contact, interest, verbal encouragement and empathy – correlated positively with patient satisfaction with a consultation. GPs with higher levels of affective behaviour were also found to write fewer prescriptions and to carry out fewer technical interventions. Using multiple regression analysis, only three variables were predictive of patients' satisfaction overall; these were affective behaviour on the part of the GP, discussion of psychosocial topics and referrals to medical specialists. This last element had a negative effect on patients' satisfaction. Since GPs showing high levels of affective behaviour are also incurring lower medical costs because they do not write so many prescriptions and do not refer patients for further interventions so frequently, then, for once, patients' choice and health service preferences may coincide.

Making a diagnosis

Tate (1994) suggests that Sherlock Holmes remains one of the finest role models for doctors. Indeed, Conan Doyle based the character on a leading medical practitioner in Edinburgh. Holmes applied logic to problems and, by paying attention to tiny details, consistently astonished the medical man, Watson, by his ability to come to the correct solution. From this point of view, the doctor is required to solve a problem – by making a diagnosis or providing an explanation for the problem presented by the patient. Notice, though, that Holmes was rarely swayed by emotion and was universally regarded as 'a cold fish'. One of the problems identified by researchers is that errors may result from a diagnosis made too early in the consultation. Tate gives an estimate of the first thirty seconds of a consultation as the time taken to arrive at the first diagnostic hypothesis. Given the likelihood that patients may not present their most serious concerns first, doctors can be led astray by early, less central complaints. Wallston (1978) has reported that doctors systematically distorted information presented late in an interview in order that it be made to fit with an already established opinion or diagnosis. Tate advises allowing the patient 'a minute or two of *relatively* uninterrupted dialogue at the beginning of a consultation' (p. 40, my italics). Relatively uninterrupted dialogue is an interesting construct!

Much research has considered the tendency on the part of problem solvers, doctors included, to seek confirmatory instances for their hypotheses. Wason and Johnson-Laird (1972), and many others since, have charted the strategy to look for positive instances rather than the more efficient one of seeking negative instances to disconfirm tentative hypotheses. The work of Tversky has also shown that thinking probabilistically does not come any more easily to doctors than to the rest of us. McNeill *et al.* (1982) studied three groups of people, including a group of doctors who were presented with imaginary problems concerning choice of treatments for cancer. They were given information on immediate and longer term risks and survival rates following the two treatments: radiation and surgery.

They found that all groups of subjects were swayed in their choice of treatment by the labelling of the treatments, and all groups also paid more attention to short-term risks of treatments than longer term survival rates. Diagnosis often involves the assessment of statistical risks; the studies by Tversky and Kahnemann (1974) showed that people have difficulty in assessing the statistical relationship between symptoms that arise with differing incidence rates.

Weinman (1981) suggests that the generation and choice of hypotheses during diagnosis are governed by:

1   the clinician's own concepts about the nature of clinical problems; i.e. the extent to which he or she espouses biological or psychosocial explanations of disorder will obviously guide the questions asked;

2   the clinician's estimate of the probability of a given disease; as we have already seen, probability estimates are subject to many influences;

3   the seriousness and treatability of the disease. Here Weinman offers the example of acute abdominal pain in children: acute appendicitis would of course be considered early as an hypothesis because of the costs and benefits associated with correct diagnosis of that disorder – it is relatively easy to treat and not to treat would have serious consequences;

4   personal knowledge of the patient; a person's past medical history but also past encounters with the GP will guide his or her decisions. The 'frequent complainer' is likely to generate different hypotheses from a 'rare attender'.

Eddy and Clanton (1982) analysed the psychological process by which doctors solve complicated diagnostic problems. They suggest the following six steps are taken to arrive at a diagnosis:

- the aggregation of groups of findings into patterns;
- the selection of a 'pivot' or key finding;
- the generation of a cause list;
- a pruning of the cause list;
- the selection of a diagnosis;
- the validation of a diagnosis.

At the first stage a number of elementary findings are combined to form a higher order aggregate. Next, one or two key findings are focused upon: this is the selection of the 'pivot'. After selecting a pivot, all other details of the case are temporarily ignored and a list of diseases is constructed which could have caused the pivot. The next step is to inspect the diseases on the cause list one at a time and to measure them against the case, noting the presence or absence of critical findings. This list is pruned by searching for the most probable diagnosis. This is not done statistically: rather, the doctor determines whether the pattern of findings in the case could have been caused by the disease under consideration, i.e. it is a comparison rather than a calculation. Next, possible diseases are compared two at a time throughout the pruned cause list. Eddy and Clanton (1982, p. 1266) remark: 'The beauty and power of this approach is that it allows selection of the most probable disease without requiring estimation of a single

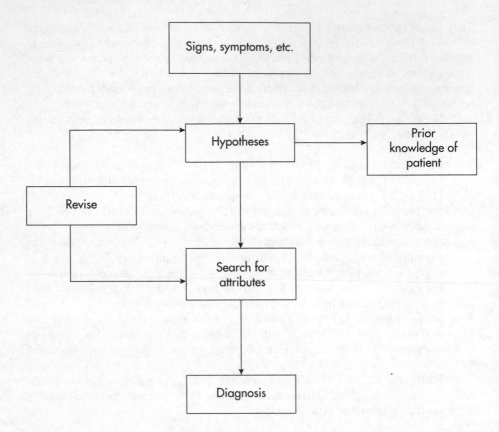

Figure 4.2 Stages in making a diagnosis
Source: Weinman (1981)

probability.' Finally, the clinical diagnosis is considered against all the findings of the case. This allows for a review of the diagnosis and the evidence in support or against it. Figure 4.2 illustrates parts of this process.

This account was derived from a consideration of clinicopathological exercises, and it is not clear to what extent these stages are used by doctors in practice. Nevertheless, it is apparent that diagnoses are not absolute entities; rather, they are predictions made with varying degrees of certainty about prognosis. These predictions can be changed as a result of new information or further developments of symptoms. This aspect of diagnosis is often felt to be unsatisfactory from the patient's point of view. The suggestion to 'come back and see me if it doesn't clear up in a day or two' is one that is perhaps seen as a 'fob-off' when a clearer statement of cause or prognosis is expected. This attitude is represented at its extreme by one of the doctors in Stimson and Webb's (1975) study who ignored a problem raised by a patient towards the end of the consultation. He remarked: 'Well, it obviously wasn't anything very important. And if it is, then he'll be back again before very long.'

The ending of consultations is also a matter for negotiation between doctor and patient. A doctor may signal that the consultation is drawing to a close by offering a summary, repeating a reassurance or set of instructions, or by physically distancing him or herself from the patient – pushing a chair back, closing a pad, putting down a pencil or even standing up. The issuing of a prescription is often the main signal. The patient may seek to prolong the consultation by asking another question or by introducing a new topic, or by taking a longer time than necessary to gather clothes or belongings together – but these delaying tactics are unlikely to be particularly successful if the doctor has decided to terminate, since he or she represents the 'powerful' half of the encounter.

Computers are undoubtedly a blessing for the efficient management of a general practice. However, they can also have negative influences on the consultation process. It is difficult to maintain eye contact with a patient and to enter and read data from a screen, and all too often the patient finds him or herself recounting problems to a face in profile.

The frequent consulter

Robinson and Granfield (1986) examined the characteristics of the 'frequent consulter'. They describe a picture of the frequent consulter as having a large number of symptoms which recur. These symptoms are of the kind which do not usually indicate major illness and are, in fact, often ignored by other people. They found that these frequent consulters also take many more self-prescribed medications; these include health foods and vitamin supplements, pain-killers, inhalers and a wide range of other preparations. It would seem however that these preventive steps do not alleviate their ailments and they consult again. There is also a group of people who believe they are suffering from a serious organic disorder even though tests and investigations produce consistently negative results.

Andersson *et al.* (1995) examined frequent attenders at primary health care clinics in Sweden. They found that, compared with a comparison group, frequent attenders were more likely to be women, and that this preponderance was especially marked in the age group 25–64. They suggest that the frequent attendance of middle-aged women relates to the burdens of wage-earning and family care. They support this suggestion by their finding that a large number of the women in the study were divorced and consulted most frequently for musculoskeletal, social and psychological problems. Other frequent attenders were women over the age of 75, many of whom were widows. These findings accord with those from other studies of frequent attenders (Schrire, 1986; Westhead, 1985).

The difficult patient

A small number of studies have considered the characteristics of patients whom doctors find it especially difficult to help. All studies used similar methodologies asking doctors to rate consecutive patients on the difficulty of their management and then to compare the characteristics of those identified as difficult with those not so described. A study by Hahn *et al.* (1994) showed that between 10 and 20 per cent of doctor–patient relationships could be regarded as 'difficult'. Patients involved were most often presenting as somatisers or suffering from mood and anxiety disorders. Hahn characterises 'the difficult patient' as 'one with three to four psychosomatic complaints and a mild to moderate depression, all embedded in a moderately abrasive personality' (p. 655).

A study in a primary health care clinic in Seattle found that patients who were distressed and used the health care clinic a great deal were viewed as frustrating by the doctors (Lin *et al.* 1991). The patients were likely to have unexplained disability and somatic complaints. Sharpe *et al.* (1994) considered patients in Oxford. Twenty per cent of repeat attenders at specialist clinics were described by the doctors as difficult to help. These patients, as those described above, were more frequent attenders, more distressed, and more likely than comparison groups to have unexplained somatic symptoms.

Mayou and Sharpe (1995) identify the underlying problem as that of different expectations within the doctor–patient encounter. There is in particular a mismatch when the patient's expectations of care are unrealistically high and yet no effective treatment is suggested. 'The shortfall in care is often in the provision of effective psychological and social interventions' (p. 324).

The problem with this account of the somatic patient is that it is potentially circular. Psychosomatic patients are, by definition, those who suffer from chronic, distressing or disabling symptoms for which no organic explanation can be found (Royal College of Psychiatrists and Physicians, 1995). Such patients have been referred to as 'heart sink patients' (O'Dowd, 1988), or 'chronic complainers' and 'the albatross syndrome'. Doctors have failed to find any organic basis for their distress, and patients have failed to accept a diagnosis of no disease in the presence of symptoms. Much heat is aroused from the discussion of these problems, namely chronic pelvic pain, irritable bowel syndrome and chronic fatigue syndrome. A recent report on chronic fatigue syndrome identified the need to treat physical and psychological symptoms in parallel and recommended that 'the whole person' should be considered (Royal College of Psychiatrists and Physicians, 1995) – a recommendation that could usefully be applied to any person undergoing a medical consultation.

A rather different aspect might be to consider those patient characteristics that are negatively stereotyped by doctors. Najman *et al.* (1982) report findings from both Australia and North America which indicate that there is a consensus amongst doctors about which medical conditions or characteristics of patients they find arouse most negative feelings. Those most frequently mentioned were alcohol abusers, unhygienic patients, angry patients, drug abusers, obese patients and patients with minor mental disorders. They found that about half of the responses from 2421 doctors fell into the category of reactions to individuals who might be seen to be 'culpable' insofar as their problems are the result of their own behaviour; this category, which contains alcohol and drug abusers, is likely now also to include people with sexually transmitted diseases, smokers and others. Increasingly, health promotional material and advice locates responsibility for ill health with the individual (Pitts, 1996), ignoring the impact of sociodemographic variables upon behaviours, including those related to health (see Chapter 16).

Communicating good and bad news

Much research has considered communicating to a patient the diagnosis and prognosis of cancer. This is probably because cancer is viewed as the disease engendering most fear in patients (Keesling and Friedman, 1995; McCaul *et al.* 1996). These reactions can be exacerbated by doctors avoiding the use of the word. Smith (1976), cited in Fallowfield *et al.* (1995) comments: 'The malignant reputation of cancer is enhanced by the secrecy surrounding it.'

Several studies (Cassileth *et al.*, 1980; Fallowfield *et al.*, 1995) have shown that doctors generally underestimate not only the amount of information, but also the kinds of information that their patients desire. Fallowfield *et al.* (1995) carried out a study of 101 patients attending a medical oncology outpatients' department. Patients had previously seen an oncologist at least once and were about to receive potentially distressing news confirming their diagnosis or the recurrence of their disease. About half of the patients had poor prognosis and the other half had a relatively good prognosis. Patients completed a number of questionnaires, including one which investigated their preferences for receiving information. The overwhelming majority of the patients (94 per cent) expressed a general desire for as much information as possible, be it good or bad. The small minority who indicated preference to leave things up to the doctor were elderly patients with a poor prognosis. Patients showed a particularly strong desire to know what were the chances of cure, all possible treatments available and side-effects of treatment. Sixty-two per cent indicated an *absolute need* to know if it was cancer. This study showed a strong need for information, whether positive or negative. Cassileth *et al.* (1980) also found the desire for information to be strong – in their study only 2 per cent did not want to know if the problem was cancer. Doctors may shy away from offering information, particularly about prognosis, since a consequence may be that the patient loses hope, but Fallowfield argues that 'honest, positive communication about what is attainable allows the maintenance of hope, whereas avoidance, evasion and secrecy may contribute to a sense of hopelessness' (p. 201). A culture of silence and secrecy can lead to despair. 'What is unspoken is unspeakable' (Simpson, 1982).

An even more difficult issue, perhaps, is the communication of the diagnosis of Alzheimer's disease. Alzheimer's disease, along with other degenerative disorders, carries with it particular dilemmas. On the one hand, people might wish to receive news of this diagnosis so that they are able to put their affairs in order, make their long-term wishes known, and perhaps prepare for the degeneration. On the other hand, one cannot overestimate the devastation and depression such a diagnosis could engender, and to date, little can be done to delay or diminish the onset of symptoms. Conor *et al.* (1996) reported that 83 per cent of family members of Alzheimer's disease sufferers did *not* want the patients informed of the diagnosis; but, in the same group of family members, 71 per cent stated that they would themselves wish to be told if they were sufferers. Rice *et al.* (1997) report a relationship between the severity of the dementia and whether psychiatrists would share the diagnosis with the sufferer. Over 80 per cent of psychiatrists in this sample stated that they rarely informed severely demented patients; in contrast, they would frequently share the diagnosis with patients suffering from mild dementia. Ethical and legal issues apart, it can be seen here that the issue of doctor–patient communication is complex; hard and fast rules can rarely be given as to what is most beneficial for all concerned.

Adherence and non-compliance

Compliance can be defined as 'the extent to which a person's behaviour (in terms of taking medications, following diets or executing other lifestyle changes) coincides with medical or health advice' (Haynes *et al.*, 1979). Non-compliance is therefore when medical or health advice is not followed. Clearly this is rarely all or nothing – we may follow some parts of advice and ignore others. Hussey and Giliand (1989) suggest there can be two kinds of non-compliance: an unintentional type when the person/patient has an inadequate understanding of the disease or condition being treated, or when they fail to understand the advice being given to them. The second kind is intentional non-compliance when the patient consciously chooses to find an alternative or simply decides to do nothing. The term 'compliance' carries an authoritarian ring to it, and increasingly in the literature there is a preference for 'adherence', or even 'therapeutic alliance', to suggest a more co-operative approach on the part of both the patient and the health professional. There is now a vast literature on the subject and concern about the 'problem' of non-compliance is understandable. Non-compliance can at the very least be expensive in the wastage of expensive drugs and the use of hospital facilities, but it can also be potentially dangerous or even lethal in its repercussions for the health of individuals.

Non-adherence can occur at any stage of the medical process. A person can fail to attend a clinic or hospital appointment; he or she can attend but fail to complete the prescription or fail to take all the medication prescribed; he or she can also fail to attend follow-up sessions or to adhere to specific regimens. More generally, adherence to much of the health advice with which we are all now bombarded would be impossible – especially in the area of preventive health, we are harangued daily about our duty to remain healthy by engaging in health behaviours and avoiding risks to health. Recent campaigns to persuade us to eat more fruit and vegetables or to stay out of the midday sun would be examples.

The extent of non-compliance

Measuring what is, in essence, the absence of behaviour is particularly problematic. Some aspects of non-compliance are more easily measured than others however. Sackett summarises it thus: 'accurate measurement of compliance is not easy; easy measurements of compliance are not accurate' (cited in Haynes,

1987). We will deal first with a relatively straightforward area – the non-atten-dance at medical appointments. Sackett and Snow (1979) reviewed several studies of attendance rates in the USA and derived figures of 50 per cent show-up if the appointments were initiated by health professionals, rising to 75 per cent show-up if the appointments were made by the clients themselves. There were seasonal variations and marked differences between clinics – antenatal clinics had the best attendance rates, and geriatric clinics the worst. The reasons for these differences are likely to be many and various: the degree to which attenders are self-reliant for transport to and from the clinic, are relatively well and fit, are aware of possible subsequent repercussions of non-attending, are attending for themselves or for others such as babies or children – all these are likely to be strong influences on the attendance rate. Many measures have been tried to improve these rates: Hochstadt and Trybula (1980) showed that a reminder in the form of a letter or telephone call improved appointment keeping substantially at a community centre. Many dentists issue reminder postcards about a week prior to a six-month dental check-up, again in the hope that this will improve attendance.

Taking the medicine

Ley (1988) defines non-compliance for medication uptake as:

- not taking enough medicine
- taking too much medicine
- not observing the correct interval between doses
- not maintaining the correct duration of treatment
- taking additional unprescribed medicines

Again, the implications of these failures to comply with medical advice are poten-tially extremely serious. The most popular method for assessing the extent of non-compliance with medication regimens is by patient interview. This method has many problems associated with it: there is some social pressure not to admit to forgetting or to failing intentionally to follow medical advice; in addition, patients may simply not recall whether or not they have taken the medication. It is extremely important therefore that information gathered by interview be collected in a manner most likely to elicit accurate responses. Haynes *et al.* (1980) began their interviews by saying, 'People often have difficulty in taking pills for one reason or another and we are interested in finding out any problems that occur so that we can understand them better.' The implication that this is a problem which occurs for most people is more likely to elicit answers than one which stresses how unfortunate it is that pills are not taken and then invites patients to 'confess their failures'. A study by Morisky *et al.* (1986) reports the development of a short series of questions which cover general aspects of compliance and they have claimed validity over five years in predicting blood pressure control.

A study reported by Roth (1987) examined patients with peptic ulcers for their intake of antacid medication. They compared patients' stated intake with the number of empty bottles of antacid which they returned. For those patients who claimed to have followed directions one hundred per cent of the time the correspondence with returned bottles was extremely poor, varying from 2 per cent upwards with a mean of 59 per cent. For those who indicated that they had missed the very occasional dose, i.e. 80–90 per cent compliance claimed, the correspondence with bottles returned remained extremely poor. Only for those who reported taking no medication was the correspondence good. Roth concludes (p. 114):

> When a patient states that the medication is taken regularly, it often is not. When a patient states that occasional doses are being missed, that is usually an understatement of the extent of deviation from the regimen. However, when a patient states that the drug is not being taken, this is usually corroborated.

It has been shown to be particularly pointless to use doctors' estimates of compliance. Both Davis (1966) and Caron and Roth (1968) found doctors to be poor judges of the extent of non-compliance. Roth (1987) reports that doctors overestimate patients' intake of medication by 50 per cent; they are also poor at identifying which patients in particular do not comply. The majority of GPs do not enquire about this aspect of the process at all, perhaps assuming that their responsibility ends with the writing of the prescription and the end of the consultation.

Other measures of medication uptake include pill counts, and blood and urine tests. Whilst these have the aura of greater objectivity, results from such studies need also to be treated with caution. Pill counts do not indicate exactly when the pills are taken, the fact that a pill has left a bottle does not necessarily imply that it has been consumed by the appropriate person, and even blood and urine tests do not guarantee the same dosages were being consumed in the periods between testing as were being consumed immediately prior to testing. Only direct observation can really be regarded as approaching a reliable method, and that, in most cases, is not a practical option.

When studies compare these various measures of non-compliance it is nearly always the case that both pill counts and urine and blood tests reveal higher incidences of non-compliance than patients report. Ley (1988) cites nine studies where both methods have been used and finds overall that patients report an average of about 22 per cent non-compliance, whilst the 'more objective methods' from the same studies yield an estimate of 54 per cent.

Compliance rates of a number of specific groups of patients have been studied. Of particular interest are the studies which deal with elderly patients. There are many aspects of the aged which could lead to particularly poor compliance with medical regimens – they may have failing memory or sight and may have fewer people around to remind them. In general, however, despite the fact that much of the research has focused on patients' personal and demographic characteristics, the search for characteristics that are unique to non-compliers has been singularly unproductive, and it is worthwhile remembering that compliance amongst health professionals and doctors themselves is no better than that of people in general (Leventhal and Cameron, 1987).

Little research has examined whether characteristics of health professionals influence adherence to medical treatment and advice. However, a study by DiMatteo *et al.* (1993) did exactly that. They found that characteristics of the physician's practice and practice style influenced patient adherence; interestingly there was a positive relationship between how satisfied with their work the *doctors* rated themselves and how likely their *patients* were to follow their advice. This intriguing finding can probably be explained by the notion that a happy doctor makes for happier patients, and we know that satisfaction with consultation is a good predictor of later adherence to medical advice.

Most of this research regards non-compliance as 'a problem', and indeed it often is. But it should be remembered that there is sometimes a rational basis for a patient's non-compliance; the patient may feel that the medicine is inappropriate, that it has been ineffective in the past or that the side-effects are more troublesome than the disorder under treatment. The important aspect is that GPs should be made aware of these doubts at the time of prescribing and either alter the prescription or spend some time discussing the reasons governing the necessity for complying. Non-compliance is not simply a medical problem; all of us regularly receive advice about what might be in our best interest, from having the roof fixed to making a will; the extent to which we choose to follow such advice is part of our right as free individuals to take decisions for ourselves about our own affairs, including our own health and lives.

Factors influencing compliance

Homedes (1991) reports that more than 200 variables have been found to affect compliance. He categorises them as:

a)   characteristics of the patient
b)   characteristics of the treatment regime
c)   features of the disease
d)   the relationship between the health care provider and the patient
e)   the clinical setting

Characteristics of the patient

Davis (1966) found that 60 per cent of doctors and medical students ascribe non-compliance to the patients' 'unco-operative behaviour'. Whether or not this is the case there is little that can be done to alter patients' personalities, and it is more productive to examine other factors which can be manipulated to improve matters.

A major influence upon adherence is the knowledge which patients bring to a consultation and their understanding of what is said to them during the consultation. Boyle (1970) and Hawkes (1974) reported clear differences between doctors and patients in their understanding and use of anatomical terms. A phrase like 'sciatic nerve' will be interpreted differently when anatomical knowledge is sketchy or absent. Samora *et al.* (1961) took fifty common items of medical vocabulary such as malignancy, cardiac, tendon, and so forth, and embedded them into sentences. When the sentences were given to patients to explain what was meant, fewer than thirty were correctly explained by the majority of patients.

It is probable that these differences are decreasing; many people now have a modicum of medical terminology, if only from watching the large number of hospital-based programmes on television. This knowledge is likely to be superficial, and there may remain several 'key' medical terms which are not adequately understood by many patients. Many words have both a medical and a 'lay' meaning and when these become confused the patient is even less likely to understand what is being said: psychological expressions such as depression or hysteria would be cases in point (Hadlow and Pitts, 1991). Ley (1988) summarises a number of studies which examine patients' understanding of the diagnosis of their condition and the medical regimen prescribed. He estimates that the percentage of patients failing to understand their medication varied from 5 per cent to as much as 53 per cent. Most especially, patients are found to have patchy knowledge about dosage and timing of medication.

Even if patients can understand what they are told during a medical consultation, the amount that they are able to recall after the consultation has been shown repeatedly to be fairly small. Studies have investigated 'real life' situations where patients are interviewed after a consultation and their recall is measured. Furthermore, 'analogue' studies have been carried out where healthy volunteers are tested for recall of 'dummy' medical information, which does not relate to them personally. There are quite strong similarities between the findings from these two methods of research. Ley and Spelman (1965, 1967) found that approximately 40 per cent of what had been said during a consultation was immediately forgotten: diagnostic statements were best remembered, followed by information about the illness, with instructions poorest recalled. Other studies have not found this same order but this is probably because there is a strong primacy effect which operates during a consultation. In general, the amount forgotten increases with the amount of information given. Ley suggests that if recall is absolutely essential, then only two statements should be made to the patient.

Ley has developed a 'cognitive' model to describe the relationships between memory, understanding, satisfaction and compliance (Figure 4.3). He describes it thus:

> Understanding will have direct effects on memory, satisfaction and compliance, and, through its effect on satisfaction, an additional indirect effect on compliance. Similarly memory will affect compliance directly and also exert an indirect effect through its effect on satisfaction. Finally, satisfaction will have a direct effect on compliance.
>
> (1988, p. 72)

There have been several practical attempts to combat forgetfulness amongst patients. Meichenbaum and Turk (1987) compiled a list of suggestions which included the provision of wrist watches with alarms, drug reminder charts, written memory aides, tear-off pill calendars, special dispensers which provide feedback, prescription stickers, and supervision. These suggestions may be helpful, but

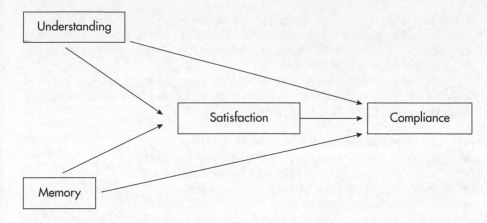

Figure 4.3 Ley's cognitive model
Source: After Ley (1989)

frequently the best aid is a second person to remind and check; that person may be a family member, or could be a health care provider. Many of us are familiar with the problems associated with the multiple medications that those suffering from chronic disease have to endure, and the balance required between administering tablets to be taken three times a day with food, those to be taken after eating and those to be taken at four-hourly intervals. No wonder there can be confusion!

Treatment variables

Geersten *et al.* (1973) considered the relationship between time spent waiting to see the doctor and compliance. Sixty-seven per cent of patients who had waited less than half an hour were compliant, 48 per cent who had waited from thirty minutes to one hour and only 31 per cent who had waited longer than an hour were compliant with subsequent medical advice. This matches well with the study by Stimson and Webb (1975) who comment on means of controlling access to the doctor. Ancillary staff such as receptionists are placed between patient and doctor to control flow; they are, though, often seen more powerfully as decision makers on whether access to the doctor should be granted at all. They quote a mother:

> 'the receptionist always asks me what is wrong with the child. But I've got so used to her now that I've got a bit catty and I say, "well if I knew that, I wouldn't be calling the doctor out would I?"'

Arber and Sawyer (1985) surveyed over 1000 adults about their experiences of receptionists. They concluded: 'the hostility expressed by the public towards receptionists is grounded in the reality of receptionists' actions' (p. 919). They found that large practices tended to operate by more rigid rules, and that parents with dependent children were those who expressed most antagonism about the receptionist's role as 'gatekeeper' – or, as Arber and Sawyer rather more vividly label it, 'a dragon behind the desk'.

A major study by Korsch *et al.* (1968) reported a strong link between patients' satisfaction with the consultation and compliance with advice stemming from that consultation. 'Satisfaction' was associated with:

- the doctor being friendly rather than business-like;
- the doctor seen to understand the patients' concerns;
- patients' expectations of treatment being met;
- the doctor being seen as a good communicator;
- the provision of information.

They conducted a series of studies at a Los Angeles outpatients' paediatric clinic and their findings have formed the basis of much later work on satisfaction. Overall, they found that mothers who said they were satisfied with the consultation were three times more likely to comply with medical advice than dissatisfied mothers. They also found no relationship between length of consultation and satisfaction level – a finding which has since been disputed.

Buller and Buller (1987) found that patients' evaluations of a doctor's communication were associated strongly with their evaluation of the medical care that they received. A style of interaction which they describe as 'affiliative' received more favourable evaluation than a 'controlling' style. They also report a relationship between the amount of time spent waiting to see the doctor and the satisfaction with medical care.

The measurement of satisfaction is in itself very complicated: the phrasing and emphasis of the questions can greatly influence the levels of satisfaction found. Wolf *et al.* (1978) devised a medical interview satisfaction scale which seeks to provide a valid measurement instrument for this rather broad concept. Ley (1972) reports a curvilinear relationship between time after discharge from treatment and level of satisfaction. In other words, those studies which examine satisfaction immediately on discharge from hospital and those which measure satisfaction eight weeks after discharge are likely to find higher satisfaction than those sampling satisfaction three to four weeks after discharge. This needs to be remembered when comparing studies, as only rarely has satisfaction been measured across several time periods. Finally, Mirowsky and Ross (1983) regard patient satisfaction and visiting the doctor as a 'self-regulating system'. They seek to account for the discrepancies between previous studies by this means. They find that satisfaction with the doctor increases the frequency of visiting the doctor, which, in turn, decreases satisfaction. This is presumably because there is an increased chance of an 'unsatisfactory' encounter as the number of visits increases. Nevertheless, patients' satisfaction is still held to be one of the most important influences on compliance.

SYMPTOMS AND CONSULTATIONS

Think about the last time you experienced 'an illness episode'.

What action did you take? Did you discuss your symptoms with anyone? If so, with whom?

Think about the last time you visited your general practitioner.

Why did you attend? Did the interaction match the descriptions given in this chapter? Did you receive any advice or medication? Did you follow that advice, did you complete the course of medication? Did you 'get better'?

You may like to compare your experiences with those of others to gain an idea of the similarities and differences between your medical encounters.

Key point summary

- The experience of symptoms is not the only reason that people decide to consult a doctor. Many other factors will influence the decision, such as beliefs and attitudes towards health and illness.
- The medical consultation is a particular form of social interaction which is distinguished from other dyadic interactions by its setting, function and the powerful relationship of doctor to patient. There are different patterns of consultation between men and women, old and young.
- Doctors and patients may have different expectations of purpose and outcome of the consultation. Certain kinds of patient are negatively regarded by some doctors.
- Adherence to medical advice is a major concern of health psychologists. Factors such as satisfaction with the consultation and understanding of the medical advice will influence compliance.

Further reading

Ley, P. (1988) *Communicating with Patients*. London: Croom Helm. Ley outlines work on patient compliance and factors which are influential in determining compliance.

Ong, L. M. L., Dehaes, J. C. J. M., Hoos, A. M. and Lammes, F. B. (1995) Doctor–patient communication: a review of the literature. *Social Science and Medicine*, 40 (7), 903–918. A useful overview of recent literature concerning communication during consultations.

Tate, P. (1994) *The Doctor's Communication Handbook*. Oxford: Radcliffe Medical Press. A fun read, even though it is written primarily for doctors. It is concerned with developing communication to improve the outcomes of medical consultations.

Chapter 5

The experience of treatment

Marian Pitts

Introduction

This chapter will consider the experiences of hospitalisation, surgery and treatments. It will examine the extent to which psychological factors play a part in how we react to these events and whether health psychologists can play a part in reducing the distress associated with going into hospital, and in aiding a speedy recovery.

Reactions to hospitalisation

Most people in industrialised societies will be admitted to hospital at least once in their lives and, for a few, hospitalisation is a relatively regular feature of their lives. For almost everyone, though, the first admission to hospital signals major changes in the pattern of their daily routines.

There are a number of social changes which inevitably accompany admission to hospital; obvious ones are the loss of privacy and independence. In most hospitals it is still the case that the person becomes the patient and takes on the characteristics of that role. Independence is given up; it is no longer expected that one can choose when and what to eat, when to sleep, when to read, bathe and so forth. Most adults do not normally allow themselves to be seen by strangers in a state of undress and do not normally take their meals to order. All these aspects of a person's individual lifestyle become subsumed to the hospital regime. Also lost are the usual social opportunities for distraction or enjoyment. At home, if you feel bored, you can go out, telephone a friend, read the paper, go to the pub, listen to a record or to the radio. These distracting activities are only available to a very limited extent in hospital; it is probably not surprising therefore that one of the most frequent reactions to hospitalisation is to become increasingly preoccupied with the hospital regime itself and with one's own clinical signs and symptoms.

These changes need not be regarded negatively by all patients. If they have been in great pain or distress, the relinquishing of decision making to powerful and competent others can be reassuring. For an increasing number of people though, entry into hospital is not because of serious illness but for rather more routine procedures to be carried out on an otherwise healthy individual; giving birth is an example of this, and the change from person to patient may not be entirely welcome.

A number of studies have examined psychological reactions to hospitalisation. Taylor (1979) examined patients' reactions in detail. She suggests that loss of control and depersonalisation are common features of hospital experience. She describes the 'good patient' role which staff may reinforce. The good patient is passive, undemanding and cooperative. This patient does not ask questions or make demands on staff time. In contrast, the 'bad patient' may indulge in what Taylor describes as 'petty acts of mutiny' such as wandering around, smoking or drinking, or trying to flirt with staff. These are perceived as acts of defiance and place demands on both time and attention of the staff. 'Bad' patients frequently ask questions or query their treatment. Although hospital staff may reinforce the behaviours of the 'good patient', Taylor lists several ways in which being a good patient can be detrimental to recovery – such persons may be in a state of learned helplessness. Seligman (1975) showed that, when people are in conditions where their actions do not give rise to the desired outcomes, they may learn to be help-less – that is, they learn that their attempts to control will not be successful because response and outcome are independent of each other. Taylor suggests that such a state is not uncommon following a long stay in hospital and that hospital regimes often inhibit the patient from taking active steps towards recovery. Patients may fail to report new or changing patterns of symptoms; the patient may remain relatively uninformed about his/her condition and may find the process of rehabilitation back to independence particularly difficult to achieve. In Goffman's (1961) terminology, the 'good patient' may become 'colonised' within the hospital regime.

The bad patient is not necessarily better off; the demands for attention and the refusal to comply with the hospital regime may result in staff ignoring the 'necessary' complaints along with the 'unnecessary'. There is one area where the bad patient does seem to benefit however. By retaining at least some control over their lives and emotions, leaving the hospital is welcomed and adjusted to quickly and well. Karmel (1972) reported higher morale and fewer instances of depression amongst a group of patients he labelled 'intransigent' – those who challenged staff and the hospital routine.

Hospital language is a particular example of the changes which can happen. Often the language used, most especially by senior medical staff, reflects a style of speech more commonly associated with children. Patients are invited to 'pop' in and out of bed, to 'slip off their clothes', women are frequently referred to by terms of endearment – 'dear', 'love'; stomachs become tummies, backsides become bottoms, and so on. Older patients are particularly likely to be the recip-ients of such speech – an old man becomes 'a naughty boy who wouldn't eat his tea'. There are aspects of this scenario which can be regarded as reassuring – nursery language carries the implications of safety and care; but it is not always received as well as it is apparently meant.

Anxiety and stress in hospitals

There are many aspects of the hospital situation which are likely to induce anxiety or stress in patients; evidence suggests that such negative feelings are common. To what extent such emotions are the inevitable consequence of a novel situa-tion has become the focus of much research. Volicier and Bohannon (1975) devised a hospital stress-rating scale and asked patients to rank order a large number of events related to hospitalisation. They concluded that events which could be directly affected by the behaviour of hospital staff were ranked high; these included knowledge about the nature and prognosis of the illness, and getting pain medication when it was needed. Wilson-Barnett (1976) found during interviews with hospital patients that issues of separation from family, friends and work were major sources of anxiety and concern. Johnston's (1982) study is one of a number to investigate in detail the areas of concern of hospital patients. Johnston compared patients' worries with those that were estimated by staff to be of major concern to their patients. She found that on the whole, nursing staff overestimated concerns about aspects of medical care; patients were more concerned with aspects of their lives beyond the ward. In a later study, however, Johnston (1987) reports that worries about the outcome of the operation were most frequently reported as concerns by patients.

Van der Ploeg (1988) investigated a range of medical stressors in terms of their frequency and intensity. He found anaesthetics, operations and hospital admissions to be amongst the most highly stressful medical events; but also that poor communication by the doctors could produce equally high levels of stress. In particular, 'doctors not giving proper answers to questions', 'having the feeling that the doctor is not listening', and 'insufficient information about the illness and treatment' were all rated as highly stressful. Patients from different ethnic groups may find the experience particularly stressful, and health advocates are sometimes used to aid the effectiveness of cultural exchanges.

There have been various estimates of the degree of depression found amongst medical patients hospitalised on general wards. Moffic and Paykel (1975) found a 24 per cent prevalence of depression as measured by the Beck Depression Inventory (BDI); Fava et al. (1982) and Cavanagh (1983) estimate around 33 per cent of medical inpatients to be depressed. There have been many attempts to link this depression with aspects of the disorders which have resulted in hospital admission. Some studies have reported a relationship between severity of illness and depression (Moffic and Paykel, 1975; Schwab et al., 1967), but not all studies have found this (Wise and Rosenthal, 1982). Length of illness does not seem to be directly related to depression, nor does the experience of pain. It is generally considered to be more fruitful to examine social aspects of the experience as an explanation of these high levels of depression. Taylor, as we have seen, links depression with learned helplessness in patients. A study by Rosenberg et al. (1988) employed a multivariate design to try to tease out the major variables influencing incidence of depression among medical inpatients. They focused particularly on the role of social support. Thirty-eight per cent of their sample of medical inpatients were judged to be clinically depressed. No significant sex, race or age differences in the sample were found to be related to level of depression. The most powerful predictor of inpatient depression was the self-rated index of pre-hospitalisation depression. This is not surprising, since current depression could be a continuation of a previous state or could induce a negative set in recall of previous affective states. Other important determinants were the patients' perceptions of the supportiveness of the doctor and their perceptions of the severity of their illnesses. The *actual* severity of the illness was not related to level of depression; once again it is the perception of the situation which is important. Other studies, such as that of Dimatteo and DiNicola (1982), have also stressed the importance of the doctor–patient relationship. Rosenberg et al. (1988) conclude that 'the physician is uniquely qualified to provide the social support which would mitigate the effects of learned helplessness within the hospital'.

Increasingly, it is acknowledged that all illnesses carry both psychological and physical features. Care is best when the patient is treated in an environment where all involved with that care recognise the social and psychological aspects of their illness as well as the physical. A recent joint report by the Royal College of Physicians and Royal College of Psychiatrists (1995) emphasised the need for psychological care of medical patients. They acknowledge that, unsurprisingly, patients often become miserable and upset in response to both physical illness and hospitalisation and that it can be difficult to decide when a more serious reaction which requires psychiatric intervention may have developed. The report estimates that adjustment disorders occur in approximately a quarter of all medical inpatients; and anxiety and depression in a further 12–16 per cent. These rates are raised in particular groups who are at increased risk of anxiety and depression. These groups include those who have suffered an illness affecting the brain such as a stroke, those with acute painful and possibly life-threatening illnesses such as myocardial infarction, those with a chronic disabling or disfiguring illness such as rheumatoid arthritis, those undergoing particularly unpleasant treatments such as chemotherapy, and elderly people (Joint Report, Royal College of Physicians and Royal College of Psychiatrists, 1995). This is quite a substantial list, and includes many of the reasons why people find themselves in hospital for any period of time. In addition, substance misuse problems are common in both outpatients and inpatients. It is estimated that about one-fifth of male inpatients have alcohol-related problems, and this proportion is often higher, especially in inner city areas (Joint Report, Royal College of Physicians and Royal College of Psychiatrists, 1995).

Recognising psychological problems

Several studies have shown that psychological problems frequently go undetected in general hospitals (Mayou and Hawton, 1986; Feldman *et al.*, 1987). Doctors and nurses have been shown to overestimate the extent of anxiety disorders, but to underestimate the extent of depressive disorders in medical inpatients (Derogatis *et al.*, 1976; Hardman *et al.*, 1989). In the latter study, nurses were shown to recognise depressive disorders more frequently than medical staff, but still recognised only half of those patients suffering from depression. In some ways this is understandable; depression may be seen as a natural and normal reaction to physical illness, rather than the potentially disabling condition it may become. It has been shown repeatedly that doctors underestimate the extent of problem drinking in their patients (Chick *et al.*, 1985; Rowland *et al.*, 1987).

Why are psychological problems detected so infrequently? It is probably due to a combination of reasons: patients are unlikely to disclose their psychological problems unless asked direct questions concerning their state, they may consider such aspects as part of their medical condition, they fear being considered troublesome by staff; in parallel, doctors and nurses employ 'distancing' strategies which keep them at a safe distance from patients' problems. The Joint Report identifies a number of distancing strategies employed by health professionals, regardless of discipline or experience. When faced with distress or concerns by the patients they tend to:

- 'jolly the patient along by explaining away the distress as normal
- offer advice before the problem had been fully understood
- offer false reassurance and
- switch the discussion to safer topics.'

(Joint Report, Royal College of Physicians and
Royal College of Psychiatrists, 1995, p. 21)

Staff employ these strategies because they are afraid that direct questions might open the floodgates of patients' emotions and begin something which their work schedules and training have not equipped them to incorporate (Wilkinson, 1991).

Recognising pain

In order for pain to be treated it needs to be identified. There is a small literature which examines different health professionals' estimations of pain. Usually, these studies have used vignettes – short stories – as their means of presenting information. Whilst this is clearly not as close to real life as evaluating an actual patient, it does ensure that everyone in the study receives the same information on which to make their estimations. An early study by Davitz and Davitz (1981) found that there were differences in the estimations of patients' pain according to 'ethnic group' – Oriental, Anglo-Saxon and Germanic patients were seen as suffering less than Jewish and Spanish patients. Caution must be exercised as to whether these perceived differences would manifest themselves when dealing with actual patients. The ethnic origin of the nurse may also play a part. Davitz and Davitz studied nurses in a number of different countries. They found marked differences in their inferences of pain, with South Korean nurses inferring greatest psychological distress whereas Nepalese, Taiwanese and Belgian nurses inferred the least; with regard to pain, Korean nurses again inferred the greatest amount of physical pain and English nurses the least. Anecdotally, Davitz and Davitz also report that English nurses are surprised when working in the USA at the low tolerance levels of pain. Obviously, these findings are open to numerous interpretations; nevertheless, there may still be remnants of the 'stiff upper lip' in the British Isles!

Pitts and Healey (1989) compared students of nursing with students of physiotherapy and medical students on their ratings of a number of vignettes. Overall, nurses inferred the greatest degree of pain, then physiotherapists, with medical students inferring the least pain. Female medical students inferred more pain than did male medical students. Johnston *et al.* (1987) compared the assessment of 'real' patients by physiotherapists, occupational therapists and nurses. Their findings again suggest differences between health professionals in their estimations of patients' pain.

Seers (1987) assessed the pain experience of a convenience sample of patients undergoing abdominal surgery. Nurses consistently rated patients' pain as lower than did the patients themselves. Calvillo and Flaskerud (1993) also found that nurses underestimated the pain of women undergoing cholecystectomy (surgery on the gall bladder). They found that nurses particularly regarded white middle-class patients as experiencing more post-operative pain than less well-educated, ethnic minority patients. They suggest that 'nurses assign a greater amount of pain and more credibility to the expression of pain to those patients with more social value' (cited by Allcock, 1996). Other studies have not found these nurse–patient discrepancies however (Thompson *et al.*, 1994). It is a truism that we cannot know the pain of others, and this literature suggests that we have low accuracy in estimating it. The area of pain is covered in more depth in Chapter 6.

Patient controlled analgesia (PCA) has become widely used in recent years. A patient can inject a bolus of analgesia by the press of a button; in principle therefore, a patient can receive pain relief rapidly and without the intervention of a nurse or medical staff. Delivery of the analgesic is monitored so as not to exceed safe levels. There is a large increase in patient satisfaction associated with this procedure and the assumption has been that this is because patients prefer the degree of personal control that the procedure confers. However, recent evidence from Taylor *et al.* (1996) challenged this assumption. They carried out semi-structured interviews post-operatively with twenty-six patients. They demonstrated that the procedure had negative as well as positive aspects. PCA was not always valued as a way of gaining control over pain relief; rather, it was seen as a way to avoid the difficulties of disclosing pain or securing pain relief from nursing staff. PCA could also impair the patient–nurse relationship by restricting contact with nursing staff. Once again, the estimation and acknowledgement of pain by health professionals becomes crucial to effective recovery.

Psychological responses to surgery

Patients about to undergo surgery experience greater disturbance and stress than in almost any other medical situation. It is not entirely clear what it is about surgery that makes it particularly stressful but there are probably at least three important elements: first, the experience of anaesthetic is in itself frightening; it involves the losing of consciousness and control and there are associated fears of 'not waking up' or of 'being aware and unable to communicate the fact'; a second element is the degree of pain anticipated post-operatively, and it would be unrealistic to imagine that any surgical operation could be pain-free; the third element involves perhaps the very nature of surgery – the fact of incision, the opening of flesh and the use of needles and knives. It may be that each of these separate elements is stressful, but their unique combination in surgery is particularly difficult to anticipate and cope with.

There have been numerous studies of reactions to surgery, many of which have focused on the relationship between anxiety, preparation for surgery and recovery. The first studies of pre-operative anxiety and its relationship to successful recovery were carried out by Janis (1958, 1969). He interviewed patients prior to surgery and assessed them for their degree of anticipatory fear; he then assigned them to one of three groups: low, moderate or extreme fear. He then assessed all of them post-operatively and rated their recovery. He reported a curvilinear relationship between pre-operative fear and recovery. That is, those whom he assigned to the high and low fear groups recovered less well than those in the moderate fear group. Janis interpreted these results as indicating the necessity for some of the 'work of worrying' to be carried out before surgery. In other words, he regarded moderate fear as a realistic response to the prospect of surgery and thought that this worry enabled people to prepare themselves for the outcome difficulties. In contrast, those people with extreme fear were unable to use their worry constructively as a preparation, whilst those with only low fear were denying the reality of difficulties associated with surgical recovery. This was a very influential study which led to much work being done on how best to prepare people for the experience of surgery. The most important element was the notion that there was a group of patients whose pre-operative anxiety was too low and who would benefit from increased anxiety. Janis's findings have not been replicated and the original study is open to the criticism that both assessments were carried out by the same interviewer, who was already aware of the patients' classifications. Other studies by Johnston and Carpenter (1980) and Wallace (1984) have failed to find this curvilinear relationship. Instead, they report a more direct, linear relationship between degree of pre-operative fear and anxiety and success of recovery. The debilitating effect of extreme fear remains, but the idea of the drawbacks associated with denial no longer seems to hold. The benefits of an attitude of denial are increasingly becoming apparent in the health literature (Gentry *et al.*, 1972; Hackett and Cassem, 1975; Maeland and Havik, 1987). The mechanism by which pre-operative anxiety can influence recovery has rarely been spelt out; there is the clear implication that anxiety affects the patient's physiology in a way which endures after the operation.

One of the difficulties in drawing firm conclusions from studies in this area are that they rarely compare like with like. A review article by Mathews and Ridgeway (1984) lists some of the ways in which studies of responses to surgery may differ:

- *Surgical procedure studied*: a wide variety of procedures has been examined, from fairly minor surgery such as dental surgery to major cardiac and abdominal surgery. Different surgical operations will have different outcomes associated with them – will surgery restore function, increase life expectancy, decrease pain or remove evidence of mutilation? Combinations of these outcomes are likely to produce differences in psychological outcomes (Kincey and Saltmore, 1990). This makes comparisons across studies which concern different surgical procedures extremely difficult.
- *Measures of anxiety used*: these also vary greatly from study to study. Some studies use self-ratings, others staff ratings; physiological indices such as palmar sweating are also sometimes taken. It is not certain whether each of these anxiety measures would correlate highly with the others and so again cross-study comparisons are made difficult.
- *Recovery measures*: Mathews and Ridgeway identify seven major types of recovery measure: behaviour, clinical ratings, length of time between surgery and discharge from hospital, medication counts, usually of analgesics, mood ratings, pain ratings, and physical indices such as blood pressure or medical complications (see Table 5.1). Once again, there is

TABLE 5.1 Assessing recovery

Clinical ratings	Rating systems used by health professionals assessing, say, mobility.
Behaviour	Observations of specific behaviours relevant to recovery, e.g. walking unaided.
Length of stay	Time from surgery to discharge.
Mood ratings	Depression, anxiety, etc.
Pain ratings	Visual analogue scales.
Physical indices	Rates of complications following surgery, blood pressure.
Medication	Measures of amounts of medications required, often analgesics (pain killers).

scant evidence that these different measures correlate with each other in any way and so studies incorporating different numbers and types of recovery measures are likely to give different results.

Preparation for surgery

Despite the difficulties outlined above, there is an increasingly large literature which documents the beneficial effects of preparing people for surgery and other stressful medical procedures. The kind of preparation offered has varied a great deal (see Table 5.2), but the most common kind has been the provision of information of some kind concerning the surgical experience. Two main types of information provision emerge.

The first type, called *procedural information*, describes interventions that employ information about the procedures that the patient is likely to undergo; for example, informing the patient of the timetable of events that will take place on the day of the operation. The second type, termed *sensory information*, gives patients details about the sensations they can expect to experience, such as the nature and duration of pain associated with the surgical incision site. A further preparation method that is related to information giving actually instructs the patients about the types of behaviour they should engage in to promote recovery. This method is sometimes referred to as *behavioural instructions*. One reason for distinguishing between types of information in this way is that it is possible that there may be differences in the power of each of these methods to promote recovery. Obviously, these different procedures are aimed at eliciting different reactions from patients. Procedural and sensory information are generally thought to act through the same mechanism of anxiety reduction. However, Johnson and Leventhal (1974) and Johnson *et al.* (1978) argue that this may not be the case. They present evidence which suggests that sensory information is the more effective of the two methods; they offer an explanation for why sensory information would be effective. It is difficult to evaluate these claims, since most researchers have designed interventions with pragmatic considerations in mind so that they often contain mixtures of these three types of information (O'Halloran and Altmaier, 1995; Burton *et al.*, 1995).

TABLE 5.2 Psychological interventions before surgery

Giving information	
Procedural	'First you will go to the preparation room, where you will be given an anaesthetic'
Sensation	'It is normal to feel very thirsty when you come round from the anaesthetic'
Giving behavioural instructions	'Try to cough once or twice to clear your chest'
Modelling	'Here is a short video showing someone like you after surgery'
Training	
Relaxation training	'Concentrate on breathing deeply'
Stress inoculation	'Remind yourself of the relaxation techniques you have learned'
Cognitive coping training	'You say you are worried about the operation, how might you make these thoughts more positive?'

Other interventions are more varied. These include various forms of preparation which focus on the patient's emotional reactions to hospitalisation, training in relaxation skills and the teaching of specific cognitive coping techniques. Reassurance has rarely been examined on its own; more often it is combined with some form of information giving, so again estimates of its efficacy are difficult to give. Cognitive coping methods attempt to train patients to deal with their anxiety-provoking thoughts in ways that are more adaptive. They may be encouraged to summon up distracting images and thoughts when they find themselves dwelling on unpleasant aspects of their hospitalisation (Pickett and Clum, 1982), or they may be encouraged to re-evaluate their threatening cognitions in a more positive manner (Ridgeway and Mathews, 1982).

There have been several major literature reviews which have attempted to evaluate the differential effects of these different preparations, of which probably the most wide-ranging has been that of Mathews and Ridgeway (1984). There have also been a number of meta-analyses. These synthesise the quantitative findings of separate studies through formulae for averaging either significance levels or effect sizes. The meta-analyses of Mumford *et al.* (1982), Devine and Cook (1983, 1986) and Hathaway (1986), as well as Johnston and Vögele (1993), all report moderate effects across a range of interventions. Reviewers have then tried to establish which of the various preparation techniques is most effective. Dunbar (1989) concludes that the two preparation types associated with greatest improvement in recovery are behavioural relaxation training and cognitive coping training. This latter method was also found by Mathews and Ridgeway to be the single most effective preparation technique. Kanto *et al.* (1990) specifically considered the fear of anaesthesia in a study involving women about to undergo caesarean sections. Before the operation, patients in the treatment group were given procedural and sensation information by a nurse; post-operatively the treatment group showed faster behavioural recovery. However, it is increasingly rare that a particular preparation method is used in isolation, and the search for a 'single best one' may prove in the end to be fruitless.

Increasingly it is recognised that there may be many 'informal' ways of preparing for this potentially distressing event. Most people in hospital will spend some considerable time discussing their circumstances with other patients. In an interesting study, Kulik and Mahler (1993) manipulated these interactions. Patients who were about to undergo cardiac surgery were placed with a room-mate who was also waiting for surgery (pre-operative condition), or with one who had already undergone surgery (post-operative condition). In addition, room-mates had either already experienced or were about to experience the same surgical procedure, or a different kind of surgery. Patients with a post-operative room-mate were less anxious before their own operation, walked about more after the operation and were discharged earlier than those whose room-mate had also been awaiting surgery. There was no difference between those patients whose room-mates had undergone similar operations and those who had experienced different surgery. It is not clear why these differences occurred; could the post-operatives have been acting as role models? In which case we would expect to see correlations between the two room-mates' recovery scores: being with a slow recovery room-mate should predict a slow recovery also; or, as the lack of difference in the kind of surgery involved would suggest, is it simply the relief of seeing someone come through the process relatively unscathed that is important? Either way, this is an interesting finding which deserves further investigation, and it reinforces the power of informal preparation, as well as the more formal preparations for surgery outlined above.

Individual differences and preparation for surgery

Many of the effects described above show great variability both between and within studies. Some of this variability may be the result of personality differences. These differences may be particularly important in the area of preferred style of coping with threat. It has been suggested by a number of authors (Evans *et al.*, 1984; Miller and Mangan, 1983) that individuals can be distinguished by the extent to which they seek information about an impending threatening event. Miller and Mangan (1983) studied patients undergoing colposcopy (a mildly invasive medical procedure) and found interactions between coping style and the amount of information given on dependent measures of self-reported stress and physiological measures of arousal. Results showed that individuals who prefer to remain ignorant about the details of the impending procedure (blunters) but who were nevertheless given large amounts of information, were found to have higher heart rates and reported greater increases in distress than those individuals with the same predisposition who were given only the barest details about the procedure. As yet, possible interactions between personality type and information given in surgical situations have not been fully investigated; but it is likely that the variation found between studies of the effect of information giving may well be due in part to personality differences.

Control and predictability have also been extensively studied (see Phillips, 1989). It is usually the case that we need to be able to predict an event in order to be able to control it; but the reverse does not follow – being able to predict an event does not necessarily mean that we can control it. Accurate expectations have sometimes been found to reduce the stress of surgery (Johnson and Leventhal, 1974), but sometimes not (Johnston, 1980). Studies of control for surgical patients have not often been carried out – controlling a ward or theatre environment is often regarded as unrealistic; none the less, at least one study (Atwell *et al.*, 1984) has reported some beneficial effects from enabling patients to control their own anaesthetic administration. There is some evidence that locus of control may be important, with internals requiring more post-operative analgesia (Johnson *et al.*, 1971). Once again, however, not all studies have reported the effect (e.g. Levesque and Charlesbois, 1977). Mathews and Ridgeway (1981) review the impact of personality differences on responses to surgery. They suggest there is evidence that high levels of neuroticism and trait anxiety are associated with poor recovery. Wilson (1981) divided patients into high and low fear groups, and characterised their primary coping style as aggressive or denying. Treatment conditions were a sensation and procedural information group, a relaxation treatment group and a combination group. These were compared with each other and against a routine care control group. All the patients in the treatment groups had reduced hospital stays compared with the routine care group. There were also significant interactions between individual differences and treatments. 'Low fear' patients tended to be discharged earlier if they were in a treatment group which included relaxation training, but relaxation did not have a similar effect on those with high levels of fear. Those with an aggressive coping style responded best in the procedural/sensation treatment group, and those with a denial strategy performed worse in this group. One or two studies (Johnson *et al.* (1971) and Viney *et al.* (1985)) have considered possible gender differences in reactions to psychological preparation. Unfortunately, these studies suffer from a number of methodological flaws and definite evidence either for or against gender differences is not available. It is not clear from the research carried out so far if there is a group of patients who respond particularly poorly to surgery, or whether there are simply individual differences in responses to life stresses in general, surgery being one such stress. This distinction is important when designing interventions for surgery. Chapter 3 considers individual differences in styles of coping and reacting to stress in a broader context.

Personality differences may not be the only reason for the finding that information is relatively ineffective as a method of preparation. The evidence from Ley (1988) (see Chapter 4) shows that patients have difficulty in understanding and remembering information given during medical consultations. If these findings hold for patients receiving information prior to surgery, then whatever effect the provision of information is supposed to have will inevitably be restricted. Few studies have checked to see which aspects of the information or instructions given pre-surgically were remembered, or whether the information was understood. Byrne *et al.* (1988) found that out of a hundred patients who had given informed consent prior to surgery, twenty-seven were unable to indicate which organ was involved in the operation and forty-four did not understand basic procedural elements of their surgery (cited in O'Halloran and Altmaier, 1995).

There have been two types of explanation advanced concerning the mechanisms by which preparation might promote recovery. Most explanations invoke the suggestion that preparation reduces stress; such stress reduction should be accompanied by a reduction in sympathetic arousal and by improvements in a patient's immunological response. Baker (1987) reviewed the evidence that external stressors could affect a person's immunological status, and concluded that such evidence was strongly indicative of such effects. Evans (Chapter 3) considers this evidence in rather more detail.

Mathews and Ridgeway (1984) advance a different explanation. They argue that preparations exert their effects by reducing the frequency and extent of maladaptive behavioural reactions that an unprepared patient might exhibit. These two explanations are not incompatible. Evidence suggests that physiological responses are improved by psychological interventions that may be the result of a chain of events which begins with a reluctance to engage in health-promoting behaviours (such as mobilising quickly after an operation). Studies such as those of Kiecolt-Glaser *et al.* (1985), and Linn *et al.* (1988) indicate that the measurement of effects of preparation on the immunological functioning of surgical patients will in future enable us to examine the mechanisms more directly.

Other stressful medical procedures

Weinman and Johnston (1988) point out that inherent in most of the preparation literature is the idea that 'stressful medical procedures' can be considered together and equivalent in terms of their psychological impact. They suggest that a useful way of distinguishing between the various procedures would be by considering the function of the procedure and the time line and nature of stress associated with the procedure. Some stressful procedures may be regarded as having a diagnostic or investigative role, such as amniocentesis or a barium X-ray, whereas others have a treatment function (for example, tonsillectomy, cardiac catheterisation). Other surgical procedures incorporate both treatment and investigative functions; for example, treatment surgery which also incorporates further exploratory investigations.

Weinman and Johnston (1988) distinguish between *procedural stress* and *outcome stress*. Procedural stress refers to the negative aspects of the actual procedure itself, the associated pain or discomfort. Outcome stress describes the longer term fears and concerns associated with the results of the treatment or procedure. Johnston (1982) examined worries of surgical patients and found most to be concerned with longer term, outcome concerns; she found that relatively few expressed concerns about the procedure itself. Allan and Armstrong (1984) studied reactions to different radiological procedures. They identified outcome concerns as more prevalent for all patients apart from the aged (more than 70 years), who were more concerned about the unpleasantness of the procedure itself.

This concern with both outcome and procedure may serve to explain the finding by Johnston (1980) that anxiety in surgical patients did not diminish as soon after surgery as would be anticipated if the major source of worry was the operation itself. It also points to the possibility of effective interventions *post-surgery* as well as pre-surgery. Weinman and Johnston (1988) suggest that a

combination of sensation information and cognitive coping might prove beneficial following an investigative procedure. They suggest that encouraging patients
to identify particular sensations and interpret them as normal may help to reduce
persistent anxiety and misattribution of internal sensations.

Children in hospital

There has been a great deal of work done concerning children in hospital. It is
beyond the scope of this chapter to consider the long-term effects of hospitalisation during childhood (see Chapter 15 for a fuller discussion). Instead, the
focus will be on attempts to reduce stress in children undergoing elective surgery.
Melamed and her colleagues have carried out a number of studies investigating
the beneficial effects of film modelling as preparation for surgery (Melamed, 1974;
Melamed and Siegal, 1975). She describes the task as to answer the following
practical questions (Melamed 1984):

- What does the child need to know in order to co-operate with the physician?
- Given the child's age, previous experience and level of anxiety, which
  preparatory treatment would be most effective?
- When should preparation take place?
- Should the parents be included in the preparation; if so, what role should
  they play?

Melamed's work is within the social learning tradition and an early study
looked at the effects of a short film *Ethan has an Operation* (Melamed, 1974;
Melamed and Siegal, 1975). This film depicted a 6-year-old boy from the time he
entered hospital through his tests and operation and his interactions with staff
and other children. Ethan is seen as a positive model who, although initially
anxious, is able to cope with the medical situation and procedures. It also
contained information about the nature of preparation for surgery. Children
between the ages of 4 and 12 who saw this film the evening before their operations
showed less anxiety both pre- and post-operatively than did children who watched
a control film about a boy going fishing. Similar results came from studies to
prepare children for dental visits. A film showing a child receiving a novocaine
injection was more effective in reducing anxiety than a similar film with no peer
model. It was important to show the injection within the context of the whole
treatment session. In fact, simply showing the injection sequence was found to
result in more disruption from the child during the dental procedures (Melamed
et al., 1978).

Melamed cautions against the assumption that the provision of information
is uniformly beneficial for children. In a study of slide show presentations for
children between the ages of 4 and 14, Melamed found that younger children
(under 7 years) and those with a previous hospital experience reacted negatively
to the presentation and were more disruptive. They argue for the use of a
distracting film for these children (Melamed *et al.*, 1983) and stressed the need
to consider the age of the child and their previous relevant experiences. Ellerton

and Merriam (1994) investigated preparations for children and their families attending for day surgery. They found that the highest rates of anxiety occurred during waits in the operating room corridor immediately prior to surgery. This is possibly because both parent and child are left, in this study for up to half an hour, without the range of activities which can serve to distract in other waiting areas and in the wards. With nothing specific to do, both parent and child have the opportunity to dwell on their fears and anxieties.

We should also not underestimate individual differences in coping styles in children. Field *et al.* (1988) characterised children as either using a vigilant coping style or a repressive one. The former were more talkative during hospitalisation, actively sought more information and protested more than the latter. Vigilant copers also required fewer hours of intensive care.

These studies have had their impact; preparation for hospitalisation of children is now almost always the rule, often involving a visit with parents and siblings to the ward, a video, and a briefing session. 'Party packs' are sometimes offered, and children emerge from the sessions with their own face masks and shoe coverings. Play areas are provided and distractions arranged; computer games are effective in distracting children awaiting surgery. Whilst it would be wrong to imply that we now know all there is to know about how best to prepare children for hospitalisation, it is the case that we have come a long way in the last two decades from the formal, impersonal style which used to dominate hospital wards for children. Adolescents are probably now the most neglected group. Teenagers may feel extremely uncomfortable in the highly colourful, cartoon character decorated wards which dominate children's areas, yet they are not yet fully prepared for the relative starkness of adult wards. Getting the setting and preparation for treatment right for adolescents is perhaps the next challenge.

We can see from these trends in recent research that the emphasis of most studies of surgical recovery has moved from simple considerations of 'the best preparation method' to a recognition of the need for differing patient preparations. Ideas of 'tailoring input' and 'targeting information' are now discussed and attempts are made to provide a theoretical framework for the findings. As yet though, it is not apparent, given hospital procedures, how such individual treatment can be achieved. How will these patient preferences be identified? And what of the interactive nature of patient, expectations and treatment? It begins to look as if the doctors have been right when they assert they tell the patient, 'if he or she asks . . .'.

You are a health psychologist. You have been employed by the new management team of the local hospital. They are concerned to improve patient satisfaction with their care at the hospital.

1   Describe what practical steps you might take to minimise feelings of depersonalisation and enhance patients' perceptions of control.
2   Your second task is to design a preparation programme for all children coming into the hospital for surgery. What form would this programme take?

Key point summary

- Hospitalisation and surgery are sources of stress for most people. Many different elements contribute to these problems and psychologists have considered ways in which these stresses may be reduced. It is important that medical and nursing staff recognise signs of distress in patients.
- Effective preparation for invasive medical procedures can reduce the degree of anxiety and depression experienced by medical inpatients. Some anxiety is, of course, normal, but evidence suggests that high levels of both anxiety and depression may hinder recovery.
- Recovery from surgery may be affected by psychological preparation offered prior to surgery. Preparation may take a number of forms, from simply providing information about the procedures to be undergone to providing stress management training and coping skills. Meta-analyses have confirmed the effectiveness of preparation but there are many problems encountered when comparisons are made between different studies.
- There are individual differences in ways of coping with these stresses; some people prefer to know a great deal about what is going on, whilst others prefer to leave the knowledge and decision making 'to the professionals'. These individual differences need to be considered when designing effective interventions.
- Children have special needs during hospitalisation and perhaps should be prepared for invasive medical procedures rather differently from adults. Adolescents are rarely considered when designing hospital settings and interventions. They, too, have preparation needs which should be addressed.

Further reading

Johnston, M. (1988) Impending surgery. In S. Fisher and J. Reason (eds), *Handbook of Life Stress, Cognition and Health* (pp. 79–100). Chichester: John Wiley & Sons. This chapter reviews and evaluates studies on preparation for surgery. It considers the range of preparations encountered.

Royal College of Physicians and Royal College of Psychiatrists (1995) *The Psychological Care of Medical Patients*. London: Royal College of Physicians and Royal College of Psychiatrists. This is an important report which outlines the need for an awareness of the psychological needs of medical patients.

Wilson-Barnett, J. (1994) Preparing patients for invasive medical and surgical procedures. Policy implications for implementing specific psychological interventions. *Behavioral Medicine*, 20(1), 23–26. This is a recent review which applies the findings from psychological studies to the medical setting.

Chapter 6

Pain: psychological aspects

Tara Symonds

Introduction

This chapter considers how psychological factors can affect our experience of pain, and will be demonstrated by a review of the early theories of pain and the most prominent explanation of the pain process, gate-control theory. Specific psychological factors in the experience of pain will then be considered, namely personality, pain behaviours and coping strategies. The chapter will also show how psychological theory has been applied to the management of pain for both chronic and acute patients.

Before discussing the theories of pain it is imperative that the problem of defining 'pain' is highlighted. The term 'pain' can be preceded by a whole host of words in an attempt to distinguish one type of pain from another. Pain is usually defined initially in terms of the site of the pain, for example toothache, headache, upper limb pain. But a common categorisation system which is also used is one that distinguishes between acute, subacute or chronic pain. This was highlighted by Spitzer *et al.* (1987) when they used such a system to distinguish between different types of spinal disorders. However, researchers often use these terms differently. For example, chronic pain has been defined as pain that has resisted treatment for at least six weeks yet others state that pain is not chronic until more than six months have elapsed. Thus when considering research that discusses pain, one should be aware of what definitions the researchers are using for terms such as acute and chronic pain.

The focus of this chapter will be on back pain, which not only has serious consequences for individuals' lives but also for the health service. It was estimated in 1993 that the annual cost of back pain to the National Health Service (UK) was approximately £480 million (CSAG, 1994) and that there is an estimated annual loss of work production caused by back pain of £3.8 billion (Frank, 1993). The study of back pain is an area that has been focused primarily on adults, and as such this chapter will not be reviewing work on children's experience of pain (see Skevington (1995) for more details of this area).

Theories of pain

The experience of pain as a sensation, however unpleasant, is a necessary one. If we were unable to feel pain we would be in danger of permanently damaging or even killing ourselves. For example, imagine breaking your leg and, because you feel no pain you continue to use it; eventually the leg will become disabled. Pain as a sensation is thus very important for our continued functioning and ultimately our survival.

Initial acute pain signals injury to our body and the sensation forces us to stop using the injured part until it has recovered. Early theories of pain concentrated on explaining the physiological processes that occurred during acute pain, but a purely biological explanation was not adequate to unravel problematic pain phenomena such as chronic pain (persistent pain, often with no physical sign of injury) or phantom limb pain (pain experienced in an amputated limb). More sophisticated theories were therefore advocated which also considered the importance of psychosocial factors in the pain experience.

Specificity theory

One of the earliest theories proposed to explain the experience of pain was specificity theory. Specificity theorists advocate that there is a direct relationship between nerve endings and so-called pain 'spots' which can be found almost anywhere on the body. Bishop (1946) and Rose and Mountcastle (1959) demonstrated a direct one-to-one relationship between receptor type, fibre size and the quality of the experience, implying that the intensity of the initial pain stimulus is directly proportional to the pain experience. However, the theory was criticised because to suggest that all nerve fibres are 'pain' receptors is an over-simplification; rather, nerve fibres should be seen as specialised (Melzack and Wall, 1991). If all nerve fibres were pain receptors, the pain experience would have to be proportional to the stimulus intensity, but this is often not the case. There are numerous instances of pain experience where intensity and stimulus are disproportionate; for example, pain is often found where there is no apparent pathology, such as some types of low back pain and headaches. Furthermore, Beecher (1959) found that men who were seriously wounded in battle felt little pain, yet paradoxically complained bitterly at other times about a minor injury. All this indicates that a direct relationship between the level of experienced pain and the severity of the injury is simplistic and that other factors may mediate the relationship between initial injury and the perception of pain.

Pattern theory

Pattern theory was developed as an alternative to specificity theory: it relates to patterns of nerve impulses. One such theory was proposed by Livingston (1953), who advocated the idea of central summation where stimulation of sensory nerves, through some peripheral damage, activates reverberatory circuits (self-excitatory loops of neurons) of activity in the grey matter of the spinal cord. These circuits are then 'open' to any further patterns of stimulation from the body, even non-noxious stimuli, which may then be interpreted as pain. It is believed that once there is activity in the spinal cord it is difficult to prevent further stimulation from causing pain. Both phantom limb pain (some amputees feeling pain in the amputated limb), and causalgia (burning sensations unrelated to a heat source) could now be explained by central summation. The stimulus intensity does not have to equal the pain felt, since the excitation in the reverberatory circuits within the spinal cord could cause a pain response from even the mildest of stimulations (Livingston, 1953).

Livingston's idea of central summation has influenced later theories of pain, especially the gate-control theory. However, the 'reverberatory circuits' that he describes have yet to be identified in the nervous system. Furthermore, the theory does not consider how psychological factors may also play an important part in the experience of pain.

Gate-control theory

Melzack and Wall (1965) have since proposed a third theory of pain recognising that, whilst aspects of both specificity theory and pattern theory could help the general understanding of the pain process, they do not, on their own, adequately explain the complexities of the total pain experience. Melzack and Wall (1965) were the first to consider psychological factors in the experience of pain.

Gate-control theory suggests that stimulation of the skin (for example injury, burns, grazes) initiates nerve impulses which are then transmitted to the spinal cord. In the spinal cord there is a 'gate' that controls the incoming impulses and integrates this incoming information with details from the brain. The brain provides information about the psychological state of the individual, including behavioural and emotional states, as well as information about previous similar experiences. The gate receives and combines all the information and decides whether to open or close; an open gate results in the perception of pain. Further opening and closing of the gate is believed to be dependent on numerous factors such as the person's attention to the pain source, emotion, anxiety, coping ability, and physical damage to the body.

The gate-control theory has undoubtedly been the most influential working model of pain to date (Skevington, 1995), and provides a conceptual framework in which physiological and psychological factors are brought together to provide a fuller understanding of pain sensation. However, over recent years, criticisms have been levelled at the theory. In fact, much of what Melzack and Wall (1965) first proposed has remained unsubstantiated. For example, there is no direct evidence of a 'gating' system in the spinal cord. Furthermore, reaction to pain is not fully explained by the theory. Reaction to a painful stimulus is seen as the direct outcome of the interaction between the sensory and the psychological components. If this is true then there should be a positive correlation between pain sensation (sensory) and high avoidance of activities that will cause pain (psychological). However, Philips and Jahanshahi (1986) were unable to show this positive correlation. They found in a group of chronic pain patients that those who avoided painful activities did not show significantly higher pain sensation scores than those who did not avoid painful activities. The gate-control theory still relies on the pain ultimately being an organic problem with psychological inputs coming at a later stage. It may be that psychological factors play a more prominent role in the pain process than either Melzack and Wall (1965) originally thought.

Psychological aspects of pain

The mere mention that psychology is being used in the management of a pain problem may, perhaps understandably, elicit a vehement response from the sufferer that their pain is not 'all in the mind'. However, psychological explanations do not necessarily assume pain is 'all in the mind'. The main psychological factors which have been highlighted as playing an important part in pain experiences are personality, inappropriate behaviours and incorrect cognitive processing.

Personality

Early work carried out by the psychiatric profession explained the problem pain phenomenon in terms of a personality or emotional disorder. Breuer and Freud (1893) were two of the early psychiatrists to try to explain non-specific pain (i.e. pain where no organic problem has been found). They believed that the problem lay in what they termed 'conversion hysteria'; this is where psychic conflict is converted into a somatic problem (bodily symptoms). In 1959 Engel followed on from and extended Breuer and Freud's work. The clinical problem, Engel believed, was in determining how individuals experience their pain. He believed that there are some individuals who are 'pain prone' where psychological factors are the main contributor to the pain experience, whether or not there is a peripheral stimulus present. The 'pain prone patient' is the one who continually suffers from one chronic type of pain or another.

Engel reasoned that the pain behaviour was displayed because of guilt feelings (unconscious or conscious) and that some patients are chronically depressed and pessimistic with their guilt being very apparent. Engel believed that these individuals generally do not succeed in life because when they do start to succeed they produce a painful symptom; only when they are doing badly are they happy. Engel stated that these individuals subconsciously believe they do not deserve success or happiness, and feel they have to pay a price for it.

The majority of 'pain prone patients' are those whom Engel would say fall into the 'conversion hysteria' category. The conversion hysteria patient converts the symptoms that a parent (or significant other) had into a manifestation of the symptom in themselves. Thus if a mother experienced severe leg pain the patient may feel it was their fault and so would produce the symptoms of leg pain in order to ease their guilt. Other patients suffer from depression, and it is often assumed that the depression results from the pain, but Engel believed, on closer analysis, that the pain lessens the person's guilt and the shame of the depression. Thus the pain often helps to prevent deeper depression or suicide. Yet other pain patients are believed to be hypochondriacal. These patients describe their pain in a very distinct manner, the pain being reported as very intense and persistent. The patient is intent on gaining instant relief and is concerned about what the pain really means. Finally, some patients are classified as schizophrenic and, according to Engel, they are similar to the hypochondriacal patients. However, the pain is really a delusion, even though the patient feels that the pain is unrelenting, annoying and inescapable.

In Engel's theory the underlying assumption is that the pain is not real but is a manifestation of some other personality problem. However, this view has not been accepted totally by other researchers; instead it has been suggested that personality may influence our response to a painful experience rather than determine our behaviour.

The idea that personality might influence our experience of pain has led to numerous measuring instruments being designed for use as screening and/or diagnostic tools. These include the Hospital Anxiety and Depression Scale (Zigmond and Snaith, 1983), the Zung Depression Inventory (Zung, 1965), the

Modified Somatic Perception Questionnaire (MSPQ) (Main, 1983), and the Minnesota Multiphasic Personality Inventory (MMPI) (Dahlstrom and Welsh, 1960). All the above instruments have been designed and used to try to identify individuals who may become chronic sufferers of pain and have been used also to determine if an individual with non-specific pain has confounding factors such as depression or hypochondriasis. Take, for example, work carried out on back pain patients. It has been found that up to 41 per cent of patients presenting with non-specific back pain at an outpatient clinic have some form of psychiatric overlay (Coste *et al.*, 1992). Polatin *et al.* (1993) have corroborated such findings with their own work, showing that 59 per cent of chronic back pain patients demonstrated symptoms for at least one psychiatric diagnosis. The most common diagnoses were major depression and anxiety disorder. It is still unclear, though, what the causal relationship is between psychiatric overlay and chronic pain; does the psychiatric disorder cause the chronic pain or does the chronic pain cause the psychiatric disorder?

Behaviourist approaches

Fordyce *et al.* (1973) have argued that pain is related to behaviour and environmental factors rather than to some inherent personality disorder. The idea of chronic or non-specific pain being dependent on environmental factors is based on Skinner's (1971) theory of operant conditioning. Generally, when a person consults a doctor to report pain they have to demonstrate that they are in pain, and this often leads to a display of pain behaviours. Pain behaviours are important because they demonstrate to the doctor how well someone is coping with the pain. However, pain behaviours can become conditioned, i.e. contingent on reinforcements in the person's social world. Conditioning can depend upon two types of reinforcement: the first is 'positive reinforcement', i.e. the occurrence of pain behaviours will increase if followed by positive consequences such as special attention, medication and rest; the second type of reinforcement is 'negative reinforcement', for example, withdrawal of privileges or ridicule from a significant other (Fordyce *et al.*, 1982).

Fordyce *et al.* (1973) have stated that the original pain could have been caused by a noxious stimulus; pain behaviours may result and these may then be reinforced (perhaps by a wife paying her husband unusual amounts of attention) and so eventually the pain behaviours will continue without the noxious stimulus being present. The doctor then has a problem, because he or she will not be able to distinguish between pain behaviours caused by a noxious stimulus and pain behaviours under the control of reinforcement contingencies (i.e. the wife's attention).

One area that Fordyce and colleagues (1982) have focused on is resting, which is thought to be contingent upon environmental reinforcers. Individuals discover 'avoidance learning', where behaviours become a means to avoid aversive consequences. An individual may think that by avoiding physical activity this will reduce the likelihood of more pain, i.e. the individual uses the pain behaviours to avoid adverse consequences: avoidance behaviours have now become pain contingent. For example, a person may limp to lessen the pain from a twisted ankle, but this limping may continue even after the ankle has recovered, because the individual does not want to risk feeling pain. Fordyce *et al.* (1982) have suggested that pain behaviours may persist because of some social consequence such as work avoidance, or social activities which the patient does not like. They have, however, found that an individual continues with the pain behaviour, not because of social consequences but because of anticipated 'internal' nociceptive stimuli and so feelings of pain (Fordyce *et al.*, 1982).

There has been a steady move away from the purely behavioural approach to the explanation of pain to a more cognitive and social approach. This move was initiated because it was increasingly becoming apparent that how people view their pain and how they make sense of the problem are also important in the experience of pain. The cognitive-behaviourists use the same theoretical basis as the behaviourists but also highlight the importance of individuals' beliefs and thoughts. The basic assumption of the cognitive-behavioural approach is that the pain behaviours of individuals are not formed purely by environmental consequences but also by the way individuals construe and make sense of their world (e.g. Turk and Flor, 1984).

Locus of control and cognitive coping strategies

There has been widespread analysis of how individuals cope with pain. The idea of 'locus of control' is based on social learning theory (Rotter, 1954), which also uses the principles of behaviourism, and has been important in studying how attitudes and beliefs relate to behaviour (Main and Waddell, 1991). Rotter (1966) devised a questionnaire to determine individuals' expectations about sources of control in their lives. He stated that there were 'internals' and 'externals', the 'internals' expecting reinforcement to come from their own behaviours and the 'externals' expecting reinforcement to come from external forces which are outside their control. It was not until 1976 that health issues in particular were analysed in relation to locus of control (Wallston *et al.*, 1976) which led to the development of the Multidimensional Health Locus of Control scale (Wallston *et al.*, 1978). It was some years before it was found that perceived control was important in both experimental and acute pain (Chapman and Turner, 1986). Crisson and Keefe (1988) adapted the multidimensional health locus of control scale for use with pain patients by substituting 'pain' for 'health' in the questions. In their study they found that patients who saw outcome as simply owing to chance believed that their ability to control and decrease their pain was poor. Furthermore, patients who had a tendency to use an internal locus of control showed lower levels of both physical and psychological symptoms, and responded better to treatment than did individuals who had a tendency towards an external locus of control.

Over recent years there has been a growing interest in the role of particular coping strategies used by people experiencing pain. Different types of coping strategies have been identified which have been broadly categorised by Fernandez (1982) as imagery techniques, self-statements and attention-diversion techniques.

Rosensteil and Keefe (1983) describe similar types of coping strategies used by chronic pain patients: (1) cognitive coping and suppression (for example reinterpreting pain sensation, coping self-statement, ignoring pain sensation); (2) helplessness (for example catastrophising, little perceived control over the pain); and (3) diverting attention and praying. Burton *et al.* (1995) found that catastrophising (for example that pain will never get better) was the most important factor when predicting the outcome of acute back pain patients.

Locus of control and cognitive coping strategies both seem to be important in influencing individuals' coping ability. The importance of coping strategies in the experience of pain has gained general acceptance by health professionals. However, the diversity of coping styles/strategies makes it difficult to identify which in particular should be challenged to maximise recovery. The following section will look at how two particular types of coping can affect rate of recovery from an acute episode of acute pain.

Fear-avoidance model (FAM)

The fear-avoidance model of pain (Letham *et al.*, 1983; Slade *et al.*, 1983) is a comprehensive explanation of the pain process, drawing on recent theories from both physiology and psychology to explain how acute pain may become chronic. More specifically, the fear-avoidance model (FAM) tries to demonstrate how 'pain experience' and 'pain behaviour' become separated from the 'pain sensation' in some individuals who show 'exaggerated pain perception'.

The core concept of the FAM model is the notion of 'fear of pain' and subsequent pain avoidance. Fear is seen as influencing an individual's responses to acute and chronic pain. In fact, Troup (1988) stated that 'so far as individual psychological factors are concerned probably the most important is the fear of pain'.

When an individual experiences pain there are four ways the experience may proceed (see Table 6.1). Letham *et al.* believed that the pain could go into 'natural remission' where the organic problem heals, resulting in a reduction of the sensory component and therefore the emotional response. The second course can be 'progressive organic' where the organic factor gets worse, as do the sensory and emotional components. Third, there is 'static organic' where the organic and the sensory component are static but the emotional component intensifies. Finally,

TABLE 6.1 Examples of exaggerated pain perception as suggested by the fear-avoidance model of pain

	Organic	*Emotional*	
Natural remission	↑	↑	Pain is getting better
Progressive organic	↓	↓	Pain is getting worse
Static organic	=	↓	Examples of exaggerated pain perception
Organic resolving	↑	↓	

Notes: ↓ indicates getting worse; ↑ indicates getting better; = indicates remains the same there is the 'organic resolving' where the sensory and organic are resolving but the emotional factor is still intensifying.

Both 'static organic' and 'organic resolving' are examples of 'exaggerated pain perception' because there is desynchrony between the sensory and the emotional components. The fear-avoidance model (FAM) was devised to explain these two forms of exaggerated pain perception.

If a person experiences an episode of severe pain, both the sensory and motivational components are used for interpreting that pain. A fear response to the pain leaves the individual with two options: 'confrontation', or 'avoidance'. The former usually leads to a reduction of the fear and the latter to the intensification or maintenance of that fear, sometimes resulting in a phobic state. An individual who confronts the pain is more likely to view pain as temporary, to be motivated to return to normal work, social and leisure activities, and to be prepared to confront their personal pain barrier. The 'confronter' gradually increases social and work activities to test their pain experience against the sensory-discriminative stimulus. The 'confronter' is therefore maintaining synchrony between the pain experience and pain behaviour (Letham et al., 1983).

The pain 'avoider' is fearful, and this avoidance, motivated by fear, is based on two things: avoidance of the pain experience (cognitive component), and avoidance of painful activities (behavioural avoidance). Behavioural avoidance can cause a number of physical and psychological problems. A decrease in physical activity, for example after surgery, can result in reduced flexibility and loss of muscle strength. This avoidance will eventually lead to more pain and will reinforce the avoidance cycle. The psychological consequences of avoiding activity mean there is less chance to calibrate the pain sensation with the pain experience. Avoidance leads to a state of desynchrony between the pain sensation and the pain experience/pain behaviour. Thus avoidance behaviour is thought to be inappropriate and detrimental to the recovery process (Letham et al., 1983).

Letham et al. stated that there are certain factors which are important in determining the type of response (confrontation or avoidance) which an individual will display when in pain. Stressful life events are important because stress lowers an individual's ability to cope with pain and so may lead to avoidance rather than confrontation. Personal pain history is important because previous experiences of severe pain will influence the amount of fear and ability to cope with subsequent pain, those having experienced more severe pain episodes being more fearful of subsequent experiences. A third factor which is important is an individual's personal coping and response strategies. There are individuals who cope more easily with pain than others; this is based on personal experience, imitating coping strategies, and also personality factors. Finally, Letham et al. suggested that 'characteristic behaviour patterns' are important. They draw on the 'neurotic triad' of personality types (hysteria, hypochondriasis and depression) to explain individuals' differing responses to pain.

It can be seen that the FAM has incorporated many of the concepts highlighted in the previous psychological theories, showing the importance of avoidance behaviours – fear, personality and maladaptive coping strategies – when considering why an individual may be more susceptible to chronic pain (exaggerated pain). Rose et al. (1992) carried out a study to determine if the FAM could, in fact, identify chronicity. They compared three chronic pain groups (post-herpetic neuralgia patients, reflex sympathetic patients and low back pain patients) with three recovered and pain-free groups (fracture patients, shingles patients and low back pain patients) on the four components originally suggested to be important in influencing an individual's fear of pain. All patients were questioned about their pain history and coping strategies. Patients' personality and stressful life events in the previous year were also assessed.

Rose *et al.* used discriminant function analysis to test the ability of the FAM to discriminate between the chronic and recovered groups and found that 82 per cent of the participants were correctly identified in terms of recovery or chronicity by using FAM as the classification system. However, Rose *et al.*'s study was retro-spective, i.e. patients were asked about stress, personal pain, history, etc. after the chronicity had already started or they had recovered. But a recent one-year prospective study, looking at acute back pain patients, found that fear-avoidance variables alone could predict future outcome in 66 per cent of patients, regard-less of physical factors (Klenerman *et al.*, 1995).

More work now needs to be carried out to identify what particular person-ality traits, stressful life events and previous pain histories are important in developing chronicity. When these factors are more clearly defined, interventions can be developed to reduce the likelihood of future chronicity. Furthermore, consideration should also be given to whether the fear-avoidance model relates to other pain phenomena or is particular to back pain patients only. Also to be considered is whether the model is culture specific.

Culture and gender

Looking more widely than at the individual level, it has been observed that cultural styles may influence pain tolerance. Melzack and Wall (1991) state that the actual sensation of pain is similar across cultures but pain tolerance levels do differ. A classic example was given by Zborowski in 1952. He found that 'Old Americans' displayed little pain in public and tended to show signs of pain (crying, moan-ing) only when they were alone. However, Jews and Italians were much more demonstrative, openly showing their discomfort. The cultural difference found for the reporting of pain is one area that generally shows consistent results. More recent work has shown differences between other cultures, such as between Americans and Puerto Ricans for chronic pain intensity (Bates and Rankinhill, 1994), and between Americans and Asians for pain associated with cancer (Kodiath and Kodiath, 1995).

Are there differences in pain tolerance between the sexes? Both sexes believe that women have a greater capacity to cope with pain (based on biological and repro-ductive factors) than do men (Bendelow, 1993). However, the research literature would suggest that this assumption is not necessarily correct. In an early study, Woodrow *et al.* (1972) found that tolerance to pressure on the Achilles tendon was greater in males than in females. Furthermore, Ellermeier and Westphal (1995) found that females, in a finger pressure test, reported more pain at high levels of stimulation than males. Yet other studies suggest that pain tolerances do not differ between the sexes (e.g. Fillingim and Maixner, 1996; Harkins and Chapman, 1977; Maixner and Humphrey, 1993). The discrepancy in the findings may be due to males and females experiencing differing tolerances to various types of pain, for example finger pressure, childbirth. Tolerances for females may also change over time. Hapidou and De Catanzaro (1992) found that females become more tolerant of pain after they have experienced childbirth; the pain experienced in childbirth being used as an anchor point to judge subsequent experiences of pain.

Pain assessment

The acceptance that the experience of pain has not only physiological but also psychological influences has led to various ways of measuring pain. The assessment method used will be dependent on what aspect of pain you are wanting to measure, i.e. physiological or psychological aspects.

Physiological measures

Physiological measures have been developed to try to quantify differences in the pain. For example, the electromyographic (EMG) machine was developed to measure muscle tension. Blanchard and Andrasik (1985) found that headache patients show different EMG readings when they are in pain than when they are pain-free. However, EMG patterns do not always correlate with reported severity of pain. Wolf *et al.* (1982) found that EMG ratings differed between a group of individuals who ranged quite considerably in their verbal reports of intensity of pain. More work needs to be carried out using the EMG to clarify if it is really that useful in the quantification of levels of pain.

Another physiological area that has been assessed to distinguish differences between pain patients is that of autonomic measures, for example heart rate, hyperventilation, skin temperature. This area of research has also had mixed results. Dowling (1983) found a correlation between autonomic response and pain tolerance, but Andrasik *et al.* (1982) found no difference between people with and without headaches on skin temperature measures. It may be that autonomic responses are better for testing the emotional response to pain rather than anything more elaborate (Chapman *et al.*, 1985).

Self-report measures

It is now acknowledged how important it is to identify how patients understand and interpret their pain. Therefore a whole variety of self-report instruments have been developed including, for example, the sickness impact profile (SIP) (Bergner *et al.*, 1981), illness behaviour questionnaire (IBQ) (Pilowsky and Spence, 1975), and multidimensional pain inventory (MPI) (Kearns *et al.*, 1985). A widely used self-report measure is the McGill pain questionnaire (MPQ) developed by Melzack (1975) to measure the sensory, affective and evaluative components of the experience of pain. It has twenty word descriptors and respondents are asked to choose words that best describe their pain. The advantage of the MPQ is that it measures pain along more than one dimension, i.e. not just physiological but also psychosocial. However, the disadvantages that have been cited are that the complexity of the words makes it difficult for respondents to complete the questionnaire reliably and the words used are culture specific.

To overcome problems of complexity and culture specificity, other, easier assessment tools have been developed such as the visual analogue scale (but, being simple, they only measure one dimension of the pain experience). This usually takes the form of a 10-centimetre line where the patient can indicate, by marking somewhere along the line, what level of pain they are experiencing, from no pain to the worst possible pain. This instrument is quick and easy to administer and is simple enough for children to use.

Behavioural assessment

The measurement of observable pain behaviours was developed as an alternative to measuring individuals' subjective feelings. The best feature of behaviours is that they are observable and therefore measurable. Chapman *et al.* (1985) summarised the behavioural measures that might be taken by a clinician: (1) activity levels; (2) amount of standing and sitting (uptime vs. downtime); (3) sleep patterns; (4) sexual activity; (5) medication demands and intake; (6) food consumption; (7) normal household activities; (8) leisure time activities.

With such a wide array of behaviours to be observed it has been argued that this is a better way of assessing pain than self-reports. However, Turk and Rudy (1987) state that the first attempts at measuring patients' behaviour was by self-report, for example, diaries detailing activity levels, medication use, and so on. There has since been a move to observing behaviours in a more structured manner, such as in an interview situation. Turk and Rudy (1987) still believe that there are fundamental flaws with observing behaviour, i.e. who makes the observation, are the observations reliable, and so on; more importantly, observation of behaviour is only one way of assessing a person's pain experience.

Pain assessment is a complex process. Researchers have so far tended to use either one or other of the above methods. Turk and Rudy (1987) believe that the underlying flaw of all pain assessment is that it is often measured only unidimensionally. They believe that pain should be measured multidimensionally, i.e. medical/physical, psychosocial and behavioural, in order to give a comprehensive assessment of the patient's experience of pain.

Pain management

Pain management initially meant prescribing, medication and rest. Psychological intervention, when considered, has tended to be used in the management of chronic pain. However, the importance of psychological intervention in acute pain is slowly being realised.

Management of chronic pain

The management of chronic pain patients incorporates a variety of methods such as psychological, medical and occupational. Pain centres were developed to bring together a multidisciplinary team to meet the chronic pain patients' needs. Pain centres are usually inpatient and are generally run over a two- to four-week period. The aim is to make individuals more functional in both everyday life and a working capacity, but also to teach them how to live with the pain more effectively. The following section will look at how two psychological theories (behaviourism and cognitive-behaviourism) have been used in the pain centre to increase function and coping in chronic pain patients.

Behavioural approach

The behavioural approach has been used in treating various types of pain behaviours (for example headaches, phantom limb pain and back pain) to reduce 'excess disability and expressions of suffering' (Fordyce *et al.*, 1985). This is attempted by changing the relationships between the pain behaviours and positive and negative reinforcements. Fordyce *et al.* (1985) wanted to make it clear that the behavioural approach is *not* concerned with modifying nociception, nor with the modification of the experience of pain, but it attempts to increase the behavioural functioning of chronic pain patients.

Take, for example, the use of bed-rest as a treatment for back pain. It is one of the treatments most likely to be prescribed by a practitioner for back pain (Frazier *et al.*, 1991), in the belief that activity may increase the pain. However, it has been found that the presumed correlation between an increase in activity and an increase in pain has not been corroborated (Doleys *et al.*, 1982; Fordyce *et al.*, 1981; Linton, 1985; Rainville *et al.*, 1992). In fact it has been found that there is no correlation between pain intensity and actual activity level as measured by self-monitoring or observed behaviour in a test situation (Linton, 1985); indeed, some back pain sufferers continue to engage in sports activities (Burton and Tillotson, 1991). These studies highlight how it is possible to exercise when experiencing pain without inflicting any further damage. Thus behavioural assessment is of importance in determining the level of activity a pain patient is engaged in. Indeed, the rehabilitation of the chronic pain patient will often involve increasing their 'up time', that is, increasing their activity levels. Patients will be given a programme where they are expected to increase their physical activity. In severe cases this may mean initially getting a patient to walk a few paces. The next session might involve increasing the patient's activity level from a few steps to walking around the gym. At the same time as trying to increase activity levels, the nurses are advised to give positive reinforcement for 'activity' behaviours (for example encouragement, congratulations) and negative reinforcement for inappropriate pain behaviours (for example ignoring moaning, grimacing).

Criticisms of the behavioural approach have been directed at the generalisability of the change in activity levels and the lack of continuation in the early increased activity effects. Cairns and Pasino (1977) showed how walking and bike-riding activities could be increased by setting patient quotas to perform; whether or not they were in discomfort they had to complete the quota. However, if verbal reinforcement was withheld for the walking activities the progress of patients on this activity began to decline and eventually became extinct. It was also noted that patients were doing other activities that were not part of the quota system but they did not make any attempt to generalise the system to the other exercises, resulting in little real increase in activity. The concern of Cairns and Pasino was that when patients left the hospital environment they might revert to their previous level of disability.

Cognitive-behavioural approach

The cognitive-behavioural approach is much like the behavioural approach, but the cognitive-behaviourists also take into account the importance of an individual's beliefs and thoughts about the pain experience.

Cognitive-behaviourists advocate the alteration of inappropriate thoughts, feelings and behaviours as well as dysfunctional sensory phenomena to help alter the pain experience (Turk *et al.*, 1983; Turk and Flor, 1984). Turk and colleagues have formed a six-stage cognitive-behavioural approach for the management process:

1   Initial assessment which includes medical as well as psychosocial and behavioural factors (Turk *et al.*, 1983; Turk and Meichenbaum, 1989).
2   Stage two is the reconceptualisation process where the therapist tries to change the patient's conceptualisation of his or her problem from one based purely on a sensory view of pain to one that is more multifactorial including cognitive, affective and social factors. Turk and Meichenbaum (1989) suggested this process was used to educate the patient to think of treatment in terms that would enable them to have more control over their lives, even if the pain is not eliminated totally.
3   The third stage is referred to as 'skills acquisition and consolidation'; this begins when the basic goals of the programme have been agreed. The therapist begins to teach the individual specific coping strategies to deal with the pain in everyday situations. It is the aim of the approach to deal specifically with the self-statements and environmental factors that may start or maintain disability, and therefore make the pain problem worse (Turk and Meichenbaum, 1989). By giving the person new behavioural and cognitive skills this can lead to a change in behaviour, self-communication, and ultimately to changes in cognitive structures, for example, beliefs or meaning systems (Turk *et al.*, 1983).
4   The fourth stage involves rehearsing and applying the new skills that the patient has acquired; this is done through role plays between the therapist and the patient, including role reversal where the patient is able to see what the therapist is trying to achieve (Turk and Meichenbaum, 1989).
5   The penultimate stage is concerned with the maintenance and generalisation of the new coping skills and behaviours; the patient is advised to try the

new behaviours in different situations and to identify any problems which may arise. Then by working with the therapist they can try and resolve the problems.

6   The final stage involves reviewing all parts of the training. After two weeks the patients may return to ensure that there are no problems and there are usually further follow-ups at three and six months (Turk and Meichenbaum, 1989).

Gottlieb *et al.* (1977), using the cognitive-behavioural approach, started a comprehensive inpatient pain programme that included stress management, biofeedback, psychological counselling, assertiveness training, self-regulated medication reduction, physical therapy, and vocational rehabilitation. Gottlieb *et al.* stated that 79 per cent of patients showed better physical functioning at discharge and 95 per cent had satisfactory vocational rehabilitation at one-month follow-up. Of the patients contacted after six months, 82 per cent had achieved satisfactory vocational rehabilitation. However, even when cognitive factors are considered, as well as behavioural, the rehabilitation of a patient is not necessarily guaranteed. Cohen *et al.* (1980) compared the effectiveness of cognitive-behavioural therapy and physical therapy in rehabilitating chronic back pain patients in an outpatient clinic. After a ten-week period they found that neither the physical therapy group nor the cognitive-behavioural group had improved activity levels or pain levels. One reason why the cognitive-behavioural treatment failed to reduce pain levels and increase activity may have been because it was run as an outpatient clinic (Cohen *et al.*, 1980).

The cognitive-behavioural approach has similar drawbacks to those suggested for the behavioural approach: (1) the patient's newly acquired behaviours become extinct once they have left the rehabilitation unit; and (2) new techniques learned to alter inappropriate behaviours (such as inactivity) do not generalise to other behaviours not specifically targeted in the pain centre.

Biofeedback and hypnosis

Some chronic pain is attributed to stress, that is, the stress produces muscle tension and when the muscle tension reaches a critical point it is experienced as pain. Thus researchers have tried to develop techniques to reduce muscle tension and, in turn, the experience of pain. One such technique has been the development of biofeedback techniques. (See Chapter 2 for a more detailed discussion of biofeedback.) Patients learn how to control muscle groups voluntarily so that they can learn to relax them in order to reduce the pain. Biofeedback has been widely used in both migraine sufferers and chronic back pain sufferers. The most common biofeedback tool is the electromyograph (EMG) which can measure electrical activity in muscles. The amount of electrical activity indicates the level of muscle tension. A signal from the machine indicates changes in electrical activity. Patients can learn to relax tense muscle groups by monitoring the signals from the machine. But does altering muscle tension actually relieve pain? From various reviews of the literature by Feuerstein and Gainer (1982), and Chapman

(1991) almost a decade later, the conclusion is positive. However, this conclusion is based on most of the research being carried out on headache sufferers. There is some evidence that it works for other pain experiences, for example arthritic pain (Bradley *et al.*, 1987). However, more research needs to be carried out to determine if this effect is generalisable to other pain problems.

Hypnosis is still a controversial technique, with some believing that it is nothing more than an elaborate show, whilst others believe that it is an altered state of consciousness (Hilgard and Hilgard, 1975). If we accept the altered state theory, how does this help in pain management? Hilgard (1975) believes that the altered state allows the individual to respond to suggestion and to control physiological reactions that he or she is unable to do in a 'normal' state of consciousness.

Hypnosis has been practised to treat many different types of pain but has mainly been used for acute pain, for example childbirth, headache, cancer pain, low back pain. The efficacy of hypnosis for treating pain does not appear to be dependent on the type of pain treated but on the type of patient. A patient has to be 'suggestible' to hypnosis for it to be effective and not all patients are. Hilgard (1978) found that highly suggestible patients could have laboratory-induced pain completely eliminated by hypnosis. The reason why hypnosis should work is still hotly debated with no concrete answers yet available. Sarafino (1994) suggests that it may be because of the deep relaxation which people experience when they have been hypnotised.

Management of acute pain

Management of acute pain has mainly involved traditional medical management (for example rest, medication) without generally considering the psychological impact. However, Main *et al.* (1992) stated that distress was apparent at the acute stage of pain and so is not just a function of chronicity. Thus education about pain problems may be important in reducing early worries and anxieties that patients may have at the onset of a pain episode, and more specifically a back pain episode.

Roland and Dixon (1989) were the first to consider using an educational pamphlet in the management of acute back pain. The aim of their study was to provide patients with more information about back pain to determine whether this would alter consultation rates. They wrote a booklet specifically designed to teach patients about their backs. The booklet contained information about general anatomy and biomechanics of the back, advice on managing acute pain attacks, advice on long-term prevention of pain, exercises, and when to seek medical attention. The allocation to a 'booklet' and a 'no booklet' group was achieved by placing alternate patients who presented with back pain at five clinics, into the booklet group. Initially, the booklet seemed to have little effect in reducing the number of consultations, but between two weeks and one year after receiving the booklet, these patients not only required fewer consultations with the doctor, they also needed fewer hospital visits and less physiotherapy. In a questionnaire distributed one year after the study began, 84 per cent of respondents thought that the booklet was useful, and the booklet group's knowledge about back pain was significantly higher than those who had not received the booklet.

Two studies carried out more recently, in primary care settings, have had differing success in educating patients about back pain. Burton *et al.* (1996), when piloting a new booklet developed by a group of health professionals based on the clinical guidelines for management of acute low back pain (CSAG, 1994), found that it was easily understood, well received, imparted the relevant messages and promoted positive shifts in beliefs about future consequences with back pain. However, the utility of this booklet for altering actual consultation rates, return to work rates and recurrences has yet to be tested. Cherkin *et al.* (1996), in a more comprehensive study, looked at the benefits of providing a booklet about back pain compared with a usual care group and a group which was given a fifteen-minute talk by a nurse. They found that patients in both the 'booklet' and 'nurse' groups had significantly higher levels of perceived knowledge than the 'usual care' group, but in the 'nurse' group there was a greater impact on reporting of regular exercise than the 'booklet' group or the usual care group. When comparing the groups for increased functioning there was no difference between them, usual care being just as effective as both the 'booklet' and 'nurse' groups. They concluded that patients appeared to like the educational interventions and may have benefited from them in some general ways, but the interventions had little or no impact on symptoms, function, disability, or health care use. The apparent contradiction in results between studies may be due to differing information given in the booklets.

In a more direct attempt to reduce anxieties about initial back pain, Symonds *et al.* (1995) designed a pamphlet based on a fear-avoidance model of pain. It advocated a positive and active approach to back pain, with messages stating that manufacturing workers should continue with their normal everyday activities and return to work sooner rather than later. The aim of the pamphlet was to reduce fears and anxieties about back pain and avoidance of activities rather than to provide information about posture, specific exercises or biomechanics of the spine. To test its effectiveness they carried out a one-year prospective study in a food manufacturing company. The results from this simple intervention are very encouraging. They found positive shifts in beliefs about the inevitable consequences of back pain and beliefs about pain in general. However, beliefs about the fear of pain were not altered. The changes in beliefs mirrored a large reduction in spells of protracted absence and in days of protracted absence due to low back trouble; similar changes were not observed in back pain sufferers in the control companies.

Pamphlet education applied to the problem of back pain has had positive results. Pamphlets should be considered more by health professionals, for use with all types of pain problems, in an attempt to allay initial anxieties and worries that individuals may understandably have.

Final thoughts

It has been established that pain is a necessary sign of physical injury. However, what is now apparent from this brief look at the role of psychology in the experience of pain is that individuals will react in differing ways depending on previous experiences, coping styles, behavioural styles and understanding of the problem. This diversity of reaction to a pain problem means that two individuals, with similar injuries, may have different courses of recovery. One may recover quickly, whilst the other may continue experiencing the pain for months, even though the injury may have healed.

Management of pain, therefore, should consider not only physical symptoms but also psychosocial factors. Furthermore, consideration of psychological factors should not be confined simply to the rehabilitation of chronic sufferers of pain. Health professionals should also consider the impact of psychological factors on acute pain in an effort to prevent development into chronicity.

Key point summary

- The recognition that psychological factors are important in a pain experience has, arguably, gained general acceptance.
- An individual's personality, pain behaviours, coping strategies and social environment are all important in determining how pain is experienced and reported.
- To assess fully the extent of pain experienced, not only physiological factors should be considered but also psychosocial and behavioural expressions of pain.
- Increased psychological intervention at the acute stage of pain is imperative because psychological factors do not begin to operate only when the pain becomes chronic. Our reaction to acute pain may, in some cases, actually be more important in determining rate of recovery than physiological symptoms.
- The future of pain research lies in a multidisciplinary approach where not only physiological processes but also psychosocial factors are included in understanding, managing and planning the rehabilitation of *all* pain patients.

Further reading

Melzack, R. and Wall, P. D. (1991) *The Challenge of Pain*. London: Penguin. This book is the classic pain textbook. It describes puzzling pain phenomena showing how some pain cannot be explained in terms of physiology alone. There is an in-depth description of the authors' gate-control theory, highlighting psychological factors as important in the perception of pain. There is also a small section describing the use of the pain clinic.

Skevington, S. M. (1995) *Psychology of Pain*. Chichester, Sussex: John Wiley & Sons. This text expands on some of the areas mentioned in this chapter and also covers important areas not mentioned due to space constraints, such as the consultation process and children's pain.

We know that the fear of pain can have detrimental effects on recovery from an episode of acute pain. How do you view back pain? Are you fearful of the consequences of experiencing an episode of back pain? Complete the back belief questionnaire (BBQ) (Symonds *et al.*, 1996) below to find out.

Answer ALL statements and indicate whether you *agree* or *disagree* with each statement by circling the appropriate number on the scale: 1 = completely disagree 5 = completely agree

		Disagree	Agree
1	There is no real treatment for back trouble.	1 2 3	4 5
2	Back trouble will eventually stop you from working.	1 2 3	4 5
3	Back trouble means periods of pain for the rest of one's life.	1 2 3	4 5
4	Doctors cannot do anything for back trouble.	1 2 3	4 5
5	A bad back should be exercised.	1 2 3	4 5
6	Back trouble makes everything in life worse.	1 2 3	4 5
7	Surgery is the most effective way to treat back trouble.	1 2 3	4 5
8	Back trouble may mean you end up in a wheelchair.	1 2 3	4 5
9	Alternative treatments are the answer to back trouble.	1 2 3	4 5
10	Back trouble means long periods of time off work.	1 2 3	4 5
11	Medication is the *only* way of relieving back trouble.	1 2 3	4 5
12	Once you have had back trouble there is *always* a weakness.	1 2 3	4 5
13	Back trouble *must* be rested.	1 2 3	4 5
14	Later in life back trouble gets progressively worse.	1 2 3	4 5

Scoring of the questionnaire

Before calculating your score all items should be reversed (i.e. 5, 4, 3, 2, 1). The score is calculated by adding together the following items: 1, 2, 3, 6, 8, 10, 12, 13, 14.

The lower the score the more negative the individual is about future consequences which back pain may have on their life. Those who score low on this questionnaire would be an obvious choice for early intervention to try and reduce unwarranted fears.

How might completing this questionnaire help in the management of an episode of acute back pain?

Health issues

IN PART THREE we consider a range of topics which have been the focus of interest for health psychologists. It would not be possible to offer a comprehensive account of each and every illness, disease or disorder, or health concern which psychologists have considered. Instead we have chosen topics which illustrate different aspects and approaches. The issues selected include most of those highlighted by the British government's approach to health in The Health of the Nation programme (1992) which has identified areas where prevention efforts are to be targeted. Other chapters reflect issues that are receiving increased attention in relation to health and which require specific action and interventions. These include nutrition and exercise, diabetes, contraception, and abortion. The concepts and processes outlined in Parts One and Two re-emerge within the particular topics included in Part Three. You will thus find chapters on the prevention of transmission of HIV, chapters on diseases related to issues about lifestyle which include cancers, coronary heart disease and hypertension, and smoking and drinking (and other social drugs). The emphasis in all these chapters is less to do with the medical aspects of the health issues described than with the psychological factors which can influence onset, progression and treatment of diseases and disorders.

Chapter 7

Social drugs: effects upon health

Andrew Parrott

Introduction

People of every race and culture have used psychoactive drugs to alter their mood and behaviour. Aborigines smoked Dubiosa leaves for their narcotic effects; Aztec Indians used an impressive pharmacopoeia of plant materials for religious and medicinal purposes, while Khat leaves are still chewed for their stimulant effects in Yemeni culture. However, the use of two particular psychoactive drugs predominates across the globe: alcohol and nicotine. Their consumption is also on the increase, despite causing high levels of mortality and morbidity. The World Health Organization estimates that tobacco causes three million deaths each year, while: 'On current smoking patterns this will reach 10 million deaths per year (3 million in developed countries, 7 million in developing countries), by the time the children of today reach middle age' (Peto *et al.*, 1994, p. 3). Small amounts of alcohol have a cardioprotective effect, but increasing doses have adverse effects on many other areas of health and well-being. This chapter will review the health psychology of nicotine and alcohol, outlining their modes of consumption, psychological effects, health consequences and ways for reducing intake. The chapter will conclude with brief sections on the health psychology of three other widely used psychoactive drugs: caffeine, cannabis and MDMA (ecstasy).

Nicotine

In 1604 James I described smoking as: 'A custome lothsome to the Nose, hermful to the braine, dangerous to the Lungs, and in the blacke stinking fume therof, neerest resembling the horrible Stigian smoke of the pit that is bottomlesse' (Mangan and Golding, 1984). He imposed a heavy import duty because 'The health of our People is impayred and their bodies weakened.' However, others claimed that tobacco was medicinal: it cured headaches, healed wounds, removed ulcers, got rid of 'naughty breath', and acted as an aphrodisiac. Its addictiveness was already recognised. One Spanish bishop reprimanded the conquistador soldiers for 'drinking smoke', but they replied that it was not in their power to refrain. Tobacco chewing is a major health concern in the USA, with around 12 million users, and increasing rates of oral cancer, which requires surgical removal of the jaw (Surgeon General, 1988). However, most tobacco is consumed as cigarettes. The percentage of UK males who smoke has reduced from 65 per cent in 1950 to 40 per cent in 1980, and 30 per cent in the 1990s. But female smoking has not shown a similar rate of decline. Rigotti (1989, p. 931) noted:

> An estimated 56 million Americans still smoke, and the rate at which young people take up the habit has not declined since 1980. Rates of smoking are higher among less-educated, lower-income, and minority groups – groups already disproportionately burdened with illness. Equally disturbing, the gender gap among smokers is narrowing. If trends continue, women will out smoke men by the mid-1990s.

This prediction has now come true, and the proportion of British adolescent females who smoke is now greater than adolescent males.

Psychoanalytic theories describe smoking as oral self-gratification, a penis/breast substitute, or a death-wish. Ethologists see smoking as a purposeful act during uncertainty, or the assertion of social dominance. However, these notions are negated by the unpopularity of herbal cigarettes, which could fulfil all these functions. The real reason for smoking tobacco is for the intake of nicotine, since the only plants which are smoked all contain psychoactive substances such as cannabinol or opiates (Surgeon General, 1988). Nicotine generates feelings of pleasure and relaxation, particularly after a period of abstinence (Fant *et al.*, 1995). Some models of smoking behaviour suggest that cigarettes generate real psychological advantages (Warburton, 1992). Other explanations have focused upon the negative effects of abstinence (irritability, stress, impaired concentration), suggesting that smoking simply reverses unpleasant abstinence effects. These contrasting models have been compared in a series of studies at the University of East London, and most findings have supported the deprivation reversal model (Parrott, 1994, 1995a). When the moods of deprived smokers, non-deprived smokers and non-smokers are compared, deprived smokers report significantly worse moods than the other groups (Parrott and Garnham, submitted). After smokers have had a cigarette, and non-smokers have undergone an equivalent period of rest, the moods of all three groups become very similar (Figure 7.1). Smoking only seems to improve the mood of abstinent smokers, suggesting that its main function is to relieve abstinence effects (Parrott, 1994, 1995a). The repetitive experience of irritability in between cigarettes also helps to explain why smokers suffer from above-average levels of daily stress (Jones and Parrott, 1997). Longitudinal studies therefore find that when smokers successfully quit, they report *reduced* levels of daily stress (Cohen and Lichtenstein, 1990; Parrott, 1995b). Nicotine is therefore a subtle drug of addiction; regular smokers need nicotine simply to remain 'normal'.

Tobacco smoke contains not only nicotine, but also tar and carbon monoxide. Russell (1989) stated: 'People smoke mainly for nicotine but die mainly from tar, carbon monoxide and other components.' Tar comprises a mixture of organic chemicals which form the fine mist of tobacco smoke. Nicotine is delivered into the lung on these tar droplets, hence the high correlation between the tar content of a cigarette and its ability to deliver nicotine. When the tar content is reduced, less nicotine is delivered into the lungs. Thus when smokers change to a low-tar brand they tend to smoke more cigarettes, and to inhale more frequently and deeply. This behavioural compensation means that switching to a low-tar brand fails to deliver much in the way of health gains. Instead it simply results in more cigarettes being sold!

On smoke exhalation, much of the tar remains in the lung as a sticky brown residue. It is this tar which leads to cancers of the lips, mouth, tongue, throat and lungs. Mangan and Golding (1984, p. 18) stated: 'The position of tar as a cancer agent is clear . . . various tar components are cancer-initiating and cancer-accelerating.' There is a direct causal relationship between cigarette consumption and lung cancer. Doll and Peto (1976) found that smokers of between fifteen and twenty-four cigarettes per day had ten times the lung cancer rate of non-smokers,

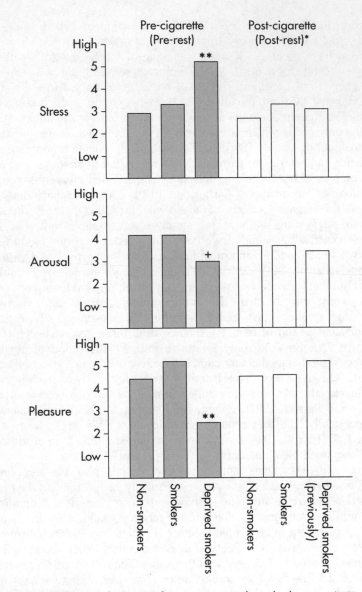

Figure 7.1 Self-rated feelings of stress, arousal and pleasure (UEL brief mood scales) in non-smokers, non-deprived smokers and overnight deprived smokers, before and after a rest/cigarette break

Notes: + p<0.10
* p<0.05 Dunnet test comparison between non-smokers and smokers
** <<0.01

Source: After Parrot and Garnham (submitted)

while smokers consuming more than twenty-five cigarettes per day had twenty-two times their incidence of lung cancer. Lung cancer takes time to develop, but other lung disorders can be seen in novice smokers. Thus lung capacity is reduced from the time smoking is started, and decreases the longer it continues (Royal College of Physicians, 1983). This decline can however be halted by quitting smoking. Shortness of breath is also reported by regular smokers, but this also reverses on smoking cessation. Chronic obstructive lung disease is also caused by smoking; here the airways become constricted, lung tissue is destroyed, and breathing is difficult. Bronchitis and other lung infections are also far more common in smokers (Table 7.1). Pipe and cigar smokers generally retain the smoke in upper respiratory areas, and therefore develop cancers of the mouth and lip rather than the lung (Table 7.1). Tobacco chewers tend to develop cancers of the gum or jaw where the soggy tobacco is habitually wedged, since this is where the nitrosamines and other tar residues become concentrated.

Carbon monoxide (CO) comprises around 4 per cent of tobacco smoke (similar to diluted car exhaust fumes). This carbon monoxide readily combines with haemoglobin in the blood to form carboxyhaemoglobin, so that by the end of the smoking day around 15 per cent of haemoglobin is carrying CO. This reduces the oxygen-carrying capacity of the smoker's blood, and impairs the peripheral circulation. Arteriosclerosis tends to develop in the lower limbs, resulting in leg pains, tissue death and gangrene. Over 90 per cent of patients suffering from peripheral arterial disease are moderate or heavy smokers. Furthermore, when arterial bypass surgery is attempted, the success rates are far lower in those who continue to smoke, and leg amputation may be required (Table 7.1). Around 500 smokers' limbs are amputated in the UK each year for this reason. Arteriosclerosis may be followed by haemorrhage, thus cerebrovascular strokes are also more frequent in smokers. The blood supply to the penis is also reduced, so that male smokers suffer from increased rates of impotence. Female smokers experience various problems during pregnancy: more spontaneous abortions, larger and more abnormal placentas, and 200 gm lighter babies. These impairments in foetal development are caused by the reduced oxygen supply through the placenta (Royal College of Physicians, 1983). The most serious effects of smoking however, are upon the heart. Auerbach *et al.* (1976) reported the following incidence rates for 'severe thickening' of the smallest arteries supplying the heart: 0 per cent of non-smokers; 48 per cent of moderate smokers, and 91 per cent of heavy smokers. This leads to various cardiac problems. Doll and Peto (1976) investigated the rates of heart disease in British doctors. With the under 45-year-olds, seven per 100,000 of non-smokers had heart disease; this increased to forty-one per 100,000 for smokers of between one and fourteen cigarettes per day, and 104 per 100,000 for smokers of more than twenty-five cigarettes per day, a relative morbidity rate of 15:1. Similar trends were apparent in all the other age groups. Overall, heart disease causes more deaths in smokers than lung cancer, but again, smoking cessation leads to an immediate reduction in the incidence of cardiac problems.

Passive smoking is the uptake of smoke-impregnated air by non-smokers. Smoking in an average-sized room can increase the concentration of carbon monoxide (CO) threefold, while in small confined spaces such as cars or

TABLE 7.1 Medical and psychological effects of tobacco constituents: nicotine, tar and carbon monoxide

Nicotine

Nicotine abstinence in regular smokers leads to stress, tension, anger, irritability and reduced alertness. Smoking then restores normal levels of psychological functioning. Nicotine addiction makes the smoker feel more irritable and stressed each day than non-smokers. This explains why regular smokers experience better moods when they quit smoking. Nicotine has few direct effects upon health, although it does increase heart rate.

Tar

The tar in tobacco smoke causes numerous types of cancer:

- Cancer of the mouth, throat and lung in cigarette smokers.
- Cancer of the lips, gum and throat in pipe/cigar smokers.
- Cancer of the gum and jaw in tobacco chewers.

Lung capacity shows a progressive decline from the initiation of smoking.
Bronchitis and chronic obstructive lung disease are increased.
Colds and coughs are more frequent, and longer in duration.

Carbon monoxide

The oxygen-carrying capacity of the blood is reduced.
The peripheral circulation is impaired, leading to tissue death and gangrene, which then necessitate limb amputation.
The blood supply to the heart is reduced, leading to cardiac problems including heart attack.
The arteries become narrowed, leading to fatal haemorrhage, or cerebrovascular stroke.
The foetal blood supply is reduced, leading to impaired foetal development, increased still-births and below-weight live births.

submarines, the CO increase can be thirtyfold. Carcinogenic tars enter the lungs of anyone breathing in this smoky air, while nicotine can be measured in their urine. If a non-smoker breathes in smoky air for eight hours, it is equivalent to smoking one or two cigarettes. This explains why non-smokers who have to work with smokers, or children whose parents smoke, suffer from the same smoking-related diseases. Hirayama (1981) found that non-smoking wives had a doubled incidence of lung cancer if their husband was a smoker, compared to when he was not. The health effects of passive smoking were reviewed by the National Institute of Health (1993). An extrapolation of their USA conclusions to Britain predicts the following annual UK health toll: approximately 1000 lung cancer deaths in adult non-smokers; around 50,000 to 100,000 cases of pneumonia or bronchitis in children aged under 18 months, caused mainly by parental smoking, and increased asthmatic attacks in children. Passive smoking also leads to a slight reduction in lung functioning, and increased rates of respiratory illness (Royal College of Physicians, 1983). Sudden infant death syndrome (cot death) is also linked to smoking: 'The World Health Organization estimate that more than 700

USA infant deaths per year are attributable to maternal smoking' (National Institute of Health, 1993, p. 17). Parents are therefore recommended never to smoke anywhere near their baby.

Smokers generally have their first cigarette between the ages of 11 and 15, with smoking before age 13 being a strong predictor of later smoking (Fergusson *et al.*, 1995). Peer influence is an important factor, with youngsters copying slightly older role models in both smoking and other drug-taking behaviours (Newcombe and Bentler, 1989). However, these social factors can work in many different ways. Peer pressure (the encouragement to conform), and peer selection (choosing friendship groups of like-minded others) are equally important for those who decide to be non-smokers (Fergusson *et al.*, 1995). Other factors which lead to increased adolescent smoking include: parental smoking, poor socioeconomic status, low self-image, and cigarette advertising, which is effective in generating positive images about smoking. Factors which lead to the reduced uptake of smoking include: higher tobacco taxes, enforcement of laws stopping under-age purchase, and school-based anti-smoking programmes (USA Department of Health, 1994). However, the educational programmes need to be well constructed, student centred and given on a regular basis, since their protective influence does decrease over time. Their main aim is to prevent tobacco experimentation, since if youngsters can remain cigarette-free until they are age 16, they are unlikely to become adult smokers (USA Department of Health, 1994).

The majority of adult smokers state that they wish they had never started and would like to quit. Indeed, many do so, but relapse soon afterwards, often 'stopping' three or four times before eventually succeeding. This raises the question of how 'cessation' should be defined. Most scientific trials use the following criteria: a follow-up period of six or twelve months; no smoking during this period; and biochemical confirmation of abstinence. Viswesvaran and Schmidt (1992) undertook a meta-analysis of 633 published smoking cessation studies involving over 70,000 subjects. Various cessation programmes were reviewed: health education; relaxation training; social skills training; hypnosis; acupuncture; nicotine replacement; aversive smoking; minimal intervention, and many combined programmes. Control subjects from the 633 studies reported an annual success rate of 6 per cent. Brief advice to quit from a physician led to the slightly higher success rate of 7 per cent. Basic counselling combined with information on the health effects of smoking increased success rates to around 17 per cent. However, the most successful outcomes were achieved with multi-component packages, where 35 per cent abstinence at one year was often achieved. The Surgeon General (1988) similarly concluded that integrated pharmacological and psychological programmes were the most effective. For instance, nicotine chewing-gum to alleviate withdrawal symptoms, combined with social skills training to develop coping skills, led to annual success rates of 30–40 per cent.

Three forms of nicotine substitution are available: nicotine chewing-gum, the transdermal skin patch and the nicotine inhaler. West (1992) noted that in professional smoking cessation clinics 'Nicotine gum ... doubled success rates from about 15% to 30%.' However, when the gum was used in less intensive programmes, the success rates tended to fall to around 10 per cent, and became closer to the rates achieved with placebo gum (Jorenby *et al.*, 1995). This empha-

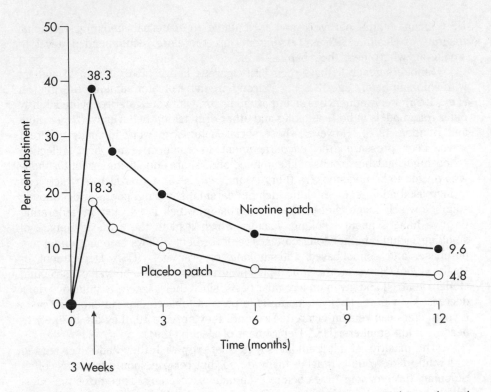

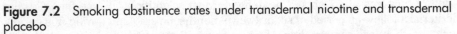

Figure 7.2 Smoking abstinence rates under transdermal nicotine and transdermal placebo

Source: Stapleton *et al.* (1995)

sises the need to educate each smoker about nicotine substitution, and to train them on the appropriate use of the gum. High success rates can then be achieved even in non-specialist general health centres (Parrott and Craig, 1995). Transdermal nicotine was the second device to be marketed. It is easy to use, involving the application of a fresh nicotine skin patch each day. Moreover, unlike the gum, it is suitable for those with false teeth! A graded withdrawal programme involves large initial patches, followed by smaller patches over the next two or three months. Transdermal nicotine doubles the rate of quitting success, in comparison with placebos (Stapleton *et al.*, 1995; and see Figure 7.2). One problem with both the gum and patch is that neither provides the 'bolus' of nicotine which is delivered by smoke inhalation. The nicotine inhaler was designed to overcome this problem, and provides an immediate 'hit' of nasal nicotine. It similarly increases smoking cessation, but does generate side-effects such as throat irritation, while there are also concerns over its abuse potential (Schneider *et al.*, 1996).

Another important factor is the intention of the smoker regarding cessation. Prochaska *et al.* (1992) identified five stages of change (see Chapter 1): pre-contemplation, contemplation, preparation, action and maintenance. Those at the pre-contemplation stage have no plans to quit smoking. Most are content being smokers, and may be strongly opposed to anti-smoking pressures. The majority of smokers are at the contemplation stage. They admit that smoking is unhealthy, wish they had never started and would like to stop, but see quitting as too difficult and therefore don't want to stop just yet! Smokers at the preparation stage are reducing their daily consumption, informing colleagues of their intention to stop, and planning a suitable date for quitting. Those at the action stage have recently quit, and may be suffering from intermittent abstinence/withdrawal symptoms. Finally, those at the maintenance stage have been abstinent for several months. They may feel confident that they have succeeded in quitting, but are still in danger of relapse. Around 15 per cent of former smokers who have not had a cigarette for two years eventually relapse (Parrott, 1996; Prochaska *et al.*, 1992). Farkas *et al.* (1996) investigated the predictive validity of the stages of change model, with pharmacological aspects of nicotine addiction (for example smoking intensity). The addiction measures displayed the strongest predictive validity, although the stages of change also proved useful, confirming the importance of considering both psychological and pharmacological factors.

Finally, the sociocultural characteristics of tobacco smokers have recently undergone a subtle change (Hughes, 1996; Warburton *et al.*, 1991). Smoking used to be seen as normal adult behaviour. Initiation during adolescence was a rite-of-passage, with smoking seen as a marker for maturity. Thus by the end of the Second World War, around 70 per cent of adult males in Western countries were smokers. Now however, its unhealthy nature is widely recognised, and only during adolescence is smoking seen as desirable. Around half of all UK adults who have ever smoked have managed to quit, while those remaining tend to be poorer and less well educated: 'This is due not only to continued high rates of initiation of smoking among the poor and less educated, but also to a lower rate of smoking cessation in these groups' (Hughes, 1996, p. 1798). Smoking is now widely recognised as a form of drug addiction (Surgeon General, 1988). Tobacco use is increasingly associated with other psychoactive drugs, both legal (alcohol, caffeine) and illicit, for example cannabis and heroin (Hughes, 1996). Smokers tend to report higher neuroticism scores and poorer everyday moods (i.e. greater stress and anger) than non-smokers (Jones and Parrott, 1997; Parrott, 1995b; Warburton, 1992; Warburton *et al.*, 1991). There is also a link between smoking and psychiatric disorders (Glassman, 1993). The incidence of smoking is high amongst schizophrenics and depressives, who also tend to smoke very heavily. It is unclear whether they are using nicotine as a self-medication (for example to reverse the sedation induced by antipsychotic/antidepressant drugs), or whether they develop nicotine addiction more readily and/or severely (Glassman, 1993; Parrott and Grimwood, 1996).

Alcohol

Most civilisations have discovered the pleasures and pains of alcohol, since any sugary juice left in an open container will be fermented by airborne yeasts within a few days. The earliest known laws concerned the regulation of Babylonian drinking taverns, and restrictive rules for its consumption have been implemented in most societies. These follow the recognition of its pleasant effects in low doses, but deleterious consequences when taken too liberally. Alcohol is a central nervous system (CNS) depressant. Low doses lead to feelings of relaxation and talkativeness, with slight reductions in alertness and vigilance. Further drinking leads to stronger subjective effects, and greater behavioural impairments. Car accidents therefore increase with alcohol consumption in an exponential dose-related manner. At 80 mg/100 ml blood alcohol concentration (BAC) the incidence of accidents is doubled; at 150 mg/100 ml BAC it is ten times higher, while at 200 mg/100 ml BAC it is increased twentyfold (Royal College of Psychiatrists, 1986). Large doses of alcohol lead to intoxication, severe decrements in skilled behaviour, and slurred speech. This may be followed by deep sleep or coma, where breathing is slow and shallow, and the vomiting reflex is impaired. A frequent cause of accidental death after drinking is the inhalation of vomit.

The effects of alcohol are modified by various factors: gender, body weight, proportion of body fat, speed of drinking, time of day. Thus a standard alcohol drink will lead to a higher blood alcohol concentration in lighter people with a higher proportion of body fat (explaining gender differences); also when drinking fast on an empty stomach, and at lunch-time rather than during the evening (Lowe, 1984). Two further modifying factors are acute and chronic tolerance. Acute pharmacodynamic tolerance is the reduction in subjective effects during a brief period of drinking. The drinker becomes adapted after the initial drink, so that within a short time the drinker feels less affected by the drink (Lowe, 1984). Acute tolerance explains why alcohol leads to impaired judgement, since the drinker routinely underestimates his or her own intoxication. Chronic pharmacodynamic tolerance develops in regular drinkers, who feel normal after their usual amount of alcohol, and need to indulge in 'binge' drinking in order to feel intoxicated (Ashton, 1987). Chronic tolerance provides a neurochemical explanation for 'alcohol dependency'. The drinker gradually increases his or her daily intake to achieve inebriation, and suffers increasingly from withdrawal symptoms without it. The symptoms of abstinence include sleep disruption, irritability, nausea, panic, delirium tremens, drug craving, hallucinations, and epileptic-like convulsions (which can be fatal).

Alcohol disinhibits all types of behaviour, so that drinkers tend to feel more confident in social situations. Leifman *et al.* (1995) found that moderate drinkers (between three and twelve units per week), had the lowest scores on various measures of social isolation. In contrast, total abstainers (zero units per week), and heavy drinkers (more than thirty units per week) reported the highest social isolation scores (for example never having an intimate conversation; having no or only one friend; feeling insecure, etc.). Moderate drinking is therefore associated with various aspects of social integration. However, the disinhibition engendered by alcohol can also have negative effects, since social functioning is dependent upon behavioural inhibition (the suppression of primary selfish urges). By loosening these restrictions, drinking causes considerable social disruption: verbal arguments, physical violence, property damage, rape and murder. The Royal College of Psychiatrists (1986) stated: 'The more one considers the woman who steals, the accountant who embezzles, the man who knifes his wife in a quarrel, the more one sees common elements ... lack of impulse control ... which brings the individual nothing in the way of real gain or satisfaction.' Domestic and business fires, deaths by drowning, transportation accidents, are also more common under the influence of alcohol. Several major disasters have also been caused by drunkenness. The most costly was the Exxon Valdiz disaster, when the drunken crew of a supertanker crashed into the Alaskan coast, spilling its crude oil into the sea and causing $8 billion of environmental damage.

Alcohol has a mixture of positive and negative effects upon health. It has a beneficial effect against risk of coronary heart disease (CHD), which is reduced in moderate drinkers (British Medical Association, 1995; Skog, 1996). This cardio-protective effect follows from the following biochemical changes: reduced athero-sclerotic plaque formation, through altered lipid metabolism; reduced thrombus (clot) formation, through reduced aggregability of blood platelets; and the removal of new clots, through increased fibrinolytic activity (Bondy, 1996; Skog, 1996). Cardioprotection occurs after just one drink every couple of days. In most other respects alcohol has detrimental effects upon health: 'Alcohol has direct toxic effects on numerous body organs including the liver, heart, pancreas, and nervous system' (Bondy, 1996, p. 1665; Edwards *et al.*, 1994). Regular drinking leads to a progression of liver diseases. Fatty liver is often indicative of early disorder, although it is often symptomless. This can progress to liver inflammation, or alcoholic hepatitis, which may then cause jaundice or abdominal pain. Continued regular drinking will often lead to cirrhosis, when the liver becomes shrunken, hard and knobbly with scar tissue. Liver functioning will now be severely impaired, leading eventually to death. This progressive decline in liver functions can how-ever be halted by quitting drinking. The national incidence of liver cirrhosis shows an almost perfect correlation with per capita alcohol consumption. Thus cirrhosis is most frequent in those countries with the highest alcohol consumption (for example France), and is increasing in those nations where consumption is rising (for example the UK).

The incidence of several types of cancer is increased by alcohol consump-tion in a dose-related manner: cancers of the liver, throat, mouth and larynx, and breast cancer in females. The stomach and intestine can be affected by binge drinking (rapid intake of high doses), or moderate regular drinking. The endothe-lium (lining) of the gut may become inflamed, lesions in the gut wall may develop, or ulcers may be exacerbated. The pancreas can also be damaged leading to potentially lethal pancreatitis. Regular drinking is often associated with irregular meals and poor nutrition, leading to general debilitation and proneness to disease. In extreme cases thiamine deficiency can develop, leading to Korsakoff's Psychosis, where irreversible brain lesions lead to mental confusion and memory loss. Impaired brain function can also occur in heavy drinkers with no clinical signs of intellectual decline, with Leonard (1989) describing alcohol as a neuro-toxin. Heavy drinking in pregnant females can also lead to 'foetal alcohol syndrome', characterised by foetal maldevelopment, particularly of the central nervous system (Ashton, 1987).

While moderate drinking may often be seen as 'normal' in many societies, many drinkers increase their consumption to levels where it becomes trouble-some (Leifman *et al.*, 1995). Thus 9 per cent of all adult Americans have attended an Alcoholics Anonymous meeting at some point. Two types of model have been proposed for problem drinking and alcoholism: the medical model, and the social learning explanation. The medical model sees the problem drinker as having lost control over his or her alcohol intake, following years of chronic tolerance (see above). Certainly, numerous changes in the brain chemistry of alcoholics have been described, some of which remain after years of abstinence (Ashton, 1987, pp. 176–188). The medical model therefore advocates total abstinence. An initial period of detoxification or 'drying out' is followed by group support, and the sharing of personal experiences with former alcoholics as the co-therapists. Once stabilised as a non-drinker, further support is provided at regular contact sessions. The self-help approach advocated by Alcoholics Anonymous has provided a clear model for many other addictive behaviours. The social learning model sees excessive drinking as the problem, rather than drinking per se. It advocates 'controlled drinking', where the drinker relearns how to drink sensibly, rather than abstain completely (Heather and Robertson, 1981). It has been suggested that abstinence may be best for the very heavy drinker or true alcoholic, whereas controlled drinking may often be most appropriate for heavy drinkers who have not yet reached the extremes of alcoholism.

Overall, the relationship between health and alcohol consumption is J-shaped. Abstainers have poorer health than very light drinkers, who have the best health; but any increase in alcohol consumption generates health impairments in a dose-related manner (Marks, 1995). This leads to the question of why the UK government raised the recommendations for 'safe' drinking, from twenty-one to twenty-eight units of alcohol per week for men, and from fourteen to twenty-one units per week for women. There is no clear scientific answer to this question. Various health bodies have emphasised the deleterious effects of higher rates of alcohol consumption (British Medical Association, 1995; Edwards *et al.*, 1994), although the Portman Group, funded by the alcohol industry, lobbied for a rise in the recommended limits (Casswell, 1996). Indeed, the alcohol industry around the world has been active in influencing both scientific research, and government alcohol policies (Babor *et al.*, 1996). But it is disheartening that the UK government sided with the alcohol industry, and ignored the advice of its own medical experts.

Caffeine

'Caffeine is the most widely used behaviourally active drug in the world' (Griffith and Woodson, 1988, p. 437). It is present in tea, coffee, chocolate, cola-flavoured drinks, and many over-the-counter medicines. Around 80–90 per cent of adults consume caffeine in one form or other. Regular caffeine users tend to feel awake after caffeine, but sleepy when their normal beverages are substituted for decaffeinated versions. In contrast, low caffeine users tend to become anxious and jittery when given a moderate dose of caffeine. The behavioural effects of caffeine are slight and subtle, although sensitive laboratory tasks can generally detect vigilance improvements following a nicotine challenge (Bruce and Lader, 1986).

In terms of health effects, three areas of concern have been raised: impaired sleep, increased anxiety, and exacerbated heart disease. Caffeine increases the time taken to fall asleep, and shortens sleep duration, while sleep tends to be rated as less sound (McKim, 1991). High rates of coffee consumption (700 mg to 1000 mg per day) can produce a state of high nervousness and tremor, although this 'caffeinism' can be remedied by reducing the amount of caffeine consumed (Bruce and Lader, 1986). Some psychiatric inpatients suffer from aspects of caffeinism following high consumption of tea and coffee. This frequent drinking compensates for the anticholinergic side-effects (for example dry mouth) of their antidepressant or antipsychotic medications. When hospital supplies of normal coffee are changed to decaffeinated coffee, there have been some indications of improved patient behaviour (De Freitas and Schwartz, 1979). The third area of medical concern is cardiovascular problems. Several large-scale studies have been undertaken, and the current position is that the earlier findings of increased cardiac risk have not been confirmed. The early positive findings were probably due to uncontrolled factors, such as differences in cholesterol intake, cigarette smoking, social class, or blood pressure. When these factors were controlled, the former association between caffeine intake and coronary heart disease largely disappeared (Robertson and Curatolo, 1984). Occasional reports of links between caffeine and other illnesses have emerged, but again these have generally not been replicated. Thus Bergman and Dews (1987, p. 199) were able to conclude: 'There has continued to be a perhaps never-ending series of suggestions of adverse effects which further investigation shows to be ill founded. ... There is much more substantial evidence that dietary consumption is harmless in normal people.'

Cannabis

Cannabis is the most widely used of all the illicit psychoactive drugs. Its use was recorded in ancient China and India, and it was taken as a medicine during the Victorian era. Government crackdowns commenced during the first half of this century, and have continued ever since (Adams and Martin, 1996; McKim, 1991). Despite this, it is still widely used, so that a recent National Institute for Health survey found that 50 million Americans stated that they had smoked cannabis, although only 49,999,999 admitted inhaling! Cannabis can be smoked, eaten in cakes or omelettes, or drunk as a liquid infusion (for example bhang). The main active ingredient is delta-9-tetrahydrocannabinol (THC), with THC uptake being most efficient after smoking. Its mood effects are generally pleasant, with low doses leading to relaxation and contentment, and higher doses leading to heightened sensory perception and euphoria. However, negative moods sometimes occur, with anxiety, panic or paranoia occasionally reported by novice users, or following high doses in regular users (Adams and Martin, 1996). THC leads to various skill impairments, with memory and information processing both adversely affected. Car drivers tend to be aware of their impaired car-handling ability, and therefore tend to drive carefully and slowly (Hansteen *et al.*, 1976).

The behavioural effects of cannabis are related to cultural practices and expectations. In Western countries cannabis is generally taken for relaxation, whereas in other societies it is often used as a work aid. In 1898, the Indian

Hemp Commission concluded that farmers and labourers in the Indian subcontinent were not impaired while using cannabis (hemp) during their manual work. Comitas (1976) came to similar conclusions with sugar cane cutters in Jamaica. Some labourer gangs used cannabis (ganja), whereas others did not. However, the overall work productivity of the two types of gang was very similar. The main difference was in their everyday work pattern. Ganja users generally started the working day by smoking and getting high together, then undertaking long and arduous periods of cane cutting while feeling good.

Cannabis smoke contains similar health-impairing constituents to tobacco, namely tar and carbon monoxide; a fresh cannabis joint can have as much tar as twenty cigarettes. Regular cannabis smoking therefore probably causes similar respiratory and circulation/cardiac problems as tobacco. However, the actual incidence of lung cancer, heart attack and other long-term illnesses in cannabis users is unknown, since the appropriate epidemiological research has not been conducted. However, a recent Australian government review concluded that respiratory diseases were 'probably' associated with cannabis (Hall *et al.*, 1996). Certainly in the short term, asthma is exacerbated by smoking, 'hash-throat' (chronic sore throat) can develop, and cardiovascular output is increased, thus exacerbating pre-existing heart diseases. Cannabis smokers often develop blood-shot eyes, caused by the dilation of the corneal blood vessels, although this does not seem to generate long-term visual problems (Adams and Martin, 1996). There is however an increased risk of psychiatric breakdown, particularly in regular users with a family history of psychosis (Hall *et al.*, 1996).

Cannabis has several therapeutic uses. THC reduces the fluid pressure within the eyeball, and therefore relieves the symptoms of glaucoma. In the 1970s an American youth was prosecuted for growing cannabis, but won his case because it relieved his glaucoma (McKim, 1991). Cannabis alleviates pain and reduces nausea, and is therefore effective as an anti-emetic for cancer patients undergoing chemotherapy. It also relieves the symptoms of multiple sclerosis. Several pharmaceutical companies have developed artificial cannabinoids, which are available on prescription (Adams and Martin, 1996). However, those who prefer the real thing still need to indulge in criminal behaviour. Thus of 42,000 recorded drug offences in the UK each year, around 40,000 are for possession of cannabis. The costs in police manpower, legal proceedings, probation and prison services are enormous. Yet the gains to society are unclear, since cannabis causes few real problems.

Ecstasy (MDMA)

Ecstasy or MDMA (3,4-methylenedioxymethamphetamine) is a synthetic amphetamine derivative. In 1990, Peroutka estimated that several million Ecstasy tablets had been taken worldwide. Since then its use has become even more pervasive, so that during the mid-1990s around half a million tablets of MDMA were being taken each weekend in the UK (Saunders, 1995). The typical mood effects of MDMA include alertness, elation, happiness and emotional calmness (Davison and Parrott, 1997). Australian drug users similarly noted: 'The most frequently reported effects of Ecstasy fell into the Positive Mood and Intimacy categories, followed by Activation and Insight' (Solowij *et al.*, 1992, p. 1166). Coming down off MDMA leads to feelings of depression, lethargy, moodiness and insomnia. This mental and physical exhaustion is caused by depletion of the stores of the neurotransmitter serotonin (Solowij *et al.*, 1992). Unpleasant or frightening experiences can occasionally develop on MDMA, with confused thought, panic, feeling out of control, or paranoia (Davison and Parrott, 1997).

MDMA has strong sympathomimetic actions, leading to increased heart rate, dilated pupils, increased body temperature, sweating and dehydration. Hyperthermia can occur in the hot and crowded conditions of clubs and raves. MDMA has therefore caused a number of deaths through heat-stroke. Most clubs now provide leaflets describing the dangers of over-exertion, and have quiet areas where ravers can 'chill-out'. The reverse problem is hyponatraemia: the dilution of body fluids following excess water intake. This can occur when the person drinks too much liquid in over-compensation; again this can be fatal (Maxwell *et al.*, 1994). Dancers who take MDMA are now recommended to maintain a steady but not excessive fluid intake. But this balance may be difficult, particularly when the confused person feels unclear whether he or she is suffering from too much or too little fluid intake.

Health concerns have also been raised over the long-term effects of regular MDMA use. Weight loss is sometimes reported, which is consistent with the regular consumption of anorexic drugs from the amphetamine class. Various types of psychiatric breakdown may also occur, which again is characteristic of chronic stimulant abuse (Series *et al.*, 1994). Perhaps the most worrying effect of MDMA is upon serotonin (5-hydroxytryptamine) neurotransmission. Animal research has shown that a few doses of MDMA can lead to long-term serotonergic depletion (Ricaurte and McCann, 1992). Neuropsychological impairments have also been demonstrated with recreational MDMA users. Using sensitive cognitive test batteries, four studies have now found evidence of selective memory impairments in regular MDMA users (Krystal *et al.*, 1992; Parrott *et al.*, unpublished; see also summaries in Parrott, 1997). Animal research has shown that the hippocampus and frontal cortex are particularly affected by MDMA, so the human memory impairments may follow from neurodegeneration in these brain areas.

DISCUSSION TOPIC

Most psychoactive drugs have a range of positive and negative effects. The positive effects provide reasons for using the drug, while the negative side-effects give reasons for not using it. Outline the positive and negative effects for each drug covered within this chapter. Summarise both psychological and health effects. Now overview all five drugs.
Which drug has the strongest ratio of positive to negative effects?
Which drug has the weakest ratio of positive to negative effects?
Is there an absence of crucial information for some questions? If so, draw up plans for research trials to answer them.

Key point summary

- Tobacco consumption is on the increase worldwide, and is the major preventable cause of death. In the UK smoking causes around 130,000 deaths each year.
- Carbon monoxide in tobacco smoke reduces the oxygen-carrying capacity of the blood, and causes heart disease, gangrene in limb extremities, impotence and foetal death in the womb. Tars in tobacco smoke cause cancers of the mouth, lips, throat and lung. Smoking cessation leads to immediate gains in health, and prolongs life-expectancy.
- Nicotine addiction leads to repetitive mood fluctuations over the day, so that regular smokers are generally more stressed than non-smokers. The supposedly 'relaxant' properties of nicotine/smoking only reflect reversal of the irritability caused by abstinence. The moods of smokers therefore improve gradually when they quit smoking.
- The relationship between alcohol and health is J-shaped, with very light drinkers having the best health. Complete abstainers and moderate drinkers have poorer health, while heavy drinkers have the worst health.
- Caffeine is the most widely used psychoactive drug, with 80–90 per cent of UK adults regularly consuming caffeine in various food products. Caffeine can lead to slight alertness gains, but also impaired sleep and exacerbated nervousness. However, it seems to have few adverse effects upon health.
- Cannabis smoking causes similar respiratory/cardiac diseases to those caused by tobacco smoking. However, their overall incidence is unknown, since the appropriate epidemiological research has never been undertaken. The active ingredient in cannabis, tetrahydrocannabinol, has various medicinal uses: relief of glaucoma, and pain reduction in multiple sclerosis, or during cancer chemotherapy.
- MDMA or 'Ecstasy' is widely used as a recreational drug. It has powerful mood elevating effects, but also has several potentially fatal side-effects (for example, hyperthermia, hyponatraemia). It may also cause neurodegeneration in the serotonin (5-HT) system, which may lead to long-term memory/cognitive impairments.

Further reading

Adams, I. B. and Martin, B. R. (1996) Cannabis: pharmacology and toxicology in animals and humans. *Addiction*, 91, 1585–1614. A general review of cannabis, including recent findings into the neuropharmacological basis for its psychoactive properties.

British Medical Association (1995) *Alcohol: Guidelines on Sensible Drinking*. London: British Medical Association Publication. An excellent review on alcohol, including its behavioural and health effects.

McKim, W. A. (1991) *Drugs and Human Behaviour* (2nd edn). New Jersey: Prentice-Hall. This volume covers the human psychopharmacology of each drug included in this chapter, and many other types of social drug and psychoactive medicine.

Parrott, A. C. (1995a) Stress modulation over the day in cigarette smokers. *Addiction*, 90, 237–244. A review of some recent studies into the psychological changes which help explain nicotine addiction.

Saunders, G. (1995) *Ecstasy and the Dance Culture*. London: Neal's Yard Desktop Publishing. A general introduction to the disparate research into MDMA although with a slight 'pro-Ecstasy' slant.

Chapter 8

The primary prevention of AIDS

Keith Phillips

Introduction

The human immunodeficiency virus (HIV) destroys the Helper T-cells of the immune system which normally provide resistance to disease. Infection with HIV makes the body vulnerable to several opportunistic infections such as Pneumocystis carinii pneumonia, protozoal and fungal infections, and tumours, including a rare form of skin cancer named Karposi's sarcoma, and lymphomas. Acquired Immune Deficiency Syndrome (AIDS) is diagnosed by the presence of such specific diseases in the absence of any other known cause of immune system deficiency. HIV may give rise to a range of symptoms such as fevers, fatigue, sore throat which may be diagnosed as AIDS-related complex (ARC) and persistent swollen lymph nodes. Many people with HIV infection show no symptoms at all for several years and the epidemiological statistics indicate that the progression from infection with the virus to the development of AIDS is between five and eight years. It is also generally accepted that several co-factors such as poor nutrition and stress assist the progression to AIDS (Siegel, 1988). The presence of these and other co-factors account in part for the differences that exist for epidemiological patterns and risk factors in different countries. However, the importance of social and cultural factors should not be overlooked (Ford, 1994).

AIDS was first reported among young homosexual men in the USA in 1981 (CDC, 1981). Since then it has been reported in countries worldwide in heterosexuals as well as homo- or bisexuals, and among injecting drug users, prostitutes, and recipients of untreated blood products including haemophiliacs. By 1992 it was estimated that there had been 1.5 million cases of AIDS and up to 11 million cases of HIV infection worldwide (WHO, 1992). It is estimated that there will be 30 to 40 million people infected by the end of the century (WHO, 1995). Because of the slow progression from HIV infection to the development of AIDS, the full impact of deaths attributable to AIDS has yet to be felt. In the UK, the number of cases of AIDS in 1996 reached 13,720 and, though the incidence now seems to have reached a plateau, the incidence rate per million population was the ninth highest among forty-four European countries (*Communicable Disease Reports*, 1995).

The medical facts concerning HIV infection and AIDS are well known (Hersh and Peterson, 1988), and yet the prevalence of AIDS continues to grow and no vaccine for HIV is currently available. In 1987 the first effective anti-HIV drug, AZT, became available and it was found to improve the life expectancy of people with AIDS. Recently it has been reported that combinations of drugs can be more effective in erasing the virus from a person's bloodstream, though on halting drug treatment the virus returns to its previous levels within two weeks (Perelson *et al.*, 1997). It is estimated that the annual cost of the drug treatment is $20,000 per person and, though this is cost-effective by eliminating costly hospital care, it is unlikely that it can be afforded worldwide.

In the absence of any medical solution, the best strategy against AIDS is its primary prevention through reduction of those behaviours that allow transmission of the HIV virus (Phillips, 1988). Unfortunately, the research into AIDS prevention shows that thus far the strategy has had only limited success. This is not surprising when one examines the literature from other areas of health psychology in which behaviour change is required to avoid illness, or more significantly, the risk of future illness in individuals who are currently well, as the statistics about smoking or drinking show (see Chapter 7).

This chapter will examine the behaviours associated with the transmission of HIV, and will consider interventions which may be used to persuade people to adopt behaviours that will limit the spread of HIV, and assess their prospects of success in the future. Its emphasis is upon studies from North America and Europe, and it should be understood that transmission differs in other countries depending upon 'regional and local historical, cultural and developmental conditions' that affect sexual and drug using behaviours (Ford, 1994).

Behavioural transmission of HIV

Mere exposure to HIV does not result in infection. There are only three effective routes of transmission of the virus from an infected to a non-infected individual: by transfer of either blood or sexual fluids, or by perinatal transfer from mother to foetus. The virus has been identified in other fluids including saliva and tears but there is no evidence that infection has occurred from contact with these fluids (CDC, 1985). There is some risk of infection for breast-feeding infants from the milk of an infected mother (Ziegler et al., 1985) and though recent estimates suggest that this risk is low, HIV seropositive women are advised to bottle-feed their infants (Mok, 1988).

Efforts to prevent AIDS have concentrated attention upon those behaviours that allow transfer of blood and sexual fluids between individuals. The particular behaviours that are significant vary from country to country. The patterns of transmission are not the same and it is important that primary prevention programmes recognise this fully (Piot et al., 1988). In some countries the greatest risk of transfer via blood may come from untreated blood products used in surgery, or from unsterilised injecting equipment used in hospitals. In the USSR, for example, there was reported an instance of seventy Russian children and their mothers becoming infected with the virus via contaminated syringes where the source could be traced to a single child born with HIV (Guardian, 5 June 1989). In Western countries that risk no longer exists, though of course in the early days of the AIDS era many haemophiliacs were infected with HIV via untreated blood extracts. In Western countries the greatest risk of transfer of HIV via blood is by intravenous drug users sharing inadequately sterilised injecting equipment.

Intravenous drug use

Intravenous drug users (ivdus) are seen as key individuals in the fight against AIDS, as they expose themselves to risk of HIV infection through their drug practices, and their sexual behaviours may present further risks to their sexual partners and their unborn children.

The initial spread of HIV infection among homosexual males in the USA has slowed as several homosexual communities have altered their behaviours to reduce high risk sexual activities (Winkelstein *et al.*, 1987). However, HIV infection continues to increase among intravenous drug users, their partners and increasingly their children. In the USA 17 per cent of AIDS cases are attributable to heterosexual ivdus. In Western Europe the problem is equally large – the proportion of AIDS cases accounted for by heterosexual ivdus has risen from 1 per cent at the end of 1984, 7 per cent at the end of 1985, to 15 per cent at the end of 1986 (Conviser and Rutledge, 1989).

Ivdus and the subculture that supports their behaviours present a major challenge for those involved in AIDS prevention (Mulleady, 1987). Innovative policies are called for that decriminalise drug use in favour of public health education for safer drug use. The potential impact of this approach has been seen by comparing the seroprevalence in Glasgow and Edinburgh during the 1980s (Conviser and Rutledge, 1989). In both Scottish cities it was legal for pharmacists to sell syringes and needles to ivdus, but in Edinburgh police pursued a policy of arrests for those found carrying injecting equipment, whereas in Glasgow no such policy existed. Sharing of equipment occurred in both cities but because of this difference in policing, sharing occurred in small local groups in Glasgow, whereas in Edinburgh sharing existed between many more drug users in so-called 'shooting galleries' (these are places where drugs are sold and buyers share or rent the injecting equipment with several others). In Glasgow the rate of HIV infection among ivdus at the end of 1986 was around 5 per cent, while in Edinburgh the rate grew from 3 per cent in 1983 to 50 per cent in 1984, and is currently endemic among the city's ivdus (Robertson *et al.*, 1986).

One approach to reduce the spread of HIV infection among ivdus is to encourage safer drug injection practices by policies operating at a national level, for example, through needle exchange schemes. These schemes were pioneered in Amsterdam in 1984 and have become established in the UK (Stimson and Donaghue, 1996) and other European countries, along with pharmacy exchange schemes. They allow ivdus legally to exchange used needles and syringes for sterile ones. In addition, they bring ivdus into contact with counselling, primary health and advice services which allows the opportunity for health education messages to be conveyed. These include messages for 'harm minimisation' (Landrey and Smith, 1988) which involve a hierarchy of behavioural changes for ivdus to reduce the risk of HIV infection:

- do not use drugs
- if you must use drugs, do not inject
- if you must inject, do not share injecting equipment
- if you must share, sterilise the injecting equipment before each injection.

Though this strategy has been criticised for condoning drug use, there is no evidence that further drug use is encouraged and it does recognise the realities of factors in the ivdus' lives that increase personal and public risks of HIV infection (Mulleady and Sher, 1989). It is an approach based upon what Stimson and Donaghue (1996) have called 'knowledge and means', where ivdus are treated as individuals able to make rational choices about their health. The USA has resisted the introduction of syringe exchange schemes but evidence from community-based 'outreach' programmes where ivdus are taught how to sterilise injecting equipment using a bleaching agent indicates that ivdus can reduce the risks of HIV infection within their local community (Watters, 1988, 1989). This approach for ivdus involves a shift from treating their chemical dependency upon drugs by trying to achieve abstinence to educating users about safe practices they can adopt to minimise the risks to themselves and others. To be successful, national policies must necessarily reflect that shift to decriminalise drug use in favour of health education programmes.

The evidence of the UK experience is that public health HIV campaigns can be effective. Research shows that the campaign against sharing has success-fully reduced its extent to less than 20 per cent and made it more restricted and discriminant (Mulleady *et al.*, 1990; Stimson, 1995). Most countries (for example Holland, the UK, Australia) that have introduced exchange schemes or similar interventions have stabilised levels of HIV infection among ivdus in contrast to those countries where these are not available (for example Thailand, Brazil). This is not to say that this has been a totally effective intervention. For example, some ivdus remain beyond contact with services and untouched by the health promo-tion messages; in the UK this is particularly true for users from ethnic minorities and for women (Abdulrahim *et al.*, 1996). Furthermore, health education messages may be only partially understood. For example, a recent study by Power *et al.* (1994) found that despite not sharing syringes or needles some ivdus do continue to share the other injecting paraphernalia such as filters or mixing liquids which may be cross-contaminated by blood and thus present a risk of transmis-sion (Koester and Hoffer, 1994).

The dangers associated with injecting drugs also threaten the sexual part-ners of ivdus and their unborn children. It is a fact that most women diagnosed with AIDS in the UK and USA are either ivdus or the sexual partners of male ivdus. It is becoming increasingly recognised that women-ivdus and women sharing relationships with ivdus require specific policies to protect themselves and their children against AIDS including not only advice upon safer drug use *and* safer sex, but also advice upon contraception, pregnancy and child care (Mulleady *et al.*, 1989). It is vitally important that women in these circumstances are not regarded as 'transmitters' of HIV either to men by prostitution or by pregnancy to infants, but as a special group that needs protection against their own drug-using behav-iours or the behaviours of their sexual partners (White *et al.*, 1993).

In Britain, the government's Health of the Nation Report (1992) identified as one of its targets a reduction in the percentage of ivdus who share equipment by at least 50 per cent by 1997 and by a further 50 per cent by the year 2000. To achieve these targets, interventions based upon well-established theoretical principles will be essential and health psychologists will play a major role in iden-tifying those principles.

Sexual behaviours and AIDS

The risks of transmission of HIV through sexual activities have been well publi-cised. Some degree of risk is associated with any practice that transfers bodily fluids, although the greatest risks are associated with penetrative sex including anal intercourse (particularly for the receptive partner), transfer from man to woman and to a lesser extent from woman to man during vaginal intercourse (Cohen *et al.*, 1989). The risks can be substantially reduced by the precaution of using a condom as a barrier to transfer of HIV. The risks are not eliminated totally however, as condoms may fail or be used inappropriately, and they do not present the complete answer since a couple may wish to avoid their contraceptive effect if trying to achieve conception. Others may have firmly held religious objections to their use. Monogamy for non-infected partners or celibacy offer complete protection of course, but their costs are clearly unacceptable for many individuals. This illustrates the dilemma facing health educators; preventive behaviours have benefits in protecting an individual against future illness but they also have costs associated with them. Decisions to adopt healthy behaviours will depend in part upon the individual's perception of the reward–cost pay-off. Effective health education must maximise that pay-off.

Since sexual transmission is a common cause of HIV infection it is important that health education messages provide accurate and appropriate information about the risks associated with unprotected sex and the opportunities for safer sex practices among individuals of different sexual preferences. In this context safer sex can be interpreted as minimising the risk of HIV transmission which means in most cases avoiding the exchange of body fluids from one individual to another (Aggleton *et al.*, 1989). HIV/AIDS has had a huge impact upon the public debate and scientific research on sexual behaviours. In Britain, for example, a major survey funded by the Wellcome Trust of 'sexual attitudes and lifestyles' of 20,000 adults was undertaken despite governmental opposition (Johnson *et al.*, 1994). In relation to HIV infection they found evidence that there was widespread uptake of the message that condoms are an effective means of safer sex, much more so than messages to restrict the number of sexual partners (see Table 8.1). However, the authors concluded: 'there is little sign yet of widespread adoption of other safer-sex practices amongst those reporting heterosexual behaviour.'

The difficulties of persuading people to alter their sexual behaviours are enormous, but changes are possible (Becker and Joseph, 1988). Statistics from some American cities did show that local groups of homosexual males have reduced high risk sexual activities and adopted safer sex practices (Hart, 1989), suggesting that they had recognised the risks and adjusted their behaviour accordingly. This does not mean however that high risk behaviours have been abandoned by *all* individuals, and the Day Report (1993) indicates that, in the UK, transmission of HIV infection between gay men is continuing. One area of argument concerns the notion of 'relapse' – referring to men who had adopted safer sex behaviours only to engage later in risky behaviour such as unprotected anal intercourse (Hart *et al.*, 1992).

Public education campaigns to persuade heterosexuals to alter their behaviours have not been obviously effective. There may be many reasons for this. One reason is undoubtedly the fact of the myth that AIDS is a disease associated with minority groups – homosexuals and drug users – rather than the reality that it is associated with particular risk behaviours and that there are no 'risk groups'. The existence of this myth allows people who do not regard themselves

TABLE 8.1 Proportions (per cent) who report sexual lifestyle change because of AIDS (by age group)

	Men				Women			
	16–24	*25–34*	*35–44*	*45–59*	*16–24*	*25–34*	*35–44*	*45–59*
Having fewer partners	12.0	8.0	4.1	1.8	9.1	4.6	2.0	0.8
Know partner before having sex	20.1	11.1	5.5	2.0	18.0	7.5	3.9	1.8
Using a condom	26.4	13.7	7.0	2.1	16.8	7.5	4.1	1.5
Not having sex	3.6	3.2	1.7	0.9	4.2	2.8	1.6	1.4
Sticking to one partner	15.6	11.2	6.5	3.1	16.3	9.2	4.7	1.7
Avoiding some sexual practices	5.0	3.6	2.4	0.8	3.2	1.3	1.1	0.6
Other change(s)	1.1	0.8	0.8	0.2	1.0	1.1	0.7	0.2
Base	1983	2153	2042	2172	2233	2889	2572	2754
Any change in lifestyle	36.2	22.9	13.9	6.2	29.7	15.7	9.4	4.5
Base	1983	2154	2042	2173	2236	2892	2572	2758

Source: Johnson *et al.* (1994, p. 236)

as belonging to those minorities to deny any risk to themselves. A damaging side-effect of the myth is that it encourages blaming of those groups and stigmatisation of individuals with AIDS. People's perceptions of AIDS are determined by a complexity of beliefs, attitudes and values that may be shared with others and which collectively form a social representation of the disease (Phillips, 1989). At the same time it is the case that HIV transmission through heterosexual sex has not increased as rapidly in the industrialised world (unlike Africa) as had been predicted. The social representation of AIDS needs to be changed if individuals are to make realistic decisions about their own behaviours (Markova and Wilkie, 1988).

A further obstacle to change is that individuals are unrealistically optimistic about their own health and see themselves as being at less risk than others in a similar situation (Weinstein, 1987). This 'illusion of invulnerability' prevents people from making realistic estimates of personal risk which in turn acts against the adoption of preventive behaviours. This is a fundamental problem for preventive health programmes and, though not unique to AIDS, its impact can be seen in studies of sexual behaviours and contraceptive use (see Chapter 9). A study of Oxford University undergraduates (Turner *et al.*, 1988) found that these students estimated their own personal risk of AIDS to be less than that for others of their age and sex. This was true even for individuals who were engaging in activities associated with greater risk for AIDS such as unprotected intercourse with bisexual partners, ivdus and prostitutes.

It is not only estimates of personal risk that are important however. Even when the risks are recognised, individuals may not take appropriate precautions to reduce the risks. Our studies with students and young people found that the precautions against AIDS that are favoured by many are mandatory screening for HIV, and vetting of partners' past sexual history. The obvious unreliability of both of these measures is denied by these young well-informed people (e.g. White *et al.*, 1989). A number of studies have found little evidence of changes in the behaviour of young heterosexuals by adoption of the simple preventive measure of condom use for penetrative sex (Baldwin and Baldwin, 1988; Kegeles *et al.*, 1988). This may reflect the difficulty in persuading people to alter attitudes to practices that are perceived as having excessive costs, for example loss of pleasure (Chapman and Hodgson, 1988).

Adolescents are a particularly important group for AIDS education campaigns. An American report on AIDS (NRC, 1989) recognised the special importance of effective health education messages for adolescents, recommending that all teenagers should receive sex education in school including information about prevention of HIV infection. The report states that 'young people are not particularly skilled in managing their sexual lives'; inevitably this places them at risk of HIV infection and health educators need to recognise this as being so. It must be acknowledged, however, that they need more than information alone: they also require opportunities for learning about relationships and the social skills needed to manage the dynamics of relationships. It is self-evident that intimacy involves social interactions between partners and negotiations about sex may not be equitable (Byers and Lewis, 1988). For example, coercion or compliance may cause an individual to disregard his or her intention to allow sexual intercourse or to use a condom during intercourse. Information encouraging safer sex must be accompanied by education about adhering to intentions for preventive health. Much more research upon this aspect of adolescents' behaviour is necessary.

Paediatric AIDS

Paediatric AIDS was first identified in 1982 in the USA in cases of children under 13 years old showing signs of cellular immunodeficiency without obvious cause (CDC, 1982). Since then an elaborate and comprehensive classification system has been developed to identify HIV infection in children (CDC, 1987). Infants may become infected with HIV perinatally, during the birth itself, or postnatally through their mothers' breast milk (Newell *et al.*, 1996). The risk of vertical transmission of HIV from an infected mother has been estimated to be around 20 per cent (Bertolli *et al.*, 1996). The prognosis for children with AIDS is poor. Women who are HIV positive should receive specialist counselling concerning the effect of their pregnancy upon their own health as well as the health implications for their infant and its future health care. As women progressively account for a greater proportion of individuals with HIV, the instances of paediatric AIDS will increase. This tragic consequence requires urgent consideration of policies for women and their infants. It is a particular problem in parts of Africa where a high proportion of AIDS cases result from heterosexual transmission and a much higher percentage of women are among the HIV positive population.

Changing risk behaviours

Epidemiological studies of AIDS have clearly identified the particular behaviours that present to the individual risks of contracting HIV infection. The success or otherwise of behavioural approaches to the prevention of AIDS depends upon persuading people to take responsibility for actions they may regard as private, personal, and which they do not perceive as a threat either to their own health or that of others. Interventions to promote changes in behaviour for reducing the risk of future illness should be based upon theoretical models that identify the determinants of behaviour change but also recognise the importance of the person's social context. Unfortunately, modelling preventive health behaviour has proved to be an enormously difficult task. Several models focus upon the importance of socio-cognitive variables in preventive health. Among these are the health belief model (Becker, 1974; Rosenstock, 1974), the theory of reasoned action (Ajzen and Fishbein, 1980) or its later version – theory of planned behaviour (Ajzen, 1985), and protection motivation theory (Rogers, 1983), which emphasise the importance of volitional decisions by individuals about the perceived utility of their actions. (See Chapter 1 for further explanations of these models.)

According to the health belief model, the significant variables that influence the adoption of precautions against a perceived threat to health are a person's perceived vulnerability to the threat, the perceived severity of the threat, and the cost–benefit pay-off that is associated with adopting preventive behaviours. Consideration of these variables in relation to AIDS indicates the difficulties faced by health educators. Despite public education campaigns there is little evidence that the bulk of the population see themselves as personally vulnerable to HIV infection. Furthermore, in the absence of perceived personal risk, individuals may estimate that the costs of safer sex such as using a condom are greater than the benefits which would mitigate against the adoption of effective preventive measures.

The theory of reasoned action/planned behaviour identifies intention as the most immediate determinant of behaviour. Intentions are themselves a function of privately held attitudes towards the particular behaviour and socially determined subjective norms that represent a person's belief that others think he or she should behave in a certain way. The model attaches values to each of these factors. The particular values attached to each of these factors will depend upon the individual's beliefs, and thus in many ways this model is similar to the health belief model.

One difficulty with this model is that it identifies a direct link between intentions and behaviours but intentions are not always translated into actions. Even when an individual holds an intention towards some behaviour, action does not necessarily result (Abraham and Sheeran, 1993). When considering sexual behaviours and safer-sex practices there may be one or several reasons for individuals' failures to carry out intentions to act in ways that are perceived as beneficial. An action may not be possible in a particular situation or at a particular time; it may be difficult or time-consuming or it may simply be suppressed, for example if the use of intoxicant drugs accompanies the behaviour (Stall *et al.*, 1986). Much greater consideration needs to be given to the impact of situational influences of this kind upon adherence to intentions to act in accordance with prevention. As pointed out elsewhere (Phillips, 1989), adherence to intentions for safer sex may be particularly vulnerable since sexual relationships involve a partner. What happens when one partner's intentions for sex do not coincide with those of their partner? Inevitably, social processes will occur which may involve one partner abandoning their intentions in deference to the wishes of the other.

Protection motivation theory identifies four components of fear as the initiators of a coping process: perceived severity of the feared threat, perceived likelihood of the event occurring, perceived efficacy of the coping behaviour, and self-efficacy. The model implies that health can be improved by interventions that focus on the harmful consequences of maladaptive (or risky) behaviours and recommend alternative behaviours that reduce risk. A number of studies have investigated components of the model in relation to sexual behaviour. For example, Abraham *et al.* (1994) found that of the PMT components self-efficacy was the best predictor of teenagers' anticipated condom use.

There is a clear need for further empirical studies that test these models for the adoption of preventive health behaviours, since interventions have implicitly accepted the assumptions contained within them. If the determinants of precautionary behaviours could be identified this would be a significant step forward in campaigns against AIDS and other behavioural diseases. There is little doubt that the principal variables identified by these models – perceived risk, perceived severity of the disease, perceived effectiveness of precautions, and cost–benefit pay-off – are important predictors of preventive health behaviours of many kinds (Janz and Becker, 1984). However, these models have their limitations and a more recent approach emphasises the dynamic aspects of preventive behaviours.

The precaution adoption process

Weinstein suggests that the precaution adoption process involves a progression through distinct stages which differ qualitatively from each other. The factors that are important at any particular time therefore depend upon which stage of the adoption process an individual has reached (Weinstein, 1988). One of the advantages of this model is that it recognises that as people move through qualitatively different stages towards adoption of preventive behaviours, the interventions that are appropriate also change. In Weinstein's words (p. 380), 'The idea of matching the communication to the audience follows naturally from a stage model.'

Though this model remains to be tested, it offers a wider perspective upon the adoption of preventive behaviours and may be more compatible with the fact that target behaviours do not exist in isolation. Attempts to modify an individual's sexual or drug-using behaviours will inevitably impinge upon other significant aspects of that person's life. The process of precaution adoption will reflect this interdependence of behaviours.

Interventions that are planned on the basis of theoretical models of behaviour change must also be prepared to provide the resources required for those changes in behaviour to be realised. Interventions that encourage safer sex, for example, might require that condoms are widely available and at an affordable cost. Similarly, harm minimisation programmes for safer drug use will involve making available sterile needles and syringes for those who wish to use them. Psychologists and educators promoting interventions must be prepared to address the social and political implications of their interventions (Ingham, 1988).

Policies for protecting against AIDS

Worldwide, many different policies to prevent the spread of AIDS have been adopted, including programmes for international co-operation and collaboration, national measures including legal restrictions upon all or some citizens or mass health education campaigns and local and community-based projects for selected groups of individuals. Each of these policies is concerned with altering people's behaviour in some desired direction: each may have several impacts upon individuals' behaviours and their perceptions and the social representation of AIDS. Some of the policies also raise significant questions, including the relationship between individual rights and public welfare, and the objectives and policies for health education. The following section considers the value of some of the measures adopted as precautions against AIDS.

HIV testing

Governments' reactions to the AIDS health crisis have varied. Some have adopted mass education campaigns designed to alert the public to the existence of HIV infection and to encourage changes in behaviour that would reduce individuals' personal risk of exposure to the virus. Others have adopted authoritarian measures that seek to legislate against individuals with HIV, against groups who are perceived as presenting a risk for transmission of the virus, or against behaviours that might transmit the virus. Legislation against particular individuals or against groups is discriminatory and may abuse individuals' rights as well as presenting a threat to civil liberties; measures against particular behaviours will inevitably be ineffective since the behaviours concerned – sexual and drug practices – are private and beyond effective control by authorities. In the midst of these various measures there has been great debate about the merits of screening and testing for HIV or rather antibodies to the virus since their presence is indicative of infection.

A number of countries, including Cuba and Bulgaria, have expressed a wish or intention to have mandatory screening for HIV of their entire population. Others require testing of citizens returning from abroad, for example Iraq, or of some visitors to the country, for example the USSR, or immigrants, for example the USA. Many more countries have introduced legislation that allows mandatory testing of selected individuals including prostitutes (Austria, Israel, South Korea and others), injecting drug users (Hungary, Bavaria), or in some instances individuals suspected of these activities (Hungary). Some countries have introduced mandatory notification of HIV infection (Japan). In all of these instances the authorities have dismissed the danger inherent in all such measures, namely that the problem is not eliminated but simply driven underground, causing the emergence of marginal groups outside the reach of health services and beyond the scope of educational programmes. Appeals for mass screening also ignore the prohibitive financial cost that would be involved, particularly as, to be effective, screening would need to be repeated at regular intervals. Long-term reliance upon screening or testing for HIV is a recipe for the continuing increase in the prevalence of HIV infection.

Anonymous HIV testing has also been a contentious issue. In the UK there has been considerable debate amongst doctors and politicians as to whether blood taken from a patient for other tests should be tested anonymously for HIV. Anonymous testing would mean, of course, that the donors could not be informed of the outcome of the test and could not be advised of their own health status. However, anonymous testing would allow statistics to be gathered to show the true incidence of HIV infection in the population, something that is otherwise difficult to establish. These statistics are needed to allow accurate projections of health provision for AIDS patients and their likely health costs. Critics, however, argue that anonymous testing would be an abuse of individual rights. Even though it might establish the prevalence of HIV, anonymous testing would be of extremely limited value for planning policies for prevention since it provides no information at all about the way in which the virus is being transmitted within a population. This information is critical for planning measures that may be effective against further transmission in that population. As discussed below, it cannot be assumed that modes of transmission will be identical for all populations; preventive measures must take account of different patterns of transmission and the ecology of AIDS.

Voluntary testing with informed consent of the client is offered by health services in several countries and may be regarded as a compassionate measure that should be available on demand to individuals who see themselves at risk. Even in this instance however, there may be costs for the individual: someone whose test is negative on one occasion may continue to engage in behaviours that place him or her at risk for the future. There must be guarantees of confidentiality if discrimination against individuals is to be avoided, and counselling must be provided for all volunteers, not only after their test results are known but also before in order to explore the meaning of the test and the possible social, health and employment consequences for someone following the test outcome (Acton, 1989). In some instances of course, voluntary testing may be of considerable value. For example, pregnant women may wish to know their HIV status if they consider themselves at risk and would wish to consider therapeutic abortion if they found themselves to be infected. Similarly, women injecting drugs may wish to know their HIV status in consideration of contraception and planned pregnancies.

Adults (e.g. Moatti *et al.*, 1988) and young people (White *et al.*, 1989) have identified screening for HIV as an effective preventive measure against AIDS without apparently recognising the difficulties and uncertainties outlined above, and many express the opinion that they would be prepared to take a test themselves. This may simply reflect anxieties about their own behaviours. It certainly indicates a failure to recognise effective precautions against HIV and suggests the need for further education about prevention of HIV transmission.

Public education campaigns

Several countries including the UK have introduced national AIDS campaigns, which provide public education by means of messages distributed via delivery of leaflets to individual homes, television, radio and print media. Evaluations of these campaigns clearly show that they have been highly effective in increasing awareness of AIDS amongst the general populations of the UK (DHSS and Welsh Office, 1987), Sweden (Brorsson and Herlitz, 1988) and the USA (Singer *et al.*, 1987). Of course, awareness of an issue is far removed from action by individuals in respect of that issue; knowing that AIDS may be life-threatening will not have any impact upon the behaviour of someone who does not consider themselves at any risk of having AIDS. There is little evidence that mass campaigns have been effective in bringing about changes in behaviour that are effective precautions against HIV infection (see Phillips, 1989). This is not surprising when one considers the psychological processes that underlie behaviour change and the precaution adoption process discussed above.

The assumption underlying mass education campaigns has been that knowledge about AIDS will cause people's attitudes to change, which in turn will lead to changes in behaviour. This simple sequential process, where knowledge leads to a rational decision to alter behaviours in favour of prevention without any regard to costs that may be incurred as a result of those changes, is clearly inadequate. It fails to take account of both the interacting complexities of variables that determine people's behaviours and the fact that behaviours do not exist in isolation; change in one behaviour has implications for other aspects of an individual's life that may be unacceptable (Hunt and MacLeod, 1987). Moreover, there is no compelling evidence that mass education campaigns have been altogether effective in communicating accurate information and increasing knowledge about HIV and AIDS. One difficulty is that the audience are not passive receivers of information. They have 'lay beliefs' that will influence their attention to the messages and their willingness to accept or reject the 'truth' of those messages (Aggleton *et al.*, 1989). In part, individuals' lay beliefs may be determined by information received from other sources including media messages that distort the facts or confirm myths and stereotypes associated with AIDS or persons with AIDS (Wellings, 1988). Furthermore, they do not share equal amounts of knowledge about AIDS, and messages that contain no new information for some may be beyond the comprehension of others. This is a particular problem when trying to present material that is appropriate for young people who may, for example, have limited experience of sexual practices. Lay beliefs may further interfere with accurate perceptions of risk and provide obstacles to the adoption of preventive behaviours. Education involving personalised learning experiences which is beyond the scope of mass campaigns is necessary to bring about changes in behaviour. For young people, greater opportunities could be made of learning within its traditional context, i.e. schools.

If increasing knowledge is difficult, then altering attitudes may be yet more problematic. Several survey studies in different countries have examined people's knowledge and attitudes towards AIDS both before and after particular education campaigns (e.g. Mills *et al.*, 1986; Sher, 1987) or as trends over time following cumulative exposure to educational messages about AIDS (e.g. Singer *et al.*, 1987). They find that though the general level of knowledge has increased, particular gaps in knowledge may remain. For example, there remains uncertainty about the risks of transmission of HIV associated with casual contacts or by oral sex. However, attitudes have changed much less. In particular there is little indication that the population as a whole recognises the need to change behaviour. Many studies have shown that individuals and particularly heterosexuals are not adopting effective preventive measures and do not intend to alter their sexual behaviours. Further interventions are required to bring out the desired alterations.

School-based education

There are opportunities for many different kinds of learning experiences for young people within school settings. Effective health education could easily be included in the school curriculum. The advantage of using schools for health education is that young people's beliefs, values and attitudes may be malleable, unlike the more firmly held attitudes of older groups. If so, appropriate attitudes towards social responsibility can be encouraged that enable precautions against AIDS to be taken. Learning experiences of this type could make use of person-centred approaches rather than simple exposure to information. This would allow youngsters to develop their own knowledge structures, at their own rate and within the context of experiences within their own lives. It is quite clear that adolescents do require more information about HIV and AIDS (White *et al.*, 1988, 1989), but information is not enough; they also need the opportunity to make use of that information for risk assessment and decision making and most importantly they need to acquire social skills that allow them to adhere to their decisions, even in social contexts that exert pressures against those decisions. AIDS education in schools should be a major aspect of policies for preventing HIV infection (DiClemente, 1993). Unfortunately, studies of school-based health promotion have been poorly evaluated and it is difficult to make firm recommendations for interventions.

Community programmes

Just as schools are an appropriate context for encouraging preventive behaviours in young people, so community groups and local social networks are appropriate for other groups. Rather than aiming for educational messages suitable for all, which inevitably will be unsuccessful, a social marketing approach can stratify groups and develop messages that are tailored to the needs, interests and existing knowledge and beliefs of specific groups and communities (Lefebvre and Flora,

1988). Within a community there is then the possibility of adopting new ideas or practices that can be spread by social diffusion. A model derived from communication studies (Rogers, 1987) predicts that the adoption of new ideas such as 'safer sex' takes time. Following introduction of the innovation the time course of its adoption is influenced by the way in which it is perceived, the means available for its transmission: Can it be advertised by media or does its spread depend upon interpersonal communication? Is there sufficient time available to allow its effectiveness to become confirmed, or will it be rejected? And is the innovation compatible with the social norms that exist within that community? The characteristics of the community, its social structures and social norms, will determine the response to the innovation and whether it becomes adopted by the majority within that community. Each community will differ, and advocates of innovations should take account of this and present their messages accordingly. It may be that particular communities require special initiatives (for example prisons), and it may be that aspects of a community could become more involved in promoting educational messages, for example the workplace, trade unions, health clinics and church organisations.

Peer education

An approach recently developed in the UK makes use of 'peers' (identified by demographic characteristics such as age, gender and ethnicity, as well as 'special characteristics' such as knowledge, experience or access to target communities) who are recruited to help deliver a planned intervention (e.g. Broadhead *et al.*, 1995). For example, former injecting drug users may be recruited to a project that aims to reduce injecting drug use because they have knowledge of the local circumstances and practices of drug use and are accepted by current drug users. Once recruited, the 'peer workers' can be trained in delivery of health education messages (such as harm minimisation) and can provide practical help too by distributing sterile injecting equipment, for example, or can participate in research by conducting interviews with 'at risk' targets (e.g. Abdulrahim *et al.*, 1996). Early indications are that this approach is a useful addition to standard interventions, but full evaluation of its impact has yet to be completed.

The ecology of AIDS

It is important to appreciate that though some groups are over-represented in the statistics upon AIDS, there are no high risk groups, only high risk behaviours. The key to preventing AIDS is changing behaviours. Many of the research studies on AIDS have focused upon investigating individuals' attitudes, knowledge and beliefs, but though these are important variables in models of behaviour change they do not act in isolation. Perceptions of risk, the illusion of invulnerability can be significant obstacles to change. In addition, decision making does not occur in isolation – it involves social influences and social comparisons also, and these will affect behaviour. Individual behaviours are influenced by the social and cultural contexts in which they occur and interventions to prevent AIDS must reflect this (Rhodes and Hartnoll, 1996).

It should also be appreciated that patterns of transmission of HIV are not identical across different countries (Piot *et al.*, 1988) and interventions to limit the spread of HIV should reflect this fact. Unfortunately, because much of the research into HIV/AIDS has come from the USA and Western Europe, health promotion messages often have reflected the patterns of transmission seen in those countries, even when as for some African countries those messages may be incorrect or inappropriate (Hubley, 1988; Pitts and Jackson, 1989). International programmes that are sensitive to cross-cultural differences and similarities and the ecologies of different countries are needed for effective worldwide strategies against AIDS.

Despite this there is cause for some optimism, since other studies do indicate that risk behaviours can be changed, but to be successful interventions must become more sensitive to the characteristics of target groups and their own particular social conditions. Because of the nature of HIV transmission, by sexual intercourse or by injecting drugs, interventions clearly cannot expect to eliminate all transmission. They can only work to reduce the risk of transmission as far as possible.

Once HIV exists within a community, the local conditions within the social and environmental parameters of that community will determine the spread and prevalence within the community. As discussed above, ecological factors can account for the situation in the UK where there is a much higher seroprevalence for HIV in some Scottish cities than others. Similar factors may explain why two American cities in 1987 which both experienced drug use showed very different patterns of HIV infection. In New York City seroprevalence was more than 50 per cent among the clinical population of ivdus; yet in San Francisco the equivalent figure was around only 15 per cent (Watters, 1989). Watters has suggested that though needle sharing occurred in both cities there were particular ecological factors in New York City that encouraged the use of 'shooting galleries' which presented such extreme risks that their use was predictive of HIV infection. The social conditions that encouraged use of shooting galleries did not exist in San Francisco, where needle sharing occurred within more localised and stable social networks.

A further ecological factor is indicated by the variations in HIV prevalence that exist between different ethnic groups in the USA. Studies suggest that Hispanic and black ivdus are at greater risk than their white counterparts (Peterson and Bakeman, 1989). Why should this be so? It has been suggested that it might depend upon some genetic susceptibility to the virus, but it is more likely that it reflects the isolation of these ethnic communities and their associated relative social and economic deprivations, for example health resources, educational attainment. In addition, the particular social representations that exist within these communities including the perception that AIDS is a homosexual problem and the associated homophobia within black and Hispanic communities act as obstacles to the adoption of precautions by heterosexuals (Friedman *et al.*, 1987).

Culturally sensitive intervention programmes are needed which recognise the differences and seek to devise appropriate educational strategies and messages which are compatible with the social representations which exist within those communities. Further research is required to identify why some individuals comply with messages for risk reduction while others do not. In addition, risk reduction must be maintained over time. Some individuals who generally adopt safer practices (drug using and/or sexual) will on occasions fail to adhere to those guidelines and increase their personal risks. Such recidivism is commonly encountered in other types of health behaviours and the reasons underlying it must also be investigated further in longitudinal studies. Once achieved, risk reduction must be maintained and interventions must aim not only to modify behaviour but also to support and maintain desirable behaviours once adopted.

There is a danger that as drug treatments become more effective AIDS will become regarded as a treatable disease and that health promotion messages will be ignored and previous progress on primary prevention overturned. Drug treatment or vaccines will not be a solution to AIDS; there will be a continuing role for primary prevention and for interventions based upon sound psychological models for health adoption.

The Head of an inner city, multi-ethnic, sixth form college is surprised by the results of a survey carried out by the local drug advisory service which shows that around one-third of students attending the college have used one or more illegal drugs during the past six months. She was less surprised, but nevertheless concerned, that one-tenth of the male students and almost as many female students were drinking alcohol at levels above the recommended safe limits and were regularly getting drunk through binge drinking. She had read that in Britain 20 per cent of the reported cases of HIV infection are in people under the age of 25 years and she knows that many of her students are having sexual relationships. She is worried that if many students are taking risks with their health through consumption of drugs including alcohol, they may also be risking threats to their health through unsafe sexual practices. She decides to launch an education campaign about drug use, safer sex and avoiding HIV infection.

- Is the Head correct to be concerned about links between risky behaviours and HIV infection?
- If so, what should she do to make her education campaign successful?
- Whose help should she enlist to present her campaign?
- What more could the college do to help students avoid the risk of HIV infection?

Key point summary

- The human immunodeficiency virus (HIV) reduces the effectiveness of the body's immune system, making it vulnerable to infections and tumours that define Acquired Immune Deficiency Syndrome (AIDS).
- HIV is transmitted from one person to another by the transfer of fluids – blood, sexual fluids, breast milk, or by perinatal transfer from mother to foetus.
- Efforts to prevent AIDS have focused on behaviours that allow transfer of blood and sexual fluids – in particular, unsafe injecting drug use and unsafe sexual behaviours.
- The emergence of AIDS has crystallised the central issues of the precaution adoption process for health psychology. In the absence of an effective medical solution, behavioural strategies must be devised that promote modification of behaviours for risk reduction and maintain those behaviours once adopted.
- It has become apparent that little is known about the determinants of risk reduction, but what is clear is that educational messages must be sensitive to the ecological balance of specific communities and groups and to the particular patterns of transmission of HIV that exist in different countries.
- Studies of gay communities and ivdus have shown that behaviour change is possible, though its long-term stability has yet to be demonstrated.
- To persuade others in the population that they must change their behaviours for risk reduction will require innovative programmes, beginning with education for young people and establishing new patterns of social responsibility.

Further reading

Aggleton, P., Homans, H., Mojsa, J., Watson, S. and Watney, S. (1989) *AIDS: Scientific and Social Issues. A Resource for Health Educators.* London: Churchill Livingstone. As the title indicates, this book provides a very useful introduction and overview of the medical issues, epidemiology, testing, and the social aspects of sexual and drug behaviours.

Green, J. and McCreaner, A. (1989) *Counselling in HIV Infection and AIDS.* Oxford: Blackwell Scientific Publications. The focus of this chapter has been primary prevention, but of course psychologists are also involved in the support and treatment of those diagnosed as HIV positive or as having AIDS, and their friends, relations and carers. For anyone interested in this aspect this edited collection provides a comprehensive account of all aspects of counselling for different groups of people in different settings.

Rhodes, T. and Hartnoll, R. (eds) (1996) *AIDS, Drugs and Prevention: Perspectives on Individual and Community Action.* London: Routledge. This edited collection brings together views of researchers from different countries upon the contemporary research and theory of developing community-based interventions to prevent HIV transmission.

Wellings, K., Field, J., Johnson, A.M. and Wadsworth, J. (1994) *Sexual Behaviour in Britain: The National Survey of Sexual Attitudes and Lifestyles.* London: Penguin. Though not concerned specifically with HIV/AIDS, this accessible account of the National Survey highlights many of the issues that are relevant to the transmission of HIV infection. It also provides useful further reading for the chapter on contraception and abortion (Chapter 9).

Decision making for contraception and abortion

Mary Boyle

Introduction

> for something like three-quarters of that part of the professional abortionist's business that derives from urban American married women, he can thank the birth controllers and the current imperfections in the technique of their art.
>
> (Pearl, 1939)

> it appears to be common practice that women will resort to abortion (whether legal or illegal) if the contraceptive method they are using fails.
>
> (Potts, 1977)

If these statements conveyed a full and accurate picture of the relationship between contraceptive use and unwanted pregnancy, psychologists would have little to contribute to the area. For the statements imply that if an unwanted pregnancy occurs, attention should be directed to the method of contraception and not to the method of use. There is, however, abundant evidence that this picture is incomplete. In spite of the availability of reliable contraception, often at little or no financial cost, the rate of legal termination of pregnancy in England and Wales rose each year between 1971 and 1990 and has fallen by only a small amount between 1991 and 1994 (Office for National Statistics, 1996a). The figures for the first quarter of 1996, however, were the highest for five years (Office for National Statistics, 1996b). Ryan and Sweeney (1980) reported that 63 per cent of a sample of pregnant teenagers claimed to have made a conscious decision not to use contraceptives, in spite of the fact that less than one-third of the sample intended to become pregnant. Similarly, Braken *et al.* (1978) found that 68 per cent of young, unmarried women having abortions had not used any contraceptive around the time of conception. Using a wider age range, Allen (1981) found that 39 per cent of a sample of women granted terminations reported either never having used contraception or not having used it at the time of conception, while Duncan *et al.* (1990) reported that 43 per cent of their sample of women requesting abortion had not used contraception during the conception cycle. There are, moreover, several reasons for supposing that these figures may overestimate the strength of the relationship between the desire to avoid pregnancy and efficient contraceptive use. First, some of the figures are based on the self-reports of women seeking or granted abortions. If abortion is not available on demand, then it would be surprising if some women did not report using contraception when they had not, in the hope that this might increase their chances of being offered a termination. They might then maintain this report if questioned afterwards by researchers. Griffiths (1990), for example, found that many of the women in his study who initially reported using contraception, later, 'with careful questioning' and after their abortion request had been agreed, reported that the method had not been used at the probable time of conception. It is interesting to note, then, that the highest figure for the reported non-use of contraception by women seeking abortion (70 per cent), should come from a Scandinavian study (Holmgren, 1994), where abortion is perhaps a less contentious issue. A second reason for suspecting that many available figures overestimate the relationship between the desire to avoid pregnancy and contraceptive use is that figures for use or non-use of contraceptives tell us little about the *pattern* of use: was the pill taken every day? Was the cap used with a spermicide? Was the condom put on before any contact was made? And, third, Ryan and Sweeney's report that around 30 per cent of pregnant teenagers said that they wished to become pregnant seems rather high in comparison with a figure of 10 per cent from a national sample of sexually active teenagers (Zelnick and Kantner, 1977). It is possible that some of Ryan and Sweeney's sample, having not used contraception and then found themselves pregnant, decided in retrospect that the pregnancy was intended, thus providing an obvious explanation for their non-use of contraception.

What is clear from these figures is that the relationship between contraceptive use and the desire to achieve or avoid pregnancy is not straightforward. This chapter will consider some of the factors which are related to the decision to use or not to use contraception. It will also examine the processes surrounding decisions about the termination of pregnancy. Finally, the chapter will look at patterns of contraceptive use after a termination has been carried out.

Before this is done, however, there is a feature of the literature which is worth noting, and that is that the vast majority of research subjects are female. Indeed, an alien reading some of the research would have to conclude that men have nothing to do with either contraception or conception. One possible reason for this bias is that women are more likely than men to form a 'captive' subject pool at family planning clinics, at pregnancy advisory services and termination clinics, or at mother and baby homes. As Chilman (1985) has pointed out, however, another plausible reason is that contraception and the avoidance of pregnancy are, in our society, seen as the responsibility of women and that the structure of research is a reflection of this deeply held view. She suggests that this selective attention to women places an unfair burden on them and makes it more difficult for men to share the responsibility for contraception, even if they wish to do so. Similarly, Schinke (1984) has suggested that, because males are less victimised by pregnancy, they are forgotten in most research directed at the prevention of unwanted pregnancy. It is perhaps not quite as bad as this, but of fourteen studies aimed at encouraging teenagers to use contraception, and reviewed by Beck and Davies (1987), seven were aimed exclusively at females and only one exclusively at males.

Decision making and contraception

Much of the research into contraceptive decision making has proceeded outside of any particular theoretical framework. This is not necessarily a disadvantage, as valuable descriptive data may be gathered and can form the basis of theoretical models. Some of the models which have been suggested have not been subjected to rigorous evaluation and present considerable measurement problems. Some, too, such as the Health Belief Model (Becker, 1974; Rosenstock, 1974) were developed in other health areas, and their applicability to contraceptive decision making is still the subject of debate (Fisher, 1977; Herold, 1983). The

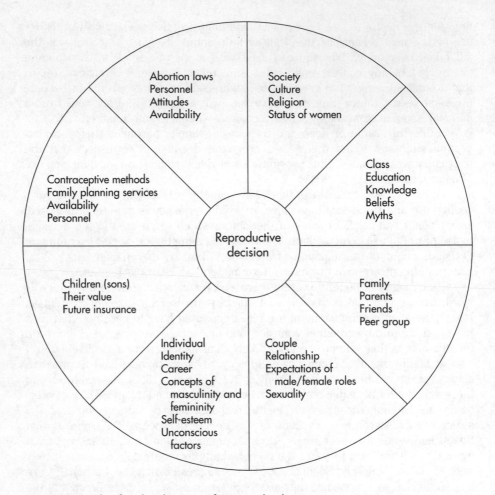

Figure 9.1 The family planning 'factors wheel'

Source: Christopher (1991)

models which have been suggested range from those which emphasise individual factors, such as emotional state or personality characteristics, to those which stress situational and social variables (see Figure 9.1): see Beck and Davies (1987) and Morrison (1985) for brief reviews; no attempt will be made here to repeat these reviews. Rather, one of the models, the subjective expected utility model suggested by Luker (1975, 1977), will be used as a framework for the presentation of research findings.

Luker's model suggests that whether people will perform a particular behaviour depends on their evaluation of the outcomes and on their expectation of the likelihood of any particular outcome. The behaviour chosen will be that which has the greatest subjective expected utility. Applied to contraceptive decision making, the model has four elements: the assignment of costs and benefits to contraceptive use; the assignment of costs and benefits to pregnancy; the assignment of probabilities to becoming pregnant and, finally, the assignment of probabilities to the termination of pregnancy. This model emphasises the social and environmental factors which may influence the decision to use contraceptives. This fits well with the idea of contraceptive use as self-regulation, i.e. an example of behaviour which may involve short-term costs for the sake of long-term gains. As Mischel (1974) has demonstrated, there is considerable evidence that situational factors can strongly influence self-regulatory behaviour. In line with this, Luker explicitly rejects the idea that certain types of people consistently do or do not use contraceptives and the model suggests that, for any one person, usage may vary considerably in different situations or at different stages in life. The factors suggested as having significance by Luker do repeatedly appear as elements in people's accounts of their contraceptive decision making, and manipulation of some of them appears to alter the likelihood of contraceptive use. Finally, the model is comprehensive and incorporates many elements of other models, particularly the Health Belief Model and Fishbein's Attitude Model (Jaccard and Davidson, 1972; Pagel and Davidson, 1984). The same framework can usefully be used to examine both female and male contraceptive use, although, of course, the values assigned to the particular elements in the decision-making process may differ considerably for the two groups.

The costs and benefits of using contraceptives

Luker (1975) has suggested that many researchers assume that the benefits of using contraception outweigh the costs and that the costs of non-use outweigh the benefits. The probable benefits of use are obvious: the avoidance of unwanted pregnancy and, for some methods, the avoidance of sexually transmitted diseases. The costs, however, may be less obvious and will vary with individuals, situations and methods. The costs which appear to contribute to non-use, or the use of unreliable methods, can be divided into a number of types.

Side-effects

A number of studies (e.g. Cobliner *et al.*, 1975; Ingelhammer *et al.*, 1994; Metson, 1988; Washington *et al.*, 1983) have found that complaints about side-effects are frequently associated with young women's failure to adhere to a contraceptive regime. It is oral contraceptives and intra-uterine devices that are most strongly associated with negative side-effects. The apparent relationship between worry over side-effects and non-use of contraception is of particular concern when considered alongside Allen's (1981) finding that many women who obtain birth-control services from their general practitioners are offered only oral contraceptives. Allen also noted that a number of the younger women in her sample of those seeking terminations reported that they did not want to use the pill because of possible health risks. They saw other methods as unreliable, however, and therefore used no method at all.

It is not clear from these studies where the women obtained information about side-effects, or how accurate that information was. Information about risks, however, may be given in a form which is extremely difficult to apply to individuals. A statement such as, for example, 'the pill increases risk of breast cancer by 50 per cent', may entirely misinform of the risk for any particular individual. Women may therefore rely on their own experience, the experience of friends, or on media reports of individual cases of the assumed consequences of contraceptive use. The possible influence of media reports on contraceptive use is illustrated by the 6.2 per cent increase in abortions carried out in the first quarter of 1996, compared to the same period in 1995 (Office for National Statistics, 1996b). Although these figures need to be interpreted with caution, it seems that some women stopped using their contraceptive pills a few months earlier following media reports of their possible links to thrombosis, but without them or their partner adopting an alternative method. There is, however, no evidence that the women who stopped using the pill were actually those at highest risk or that the women had been given enough information about, for example, the comparative risks of their contraception and of pregnancy, to make an informed judgement. This again emphasises the difficulties which individual women face in trying to take into account information about health risks in making decisions about contraception.

It has also been suggested that women are expected to endure more side-effects from contraceptives than are men. Reading *et al.* (1982) have commented on the far greater concern surrounding the effect of a male chemical contraceptive on sexual functioning than was apparent during the development of female oral contraceptives, in spite of indications that they could affect women's sex drive.

Problems in obtaining contraceptives

It is now relatively easy to obtain condoms and spermicides. Obtaining other contraceptives, however, can involve considerable time, effort and anxiety for women. In a study of women who had attended family planning clinics, Allen (1981) found that a substantial proportion said that they had been nervous or even terrified before their first visit. Some were pleasantly surprised and found the staff friendly and sympathetic; others were dismayed by long waiting times, complicated appointment systems, examinations and lack of privacy. Some found the experience so negative that they never returned, although it is not known whether this led them to abandon contraception entirely or to use less reliable methods. It is perhaps not surprising that it is young, single women who appear to be most vulnerable to these negative experiences, although the mothers of young children were most critical of the lengthy waiting times. These results are particularly dismaying when it is considered that it is only at these clinics that women – and men – are routinely offered the whole range of contraceptive methods, and can discuss problems in using them.

Social sanctions

Morrison (1985) has suggested that part of young people's negative attitudes towards contraception involves the anticipation of guilt feelings and fears of others, particularly one's family, knowing about contraceptive use. Allen's (1981) findings strongly support this. It was single women aged under 20 who were most likely to report high levels of anxiety before their first clinic visit, and who were most likely to mention anonymity as a reason for obtaining supplies from a family planning clinic rather than from their general practitioner. Similarly, Allen's sample of those aged under 20 who were seeking termination of pregnancy had made far less use of family planning clinics than had the older women. These young women reported that they were too shy, afraid of being turned away or lectured at or of the lack of privacy, to use these services. Other studies support the importance of confidentiality for young women using contraceptive clinics (e.g. American Psychological Association, 1987; Zabin and Clarke, 1983). Sanctions for using contraceptives may also be anticipated from peers and partners. Two-thirds of teenage subjects in a study by Freeman *et al.* (1980) agreed that a girl would feel 'used' if her partner knew she used contraception. It is difficult to know what this figure means, however, because a similar proportion also agreed that 'A boy respects a girl who uses birth control'. The strength and extent of these sanctions will vary in different cultures. Contraception use is, for example, explicitly forbidden, or at least regarded as sinful, by the Roman Catholic Church, although the rhythm method may be excepted. In other cultures, multiple pregnancies may be valued for economic reasons, because of a high infant and child mortality rate, or as a sign of a man's virility.

The anticipation of sanctions for using contraception may be related to the finding that unwanted pregnancy and unplanned sexual activity are often associated. Zelnick and Shah (1983), for example, found that both male and female teenagers were more likely to use a reliable method of contraception if their first intercourse was planned. It seems, however, that many young people prefer not to plan sexual encounters and give as a reason for negative attitudes to contraception that it makes sex seem pre-planned and less natural and spontaneous (Morrison, 1985; Schinke, 1984). It may be that some people derive more enjoyment from unplanned sexual activity and do not arrange contraception for this reason, but this is unlikely to be the whole story. Certainly it does not fit with the oft given advice in agony columns to revive a flagging sex life by planning and anticipating sexual encounters! It seems more likely that people who do not belong to groups in which regular sexual activity is sanctioned may be reluctant to be *seen* to be anticipating sexual encounters by carrying or using contraception. In other words, for many people it is not so much that sanctions operate against contraception, but against the sexual activity which its use implies.

Interpersonal anxiety

Schinke (1984) has suggested that one cost associated with contraceptive use is having to discuss the matter with a partner, health professional or even just mentioning it to a shop assistant. The problem of discussion with partners is particularly severe with methods such as the condom, withdrawal and, possibly, the cap, which are likely at the very least to be commented on during sexual activity. It is perhaps not surprising that anxiety about heterosexual relationships should have been found to correlate negatively with use of effective contraception at first intercourse (Bruch and Haynes, 1987), or that embarrassment about birth control should be related to less reliable use (Herold, 1981). Indeed, Morrison (1985) notes the 'unanimous conclusion' that 'high sex guilt' is associated with less use of contraception.

In an attempt to deal with this problem, Schinke designed a number of programmes to teach young people the interpersonal skills needed to discuss contraception. The participants were asked to provide information about the specific problems they had encountered, and the skills were taught in those contexts. At follow-up these people, in comparison with a control group, were using contraceptives more consistently and were more likely to have used a reliable method at last intercourse.

Costs and benefits of the AIDS campaign

In theory at least, the cost–benefit equation for one type of contraceptive has altered considerably with the risk of HIV infection. An analysis of people's response to this risk may help to clarify some of the processes underlying contraceptive use in general.

In a study of 234 male and ninety-one female teenagers living in the San Francisco area, Kegeles *et al.* (1988) found that the majority of subjects agreed that using a method which prevents both pregnancy and sexually transmitted diseases was of great value and importance. In spite of these perceived benefits, however, only 2.1 per cent of females and 8.2 per cent of males reported using condoms each time they had intercourse during the study year. In addition, males' intentions to use condoms decreased during the study, while females' remained at the same very low level. Unfortunately, the authors did not collect data on the use of other contraceptives, so that it is not clear what benefits would have accrued to this sample had they used condoms. What may be the case, however, is that the sample saw themselves as at low risk of HIV infection and saw condom use as having costs which outweighed the perceived benefits. One cost, of course, is interpersonal anxiety, and condoms are probably the least likely of any contraceptive method to be used without discussion. Indeed, Holland *et al.* (1990) reported that they found embarrassment 'at every stage of condom use'. Research on condom use has also highlighted an issue which has often been neglected in psychological research on contraception: that of the ways in which male–female power relations constrain choices and decisions about contraception. Sexual activity has traditionally been looked at from a male viewpoint, with women's pleasure subordinated to men's. The importance of this bias for contraceptive use is made clear by research on condom use in which concern over a reduction in male pleasure is one of the major reasons given by men for disliking condoms (Pleck *et al.*, 1990; Wilton and Aggleton, 1991). Holland *et al.* (1990, 1991) and

Maxwell and Boyle (1995) have shown some of the difficulties this creates for women in securing condom use in a situation where male pleasure may be paramount or where the woman may fear she will be coerced to have intercourse. Some men, of course, are unsure of how to use condoms and refuse to wear them in order to avoid embarrassment. They can, however, use arguments about their sexual pleasure to excuse their dislike and thus avoid discussion of their fears about sexual performance.

This research, and that discussed above, emphasises that contraceptive use cannot be seen as a straightforward choice of suitable methods by people who want to avoid pregnancy. Rather, the research shows that many social processes may be involved in sexual intimacy, including negotiation, bargaining, coercion and compliance. Each will have implications for the willingness of one or both partners to adopt an effective contraceptive method.

The costs of practising contraception may be immediate. The benefits are always in the future (when it is clear that pregnancy has not happened) and uncertain (pregnancy might not have happened even without contraception, or might happen even with it). Theories of self-regulation have emphasised the importance of the balance between immediate costs and future benefits; it is exactly under these conditions of high immediate costs and uncertain future benefits that we should expect inconsistent self-regulation. Given the potentially high costs of using contraception, the values assigned to the remaining factors in the equation become extremely important.

Costs and benefits of pregnancy

There have been few detailed studies of the relationship between the perception of pregnancy and contraceptive decision making, although, as might be expected, a positive relationship has been found between young women's educational and career aspirations, the desire for pregnancy and the consistent use of contraception (Herold, 1983; Morrison, 1985). Smith *et al.* (1984) compared pregnant teenagers, who claimed that their pregnancies were desired, with a group whose pregnancies were unwanted. The first group had more positive expectations for improved relationships with their families and friends after delivery. But the relationship between perception of pregnancy and contraceptive use is not clear, because the patterns of non-use were similar in the two groups. This raises the question of whether the first group's failure to use contraceptives was for quite other reasons than the desire to become pregnant, and whether they only later anticipated or experienced benefits to make the pregnancy desirable. Ryan and Sweeney (1980) studied a sample of pregnant teenagers, most of whom had not used contraceptives. Forty-seven per cent claimed to feel 'happy' or 'OK' about their pregnancy. Only 10 per cent claimed that their parents were 'sorry' or 'upset' about the pregnancy. Eighty-six per cent expected to complete their high school education, although 38 per cent claimed that either they alone, or they and the father, were going to look after the child. As with the previous study, however, it is difficult to know the relationship between contraceptive use and these rather positive views of pregnancy.

In both these studies, participants had not yet given birth, so that they had not had the opportunity to match the anticipated benefits of having a child with the reality. But it is presumably the anticipated costs and benefits which operate at the time of contraceptive decision making and it is not difficult to see how these might differ from the real costs and benefits. But even if the anticipated costs are high, contraception might still not be used in some situations. For example, the costs of obtaining and using contraception might be seen as even higher, or cues signalling the likely outcome of unprotected sex may be absent. The influence of the anticipated costs and benefits of pregnancy will also be modified by the values placed on the final two aspects of Luker's equation.

The probability of becoming pregnant

A number of researchers have noted that the belief that pregnancy won't happen is frequently offered as a reason for not using contraception (Goldsmith *et al.*, 1972; Morrison, 1985; Washington *et al.*, 1983). In fact, it is estimated that although the overall probability of pregnancy resulting from any one act of intercourse is about 0.04 (Bongaarts, 1976), the probability of a woman becoming pregnant during a year of unprotected intercourse is 0.8 (Potter, 1963). Morrison (1985) has noted the interesting finding that adolescents often overestimate the overall probability of pregnancy from a single act of intercourse, giving figures ranging from 0.17 to 0.50. Cvetkovich and Grote (1981) have suggested that any estimate which is less than one may be seen as low or uncertain or may encourage women to see themselves as sub-fertile if they do not become pregnant. For any particular couple, estimates of the likelihood of pregnancy may depend on their prior experience of the outcome of unprotected intercourse and their beliefs about the timing of and circumstances surrounding their sexual activity.

Morrison (1985) has reviewed studies of teenagers' knowledge of the risk periods for conception and found that fewer than half the subjects in these studies were able to answer correctly. Knowledge was related to age, social class, race and sexual experience with attendance at sex education classes appearing only as a weak predictor. In addition, many young people appear to hold beliefs which encourage the idea that pregnancy is unlikely. Kantner and Zelnick (1972), for example, reported that 40 per cent of their national sample of 15 to 19 year olds believed that fertility does not begin at the menarche. About one-third of Sorensen's (1973) sample agreed with the statement that 'If a girl truly doesn't want a baby, she won't get pregnant, even though she may have sex without taking any birth control precautions.' Ten per cent of a sample studied by Cvetkovich and Grote (1983) did not believe that pregnancy was possible the first time a woman had intercourse, while Allen (1981) noted that a number of her sample of women seeking termination of pregnancy claimed that they had not thought they would become pregnant so soon after starting to have sex.

It would be easy to conclude from these findings that young people have unprotected intercourse because they do not know the risks. But there is no logical reason why lack of knowledge should lead to underestimates of risks and unprotected sex, rather than overestimates and overprotected sex. The beliefs are, in fact, notably self-serving, in that they allow the performance of a wanted activity without incurring any immediate costs. There is no reason to suppose that if these beliefs were challenged, another equally self-serving set would not emerge to replace them as long as, for some people, the costs of using contraception remain high.

The probability of the reversal of pregnancy

There has been virtually no research into how women, or men, perceive the likelihood of an unwanted pregnancy's being terminated, or how this might affect the decision to use contraception. The likelihood of being offered a National Health Service termination appears to vary considerably across health regions (Office for National Statistics, 1996a) and it is difficult to know how an individual woman would be able to predict whether she would be successful. Allen (1981) noted that the women in her sample had been unable to judge how their general practitioner or consultant was going to react to their request, and that they knew very little about the abortion services beforehand. Hamill and Ingram (1974), however, concluded that 'the bulk of women seeking an abortion achieve their end if not in one centre, then in another; if not under the NHS, then privately'.

Conclusions

It is notoriously difficult to collect information about their sexual behaviour from any group and the data we have on contraceptive use must be interpreted with some caution. Much of the data, for example, consist of self-reports given after contraception has or has not been used. It is therefore difficult to know how accurate usage figures are or, indeed, what 'usage' might mean to different people. It is also possible that some of the reasons given for non-use are *post hoc* rationalisations which had little to do with the actual decision not to use contraception, or are given as the more socially acceptable reasons.

Nevertheless, the results do suggest that, for some people, using contraception may involve considerable costs and the mere availability of reliable methods, or knowledge of their benefits, will not be sufficient in themselves to reduce the rates of unwanted pregnancy.

Decision making and the termination of pregnancy

As Adler (1982) has pointed out, abortion is unusual amongst medical procedures in that it involves not only interpersonal interaction between patients and health professionals but also legal, political, economic, theological and moral issues which impinge on the woman undergoing the procedure. That this is indeed the case is made clear by an analysis of the decision-making processes surrounding abortion. This section will briefly examine these from the point of view of social policy, of the woman seeking a termination and of the professionals who decide whether she should have one. Finally, the section will return to contraception, to look at the use of birth control methods after abortion.

Abortion and social policy

Abortion in Britain (but not in Northern Ireland, where the highly restrictive 1861 Offences Against the Person Act still applies) is regulated by the 1967 Abortion Act and the 1990 Fertilisation and Embryology Act. Under this legislation, a woman may be granted an abortion if, in the opinion of two registered medical practitioners, the pregnancy has not exceeded twenty-four weeks and *either* the continuation of pregnancy would involve a risk to the life of the pregnant woman or injury to her physical or mental health or to that of any existing children, greater than if the pregnancy were terminated, *or* there is a substantial risk that if the child were born, it would suffer such physical or mental abnormality as to be seriously handicapped. The 1967 Act also stipulates that in determining whether the continuation of pregnancy would involve such risks to health, account may be taken of the woman's actual or reasonably foreseeable environment.

A number of writers have examined some of the problems of this form of legislation and the assumptions which appear to underlie it. For example, the legislation involves negative beliefs about women which depict them as unable to decide responsibly for themselves whether to have an abortion (Boyle, 1992, 1997). In addition, Watters (1980) has pointed out that mortality and morbidity rates following a first or second trimester termination are lower than those following normal childbirth. He also points out that those few studies which have followed up women who were refused abortion suggest that this group fares worse on a variety of psychological and behavioural measures than do those granted abortions. These two sets of evidence, Watters suggests, mean that anyone who prevents a woman having a safe, legal abortion, if that is what she wishes, is placing her in a situation where, statistically, her physical and mental health are at greater risk than if she is allowed to have an abortion. But what would be effectively abortion on demand is presumably not the intention of the legislation, and is apparently not the way in which it operates.

It might be suggested that although the population risk of refusing termination is greater than granting it, the risk to an individual woman might not be so. This argument, however, is difficult to apply to abortion legislation, because there is no set of rules which allows us accurately to predict in the very early weeks of pregnancy what complications might arise in childbirth, or how happy or unhappy any particular woman might be with her situation in a few years' time, as compared to her state had the termination decision been different.

Radcliffe Richards (1982) has highlighted a further complication of this form of legislation: it conflates two types of decision which ought to be clearly separated. The first is a *descriptive* statement that, if abortion is granted or refused, certain consequences are likely. The second is a *prescriptive* statement as to whether these consequences ought to justify the sacrifice of a child. Radcliffe Richards suggests that, even if we assume the first type of decision lies within the competence of a medical practitioner, there is no good reason to suppose that the second type does also.

It is not clear to what extent beliefs about the harmful effects of abortion have been influential in framing this legislation. Adler (1982) suggests that research on abortion, or, at least the conclusions drawn from it, have mirrored historical and social trends in attitudes and legislation. From the 1940s to the 1960s, when legislation was generally restrictive, it was often concluded that abortion was a traumatic experience likely to result in psychological disturbance; it has, however, proved extremely difficult to find data to support the idea of abortion as a generally harmful experience. (Adler *et al.*, 1992; Clare and Tyrrell, 1994; Lazarus, 1985; WHO, 1978). This is not to suggest that some women do not suffer afterwards. It has, however, been found that a negative outcome tends to be associated with, amongst other variables, lack of social support and negative attitudes of family, and also with terminations carried out for medical reasons. These negative consequences, however, must be considered in relation to the possible negative results of having the termination refused.

Decision making by the woman

Allen (1981) reported that 73 per cent of her sample of women who had had abortions had visited their general practitioners before the eighth week of pregnancy, and over 90 per cent before the eleventh week. The majority of these women had already made a definite decision before the consultation. Holmgren (1994) found that 70 per cent of the women in her sample had made the decision to have an abortion before the pregnancy was confirmed. Research has emphasised the importance of discussions with friends, relatives and partners, rather than with medical professionals, in the decision to have an abortion. Braken *et al.* (1978) suggested that, having reached a tentative decision, the woman then seeks support by discussing the decision with people who might agree with her. Particular importance may be attached to role models; for example, to other women who have had abortions without apparent ill effects. Although a decision may be reached early in the pregnancy, the woman may still be ambivalent. Braken *et al.* found that about 40 per cent of each of their samples of young women who terminated or continued their pregnancies changed their minds at least once in the early stages. Allen reported that, although more than half of her sample never had any doubts about wanting a termination, there was greater ambivalence amongst very young women and divorced and separated women. Amongst the young women, this seemed to be associated with what Allen calls 'romantic notions' of what it would be like to have a child. The ambivalence also may be reflected in the greater contraceptive risk taking which Allen noted in both these groups. Their non-use of contraceptives could, however, be related to unplanned sexual activity.

Smetana and Adler (1979) studied the decision-making process using Fishbein's model of behavioural intention (Fishbein, 1972). This model predicts that the intention to perform an act, and its actual performance, are a multiplicative function of the attitude towards performing the behaviour in a particular situation, of beliefs about what others expect to be done and of the person's motivation to comply with these expectations. Smetana and Adler found that the intention to have, or not to have, an abortion, stated before the results of a pregnancy test were available, correlated very highly with actual behaviour. In line with the model's predictions, the intention to have an abortion was related to beliefs about the expectations of significant others (mother, partner, clergyman) and to beliefs about the consequences of having a child. Thus, women choosing either action claimed that others wanted them to follow their chosen alternative. The two groups saw the consequences of having a child in very different terms: the group who chose abortion stressed the burden and long-term commitment of child rearing, while those who continued their pregnancies stressed their emotional well-being and fulfilment. The groups did not differ in their moral attitudes to abortion.

These results support Allen's finding that the decision to have an abortion is made relatively quickly; indeed, in Smetana and Adler's and Holmgren's studies, the women did not yet know for certain if they were pregnant. The results also emphasise the perceived role of partners, family and friends in the decision-making process. The results do not, however, offer direct evidence about the nature of this role, as no data were collected from these people.

Decision making by professionals

The majority of abortions in England and Wales are carried out because it is claimed that continuation of the pregnancy would involve greater risk of injury to the physical or mental health of the pregnant woman than if the pregnancy were terminated. It appears that it is the mental health of the mother which is thought to be at risk in the vast majority of these cases, because 'neurotic disorders' or 'personality disorders' are the conditions most frequently given as justification for the termination (Office for National Statistics, 1996a). This means that the majority of abortions (and, presumably, the majority of refusals) involve doctors' judgements about the woman's likely psychological state, taking into account her 'actual or foreseeable environment'. It was pointed out earlier, however, that there is no set of rules by which these judgements might be made, nor have representative data been provided on their reliability. This places those who must make the judgements in a very difficult position. It also, as Radcliffe Richards (1982) has pointed out, leaves open the way for the operation of personal beliefs.

Qualitative data presented by Allen (1981) emphasise this problem. Although she found that many of the general practitioners in her sample referred for consultation all women who requested a termination, some did not. One commented:

'They're entitled to the benefit of the law. I've given up moral judgement. If it's for a reason like they have a heavy mortgage etc., I forget to write sometimes. I say, "Too late, love, sorry. It's the hospital appointment system. You'll have to have the baby".'

Most of the consultants interviewed claimed that they very rarely refused to perform abortions, but it was clear from Allen's interviews with general practitioners that certain consultants were avoided when referrals were made, presumably because they were less likely to agree to perform abortions.

The liberalisation of abortion legislation in 1967 led to a number of studies of doctors' decision making about abortion. Hamill and Ingram (1974), for example, examined the decisions reached in 132 referrals for psychiatric opinion on termination. A questionnaire covering general information, clinical and social findings, contraceptive history and whether the termination was allowed or refused was completed by each consultant at the time of examination. Sixty-four per cent of the women were granted a termination and 36 per cent refused. The questionnaire data for these two groups were then compared. Those granted terminations were significantly more likely to be older, married, to already have children, to have claimed to use contraception regularly, and to be rated as showing psychiatric symptoms. There was no significant difference in the overall number of social problems rated in the two groups, but the women who were refused terminations were significantly more likely to have been deserted by their partners. The finding here that women who claimed to use contraception regularly were more likely to be granted an abortion is in line with Allen's (1981) report that women who had been 'unlucky' because of contraceptive failure were usually granted a termination without difficulty, and were sympathetically treated by their doctors.

In introducing their research, Hamill and Ingram (1974, p. 119) noted that 'the assessing doctor tends to show bias by labelling psychiatric disorder in those he recommends and vice versa. We hoped to diminish this by avoiding formal diagnoses on the questionnaire and asking instead about the presence or absence of specific symptoms.' There is, however, no reason to suppose that any biases in psychiatric diagnoses would not equally apply to judgements about the presence of the 'specific symptoms' rated on the questionnaire and which included 'emotional immaturity' and 'personality disorder'. Hamill and Ingram's results do raise the question of whether those women who were granted termination were somehow seen as more 'deserving' and of whether this judgement might have biased judgements of symptoms. It is, however, very difficult to research this question because the details of doctors' decision making, and much of the information gathered by Hamill and Ingram, are not officially recorded, nor are the numbers or characteristics of those refused terminations. Other research, however, emphasises the inconsistency in medical decision making for abortion (see Boyle, 1997).

Contraception following abortion

It seems reasonable to suppose that the values assigned to various elements in contraceptive decision making would alter following the termination of a pregnancy, although we cannot assume that this will always lead to increased, or more efficient use of contraception. There have been no direct studies of this process, but a number have examined the extent of women's use of contraception after abortion.

Beard *et al.* (1974) found that 81 per cent of their sample reported using some form of contraception one to two years after a termination, and that some of the remainder wished to become pregnant. This figure compares favourably with that of 41 per cent who claimed to be using contraception previously. Using a sample of 10 to 18 year olds, Abrams (1985) reported that 79 per cent of those followed up for two years after a termination were using reliable methods of contraception. Lask's (1975) figures are much lower: of a sample of forty-one women followed up six months after the abortions, sixteen were regularly using some form of contraception and five had been sterilised. It is not clear, however, how many of the women were sexually active nor whether any were trying to become pregnant.

These figures present similar problems of interpretation as those mentioned above: they are based on self-report and give little indication of the pattern of use. Some researchers, however, have reported figures for requests for subsequent abortions. In Abrams' study, these were 7 per cent in the first year of follow-up and 11 per cent in the second. Rovinsky (1972) reported a rate of 5 per cent even with intensive advice about contraception, though some requests for repeat abortions would be expected simply from rates of contraceptive failure.

Allen (1981) has noted that advice about contraception has apparently become standard practice following, or even prior to, abortion. As she points out, promises to use contraception may be used as part of a 'bargaining procedure' before the termination is carried out. There is, however, little evidence that this advice is based on a systematic analysis of the personal and situational factors which may influence a woman's – or her partner's – decision to use contraception. Rather, some of Allen's professional respondents appeared not to acknowledge the difficulties women might experience in obtaining and using contraception. One gynaecologist claimed that it was necessary to 'put the squeeze' on women before the termination because afterwards they 'don't give a damn'. One general practitioner spoke of a 'hard core' who 'like to live with the risk', while another claimed that women did not experience two unwanted pregnancies 'unless they're hopeless'. This last comment was said by Allen to sum up the feelings of many respondents.

Conclusions

Research on abortion has tended to concentrate on the outcome of the procedure in terms of 'psychiatric complications', even if this has been in attempts to show that these are rare. It is, of course, important to know about the outcome of abortion and about the factors which influence it, provided that this research is matched by research on the outcome of refusals to grant terminations. But this implicitly pathological bias has led to a relative neglect of other important aspects of the subject, particularly of the relationship between social attitudes and abortion legislation, of professional decision making and of the application of research on contraception use to post-abortion counselling. The neglect of male subjects is even more marked than in the literature on contraception use. Their attitudes and reactions to their partners' experiences are rarely studied, while they do not appear to be expected to take much responsibility for contraception immediately after a termination. Future research needs to redress the balance and to place abortion in the wider social context in which it belongs.

Elective abortions are carried out legally in the UK because of risks to the mother's physical or mental health, or risk to her family. The criteria for medical termination of pregnancy identified in the Abortion Act (1967) are that two or more medical practitioners must agree that:

1   The pregnancy has not exceeded its twenty-fourth week and that continuance of the pregnancy would present risk of injury to the physical or mental health of the mother or any existing children of her family; or
2   Termination is necessary to prevent permanent injury to the physical or mental health of the pregnant woman; or
3   Continuance of the pregnancy would involve risk to the life of the pregnant woman; or
4   There is a substantial risk that if the child were born it would suffer from such physical and mental abnormalities as to be seriously handicapped.

To what extent do these 'legal' criteria reflect the decisions that a woman must take when deciding to seek an abortion? What other factors are important?

Key point summary

- A great deal of attention has been paid to the reliability of contraception, to its availability and to knowledge about it, in trying to explain unwanted pregnancy. But although these factors are important, they give a very limited picture of contraceptive decision making because they overlook important social and interpersonal processes involved in using contraception.
- Psychological analysis has increased our understanding of what might seem like paradoxical behaviour: why do people who do not want pregnancy have unprotected intercourse? But psychologists have often paid too little attention to important factors such as the unequal power which men and women have in sexual encounters and the implications of the cultural bias which sees women as more responsible for contraception than men. Psychology has actually reinforced this bias by concentrating on women in research on contraception.
- Abortion legislation requires that doctors decide whether a woman should continue with an unwanted pregnancy. Most abortions are granted on mental health grounds and this raises important issues about the validity of doctors' judgements and about the extent to which personal beliefs can influence their abortion judgements.
- Because using contraception is a complex social and psychological process, the effects of having an abortion on later use of contraception are not easy to predict. Efforts to increase contraceptive use after abortion need to take

social and interpersonal aspects into account and to pay more attention to men's role in shared contraceptive decision making.

Further reading

Boyle, M. (1997) *Re-thinking Abortion: Psychology, Gender, Power and the Law*. London: Routledge. This book provides a detailed analysis of psychology's relationship to abortion through discussion of the development of abortion legislation, of women and men's experience of abortion and of ways in which psychological analysis can clarify why abortion is such a contentious social issue. It includes a chapter on contraception and a critique of traditional psychological research on abortion.

Morrison, D. M. (1985) Adolescent contraceptive behaviour: a review. *Psychological Bulletin*, 98, 538–568. A useful, if traditional, review of research which highlights some of the reasons why so many young people might not use contraception.

Schinke, S. P. (1984) Preventing teenage pregnancy. In: M. Hersen, R. M. Eisler and R. M. Miller (eds) *Progress in Behaviour Modification 16*. New York: Academic Press. An interesting discussion of the practice of psychological ideas in encouraging young people to use contraception.

Chapter 10

Essential hypertension

Keith Phillips

Introduction

Hypertension is a chronic disorder characterised by sustained elevation of blood pressure level (BPL). It may result from a specific physical cause such as renal failure, adrenal tumour or aortic disease in which case the disorder is termed secondary hypertension. The treatment of secondary hypertension involves purely medical interventions. Temporary BPL elevations may be caused by the actions of some drugs or may occur during pregnancy. Commonly, however, chronic elevation of BPL is not associated with any identifiable physical cause and in this instance the condition is termed primary or essential (meaning of unknown origin) hypertension. This chapter will be concerned solely with essential hypertension whose treatment may involve pharmacological or behavioural methods, or both. (Further references to 'hypertension' should be understood as meaning essential hypertension.)

Hypertension is said to be asymptomatic and although a variety of symptoms are reported by hypertensive patients, such as headache, dizziness, fatigue and breathlessness, these are neither consistently reported and nor are they exclusive to hypertension. It has been found that hypertension affects around 20 per cent of adult populations in many countries (WHO, 1996) and it is a major threat to health since although itself asymptomatic, hypertension is a risk factor for other diseases including kidney failure and cardiovascular disorders such as myocardial infarction, congestive heart failure and cerebrovascular stroke (see Chapter 11). The objective of treating hypertension is to reduce the morbidity and mortality associated with renal and cardiovascular diseases of these types.

Definition of hypertension

The diagnosis of hypertension depends upon measurement of BPL within the arterial blood system. Blood circulates within a closed circulatory system and has to be forced around the system under pressure. Its movement within this system is determined by several haemodynamic factors and the BPL within the arteries is a product of the cardiac output from the heart and the resistance to flow presented by peripheral blood vessels. Pressure varies according to the cycle of activity of the heart: peak pressure, which coincides with the contraction of the heart, is called systolic blood pressure and pressure reaches its minimum level in the arteries, the diastolic blood pressure, as the heart relaxes before its next contraction. Within populations BPL shows a normal distribution and varies according to demographic factors including age, sex and ethnic origin (WHO, 1996). Within many populations BPL shows a systematic increase with age, but this is not true of all populations, which suggests that age-related increases are not a direct function of ageing but reflect other, perhaps psychosocial, factors (Steptoe, 1981).

Clinically hypertensive individuals are categorised according to the severity of their illness on the basis of either diastolic or systolic blood pressure (measured by the physical pressure unit of millimetres of mercury (mmHg)). The precise

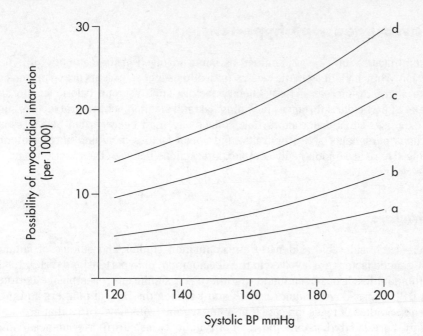

Figure 10.1 Risk of myocardial infarction occurring in next six years per 1000 men at different levels of systolic blood pressure

Notes: a Risk in absence of smoking and elevated serum cholesterol
b Risk in smokers
c Risk in men with elevated serum cholesterol
d Risk in smokers with elevated serum cholesterol

Source: After Strasser (1992)

cut-off points are arbitrary and vary between different classification systems, but generally individuals with systolic BPL greater than 140 mmHg or diastolic BPL greater than 90 mmHg are diagnosed as mild hypertensive. A systolic level greater than 160 mmHg or a diastolic level greater than 115 mmHg is classified as severe hypertension.

A large-scale study in the USA, multiple risk factor intervention trial (MRFIT), has shown that elevation of either systolic or diastolic pressure is associated with greatly increased risk of cardiovascular and renal diseases (Stamler *et al.*, 1993). Moreover, the association between BPL and risk is continuous, i.e. the higher the pressure the greater the risk (Kaplan, 1982); thus any reduction of BPL is beneficial in reducing the risk.

Though BPL is an independent risk factor it can combine with others to produce even higher risks of cardiovascular illness as shown by Strasser (1992), whose findings in relation to two additional risk factors – serum cholesterol and smoking – are illustrated in Figure 10.1.

Factors associated with hypertension

Several factors have been identified as being involved in the aetiology of hypertension. They include: genetic factors (individuals whose parents are hypertensive have a greatly increased risk); dietary factors such as total caloric intake and intake of particular substances including salt and alcohol; behavioural factors such as exercise; situational factors that collectively may be regarded as stressors, perhaps personality styles or traits; and social factors including socioeconomic status. There are undoubtedly complex interactions between these various factors (see Steptoe, 1981).

Genetic factors

There is considerable evidence from population studies and studies of families that genetic factors are involved in the development of hypertension (WHO, 1983). Within families it has been found that there is a significant resemblance between the BPL of first-degree adult relatives and between the BPL of mothers and their infants. Studies of twins indicate that monozygotic twins have BPLs that are more highly correlated than are those of dizygotic twins. Further evidence comes from the finding that there is no significant correlation between BPLs of adopted children and either their adoptive parents or their adoptive siblings despite the fact that they share the same environment, diet and so forth. Within populations, BPL shows a continuous distribution which is indicative of multifactorial determination. It is generally accepted that though BPL cannot be inherited through transmission by a single gene, some form of polygenic inheritance is likely, though the exact mode of inheritance has yet to be identified.

Though genetic factors may account for some of the variance in arterial pressure it does not account for them all, and the remaining variation must be determined by other factors in the environment.

Dietary factors

Obesity has been established as an independent risk factor for hypertension and obese individuals are between two and six times more likely to be hypertensive than non-obese individuals (MacMahon et al., 1987). It has been suggested that the physiological mechanisms producing this increased risk involve either activity of the sympathetic nervous system or increased insulin secretion and other disturbances of the endocrine system (Modan and Kalkin, 1991).

An obvious treatment intervention for hypertensives who are overweight is to lose weight by changing diet, reducing caloric intake and increasing exercise, as weight loss is reliably associated with blood pressure reduction (Rosenfeld and Shohat, 1983). Unfortunately, there are problems in achieving adherence to weight reduction programmes and in maintaining weight loss over time and there is a need to investigate behavioural strategies to improve compliance in this area.

Sodium levels in the body are influenced by dietary intake of salt and there are indications that high salt intake may contribute to increased BPL. Experimental studies with rats have shown that feeding with a high salt content diet does lead to increases in BPL (Dahl, 1961). It is also possible to produce a strain of rats with hereditary sensitivity to the pressor effect of salt through selective breeding and it may be that it is salt tolerance rather than salt intake that is the critical factor.

Research from population studies such as INTERSALT, which involved 10,000 men and women from thirty-two different countries, has found that reducing sodium intake by 100 nmol per day would result in a 9 mmHg smaller rise in BPL between the ages of 25 and 55 which represents a reduced risk of death between these ages by 13 per cent (Stamler, 1991). However, research has not provided conclusive evidence for a role of sodium in the pathogenesis of hypertension. For example, there are differences in salt intake between different populations, and cross-cultural studies find a positive relationship between salt intake and incidence of hypertension (Dahl and Love, 1957). Yet other studies have failed to find any clear difference between the salt intake of normotensive and hypertensive individuals within a particular population (Laragh and Pecker, 1983). However, despite such inconsistencies, recommendations for treatment of hypertension do include restriction of dietary intake of salt. Belief in the effectiveness of sodium intake restriction has existed since the studies of Kempner (1948) showed that severe dietary restriction based upon a diet of low sodium foods such as rice and fruit could reduce blood pressure. Unfortunately this conclusion may be too simple, since diets of this kind additionally produce weight loss which is itself associated with blood pressure reduction, and they also affect the intake of other nutrients and minerals such as potassium and calcium. In a review of studies of salt restriction, Laragh and Pecker (1983) question the assumption that salt restriction is of benefit to all hypertensives: although it does seem to benefit some, it may actually increase BPL in other severe hypertensives. The issue is not yet resolved.

Population studies have shown a direct linear relationship between alcohol consumption and BPL and high consumption of alcohol is also associated with hypertension (Pearce and Furberg, 1994). Heavy alcohol consumption is also associated with increased incidence of coronary heart disease. Fortunately, the effect of alcohol on BPL is reversible; that is to say, when alcohol intake is reduced, BPL decreases (Potter and Beevers, 1984).

Clearly, diet can influence BPL and may be causally implicated in the development of hypertension. If so, individuals' risk could be modified by behavioural interventions that allow self-management of dietary factors.

Exercise

There is evidence that regular exercise has some slight beneficial effect for lowering BPL in adults, though the changes are generally small. However, there are additional benefits in that regular exercise is generally accompanied by lower body weight, less smoking, and lower blood cholesterol levels (Epstein and Oster,

1984). Beneficial effects of exercise upon BPL may reflect these changes or may be related to psychological effects, since regular exercise is also associated with increased self-efficacy and positive mood states, as well as providing an escape from the experience of daily stressors. It has been demonstrated in animal studies that exercise is beneficial as a coping mechanism to buffer the reaction to stress (Mills and Ward, 1986). This was independent of fitness effects associated with exercise and it may be that only very moderate levels of exercise are required for beneficial reductions of BPL in humans (Jennings *et al.*, 1986). In addition to altering mean BPL, aerobic exercise has been found in experimental studies to be effective in reducing hypertensives' cardiovascular reactivity to external stressors such as mental arithmetic tasks and playing a video-game (Perkins *et al.*, 1986). Since excessive cardiovascular reactivity has been implicated in the aetiology of hypertension (see below) it is possible that aerobic exercise may be of value in preventing the onset of hypertension.

Personality traits

There have been many studies that have attempted to find associations between individuals' personality characteristics or traits and hypertension following Alexander's (1939) hypothesis that suppression of hostile feelings leads to elevated BPL. One approach has been to investigate the personality profiles of diagnosed hypertensives. Unfortunately, this approach suffers from the methodological flaw that any factors exhibited by hypertensives may reflect and be a reaction to their diagnosis, rather than a characteristic that is causally related to development of the disease. Robinson (1964), for example, found that hypertensive patients attending a clinic had higher neuroticism scores than individuals participating in a programme simply screening BPL, but their neuroticism scores were no higher than those of other outpatients attending a psychiatric clinic. It would seem that it is attendance at a clinic that is the critical feature and that 'any excess of psychiatric morbidity .. is not part of the hypertensive state but follows upon diagnosis' (Mann, 1986, p. 534).

A superior methodology involves screening a population and identifying the characteristics of those individuals who emerge as the hypertensive sub-group. Using this approach there have been few findings of consistent associations between personality measures and high BPL. For example, Waal-Manning *et al.* (1986) found that among 1173 citizens of a New Zealand town neither neuroticism, nor affective factors such as anxiety or depression, were associated with high BPL. In another study of this type Mann (1977) did find that hostility was a feature of people with high diastolic BPL. This is of interest, as hostility and anger are components of the Type A behaviour pattern which is associated with risk of cardiovascular disease (see Chapter 11). Several studies have indicated that anger may be associated with elevated BPL in high-stress urban environments (Gentry *et al.*, 1981; Harburg *et al.*, 1979), but this finding is not universal and was not found in a rural setting (Waal-Manning *et al.*, 1986). A direct link between Type A behaviour pattern and hypertension has not been established (Shapiro and Goldstein, 1982).

To demonstrate a causal relationship between personality and hypertension it is necessary to conduct prospective and long-term longitudinal studies and it would be interesting to examine further the role of some of these constitutional factors in hypertension; for example, the relationships between BPL and styles of expressed anger and hostility. Unfortunately studies of this type are lacking. In their absence there is no evidence for a clear link between personality traits and hypertension and certainly no evidence that there exists a certain 'hypertensive personality' (Mann, 1986).

Psychological risk factors: stress

External and environmental factors are assumed to operate through psychological processes that have an impact upon physiological responses including elevation of BPL. Factors that have been implicated include migration, rapid modernisation, and the experience of major life events. Epidemiological and laboratory studies have been conducted to investigate the impact of these factors.

Epidemiological studies have looked at the changes involving migration to a new environment or rapid changes within a local static population. In general these studies have shown that the experience of rapid cultural change, or change from rural to urban environments, is associated with increased BPL (Cassel, 1975). However, in at least one instance involving Japanese migrants to the USA, Marmot (1984) has shown that the expected increases in BPL did not occur and though there was an increased prevalence in coronary heart disease among the migrants this probably reflects changes in diet and exercise pattern rather than the process of urbanisation *per se*. It may also be the case that migrants from any population are a self-selecting group with particular characteristics that predispose them both to migrate and also to develop increased BPL.

Other studies have concentrated upon environmental factors within non-migrant communities and again factors have been found that are apparently associated with elevation of BPL. Animal studies, for example, have shown that environmental crowding causes elevated blood pressure in rat communities (Henry and Stephens, 1967). Similarly, D'Atri and Ostfield (1975) found that crowding of humans within prisons elevates BPL. Occupational factors may also have a significant effect upon BPL. These may be caused either by direct effects of the work environment or by the demands imposed upon the individual by the nature of the work itself. In the former instance, for example, it has been found that chronic exposure to noise at work is associated with elevated BPL (Johnsson and Hanssen, 1977). Environments, including work, have great potential for influencing individuals' health, and the impact of environmental factors upon workers' health including hypertension deserves greater consideration. More attention has been given to the influence of work-task characteristics upon morbidity and mortality and it is recognised that many factors can influence health including work overload or underload, occupational change, responsibility, social support, and so on (Fletcher, 1988). It is likely that factors of these types interact with the internal characteristics of particular workers to produce effects that have consequences for individuals' BPLs (Theorell, 1976).

Laboratory studies have looked at the responses to physical and psychological stressors of normal, borderline and hypertensive subjects. These studies indicate that in many different situations, particularly those involving challenging or provoking demands that require active coping responses, hypertensives exhibit greater blood pressure responses than do normotensives (Obrist, 1981; Steptoe, 1981). Exaggerated cardiovascular responses to challenging tasks may depend upon excessive sympathetic reactivity which has been implicated as a mediator in the pathogenesis of hypertension. This issue is discussed more fully below.

Socioeconomic status

Socioeconomic status is an imprecise construct that relates social class with income (often measured by reference to occupation). It gives a broad measure of material benefit within a society. In industrialised countries it is found that higher BPL are found in the lower socioeconomic groups (Anderson, 1989; Wilkinson, 1996). There exists an inverse relationship between BPL and each of educational attainment, income and occupation. In other less developed societies there may be higher BPL in the upper socioeconomic groups. The mechanisms linking socioeconomic status with health are poorly understood but are discussed more fully in Chapter 16.

Cardiovascular reactivity and the aetiology of hypertension

Exposure to stressors of many kinds provokes physiological changes in animals and humans beings. One aspect of those changes is cardiovascular activation indicated by increased heart rate and elevation of BPL. The extent of such activation and its duration of effect varies from individual to individual and one hypothesis is that exaggerated cardiac reactivity is implicated in the pathogenesis of hypertension (Obrist, 1981).

Elevated blood pressure is a symptom. By itself it simply indicates that the usual regulatory mechanisms which maintain homeostasis within the cardiovascular system are not functioning appropriately. Psychophysiological studies have sought to identify the mechanisms by which behavioural factors can affect the control mechanisms that regulate blood pressure. In a healthy organism, when blood pressure rises, the cardiovascular system compensates to reduce pressure to normal levels. In hypertension, complex physiological changes involving renal, autonomic and cardiovascular systems occur and become fixed as a response to idiopathic states involving high cardiac output. The result is sustained high BPL (Guyton et al., 1970). In established hypertensives cardiac output can return to normal levels, but in this case the process is accompanied by increased peripheral resistance of the vasculature and this again operates to maintain the pressure within the circulatory system at a high level. In this case although the symptom, namely high blood pressure, has remained the same, the physiological mechanisms sustaining it are different from those that initially gave rise to it. The key to recognising the disorder is to understand how behavioural factors can influence these various regulatory mechanisms.

One mechanism involved in controlling variability of blood pressure is the baroreceptor reflex arc. The sensitivity of this reflex is suppressed in hypertension. This reflex also influences the central nervous system and individuals' pain thresholds. It has been proposed that the stress of exposure to chronic pain or anticipation of pain causes the sensitivity of the baroreceptors to become reset, and as this learned response becomes established there is a consequent rise in blood pressure which eventuates in hypertension (Dworkin, 1988). It has been found that baroreceptor reflex sensitivity increased for normotensive subjects during relaxation and was reduced during performance of a stressful task demanding active engagement by subjects, namely mental arithmetic, though not during exposure to a passive stressor, the cold pressor test (Steptoe and Sawada, 1989). Thus a link has been established between behavioural demands of a particular kind known as active coping and changes in circulatory regulation that are mediated by the baroreceptor reflex arc and which are associated with hypertension. It remains to be confirmed whether baroreceptor reflex sensitivity is selectively suppressed in individuals at risk for the development of hypertension.

Changes in BPL are a ubiquitous feature of everyone's daily lives. Why is it then that some individuals develop hypertension but others do not? It may be that those who are predisposed to develop hypertension are, in certain situations, prone to excessive cardiac reactions mediated by sympathetic nervous system actions upon the heart. Young adults who show exaggerated cardiac reactivity experience the high cardiac output state that precedes development of hypertension. The exact processes involved remain unclear but are believed to involve central and autonomic nervous system mechanisms, though renal and endocrine systems may also be involved (Guyton, 1977). What is clear is that excessive sympathetic influence upon the heart is at least one of the factors involved in the aetiology of hypertension.

Many studies have demonstrated that hypertensives do show cardiac responses, including BPL responses, of greater magnitude than normotensives during performance on a variety of tasks such as a ball-sorting task, mental arithmetic, competitive games, and reaction-time shock avoidance. These tasks and others that provoke this hyper-reactive effect involve active behavioural involvement by the subject. Passive tasks such as the cold pressor task where the subject plunges a limb into a mixture of freezing ice and water and passively endures the pain do not reliably distinguish the cardiac reactions of hypertensives and normotensives (Steptoe, 1983). This suggests that it is the active engagement in a task that may be the critical component for hyper-reactivity. It is not the case that hypertensive individuals are over-reactive in all situations but only with respect to certain environmental challenges which provoke excessive sympathetic activation of the heart (Johnston et al., 1990).

In summary, it seems that it is those individuals who respond to challenging tasks with exaggerated increases in heart rate and blood pressure who are at risk of progressing from a state with normal blood pressure regulation to one with maladaptive physiological changes that underlie sustained elevation of blood pressure. Consistent with this hypothesis is the finding that the normotensive children of hypertensive parents have a greatly increased risk of themselves becoming hypertensive as adults and they show excessive cardiac reactions to psychological challenges that require active coping even during their normotensive state (Carroll *et al.*, 1985; Manuck and Proietti, 1982). Thus it may be that exaggerated cardiac reactivity in childhood becomes translated into higher than normal BPL later in life (Malpass *et al.*, 1997).

Behavioural treatments for primary hypertension

Drug therapy with one of the many available antihypertensive agents is currently the major form of treatment for hypertensive patients. However, the effectiveness of these drugs is uncertain. Some patients who are prescribed antihypertensive drugs do not show BPL reduction (MRC, 1985) and compliance with medication may be poor, particularly as many of the drugs have side-effects that can be both distressing and harmful. Adverse symptoms reported by patients taking antihypertensive medication include, for example, insomnia, fatigue, lethargy, impotence, and reduced glucose tolerance (MRC Working Party, 1981). In recent years there has been increased interest in non-pharmacological treatments for hypertension involving self-management through behavioural methods. These non-pharmacological methods are most appropriate for the mild hypertensive patient, and those who are severely hypertensive will almost certainly remain on medication for treatment of their condition. Even in these cases however, behavioural measures may provide useful adjuncts to drug treatment.

It will be clear from the earlier section upon factors associated with hypertension that there is considerable scope for behavioural management of this disorder. Recommendations for treatment by modification of lifestyle factors include taking regular aerobic exercise, reducing weight, restricting salt intake and reducing alcohol consumption. In addition to these direct interventions, considerable interest has developed in self-management of hypertension based upon stress reduction techniques which include various forms of relaxation and biofeedback training.

Biofeedback

As described in Chapter 2, biofeedback training is used to allow an individual to gain control over some specified physiological response. Training can be used either to modify some particular symptom (direct symptom control approach) or to produce generalised relaxation. Since hypertension is defined by reference to one particular and easily identifiable symptom, namely BPL, it would seem ideally suited as a candidate for biofeedback treatment using the direct symptom control approach. Experimental studies using normotensive volunteer subjects have shown that biofeedback can be used effectively to train both increases and decreases in BPL (Shapiro *et al.*, 1972). The results of blood pressure biofeedback from clinical studies have been disappointing, however. Though some applications of biofeedback training to reduce high blood pressure have been successful (e.g. Kristt and Engel, 1975) in general the reductions achieved in hypertensive patients have been modest and offer little clinical value. Similarly, biofeedback training for generalised relaxation using feedback based upon responses other than blood pressure has had only limited clinical success, though one controlled comparison study has found thermal biofeedback to be superior to relaxation training for the reduction of blood pressure in hypertensive patients (Blanchard *et al.*, 1986). Having reviewed the extensive literature, Johnston (1984) concludes that there is no evidence that cardiovascular biofeedback has any specific effect upon BPL in hypertensive patients.

Stress management

As has been already described, both epidemiological studies and experimental laboratory studies have implicated hyper-reactivity to acute or chronic stressors in the development of hypertension. As a consequence, several studies have investigated the effectiveness of stress management programmes for treatment of hypertension. The precise methods involved differ considerably but the majority include some form of relaxation training such as meditation, yoga, muscle relaxation and biofeedback. In an excellent review of this topic, D. W. Johnston (1987) has identified twenty studies carried out since 1975 which have used stress reduction methods within clinics; he states (p. 100): 'in the majority of studies stress reduction techniques are associated with reductions of blood pressure and that these persist for as long as four years.' He argues that the effects are specific to stress management and are significantly greater than for control procedures. Extending this analysis, Johnston (1989) has pooled data from twenty-five randomised controlled trials of relaxation-based stress reduction studies. In total, 834 patients received some form of stress management procedure and achieved substantially greater reductions in both systolic and diastolic BPL than the 561 equivalent subjects represented within control conditions. A similar analysis of other groups of patients whose BPLs were measured outside the clinic in home or work environments again found significantly greater BPL reductions in patients given stress management rather than control procedures (see Table 10.1).

It seems that stress management is effective in producing long-term reductions in blood pressure though the mechanisms involved are poorly understood. Some studies however have suggested that the effects of relaxation are mediated by the patients' expectations of benefit and that the BPL reductions achieved are attributable solely to this non-specific effect (Agras *et al.*, 1982; Wadden, 1984). In a direct test of this hypothesis, Irvine *et al.* (1986) compared for hypertensive patients the effects on BPL of stress management using relaxation with a control procedure involving physical exercise in which similar expectations of benefit were encouraged. Patients' responses to an expectancy questionnaire showed no difference between the two conditions prior to treatment. Following ten weeks of treatment they found that the relaxation condition was superior to the control procedure, both immediately post-treatment and at three months' follow-up, indicating some specific advantage for the relaxation condition. Whether caused by specific or non-specific effects or both, what is impressive about relaxation training

TABLE 10.1 Comparison of blood pressure reductions following stress management versus control procedures in clinic and non-clinic studies

	Clinic			Non-clinic		
	No. of patients			No. of patients		
		SBP	DBP		SBP	DBP
Stress management	834	−8.4	−6.1	313	−6.3	−4.5
Control	561	−2.7	−2.1	142	−2.1	−1.9

Note: The figures are adapted from Johnston (1989) and show mean reductions of systolic blood pressure (SBP) and diastolic blood pressure (DBP) measured as mmHg for subjects pooled from 25 separate studies

Source: Johnston (1989)

is that reductions in BPL achieved in the clinic do generalise to patients' home and working environments and the beneficial effects have persisted when measured at fifteen-months' follow-up (Agras *et al.*, 1983; Southam *et al.*, 1982). Clinicians using relaxation therapy for blood pressure reduction frequently complement clinic-based training with the addition of home relaxation tapes to be used by the patient. However, a controlled comparison study found no evidence that their use offers any additional benefit for BPL reduction over and above that achieved in the clinic training (Hoelscher *et al.*, 1987). Considerably more research is needed to identify the presentation and components of relaxation training for optimal effectiveness for reducing BPL in hypertensive patients.

By far the most impressive and systematic research into the value of relaxation therapy for hypertension has been carried out by two groups of workers led respectively by Patel, and Agras and Taylor. Agras and colleagues have developed a self-management programme based upon progressive muscle relaxation trained in the clinic, together with home exercises and instruction as to the application of relaxation for stress reduction in patients' everyday lives. In controlled comparison studies they found that this relaxation programme is more effective for reducing BPL than control procedures such as no treatment, psychotherapy and self-monitoring of blood pressure and follow-up studies have shown that the effect of lowering BPL persists for at least a year after training (Agras *et al.*, 1983). Other studies by this group have demonstrated that relaxation training can be applied effectively in the worksites of newly diagnosed untreated hypertensives (Chesney *et al.*, 1987) and also established hypertensives who were responding poorly to antihypertensive drug medication (Agras *et al.*, 1987).

Patel and her colleagues in London developed a highly successful approach to treating hypertension using an eclectic stress management programme that includes relaxation, breathing exercises, meditation, and both EMG and skin resistance biofeedback. Patients are also given instruction upon applying relaxation to manage stressful situations within their everyday lives (Patel and North, 1975). Comparison of eighty-nine patients trained in this way with eighty-two matched controls showed that those in the relaxation condition achieved significant reductions in both systolic and diastolic blood pressure which were evident after training for only eight weeks. Follow-ups conducted at eight months and four years found that the substantial BPL reductions were maintained over time. The importance of the relaxation training itself is indicated by the fact that those patients who reported using relaxation to self-manage their condition on a regular basis showed greater reductions in blood pressure (10.9 systolic, 7.0 diastolic) than did those whose adherence was poorer (6.3 systolic, 1.7 diastolic). Even more significant is the fact that on the basis of changes in standard risk factors (smoking, blood cholesterol level, blood pressure), the risk of developing coronary heart disease for the patients receiving relaxation training was substantially reduced by around 12 per cent (Patel *et al.*, 1981, 1985). At the four-year follow-up patients were also questioned about the effect of the treatment upon other aspects of their lives including social life, sexual life, work relationships, general health and enjoyment of life. The results showed that compared to controls the treatment group showed beneficial changes in many aspects of their life and significantly so for general health, enjoyment of life, personal and family relationships, and work relationships. These non-specific improvements may be additional health benefits that result from the relaxation training received by these patients, or it could be that the improvements have themselves contributed to the reductions in BPL achieved (Steptoe *et al.*, 1987).

Stepped-care approach

Although the immediate goal of treatment for hypertension is to reduce BPL by as much as possible and ideally to within the normotensive range, the longer term objective is to reduce the incidence of renal and cardiovascular disease for hypertensive patients. Appel (1986) suggests that the objectives of self-management programmes can best be met by considering hypertensives as a heterogeneous group whose treatment package should adopt a 'stepped-care approach' starting with procedures that are least costly and best suited to each particular patient, for example weight loss for an overweight patient or alcohol reduction for someone with high alcohol intake, and more costly or effortful procedures introduced only as necessary. Using this approach, Glasgow *et al.* (1989) carried out a controlled study of a stepped-care approach that compared fifty-one patients given a stepped-care treatment involving, first, blood pressure monitoring followed by blood pressure biofeedback training, and finally relaxation training as required with fifty-one control patients. Both groups received medication to keep their BPLs within normal limits. However, the medication of those patients in the stepped-care condition receiving behavioural treatments was reduced as far as allowable to maintain their BPL within the normotensive range. Comparisons between controls and stepped-care patients were made over nineteen months and it was found that the stepped-care group required less medication to control their blood pressure than did the control patients, and their cost of care was also significantly lower. This study shows that patients with moderate hypertension are able substantially to reduce their antihypertensive medications without any increase in BPL by the introduction of behavioural treatments to complement the drug therapy. Combined behavioural and drug treatments using the stepped-care approach may offer the most cost-effective therapy for hypertensive patients.

Primary prevention of hypertension

Thus far, behavioural treatments have been used for diagnosed hypertensives. However, it could be the case that it is also appropriate to use self-management for individuals who are judged to be 'at risk' for hypertension on some criterion, for example family history of hypertension, to prevent the development of the disorder. It should not be forgotten that though hypertension affects adults, the conditions that give rise to it are associated with factors that may well be established in infancy or adolescence, i.e. lack of exercise, poor diet, and drinking alcohol. Though BPLs are lower in children than in adults, there is clinical and epidemiological evidence that hypertension begins early in life (Berenson, 1986). A longitudinal study of BPLs in adults (Tecumseh Study) has shown that people with high blood pressure in their forties had higher than normal BPL at age 7 (Julius *et al.*, 1990). Future research should examine the possibilities for behavioural interventions introduced during childhood or adolescence for the primary prevention of hypertension in adulthood (Coates, 1982). Those interventions would probably be based upon modification of physical factors but might also include stress management programmes. For example, the package of treatment for stress management introduced by Patel is estimated to require only one hour per patient which is highly cost-effective, since its beneficial effects persist for at least four years. The difficulty, of course, is identifying those individuals who are at risk and who should be recruited to treatments for preventive care. This can only be done by large-scale community screening of BPL but, given the prevalence of hypertension in the adult population and the associated mortalities by renal and cardiovascular diseases, primary prevention could be more beneficial than trying to treat the disorder (Hart, 1987).

Problems of adherence to treatment

Chapter 4 has discussed the issue of compliance in medical settings. Non-compliance is a problem for behavioural as well as pharmacological treatments and particularly so for hypertension. One of the difficulties encountered with hypertension is that being a symptomless disorder, patients may ignore or deny their condition and fail to comply with the treatments advised. It is well known that many hypertensives do not adhere to their treatment regimen, probably because they do not experience any symptoms to convince them that they are 'ill'. One further problem is that the diagnosis itself can become a stressor, which may lead to behavioural and psychological problems that would not have existed in the absence of a diagnosis. The benefits of adherence to medical treatment for mild hypertension may be poor compared to the adverse side-effects (including impotence and diabetes). This is particularly so when the medication causes distressing symptoms; Sackett and Snow (1979) reported that as many as 50 per cent of hypertensive patients do not comply with their medication regimens. There may also be intolerable costs for the patient associated with behavioural treatments. For example, patients may be unwilling to reduce their alcohol consumption or to change their diet to treat their disorder. Hypertension within a lifestyle that includes smoking, excessive alcohol consumption, perceived 'stress', high cholesterol, etc. will demand antihypertensive treatment. However, mild hypertension, with no other risk factors for morbidity, may be no more than a percentile of the distribution of blood pressure within a population that is best left not diagnosed as a medical condition requiring treatment.

Behavioural methods may be used not only as direct interventions to alter individuals' behaviours but also indirectly to improve adherence to either pharmacological or non-pharmacological therapies. Several strategies have been adopted to improve hypertensive patients' compliance including self-monitoring of blood pressure and education about the disorder. Self-monitoring of blood pressure is often recommended as a useful component of self-management programmes, though the evidence that it is useful is inconsistent and some studies have found that self-monitoring by hypertensive patients did not lead to BPL reduction (e.g. Goldstein *et al.*, 1982).

Similarly, it has been assumed that education about hypertension and its management will increase patients' adherence to treatment, but again this may not be so. Kirscht *et al.* (1981) developed an educational programme for hypertensive patients but although it increased their knowledge about the disorder it did not improve their adherence to treatment. Similarly, Haynes (1979) has found that education increased knowledge but not adherence to medication.

Other strategies that may be used to improve adherence include verbal and written contracts between patient and doctor, social support, and individualised treatment programmes that allow the patient maximum flexibility in managing their disorder. Haynes (1979) found that combinations of several such strategies are necessary to improve compliance and any one alone is insufficient.

Although there is little evidence that either mood states or particular symptoms are consistently associated with hypertension, hypertensives themselves often believe that they can tell when their BP is elevated and take medication accordingly (Meyer *et al.*, 1985). Unfortunately this can be effective only when hypertensives' beliefs about their illness are correct and these are not always so (Pennebaker and Watson, 1988). However, it may be possible to encourage correct beliefs and to train hypertensives more accurately to detect changes in their BPL by using blood pressure feedback (Barr *et al.*, 1988). Certainly accurate blood pressure discrimination has been shown to be possible with feedback training (Greenstadt *et al.*, 1986). Accurate detection of changes in BPL, if it could be achieved, might assist patients to adhere to treatments and to employ behavioural and pharmacological treatments to self-manage their disorder more effectively.

Mrs Patel has visited her GP complaining of headaches and breathlessness. The GP takes Mrs Patel's blood pressure and records it as 150 mmHg systolic and 105 mmHg diastolic. During the consultation the GP finds that Mrs Patel is aged 36 years and has two sons aged 15 and 12 years. She is employed as a senior administrator in local government with considerable responsibility for her own work and that of eleven junior administrators in her department. The job is largely sedentary and involves working to tight deadlines. In addition to looking after her family and her career Mrs Patel also does voluntary work for a local hospital and is a School Governor.

It appears that Mrs Patel has elevated blood pressure:

- What additional questions should the GP ask about Mrs Patel's lifestyle?
- Should the GP diagnose Mrs Patel as 'mildly hypertensive'?
- Are there any recommendations for treatment?
- Would there be any value in examining Mrs Patel's sons and taking their blood pressures?

Key point summary

- Essential hypertension is a chronic elevation of blood pressure where the cause cannot be identified. It is a significant risk factor for cardiovascular disorders.
- Factors associated with hypertension include heredity, obesity, excessive alcohol and sodium intake, reactivity to environmental stressors, and socio-economic status.
- Laboratory studies have sought to identify the mechanisms that give rise to sustained blood pressure elevation and there is strong evidence to suggest that they involve excessive sympathetic reactions to challenges that demand active coping responses.
- Treatment may be by antihypertensive drugs or behavioural management or both. Interventions based on lifestyle factors can reduce blood pressure – reducing salt and alcohol intake, taking more exercise and dieting if over-weight, or using relaxation techniques to manage stress.
- Primary prevention of hypertension may be preferred over secondary treatment and there is evidence that risk of high blood pressure in adults is established in childhood.
- Detection of high-risk individuals should be encouraged and these individuals provided with information about risk factors and effective interventions.

Further reading

Carroll, D. (1992) *Health Psychology: Stress, Behaviour and Health*. London: Falmer Press. This book by a leading researcher includes a variety of topics in health psychology, several of which are relevant to the discussions in this chapter including 'hypertension and cardiovascular reactions to stress', 'exercise fitness and health' and 'stress management'.

Obrist, P. (1981) *Cardiovascular Psychophysiology: A Perspective*. New York: Plenum Press. Despite its publication date this book illustrates the value of a sustained programme of research by a man who contributed much to the development of cardiovascular psychophysiology and the discovery of mechanisms by which external factors become translated into illness and disease.

World Health Organization (1996) *Hypertension Control*. WHO Technical Report Series 862. Geneva: WHO. This report by an expert committee of the WHO provides a comprehensive review of the epidemiology and pathophysiology of hypertension and its management. It includes recommendations for controlling hypertension in individuals and populations.

Chapter 11

Coronary heart disease

Philip Evans

Introduction

Coronary heart disease (CHD) is one of the major causes of death in modern industrialised societies. It is also a disease which often kills prematurely or leaves its middle-aged victims with a reduced quality of life. Not surprisingly, therefore, much research has concentrated on knowing more about the risk factors for CHD.

As a disease concept CHD embraces two major types of coronary disorder: *angina pectoris* and *myocardial infarction*. In order to understand both of these, however, we need first to understand the term *atherosclerosis*. This is the technical way of referring to the process whereby arteries become narrowed as a result of fatty material being deposited on their walls. In some people the coronary artery, which is responsible for feeding blood to the heart muscle itself, becomes so narrowed that the heart can be temporarily starved of oxygen giving rise to *ischaemic* pain. This is usually noticed following a period of exertion and constitutes an attack of angina. Atherosclerosis, however, can also lead to a more serious eventuality. A narrowed artery is more easily blocked by an obstructing deposit or blood clot. Such an event is called *coronary occlusion*, and it can cut off the supply of oxygen sufficiently for parts of the heart muscle (the myocardium) to die. Such an acute emergency is called a myocardial infarction, or less technically a heart attack. A severe attack often proves fatal unless emergency treatment is immediately given.

Traditional risk factors

Of course we must all die eventually of some disorder or other, but the distressing aspect of CHD is that many victims are only just entering middle age and are in the full swing of career and family life. What makes these people vulnerable to such illness? In terms of premature CHD there are several well-recognised risk factors: smoking, high blood pressure, family history of heart disease, high levels of cholesterol, and diabetes. Gender is also a significant factor. Women are at less risk than men, at least premenopausal women, although this should not be allowed to obscure the equally true statistic that coronary heart disease is still the leading cause of death in women. It seems probable that hormonal factors inhibiting atherosclerosis are responsible for the relative protection seen in premenopausal women (Kaplan *et al.*, 1996). Finally, there is the possibly good news for some that alcohol, at least in moderation, may actually be protective, although the mechanisms for such an effect remain unclear (Roberts *et al.*, 1995).

Despite the array of traditional risk factors, it has to be said that any one of them by itself explains only a minuscule portion of the variability in who does or does not suffer CHD, and epidemiological evidence often points to complexity in the way that risk is translated into effect. A high-smoking country, for example, may 'buck the trend' and produce low CHD statistics; similarly, a community known for its high consumption of saturated fats might nevertheless prove to have a low incidence of disease. Some of the anomalies disappear when we look at multiple risk. The risk factors do not simply add to each other but interact such that overall risk is considerably increased for an individual who scores unfavourably on more than one single factor. However, even the best predictive equation using traditional risk factors leaves most of the aetiology of CHD unexplained and this has led some researchers to ask whether additional *psychological* factors may exist.

CHD and 'stress'

An obvious candidate, but one difficult to define with any exactitude, is social stress. Certainly early research established that exposure to certain life events might be broadly predictive of CHD, particularly events which involve substantial and potentially stressful change in a person's routine and which require a good measure of adjustment. Theorell (1982) showed that a measure of such life change effectively doubled in the three months prior to occurrence of ischaemic heart disease. Similar findings were reported by Rahe and Lind (1971). More recently, researchers have been able to illuminate mechanisms that may be involved. Thus Theorell and Emlund (1993) in a longitudinal study showed that significant negative life change over the course of a year was accompanied by rises in levels of both diastolic blood pressure and serum triglycerides (fatty materials, including the so-called saturated fatty acids which are implicated in increased blood cholesterol). A major negative life experience for many is prolonged unemployment. It has been reported (Arnetz et al., 1991) that this particular stressor is associated with lower levels of high-density lipoprotein (HDL). HDL is responsible for transporting cholesterol from the arteries and back to the liver, and is considered protective in terms of heart disease risk.

Stressors such as overload at work and chronic conflict have also been implicated as risk factors for heart disease (Jenkins, 1971, 1976). More recently there has been an emphasis in occupational-based research on so-called 'decision latitude', which relates to the controllability inherent in a job. Controllability is of course a key factor in most current theories of stress. Low-decision latitude has been linked to both CHD incidence (Alterman et al., 1994) and higher scores on the CHD risk factors of high diastolic blood pressure and serum cholesterol (Sorensen et al., 1996). In the United Kingdom, two major studies of occupational grade within the Civil Service and health (the Whitehall Studies I and II) has been generating substantial data over many years. Not only is there a well-established *inverse* gradient between overall morbidity and mortality (including CHD) on the one hand and employment status on the other, it is also evident that low controllability over work environment, less job satisfaction, and having to work at a faster pace, all characterise the lower status jobs (Patel, 1994). It seems increasingly likely from Whitehall and other studies of social class inequalities in health that stress exposure factors, rather than simply differences in health behaviours such as smoking and dietary habits, are significantly implicated in the greater risk of serious illness, including CHD, found in lower social classes (see Chapter 16 and Figure 11.1).

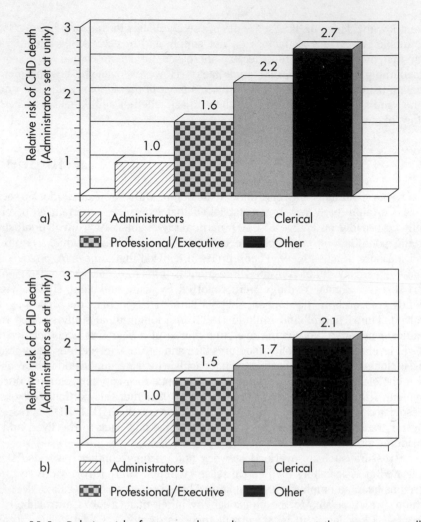

Figure 11.1 Relative risk of coronary heart disease among civil servants, controlling for (a) age, and (b) age, smoking, blood pressure, plasma cholesterol and obesity
Source: Carroll *et al.* (1994, p. 124)

Fisher (1986) cites indirect evidence of the role of stress by showing that heart disease rates in the United States show a distribution pattern which parallels suicide rates rather than infant mortality rates. Insofar as suicide rates can be taken to reflect stress levels, whereas infant mortality rates provide a control level of general deprivation, one can plausibly infer that stress levels in different communities rather than differences in levels of physical deprivation partly underpin observed differences in the distribution of heart disease.

Finally, if stress is a factor in CHD, one might expect that variables which reduce or provide a 'buffer' against the impact of stressful experiences would be protective. One such variable is social support, the degree to which a person can rely for emotional or practical support on colleagues, friends and family. It does seem that social support is important. In the Whitehall study just mentioned, lower status participants, at higher risk for CHD, reported less social support. In addition, several prospective studies indicate a protective effect of social support in relation to CHD (Eriksen, 1994).

The Type A behaviour pattern

Stress, assessed in various ways, has generally been implicated in illnesses of many kinds. The possibility of linking psychological factors to CHD in particular has arisen from the notion that certain people, by dint of certain characteristic behaviours, are more at risk of CHD than others. From such a notion has sprung the concept of a Type A person. Although it is possible that Type A itself may have wider implications for risk of illness in general (see e.g. Evans and Edgerton, 1992; Rime *et al.*, 1989; Woods and Burns, 1984) this is an avenue which has remained relatively unexplored and most research has concerned the relationship between Type A and CHD in adults.

The Type A construct was invented by two cardiologists, Friedman and Rosenman, to describe a certain kind of individual who, they believed, tended to be over-represented as clients in their clinical practice. Type A individuals were depicted as people with a highly competitive craving for achievement and recognition, together with a tendency towards hostility and aggression, and a sense of tremendous time urgency and impatience. The Type A individual sees goals and challenges everywhere, wants to win every 'game' in life, speaks fast, acts fast, interrupts and manifests impatient gestures when faced with slower mortals, cannot abide queues, is only superficially interested in the aesthetic aspects of life and tends to measure success in terms of material gains, and number rather than quality of goals achieved.

One of the difficulties with the Type A construct is that it is a broad outline portrait which includes or suggests the presence of a number of different but perhaps interacting personality traits. Psychologists who have spent many years refining and measuring traits are prone to regret that the research in this area has not developed around more tried and tested measures, which avoid the artificiality inherent in dividing people into broad types – a practice which is bound to ignore the dimensional nature of real traits (see Eysenck, 1985). However, insofar as Type A has been measured as a general *behaviour pattern* rather than a personality measure in the true sense, we shall see that it has had some real success in predicting incidence of CHD. How then has Type A been measured and are such measures reliable and valid?

The measurement of Type A

Friedman and Rosenman originally assessed Type A using a structured interview (SI) method. The interviewer in this procedure not only asks subjects about their behaviour but also observes and elicits behaviour in the actual interview. Thus the subject's style of speaking – how fast or explosive it is, the subject's reactions to pauses by the interviewer, and other behavioural characteristics are all noted and recorded as part of the assessment. The structured nature of the procedure means that with adequate experience two independent raters can achieve respectable reliability in terms of classification agreement. Raters have traditionally favoured the use of four categories. Type A1 and A2 simply differentiate degree of Type A and are often collapsed into a single category. Type B indicates a notable absence of Type A characteristics. Finally, Type X is an 'unsure' middling category where Type A characteristics are not sufficiently in evidence to justify a Type A judgement but not so totally absent as to indicate a Type B judgement.

Although the SI method of Type A assessment remains a sort of 'gold standard' against which other measures are judged, many self-report measures have been used by researchers, not least because self-report instruments are less time-consuming, more convenient to use, and their reliability is often, superficially at least, more easily established. Their validity has, as we shall see, proven in some cases to be more problematic. The most widely used self-report instruments have been the Jenkins Activity Survey (JAS), the Framingham Type A Scale (FTAS), and the Bortner Rating Scale (BRS).

The predictive validity of Type A

The fact that so much research has been done on the Type A construct may lead one to suppose that its predictive validity as a genuine coronary risk factor has been established beyond doubt. Indeed, this was the authoritative view expressed by a review panel of distinguished American scientists gathered together in 1981 under the auspices of the National Heart, Lung and Blood Institute. Type A was duly added to the official list of traditional coronary risk factors mentioned above. Since then however, there have been a number of negative findings in relation to Type A and CHD which has meant that any interpretation of the research as a whole is considerably complex and far from definitive in its conclusions. If we restrict ourselves solely to an examination of prospective research projects – ones which have taken measures of Type A and then followed up subjects over a number of years – what findings emerge?

The first major prospective study was the Western Collaborative Group Study (WCGS) in which a sample of over 3000 Californian males, initially free of CHD and between the ages of 39 and 59, were followed up over a period of eight-and-a-half years. It was found that the subsequent incidence of CHD was twice as great among Type As (assessed by SI) than among Type Bs (Rosenman *et al.*, 1975). To put this relative risk into some absolute perspective we note that 7 per cent of the entire sample developed some signs of CHD and that two-thirds of these were Type A. This degree of risk is comparable with the traditional physical risk factors to which we referred above. Moreover, statistical analysis revealed that the risk associated with Type A was 'independent' risk. In other words, researchers had not simply discovered something which predicted a traditional risk factor thereby suggesting a spurious link with CHD (for example, the Type As in the study might have been heavier smokers). It seemed that there was something about the Type A behaviour pattern itself which made people vulnerable to CHD. It should be noted, however, that Type A must ultimately express itself as a risk factor via some physiological pathway, and while in the early research Type A prediction of CHD was independent of cholesterol, some more recent research suggests, for example, that the Type A and CHD link is much attenuated when HDL differences are statistically controlled (O'Connor *et al.*, 1995). It will be remembered that HDL is seen as CHD-protective and carries cholesterol from the arteries to the liver.

Further support for the role of Type A as a coronary risk factor soon came from the opposite side of the United States, in Framingham, Massachusetts, where a large-scale investigation of CHD was under way. These researchers had asked their subjects to fill in several psychosocial rating scales at the beginning of the study and certain key ratings were grouped to form a Framingham Type A measure. This measure succeeded to a similar extent in predicting CHD over a period virtually identical to that of the Californian study (Haynes *et al.*, 1980). Two points can be added in regard to the Framingham study. First, it recruited both male and female subjects; thus it was the first major study to show Type A as a risk factor for women. Second, its predictive power in regard to CHD was better for angina than myocardial infarction.

Since these first major studies, further prospective investigations have been reported and reviewed (Booth-Kewley and Friedman, 1987; Matthews, 1988). Since several investigators have reported negative or even contradictory results in relation to Type A, it is necessary to try and determine what features distinguish supportive and non-supportive studies. Two such features seem to stand out.

First, studies which have used the SI method of assessing Type A have tended to indicate that it is a genuine risk factor, whereas studies that have assessed Type A using JAS have been particularly prone to negative conclusions. Since the classificatory agreement of the JAS with the SI is known to be little better than 60 per cent (one would expect agreement 50 per cent of the time by chance), we might expect this measure to be problematic. Estimates of the variance shared by SI and the JAS seldom exceed 10 per cent and many researchers have explicitly cautioned that they should not be seen as substitute measures (Mayes *et al.*, 1984). In at least one report JAS mean scores did not even relate linearly to SI categorisation (Byrne *et al.*, 1985). Both the FTAS and the BRS fared appreciably better in their agreement with the SI. Little wonder then that Friedman and Booth-Kewley (1988) called for the virtual abandonment of the JAS as a research instrument.

The second distinguishing feature of the studies which have failed to show Type A as a risk factor for CHD is that they tend to be so-called 'high-risk' studies. Such studies typically select subjects who are already known to be at risk for CHD. The advantage of such studies is that they enable researchers to utilise smaller samples and still obtain enough CHD incidence to make statistical analysis possible. Many of these studies have taken subjects who have already suffered one episode of CHD and have followed them up over a further period in which subsequent mortality rates and recurrences of myocardial infarctions can be recorded. Other studies have selected subjects who are at greater risk of CHD by reason of another risk factor. One such British study reporting negative findings (Mann and Brennan, 1987) used subjects exhibiting mild hypertension.

High-risk studies lead to several interpretative difficulties. For the most part the Type A measure is taken from subjects who are already aware of their greater risk and this may affect their response to assessment, particularly self-report measures. Some studies have indicated that there may be a higher prevalence of Type A persons in high-risk studies, thus perhaps limiting Type A differences to a degree where associations with CHD are difficult to demonstrate.

Survival itself may be a consideration. Type A subjects who have survived an initial episode of CHD may actually represent a sub-sample of Type A individuals who are different in important respects from those who did not survive. They may be more likely to seek help for early warning symptoms; they may generally be better health monitors, or even complainers. This may be a particularly salient consideration when mortality rate is used as a key variable. Survivor Type As may also be precisely those who have suffered less atherosclerosis and therefore may not differ from Type Bs in regard to future CHD indices, or may even be at less risk.

On that note, one particular high-risk study (Ragland and Brand, 1988) is worthy of special mention since it reported an apparently contradictory finding of greater risk for Type B subjects. It is particularly interesting because the group followed up were the survivors of the original WCGS. Although this group included more Type A people, by virtue of the original findings, it was nevertheless found that over a further follow-up period mortality from CHD incidence was actually higher among the Type B persons who had survived their original incident. How can we account for this result? At least two possibilities, not mutually exclusive, can be considered.

The first takes up the point that Type A survivors may be crucially different from Type As having fatal first incidents. Let us assume that Type A has two endangering effects in regard to CHD: first, a chronic effect which aids the process of atherosclerosis, and second, an effect which makes the eventuality of an obstruction or blood clot more likely. The second effect may only be of major significance if atherosclerosis has advanced to a certain degree. If we suppose that the Type A individuals who survived their first incident were those with less atherosclerosis and, perhaps for a variety of reasons, were less prone to develop atherosclerosis then we have invented a scenario in which the results of Ragland and Brand become more understandable.

The second line of reasoning suggests that the psychological impact of a heart attack may be different for Type As than it is for Type Bs. Type A may be more prone to reassess their lifestyle, modify their values and behaviour, etc. At the very least one may argue that they have scope to do so, certainly more scope than their Type B opposites who seem to have suffered despite their laid-back manner! Although this may seem extremely speculative, it is worth noting that when we look at the figures provided by Ragland and Brand in more detail, it seems that their reported effect is apparent only for cases where an original myocardial infarction was 'overt', that is to say consciously registered at the time. The figures for so-called 'silent' myocardial infarctions, where damage only comes to light at some later time, when, for example, an electrocardiographic record (ECG) is obtained, seem to show no difference between Type A and B subjects. Given that anecdotal reports from individuals who have consciously suffered a heart attack often indicate a great sense of 'life-endangerment' it is not beyond the bounds of belief that Type A may resolve to reassess their lifestyle and reduce their risk factors.

What then, in general, should we conclude regarding the status of Type A as a risk factor for CHD? We could say that in population studies, as opposed to high-risk studies, and using Type A measures other than JAS, but preferably the structured interview (SI), the evidence is still supportive. However, there is bound to be a subjective element in deciding how convincing one finds a body of evidence. Reviewing essentially the same evidence, Friedman and Booth-Kewley (1988) conclude: 'By our reckoning, this adds up to convincing evidence that we should be asking how, why and for whom, not whether, Type A behaviour is an important element in heart disease.' Questions of 'how' and 'why' neatly take us on to a consideration of the more general construct validity of Type A. The measure not only seems to relate to CHD but to mechanisms which may explain the link with CHD. In other words the Type A literature has addressed the issue: how does behaviour influence physical pathology?

Type A, psychophysiological response and CHD

It has been thought for some time that psychophysiological response to stressors, particularly excessive neuroendocrine activity, may be implicated as a mechanism promoting premature CHD (Williams, 1978). There is certainly growing hard evidence from animal studies that behavioural stressors can impact not only on neurohormonal systems but also on atherosclerosis (Kaplan et al., 1996). Earlier reviews (e.g. Krantz and Manuck, 1984) suggested on the one hand that psychophysiological response may indeed be an important factor, and on the other hand cautioned us against accepting as meaningful any simple construct such as 'reactivity to stress'. That caution is if anything even more warranted in the light of the large body of psychophysiological findings which has since accumulated in the field of reactivity. Different patterns of physiological response exist and often vary according to the exact nature of the task, challenge or situation, making the investigation of stable individual differences a difficult undertaking. Such caution ought to be especially exercised before making the over-simplistic leap to the assertion that Type A people are at risk because they are physiologically over-reactive to stress.

That said, suspicion has attached itself to neuroendocrine response for good reason, and enough is known at a more 'molecular' level (e.g. effects of catecholamines on platelet aggregation) to draw plausible links with pathological processes such as atherosclerosis. Current understanding in this area has to an extent been aided by research strategies which have fractionated some or all of the three 'mixed bag' constructs which have variously been linked: Type A, reactivity, and coronary heart disease. But such dissection will be more profitable if it proceeds in an organised manner. Flawed global positions with some apparent truth in them may indeed need refinement but at least they are temporary structures. In that spirit, we now consider the evidence from laboratory studies that Type A subjects on some physiological measures and in some situations do show heightened reactivity.

Numerous studies have now been done using SI or JAS assessment of Type A. They form the major focus of earlier reviews (Houston, 1983; Matthews, 1982). Most, but by no means all, have tended to differentiate Type A subjects from Type B subjects in the predicted direction. Measures have included heart rate, blood pressure, skin conductance and catecholamine response. The most consistent results have come from measures of systolic blood pressure. Positive results have also been found using the FTAS: Significant A/B differences have been found in systolic blood pressure (Smith *et al.*, 1985) and heart rate (Evans and Fearn, 1985; Evans and Moran, 1987a).

An important question, given that positive findings have not been universal, is whether there are particular kinds of laboratory situation which favour the emergence of Type A/B differences. Broadly speaking, reviewers have emphasised the need for the task or situation to challenge the subjects sufficiently. In an interesting recent study, Frankish and Linden (1996) followed up in the laboratory on some epidemiological research which had shown that Type A men who were married to well-educated women seemed to have a particularly increased risk of CHD. They indicated that a sample of such men showed greater blood pressure reactivity to a particular stressor, namely provocation in the context of a social interaction with their spouse. Differences were not however apparent for individual testing using a standard laboratory stressor. This study serves as a typical example of more recent research which seeks to widen the perspective for looking at Type A phenomena. Potentially pathophysiological processes may only become apparent if, in this case, we know to whom the Type A person is married, and witness a suitable piece of social interaction! More broadly we need a theory as to what constitutes challenge for Type A subjects. Indeed it is time to consider theories of what essentially it is to be Type A.

Type A and the need to be in control

That an overdeveloped need to control events lies at the core of the Type A behaviour pattern is a theory associated with Glass (1977). He suggests that in situations of challenge but where control is lacking or ambiguous, the Type A person exhibits relentless striving leading to frustration and exhaustion, when lack of control is eventually recognised. Type As will then decline into greater 'helplessness' than Type Bs. Thus he predicts that Type As will tend to be the victims of cycles of *hyper-responsiveness* and *hypo-responsiveness* which are both associated with a pattern of physiological response linkable to processes which would favour the development of CHD.

Glass (1977) presents evidence using laboratory studies of induced 'helplessness' to support his theory. Brunson and Matthews (1981) similarly report that Type As who are exposed to repeated failure tend to exhibit significant helplessness effects. In our own laboratory we have also shown that Type A subjects will choose to monitor for a warning stimulus of a low probability electric shock even when they have little or no control over it and even though such monitoring is associated with higher cardiovascular arousal (Evans and Fearn, 1985; Evans and Moran, 1987a). Interestingly, in the same paradigm we have found (Evans and Moran, 1987b) that the slow decline in heart rate at the end of the trial (slow 'unwinding') is particularly characteristic of those high on Type A and high on internal locus of control, i.e. a heightened tendency to see oneself as able to control events.

Although the control theory of Type A seems to capture an essential ingredient in the behaviour pattern, in practice it is not always easy to be precise as to what constitutes 'control' (see Phillips, 1989b; Thompson, 1981). This was apparent for some male subjects in our own experiments who behaved counterintuitively: they proved more likely to *reject* control the more it was offered. This meant that our predictions about Type A and control seeking were effectively only confirmed for the female subjects in our sample. Similar seemingly irrational behaviour by male subjects has been reported before in a similar experimental situation (Averill *et al.*, 1977). What are we to make of it? One possibility which we suggested (Evans *et al.*, 1984) was that these subjects may have been trying to show superordinate control over the situation and the experimenter by not doing what was expected of them. At the time we saw this in terms of Brehm's (1966) theory of 'reactance', i.e. that people react in certain predictable ways when they perceive a threat to their freedom. This in turn indicated to us, in regard to Type A hypotheses, that what subjects may at root be most concerned with controlling is the 'image' that they present and that control-seeking theories of Type A are perhaps secondary to theories which emphasise the importance of self-concepts. Such theories have in fact been developed.

Type A and self-esteem

Price (1982) puts forward a cognitive theory of Type A which seems to have parallels with Ellis's rational-emotive view of much neurotic disorder (Ellis, 1984), in that the competitive relentless striving of Type A subjects, their hostile emotions and so forth, stem from a belief that self-esteem is to be measured exclusively by accomplishments. Recognition by others is seen as a scarce and fluctuating resource for which a person must constantly battle. Beneath the superficial achievement-striving, there lies, in this view, a more profound sense of inadequacy and perhaps low self-esteem, although predictions in regard to such measures have to contend with the fact that Type A individuals may be highly motivated not to reveal such weakness to others.

There is certainly evidence, direct and indirect, to support the sort of cognitive theory outlined by Price. In a study which actually used threat to self-esteem, Pittner and Houston (1980) showed that Type A subjects showed more denial responses than Type B subjects. Furnham and Linfoot (1987) report that Type As reveal a stronger need than Type Bs to 'prove themselves'. Henley and Furnham (1989) have demonstrated that Type A subjects show higher actual–ideal self-discrepancy scores than do Type Bs when asked to rate themselves, and their ideal selves on a list of forty trait-like adjectives. Interestingly, however, the study also suggests that low self-esteem is not necessarily synonymous with negative self-evaluation. It was found, for example, that Type A subjects were more likely than Type B subjects to rate their ideal selves as 'dominating', 'demanding' and 'conceited'.

Beyond the Type A construct

We have so far only considered Type A as a global construct. In doing so we have found that the crucial relationship with CHD is far from clear. The theories of what might underpin Type A which we have just considered might further suggest to us that certain more clearly defined personality measures, implicit in global Type A assessment, may be more important than others in predicting CHD. What findings emerge from the literature which give support to such a view?

The well-known theory of personality put forward by H. J. Eysenck proposes three principal and fundamental dimensions of personality, which are purported to have innate biological roots. Those dimensions are neuroticism ('anxiety-proneness'), extroversion and psychoticism (tough-mindedness). Eysenck and Fulkner (1983) identify Type A individuals as high on neuroticism and extroversion, while Eysenck (1985) suggests that high psychoticism may also be linked to certain of the 'hostility' aspects of Type A behaviour pattern. From this perspective, however, we are still left with the question of trying to be more precise about CHD risk.

If Type A persons are more anxiety prone, this does not of itself seem related to risk of myocardial infarction, although anxiety measures do seem to predict angina (see Eysenck (1985) for a review of relevant studies). Interestingly the large Framingham study, described above, but not cited by Eysenck, could be interpreted as supporting his case. The overall significant predictive relationship between the FTAS and CHD relies heavily on incidence of angina. Moreover, the FTAS is more strongly and consistently correlated with anxiety measures than any other Type A scale (Byrne *et al.*, 1985; Evans and Moran, 1987a). Unfortunately the diagnosis of angina is far more 'subjective' than myocardial infarction and may be influenced by how much the person complains. Since anxiety-proneness measures such as Eysenck's neuroticism scale are also measures of 'complainer's syndrome', the interpretation of findings in this area is fraught with problems. Eysenck (1985) even cites one study (Elias *et al.*, 1982) which reports a negative correlation between anxiety and the degree of arterial stenosis ('narrowing') objectively assessed by angiography, an invasive technique whereby the condition of artery walls can be directly inspected. Angiographic studies, in which the degree of coronary atherosclerosis is objectively determined, have however shed light on the role of other components of the Type A behaviour pattern. The background to such studies is similar to that in relation to CHD itself as an end point measure. About half the angiographic studies have found that global Type A measures do relate to degree of atherosclerosis and about half have found no significant relationship. In an important angiographic study using audiotapes of SI assessments of Type A, Dembroski *et al.* (1985) rated their subjects on twelve distinct components of the global profile. Of these, only two significantly predicted degrees of atherosclerosis. They were: 'potential for hostility' and 'anger-in'. Moreover, the two interacted so that atherosclerosis was particularly pronounced in subjects high on both measures: someone with a lot of potential for hostility but uncomfortable about openly expressing angry emotions.

This study is important for two reasons. First, it does seem to offer some resolution of the ambiguities posed by angiographic findings as a whole. Second, it is in broad agreement with re-analyses of WCGS data concerning the relationship between Type A and CHD. Matthews *et al.* (1977) report that CHD cases in the original WCGS were primarily distinguished from controls on the basis of hostility, anger, irritation, competitiveness, and vigorous voice stylistics. Prospective studies have also implicated a quite separate (MMPI) measure of hostility in CHD (Barefoot *et al.*, 1983; Shekelle *et al.*, 1983). It is therefore not surprising that most recent writers on the subject of Type A have tended to mention hostility as the most promising 'active' component of the Type A global pattern, perhaps especially what has been termed 'cynical' hostility (Williams, 1989). More recent studies have continued to implicate the Type A components of anger and hostility in CHD. Bitti *et al.* (1995), in a case-control study, showed an association between CHD and both anger and hostility measures. However, not all studies are supportive. O'Connor *et al.* (1995) found, as reported above, an association between Type A and CHD, but only a weak and insignificant relationship for their anger measure, in this case suppressed anger. In the Whitehall study, also referred to above, anger and hostility but not Type A were associated with lower status. Lower status, as reported above, was associated with CHD. However, there was no clear relationship between anger, hostility and prevalence of angina or ECG ischaemia.

In fact the unclear picture that emerges from research as a whole suggests that a totally molecular approach of breaking down Type A into smaller and smaller components may actually obscure the true picture. Results are not clear-cut, and concentrating only on hostility may actually underemphasise the value of keeping a larger albeit fuzzy construct where different behavioural aspects of Type A may be illustrating a coherent but usually covert dynamic. We have mentioned candidates for this role already: underlying concerns about self-esteem (Price, 1982) or the need to be in control (Glass, 1977). Both these 'theories' of Type A have over the years accumulated much supportive evidence, are not mutually exclusive, and in theory can be considered apart from the issue of whether Type A is a coronary risk factor. Global theories of Type A, particularly involving controllability and threats to self-esteem, fit better with the way that psychologists currently construe the all-important notion of psychological stress (see Chapter 3), and stress, as we have seen, is itself strongly implicated as a possible aetiological factor in CHD. Thus stress is a transaction between a person and the environment, and Type A behaviour should be seen likewise. Type A behaviour, like stress, does not occur in a vacuum; rather it is embedded in a social context. It could indeed be argued that the primary and unfortunate role of Type A is to aggravate ultimately biological stress processes by exacerbating negative cognitions and emotions. As we shall see below, such cognitions and emotions have been at the heart of attempts to intervene therapeutically in this area.

Behavioural intervention

Even without considering Type A as a risk factor for CHD, it is readily apparent that health psychologists could have a role in cardiac care and prevention. Several so-called health-related behaviours are important in CHD risk: smoking status, dietary habits and physical exercise. Motivating helpful behavioural changes in these regards could therefore be important. The currency of the controversy in respect to Type A can be seen in the very title of one recently published paper in the literature, which is put in the form of a question: 'Should we intervene to modify Type-A Behaviour Pattern in patients with manifest heart disease?' (Bennett, 1994).

I can think of three classes of reason to support the principle of Type A intervention studies, and they are based on (1) interpretations of existing studies of CHD risk, (2) evidence that Type A behaviour pattern may be negatively related to other health outcomes, not just coronary heart disease, and (3) the fact that intervention studies themselves constitute powerful experimental testing of risk-related hypotheses. The last point should be self-evident: only in intervention studies is an attempt made to manipulate the key independent variable. We address the two remaining points below.

Broadly speaking, it is probably true to say that the validity of Type A as a risk factor should properly lie with prospective population studies, which, as we have seen, is precisely where the results are most encouraging and consistent. Other methodologies can perhaps shed light on mechanisms by which Type A may exert its effects, or perhaps, and more to the point, they may cause us to modify or even abandon what at first may be our most plausible hypotheses concerning mediation. In terms, then, of the controversial question asked by Bennett (1994), the answer given here is that Type A behaviour pattern is probably a risk factor and the case for attempting treatment of it is a plausible one. Having said that, researchers must still endeavour further to substantiate and if necessary refine the notion of a behavioural risk factor for coronary heart disease.

And so to our final reason for looking favourably on intervention efforts. We have already made the point that no one would be very interested in treating Type A behaviour pattern as a 'disorder' if it were not for the fact that it has been shown to be a risk factor for coronary heart disease. Although that is broadly speaking true, there is a question of specificity of risk. We mentioned above that some researchers have raised the question of whether Type A behaviour pattern is really a specific risk factor for just coronary heart disease (Evans and Edgerton, 1992; Rime *et al.*, 1989; Woods and Burn, 1984). Insofar as Type A behaviour may indeed be a risk factor for more general illnesses, this may at least be one area of controversy which can be seen as further legitimising the endeavour of intervention. It will be evident that I suspect that the toxic effects of Type A may be in modulating (to bad effect) the impact of potentially stressful experiences, or, indeed, in causing stressful appraisals in circumstances where others remain relatively unconcerned. This view theoretically draws together two risk factors, stress and Type A. However, since stress is commonly seen as increasing vulnerability to a range of illnesses, it also emphasises the non-specific risks that might attend chronic Type A behaviour.

The Recurrent Coronary Prevention Project

Undoubtedly the single most compelling case in favour of intervening to modify Type A behaviour pattern comes from the Recurrent Coronary Prevention Project (Friedman *et al.*, 1986). This study was extensive enough to supply objective outcome data, in terms of cumulative re-infarction and mortality rates over a period of four-and-a-half years by the time of the final assessment.

The key comparison was between two groups: a cognitive / behavioural treatment group and a control treatment group. Participants in the control condition received standard cardiac counselling procedures, consisting largely of group discussions designed to improve adherence to the sort of traditional advice about diet, exercise, etc., given in cardiac rehabilitation programmes.

In the treatment group, instructors additionally attempted directly to modify Type A behaviour by using a diversity of techniques, both behavioural and cognitive in nature. Cognitive restructuring approaches were used to attack what are often seen as core aspects of Type A behaviour pattern (see above). Thus, participants were asked to examine and question their belief systems about such core constructs as challenge, success and ambition. Examples of targets for behavioural intervention were conversational habits: talking more slowly, listening rather than interrupting, etc. Vigorous voice stylistics had of course been one of the diagnostically salient components in the original structured interview approach to Type A measurement. It also appeared to be a particularly good predictor of coronary heart disease in re-analyses of the Western Collaborative Group Study data, when researchers examined particular sub-components of global Type A (Matthews *et al.*, 1977). Direct training in relaxation was also part of the package.

In terms of outcome measures, at the final assessment four-and-a-half years later, the re-infarction rate was considerably less in the Type A behaviour intervention group (13 per cent in the combined counselling treatment group, compared to 21 per cent in the cardiac counselling only group). Cumulative mortality from myocardial infarction was also significantly reduced in the treatment group compared to the control group (5 versus 7 per cent respectively).

However, it is pertinent to ask not only whether the intervention was effective, but also whether the key manipulated variable, Type A behaviour pattern, was modified successfully. Mendes De Leon *et al.* (1991) reported results from the project which indicated significant differential changes in the two groups on quite a number of psychosocial, behavioural and affective measures, covering but extending beyond what would generally be agreed to be core coronary prone behaviours.

Certainly, the Type A components of hostility, time urgency and impatience showed significant reductions among the participants in the intervention group compared with those in the control group. Affectively, there were also greater decreases in the negative emotions of depression and anger. Participants in the intervention group also showed significant relative gains in self-efficacy, and there were indications that social support and well-being were also more improved in this group compared with the controls. The authors also point out that there was a dose–response type relationship between psychosocial change and amount of treatment contact, such that those exposed to most treatment contact showed more psychosocial change.

The results from the Recurrent Coronary Prevention Group are certainly promising. They are also the most compelling results so far which address the specific issue of the efficacy of cognitive/behavioural intervention in modifying specifically Type A behaviour pattern as a coronary risk factor. Finally, the project is certainly the only stand-alone study which has been extensive enough to address coronary disease outcomes as well as behaviour change with any degree of statistical power. However, there are a number of reservations which limit the conclusions we can draw from this study. Some of these are methodological issues which would point to caution in generalising about risk reduction in the intervention group. The other set of reservations concerns interpretation of exactly what has been the essential ingredient of what appears to be successful intervention.

Dealing first with the methodological issues, a major requirement of the ideal intervention study would clearly be random assignment to treatment groups. However, in the Recurrent Coronary Prevention Project the participants were self-selected volunteers, who were also given a choice in regard to their allocation to intervention or control groups. It thus always remains possible that unknown variables could have been associated with self-selecting behaviours and the clinical prognosis of participants. It has also been pointed out (Bennett and Carroll, 1994) that, although the participants did not differ at baseline on measures of cardiac state or risk factors, there was a non-significant difference in the rate of re-infarction during the first three months, favouring the intervention group. This would arguably be before any substantial behaviour change had taken place. In the longer term it is therefore in turn arguable that prognosis was mildly enhanced for the intervention group compared to the control. However, the overall considerable magnitude of effect found in the project over its full term would seem to argue against any decisive influence of this early inequality of groups.

The other possible reservations concerned the interpretation of the results rather than their validity. Taking the relative difference in subsequent morbidity and mortality as given, it was noticeable that there was a broad spectrum of behavioural and cognitive change among the participants. It will be remembered that participants in the intervention group showed generalised improvement and relative gain on self-efficacy measures. There were also indications that social support and general well-being were relatively more improved in this group compared with the controls. Could it be that these more general improvements, relative to the control group, were responsible for better outcome in regard to the health outcomes, rather than specific changes in variables such as time urgency and hostility which are more directly relevant to the Type A construct?

Put in those narrow terms, there is clearly a problem with interpretation, and the problem is unlikely to be fully resolved by finer analysis of the data. However, this type of criticism may actually be somewhat misguided if the following line of reasoning is accepted.

We have seen above that one way of viewing the various components of the Type A construct involves construing those components as variably existing pieces of evidence for a more covert and dynamic area of concern, focusing on the self-concept. Putting the two principal theories of Price and Glass together, since they are arguably related, we may suggest that the strongly Type A person is, at root, a person troubled by self-esteem worries, and this in turn is translated into a desperate need to show that he or she is always in control of events. This underlying dynamic will typically give rise to some but not necessarily, in any individual case, all of the components of Type A behaviour pattern. It is also likely however that Type A behaviour pattern, like any other behaviour, will have certain social and personal consequences as well as symptoms and these may well come to be reflected in compromised social support, well-being and real self-efficacy.

Assuming then that the Type A behaviour pattern has certain social and personal results, that would surely lead us to suppose that changing the behaviour pattern would itself result in change on these relevant social and personal measures. Another way of putting the argument is that consideration of Type A behaviour pattern in isolation from its social context makes it a fairly meaningless concept. This harks back to our earlier discussion in which a case was made that the best psychological measure of coronary risk may continue to be obtained by assessing a global construct such as Type A (possibly measured ideally by the structured interview) rather than following the alternative route of component fractionation in search of a special super-toxic ingredient such as 'cynical hostility' or whatever. If we do subscribe to this view, it would follow that cognitive/behavioural intervention should be aimed at the same broad construct. It would then also be likely that positive change would be seen on a broad basis.

It may well turn out that change on a 'basket' of variables turns out to be the best predictor of improved prognosis. In any event, it is wise to caution against falling into the reductionist fallacy that as we move from analysis of broad construct to narrow construct, and then from component to sub-component, we are necessarily increasing the scientific rigour of our research. Molar and molecular approaches are always different, but always equally valid.

There are also strong ethical and pragmatic considerations that need to be made. There would appear to be a sound prima facie argument for staying with an apparently successful broad spectrum approach to intervention, unless and until converging evidence should point much more clearly than at present either to the overwhelming importance of one single factor, or alternatively to the irrelevance of other factors currently targeted as part of intervention strategies. However, there may well be a case for some parallel exploration in the direction of brief interventions which may hold the promise of effective but less costly intervention for more people.

Other intervention studies

We have so far tended to concentrate exclusively on the results of the Recurrent Coronary Prevention Project. This is for good reason. The project stands alone in being able to address in a single study the end-point of central interest as to whether modification of Type A behaviour pattern results in diminution of coronary risk. There are some studies which have sought to intervene to alter Type A behaviour pattern as part of wider programmes of cognitive / behavioural counselling, stress management, etc. which, though of interest, are bound to be ambiguous in regard to any diminution of risk. Nevertheless, positive results regarding reduced risk have been reported following such mixed package intervention (e.g. Oldenburg *et al.*, 1985).

Equally there are a number of studies which have addressed the feasibility of Type A behaviour change but have been unable to address issues of effects on differential risk for coronary heart disease indices. One relatively large sample study has certainly shown encouraging effectiveness for an intervention, based on the Recurrent Coronary Prevention Project approach (Gill *et al.*, 1985). The subjects were senior army officers and the allocation to treatment and control groups was randomised. Unfortunately the major weakness of this study is that no follow-up has been reported, so we do not know how permanent the apparently effective intervention was. A study by Thurman (1985a, 1985b) did incorporate a one-year follow-up. Cognitive / behavioural intervention was successful in reducing Type A behaviour pattern following an eight-week intervention, and the superiority of interventions over controls was still evident at assessment a year later. The broad conclusion to draw from these and several other studies is to confirm that the Type A behaviour pattern is indeed modifiable.

As a concluding point, it would be desirable to know whether interventions among coronary disease-free subjects were actually effective in reducing risk of future myocardial infarction or other coronary heart disease. Existing population studies have merely shown that Type A behaviour is alterable. Even where the more limited goal of examining the modifiability of Type A behaviour has been the focus of study, the lack of meaningful follow-up data is striking. This issue needs to be addressed in future research.

Finally, it should be remembered that stress is itself associated with CHD risk. Although Type A may interact significantly with stress processes, it seems likely that individuals in relatively adverse circumstances, with little control over those circumstances, will exhibit higher risk regardless of their personality or behavioural disposition. This social stress dimension is likely to be more important than individual psychological characteristics in accounting for major social class inequalities in CHD and, indeed, general morbidity and mortality.

A MEASURE OF TYPE A BEHAVIOUR PATTERN

The questions below were used to identify Type A individuals in the large-scale Framingham Project on Coronary Heart Disease (Haynes *et al.*, 1978).

Do the following statements describe you:
(1) very well, (2) fairly well, (3) somewhat, (4) not at all?

- Being bossy or dominating
- Usually pressed for time
- Having a strong need to excel in most things
- Eating too quickly
- Being hard-driving and competitive.

Do you get upset when you have to wait for something? (YES/NO)
What are your feelings at the end of an average day of work?
Answer YES or NO to each of the following:

- Often felt very pressed for time
- Work stayed with you so you were thinking about it after working hours
- Work often stretched you to the very limits of your energy and capacity
- Often felt uncertain, uncomfortable, or dissatisfied with how well you are doing.

One of the difficulties (see p. 211) for researchers is that different measures of Type A have only very limited agreement with each other. Why do you think this is so? They also lack 'purity'. This Framingham scale, for example, usually correlates quite highly with the fundamental personality dimension of neuroticism. What does this tell you about the use of self-report scales to measure Type A behaviour pattern?

Key point summary

- CHD is a major life-threatening disorder in modern society. Psychological and psychosocial variables including stress and Type A behaviour pattern have been implicated as risk factors.
- Although the Type A construct has been somewhat under siege in recent years, I would deem it premature to abandon it yet. Although there is a case for examining the role of components (such as hostility indices), there is also a case to be made for continuing to view the Type A construct more loosely and globally. It is possible that some 'toxic' psychodynamic expresses itself variously among the classic Type A behaviours with perhaps different emphases in different individuals.
- Given that a treatment approach based on modifying a broad range of Type A behaviours seems to have achieved positive results, it would seem from pragmatic, clinical and ethical perspectives arguable that future approaches

should not in the main unduly narrow the focus until they have good reason to do so from converging lines of research.

● It has been suggested here that stress and Type A behaviour pattern may interact in relation to CHD risk. Equally, and like stress itself, Type A behaviour pattern may not uniquely be associated with CHD, but with a range of illnesses.

Further reading

The following publications may help to extend and consolidate some of the themes of this chapter.

Bennett, P. and Carroll, D. (1994) Cognitive-behavioural interventions in cardiac rehabilitation. *Journal of Psychosomatic Research*, 38, 3, 169–182. This article discusses cognitive/behavioural intervention.

Rosenman, R. H. (1996) Personality, behaviour patterns, and heart disease. In: C. L. Cooper (ed.) *Handbook of Stress, Medicine, and Health*. London: CRC Press. This chapter discusses personality and behaviour patterns in CHD.

Theorell, T. (1996) Critical life changes and cardiovascular disease. In: C. L. Cooper (ed.) *Handbook of Stress, Medicine, and Health*. London: CRC Press. This chapter provides a broader approach to social stress and CHD.

Diabetes

Paula Hixenbaugh
and Laura Warren

chapter 12

Introduction

Diabetes is a chronic disease which must be self-managed. The consequences of poor management are severe; they include blindness, limb amputation, kidney failure and early death. There is evidence that careful management of the disease can enable the patient to avoid these complications. Bad management often results not from inadequate education but from poor psychosocial adjustment to the demands of the recommended self-care routine. There are clear roles for health psychology in understanding the psychological consequences of diabetes and the psychological factors involved in effective self-management of the disorder.

The nature of the disease

Diabetes mellitus is a chronic multisystem disorder defined by an abnormally high blood glucose concentration. The word 'diabetes' is derived from the ancient Greek, meaning siphon or fountain, while 'mellitus' refers to honey and sweetness. Although reference to the condition of diabetes has been found in the Ebers Papyrus, dating back to 1500 BC, it was not until 1889 that Paul Langerhan found that when specific cells in the pancreas were damaged, diabetes developed.

There was no effective treatment for diabetes until Banting and Best isolated insulin which was first used with patients in 1922. Insulin regulates blood glucose levels and is necessary to convert glucose to energy. When insufficient insulin is produced or when the body is unable to utilise it effectively, glucose accumulates in the blood and spills over into the urine. Symptoms of diabetes commonly include excessive thirst, frequent urination, weakness and weight loss.

The British Diabetic Association (BDA) reported that in 1996 there were 1.4 million people with diabetes in the United Kingdom. It is the fourth leading cause of death in developed countries (Kings Fund, 1996) and the overall life expectancy of a patient developing diabetes in childhood is only 50 per cent of that expected by a non-diabetic: even those developing diabetes in later life lose 30 per cent of their expected life span (Hill, 1987). Overall disability rates in diabetics are two to three times higher than in non-diabetics, with diabetes being the single most common cause of blindness in the UK among people of working age (Kings Fund, 1996). About 50 per cent of insulin-dependent diabetics are likely to develop kidney disease (nephropathy). Furthermore, in the USA diabetes is now recognised to be *the* major cause of disability in people over 45 years of age (Rubin and Peyrot, 1992).

The cost of diabetes is measured not only in terms of human suffering; the financial costs place a substantial burden on the National Health Service. A recent report commissioned by the British Diabetic Association (Kings Fund, 1996) presents evidence that the cost of diabetes to the NHS is 8 per cent of hospital expenditure or at least £2 billion annually.

Diabetes is classified as type 1 (insulin-dependent diabetes mellitus (IDDM)) or type 2 (non-insulin-dependent diabetes mellitus (NIDDM)). In insulin-dependent diabetes, the pancreas stops producing insulin and survival depends on daily injections. IDDM can occur at any age though it usually develops prior to the age of 30 with incidence reaching a peak during adolescence. Onset is usually rapid and symptoms acute due to severe hyperglycaemia (high blood sugar). IDDM accounts for approximately 15 per cent of diabetes (Kings Fund, 1996) and is found equally in males and females. The last decade has witnessed a significant increase in the incidence rate in children under 5 years of age (Gale, personal communication). The cause of IDDM is unclear, although genetic, auto-immune and infection factors are all thought to be involved (Cox *et al.*, 1991).

In NIDDM, insufficient insulin is produced and there may be increased resistance to the effects of insulin. While it has been estimated that 90 per cent of NIDDM sufferers could be treated only through diet and exercise (Newburgh and Conn, 1979), the significant majority of patients have to take either tablets (50 per cent) or insulin injections (20 per cent). The most recent BDA estimate (Kings Fund, 1996) is that NIDDM accounts for approximately 85 per cent of cases of diabetes. Typically it occurs in middle age, with the prevalence increasing with age. Onset is often gradual and free of symptoms, with the consequence that diagnosis is made during either a routine examination, or during an investigation for some other health complaint. As a result, approximately 50 per cent of individuals present further medical complications at diagnosis (UKPDS Group, 1990). There is a strong genetic component to NIDDM and obesity and inadequate exercise are also understood to contribute to onset.

The goal in treating both types of diabetes is to maintain blood glucose levels as closely as possible within the non-diabetic range. The Diabetes Control and Complications Trial (DCCT) (1993) was a landmark study that confirmed what most health professionals believed: that rigorous blood glucose control prevents or delays the onset of complications. However, such control must be achieved through an intensive treatment programme for IDDMs consisting of at least three daily injections of insulin, four or more blood glucose tests daily, frequent dietary instruction and a monthly visit to the clinic. Although NIDDMs were not included in the study, it is reasonable to conclude that similar requirements for good blood glucose control also apply. Though such intensive treatment may be the ideal, it is probably not practical in the normal clinical setting. However, the beneficial effects of good glycaemic control cannot be underestimated.

Diabetes is a chronic condition and unique in the extent to which patients must assume responsibility for their own care in order to maintain blood glucose as closely as possible to normal levels. To achieve this the diabetic must not only take tablets or inject insulin at regular intervals each day but also take regular exercise and follow a special diet, adjusting food timing or intake to take account of activity levels. The 'success' of their diabetes management is determined by taking regular blood or urine glucose tests: in instances where test results are outside the advocated limits, the patient must first take a decision (rightly or wrongly) as to what has caused the fluctuation (for example overeating, mistiming medication), and then make an appropriate adjustment (for example increasing medication intake). In order to be able to make the appropriate adjustments the individual has to keep a constant record of daily events relevant to their blood glucose levels (Table 12.1).

TABLE 12.1 Educational messages about insulin and its administration

A patient should be able to:
1   Identify that action times vary with different insulins
2   Recognise that short acting insulin is clear: medium and long are cloudy
3   Identify own insulin type by name, strength, dosage
4   State times of injections
5   Identify need for regularity in the timing of injections
6   Properly identify syringe used: millilitres, type
7   Recognise that problems may arise from changing syringes
8   Demonstrate proper preparation of insulin injection
9   Demonstrate proper injection techniques
10 Identify by name recommended injection sites
11 Recognise need to change injection site
12 Correctly state outcome of injecting too often in same site
13 State why insulin is taken before meals
14 Identify procedure to be followed if meal delayed after injection
15 Correctly identify when own insulins:
    (a) begin working
    (b) act most powerfully
16 State indicators for increasing / decreasing insulin
17 Identify number of units changed
18 Correctly identify action to be taken when tests remain high after increase in insulin
19 State proper insulin storage procedure
20 Recognise that insulin should never be stopped even when:
    (a) feeling unwell
    (b) unable to take required diet
21 Recognise that there may be a need to increase insulin during illness
22 Correctly identify the insulin to be increased in emergencies (short acting)
23 Recognise the importance of expiry date
24 Recognise the acceptable reuse of disposable syringes

Source: Shillitoe (1988, p. 69), after Boggan *et al.* (1984)

Models of personal control

The health belief model

Diabetic patients' adherence to medical treatment is critical for their survival. The health belief model (HBM) (Becker and Maiman, 1975) has been the subject of extensive research into patients' compliance with medical advice (Becker and Rosenstock, 1984, and see Chapter 1). This model proposes that an individual's level of self-care is influenced by a combination of readiness variables including perceived vulnerability to the disease, perceived seriousness of the disease, and the costs and benefits of action. These readiness variables will be affected by internal or external cues to action. In the case of the diabetic patient, internal cues to action might be feeling unwell due to high blood sugar while external cues include advice and information about the disease. The important assumption of the HBM is that it is the patient's subjective assessment of the model components that is of relevance to their personal self-care.

Results of investigations using the HBM have been mixed. Some have found that either individual components or combinations were positively related to self-care (Alogna, 1980; Bloom-Cerkoney and Hart, 1980) but other studies have failed to find support for the model (e.g. Harris and Linn, 1985). One of the significant weaknesses of the model has been its inability to demonstrate cause and effect (de Weerdt *et al.*, 1989). May (1991) has suggested that levels of adherence to treatment regimen determine health beliefs. Since there is evidence to suggest that there is a changing relationship between beliefs, behaviour and outcomes over time, the model is unlikely to be useful in predicting behaviour (Shillitoe and Miles, 1989).

Lewis and Bradley (1994) have investigated the use of validated diabetes-specific scales as opposed to general health belief scales. The employment of these scales has met with some success when used in studies designed to try to understand differences in choice of treatment and to assess the effectiveness of treatment. However, Lewis and Bradley observed that the association between health beliefs and self-care behaviour was weakened both by patients' lack of knowledge and the existence of competing priorities. In addition, when examining NIDDM-specific measures of disease severity, these were found to be related to control of the disease in the *opposite* direction to that which the model would predict.

Factors which may be important to consider in determining the ability of the model to predict the behaviour of diabetic patients include the possibility that health beliefs may change predictably over time and/or over the course of the disease. On the other hand, it may be that health beliefs regarding diabetes remain unchanged but that their relationship with behaviour alters systematically over time. For example, a belief in vulnerability may lead to better self-care before the development of complications; however, upon the onset of complications this same belief may have no effect on self-care. If a patient has followed advice and still develops complications, motivation for self-care may be reduced (Warren and Hixenbaugh, 1996).

Social learning models

In recent years, self-efficacy, i.e. the person's belief in his or her own capacity to perform the recommended behaviour (Bandura, 1984), has received increasing attention as a predictor of adherence to treatment. The strength of efficacy beliefs are hypothesised to determine the degree of effort that an individual will expend and how long they will persist in their coping efforts. In relation to chronic disease, the social learning model (SLM) has been expanded to include a physiological component which may act as a cue for behaviour and cognition as well as react to environmental events (Thoresen and Kirmil-Gray, 1983).

Support for self-efficacy as a predictor of adherence is mixed. In a study conducted with a largely elderly, retired population of IDDMs and NIDDMs, Kavanagh *et al.* (1993) found that self-efficacy did predict adherence to diet, exercise and blood glucose testing over an eight-week period. Similarly, self-efficacy was found to be associated with regimen adherence among a sample of inner city African-American women with NIDDM, who were studied over a five-month period. However, the results suggested that a relationship at one point in time should not be taken as evidence of a stable relationship over time, since over longer periods the initial relationships weakened or disappeared (Skelly *et al.*, 1995). A recent, well-designed study conducted by Drapkin *et al.* (1995) found that self-efficacy was not related to weight loss for a sample of ninety-three male and female NIDDM adults who took part in a control programme. They suggested that the lack of support for the model could be due to the method of assessment employed. Rather than simply asking their subjects to complete a self-efficacy questionnaire, Drapkin *et al.* presented them with a number of vivid descriptions of high-risk scenarios related to overeating and asked them to rate their confidence in avoiding these. Each scenario contained an emotional trigger and exposure to a food cue; for example, 'You are having a family celebration. You are enjoying the company and the festive atmosphere. Everyone has prepared their speciality dishes, from the appetisers through the desserts, and you really love these foods.' Although the study did not offer support for self-efficacy, what did predict weight loss was the ability to generate any coping response, rather than a certain type or number of responses. Analysis also revealed that coping strategies varied significantly across situations, with behavioural strategies being suppressed in work settings in particular, where it has been suggested that visible coping efforts may carry a psychosocial cost (Warren and Hixenbaugh, 1996; Wills and Shiffman, 1985). These results suggest that it may be productive to identify the patients' most difficult situations and devise specific coping skills accordingly.

Further evidence for the value of self-efficacy in predicting treatment adherence comes from the studies of Glasgow and colleagues (McCaul *et al.*, 1987). The aim of their ongoing research is to develop interventions that are tailored to each patient (Glasgow, 1991), and thus they are continually adding new variables to their model and designing alternative intervention strategies. Some of the more recent additions are the influence of the community (for example public opinion) and the use of problem-solving skills. Although the most recent intervention strategies are too new to have been subjected to extensive evaluation, the research team report initial results that are positive (Glasgow *et al.*, 1995). Despite significant changes in the breadth and emphasis of the model, it remains grounded in the principles of social learning theory: with a non-pathological view of the non-adherent patient and with an emphasis on 'reciprocal determinism and the inter-relationship among cognitive, behavioural and environmental factors' (Glasgow *et al.*, 1995, p. 34). To assess empirically such a complex model and confirm causal explanations is difficult. However, the fact that the model has taken the patient's perspective provides it with a clinical relevance that should produce improvements in patient outcomes beyond those achieved by the more experimentally controllable, but less relevant and complete approaches to understanding adherence.

Psychosocial consequences

Stress

The role of stress and its management in diabetes has been investigated widely. Stress has been found to have both direct and indirect effects on metabolic control in adults: a direct effect occurring as a result of an increase in counter-regulatory stress hormones, which in turn raise blood sugars (Surwit and Feinglos, 1988; Aitkens *et al.*, 1992) and an indirect effect resulting from stress affecting self-care behaviour, which in turn affects glycaemic control (Bradley, 1979). However, much of the stress research has been experimental, with stress being induced artificially under laboratory conditions (Helz and Templeton, 1990). Such experiments have yielded mixed findings. Whilst field studies have produced more consistent evidence that stress affects metabolic control directly (Halford *et al.*, 1990) and indirectly (Peyrot and McMurry, 1985), the findings are by no means conclusive, and to date there have been no such studies with a clearly defined NIDDM population (Cox and Gonder-Frederick, 1992).

What is clear from the more recent studies (e.g. Griffith *et al.*, 1990) is that high stress levels do not lead uniformly to poor metabolic control as was once believed. It would appear that in times of stress, factors such as social support can serve as an important buffer. It would also seem that the findings depend in part on the way in which stress is measured. For example, when Cox *et al.* (1984) defined stress only in terms of 'daily hassles', social support did not feature as an intervening variable. One reason for the conflicting findings may be that stress, related to support with diabetes, could be serving as a confounding variable. For example, the survey conducted by Warren and Hixenbaugh (1996) showed that regular reminders from significant others regarding self-care (often assumed by health professionals and researchers to be supportive) were not only perceived by 18 per cent of the sample as stressful but led *regularly* to them deliberately *not* performing the required behaviour. Importantly, a further 14 per cent reported that they were unsure if reminders from others led them deliberately to neglect self-care. However, in this same sample, patients reported that support from their 'significant others' did help them to cope with diabetes during the occurrence of major life events (Warren and Hixenbaugh, 1996).

It may be that, provided that the stress caused by reminders of self-care is at a relatively low level, support from 'significant others' does act as a buffer in coping with major life events. However, if the amount of stress caused by these reminders is great, then support in relation to life events loses its capacity as a buffer against stress. This is borne out by the fact that not all diabetic patients saw stress as equally relevant, the pattern being that those who reported conflict concerning their diabetes with their 'significant others' were the ones who found stress more relevant to their condition.

Clearly, more research is needed to determine the conditions under which people with diabetes are most vulnerable to the effects of stress. Such research needs to take account of demographic variables (such as age and type of diabetes) and the way in which stress is defined and measured. For example, Aitkens *et al.* (1992) found from a study with IDDMs that daily fluctuations in stress (the highs and lows) were more relevant to diabetic functioning than mean stress levels. It is the latter which have usually been investigated in the past. Future research will need to allow for the fact that what is perceived as a mediator of stress (i.e. social support) by one patient may be viewed by another as a stressor. These issues have important implications for the cost-effectiveness of stress-management interventions. Bradley (1994), having reviewed the stress literature, asserted that despite the fact that many clinics in the USA now include stress management as a part of routine treatment, stress interventions will only be of use to patients with poor control if they are currently experiencing considerable stress in their lives.

Quality of life

In recent years there has been increasing emphasis placed on patients' quality of life (QOL) as an important concern (Gross *et al.*, 1995; Rodin *et al.*, 1993), in recognition of the fact that it is of equal importance as an outcome as are the more traditional biomedical measures (Spilker, 1990). This is of particular importance in the case of diabetes because health professionals are now under even greater pressure to focus on tight metabolic control in order to reduce the risk of long-term complications. Rodin (1990) has suggested that while health professionals may view a reduction in patients' QOL as an acceptable sacrifice in return for a reduced risk in long-term complications, patients may not.

As with the concept of stress (see Chapter 3), QOL is somewhat difficult to define and thus evaluate. The difficulty arises in that it can refer to general QOL, disease-specific QOL, or to QOL within specific life domains, such as psychological status and well-being and social interactions. This is complicated by the fact that since QOL is a subjective phenomenon, a number of definitions (e.g. Calman, 1984; Diener, 1984; Goodinson and Singleton, 1989) and measurements have been developed (e.g. the Duke health profile (DUKE): Parkerson *et al.*, 1990; general health perceptions scale (GHP): Ware *et al.* 1978; the diabetes quality of life scale (DQOL): DCCT, 1988). While those measures that assess QOL in broad terms have been criticised for being unable to distinguish specific goals or behaviours that are significant to the individual (McGee *et al.*, 1991), there is some evidence to suggest that this depends in part on the aims of the research (Patrick and Deyo, 1989). Parkerson *et al.* (1993) examined this issue in detail. If valid, general instruments could have many advantages over disease-specific measures. A general measure of QOL would allow comparisons between patient and non-patient groups and between patients with various medical conditions. It would enable researchers to use one measure for patients with multiple medical difficulties. As Parkerson *et al.* (1993) maintain, this point takes on particular significance if the reference for optimal health-related QOL is established by measuring individuals without health problems. Using a sample of 131 Caucasian insulin-dependent adults they cross-sectionally evaluated three QOL self-report instruments: two general, the DUKE and the GHP, and one disease-specific, the DQOL. They took account of a number of variables including diabetes factors (for example, duration of disease), comorbidity factors (for example, other organic diseases), and demographic factors (such as gender and psychosocial factors including the quality of significant relationship). While the precise pattern of inter-relationships between the numerous variables measured was somewhat complex, overall, the general measures provided as much or more information about QOL and its relationship with both diabetes and non-diabetes factors than did disease-specific measures. Furthermore, variables that were *not* diabetes-related were found to predict health-related QOL more frequently than diabetes factors. Unfortunately, because the above study was cross-sectional it is not possible to determine the stability of such findings over time. As McGee *et al.* (1991) have contended, the items used may not have the same importance over time and across the course of the disease. Evidence does, however, exist to suggest that the DQOL is indeed sensitive to disease-related changes (Nathan *et al.*, 1991; Selam *et al.*, 1992). A further issue raised by McGee and colleagues concerns the importance of the items to the individual. It is of little clinical value to learn from a person's profile that they have a relatively limited social life, if the person concerned attaches very little importance to this. In the light of the mixed findings to date it may be that a combination of general and disease-specific measures would provide the most comprehensive picture of the needs and experiences of each individual. It is certainly the case that these findings signal the importance of consulting individual patients before clinical decisions are made about their health.

Anxiety and depression

The psychological impact of diabetes upon sufferers has been demonstrated to affect significantly their level of self-care (Hampson *et al.*, 1990). Furthermore, a negative perception of the social consequences of diabetes has been shown to be related to the risk of mortality (Davis *et al.*, 1988). Owing to the extent to which diabetes impinges on all areas of a person's life, psychosocial well-being is vital for successful management of the disease. Many investigations have been conducted into the emotional and social consequences of diabetes; however, most have focused on severe disorders such as clinical depression (Von Dras and Lichty, 1990), eating disorders (Rodin *et al.*, 1986; Steele *et al.*, 1989), and medical complications such as sexual dysfunction (Lustman and Clouse, 1990). While psychiatric problems do occur, the incidence of clinical disorders such as depression is now understood to be comparable to the general population (Wise, 1994). Many of the overestimations have been due to methodological limitations such as sampling bias (for example, hospitalised patients) and unreliable diagnostic criteria (Lustman *et al.*, 1983).

According to Tattersall and Jackson (1982), the more 'typical' social and emotional consequences of diabetes such as anxiety, sub-clinical depression, low self-esteem and diabetes-related fears and worries have often been ignored. They suggest that this may be because these difficulties are often invisible and prob-lematic to manage or assess, and because the assumption is made that these problems will be treated as part of the normal health treatment. It is important to stress that even though an emotional difficulty may not be severe enough to warrant a clinical diagnosis, it may cause significant problems for the patient and his or her family (Shillitoe, 1988). Indeed, a study with fifty IDDM adults aged between 16 and 60 years, carried out by Surridge *et al.* (1984) found that both patients (deemed in clinical terms to be 'free of depression') and their relatives frequently reported that diabetes sufferers displayed signs of depressed mood, fatigue and irritability of sufficient magnitude to cause interference in their family and social life.

Most of the studies evaluating the psychological consequences of diabetes have focused on children and adolescents. The scant research with adult populations has sometimes used clinically inappropriate measures: most notably the Beck depression inventory (Beck *et al.*, 1961) and Zung depression scale (Zung, 1965). Although well-validated inventories, their use with diabetic patients can result in artificially inflated scores, due to the inclusion of items, such as loss of appetite and tiredness, which are frequent physiologically based symptoms of diabetes. The recent development and validation of diabetes-specific scales to assess psychological functioning (Bradley and Lewis, 1990; Bradley, 1994), mark a potentially significant step forward in the area; not least because, as Bradley has affirmed, they provide a means of determining positive well-being, which in the past has been implied, incorrectly, from a low score on scales measuring negative well-being. The scales were not designed as tools for diagnosis, but rather to assess the effectiveness of new treatments or interventions.

While it is recognised that depression and anxiety add strain to dealing with both common life events and to the demands of diabetes self-care, which in turn are related to non-adherence to the regimen (Warren and Hixenbaugh, 1996) and poor metabolic control (Von Dras and Lichty, 1990), very little is known about the long-term implications of the more common psychological consequences of diabetes. Assessing these consequences is often problematic. Without measures of psychological functioning prior to diagnosis, it is difficult to determine the part diabetes plays in the psychological state. This is further complicated by the differential age of onset of NIDDMs and IDDMs. Because NIDDMs as a group are older, it may be that these patients will have experienced psychological problems such as episodes of depression prior to the onset of the disease (Lustman *et al.*, 1988). Other background factors that need to be considered include existing tensions within the family unit, as this has been found, in a study with adolescents, to influence later outcomes (Hauser *et al.*, 1985). The patients' cultural background can also have an immense impact on the way in which the disease is perceived and managed (Warren and Hixenbaugh, in press). Of considerable importance is the pre-existence of diabetes within the family, which has been found to influence significantly the psychological reaction to diagnosis. Having a family member with perceived problematic diabetes was predictive of a negative psychological reaction, which in turn was found to be predictive of long-term psychological problems (Hixenbaugh and Warren, 1996).

Future research needs to be longitudinal, in order to determine how psychological difficulties and the development of complications interact with social factors and how the outcomes of these interactions, in turn, impact upon adherence and control. Specifically, there is little understanding of how these important variables affect relationships and the type and level of support offered to the patient. Employment prospects are also likely to be related to psychosocial problems. While evidence exists to demonstrate that competency and commitment level in the workplace are comparable to non-diabetics (Lloyd *et al.*, 1992), employment discrimination and having to withhold disclosing their diabetes to work colleagues is likely to cause sustained psychological strain, neglect of self-care, poor metabolic control and thus an increased risk of health complications.

Infancy, childhood and adolescence

Young people with diabetes represent a relatively small percentage of the diabetic population. However, the incidence of childhood diabetes appears to be increasing, with rates doubling in some European countries over the last twenty years (Bingley and Gale, 1989). Disturbingly, the greatest increase has been in the under fives, where the prevalence rate has increased from one in a thousand to eight in a thousand children (Gale, personal communication).

The effects of childhood diabetes on the family has been a major focus of the psychological research in diabetes. While the initial impact of diagnosis is likely to be limited in those diagnosed in infancy or very young childhood, research suggests that the demands and stresses placed upon parents having to manage their baby's or very young child's diabetes regimen can be devastating (Banion *et al.*, 1983; Betschart, 1988). Young children with IDDM in the year following diagnosis are prone to develop severe episodes of hypoglycaemia often associated with convulsions. Regulation of blood glucose levels is difficult and this is not aided by the fact that infants and young children display erratic eating patterns and activity levels. These problems are compounded by the rapid growth taking place during this period. While there can be little doubt that diagnosis in very young childhood will, in the long term, impact upon the physical, cognitive and social development of the child (Shillitoe, 1988), to date there has been virtually no research conducted into the special needs of this age group. A recent qualitative study (Hatton *et al.*, 1995) suggests that diagnosis represents a life crisis for the parents concerned and that adaptation is a very slow process which requires tremendous psychosocial support and education from the health professionals. Parents' descriptions of their experiences suggest that effective nursing support and intervention can make a critical difference to family outcomes, such as helping to relieve the marital strain reported by parents to have been brought about by the diagnosis. Interestingly, it would appear that for the parents of very young children with diabetes in the family, broader social support system is often lacking. The parents participating in Hatton *et al.*'s study reported that family, friends and others within the family's social milieu (for example, baby-sitter/childminder) became overwhelmed by their own grief and fear and often withdrew their support.

While little is known about the very young, research has identified some factors that may help to predict psychosocial outcomes in those children aged 5 years and over. Good adjustment is most likely in those families characterised by a stable structure, supportive relationships and an ability to cope well with adversity before the onset of diabetes (Johnson, 1980; Simonds *et al.*, 1981). In contrast, poor outcomes are most frequently associated with families that are characterised by marital conflict, unstable structures, social isolation and limited financial resources (Koski and Kumento, 1977; Orr *et al.*, 1983).

Adolescence has been well documented for diabetics as a time of poor adherence and metabolic control (Anderson *et al.*, 1996; La Greca *et al.*, 1990; Mann and Johnston, 1982). Hirsch *et al.* (1983), in a survey of diabetic youths who had been self-monitoring their blood glucose levels for one year, found that nearly half were testing their BG less than once a week and that very few were using the feedback provided to make insulin adjustments. The clinical literature suggests that adolescents' desire to conform to their peer group and to be independent of their parents can interfere with their self-care (Tattersall and Lowe, 1981). These desires may reduce their willingness to follow medical advice, particularly if the restrictions are perceived as interfering with their autonomy (Prazar and Felice, 1975).

Research points also to the importance of the family environment in determining adolescents' health outcomes. Anderson *et al.* (1981) compared the family environments according to whether the adolescents were in good or poor metabolic control. They determined that families characterised by high conflict were significantly more likely to have children in poor control. In contrast, children in good control were likely to be in families where the environment was supportive, independent and less in conflict.

The role of the family and social support

Relatively little attention has been paid to the importance of the family for the adult diabetic. The diagnosis of diabetes in an adult family member affects the family as a unit and family functioning has an impact on the diabetic's self-care.

There is substantial evidence that non-supportive family behaviours are related to poor adherence and poor blood glucose control in adults. A study by Edelstein and Linn (1985) found that adult male diabetics in good control of their disease perceived their families to be low in conflict and oriented towards achievement. The orientation towards achievement was found to be the most important predictor of control and the authors speculate that this dimension encourages high self-esteem in family members and that diabetic individuals with high self-esteem would put value on their health and their ability to control the disease. In contrast, a study by Lyons *et al.* (1988) found that unlike the results for chronic psychiatric patients and undergraduate students, for diabetics it was support from friends rather than family which was related to general health status. It is possible that these findings can be explained by the failure to measure diabetes-specific support. Schafer *et al.* (1986), using the diabetes family behaviour checklist (DFBC) found that more perceived negative family interactions were associated with poorer adherence to glucose testing, diet and insulin injection. The benefit of the DFBC is that it measures family behaviour specific to the diabetic's care requirements rather than more global family behaviour. The importance of this is supported by a study carried out by Gottlieb (1992) which demonstrated that diabetes-specific as opposed to global measures of family support were better predictors of adherence across the range of self-care activities.

Bailey and Kahn (1993) usefully distinguish between different types of support from the diabetic's spouse. They differentiated between appraisal support, designed to assist with self-evaluation (for example, questioning the diabetic's decisions), emotional support, informational support and instrumental support. They found that two factors were important in the diabetic's response to help from the spouse: perceived need and perceived spousal motivation. They suggest that enhancing the quality of communication between the partners may improve the quality of help and appropriate acceptance of that help.

The role of the nurse

Effective management of diabetes is largely the responsibility of the patient. Nurses need to be trained in skills which will assist them in helping the patient to improve his or her *self-care* and *self-control* (Coles, 1990). These skills, grounded in theories advanced within the discipline of psychology, can help significantly to improve health outcomes by altering patient attitudes; increasing patient motivation; developing patient coping skills; addressing patient concerns; meeting patient needs, and overcoming barriers to treatment adherence, as it is these *psychosocial* factors that have been determined to influence behaviour (Glasgow *et al.*, 1995) and predict metabolic control (Tattersall and Jackson, 1982).

One possible reason why nursing has been perceived to be a stressful profession might be because many nurses, particularly those dealing with patients with chronic illness, have found themselves having to address the psychosocial issues mentioned above, but with only minimal support or training. While those responsible for training have begun to provide nurses with communication and interpersonal skills, the benefits of these formalised skills are unlikely to result in maximum gains in terms of patient outcomes, in the absence of a team approach (Llewelyn, 1989). Doctors, who are still largely trained in the medical model (Whitehouse, 1991) are often unwilling and unable to adopt a biopsychosocial approach to the care of patients (Llewelyn, 1989; Nichols, 1981).

Despite a lack of time, skills or support to provide psychological care to patients, nurses are ideally placed to provide such care (Nichols, 1984) and, just as importantly, *want* to be able to provide the type of care that takes account of the interrelationship between biomedical and psychosocial functioning (Bennett, 1996). One possible way to gradually change attitudes to treatment is through education. While achieving this by 'formal' education may not be an option at the present time, an alternative route is through exposure to research literature that offers empirical evidence of the efficacy of a biopsychosocial approach to patient treatment. Nurses are ideally placed to provide a holistic approach to care, and so too are they ideally placed to study and report on the process and outcomes of such care, not only because they have a unique understanding of the patients and the system under which they are treated, but also because they are able to communicate with doctors in a common language. Although nurses do frequently publish research, the majority of studies are published in nursing journals, which other health professionals may not read.

The role of psychology in treatment

At present the provision of psychological care in the UK is only available, following referral, for those who have severe problems. There are many possible reasons for this. First, there are not sufficient resources available routinely to offer specialised psychological support. Second, there is a lack of evidence regarding the effectiveness of providing psychological support on a widespread basis; and third, even if such support were available, some patients may perceive a stigma in being referred to a mental health professional.

What is gradually being recognised by those involved in the health care of people with diabetes is that a significant proportion of the diabetic population, in line with patients with other chronic diseases, experience long-term psychological problems (Royal College of Physicians and Royal College of Psychiatrists, 1995). The prevalence rates for depression and anxiety are particularly high (Nichols, 1984; Royal College of Physicians and Royal College of Psychiatrists, 1995; Warren and Hixenbaugh, 1995, 1996). The overwhelming majority of patients want psychological care and recognise its benefits (Warren and Hixenbaugh, 1995, 1996). Furthermore, research suggests that treatment approaches which emphasise only medical care and information transfer may be less effective than those taking account of patients' beliefs and incorporating psychosocial interventions, and may lessen treatment adherence (Royal College of Physicians and Royal College of Psychiatrists, 1995) and serve to reduce the frequency of clinic attendance, which in turn may lead to an increased risk of complications (Jacobson and Leibovitch, 1984; Jacobson et al., 1991).

One possible approach increasingly advocated by this problem would be to train nurses and doctors in each team in counselling skills. This method is beginning to be evaluated (Dohery and Hall, 1996; James et al., 1996; Woodcock, 1996). However, it has been argued that psychological care demands that health professionals have not only basic counselling skills, but also an in-depth understanding of the psychosocial needs of the particular patient population (Hixenbaugh and Warren, 1994). Good psychological care means recognising that each individual has different requirements in terms of their psychological needs. This is directly comparable to the needs of the patient in terms of the physical regimen prescription. Equally, just as a good treatment regimen is designed to *prevent* physical complications, so the aim of psychological support should be to *prevent*, or at least minimise, psychological 'complications' and their ramifications, rather than deal with the much more potentially complex, lengthy and costly process of intervention (Hixenbaugh and Warren, 1996). Pilot studies have shown that clinicians (i.e. doctors and nurses) can effectively take on this 'first line' of treatment (Royal College of Physicians and Royal College of Psychiatrists, 1995). It is also important to note that a counselling approach has been deemed to result in greater professional satisfaction for nurses on a number of grounds (Davis and Fallowfield, 1996).

In the absence of any formal provision, many varying types of counselling services have been set up, many in the form of self-help groups. However, there is little research which has evaluated their efficacy. It has been suggested that attending self-help groups allows people to change from feeling like naughty children who deviate from their treatment, to people who are psychologically secure and thus able to take control of their disease (Kelleher, 1994). Whether or not they are effective, for the majority of patients (who may neither recognise nor be willing to admit to experiencing psychosocial difficulties), psychological care needs to be a part of a holistic approach whereby the physical and emotional manifestations of diabetes are seen as two sides of the same coin. In the absence of properly formulated schemes of psychological care in the treatment of diabetes, it has been argued eloquently by Nichols (1993) that health care 'can only at best be second rate, and at the worst be open to the charge of negligence' (p. 200).

The exploration of alternative models of regular health care delivery is gaining ground particularly for youngsters, including peer support of the newly diagnosed and meetings away from the hospital setting, with emphasis on patient, rather than professional, domination. These have pointed to the potential benefits of psychosocial intervention, particularly at the point of diagnosis (Galatzer *et al.*, 1982; Laron *et al.*, 1979). However, the research and clinical emphasis concerning adults is not moving forward systematically. This has implications not only for those diagnosed in adulthood but also for children who, on reaching adulthood, will perhaps suffer from having a potentially vital part of their support system removed.

A recent study found that not only are a large percentage of the diabetic population unable to cope with diagnosis (31 per cent), but that being unable to cope during this period is a highly significant predictor of protracted psychological problems and non-adherence to the prescribed treatment. Critically, only 24 per cent of people diagnosed reported being given time to talk about what it meant to them to be diagnosed (Warren and Hixenbaugh, 1996). Diagnosis of diabetes involves psychological, social, and often work adjustments as well as education in a self-care routine. A system of psychological care needs to be introduced into the health care provision at the point of diagnosis and during the critical first year of adjustment. Training nurse specialists to deliver this psychological care may prove to be a cost-effective method in terms of the prevention of long-term physical and mental health complications.

LANDMARK IN DIABETES CARE – THE DIABETES CONTROL AND COMPLICATIONS TRIAL (DCCT) 1993

The results of this study confirmed what many health professionals thought to be true: that maintenance of blood glucose at near normal levels can reduce the risk of complications.

Sample 1441 North American patients with insulin-dependent diabetes were recruited and assigned to a primary prevention (726) or a secondary intervention (715) group. The subjects in the primary prevention group did not show any signs of retinopathy while all the subjects in the secondary intervention group had at least Class 2 retinopathy. Subjects within each group were randomly assigned to an intensive treatment group or a conventional treatment group.

Questions Will intensive therapy prevent the development of retinopathy in the primary prevention group? Will intensive therapy prevent the development of retinopathy in the secondary intervention group?

Treatment The conventional group received standard care which included one or two daily injections of insulin, daily blood glucose monitoring, standard diet and exercise. These subjects were seen at the clinic four times a year. In the intensive group, subjects took at least three daily injections of insulin, four or more glowed glucose tests and a period of hospitalisation to introduce treatment. These subjects had frequent support with their diet, weekly telephone calls and a monthly visit to the clinic.

Results 99 per cent of subjects were followed for a mean of 6.5 years. Intensive therapy reduced the risk of complications by: retinopathy 76 per cent, neuropathy 60 per cent, nephropathy 35–56 per cent. Cases of severe hypoglycaemia (low blood sugar) increased threefold.

Implications These astounding results make it very clear that the maintenance of near normal blood sugar levels is an important goal of treatment. However, the costs of such treatment are substantial. The restrictions placed on subjects in the intensive care group, and the increase in incidence of hypoglycaemia, raise important issues about quality of life.

Questions What do you think are the costs and benefits to the individual diabetic patient of intensive treatment? Should the National Health Service provide more resources for diabetic services? What contribution could a health psychologist make to the treatment programme?

Key point summary

- Diabetes mellitus is a chronic multisystem disorder, characterised by high blood glucose levels, which patients must self-manage.
- The consequences of poor management are reduced life expectancy and complications such as blindness and kidney disease.

- Findings from research on health beliefs and adherence to medical treatment for diabetic patients have been mixed. There may be a changing pattern in the relationship between beliefs, behaviour and outcomes over time.
- There is evidence that self-efficacy, a belief in one's own capacity to perform a behaviour, is a useful concept in understanding control in diabetic patients. Models need to consider the individual patient's perspective.
- Stress does not uniformly lead to poor control. Daily fluctuations in stress may be more relevant than mean stress levels.
- Specifically designed quality of life measures are sensitive to disease-related changes but more general quality of life measures indicate that variables which are not diabetes-related may predict health-related quality of life more frequently than do diabetes factors.
- Psychological factors critically are important in the patient's control of diabetes. A significant proportion of the diabetic population experience psychological problems.
- For children and adolescents diagnosed with diabetes, poor outcomes are associated with families characterised by conflict, social isolation and poverty.
- Nurses are well placed in the health care team to help patients adjust to diabetes. However, to be effective nurses need specific training in the psychological care of patients.
- Psychological care needs to be part of a holistic approach to health care for diabetics.

Further reading

Bradley, C. (1994) *Handbook of Psychology and Diabetes.* Chur: Harwood Academic. This book offers an excellent source of measures which have been devised specifically for diabetic patients.

Kelleher, D. (1988) *Diabetes.* London: Routledge. A good general book on the experience of diabetes.

Shillitoe, R. (1994) *Counselling People with Diabetes.* Leicester: British Psychological Society Books. This book provides an extensive discussion of counselling diabetic patients with excellent examples.

For more information contact:

British Diabetic Association
10 Queen Anne Street
London, W1M 0BD

Chapter 13

Nutrition, exercise and health

David White

Introduction

Throughout our life span the efficient functioning of our bodies, including the functioning of the immune system and susceptibility to diseases are influenced by nutritional practices. Healthy nutritional practices start pre-birth and even preconception. In this chapter a broadly chronological approach to nutrition and health is adopted, followed by discussion of specific topics including obesity, eating disorders, heart disease, diabetes, cancers and health promotion issues.

Typical diets

In Western societies the average adult uses up about 2500 calories a day, although this varies depending on individuals' activity levels and metabolism. With ageing and a reduction in activity levels the energy requirements of the elderly reduce; however, the need for vitamins and minerals remains. With a reduction in energy intake the diets of many elderly people become deficient in vitamins and minerals resulting in greater susceptibility to diseases and poorer cognitive functioning (Blumberg, 1994). People in most developed countries eat more sugar, animal fats and animal protein than is recommended and less dietary fibre and this can be seen across the life span. Men over 65 years have a lower calorific intake than younger men, but a similar distribution of fats, proteins and carbohydrates in their diets (Arnet and Zahler, 1993). Surveys of the nutrition of children point to the same trends seen in adult diet and, in particular, to the difficulty in encouraging children to consume sufficient dietary fibre. Many children consume only a quarter of the recommended amount. Even among highly knowledgeable and health-conscious families, only half of the children received the recommended amounts of dietary fibre (McClung *et al.*, 1995). There are dietary variations within each country and these are associated with income, education, gender, ethnicity and culture (Otero-Sabogal *et al.*, 1995).

Development of dietary habits

Research over the past few years clearly points to early childhood as a critical period when dietary and lifestyle patterns are initiated. The pre-school years therefore offer the best opportunity for laying the foundations for good dietary practice. When they are pre-schoolers, infants and young children attempt to influence their diet, refusing what they are offered or demanding different foods. However, at this stage the family provides, prepares and serves nearly all the food and drink that pre-schoolers consume, unless they are provided with alternative care. Once they start school, control of children's diets weakens. As children become older, peer pressure and example also influence eating behaviour. Habits and tastes developed early in life can persist into later childhood and into adult life. Parents differ in the extent to which their choice of foods is influenced by their children's preferences, convenience and their beliefs about the healthiness of foods. Some parents are more aware of nutrition than others, but even when they are aware they do not necessarily select healthy foods for their children. However, in general when parents are aware of nutrition and select foods on the basis of their health giving properties children do eat better. Children whose diets are determined by their preferences take in more calories, more fat, less fibre and fewer vitamins (Contento *et al.*, 1993).

Children's dietary practices are substantially influenced by their parents (Prout, 1996), both through the food, drink and confectionery they make available and their ability to monitor and control their children's intake. Parents also act as role models for younger children in demonstrating eating and nutritional behaviours and physical exercise patterns. Television viewing exposes young children to advertisements for unhealthy foods and allows them to witness the consumption of unhealthy foods. The majority of advertised foods are high in fat, sugar and/or salt. Commercials advertising unhealthy foods account for a large portion of children's televised viewing time (Taras and Gage, 1995). With the emergence of a more sedentary lifestyle for many children, there has been a reduction in energy expenditure and an increase in obesity. Nutritionists have identified several ways in which parents can help prevent obesity. These include: encouraging the taking of regular exercise; restricting the amount of television viewed; restricting access to high cholesterol and sugary foods; increased use of nuts and fruits as desserts; ensuring children eat a healthy breakfast; restricting access to high calorie snacks, particularly at night; avoiding using unhealthy food as a reward for eating healthy food (for example, 'if you finish all of your vegetables you can have a chocolate dessert'), and regularly monitoring children's weight.

During adolescence, young people take on increasing responsibility for their own diet and with this increased independence they may experiment with diet. For some, this experimentation is transitory, but for others poor dietary practices are established which persist into adulthood and so have long-term consequences (Kelder *et al.*, 1994). Knowledge of nutrition among adolescents is frequently deficient (Gracey *et al.*, 1996). Knowledge about healthy diet is a necessary, but not sufficient condition for the adoption of a healthy diet. Motivation for the adoption of healthy eating practices and high self-efficacy are additional determinants (Glanz *et al.*, 1993). Furthermore, poor dietary practices in adolescence are associated with drinking and smoking, both of which are associated with increased fat intake and decreased intake of fibre. Television viewing by adolescents is associated with poor diet, high cholesterol and obesity; this is associated with unhealthy nutritional messages in television advertising and in lowered activity levels (Gracey *et al.*, 1996).

Diet and health

Preconception and pregnancy

Preconceptual nutritional care has been recognised as a means of reducing the risks of conceiving a child with congenital abnormalities and improving the health of both mother and child. A variety of nutritional and non-nutritional factors can act during the preconceptual period. Pre-pregnancy body weight and gestational weight gain have an independent but cumulative influence on the birth weight. Women with a low gestational weight gain have smaller babies than women who make greater weight gains. Women who at the start of their pregnancy were of average weight are more likely to give birth to a healthy baby. Underweight women may be at increased risk of delivering a low birthweight infant and of complications of pregnancy, whilst those who are excessively obese are at greater risk of gestational diabetes and hypertension. Vitamin deficiency in the preconceptual period, especially of foliates, seems to be associated with neural tube defects. There is growing evidence that even marginal vitamin deficiencies in women may have deleterious effects on pregnancy outcome (Pickard, 1986). Several other maternal nutritional as well as non-nutritional variables are related to pregnancy outcome. Among those with harmful effects are drinking alcohol and smoking. Nutritional interventions can contribute to an increase of the birth weight. The available evidence confirms a significant impact of preconceptual nutrition on pregnancy outcome (Vobecky, 1986). It has been argued further that the quality of breast milk is affected by preconceptual nutrition and that this can only be improved by dietary measures extended over several years' preconception to reduce the entry of chemical pollutants, especially dioxins, into breast milk and so into the diet of developing infants (Koppe, 1995).

The factors that are important preconceptually continue to be of importance during pregnancy. Inadequate nutrition during pregnancy retards foetal growth and increases the risk of delivering a low birth weight infant. It is suggested that poor foetal growth has an influence on the susceptibility to diseases in adulthood and is a strong predictor of hypertension, diabetes, hyperlipidemia, fibrinogen concentrations and chronic obstructive airways disease (Goldberg and Prentice, 1994). They suggest that poor foetal growth results in deficits in the development, structure and functioning of organs and this interacts with diet and environmental stress in later life to produce increased risk of disease.

Early nutrition (neonates and young infants)

Improvement in feeding of infants reduces illness due to diarrhoea and pneumonia. Breast-fed babies are less likely to develop diarrhoea and complications such as severe dehydration arising from diarrhoea and so have a lower risk of dying. Breast-feeding is also associated with lower rates of respiratory infections. Reduction in the amount of breast-feeding is associated with progressively increased risk, so any breast-feeding is beneficial. Increasing duration of exclusive breast-feeding to six months and beyond and improving complementary feeding promote growth and reduce infection and mortality. The benefits appear to come from the reduced exposure to contaminated and non-sterile bottle feeds and to the increased exposure to maternal anti-infective agents carried in breast milk. Despite the known benefits of extending breast-feeding to six months, the duration of breast-feeding in many countries is very short, not extending beyond the first few weeks (Huffman and Martin, 1994).

Childhood is a time when food habits are acquired; it is also a time when susceptibility to later diseases may be developing. Ischaemic heart disease, malignancy, cerebrovascular accidents, hypertension and obesity can all be influenced by childhood nutritional practices and interventions in childhood may delay their onset (Kemm, 1987). For instance, recent studies have demonstrated a link between nutrition in the first year of life and later CHD mortality (Barker, 1995).

Diet and disease

Cardiovascular risk factors, such as hypertension and atherosclerosis, can be substantially modified by changes in lifestyle including changes to diet. Epidemiological evidence shows that for every 1 per cent change in serum cholesterol levels, there is a 3 per cent change in the likelihood of developing coronary heart disease. In addition, a long-term (five-year) change of 5 to 6 mmHg in diastolic blood pressure can reduce the chances of stroke by 35 to 40 per cent and of coronary heart disease by 20 to 25 per cent. The adoption of a prudent diet can reduce the incidence of coronary heart disease morbidity; however, mortality rates may be relatively stable. The benefits of lowering serum cholesterol may lie more in overall physical and psychological fitness rather than longevity (Hadley and Saarmann, 1991).

Diet and atherosclerosis

Atherosclerosis is the deposit of fatty plaques in blood vessels. This in turn is associated with increased risk of heart disease and the occurrence of strokes. Cholesterol is the fatty substance implicated in the development of atherosclerosis. It is produced naturally in blood, but is supplemented by cholesterol in the diet. Different individuals show different susceptibility to blood clotting; this is related to the presence of different cholesterol-carrying proteins in blood called lipoproteins. There are three types of lipoproteins: low density, very low density and high density lipoproteins. Low and very low lipoproteins are associated with increased cholesterol deposits and high lipoproteins are associated with a decreased build-up of clotting agents. Cholesterol carried by low- and very low-density lipoproteins moves into body cells whereas high-density lipoproteins carries cholesterol away from the cells to be processed by the liver. The higher blood cholesterol levels the greater the risk of heart disease and strokes. However, this depends on the balance between low- and high-density lipoproteins. The greater the amount of high-density lipoprotein in the blood cholesterol the lower the risk of cardiovascular disease (Gordon *et al.*, 1989). High-density lipoprotein levels may be raised by increasing exercise, but a considerable amount of exercise is required over a long period of time. Alcohol consumption and weight loss through dieting inconsistently raise high-density lipoprotein levels (Leighton, 1990).

Atherosclerosis can begin to develop in childhood and its development is determined in part by heredity. Smoking may also be involved by altering the balance of high- and low-density lipoproteins (Muscat *et al.*, 1991). The other contributory factor is diet. Cholesterol occurs in high concentrations in foods such as full fat milk products, eggs and red meat. Ensuring that the intake of cholesterol is limited to healthy levels is important both for children from school age upwards and adults. Lowering cholesterol in diet can have an impact on cardiovascular disease by lowering serum cholesterol and retarding the development of atherosclerosis. However, there is also some evidence of unforeseen side-effects of reducing serum cholesterol. Some studies have found an increase in recklessness and aggressiveness among those with markedly reduced serum cholesterol (Blankenhorn *et al.*, 1987).

Another haemostatic factor associated with atherosclerosis and heart disease is fibrinogen. Fibrinogen is involved in coagulation: it is a soluble protein in the blood which when the body is injured is converted into insoluble fibrin. However, plasma fibrinogen levels are strongly associated with coronary artery disease and it is thought that high levels of fibrinogen predispose to thrombosis and that fibrin is an important constituent of atherosclerosis plaques. The link of fibrinogen to heart disease is stronger than the link of cholesterol. The link to diet and fibrinogen levels is less clear than the link of fat intake to plasma cholesterol levels. Changing diet to reduce fat or to reduce other nutrients from within the diet has no impact on fibrinogen levels. Nevertheless, there is a link between obesity and fibrinogen levels (Meade, 1988). Smoking also has a direct impact upon fibrinogen levels.

Diet and hypertension

Hypertension, i.e. having blood pressure which exceeds 140 systolic and 90 diastolic, is common. Blood pressure can be reduced by making lifestyle changes, including changes to diet (Stamler *et al.*, 1989). Weight loss is associated with reductions in blood pressure. A meta-analysis found substantial relationships between weight loss and blood pressure reduction both in hypertensive and normatensive populations (Staessen *et al.*, 1988): they reported that a reduction in body weight of 1 kg resulted in a reduction in blood pressure of 1.2 and 1.0 mmHg respectively. This relationship between body weight and blood pressure levels appears to be independent of salt intake (Prineas, 1991). It is suggested that the acquisition of excess weight for height during childhood and adolescence adds significantly to the prediction of future blood pressure elevations. Obesity in childhood is associated with higher blood pressure and the link between weight and blood pressure is established early in life (Lauer *et al.*, 1991).

Sodium intake in the form of salt, either added to food or as a constituent of processed food, including bread, is the most commonly identified dietary risk factor for hypertension and associated cardiovascular diseases and it has an effect independent from that of body weight. Reducing salt intake lowers blood pressure among both hypertensives and normatentives, although it is clear that some people have greater tolerance of salt than others (Sullivan, 1991). Further evidence for the importance of salt intake in hypertension comes from comparison between Polynesians and Westerners with similar lifestyles. Polynesians seldom use alcohol, they are lean and active and additionally they take in very little salt. Westerners with similar virtues tend to have a higher salt intake and are much more prone to hypertension (Beard, 1990). The factors linked with hypertension are discussed more fully in Chapter 10.

Diet and cancers

Surveys suggest that adults eat too few fibre foods such as fruit and vegetables and cereals and too much red meat and processed food (Arnet and Zahler, 1993). Diets that are low in fibre and high in fat are associated with the development of cancer of the colon (Bristol *et al.*, 1985).

Appropriate weight control is vital for ensuring good health, particularly in early adult life. Experimental evidence suggests that the susceptibility of mammary tissue to carcinogenesis is greatest in early adult life, and multiple studies show that a history of weight gain in early adult life is associated with increased breast cancer risk in Western women. Nutrition and especially weight control are implicated in the onset of breast cancer and it has been suggested that preconceptual nutrition and weight control and weight control during pregnancy can be important in the prevention of breast cancer. For instance, Colditz (1993) has recently published a mathematical model of the aetiology of breast cancer pointing to the years before the birth of a first child as the crucial period in establishing the risk of breast cancer.

Vitamin A may offer protection against lung cancer. Comparisons of lung cancer patients with healthy individuals reveal differences in their diets, with the healthy eating foods rich in beta-carotene, a substance that the body converts to vitamin A (Byers *et al.*, 1987). Beta-carotene-rich foods include spinach, broccoli, lettuce, tomatoes, apricots, carrots and cantaloupe melons. Vitamin E may also have anticancer properties as a lipid antioxidant and free radical scavenger. Some animal studies support this hypothesis, although findings are contradictory. Some case-control studies, however, have shown lower concentrations of vitamin E in the serum of patients with cancer than in the controls. Cohort studies also generally show a low level of serum vitamin E associated with a slightly increased risk of cancer, though the strength of this association varies between different cancer sites (Knekt, 1991). Epidemiological studies have shown that diets rich in one or more antioxidant nutrients may reduce the risk of cancers of the lung, uterus, cervix, mouth and gastrointestinal tract (Singh and Gaby, 1991). Further discussion of cancer is found in Chapter 14.

Diet and diabetes

There is a clear link between obesity and diabetes. This link is true particularly of non-insulin-dependent diabetes (a condition that typically appears during middle age) and gestational diabetes (diabetes appearing during pregnancy), and the greater the degree of obesity, the greater the risk (Bodansky, 1994). However, these forms of diabetes can affect both the obese and non-obese. The mechanism linking obesity and diabetes is unknown. Non-insulin-dependent diabetes appears to have a genetic component since the concordance rates among identical twins is very high (Bodansky, 1994). Frequently, these forms of diabetes can be treated by diet alone to reduce weight and restore blood glucose levels to normal. This treatment may fail because of poor adherence to dietary instructions or because metabolic processes have become impaired.

Dietary control is an essential part of the treatment for all forms of diabetes and not just for obese diabetics. Non-obese non-insulin-dependent diabetics are advised to follow a diet low in refined carbohydrates and increasingly are advised to increase their intake of unrefined carbohydrates (Bodansky, 1994). The dietary treatment of insulin-dependent diabetes is to control calorific intake to balance calorific output and to distribute the intake of carbohydrates throughout the day in a consistent fashion with the aim of regularising blood glucose levels. All diabetics are advised to consume unrefined rather than refined carbohydrates, to increase dietary fibre, to reduce their intake of saturated fats, substituting polyunsaturated fats, and to consume alcohol in moderation. Complex unrefined carbohydrates are less readily absorbed than are refined carbohydrates and have less impact on blood glucose levels. The reduction in saturated fats is advised because diabetics are at particular risk of vascular disease. Over-indulgence in alcohol is to be avoided as it is high in calories. There are many complications that can arise with diabetes, but the risk of these is minimised if good diabetic control is achieved and maintained. See Chapter 12 for a fuller discussion of diabetes.

Diet and osteoporosis

As they get older, men and women usually show a negative calcium balance, losing more calcium than they ingest. This is a more serious problem for women than men since they start with a lower bone density. Childhood through to early adulthood is the period when bone density is still growing. Arresting bone loss has proved to be much more effective than rebuilding a depleted skeleton. Interventions promoting the growth of bone density through a combination of proper nutrition, exercise and lifestyle changes can help prevent the later development of osteoporosis (Licata, 1994). Calcium supplementation of the diets of pubertal girls also leads to increased bone density in adolescence (Teagarden and Weaver, 1994). Although the best time to intervene to prevent osteoporosis is while bone density is increasing, the use of diet in later life to reduce bone loss can also be effective. Women at the time of the menopause and thereafter benefit from diets high in calcium or the use of calcium supplements, although their bodies become less efficient at absorbing calcium from their intestines (Galsworthy, 1994). Exercise may also slow down the loss of bone density. However, prolonged excessive exercising that interferes with menstrual functioning for a long period of time accelerates bone loss. One way in which exercising may be beneficial is in improving muscle tone and so reducing the risk of falls and of fractures.

Obesity and weight control

Obesity is usually defined by a weight level 20 per cent or more above the weight recommended for someone of a given height and sex or in relation to a Body Mass Index (weight in kilograms divided by the square of height in metres: see Table 13.1) of 30 or over. Estimates for obesity vary, but between 5 per cent and 15 per cent of infants and pre-schoolers in Western countries are obese and between 10 per cent and 35 per cent of adolescents (Alexander and Sherman, 1991). In the USA a quarter of the adult population is obese (American Public Health Association, 1991). Obesity is more prevalent among females than males and is on the increase (Cowell *et al.*, 1989). Obesity is associated with many health problems throughout the life span. The health risks associated with obesity occur more commonly when onset of obesity is in childhood. Untreated obesity in childhood and adolescence is a major health hazard in both childhood and adulthood and includes risks of lower respiratory tract infection, risks to the functioning of the immune system, increased risk of elevated blood pressure and increased cardiovascular risk (Knowler *et al.*, 1991).

Children who are obese are at high risk of becoming obese adults. Obese adults are poor at reducing weight and at maintaining any weight loss; it is therefore desirable to develop weight control strategies for children and adolescents (Sherman *et al.*, 1992). Ideally, children should not be allowed to become overweight, but the sooner excess weight is lost the better the chances of avoiding obesity in adulthood. Few normal weight children become obese adults but 14 per cent of obese infants and 70 per cent of obese 10–13 year olds become obese adults (Alexander and Sherman, 1991). Obese children tend to come from obese families. Children with obese parents are at increased risk of obesity and if one child in a family is obese there is a 40 per cent chance that his or her siblings will also be obese (Garn and Clark, 1976). There remains considerable contention over the relative importance of physiological, psychological and sociocultural factors in the aetiology of obesity. Many studies show that heredity is implicated (Sorensen *et al.*, 1992). However, whether or how a genetic predisposition to obesity expresses itself is influenced by the family environment and its impact upon eating behaviours (Poskitt, 1993). Contemporary society has seen a number

TABLE 13.1 Calculating body mass index (BMI)

BMI is calculated by dividing your weight in kilograms by the square of your height, measured in metres.

$$BMI = W / H^2$$

For example, a woman of average height (168 cm) and weight (62 kilos) would have a BMI of:

$$BMI = 62 / (1.68)^2 = 62 / 2.82 = 22$$

The 'normal' range for women is 21–23, and for men 22–24.

of changes in lifestyle that impact on nutrition and weight control. Increases in family breakup, in women working outside of the home, with a corresponding decline in communal family meals, encourage the use of convenience foods and snacking (White, 1997). These factors, together with lower family income, parents' weight and parental attitudes to food, relate to children's weight and to their risk of obesity (Klesges *et al.*, 1991).

In adulthood, obesity is associated with high cholesterol levels and the development of hypertension, coronary heart disease and diabetes (Jeffery, 1992). The greater the degree of obesity the greater the health risk. Furthermore, the health problems arising from obesity may combine to exaggerate the risk. Thus diabetes and hypertension arising from obesity increase the likelihood that obesity will lead to heart disease (Light and Girdler, 1993). The distribution of fat on the body may also relate to morbidity and mortality. Having excess weight concentrated around hips and thighs may be healthier than having the same weight distributed around the waist. In one study of a large number of overweight women the incidence of hypertension and diabetes was 'higher among "round in the middle" women', with large waists relative to hip size, than among pear-shaped women. Other studies have replicated and extended these results finding higher mortality, coronary heart disease as well as increased hypertension and incidence of diabetes in both men and women with larger waists relative to hip size (Folsom *et al.*, 1993).

Malnutrition

Thus far, this chapter has focused upon nutritional practices in developed countries and practices of those who have the opportunity to exercise choice in what they ingest and who have access to adequate supplies of nutrients. There are, however, many living in both developed and under-developed countries who do not have such choice. It is estimated that 786 million of the 5.47 billion world population do not consume enough food to maintain body weight and sustain light activity and this figure includes 184 million children under the age of 5 (Uvin, 1994). Chronic malnutrition in children results in stunted growth and cognitive impairment, and it contributes to 56 per cent of child deaths. Even mild to moderate malnutrition (having a body weight 65 per cent or more of reference weight) is associated with increased mortality. Malnutrition affects the ability to resist infections and weakens the response to infections, but in turn the infections adversely affect the body's ability to utilise available energy and nutrients (Pelletier, 1994). Inadequate diets are also often deficient in micronutrients as well as being deficient in their energy supply. Vitamin A deficiency is associated with various forms of damage to the eye including blindness; it is also associated with reduced resistance to measles and other infectious diseases and so is linked to morbidity and mortality. It is estimated that 190 million people including 40 million pre-school children suffer from vitamin A deficiency. Another common deficiency is iron deficiency which leads to anaemia, deficits in learning abilities and, in premenopausal women, increases susceptibility to illness and to pregnancy complications (Uvin, 1994). There is a high prevalence of anaemia among toddlers, even in Western countries (12 per cent anaemia in children aged 1.5 to 2.5 years).

One group in Western countries which is frequently exposed to involuntary under-nourishment and malnutrition is the homeless. The numbers of people who become homeless is rising and mothers with dependent children make up 65 per cent of homeless people and are the most rapidly expanding group in the homeless population; most frequently they become homeless following domestic violence (Vostanis *et al.*, 1996). Food deprivation is reported particularly by mothers with children (DiBlasio and Belcher, 1995). For those living in hostels for the homeless, providing food for the family may be less of a concern, since food is often provided. However, the need for hostels to provide food on a limited budget results in a diet that is high in fat (Killion, 1995). Pregnancy rates for homeless women are twice the normal rate and pregnant homeless women have a number of experiences that are associated with complications of pregnancy, including malnutrition (Killion, 1995). Contributing factors to malnutrition among the homeless are poor access to transportation, which means the homeless obtain food from local stores that are often more expensive and stock little fresh food. The lack of usual cooking, storage and refrigeration facilities encourages them to eat more filling convenience foods that do not meet their nutritional requirements. Furthermore, food obtained is sometimes stolen from them. The most extreme under-nourishment and malnutrition is associated with high substance use (Killion, 1995).

Eating disorders

Though there is a continuum from good to poor eating practices, poor practices are common. At the extreme they become labelled eating disorders. There are a range of proposed eating disorders, but agreement about their definition is sometimes poor. Cases where there is wide agreement include anorexia nervosa and bulimia. However, probably the most common disorder is compulsive eating. There is variability in the estimates of the prevalence of eating disorders, but it is thought that in Western society about 1 per cent of women will experience anorexia at some time in their lives and 5 per cent will experience bulimia. The prevalence appears to have increased over the last thirty years.

Anorexia nervosa is characterised by a severe loss of weight and a dread of becoming fat and frequently an associated sense of guilt when consuming food. It is predominantly experienced by girls and young women. Anorexia can have a permanent impact on health. An inadequate diet leads to an inadequate supply of vitamins and minerals including low levels of electrolytes such as sodium and potassium. This can result in extreme low blood pressure, heart damage, or cardiac arrhythmia. There has been speculation that anorexic women have a distorted body image, believing themselves to be fat when they are not. Despite the diagnostic criteria of the American Psychiatric Association (Table 13.2), evidence suggests that anorexic women feel fat but are as accurate as other women in making judgements about actual body size and shape; nevertheless, there is some distortion in the body image of both eating disordered and normal eaters.

TABLE 13.2 Diagnostic criteria for anorexia nervosa

1	Refusal to maintain minimal normal weight. Body weight is less than 85% of that expected for age and height
2	Fearful of becoming fat or gaining weight
3	Disturbance in body weight and shape perception. Body image linked to self-esteem
4	Absence of at least three normal non-drug-induced consecutive menstrual cycles

Source: American Psychiatric Association (1994)

A recent study examined a number of dimensions relating to body image, including fear of fatness, preference for thinness, body size distortion, body dissatisfaction and actual body size, and looked at their relationship to restrictive eating. Fear of fatness, preference for thinness and body size distortion had an effect on body dissatisfaction over and above the effects of actual body size. Fear of fatness was the best predictor of restrictive eating (Gleaves *et al.*, 1995). Bulimia nervosa is associated with binge eating and a feeling that eating is out of the individual's control (see Table 13.3). Binge eating is accompanied by depression and self-deprecation. Self-induced vomiting occurs in the majority of cases. Bulimia can cause a wide range of medical problems including inflammation of the digestive tract and, as with anorexia, it is associated with cardiac problems resulting from low levels of electrolytes.

There are a range of theoretical proposals to account for eating disorders, in particular anorexia and bulimia. A predisposition to obesity may be part of the aetiology of eating disorders which encourages girls and women into dieting. In some women there may be hormonal dysfunction affecting the hypothalamic feeding centres or the experience of amenorrhoea. The rarity of eating disorders in men points to features of women's experiences in the development of such disorders. Some argue therefore that an understanding of the conditions requires analyses of the construction of femininity and how women experience the passage from girlhood to womanhood. Other contributory factors include the current social desirability of slenderness, especially for women, and the pressure for women to achieve success, both academically and in the workplace (Kern and Hastings, 1995). Women who perceive themselves as failing to meet these demands for the perfect woman then experience guilt or feelings of failure which encourages binge eating or denial and a sense of loss of control over eating. In a recent study, 54 per cent of 15- and 16-year-old girls considered themselves to be overweight,

TABLE 13.3 Diagnostic criteria for bulimia nervosa

1	Recurrent episodes of binge eating accompanied by a sense of loss of control
2	Recurrent compensatory behaviour, e.g. self-induced vomiting, use of laxatives or enema
3	Binges and compensating behaviours occurring about twice a week for three months
4	Body shape and weight are critical in self-evaluation
5	This experience does not only occur during a period of anorexia nervosa

Source: American Psychiatric Association (1994)

including 20 per cent of the leanest girls. Boys, too, saw themselves as overweight, but in smaller numbers: 21 per cent of boys and 8 per cent of the leanest boys (Gracey *et al.*, 1996).

Comparisons of the family functioning of bulimics and normal eaters reveal differences in family conflict, family cohesion, family recreational activities and expressiveness pointing to bulimics experiencing more family disturbance (Kern and Hastings, 1995). This association between disturbed family functioning and bulimia is often interpreted as a causal relationship with unsatisfactory family relationships leading to bulimia. However, similar family disturbances are noted among the victims of childhood sexual abuse and young people receiving psychiatric treatment. It is possible therefore that family disturbance results from the distress of coping with a vulnerable family member. It would help to determine whether family disturbance leads to emotional and behavioural difficulties or results from those difficulties if some features of family functioning were condition specific. The one feature of family life that is unique to bulimia is that bulimic families appear to emphasise to an unusual level the importance of life achievements, including social, monetary, academic and work achievement (Kern and Hastings, 1995). Intuitively, it would seem that such an emphasis is unlikely to result from the experience of living with a bulimic person and rather more likely from the demands for high achievement to overburden the individual and make them vulnerable. When bulimic young women receive treatment and reduce their bingeing and gain weight they frequently perceive the functioning of their family to improve (Woodside *et al.*, 1995).

The experience of childhood sexual abuse is sometimes linked to bulimia. A range of experiences are subsumed under the heading 'childhood sexual abuse' and different people experience sexual abuse in different ways. Moderate negative experiences relating to sexual abuse do not appear to be associated with bulimia. However, there does seem to be a link between the severity of child sexual abuse and bulimia (Hastings and Kern, 1994).

Although anorexia and bulimia nervosa are disorders most commonly affecting adolescents and young women, there is a growing number of women experiencing these conditions at a later age. A common belief about the onset of eating disorders among these older women is that the intimate relations of eating-disordered women are lacking in intimacy and cohesion and that this triggers the eating disorder and helps to perpetuate it. More specifically it is suggested that the communication between couples is superficial and they are unable to express their feelings for one another adequately. In a comparison of women with an eating disorder and their partners with non-eating-disordered couples, partial support for this notion was found (Van den Broucke *et al.*, 1995a). Couples including an eating-disordered woman were less skilled in constructive communication than other couples, but they demonstrated higher levels of self-disclosure.

It has been observed that married or cohabiting eating-disordered women and their partners have significantly more topics that have the potential to trigger conflicts than do non-eating-disordered couples. Moreover, the topics of those potential conflicts are often emotionally laden, for example sexual relationships. A frequently observed pattern when conflicts occur among eating-disordered couples is that one of the couple seeks to defuse the conflict while the other seeks to escalate it. In contrast, non-eating-disordered couples were more likely to both work to reduce conflict (Van den Broucke *et al.*, 1995b). One suggested trigger for the onset of eating disorders is conflict in intimate relationships which is not resolved because one or both partners avoid open confrontation about the aversive issues which might generate conflict. The eating disorder is seen as promoting conflict avoidance and protecting the relationship from the threat of conflict. However, in the absence of longitudinal data the direction of the relationship between conflict avoidance and eating disorders cannot be determined.

Intervening to promote health

Weight loss and exercise

Interventions to tackle obesity in children and adolescents typically include nutritional education, increased physical activity and training in behavioural techniques including cognitive restructuring, self-monitoring, development of techniques to control the act of eating and reinforcement of desired behaviours. These programmes can be effective. Relative to the weight of untreated obese children those on programmes show weight loss of between 4 and 9 kg at one-year follow-up (Brezinka, 1992). However, programmes are not equally effective for all children. When obese children with overweight parents are placed on individual weight loss programmes they are less successful in achieving weight loss than obese children of leaner parents (Israel *et al.*, 1990). Mothers' characteristics have more of an impact on child obesity and weight loss than father characteristics (Favaro and Santonastaso, 1995). In that study younger children and children with an obese mother lost least weight during a one-year weight loss programme and children's level of obesity related to the psychological distress shown by mothers.

Weight loss programmes that involve the parents are more effective than those that do not. This is partly because obesity runs in families and so weight loss is easiest to achieve when the whole family changes its eating behaviour; as has been noted above, parents influence their children's eating and activity levels. One important feature of programmes that involve parents is that fewer children drop out of the programme. Programmes that involve parents are most effective if they provide skills training, such as training parents in behaviour modification techniques and problem-solving strategies (Brezinka, 1992). Involving parents in behaviour modification programmes results in greater weight loss in children than when the family is not involved. Furthermore, involved parents also lose weight (Brownell and Cohen, 1995). The inclusion of physical exercise in weight loss programmes assists weight loss among adults, but has less impact on children's and adolescents' weight. Children achieve similar levels of weight loss and maintain weight loss equally on programmes that do and do not include exercise. The inclusion of exercise improves fitness but is not a necessary component of weight loss programmes for children and adolescents (Brezinka, 1992).

In adulthood, attempts at weight reduction through dieting are frequently unsuccessful. About 60 to 70 per cent of women who achieve a weight loss of 20 pounds or more fail to maintain the weight loss over a two-year period (Light and Girdler, 1993). While some individuals can lose weight through diet and maintain their weight loss, many lose weight and quickly put it back on again. Repeated dieting with its cycles of weight loss and weight gain may increase the risk to health (Jeffery, 1992). Furthermore, failure to maintain weight loss may lead to the adoption of strategies to control weight that have other maladaptive health outcomes. For instance, cigarette smoking may be used as a weight control strategy. Dieting is more successful when dieters have constructive support from their families and when individuals are able to make permanent changes in their lifestyle that they and their family can maintain (Edell *et al.*, 1987). Behaviour modification programmes appear to offer the highest success rate in the long term. Weight loss is not rapid, although losses of 10 to 15 kg have been achieved after six months, and this may be increased when behaviour modification therapy is combined with more aggressive treatments such as severe caloric restriction or jaw wiring. Behaviour modification is particularly beneficial in special patient groups such as the obese elderly, children or adolescents, and disabled patients. The cornerstone of therapy for most obese patients is a programme of dietary restriction, combined with exercise and behaviour modification (Caterson, 1990).

Increased exercising has a number of effects that are beneficial: exercising uses up calories; it increases metabolism so that a greater number of calories are used during daily tasks; exercise acts as an appetite suppressant; exercising focuses weight reduction on body fat; exercising improves muscle tone (Hill *et al.*, 1987). Exercising therefore assists with weight loss and improves body shape, so that even in the absence of weight loss individuals generally see an improvement in their physical appearance. Dieters who include exercise are better able to maintain their reduced weight, partly because their increased fitness allows them to be more physically active (Epstein *et al.*, 1988). Increasing physical activity also has other health benefits, particularly as regards cardiovascular health and the prevention of cancers.

There are risks and costs associated with regular exercise. Exercising takes time, and for those with other heavy commitments this is a serious disincentive. The creation of time for exercising may require assistance from others within the family, such as a renegotiation of household activities or child care arrangements. Furthermore, participating in exercising requires some specialist clothing, equipment or facilities and so incurs some expense. Even regular walking increases footwear costs. In addition, exercising exposes participants to the risk of injury and even death. These risks are greatest in contact sports, but are present with other forms of vigorous exercise. Most attention has been given to repetitive overloading injuries, cardiovascular accidents during exercising, the immunosuppressive effects of exercise and effect of exercise on reproductive health. Overuse injuries occur with the accumulation of repetitive musculoskeletal microtraumas. The most common site for these injuries is the knee. There have been epidemiological investigations of injuries to competitive (but not to non-competitive) swimmers and to runners, badminton players and aerobic dancers. These point to the high incidence of such injuries and their link to the amount of exercise taken. For instance, runners experience significantly more knee injuries than do non-exercisers. Their chance of injury increases with increase in weekly mileage run. Age, gender, obesity, speed of running and muscle stretching prior to exercise do not seem to contribute independently to the risk of sustaining an injury. Consequently, 50 per cent or more of marathon runners injure themselves during their preparation for the race (Siscovick, 1990). The risks of overuse injury through strenuous walking and non-competitive swimming are probably small.

There are concerns also about the cardiac hazards of exercising. Several studies point to the incidence of sudden deaths during vigorous exercise. Death while engaging in strenuous exercise accounts for 5 per cent of sudden deaths (Siscovick, 1990). Those who do exercise vigorously on a regular basis are between five and nine times as likely to die when exercising as they are when not exercising. For those who do not normally take exercise, vigorous exercise increases their risk while exercising fiftyfold or more. However, compared to those who do not exercise, vigorous exercise totalling as little as twenty minutes per week reduces the risk of cardiac arrest to 40 per cent the risk run by sedentary individuals (Siscovick, 1990). The benefits of improved cardiovascular health and avoidance of obesity associated with sustained exercise outweigh the short-term risk of sudden death.

The evidence as to the effects of exercise on the immune system is unclear. All forms of cancer occur less frequently among those who exercise regularly (Paffenbarger *et al.*, 1986), although this could be the result of lifestyle differences between exercisers and non-exercisers, including differences in their diet and weight control. On the other hand there is some evidence that susceptibility to infectious disease is increased among those who engage in high levels of exercise. Athletes report more frequent and more severe symptoms, particularly symptoms of upper-respiratory tract infection, than do non-exercisers (Calabrese, 1990). Very high levels of exercise may act as a stressor and begin to impair the operation of the immune system. However, the evidence for this is incomplete at present. The effects of stress on the immune system are discussed more fully in Chapter 3.

For both men and women who engage in intense exercise there is an additional risk: impairment to fertility. In women, intense exercise can interfere with menstrual functioning and this in turn may be deleterious to bone density and in the young to skeletal formation (Sutton *et al.*, 1990). It is unclear by what route exercise interferes with menstrual functioning, but amenorrhoea is seen more commonly in women who engage in intense exercise. Menstrual functioning is usually restored once the level of exercise is reduced and body mass increases. However, if women continue to exercise at a level which maintains amenorrhoea for a period of three years or more, irreversible bone loss can occur. Very high levels of physical activity appear to impair fertility of males, but it is unclear whether this has any longer term significance. Men who are highly active physically and who have a low sperm count are less successful in AID programmes (artificial insemination) than less active men with similar sperm counts. Men also report reduced libido during periods of intense training (Cumming, 1990). Reduction in libido is probably the result of chronic fatigue rather than being an enduring feature.

There are both benefits and costs associated with the use of exercise to supplement the effect of dieting in achieving weight loss. In general, the benefits outweigh the costs, but some forms of exercise, such as vigorous walking, seem to have a better balance of benefits over costs than others.

Improving nutritional health

Nutritional practices have implications for the maintenance of health and the avoidance of a number of diseases. Interventions promoting a healthier lifestyle can reduce the risk of future ill health. The earlier in life a healthier lifestyle is adopted, the easier it is to maintain. Preconceptual interventions to improve the health of women and their future children have been attempted. These target substance use, improved dietary practices and an increase in weight for under-nourished women (Alexander and Korenbrot, 1995). It is unclear whether these programmes have a long-term impact upon behaviour and health. Interventions to promote breast-feeding introduced in maternity hospitals can effectively encourage the continued use of breast-feeding to six months and be highly cost-effective. One such intervention included special incentives (prizes) to encourage women and their partners to participate in a breast-feeding class for expectant couples and an educational series on childbirth. A breast-feeding support programme was included in which peers served as role models. The incentives can attract primiparous women from lower socioeconomic groups, along with their partners, to participate in educational interventions designed to promote breast-feeding. Participation by couples in breast-feeding promotion activities can dramatically increase the rate and duration of breast-feeding (Sciacca *et al.*, 1995).

The potential use of schools as a site for the introduction of interventions is being exploited with some success in programmes promoting improved cardio-vascular health. Interventions typically include regular lessons on nutrition and increased numbers of physical activity lessons and are introduced early in children's schooling careers. Measured benefits of such programmes include reductions in blood pressure and cholesterol concentrations as well as increased nutritional and health knowledge (Gore *et al.*, 1996) and, in one study, a reduction in body fatness and an increase in aerobic fitness was also reported (Stone *et al.*, 1989). While such programmes can be beneficial, their impact is increased when the family is also involved in the intervention. A school and home educational programme would involve schoolwork, with associated homework/parental activities. Children with higher family involvement showed the greatest increase in their reported use of grain, lower reported intake of cholesterol, and strongest intentions for good nutritional practices in the future (Edmundson *et al.*, 1996).

The benefits of family involvement can be seen in other interventions. A British cardiovascular intervention aimed at 12,000 middle-aged couples showed improvements after one year in their cardiovascular health, largely by targeting diet. Couples received counselling from a nurse about healthy diet, smoking and their role in cardiac risk. Their cardiac risk was assessed (for example smoking, obesity, elevated blood pressure) and families received variable follow-up depending upon their level of risk. Couples showed lowered blood pressure and cholesterol levels (Family Heart Study Group, 1994). Men with elevated choles-terol levels also benefit from family involvement in their treatment. In one study, families received counselling about diet, exercise and smoking. Men and their wives showed improved health behaviours that were maintained at a seven-year follow up. However, their children did not show the same benefits (Knutsen and Knutsen, 1991). More intense interventions with booster sessions to reinforce messages may be needed to achieve long-term improvements in children's cardio-vascular risk-taking behaviours. Interventions that modify the behaviour of the whole family give rise to an environment that is more supportive of the mainte-nance of any changes than would be the case with individually directed interventions. Nevertheless, where this approach is not possible, targeting one family member may have spill-over effects on others in the family, improving their health too. For instance the intervention to promote the cardiovascular health of men in the USA, MR FITT, also indirectly improved the diets of their wives (Sexton *et al.*, 1987). In a similar way there is evidence that nutritional programmes delivered in schools can improve parental diet (Perry *et al.*, 1987).

The treatment with family therapy of eating disorders is relatively common practice. However, there have been few evaluations of the effectiveness of this approach compared to individual therapy. One randomised control trial found that family therapy was more efficacious than individual therapy for younger anorexic patients who had had their eating disorder for only a short period. Older patients and those with longer duration of their eating disorder responded similarly to both types of therapy (Russell *et al.*, 1987). The benefits of family therapy over individual therapy for adolescents was confirmed by Robin *et al.* (1994). Weight gain was greatest among the family therapy treated anorexics. However, another study found individual and family counselling to be equally effective (Gowers *et al.*, 1994).

- 'My grandmother is 90 and she still has all her wits about her. She has always eaten whatever she liked, lots of fatty foods. She used to be very large, but the smoking helped her to lose weight. My friend's Dad on the other hand was always worried about his health, always ate what-ever the "experts" recommended and was as skinny as a rake. He had a heart attack and died last year: he was only 42. I know which one I want to be like!'
- 'I heard that whether you end up being fat or not and whether you get cancers or heart disease is all decided by the time you are six months old. It's too late to try and do anything now to make myself more healthy.'
- 'I can't diet: I have to cook chips and bake cakes for the children; I don't have the time to cook something different for myself.'
- 'I can't lose weight by dieting and I don't seem to have the energy or the time to exercise.'
- 'You keep hearing about people who were completely healthy until they took up exercising who died suddenly while exercising. When you get to my age exercising is too risky.'

What messages has health psychology for the speakers above?

Key point summary

- Nutritional practices pre-birth, in infancy and in childhood lay the foundations for future health status. Hypertension, heart disease, cancers, diabetes, strokes, osteoporosis are all influenced by early nutritional practices.
- Nutritional habits are hard to change; good nutritional practices that are begun early in life are easier to maintain.
- Obesity is associated with health risks. Obesity in adolescence and adulthood is hard to reverse although the use of exercise to control weight can be an effective strategy.
- Under-nutrition, whether involuntary or resulting from an eating disorder, results not only in wasting of the body, but also in vitamin and mineral deficiencies which interfere with effective body functioning.
- Interventions to improve nutritional practices are most effective when they target the whole family. Nevertheless, interventions targeted at one family member frequently result in changes in nutritional practices by others in the family.

Further reading

Bouchard, C., Shephard, R. J., Stephens, T., Sutton, J. R. and McPherson, B. D. (1990) *Exercise Fitness and Health: A Consensus of Current Knowledge.* Champaign, Ill: Human Kinetics Books. Provides a comprehensive examination of the impact of exercise on the body, and on health, and its potential role in the prevention of various diseases.

Brownell, K. D. and Cohen, L. R. (1995). Adherence to dietary regimens 1: An overview of research. *Behavioral Medicine*, 20(4), 149–154. Reviews the evidence for the links between diet and health and looks at how dietary changes could reduce risk for major chronic illness such as cancer and cardiovascular disease. It also considers how cultural, environmental and psychological factors may relate to dietary management.

Epstein, L. H., Coleman, K. J. and Meyers, M. D. (1996) Exercise in treating obesity in children and adolescents. *Medicine and Science in Sports and Exercise*, 28(4), 428–435. Provides a review of the use of exercise programmes in the prevention and treatment of obesity in children and adolescents. However, it also points to the limited number of evaluations undertaken of such programmes.

Favaro, A. and Santonastaso, P. (1995) Effects of parents' psychological characteristics and eating behaviour on childhood obesity and dietary compliance. *Journal of Psychosomatic Research*, 39(2), 145–151. Considers the extent to which children's ability to change their weight on a diet may be influenced by their parents' characteristics. They conclude that mothers' characteristics are more important than those of fathers in relation to both obesity and weight loss.

Hodes, M. and Legrange, D. (1993) Expressed emotion in the investigation of eating disorders – a review. *International Journal of Eating Disorders*, 13(3),

279–288. Examines the relationship between variations in family interaction patterns and different eating disorders and their impact on responses to treatment and therefore treatment effectiveness.

Kemm, J. R. (1987) Eating patterns in childhood and adult health. *Nutrition*, 4(4), 205–215. Examines the influence of childhood nutritional practices on adult health and considers the effectiveness of childhood interventions in delaying the onset or preventing the occurrence of diseases such as heart disease, cancers and cerebrovascular accidents.

Chapter 14

Cancer

Marian Pitts

Introduction

The diminishing threat of death in the West from infectious diseases and the increased longevity of the population have enhanced the importance of cancer as a cause of ill health and death. It is estimated that one in three people will develop cancer at some time in their lives. Overall, the risk of cancer increases with age and hence the longer we live the higher the risk of developing and possibly dying from cancer. There are more than 300,000 new cases of cancer every year, and 165,000 people die of the disease each year (about a quarter of all deaths in the UK); more than 70 per cent of new cases occur in people over the age of 60. As we will see below, not all cancers carry the same mortality risk – for example, lung cancer is responsible for a quarter of all deaths from cancer. This chapter will consider the role of psychological variables in the aetiology and development of the disease and the responses to the illness and its treatments.

What is cancer?

Cancer is a group of more than one hundred different diseases; what these share is the way in which they develop. Cancer occurs when cells become abnormal and develop and multiply without regulation. Normally cells divide to produce more cells only when the body requires them and at a relatively slow rate; cells that are cancerous multiply very rapidly. If they divide without regulation, a mass of excess tissue is formed which is called a tumour. Tumours can be benign or malignant (cancerous). Cells in malignant tumours invade and destroy nearby tissue, or they can break away from the tumour and travel via the bloodstream or the lymphatic system through the body and form new tumours in different sites. The spread of cancer in this way is known as metastasis.

Cancer can be classified into two broad types: haematological (malignancies of the blood) and solid tumours. The name of a cancer describes the type of tissue or location of the site where it develops. A sarcoma describes a cancer developing in bone, muscle or connective tissue, carcinoma describes cancers arising in the cells of glands, organs and other similar locations. Cancer is rare in childhood; about one in every 600 children under the age of 16 will develop cancer; the most common is leukaemia, accounting for almost one-third of all childhood cancers. Leukaemia is a condition where too many white blood cells are found in the blood and bone marrow.

Kinds of cancer

Figures 14.1 and 14.2 show the number of deaths from cancers in the United Kingdom in 1988. As can be seen, lung cancer is the highest cause of death for men and the second highest for women after breast cancer. Figure 14.3 shows five-year survival rates for different cancers. Again, the very poor survival rate for lung cancers is important to note. With the exception of stomach cancer, survival rates have not changed greatly over the past thirty years. We will return

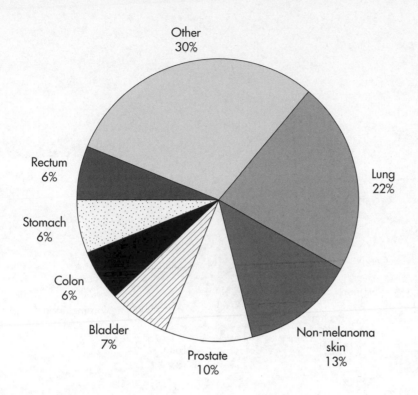

Figure 14.1 Most common cancers in men in the UK, 1988
Source: *Cancer Research Campaign Year Book (1994–1995)*

to these figures when we examine strategies for the prevention of cancer. First though we should consider people's understanding and beliefs about cancer.

Beliefs about cancer

As we saw in Chapter 1, people's beliefs and representations of illness will have a direct effect on the kinds of preventive action they will take. There is a growing body of literature concerned with 'lay representations of illness' (Lau and Hartman, 1983; Leventhal *et al.*, 1980). These studies suggest that there are four or five components which underlie our representations of illness. These are: identity, consequences, time line and causes, and possibly also cure or recovery.

Much of the work in this area has focused on lay representations and under-standings of breast cancer. Payne (1990) interviewed 286 healthy women about their beliefs surrounding breast cancer. She found that the major cause identi-fied was stress, which included a number of components such as the death of a close relative, being 'run down', being depressed and 'bottling up your emotions'. Second, there were common misconceptions about breast cancer – that it was

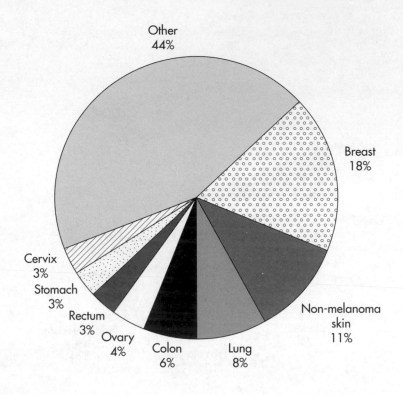

Figure 14.2 Most common cancers in women in the UK, 1988
Source: *Cancer Research Campaign Year Book* (1994–1995)

the consequence of vigorous exercise, of being hit in the breast, of having many sexual partners, not wearing a bra and having sons rather than daughters (!). Personal and environmental hazards were the next most important factor such as drinking alcohol, smoking, being overweight and being exposed to nuclear waste. Finally, there was a very small component of contact which covers statements such as 'getting older', or having close contact with a sufferer from breast cancer. Payne's findings support other earlier studies which have identified stress as the most frequent cause of illness, and the significant role ascribed to environmental factors (Taylor *et al.*, 1984). Salmon *et al.* (1996) found similar accounts for illnesses in general practice; see Chapter 4 for further details.

Some causative elements are now widely known and understood. The most obvious is the role of smoking in causing lung cancer. However, it is interesting to examine what sufferers from lung cancer understand about this behaviour. Faller *et al.* (1995) carried out semi-structured interviews with 120 diagnosed lung cancer patients and administered structured questionnaires. Both methods showed that the most frequent attribution for lung cancer was smoking; but that it was blamed less frequently than would tally with actual smoking behaviour. The next most common attributions were 'toxins in the workplace' and 'air

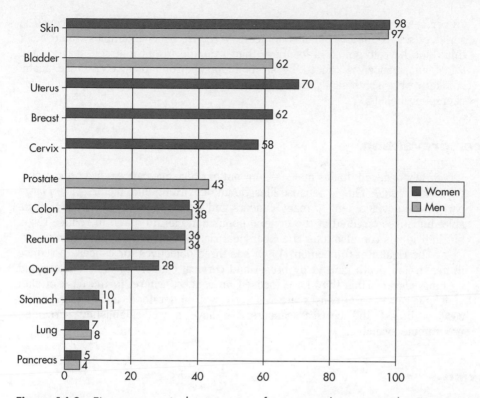

Figure 14.3 Five-year survival percentages for men and women with cancers

Source: *Cancer Research Campaign Year Book* (1994–1995)

pollution'. Interestingly, during the interviews, Faller *et al.* found that patients frequently tried to question or minimise the causal impact of smoking. More than 80 per cent put forward at least one argument which served to qualify the relevance of smoking as cause of the illness, for example, by saying that they did not really know where the disease had come from, or that they had always led a normal and healthy life, or that non-smokers can get lung cancer too. This denial of the link between behaviour and the disease is best described by Faller *et al.* as 'Obviously smoking is usually the cause, but it is not really so in my particular case!' This ties in well with the characteristic of 'unrealistic optimism' described in Chapter 1.

This self-exempting tendency was also observed by Chapman *et al.* (1993). They examined differences between smokers and ex-smokers in terms of their cognitive dissonance-reducing beliefs, otherwise known as self-exempting beliefs. Respondents to a postal questionnaire in Australia were asked to indicate whether they agreed that smokers were more likely to be at risk of six diseases. The diseases were heart disease, poor circulation, bronchitis, lung cancer, stroke and rheumatoid arthritis. All but the last are known to be smoking related; the last was included to test response bias. Forty-two per cent of ex-smokers but only

28 per cent of smokers agreed with the risks of smoking and these diseases. A series of self-exempting belief statements were also used. Examples would be: 'I think you have to smoke a lot more than I do/did to put yourself at risk', and 'Most lung cancer is caused by air pollution, petrol fumes, etc.' Once again, smokers were significantly more likely than ex-smokers to endorse such self-exempting beliefs.

Cancer prevention

It is widely believed that as many as four out of every five cancers are preventable (Austoker, 1995). This is because lifestyle and environmental factors play a large part in the development of many cancers and hence they are potentially avoidable. Initiatives targeted at the general population can do much to reduce risks, but individuals can also alter their personal risk of cancer to some extent.

The Health of the Nation (1992) has three objectives for cancer: to reduce ill health and death caused by breast and cervical cancer, by skin cancers and by lung cancer. Thus they have focused on cancers where, in the case of skin and lung cancers the causes are relatively well understood, and where, in the case of breast and cervical cancers, we have a well-established screening programme available.

Smoking

There are well-documented links between smoking and various cancers, including lung cancer, throat and jaw cancer. I will not deal with smoking in this chapter since it is discussed extensively elsewhere (see Chapter 7).

Diet

The fact that people living in different countries have different patterns of food consumption and different rates of certain cancers has highlighted the possibility that diet is related, perhaps causally, to the incidence of cancer. However, the evidence is, as we will see, sometimes very difficult to interpret and studies with animals have not always given clear-cut evidence. On the basis of current knowledge, it is not possible to formulate precisely what proportion of cancers are directly related to diet. Austoker (1995) suggests that modification in diet could reduce cancer risk by as much as one- or even two-thirds. She offers a review of the findings from a number of studies and concludes that there is now strong evidence that high intake of fruit and vegetables is protective against various cancers, with the effect most marked for respiratory and digestive cancers. Thus smokers who have high intakes of fruit and vegetables may have a 60 per cent lower risk of developing lung cancer. This protective effect would seem to be general to most fruit and vegetables, although vitamins C and E and carotenoids would seem to be particularly important in this protective role. There is no evidence that vitamin or mineral supplements protect against cancer; equally there is no evidence that food additives such as preservatives, flavouring and colourings or artificial sweeteners cause cancer in humans (CRC, 1995).

The evidence concerning fat intake is less clear. There is a suggested link between high fat intake and breast cancer, but this remains contentious. There is also evidence for the importance of starchy fibre-rich foods in the prevention of large bowel cancer. There is now a large-scale study under way known as the European Prospective Investigation of Cancer (EPIC). More than 400,000 healthy middle-aged men and women in seven European countries are being studied with a projected follow-up for ten years. This should enable us to be a good deal more confident as to some of the claims made about links between diet and cancers. The United Kingdom has the lowest consumption per person per year of vegetables and of fruit in these seven countries. Inhabitants of Italy, Greece and Spain consume, on average, about 70 kg of fruit per person per year, compared with 38 kg for the United Kingdom, and about 200 kg of vegetables per person per year compared with an average of 57 kg per person in the United Kingdom. These large differences have been linked with different rates of cancers in these countries (Austoker, 1994b). Chapter 13 discusses these issues further.

Alcohol

Alcohol is second only to smoking as a proven cause of cancer. Three per cent of all cancer deaths are directly due to excessive alcohol consumption, but a number of cancers are also now believed to be indirectly linked to heavy alcohol consumption. Cancers of the mouth, pharynx, larynx and oesophagus are definitely related to alcohol consumption, and there is some evidence that breast cancer is also related (Longnecker and MacMahon, 1988). The overall risk of cancer rises as alcohol consumption increases; with men drinking fewer than twenty-one units per week and women drinking fewer than fourteen being at lowest risk. In December 1995 the government revised these figures upwards so that recommended sensible drinking levels now stand at twenty-eight units per week for men and twenty-one for women.

There is some evidence, however, that low levels of alcohol consumption are positively related to health (Pitts, 1996). Most studies now conclude that very moderate drinking lowers the risk of heart disease; however, these findings come from studies which have concentrated on men (e.g. Marmot and Bruner, 1991) and the effect of low alcohol consumption on women is still not well established. There still remains a controversy on the benefits weighed against the risks of alcohol (Burr, 1995; Deburgh, 1996; Douds and Maxwell, 1994; Engs, 1996; Stockwell *et al.*, 1996).

Detecting cancer

Screening

At the heart of attempts to prevent cancer is the need to detect it at an early stage of development, preferably before it has spread. A major component of this attempt is the national screening programmes introduced for breast and cervical cancer. Before we consider these, however, we need to understand more about what the purposes of screening are, and for which cancers it might be appropriate to screen. The basic questions are who to screen, at what age and how frequently?

When is screening most effective?

Before a screening programme is introduced, several criteria need to be satisfied. Austoker (1994) suggests the following general criteria:

- Is the condition an important health problem?
- Is there a recognisable early stage?
- Is treatment at an early stage more beneficial than at a later stage?
- Is there a suitable test?
- Is the test acceptable to the general population?
- Are there adequate facilities for diagnosis and treatment?
- What are the costs and benefits?
- Which subgroups should be screened?
- How often should screening take place?

Cervical cancer screening

Screening for cancer of the cervix is one of the longest and best established screening programmes available in the UK. Current policy in the UK is to advocate screening at least once every five years for women between the ages of 25 and 60 (Scotland) and 20 and 64 (England and Wales). Cervical cancer is a major cause of death among women. More than 1500 women a year die from cervical cancer. If the disease remains unidentified until detected at the symptomatic stage, it is usually fatal. Early treatment of cellular abnormalities can, however, be very effective. Research indicates that 80 per cent of women dying from cervical cancer have never had a smear test (Day, 1989, cited in McKie, 1993). The aetiology of the disease is still very poorly understood; incidence of cervical cancer is positively associated with early age of first intercourse, multiple sexual partners, cigarette smoking and, possibly, a lowered immune system. Hence the disease is capable of carrying some of the stigma of sexual activity with its diagnosis. Orbell and Sheeran (1993) carried out a comprehensive survey of the psychological literature pertaining to cervical cancer screening. They found that studies which consider demographic variables show that age is almost always inversely related to uptake of screening (Beardow *et al.*, 1989; Meadows, 1987); there is a lower uptake amongst social classes four and five (Sansom, 1970) and lower uptake in socially stressed areas (Meadows, 1987). Explanations for these variations suggest that chance contact with service providers and encouragement from GPs are major factors in accounting for this difference. Women from lower social classes tend to be in less frequent contact with services and hence have fewer chances for opportunistic encouragement of the service.

Attitudes, beliefs and knowledge of cervical cancer and the cervical screening test are consistently found to be poor (Peters *et al.*, 1989). Not surprisingly, negative attitudes, low knowledge and negative evaluations are found to be associated with failure to attend for screening. McKie (1993) reports a small-scale study of seventy non-attenders; she asked these women what they knew about the causes of cervical cancer. Fifty-seven per cent did not know the causes, and the causes are indeed difficult to identify. Nineteen per cent identified promiscuity as the potential cause and a further 13 per cent identified sexual activity. Finally, 11 per cent suggested other causes such as smoking, the oral contraceptive, a virus and heredity. Clearly there are serious implications from these findings for perceived vulnerability to the disease; most especially, its perceived link with promiscuous sex will affect the likelihood of a women defining herself as potentially 'at risk' of cervical cancer.

Non-attenders for screening have become a particular focus of research study. Orbell and Sheeran (1993) collected data from ten studies reported between 1967 and 1989 and they summarise the reasons for non-attendance following an invitation for cervical screening. The highest percentage of reasons for non-attendance concerned other preoccupations at the time – holidays, being too busy, or an illness, are examples given. Nineteen per cent of women indicated a perceived invulnerability to cervical cancer – it is impossible to determine the accuracy of this perception. This perceived invulnerability may be related to the 'unrealistic optimism' described in Chapter 1 in connection with other health risks. Seventeen per cent cited practical difficulties such as problems with the time or venue for screening. Sixteen per cent reported psychological costs associated with the test procedures (for example, anxiety or embarrassment) and 13 per cent 'forgot'. Thus non-attendance is a combination both of psychological variables and aspects of how the service is made available to women. It is difficult to interpret the high percentage reporting other preoccupations; this could be influenced by more flexible service provision, but may also mask underlying emotional barriers to the screening process. The recent study by McKie (1993) asked non-attenders if there was anything that might trigger them to request a smear test. Women cited the presence of symptoms as a potential trigger most frequently (37 per cent), and social pressure, predominantly from family or friends, as the only other trigger (17 per cent). Since the presence of symptoms is an indication of serious, if not fatal progression of the disease, this finding is particularly concerning.

Three models of health behaviours have been applied to cervical cancer screening. Inevitably, the health belief model has generated much research. Hennig and Knowles (1990) and Hill *et al.* (1985) both report that intention to attend is significantly related to perceived vulnerability to cervical cancer and non-attendance is linked to perceived barriers to attendance. In both studies the amount of variance accounted for was rather low: 32 per cent and 27 per cent respectively. The same researchers have also considered the theory of reasoned action and once again found significant, but extremely modest, support for the model. Orbell and Sheeran argue convincingly that models which combine psychological variables with a consideration of aspects of service provision and delivery stand the best chance of predicting and explaining the uptake of cervical screening opportunities.

Breast cancer

Given the high mortality rate of breast cancer in the world, it is not surprising that it should be the focus of much research. Other factors make the investigation of psychological dimensions of this disease an important focus of study. If breast cancer can be detected at an early stage the prognosis is very much better. Eighty-four per cent of women with breast cancer discovered at Stage One will be alive in five years' time as opposed to 18 per cent of those who have tumours advanced to Stage Four. Various strategies for prevention of breast cancer are possible. From the point of view of this chapter, mammography and breast self-examination are important strategies to consider.

Mammography is available in the UK for women between the ages of 50 and 64; a number of studies have shown that screening these women has reduced death from breast cancer by between 20 and 50 per cent. The setting of these age limits is controversial. The argument for not extending the limit downwards to, say, age 40 concerns the cost-effectiveness of the screening programme. It also relies on evidence from the USA and Sweden that screening over the age of 50 is effective in reducing mortality (Shapiro *et al.*, 1985). There are trials being carried out in the UK now which may result in the lower limit being reviewed. The upper limit is equally problematic. A UK trial screening programme reported in 1988 showed that 69 per cent of women invited for an initial screen in southern England responded, and 63 per cent in Scotland. Vaile *et al.* (1993) found that demographic factors played little part in predicting attendance; the only exception was the finding that married women were more likely to attend than those who were single, widowed, separated or divorced. The role of 'significant others' in encouraging women to seek screening might be important here, but it is also possible that unmarried women of this age are more likely to be in full-time employment and hence might find attendance at the clinic difficult to arrange. Amongst those who did attend a screening, Vaile *et al.* identify two major sources of dissatisfaction which might impede future attendance. The first is the delay in notification of results. The second is the finding that a significant proportion of women reported discomfort and pain from the procedures. A mammographic screening is frequently described as painless in promotional literature, yet 40 per cent of Vaile's sample of over three thousand women reported discomfort and up to 20 per cent reported pain. A study by Rakowski *et al.* (1992) examines women's decisions about mammography from the transtheoretical model of behaviour change (Prochaska *et al.*, 1982). The model proposes a sequence of stages along a continuum of behavioural change and is outlined in

Chapter 1. Rakowski *et al.*'s findings support an analysis of intention to attend for mammography via the transtheoretical model. This is particularly interesting, since much early work with this model focused on the avoidance of a potentially harmful activity, i.e. contemplating giving up smoking or cutting down on fat intake, rather than on the uptake of a potentially healthy activity such as seeking screening.

A recent meta-analysis of the literature on breast cancer risk and screening was carried out by McCaul *et al.* (1993). They identified nineteen studies which collectively surveyed over 20,000 women. They found a positive effect between measures of risk – such as a family history of cancer, or high perceived vulnerability – and screening behaviour. This is important, since it indicates that public health campaigns should continue to emphasise personal vulnerability to disease. A further study by McCaul *et al.* (1996) also showed that worry about breast cancer will motivate women to breast screen. High worry is consistently associated with screening attendance. Whilst the message is not that one should intentionally create worry about breast cancer, it does make sense to provide accurate information which emphasises personal vulnerability to the disease.

Colorectal and prostate cancer

Prostate cancer is the second most common cancer among men in the United Kingdom. The incidence of the cancer is increasing, partly because of increased longevity since nearly all cancers of the colon and prostate occur in people over the age of 50. Deaths from prostate cancer peak between the ages of 75 and 79. Some increase in the rate of these cancers may also be the result of changes in lifestyle and diet. The five-year survival rate for cancer of the prostate is 43 per cent, largely because of the late stage of presentation. In the United States there have been a number of screening initiatives for these cancers; screening is often carried out via a digital rectal examination, but the method has only limited sensitivity. Austoker (1995) summarises the case against routine screening for cancer of the prostate by estimating that only a few years of life would be saved and that the reduction in overall mortality from screening would be very limited. Recent surveys have concluded that screening for prostate cancer is not to be recommended as cost-effective (NHS Centre for Reviews and Dissemination, 1995).

Self-examination

Given the costs of screening outlined above, and the difficulties in persuading people to attend such screening programmes, it is important to consider other activities related to the early detection of disease. A preventive health behaviour which has attracted much psychological interest and research is the practice of self-examination. This can be defined as the practice of examining one's body in a systematic fashion for the purpose of detecting an abnormality. Self-examination is simple, safe and economical; the questions concern whether it works as a means of detecting abnormalities at an early stage of development and whether the practice itself carries any psychological risks, such as, for example, an increase in anxiety. Currently, self-examination techniques are most appropriate for breast cancer, testicular cancer and certain kinds of skin cancer. McCaul *et al.* (1993) considered breast self-examination (BSE) applying the theory of reasoned action. They found that attitudes and subjective norms predicted intentions to perform BSE. Fletcher *et al.* (1989) examined the relationship between women's socio-demographic characteristics, knowledge, attitudes to and beliefs in BSE. They found the most important single predictor of BSE was type of employment, accounting for approximately 9 per cent of the variance, with a general interest in health matters accounting for a further 5 per cent. Studies such as these indicate that a search for single predictors of such practices as BSE are not likely to result in findings which can meaningfully be incorporated into educational programmes. This last finding also reminds us how important social and demographic, as well as psychological variables are in our search for predictors of behaviour. There has regularly been reported a negative association between age and the practice of preventive health behaviours (e.g. Gould-Martin *et al.* (1982) and others). This finding has particular importance for BSE, as the older a woman is, the more likely she is to develop a breast lump.

Hobbs *et al.* (1984) review the evidence that teaching programmes on BSE can influence the opinions and knowledge of women about the advantages of early detection and treatment. They argue that such changes in knowledge have little direct effect on the extent to which BSE is actually practised. It seems from the women's comments that the difficulties lie in knowing exactly what to do, and when and how often to do it. It is also the case that women are not particularly well informed about the risk factors associated with breast cancer; they are by and large unable to make a realistic assessment of their own susceptibility to the disease and tend to overestimate the personal risks. Such overestimation may result in fear and denial as coping strategies. Further information which seeks both to reassure and educate women as to the actual incidence of breast cancer and the relative frequency of 'benign' lumps linked with detailed information on the practice of BSE could further reduce the number of women failing to carry out this procedure.

The lessons learned from a consideration of the processes which influence the practice of BSE can be extended to other cancers. For example, testicular cancer can be cured if treated early and similar techniques of self-examination can be taught to men, or their partners, to enable abnormalities to be detected before they are at an advanced stage. Testicular cancer is the commonest cancer for men aged between 20 and 34. More than half the cases of testicular cancer occur in men under the age of 35. Testicular cancer is highly susceptible to modern treatment, with a survival rate of nearly 100 per cent if the cancer is detected early. The major risk factor for testicular cancer is cryptorchism (undescended testis). There is an increased risk of three- to fourfold with one undescended testicle and a tenfold increase in risk for two undescended testes. Consistently, relatively low levels of knowledge about testicular cancer, and testicular self-examination (TSE) in particular, are reported (Conklin, 1983; Goldenring and Purtell, 1984; Steffen, 1990). McCaul *et al.* (1993) found support for the theory of planned behaviour as a moderate predictor of intentions to perform TSE in a student sample. They also found self-efficacy to have an additional, but weak role (Brubaker and Fowler 1990; Brubaker and Wickersham, 1990; McCaul *et al.*, 1993). Unfortunately, these studies did not examine the actual behaviour of self-examination, but only the stated intention to perform it.

However, things are gradually improving. Neef *et al.* (1991) questioned college students in the US. They found that more than 41 per cent had been taught TSE, 22 per cent had examined their testicles at least once, but only 8 per cent reported practising TSE once a month. But Katz *et al.* (1995) reported that only 46 per cent of their college sample knew about TSE and less than 20 per cent claimed to practise it regularly. A comparative study of British and Zimbabwean undergraduates also reported extremely low levels of knowledge and practice in both countries (Pitts *et al.*, 1991).

Melanoma

In countries such as Australia and New Zealand, melanoma (skin cancer) is the most common form of cancer amongst adults between the ages of 20 and 45 (Morris and Elwood, 1996). There is a strong causal link between excessive sun exposure and skin cancer, with more than 80 per cent of melanomas in white populations being caused by sun exposure. Skin cancers are associated with many of the characteristics which make screening or self-examination programmes a good option. McCarthy and Shaw (1989) report that a cure rate of 100 per cent for some skin cancers can be achieved if lesions are detected early enough. Education about melanomas can lead to the seeking of medical advice at an early stage of skin cancer; however, education by itself is unlikely to lead to behavioural change. A broad-based media campaign in the UK was studied by Cameron and McGuire (1990). They found no significant change in sunbathing behaviour pre- and post-campaign. A more successful campaign was introduced in Australia and became known as 'Slip! Slap! Slop!' This catchy phrase was designed to remind Australians to cover up by wearing a shirt, to put on sun cream and to wear a hat when the sun was high. There was some evidence that this campaign achieved a degree of behaviour change as well as generally educating the public (Rassaby *et al.*, 1983).

Screening for melanoma can either be achieved via self-examination or via examination by another person, often a health professional. Hennrikus (1991) reported delay in seeking medical advice following detection of abnormalities associated with skin cancer. Reasons for such delays were usually the result of a lack of sufficient information about the significance of signs of possible skin cancer. Almost half the people surveyed by Hennrikus thought the signs were not serious, and an additional 27 per cent employed a 'wait and see' strategy. Eiser *et al.* (1993) have carried out one of the few studies based in the UK. They interviewed an opportunistic sample of 176 university students and report some interesting gender differences. Previous studies had found that men took fewer precautions against skin cancer than women (Cody and Lee, 1990) even though they were more likely to be exposed to the sun during their working day. Women in Eiser *et al.*'s study were more prepared to protect themselves appropriately, most especially by the use of sunscreens, but also tended to value sunbathing more highly than men. Carmel *et al.* (1994) examined the role of age in predicting skin cancer-protective behaviours, including self-examination. They found that younger people (15–44 years) held a number of beliefs which ran counter to self-protective behaviours. They endorsed statements such as: 'to be tanned is to be beautiful'; 'it is pleasant to sit in the sun and get tanned'; 'it is healthy to get tanned and being tanned is being more attractive to others.' They also found that women were more likely to endorse these statements.

Thus, although there are ways of protecting oneself against some cancers, and of detecting them at an early stage of development, there are also beliefs and barriers which may inhibit the development of these protective behaviours. Knowledge alone is rarely (if ever) sufficient to produce the healthy behaviours required, and studies must always pay close attention to the beliefs and attitudes of the targets of their health promotion.

Getting the results of screening

Marteau *et al.* (1993) review the evidence of the impact of undergoing screening. The time between attending for screening and receiving the result is inevitably an anxious one. Fallowfield *et al.* (1990) carried out a retrospective study of women who had attended for breast screening. Ninety-three per cent reported that they were pleased they had received an invitation, but 55 per cent also reported feeling worried. Nathoo (1988) traced women who had not attended for cervical screening and reported that twelve out of seventeen reported terror; some had the assumption that their doctor had reason to suppose they *had* cervical cancer and that was why they had been called for screening. Positive results in cervical screening very greatly, but are around 10–25 per 1000 (Wardle *et al.*, 1995). A number of studies have examined the psychological impact of abnormal cervical smear results. Beresford and Gervaise (1986) interviewed fifty women following an abnormal PAP smear and found they were all (not surprisingly) fearful of cancer, that 80 per cent feared loss of reproductive functions and half reported negative emotions. Kincey *et al.* (1991) and Wardle *et al.* (1995) both found very high levels of anxiety amongst women during follow-up after an abnormal smear, even though the majority of women will show only mild abnormality which does not of itself increase cancer risk. The way in which women are informed of their result is also potentially problematic. This is usually by letter, and women may have to wait over a weekend before they can have the opportunity to discuss the meaning of the letter with a health professional. The message that a positive smear test result is *not* a diagnosis of cancer needs to be conveyed clearly and at the earliest possible stage.

Managing cancer

Breast cancer causes 13,000 deaths per annum in England and Wales and is the most common cause of cancer death among women. If detected early, as we have seen, survival rates are good – over 80 per cent. However, England and Wales also have one of the highest age-standardised incidence and the highest mortality from breast cancer in the world (McPherson *et al.*, 1995). For the majority of women with early breast cancer there are the options of lumpectomy (conserving part of the breast) and mastectomy (removing the whole breast). Randomised controlled trials have not shown any effect on life expectancy of the two types of surgery (Care, 1996). There is some evidence that women who have breast-conserving surgery report better body image and greater satisfaction than those who undergo mastectomy. But the evidence is judged to be equivocal since many of the studies are poorly controlled. Women with early breast cancer may also undergo a course of radiotherapy, hormone therapy and chemotherapy. Once again, the evidence for the effectiveness of chemotherapy is mixed and very much depends on the age and type of cancer.

How do women cope with these treatments, which can be, in themselves, unpleasant and debilitating? The most common complaint concerns poor communication and inadequate provision of information. In Chapter 4 we considered the issues of conveying the diagnosis of cancer to women, and the problems associated with this. A number of studies have looked at the use of audiotapes of the consultation and information booklets. McHugh *et al.* (1995) studied patients with a variety of cancers and provided some of them in a randomised trial with audiotapes of their clinical interviews: 76 per cent of the patients said they found the tape useful, and 16 per cent found it upsetting. Patients provided with a tape recalled significantly more information than the controls. Psychological distress, however, was unaltered by the provision of the tapes. A similar study by Dodd (1987) provided patients with written information sheets or with standard oral information concerning the side-effects of chemotherapy. Again, the provision of information in a lasting form – this time by written means – improved patients' understanding, but did not reduce their levels of psychological distress.

Providing people with information does not necessarily involve them in decisions about treatment. The evidence about the psychological effects of providing patients with choices about their treatment is very mixed. A recent systematic review of the literature (Care, 1996) considered a number of studies. Some (e.g. Fallowfield *et al.*, 1994b; Wilson *et al.*, 1988) report a higher level of life satisfaction and reduced depression and anxiety when choices are made, particularly between mastectomy and breast-conserving surgery. However, these same studies also report that a significant proportion of women find the process of making such a choice extremely problematic. A study by Pierce (1993) analysed interviews with forty-eight women who had received a diagnosis of breast cancer, but who had yet to make treatment decisions. She characterised the women as deferrers, delayers and deliberators. 'Deferrers were immediately attracted to a particular treatment option; delayers experienced a small degree of conflict between options, whilst deliberators showed high levels of conflict and a need for more information' (p. 27). Once again, individual differences in coping styles would seem to be relevant here. It is unlikely that any one approach can be effective and the best option for all cancer patients.

Taylor (1983) has identified a search for meaning as a major aspect of adjustment to life-threatening events such as the diagnosis of breast cancer. Women with breast cancer were interviewed by Taylor and her team and only two out of seventy-two believed that they were coping worse than other women with breast cancer. The great majority reacted to their condition by developing a perception of themselves as physically better off and as coping more success-fully than other similar patients. Frequently this comparison depended on beliefs that the condition had revealed or highlighted previously under-used resources such as increased tolerance of others or an enhanced sense of the meaning of life (Taylor, 1995; Taylor and Armor, 1996; Taylor *et al.*, 1991).

Providing psychosocial support

Reviews of the literature show that psychotherapeutic counselling and educational interventions can improve quality of life and may also boost immune system functioning and hence improve life expectancy (Mayer and Mark, 1995). Such interventions can be carried out by a variety of people. Many hospitals now employ specially trained breast cancer nurses whose role is to give information and offer psychological support. This role is still evolving in the UK (Poole, 1996) and the evidence of the impact on patients' progress is variable (Jary 1996; Watson *et al.*, 1988). A recent study in Glasgow (McArdle *et al.*, 1996) examined 272 women undergoing surgery for breast cancer. Patients were randomly allocated to receive routine care from ward staff, routine care plus support from a breast care nurse, routine care plus support from a voluntary agency, or routine care plus support from both the nurse and the voluntary organisation. They found that only the group receiving the breast care nurse support alone showed reduced psycho-logical morbidity after one year; all the other groups showed similar scores. Patients turned to the nurse at times of crisis, for example, when experiencing symptoms possibly indicating a recurrence of the cancer. A number bypassed their GPs to speak directly to the nurse. This extremely interesting result points the way towards further research in the area which examines more widely the role of specialist support for other cancer sufferers.

Alternative therapies

Many people, on receiving a diagnosis of cancer, may resort to non-medical regimes and treatments. Such treatments may involve lifestyle changes in diet and exercise, and attempts to use mental imagery, visualisation and relaxation to improve immune system functioning. It is extremely difficult to evaluate the effec-tiveness of such therapies, and research has often been criticised for applying inappropriately stringent criteria such as randomised control trials. However, as the chapter on stress shows us (Chapter 3), belief in treatment, gaining a feeling of control over one's illness and a sense of optimism may go a long way in the healing process, with or without specific curative agents.

There are a number of 'self help' books available today with titles such as *Mind over Cancer* or *You can Conquer Cancer*. Such books often contain examples of the beliefs held by the writers about cancer. Ryder Richardson (1995) provides a list of possible causes of cancer which includes emotional upsets, death or divorce in the family, depression and life dissatisfaction. A difficulty with this list is that it would seem not to be possible to live on this earth and *not* experience bereavement or emotional upset – they are part of everyone's lives and to label them as 'causes' of cancer does little good for people experiencing the disease. In the same way, self-help books often overemphasise the degree of personal responsibility for the disease. Whilst a sense of control or even mastery may well aid recovery or coping with cancer, it is a short step to the allocation of responsibility – or even blame – if the disease recurs. If my cancer comes from my approach to life, 'my cancer is the sum total of my mistakes in life' (Ryder Richardson, 1995, p. 58), and I seek to modify that approach, then a recurrence is the most obvious indication that I have 'failed'. Paradoxically therefore, exhortations to take personal control and responsibility for a disease can carry with them the means of effectively undermining that sense of personal control. This is not to say that attention to diet, exercise and other aspects of lifestyle may not help a person to live and cope with the diagnosis and treatment of cancer, merely that some claims such as those illustrated here can be, at the least, extravagant, and potentially harmful.

Similarly, accounts of cancer which afford moral and spiritual aspects to the disease can also be either beneficial or detrimental to a person's ability to cope with it. The following quotations are again from Ryder Richardson's widely available book on cancer:

> Imagine a beautiful apple, ready for picking. You can smell the fruit and you savour the taste to come. . . . You hold it in your hand, the skin breaks under the pressure of your teeth. The juice runs down your chin as you begin to eat. Suddenly you are aware that all is not well. . . . You look at the partly eaten apple and see to your disgust that there has been severe bruising or that an insect has been at work, eating from the inside. Cancer is like that apple. Outwardly in body, we appear to be whole and desirable, but inwardly there are sinister factors at work. An evil force is eating you like the insect in the apple. (p. 51)

> the battle cry is the one word which I feel sums up this book —PURIFI-CATION (p. 110)

It is clear from these passages that cancer is regarded as evil, possibly immoral and certainly unacceptable. It is a short step from ascribing such attributes to a disease to ascribing them to the individual with that disease. We may be providing, via these metaphors, new ways of stigmatising what has always been a stigmatised and feared illness (Sontag, 1983).

> I often ask some cancer patients 'do you feel responsible for your cancer in any way?' The response I get can be quite angry, suggesting it is a cruel question. And yet if within themselves they feel it is cruel then it must in some way imply that there is a grain of truth which they do not wish to recognise. It is the dark side of the moon. . . . The question is cruel yet I feel I can truly say 'Yes, I am responsible for my cancer'.
>
> (Ryder Richardson, 1995, p. 133)

Quality of life

Until relatively recently, the major concern for people with cancer was length of survival. However, the success of many therapies in prolonging life has refocused interest on a consideration of the psychosocial aspects of that life, and of the experience of some of the treatments. Quality of life information can be used to compare different therapies and some of the reasons for poor adherence to treatment schedules. The development of measures specific to the effects of cancer and its treatment have resulted partly from an increase in the incidence of cancer and partly from improvements in treatment which increase longevity for people with cancer (Garne *et al.*, 1997). Quality of life (QOL) has a number of meanings: it is subjective, multi-dimensional and is likely to include aspects of the disease or its treatment which refer to physical, emotional, psychological and social functioning and to pain control, and side-effects of treatments such as nausea and fatigue. The World Health Organization defines QOL as: 'An individual's perception of their position in life in the context of the culture and value systems in which they live and in relation to their goals, expectations, standards and concerns' (WHO, 1996).

A number of scales have been developed both to measure quality of life generically, and specifically for people with cancer. The European Organisation for Research on Treatment of Cancer (EORTC) is a large group of oncologists, surgeons, psychologists and therapists. They have developed a questionnaire which considers four domains of life: physical, psychological, social, emotional and role functioning. It has been field tested on patients with lung cancer and is sensitive to changes over time. The use of such scales is increasing in clinical trials to assess the benefits of different kinds of treatment. They also help in more general policy making about chronic illness.

Personality and cancer

One of the most contentious areas of research is the relationship between personality type and a predisposition to cancer. Hans Eysenck and others have suggested there is a cancer-prone personality (Type C) who has certain personality characteristics: they react to stress with either helplessness or hopelessness; they are passive, appeasing and repress their emotional reactions (Eysenck, 1990). Eysenck quotes a turn-of-the-century doctor, Sir William Osler, who wrote in 1906: 'It is many times more important to know what patient has the disease than what kind of disease the patient has.'

Some of the most striking evidence has come from Steven Greer and his colleagues; they provide evidence from a study of women with breast cancer (Greer and Morris, 1975). They followed a group of sixty-nine women with breast cancer at five- and ten-year markers to try to distinguish survivors from non-survivors in terms of their adjustment to breast cancer measured three months after they had received their diagnosis. They found that women with short survival times were most often hopeless and helpless and that some were stoic in their adjustment. In contrast, long survivors showed 'a fighting spirit'; using a coping strategy of 'denial' also correlated well with long survival. The study claimed that, particularly at ten years after diagnosis, this outcome was independent of any biological factor which might have affected it. DiClemente and Temoshok (1985) offered some support for this finding. Looking at patients with malignant melanoma they found that women who had stoic acceptance and men who displayed strong hopelessness / helplessness had an increased risk of disease progression.

There have, however, been critics of the work who have pointed out that crucial information about the degree of cancer spread was not taken into account. Furthermore, Cassileth in a similar, but not a replication study, failed to find these differences (Cassileth et al., 1985). Cassileth is extremely critical of the interpretation of those studies which claim to show a link between personality and the development of cancer (Cassileth, 1996). It is important to establish whether different psychological attributes exist prior to a cancer diagnosis which might account for the onset of the disease. Such research is, however, extremely difficult to carry out effectively. Greer and Morris (1975) report a study which compared 160 women admitted to hospital for breast tumour biopsy. Interviews and testing were carried out one day before the operation. A comparison of data from those women who were found by operation to have breast cancer and those who were not showed personality differences associated with the degree to which emotion was released. In particular, failure to release anger was found significantly more frequently among women with cancer than among controls. Similar results were reported by Geyer (1993), who studied thirty-three women with cancer, fifty-nine with benign tumour and twenty with gallstones. Using a life events scale, Geyer reports more severe life events for those women with cancer. Most particularly, he identifies events associated with loss as being more likely to be reported by women suffering from breast cancer than women in the other two groups. In the 'malignant' group the severest events were four times more likely than in the controls. Cooper et al. (1986) carried out a large-scale prospective study on 2163 patients attending breast-screening clinics. They report that women subsequently diagnosed as having cancer had suffered significantly more loss or illness-related events than controls. There are other studies however, including those of Greer et al., which have failed to find any relationship between loss events and the development of cancer.

There is stronger evidence that depression is linked with cancer. A meta-analysis by Herbert and Cohen demonstrated a link between stress and depression. Such stress could have been the result of negative life events. McGee et al. (1994) also carried out a meta-analysis, this time on seven longitudinal prospective studies of depression and cancer mortality and morbidity. These wide-scale and long-term epidemiological studies are helpful in assessing cancer risk. One such study is known as the Johns Hopkins Precursors Study (JHPS); this is an investigation of around 1300 medical students, the large majority of whom were male; they were initially assessed between 1948 and 1964; by 1979, fifty-five of them had developed cancer and they were compared with matched controls. Twenty-two per cent of those suffering from cancer had reported depressive feelings at the time of the first assessment, compared with only 7 per cent of the controls. A similar study of men working in Chicago known as the Western Electric Health Survey (WEHS) followed a group of men for twenty years and reported that 9.5 per cent of the depressed group had died of cancer compared with 5.3 per cent of the non-depressed group.

Thus there is some evidence that certain personality predispositions may influence the development of cancer. However, we need to be extremely cautious in interpreting these findings. There is, inevitably, an interaction between the kind of personality a person has and the kinds of events that happen to that person. The idea that the link is causal and in the direction predisposing personality – life events – cancer has not yet been shown.

Cancer remains one of the major challenges for health psychology. Psychologists can have an impact on this disease at all stages from examining and detailing the predisposing factors, by attempting to change damaging lifestyle habits, by encouraging protective behaviours and by helping those who suffer from the disease to cope with its consequences. The fact remains, however, that at this stage our knowledge and understanding is exceedingly patchy and more research needs to be done.

THE MEANINGS OF CANCER

Take a number of magazines and newspapers and analyse the articles about the prevention, detection or treatment of cancer.

How are people who have cancer portrayed?
Pay particular attention to the ways in which cancer is described, the metaphors and imagery used. What does this tell us about people's beliefs about the disease?
Are some cancers featured more frequently than others?
Is this in relation to their incidence? If not, what is it that causes particular cancers to be highlighted?

Key point summary

- Cancer is on the increase, largely due to the fact that we are living longer. Different cancers have different survival rates; many cancers can be detected early and treated easily.
- Beliefs about cancers can influence our behaviour. Smokers tend to hold different beliefs about the causes of lung cancer from non-smokers and ex-smokers.
- Screening and self-examination can be effective in detecting breast cancer, cervical cancer, testicular cancer and skin cancer at an early stage. Most of the predictors of the uptake of screening are psychological.
- Psychological factors are also important in helping people cope with the diagnosis of cancer and with its treatments. Many people use a coping style which emphasises their personal effectiveness in coping with the disease.

- Alternative therapies are popular, but have rarely been examined scientifically. Self-help books may play an important role in informing people about cancer, but can also convey potentially harmful messages.
- The quality of life (QOL) of people with cancer has become an increasing concern for health psychologists. Measures have been developed which seek to assess the various aspects of QOL and to track changes over time and with treatment.
- The link between certain personality types and a predisposition to cancer remains controversial. The evidence is strongest for a link between depression and a predisposition to cancer. However, much more work is needed to determine how this link is established, and what might influence this relationship.

Further reading

Austoker, J. (1995) *Cancer Prevention in Primary Care*. London: British Medical Journal Publishing Group. This book considers a variety of cancers and the role of the general practitioner in helping to prevent them. It is both authoritative and very readable.

Cooper, C. L. (ed.) (1984) *Psychosocial Stress and Cancer*. Chichester: Wiley. This contains a number of papers on the relationship between stress and cancer.

Pitts, M. (1996) *The Psychology of Preventive Health*. Routledge: London. This book has chapters which examine in more detail screening, psychoneuroimmunology, and lifestyle factors which impact on cancer, such as smoking and drinking.

Part four

Wider social issues

IN THIS FINAL SECTION we broaden our focus. The two chapters which comprise this section look beyond the individual perspective of much of health psychology. It is right that health psychology should consider the individual, and differences between individuals' health which result from differences in lifestyle, temperament, personality and other dimensions. However, in relation to health, it is important that psychologists recognise the importance of the social, political and economic circumstances in which we live. Chapter 15 locates our interest within the family, one of the most important contexts that has influence on our lives and health. The issues considered are relevant to many different aspects of health such as the effects of hospitalisation, the role of environmental factors in shaping children's health and the impact that a sick parent or child may have on family functioning. Aspects of protecting children from harm are considered and the effect of social policy on, for example, accident rates among children is stressed.

The final chapter seeks to consider issues of gender, race and class and how they impact on health. This concern with social variations and inequalities in health is a long-standing one, but one that has recently received increasing attention. Chapter 16 identifies the effects of poverty and deprivation on mortality and on morbidity. The focus is wider than just the UK however. We show that psychological variables often underpin health discrepancies both within and between countries.

Women and people from different ethnic groups have often been excluded from mainstream medical and psychological research. We consider the impact of those exclusions on what we know and understand of health variations due to gender or race. We also highlight recent attempts to redress this neglect, such as the Women's Health Initiative in the United States.

We show that psychology can impact not only on the health of individuals, but also on the health of different groups in society and thus on the health of nations.

Chapter 15

Child health, illness and family influences

Jacqueline Barnes
and Hartwin Sadowski

Introduction

Health psychology admirably illustrates the interdependence between biological and environmental influences on development and the potential to plan preventive work that incorporates both these models of human behaviour. Issues of child health provide a particularly focused view of this process since children's use of health services, child health status, and many causes of their mortality or morbidity can be attributed in part to the behaviour of other people (Schor, 1995). Many factors within the environment may have far-reaching effects upon a child's health. Similarities between parents' and children's health reflect familial, genetic predispositions; shared physical, social and emotional environments; and learned health beliefs and values (Schor, 1995). Preventive health services therefore may be presented in ways that take account of family difficulties and build on parental strengths.

An examination of the interaction between child and parent illness, family relationships and child outcomes can highlight the role of the family both as a source of stress and as a place where members can acquire coping skills and resilience (Pearlin and Turner, 1987). One of the challenges of health psychology is to indicate ways in which to empower families and children to increase their resources and cope with stress, while promoting optimal child mental and physical health (Patterson, 1995). In this chapter a number of ways in which the behaviour or circumstances of families interact with the health status of children will be reviewed, with particular attention to potential prevention strategies.

- First, characteristics of families relevant to infant health will be examined, looking in particular at how poverty and associated parental behaviours are thought to influence child outcomes.
- Second, social disadvantage and parental behaviour will be reviewed in relation to accidents in childhood.
- Third, the relationship between family factors and illness in childhood will be described by covering the issues of coping with medical procedures; family coping with chronic illness; and the relationship between family factors and child symptoms.
- Finally, the impact on child development and child mental health problems of parental mental and physical health problems will be discussed, demonstrating general principles using breast cancer and maternal depression as examples.

Theoretical frameworks

Throughout this chapter a multi-level theoretical framework for studying the relationship between family characteristics and child health will be used to link parenting behaviour and child health in an ecological model. Given that there may not be sufficient resources to conduct individualised preventive work with large numbers of at-risk families, there has been increased interest in promoting

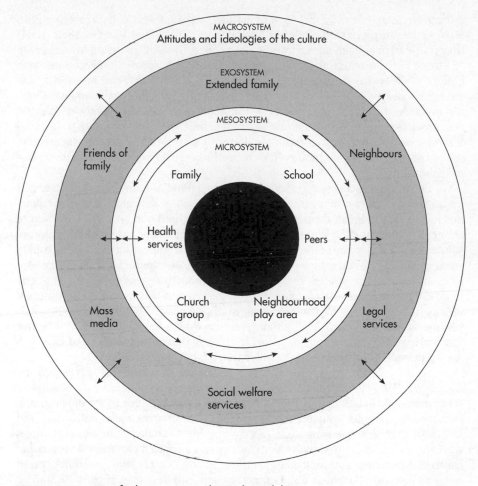

Figure 15.1 Bronfenbrenner's ecological model
Source: Garbarino (1982)

community level changes to improve child outcomes for the whole community (Connell *et al.*, 1995; Schorr, 1988; Wallerstein and Bernstein, 1994). Medical practitioners are increasingly being encouraged to think about child health in relation to the environment (Satterthwaite *et al.*, 1997). Bronfenbrenner (1979) integrates the influence of the family with the community using a model that takes account of child and parental characteristics and the impact of poverty on both the home and the broader environment (see Figure 15.1). Community characteristics, social support and the values or prejudices held in society may have important influences on children's health and well-being (Jencks and Mayer, 1990; Wilson, 1987).

The multi-level theoretical approach of Bronfenbrenner is useful for conceptualising interventions for specific problems (for example, a mother who smokes during pregnancy, a child with severe asthma, a parent who is depressed) within a larger health promotion model. It has been recommended (Green, 1983, 1986) that paediatricians take an environmental approach when assessing vulnerability to stress in the context of planning preventive or therapeutic interventions with children. Green has designed a 'Homeogram', a chart which can be used to list strengths and weaknesses of the child, the family and the environment. Thus, for instance, the child with severe asthma but a responsive family with good resources living in a town which has extra teachers available for home or hospital teaching may need to be treated quite differently from a milder case whose parents are divorced and whose mother has recently been depressed, living in a poor neighbourhood.

Social class is a concept which has been applied to many health issues, and its importance cannot be overemphasised. Social class indicators reveal inequalities in the rate of infant deaths (see Chapter 16), childhood accidents, take-up of services, extent of child illness and emotional problems of parents and children. While social class is one of the primary descriptors of families, an ecological framework can be used to investigate the processes that underlie social class differences in child health. The studies reviewed here demonstrate that poverty and social disadvantage interact with parental strengths or vulnerabilities and the community in which they live. For all families living in disadvantaged neighbourhoods, intervention at the structural level should be introduced in conjunction with other medical care, to improve housing, provide services that are accessible and effective, and to provide good-quality day care for those families who need it.

At the family level, the theoretical model of parenting developed by Baumrind (1967) is a useful way to conceptualise parent–child interactions in relation to child health (Schor, 1995). Baumrind described four styles of parenting: authoritative parents who are child-centred, accepting of child behaviour and responsive while at the same time demanding high standards; indulgent parents who are also child-centred but undemanding; authoritarian parents who are adult-centred, demanding and controlling; and neglecting parents who are adult-centred but low in control, making few demands upon children (see Figure 15.2). The authoritative style is likely to be the most beneficial during early childhood (Baumrind, 1967; Maccoby and Martin, 1983) although there is some debate about the relative advantages of authoritative and authoritarian parenting during adolescence, especially for children of minority groups who live in disadvantaged environments such as inner cities (Baumrind, 1990; Dornbusch *et al.*, 1987).

Using this model, some mothers faced with poor housing and social isolation may be overwhelmed with ways in which the circumstances affect themselves (adult-centred). They may become depressed, smoke heavily, or become critical and hostile to their children. Others, perhaps those who have a personal history with more secure attachment relationships, are able to reflect on their children's needs and behave in ways that will be more advantageous for their children's health. In Baumrind's terms they are able to be more child-centred. For vulnerable families, intervention needs to take into account their particular difficulties and to provide multiple levels of support in order that child health outcomes can be optimised. An understanding of parental characteristics and any child vulnerabilities is crucial, as the work on preparation of children for intrusive medical procedures indicates.

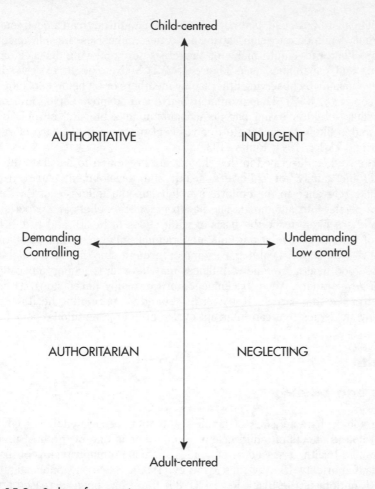

Figure 15.2 Styles of parenting
Source: Baumrind (1967)

Finally, another important aspect of the family is the way in which they cope with adversities. It has been increasingly recognised that coping strategies (or styles) play a crucial role in a family's physical and psychological health when a family member is confronted with acute or chronic illness, and the family environment has been identified as an important predictor of both parents' and children's adaptive coping (Kazak and Meadows, 1989; Sein *et al.*, 1988; Wallander *et al.*, 1989; Wertlieb, 1993). Lazarus and Folkman (1984) defined coping as 'constantly changing cognitive and behavioural efforts to manage specific external and/or internal demands that are appraised as taxing or exceeding of the person'. Coping behaviours are learned in the family context. Patterson's (1991, 1995) family adjustment and adaptation response (FAAR) model assumes that family adaptation occurs when the sources of stress (demands) and the mediators (capabilities) are balanced, but that families often go through an adjustment phase first, when demands outweigh capabilities. She emphasises the relevance of the meanings that the family make of the crisis for achieving balance between demands and capabilities (see Figure 15.3). Children begin to learn how to manage demands by observing other family members or by being explicitly taught (Patterson *et al.*, 1993). Thus promoting active and adaptive coping in caregivers can facilitate children's and parents' adaptation to acute and chronic physical illness and is likely to contribute to a resilient outcome in the face of adversity (Luthar and Zigler, 1991; Rutter, 1987).

The studies described in this chapter are presented to illustrate the importance of the family for children's health and development. Apart from the immediate relevance to the children's well-being, the influence of the family is likely to persist into adulthood. The health practices, beliefs and experiences of childhood are likely to be the basis of adult styles of health and health beliefs. Styles of parenting have strong inter-generational influences and ways in which parents risk their own health (for example, through smoking or alcohol abuse), promote good health, or cope with illness may have far-reaching implications for optimal development. Thus the influence of the family never stops, as children themselves become parents. It is a fertile ground for promoting health and there are many strategies that can interrupt cycles of inter-generational poor health.

Infant health

Social class and poverty

Demographic characteristics of families and their associated living conditions have profound effects on child health. Being poor is one of the best predictors of poor child health, assessed by outcomes such as prematurity, low birth weight and infant mortality (Botting and Crawley, 1995). Since the publication in the United Kingdom of the Black Report (1980) there has been increased attention to the relevance of disadvantage to child outcomes, looking at the influence of factors such as social class, family types (birth within marriage or not), maternal age, and parity (Townsend *et al.*, 1992).

Rates of low birth weight and infant mortality are significantly related to social class, as defined by paternal employment in two-parent families or by maternal employment (current or most recent) in single-parent homes. For example, figures for England and Wales for 1989 to 1990 show a difference of 100 grams between mean birth weights for social classes I and V (Power, 1995). This comparison of births within marriage underestimates the influences of social disadvantage in that it does not include the large number of vulnerable infants born to single, young, unsupported mothers. Low birth weight is more common for children of unmarried women (8.2 per cent) compared to children born to married women (5.9 per cent) and greater for children born to women under 20 years of age. For instance, the rate of low birth weight infants is 8.1 per cent for women aged 18–19 compared with 5.9 per cent for women aged 25–29 years and 6.3 per cent for those aged 30–34 (Power, 1995). Statistics for infant mortality are similar.

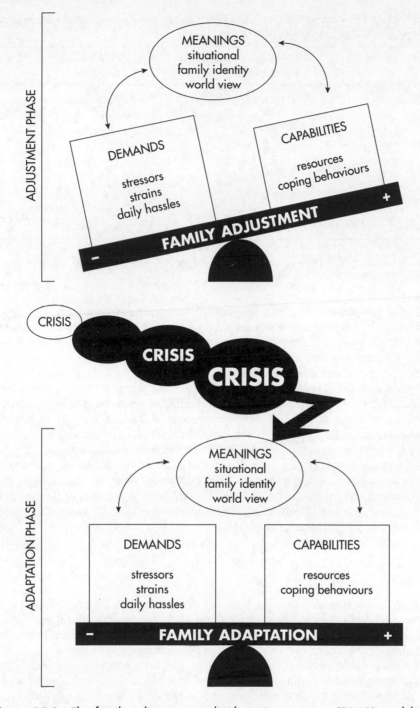

Figure 15.3 The family adjustment and adaptation response (FAAR) model
Source: Patterson (1995)

TABLE 15.1 Infant mortality by social class based on the father's and mother's occupation, 1986–1990 combined in England and Wales

Social class	Based on father's occupation	Based on mother's occupation
All stated	8.6	6.1
I	6.6	6.1
II	6.6	5.7
IIIN	7.5	5.7
IIIM	8.4	7.0
IV	10.5	7.0
V	13.1	10.8
Armed forces	7.8	6.3
Other	21.4	10.0
Not stated	*	9.9

Note: * No father's occupation means that no father's details were given at birth registration.

Source: *Population Trends* 74 (Winter 1993). Reported in Staples and Pharoah (1994), p. 550. Reproduced by kind permission of the BMJ Publishing Group.

At all ages, but particularly from 1 to 4 years, there is increased mortality with lower social class. In England and Wales the 1986 to 1990 infant mortality rate for social class V was twice that of the infants born in the most advantaged homes at 6.6 per 1000 live births in social class I compared with 13.1 for social class V, based on father's occupation (Staples and Pharoah, 1994; see also Table 15.1).

Occupational classification or classification as 'living in poverty' does not tell us about parental behaviour, but a great deal of attention has been paid to the effects of stress and to its concomitants such as smoking and use of alcohol as the explanatory factors in these class variations in infant health and well-being. There is a certain amount of debate. Some studies indicate that specific parental behaviours (such as smoking, poor diet, not breast-feeding, not taking up preventive services) have a direct impact on child outcomes, while others highlight the importance of environmental deprivation and problems at the level of the community (such as poor service provision, run-down housing, lack of transport to health care centres) (Botting and Crawley, 1995).

Smoking

Smoking is of particular interest because of the ways in which it appears to interact with both personal vulnerability and environmental disadvantage. There is substantial evidence that a significant minority of women continue to smoke throughout pregnancy. For example, a population study of more than 14,000 women giving birth between 1990 and 1991 in the Avon region of England found that 51 per cent of the women had smoked at some time in their lives, 25 per cent smoked during the first trimester, and 14 per cent smoked at least ten cigarettes a day throughout the pregnancy (Adam and Golding, 1996). Smoking during pregnancy is related to very early delivery (Peacock *et al.*, 1995), low birth weight

(Shu *et al.*, 1995), perinatal mortality, even relative to their reduced birth weight (Wilcox, 1993), and breathing problems (Toubas *et al.*, 1986). Clearly, from a public health perspective, in planning preventive interventions one needs to know whether the smoking itself, the associated poor living conditions, inadequate diet, a general rejection of advice on health behaviour, or other associated factors such as social isolation are the most important factors predicting child health outcomes.

Experts disagree about whether the chemicals produced by cigarette smoke are responsible for reduced foetal development, by constricting blood flow (Economides and Braithwaite, 1994), inadequate nutrition (Law *et al.*, 1993), alcohol intake, or psychological factors such as stress or social isolation which are associated with increased smoking behaviour. The diet of smokers is known to include less fruit, less meat and fish, more drinks such as tea, and more sugar in drinks (Power, 1995). In addition, smokers are more likely to live in poor socio-economic circumstances (Graham, 1993). Smoking during pregnancy is also a strong predictor of intention not to breast-feed (Barnes *et al.*, 1997; White *et al.*, 1990) which could have implications for infant health in the prenatal period, during infancy and in childhood (Lanting *et al.*, 1994; Lucas *et al.*, 1992; Pollock, 1994).

A study conducted in London attempted to evaluate the relative importance of smoking, alcohol, caffeine, socioeconomic factors and psychosocial stress on birth weight in a prospective study of 1513 women in an inner London borough (Brooke *et al.*, 1989). They found that psychosocial factors such as anxiety, depression, life events, social support and housing tenure, which had significant effects on birth weight, were not significant after controlling for maternal smoking. Not only was smoking identified as the most important factor, but its effect could not be accounted for by either alcohol or caffeine consumption, both higher in smokers. In fact, subsequent work showed that the effect of alcohol on birth weight was confined to the group of non-smokers (Peacock *et al.*, 1995). Thus the way in which maternal behaviour or circumstances influences child health prenatally and at birth are complex and multi-factorial.

Smoking behaviour may be a marker for ongoing maternal stress and anxiety. While there is a consensus that maternal mental state influences the foetus, the links between anxiety and infant health problems are not clear. Increase in life stress and prenatal anxiety in one sample of women was associated with increased likelihood of low birth weight and pre-term delivery (Wadhwa *et al.*, 1993), while for adolescents giving birth to their first child higher levels of cortisol and anxiety were linked with either pre- or post-mature birth, but were also related to positive indicators such as no meconium during labour, suggesting that a certain amount of anxiety is necessary for adequate perinatal outcomes (McCool *et al.*, 1994). Nevertheless, higher levels of maternal trait anxiety have also been associated with fewer foetal movements and more time in quiet sleep, which might pose risks to the foetus (Groome *et al.*, 1995).

Attitudes and expectations

The effects of prenatal maternal stress may trigger a chain of effects which, when associated with outcomes such as low birth weight, irritable or restless behaviour could elicit unfavourable attitudes from parents such as feelings of hostility and rejection, unresponsive maternal behaviour and insecure attachment (van den Boom, 1991, 1994). This is of particular importance since it has been shown that mothers-to-be are likely to form stable ideas about their child's behaviour before they give birth (McArney *et al.*, 1986; Wadsworth *et al.*, 1984). A recent study showed that there is substantial stability from the prenatal period to the first year of life in mothers' representations of their infants (Benoit *et al.*, 1997). These ideas also influence subsequent parent–child interactions. Expectant women completed temperament questionnaires at thirty-six weeks' gestation, with the instructions to imagine what their infant would be like (Zeanah *et al.*, 1987). Those mothers who imagined that their infants would be difficult to manage and unpredictable in their behaviour had children who were in fact at age four months less responsive during videotaped feeding sessions. Feeding problems and conflict during mealtimes have been found to predict growth problems and behavioural difficulties in early childhood (Stein *et al.*, 1994, 1996). Thus mothers' prenatal attitudes about their children could set in motion a sequence of developmental problems throughout childhood. Problems with feeding are the most directly relevant to future health and physical development, but the quality of interactions could be important for predicting the development of a mutually satisfying mother–child relationship, relevant to subsequent mental health.

Self-perceptions formed before having a child are also associated with the mother's subsequent feelings about her infant and her behaviour with her child (Belsky *et al.*, 1991; Smith and Pedersen, 1988) and with the infant–mother attachment relationship (Benoit *et al.*, 1997; Fonagy *et al.*, 1991). Infant characteristics such as persistence or goal directedness during play, alertness and skill in manipulation at twelve months could be predicted by a mother's self-confidence shown in responses to interview questions such as 'Can you picture yourself as a mother?' (Heinicke *et al.*, 1983). Self-perceptions, particularly those pertaining to parenthood, have been related to childhood experiences. Using the Adult Attachment Interview (George *et al.*, 1985) with a sample of 100 expectant mothers attending a London teaching hospital, ratings of the security of their attachment to their own mothers were significantly related to subsequent attachment behaviour (secure versus insecure) of their 1-year-old children (Fonagy *et al.*, 1991). This indicates strong inter-generational influences on child development identifiable prior to a child's birth. Consequently, women who have unresolved attachment issues with their mothers tend to be preoccupied with their own concerns, possibly at the expense of their children's needs. Problems with early working models of relationships will be particularly relevant when parents need to cope with multiple stresses, such as financial hardship, a child with health problems, or marital discord (Fonagy *et al.*, 1994). In these cases of multiple risk a multi-level strategy is called for. Universal interventions such as routine antenatal care and environmental changes such as housing improvement, transport provision, employment opportunities, or community social support networks need to be presented in combination with targeted work with women who have specific problems such as an eating disorder or early relationship difficulties.

Childhood accidents

Social class and poverty

Accidental injuries are the main cause of morbidity and mortality in childhood, leading the report *The Health of the Nation* (Department of Health, 1992) to identify the reduction of deaths from accidents as a national priority. There is a strong socioeconomic gradient for childhood injuries, one that is becoming steeper (Petridou *et al.*, 1994; Roberts and Power, 1996). For example, taking the 1979 to 1983 statistics, the injury death rate in England and Wales for children in social class V was 3.5 times that of children in social class I. While statistics for the period 1989 to 1992 show a general decline in deaths from injuries, the decline was greatest for children in social classes I and II (32 per cent and 37 per cent) and least in social class V (2 per cent). By 1992 the death rate for children in social class V was five times that in social class I (Roberts and Power, 1996; see also Table 15.2). Accidents have also been linked to lone parenthood, poor housing and social isolation (Roberts and Pless, 1995).

Differential accident rates are related to a number of factors including attitudes to protecting children from harm, parental educational level, inadequate housing and living conditions of poor families, or to variations in parental behaviour that can be associated with class differences (Power, 1992). The way in which poverty, lifestyle and behaviour interrelate to place children at greater or lesser risk is illustrated by investigations of childhood pedestrian injuries. An analysis of the National Child Development cohort, approximately 18,000 children born in England, Scotland and Wales during one week in 1958, showed that road traffic injuries in school age children were related to some individual characteristics (for example, fidgety behaviour) but environmental factors such as home overcrowding, family difficulties and being placed into care were more important (Pless *et al.*, 1989). The investigators concluded that the relative lack of risk associated with individual level child factors indicated that community-based environmental strategies, within the exosystem of Bronfenbrenner's (1979) model, were likely to be the most beneficial.

Roberts *et al.* (1996) similarly suggest that in many different countries pedestrian injury is a 'disease' of poverty. The exposure to risk which differentiates children in the social class groups was identified in their research as the explanatory factor in relation to child deaths from road accidents. They found in a New Zealand study that, after controlling for traffic volume and speed in their neighbourhoods, the risk of injury to children in families without a car was twice that of families with a car. Not only were the poor children more likely to walk to school and to cross more roads during the week which placed them at risk, but also, akin to the effects of secondary smoke, the greater use by affluent families of cars to transport their children to school contributed to that risk while at the same time protecting their own children from harm (Roberts *et al.*, 1996).

TABLE 15.2 Injury death rates per 100,000 children by social class and external cause, 1979–1983* (ages 1–15 years) and 1989–1992 (ages 0–15)

	Motor vehicle accidents†			Pedestrian accidents			Accidents caused by fire and flame		
	Rate per 100,000 (No)		% decline (95% confidence interval)‡	Rate per 100,000 (No)		% decline (95% confidence interval)‡	Rate per 100,000 (No)		% decline (95% confidence interval)‡
	1979–1983	1989–1992		1979–1983	1989–1992		1979–1983	1989–1992	
Social class									
I	11.3(65)	7.9(45)	30(−2 to 52)	6.1(35)	4.4(25)	28(−20 to 57)	1.2(7)	0.9(5)	28(−127 to 77)
II	12.5(280)	7.7(189)	39(26 to 49)	6.9(155)	3.5(85)	50(35 to 62)	1.0(22)	0.9(23)	5(−71 to 47)
IIIN	11.7(115)	8.8(79)	25(0 to 43)	6.1(60)	4.6(41)	25(−11 to 50)	0.9(9)	1.1(10)	−22(−200 to 51)
IIIM	17.2(594)	16.6(401)	4(−9 to 15)	11.5(398)	9.8(236)	15(1 to 28)	2.8(97)	2.4(59)	13(−20 to 37)
IV	20.4(297)	16.8(186)	18(1 to 31)	14.6(212)	9.6(106)	34(17 to 48)	4.1(60)	4.9(54)	−18(−71 to 18)
V	33.3(162)	32.9(118)	1(−25 to 22)	26.3(128)	22.3(80)	15(−12 to 36)	9.5(46)	13.1(47)	−39(−108 to −5)
P value for trend		P = 0.001			P = 0.055			P = 0.134	
Other	49.2(485)	19.8(373)	60(54 to 65)	31.7(312)	12.0(227)	62(55 to 68)	8.8(87)	6.4(115)	31(9 to 48)
Non-manual vs manual									
Non-manual	12.1(460)	8.0(313)	34(24 to 43)	6.6(250)	3.8(151)	42(28 to 52)	1.00(38)	0.96(38)	3(−52 to 38)
Manual	24.1(1538)	18.7(1078)	23(16 to 28)	16.5(1050)	11.3(649)	32(25 to 38)	4.55(290)	4.77(275)	−5(−24 to 11)

Notes: *Excludes 1981
† Includes pedestrian accidents
‡ Based on rates before rounding

Source: Roberts and Power (1996). Reproduced by kind permission of the BMJ Publishing Group.

Attitudes and behaviour

The relevance of social inequality does not necessarily imply, however, that psychological factors are irrelevant or that intervention could not take place with these in mind. Information on the rates of childhood accidents and deaths suggests that psychological factors are implicated, though it is difficult to distinguish between the contributions of children and parents. For example, Wright (1979) pointed out that in the USA one child in 500 is involved during the preschool years in a poisoning accident. The chances that a child would be involved a second time should also be one in 500, if accidents were random. However, the chance rises to one in four for a second poisoning. He suggests that since neither parental storage practices nor knowledge of toxicity seem to be related to the chance of an accident, it is likely that there are identifiable psychological characteristics of the families of repeat poisonings. For example, in a study of older children, it was found that, independent of the extent of behaviour problems exhibited by the youngsters, 15 and 16 year olds who had more conflict with their parents had more than twice as many injuries resulting in hospitalisation as the low conflict group (Bijur *et al.*, 1991).

There is disagreement about how to change parents' perceptions on the necessity for preventing illness or accident to their children. Kellmer Pringle (1980) emphasised parent education, reporting that more than 50 per cent of mothers thought their 5 year old could cross a main road safely without adult help. However, as mentioned earlier, poisonings and other pre-school accidents seem to be unrelated to parents' knowledge of toxicity or to their storage practices (Wright, 1979). Despite the relevance of parental characteristics it is more effective to intervene at an environmental level with practical changes rather than trying to change beliefs, since attitudes are notoriously difficult to alter. Intervention at an environmental level avoids the problem of which parents will respond if it is provided for everyone. Many recent examples can be identified, including the introduction of child-proof tops for many common household items such as aspirins or other medication, bleach and cleaning fluids. The rate of childhood ingestion of poisons has been reduced most dramatically in recent years following this marketing change (Cataldo *et al.*, 1986). Data on attempts to reduce child deaths in car accidents clearly illustrate the problems of changing parental behaviour. Young children are more likely to die as a result of injury resulting from a car accident, either as a passenger or pedestrian, than from serious illness or poisoning (Stylianos and Eichelberger, 1993). Parental motivation to adjust their habits seems to be lacking, in spite of knowledge of preventive methods. For example, in the 1980s a sample of parents in the USA reported knowledge of the protective capability of restraints but did not use them, giving a variety of reasons (for example, they will be able to grab the child in time if they are held on someone's lap; they only drive into town so there is no danger) (Faber, 1986). Social class was relevant, with more middle-class parents using child seats, but also the parents' behaviour in relation to their own safety was a factor. Most parents who used child seats also used seat-belts themselves and were concerned about other preventive measures such as visiting the dentist. Stylianos and

Eichelberger (1993) recommend a combination of legislation to enforce use of child seats with education about their benefits as the best way to bring about parental behaviour change to reduce childhood injury.

The complex relationship between parental attitudes and knowledge, their social and economic circumstances, and their actual child care practice is high-lighted by a recent parental survey administered by health visitors at the eight-month hearing test in five areas of Nottingham (Kendrick, 1994). Parents were asked about possession and perceptions of the importance of safety equip-ment. A sizeable proportion of families were found not to possess items of safety equipment thought to be appropriate for an eight-month-old child despite the fact that most items were perceived to be important. Perceptions of importance did not vary by sociodemographic variables but families on benefit, single-parent fami-lies, non-owner occupiers and families with only one child possessed significantly fewer items. This study indicates that, from an early stage in children's lives, there is considerable scope for educating parents about safety equipment. It also points to the importance of providing affordable safety equipment combined with support to encourage its use.

Environmental interventions

The problems of poor housing are emphasised by information on children in single-parent families, who have injury rates almost twice those of children in two-parent families, a difference which experts link with poverty, poor housing and social isolation rather than inept parenting behaviour (Roberts and Pless, 1995). Environmental change can be particularly effective for those living in poverty, as illustrated by the 'Children Can't Fly' intervention in New York City, for residents of high-rise flats. The installation of free window guard rails in a high-rise complex led to a 50 per cent reduction in children falling from windows within two years (Cataldo et al., 1986). Similarly, while childhood injuries and deaths can be significantly associated with the presence of an adult smoking ten or more cigarettes per day (Ballard et al., 1992), it is more effective to prevent childhood injury by promoting the use of smoke detectors than to attempt to change parental smoking behaviour (Stylianos and Eichelberger, 1993).

Another possible environmental, structural intervention to promote the health of young children is suggested by two recent studies in the United States which both found that pre-schoolers in out-of-home care had lower injury rates than children at home all day (Gunn et al., 1991; Rivara et al., 1989). While there may be developmental differences between children in day-care and those at home which account for differences in injury rates (Roberts, 1996), for children from disadvantaged homes this could be the most appropriate short-term intervention, in the context of improving the housing conditions and parenting practices of at-risk families.

The sick child

A number of studies have shown how psychological characteristics of the parents, and of the family, will influence the course of children's illnesses and their adaptation. Although most children with chronic illness and their families adapt to the associated stressors (Eiser, 1993; Garrison and McQuiston, 1989; Sein *et al.*, 1988), in general such children are at higher risk of being disabled by secondary social and psychological maladjustments than children without chronic physical illness (Cadman *et al.*, 1987; Rutter *et al.*, 1970; Wallander *et al.*, 1988). The outcome seems to be mediated by numerous familial and socioeconomic factors facilitating the child's adaptation to the disease process (Brown *et al.*, 1993). The burden of care, both practical and emotional, falls more heavily on mothers, and there has also been growing evidence that mothers of children with chronic illness suffer high levels of psychological stress (Engstroem, 1991; Goldberg *et al.*, 1990; Hausenstein, 1990).

Nevertheless, over the last decade it has been increasingly recognised that many children and parents successfully negotiate salient developmental tasks in spite of major stressors such as acute or chronic illness and possibly underlying emotional distress (Garmezy and Rutter, 1983; Luthar and Zigler, 1991; Rutter, 1987). The onset of serious illness in a child can bring into focus the dynamics within the family as they try to cope (Patterson, 1995). In this section we review ways in which family characteristics are implicated in coping with medical procedures, maintaining a prescribed treatment regimen, and in following the course of chronic illness, we highlight some of the adaptive coping used by families with a child with chronic illness.

Coping with medical procedures and hospitalisation

One of the key concerns of parents is the problem of helping children to accept intrusive and painful medical procedures, both to limit their suffering and to obtain the best medical outcome (Rudolph *et al.*, 1995). Chapter 4 discusses preparation for medical procedures and this discussion will focus on the role of the family as it relates to children's coping. Many hospitals routinely offer preparation for the family, frequently based on Escalona's emotional contagion hypothesis (Melamed, 1988). The central idea is that parental anxiety (usually maternal) is communicated to the child by non-verbal and verbal channels, leading to anxiety and nervousness in the child, which is likely to make him or her more distressed and less co-operative while in hospital. Visitainer and Wolfer (1975) developed a model of providing information to the child and the attending parent (usually the mother) together, explaining the role which the mother could take (for example, holding the child's hand and talking while a blood test was going on). The preparation focuses upon the mother's importance to the child and her control over him or her during the hospital visit. This has proved to be successful not only in gaining the child's co-operation during procedures but also in lowering parental anxiety.

Melamed and colleagues observed mothers and children in a paediatric outpatient clinic in a tertiary referral hospital (Bush *et al.*, 1986), measuring maternal responsiveness, use of distraction, providing information and child exploration and approach to mothers. When mothers made use of distraction, were informative on non-medical matters (for example read books or chatted about the toys) and attentive (i.e. unlikely to ignore child approaches), their children coped better and did not have separation problems. In contrast mothers who provided a lot of reassurance and talked about medical topics were likely to have children who displayed more distress, which could be displayed by either crying and running about or quiet withdrawal and unease. On the basis of this work it has been suggested that intervention in medical settings should focus principally on helping the mother (rather than the child) to cope, taking into account attachment issues and anxiety reduction (Melamed, 1988).

However, subsequent research concerning parental preparation is inconclusive. On one hand parental support enhances children's coping and adjustment (Siegel and Smith, 1989), but other studies have shown that children's distress in painful procedures such as bone marrow aspiration or lumbar punctures can be increased by parental involvement, specifically empathic comments, apologies to the child, reassurance, and criticism (Blount *et al.*, 1990). Explanations for these variable effects of parental behaviour have suggested that children's coping is influenced by pre-existing parental characteristics such as state anxiety, or child characteristics such as attachment status or temperament and the need for 'goodness of fit' is now recognised. Children with anxious mothers show greater anxiety in their parents' presence while children with low-fear mothers show more distress when their parents are absent (Fishman *et al.*, 1989; Jacobsen *et al.*, 1990). Lumley *et al.* (1993) studied pre-surgical waiting during anaesthesia induction and found that the result was determined by an interaction between parent and child. Maternal distraction and low information sharing led to more distress for children who had 'approaching' temperaments, the kind of child who is sociable and eager for new experiences. In contrast, children with 'avoidant' temperaments showed more distress when mothers did not distract but provided high levels of medical information about the procedure.

Thus it appears that children cope best when parents are child-centred in that they know their own child well enough to judge what balance of didactic or comforting behaviour would be the most effective. When, in Baumrind's terms, parents are adult-centred, concentrating upon their own distress, children will cope less well, though it is important to remember that many aspects of the child's characteristics will also have an impact on their coping behaviour (Rudolph *et al.*, 1995).

Families coping with children's chronic illness

Families of children and adolescents with newly diagnosed chronic illnesses are touched in many ways by these various illnesses (Patterson, 1995). Parents experience a range of emotions such as guilt, helplessness, anxiety, shame, anger or misery, all of which could influence child care practices. Mattsson (1972) proposed that children who cope most successfully have parents who have mastered feelings of guilt or fear and treat them as much like a healthy child as possible. Parental reactions might be particularly relevant in illnesses such as blood disorders which have a strong genetic component. In a recent study most parents with children suffering from Thalassaemia intermedia said that, in light of their experiences, they would opt for prenatal diagnosis and termination of affected pregnancies (Ratip et al., 1995). In various clinical studies a tendency to parental over-protection and over-indulgence was reported for families with Thalassaemic children (Ratip and Modell, 1996), although not for another genetic blood disorder, haemophilia (Bussing and Johnson, 1992). On one hand the results might reflect parental anxiety about a shortened life expectancy in Thalassaemia whereas modern treatment regimes ensure almost normal life expectancy for haemophilia. On the other hand the methodology used in studies of haemophilia is more rigorous and the difference between the groups may not be great. Other maladaptive outcomes of childhood illness have been reported such as powerful parental feelings of rejection or neglect, or excessive strictness, which are potentially more harmful than over-protection to the child's physical and mental well-being (Mattsson, 1972).

Coping with a child's chronic illness has not only implications for the management of the child's illness and the child's adjustment, but also for parental mental health. This is demonstrated in Thompson et al.'s study (1992) of thirty-five families with children with Duchenne Muscular Dystrophy. Parents who showed poor adjustment used more palliative coping methods (for example, avoidance, wishful thinking and self-blame), experienced lower levels of family support and had higher levels of family conflict than parents with good adjustment. Parental distress and use of palliative coping strategies were associated with emotional and behavioural disturbance in their children.

However, families can gain strength from facing the adversity of chronic childhood illness as they develop ways to cope more effectively, developing resilience and strength. Hauser and colleagues (1986) studied families with a diabetic child, comparing them with families where a child had an acute illness (for example, fractures, appendicitis, infections). The families were observed in a 'revealed differences' problem-solving task. They were given questionnaires concerned with typical parent–child dilemmas dealing with autonomy, privacy, honesty and support. Instances were found in which the mother and child agreed but the father did not and vice versa, and family members were asked to defend positions and finally to reach a consensus. Overall the mothers of the diabetic children were more 'enabling', explaining, attempting to clarify the other person's point of view and trying to come to agreement than the control mothers, while the fathers of diabetic children were slightly more judgemental than the control fathers. Hauser et al. suggest that the 'we'll fight it together' spirit of the mothers will be beneficial to parent–child relationships in diabetic adolescents, although they also mention the need to guard against moving from healthy and supportive involvement in the child's illness to 'enmeshed' over-protection.

Families who have a broad and diverse array of coping behaviours are more likely to meet individual and family needs and have good outcomes both in terms of physical and psychological health. Patterson et al. (1993) demonstrated that in families where parents scored higher on the use of three different coping strategies, children with cystic fibrosis had better pulmonary function tests over a ten-year period. The three coping strategies emphasised investing in and working together as a family, taking care of personal support needs, and getting consultation about the medical conditions from professionals.

Another area of adaptive coping is the change of perception of the life stresses imposed on the family by a chronic illness. Eiser *et al.* (1994) interviewed parents with children who had developed cancer. About half of the mothers reported that they 'value life more', and a quarter of the mothers had also become more assertive and prepared to speak their minds. About one-fifth of the fathers reported changes in their attitudes to others, particularly in their increased awareness of others with illness and disability. It seems that the formulation of positive meanings about the situation is highly adaptive (Patterson and Leonard, 1994). During interviews, coping parents with chronically ill children stressed the positive characteristics of their child (warmth, responsiveness and the ability to endure pain), of their other children (empathy and kindness), of themselves as parents (assertiveness skills in dealing with service providers), and of the family (greater closeness and commitment to each other from facing the challenge together).

Parental behaviour is important in predicting children's coping strategies. Gil *et al.* (1991) studied coping strategies in mothers and their children with sickle cell disease. Those mothers who rated themselves high on active coping attempts had children who reported significantly less negative thinking. Furthermore, mothers who reported less adaptive and passive coping strategies had children who showed a lower rate of school attendance and who had more contacts with health professionals. In another study of children with sickle cell disease (Sharpe *et al.*, 1994), mothers who reported more active strategies for coping with their child's pain were more likely to endorse greater use of techniques to prevent and effectively manage pain in their children. If families can demonstrate co-operation and mutual support they will cope more adaptively, preventing deterioration in the physical illness status and also secondary disabilities of psychological disturbance in their family members.

Child symptoms and family interactions

While the presence of a sick child within the family can precipitate effective parenting, the onset of child symptoms has been associated with parental disagreements or problems in parent–child relationships (Graham *et al.*, 1967) which in turn influence the illness outcome. Mrazek *et al.* (1991) examined prospectively the relationship between early parental behaviour and the later onset of asthma in a cohort of 150 children who were genetically at risk for developing asthma. The clinical judgement of 'early parenting difficulties' was based on concerns about some aspects of the ability of the parents to deal with the demands of their growing infant, based on an interview. About a quarter of fifty-two infants whose parents were judged to be having problems with parenting subsequently developed asthma, as compared with less than one-tenth of the infants whose parents were perceived as parenting their infant well.

Another dimension of parental behaviour is the expression of criticism and/or over-involvement as documented in 'expressed emotion' research (Vaughn and Leff, 1976). Schoebinger *et al.* (1993) interviewed mothers of twenty-eight children with bronchial asthma and twenty-three matched healthy children and found that half of the mothers of the asthmatic children showed a critical attitude towards their child as opposed to only three (13 per cent) mothers of healthy children. The mothers' critical attitude was significantly related to both frequency of asthma attacks and medication. Mothers of asthmatic children who made significantly more critical remarks had to make more effort to have their child comply with the medical requirements. Fathers' critical attitude status was not related to the severity of the child's asthma (Schoebinger *et al.*, 1992). Since the child's bronchial asthma is a chronic stressor for the parents as well, it may contribute to a negative attitude to the child. On the other hand, mothers' critical attitude can act as a chronic stressor and thus contribute to the recurrence of the asthma attacks.

The importance of the family environment in relation to illness severity was also demonstrated in children with atopic dermatitis (Gil *et al.*, 1987). The aim of the study was to see how stress and the family environment influenced indices of symptom severity (inflammation or the amount of antihistamine cream used). While stressful events such as moving house, a family member becoming ill or losing a job were not related to eczema symptoms, family relationships did predict severity. Six of the seven measures of symptom severity were significantly lower in children whose parents were said to be active and supportive with a similar, but less marked pattern for families who reported that they focused on independence and organisation. In contrast, children whose parents had a strong moral/ religious emphasis had significantly more symptoms. The authors suggest that the moral/religious families had strong views on what was right and wrong, believed in punishment and were rigid in their style of coping, relying heavily on medication. This could also be described as a demanding but adult-centred strategy, similar to Baumrind's (1967) authoritarian style.

The sick parent

Parental illness

In the same way that studies of pathological behaviour elucidate processes of normal development (Sroufe and Rutter, 1984), so the influence which the family might have upon child health and the possibilities for resilience can be highlighted by examining families in which a parent is ill. Epidemiological surveys suggest that having a parent with a physical illness is a marker for childhood psychiatric disorder and adjustment problems (Offord *et al.*, 1989). Much research has been carried out examining the influence of parental mental illness upon their children (Beardslee *et al.*, 1988, 1993; Keller *et al.*, 1986; Orvaschel *et al.*, 1988; Radke-Yarrow and Zahn-Waxler, 1990; Rutter and Quinton, 1984). Generally, children are most at risk when family interactions are disrupted and there is little communication about the illness (Lewis, 1990; Rosenfeld and Caplan, 1983) and particularly when children experience aggressive or hostile parenting, are the targets of parental delusions or are neglected for pathological reasons (Hirsch and Moos, 1985; Peters and Esses, 1985).

There is considerable overlap in the impact of parental physical illness and psychiatric illness because adults with chronic medical conditions have a high likelihood of suffering from a concurrent psychiatric disorder (Wells *et al.*, 1988). For instance, children whose parents had Huntingdon's Disease were found to be more likely to suffer from affective disorders if the ill parent also had similar symptoms (Folstein *et al.*, 1983). The importance of family relationships was also indicated by this study. The major influence on child outcomes, a greater likelihood of conduct disorder, sometimes continuing into adulthood as antisocial personality disorder, was social disorganisation in the family, where the remaining partner could not maintain effective discipline. The adjustments of families to a physically disabled parent have also identified family relationships as key predictors of child outcomes (Peters and Esses, 1985).

Certain parental conditions are of particular interest because they are widespread (for example, cancer, depression) and these selected illnesses will be discussed to illustrate the impact which family health difficulty can have on the health and mental status of children.

Breast cancer

Some researchers have concluded that parental cancer, with the threat of death, contributes to enhanced intimacy between family members and promotes family activities (Cooper, 1984; Lewis *et al.*, 1985). Nevertheless, retrospective interviews with adults who experienced maternal cancer as children indicate that long-lasting feelings of anxiety and anger sometimes exist. These are often related to poor communication within the family, and secrecy, which could have been inadvertently enhanced by the tendency for medical staff to treat their patients' children as tangential (Northouse, 1988). Thus, children of cancer patients are now recognised as a hidden, high-risk group whose problems may be minimised by overwhelmed parents, but who may suffer long-term changes in cognitive performance, personality attributes and self-esteem (Holland and Rowland, 1990). Breast cancer affects up to one in twelve women in the United Kingdom and often occurs during child-rearing years. As with other life-threatening illnesses and chronic health conditions it is associated with anxiety, depression and other emotional difficulties (Fallowfield *et al.*, 1994a; Maguire, 1994), all of which can impair parenting and place children at risk for problems. Apart from the effect of parental mental health, there is good evidence that diseases such as breast cancer may adversely affect the psychological health of the children, whether or not the disease proves fatal (Lichtman *et al.*, 1984; Nelson *et al.*, 1994).

The age of the child appears to influence the kinds of problems that develop, or the chances for good coping behaviour. Lewis and colleagues (1985) conducted a longitudinal study of 126 families whose mothers had non-mestatic breast cancer. The young children (aged 7–10) commonly reported feelings of sadness, fear and loneliness, and at times anger about what had happened to their mother, while the 10–13 year olds expressed preoccupation with their own lives. The adolescent group (14–18) however experienced the most problems, with conflict between autonomy and attachment to their mother. The child's gender is also relevant in that daughters have more problems than sons in their relationship with their mother (Lichtman *et al.*, 1984). It has been suggested that long-term problems such as depression are more likely if communication within the family about the mother's illness has been poor, with secrecy and collusion (Lichtman *et al.*, 1984; Rosenfeld and Caplan, 1983).

However, not all studies have concluded that a poor outcome is necessarily associated with maternal illness. Howes *et al.* (1994) found that levels of behaviour problems in a group of children whose mothers had recently been diagnosed as having breast cancer were no different from the general population. Contrary to what one might predict, children whose mothers were less seriously ill had more psychosocial problems than children whose mothers had serious complications. The authors suggest that in the face of their mother's serious conditions these children might have been 'over-coping' and trying hard to be 'good'. However, if their mothers described becoming depressed, children were not as successful at coping and exhibited more behavioural and emotional problems. Howes *et al.* (1994) and others (Nelson *et al.*, 1994) have noted the importance of support from sources outside the family such as the school and peer friendships in preventing children from experiencing problems such as depression.

The available evidence is inconclusive about the effects of maternal breast cancer on child outcomes. Several studies are of small samples, and many have obtained information exclusively from the mother, using instruments that may be insensitive to children's problems and with insufficient follow-up. While it has been suggested that many children have a swift return to 'normal', even after experiencing prolonged illness and the death of a parent from cancer (Siegel *et al.*, 1996), short-term positive adjustment to the diagnosis of illness can mask problems later in childhood or in adulthood and the impact of parental cancer may be quite different if the illness is not terminal. The nature of available social support and communication within the family following terminal maternal illness have been identified as key to predicting long-term outcomes (Harris *et al.*, 1986; Silverman and Worden, 1992) but there is less information about how children cope in families where the mother is seriously but not terminally ill. The studies described above highlight the complex aspects of family life that relate to coping and better outcome. In particular, improving family communication about the illness and its meaning for family members could improve children's ability to cope and avoid long-term emotional problems (Rosenheim and Reicher, 1985).

Depression

Depression and other affective disorders are public health problems of major proportions, with estimates ranging from 10–20 per cent of the population at risk for the lifetime occurrence of an affective disorder. Depression is the most widespread mental health problem experienced by mothers of young children and several studies have shown that children with depressed mothers have an

increased likelihood of experiencing emotional and behavioural disturbance themselves (Downey and Coyne, 1990; Ghodsian *et al.*, 1984; Hammen, *et al.*, 1987;
Richman *et al.*, 1982).

The situation is clearly complex and a number of explanations of child problems are possible. There is a genetic component to affective disorders (Tsuang
and Faraone, 1990) and environmentally the same stresses which undoubtedly
contribute to the mother's feelings of depression might be influencing the child,
the child might be influencing the mother, or vice versa. While all these possibilities might be operating together, recent work has highlighted the importance
of the quality of the relationship between mother and child to the child's well-
being. Nevertheless, the relationship between family interactions and children's
emotional problems is not necessarily explained by a straightforward exposure
to depressive symptoms (Cox, 1988). The best model for understanding the influence of parental affective disorder on poor child outcomes is that parental affective
disorder is a marker indicating a number of other associated family risk factors.

The psychosocial mechanism of influence appears to be concentrated in
two aspects of family functioning: marital discord within the home, and interference with parenting practices (Downey and Coyne, 1990; Fendrich *et al.*, 1990;
Rutter, 1989). There is substantial evidence of higher rates of divorce and of
marital discord in families in which one parent is depressed (Downey and Coyne,
1990). There is also considerable evidence of interference with parenting practices
across the life span in depressed parents. For instance, depressed mothers of
infants tend to be less responsive and to show more sustained negative affect
than non-depressed women (Field *et al.*, 1990; Murray *et al.*, 1993). Depressed
mothers of older children have been observed to use more verbal aggression,
criticism and negativism (Cohn *et al.*, 1990) and more physical aggression
(Zuravin, 1988). Depressed mothers tend to be less effective than non-depressed
mothers at disciplining and setting limits with their children (Goodman and
Brumley, 1990) and are less able to resolve conflicts (Kochanska *et al.*, 1987)
and feel more helpless in the belief that their children's development was determined by uncontrollable factors (Kochanska *et al.*, 1987).

Observations of interactions with young children (Mills *et al.*, 1985) have
shown that depressed mothers were less likely to respond appropriately to their
child's comments or actions than non-depressed women. Depressed mothers
with older children, aged between 8 and 16, in a family discussion about a topic
of disagreement, were more critical and negative to their children than non-
depressed mothers (Gordon *et al.*, 1988). They were also less likely to stay on
task and made fewer positive confirming statements. This style of interacting may
also be associated with ignoring symptoms of child illness such as fussiness,
lethargy or loss of appetite, or by accusing them of malingering, possibly putting
the child at risk of developing complications. Thus, children of depressed mothers
are at risk for both emotional and physical well-being.

The influence of parental depression on child problems is also related to
the chronicity and severity of a parent's depressive illness (Keller *et al.*, 1986).
A study looking at a range of child behaviour including adaptive skills, rated by
teachers, peers and parents, and cognitive ability, found that child functioning
was related to the length of time their parent had been depressed and the degree

of recovery (Harder and Greenwald, 1992). Caplan *et al.* (1989) found that children's behavioural difficulties at age 4 were related to marital discord and current maternal depression, but not to post-natal depression.

The influence of maternal depression on child development thus represents a complex interaction between individual vulnerability (including a genetic predisposition), problems with dyadic parent–child relationships, and the wider context of the parental relationship and the family's social networks in the community. In addition, the mother's mental state could reduce the availability of social support networks. There is also a developmental component to consider. In early childhood the lack of mutual responsiveness can be particularly detrimental to early language development (Cox, 1988; Mills *et al.*, 1985) while the expression of hostility and use of coercive, parent-centred control leads to increased conduct problems in older children (Panaccione and Wahler, 1986). Nevertheless, there are some innovative interventions being developed that highlight the importance of communication within families about parental illness. When children are given information about depressive illness and provided with the opportunity to talk about their parents' depression, expressing ideas about how it relates to their own behaviour, family discord is reduced and there is more open discussion (Beardslee *et al.*, 1992, 1993). In accordance with Patterson's (1995) model of coping, helping children to attribute personal meaning to parental illness is expected to be protective for them and to offer a long-term style of dealing with family problems in that communication between parents and children, and between siblings about parental illness is enhanced.

Key point summary

- The marked social class differences in child health indicators such as infant morbidity and deaths from accidents can be explained in part by the environmental stresses associated with economic disadvantage. These environmental factors in turn influence parental mental health and coping behaviour.
- Attitudes held by mothers about themselves or their infants prior to birth influence child development and are influenced by their own experiences of parenting. However, it may be more effective to use prevention methods designed to improve the environment and reduce risk than attempting to change mothers' perceptions.
- Intervention for at-risk groups such as pregnant teenagers are likely to be more effective if they are designed to boost maternal self-confidence and provide a positive image of their infants rather than attempting overtly to reduce behaviour such as smoking.
- The fit between parents' and children's attitudes and style of coping with stress and anxiety is the most important factor which medical and support personnel should take into account when thinking about how to help families and children cope with intrusive medical procedures or hospital visits.
- Families are less able to cope with chronic childhood illness if they experience guilt or self-blame and if there is discord between parents. Families

are better able to cope when parents can attribute some positive meaning to the illness.

- Parenting ability and child–parent interactions can influence the onset and severity of a chronic childhood illness and its impact on the child's emotional development. Emotional disturbance once developed can hinder subsequent compliance with treatment and subsequent illness outcomes.

- Maternal physical or mental illness does not necessarily affect children's emotional and behavioural development. Rather, the associated marital discord, ineffective discipline, criticism and hostility, or lack of responsivity to children's needs increases the likelihood of emotional or behavioural disturbance.

- Children cope more effectively with physical or mental illness of a parent if there is good communication within the family or if they have social support from peers or other adults. Long-term outcomes are influenced by factors such as ongoing parental emotional problems and the nature of care giving.

- Children can cope more effectively with parental physical or psychiatric illness if they can understand the meaning that the illness has for them personally. This can be facilitated through good communication between parents and children.

Further reading

Botting, B. (ed.) (1995) *The Health of Our Children*. Decennial Supplement. Office of Population Censuses and Surveys. Series DS no. 11. London: HMSO. This volume contains a number of useful papers that summarise historical trends and the latest national statistics on a range of child and family health issues including infant mortality and low birth weight, and health related behaviours such as breast-feeding, exercise, smoking and alcohol consumption. Useful models are presented for understanding the complexity of biological and behavioural factors that influence a number of child health outcomes.

Eiser, C. (1993) *Growing up with a Chronic Disease. The Impact on Children and their Families.* London: Jessica Kingsley Publishers. This book gives an excellent overview about the impact of and adjustment to chronic illness of the whole family at different developmental stages of children. Eiser reviews not only the research into family coping with chronic illness, but also the effects on the relationships between parents, parent and child, and between siblings.

Krasegor, N. A., Arasteh J. D. and Cataldo, M. F. (eds) (1986) *Child Health Behavior. A Behavioral Pediatrics Perspective.* New York: John Wiley. This collection of papers provides a useful introduction to the growing partnership between paediatrics and developmental psychology. It includes a section on prevention which is particularly relevant.

Schor, E. L. (1995) The influence of families on child health. *Pediatric Clinics of North America*, 42 (1), 89–102. This review, written with a practical orientation for paediatricians, reviews family effects on health and health behaviours such as exercise, eating problems or smoking, the impact of poverty, and the possible effects of family factors such as unsupported working mothers, teenage parenthood and parental learning disabilities.

PREVENTION STRATEGIES TO IMPROVE CHILD PHYSICAL HEALTH, EMOTIONAL AND BEHAVIOURAL DEVELOPMENT

Prevention of child health problems can be approached at a number of different levels. Primary (sometimes called universal) prevention seeks to decrease the number of new cases of a disorder or illness and the method of prevention is given to a whole population, a good example being immunisations for infectious diseases. Secondary (selective) prevention aims to lower the rate of established cases by providing an intervention for at-risk groups. The intervention may not be desirable, either because of cost or perhaps associated risks such as stigma, unless there is a belief that the benefits would outweigh any risks. An example is offering home visiting to pregnant, low-income teenagers to improve their antenatal care and health-related behaviour. This can improve health outcomes for their infants, lessen the chances of them becoming isolated and depressed once their infants are born, and even reduce the possibility of child abuse occurring. Tertiary prevention is given once an illness or other problem has been experienced, to prevent its recurrence or to prevent other problems from emerging. An example is family therapy for children and parents after a serious illness in the family, to reduce the likelihood of emotional and behavioural problems developing in the children. The information in this chapter is designed to help you think about prevention at all these levels, and to integrate ideas about using an understanding of risk factors in health promotion within an ecological model of child health that highlights the development of coping strategies.

1   Using the information that you have about social class differences in child health, what advice would you give to a community health project that wanted to reduce infant mortality and low birth weight in a disadvantaged urban neighbourhood?

2   You have been asked to join the committee giving advice to a support group for parents of children with asthma. What prevention programmes would you develop for them?

3   If you were asked by a local hospital in a rural area to design a programme for children whose parents had experienced serious, chronic physical illness, what would your recommendations be?

Chapter 16

Social circumstances, inequalities and health

Marian Pitts and Keith Phillips

Introduction

Much of the research reported in earlier chapters has focused upon individual differences and how they impact on health and health behaviours. Clearly such a focus is appropriate for a book concerned with the psychology of health. However, it is essential that health psychologists are aware of the effects of broader demographic, geographic and social influences upon health.

Health can be defined in many ways: either positively, where it is characterised by the presence of particular qualities such as physical and mental fitness, or negatively, where health is regarded as a state in which fitness is absent. We should return here to the definition of health offered by the World Health Organization (WHO, 1946) as 'a state of complete physical, mental and social well-being and not merely the absence of disease and infirmity'. This holistic definition clearly recognises the importance of the 'social' as well as the individual dimensions of health.

Much of the research in this area has been carried out by epidemiologists and medical sociologists but there is much too that is the concern of health psychologists. This chapter reviews inequalities in health under three headings: variations related to socioeconomic status, to gender differences, and to ethnic and racial differences, and finally consideration is given to some psychological mechanisms by which the observed variations in health may be related to these structural variables.

Social class differences in health and illness

Social class differences in health and illness in Britain have been recognised since statistics upon mortality were first collected. Macintyre (1997) has outlined the historical background, noting that by the second half of the nineteenth century, records showed that poorer sections of the population had poorer health and died earlier. She refers to a report by Edward Chadwick in 1842 that showed that in Liverpool at that time, the average age of death for the 'gentry' was 35 years, and for 'labourers, mechanics and servants' 15 years. Since then there have been changes in the major causes of death. In Britain in 1840 the major causes were infectious diseases; now they are the lifestyle diseases reviewed in earlier chapters: heart disease, stroke and cancers. Life expectancy for men and women is now much greater; men can expect to live on average to age 74 and women 77 years. Yet, the death rate for men is greater than that of women at every age group from birth onwards.

Of course, the patterns as well as the causes of mortality have changed; in 1840, infant mortality was extremely high and this was a major contributor to the statistical value of low overall life expectancy (Macintyre, 1997). However, class differences existed here too. By 1913, the Registrar General was concerned about class differences and suggested that 'at least 40% of the present infant mortality of this country could be avoided if the health conditions of infant life in general could be approximated to those met within class 1' (cited in Macintyre, 1997).

During the twentieth century infant death rates have fallen but the decline for classes I and II has been greater than for others. Titmuss (1943) concluded that the gradient of inequality had not lessened but rather had increased in comparison with the end of the nineteenth century. Concern with class differences continued through the middle part of this century and in 1977 the government commissioned a report upon differences in health status between classes from Sir Douglas Black. His report (Black Report, 1980) made use of the Registrar General's classification of social class which allocates individuals to one of six occupational groups:

- Professional   (social class I)
- Managerial and lower professional   (social class II)
- Skilled non-manual   (social class IIIN)
- Skilled manual   (social class IIIM)
- Partly skilled   (social class IV)
- Unskilled   (social class V)

The committee found, as had others previously, that not only were there striking differences in mortality rates (the most conclusive indicator of ill health!) between classes, but that the differences existed at all ages. This is strikingly shown, for example, by the statistics on infant death rates in Figure 16.1.

Worryingly, such differences are increasing rather than the reverse (Blaxter, 1987). It was further found that the utilisation of health care resources showed parallel variations, with the lower social classes accessing health care services to a lesser extent than the higher social classes. The recommendations of the Black Report (1980) for health policy and research were many, but it was its description of the inequalities in health that captured attention. As Macintyre has pointed out, the acrimony of the debates within Britain have surprised observers from other countries who are less aware of the nature of class differences that continue to exist in Britain today. When Sir Douglas Black reported, there were attempts to explain away the gradients in health as the outcome of some Darwinian process of natural selection where the sick get poorer, or by the 'poor' bringing ill health upon themselves by taking irresponsible actions towards their health. When the Black Report was published the Secretary of State for Health's foreword dismissed any suggestion that inequalities could be remedied, adding, 'I must make it clear that additional expenditure on the scale which could result from the report's recommendations ... is quite unrealistic in the present or any foreseeable economic circumstances.' Thus the problem was regarded as an irreversible fact of life.

Social class differences in health remain. In 1991 mortality in men was three times higher in social class V than in social class I. Indeed in the years since the Black Report, social class differences in mortality have increased. This has been recognised by a national research programme funded via the government through the Economic and Social Research Council (ESRC Health Variations Programme), which aims to identify the social factors that underlie class differences in health and to develop policies to reduce them. Similar programmes have been introduced in other countries including Sweden and the Netherlands.

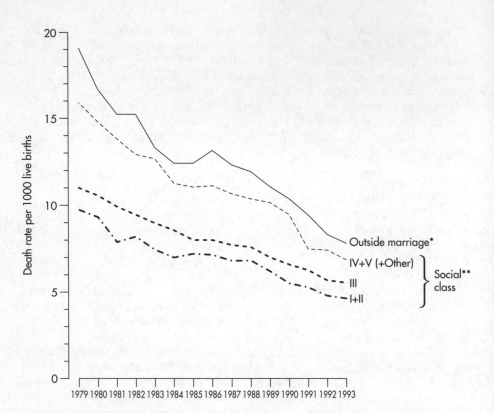

Figure 16.1 Infant death rates by social class in England and Wales, 1979–1993

Notes: * Data include births which were jointly registered by both parents
** Social class based on father's occupation (at death registration) for births inside marriage

Source: *OPCS Mortality Statistics* – perinatal and infant: social and biological factors

In 1995 as part of the UK Health of the Nation programme, a report was published called 'Variations in health: What can the Department of Health and the NHS do?' This drew together the findings from a number of important studies such as those of three national birth cohorts born in 1946, 1958 and 1970 and from other surveys including the national Health and Lifestyle Survey conducted in England, Scotland and Wales during 1984/85 (Cox *et al.*, 1987). The report considers the magnitude of variations in health and the evidence suggesting that differentials in mortality and morbidity rates are increasing between different socioeconomic groups, between men and women, and between regions of the country and different ethnic groups. Considering occupational class differences first, the report shows that (DHSS, 1995, p. 9):

- Life expectancy at birth is currently around seven years higher in the Registrar General's social class I than in social class V;

- Children in social class V are four times more likely to suffer accidental death than their peers in social class I;
- Of the sixty-six major causes of death in men, sixty-two were more common among those in social classes IV and V combined than in other social classes;
- Of the seventy major causes of death in women, sixty-four were more common in women married to men in social classes IV and V;
- Women in social class I have a registered incidence of breast cancer 1.5 times higher than women in social class V.

Several kinds of explanation for these observed variations were put forward, including:

- artefacts of measurement
- access to and use of health services
- exposure to different environmental conditions including working and living environments
- health-related behaviours
- health-related mobility
- biological (including genetic) factors
- psychosocial factors including stress.

Considering each of these explanations in turn, we find that the report concluded that while different measures of socioeconomic status or health might change the picture slightly they do not appreciably change the significant patterns. Differential use of health services may contribute to variations in health and longevity. In Britain, access to health services is free at the point of delivery. However, there are barriers to services arising from geographical location, or times of services, or for some ethnic minorities language difficulties, all of which make it difficult for some people to gain equitable access to services (White *et al.*, 1996). Having gained access to services, there is evidence that patients of higher socioeconomic status are more likely to have investigations and less likely to receive prescriptions than those of lower socioeconomic status (Scott *et al.*, 1996).

Whilst living and working conditions are important, the birth cohort studies have shown that they have only minor influence when considered independently of economic circumstances.

It has been suggested that poor physical or mental health might lead to social disadvantage through unemployment and poverty and hence to downward mobility, but the report concluded that this could not account for the broad pattern of inequalities. Recently, health behaviour explanations have been favoured. Different patterns of smoking, drinking, diet and use of preventive services have been noted between social classes and it has been suggested that these account for why and where ill health exists. However, evidence from studies such as that of Rose and Marmot (1981) shows that risk factors such as these account for only one third of the social gradient in coronary heart disease and morbidity. This is discussed in more detail below.

A similar argument can be made for genetic and biological differences. There seems to be a genetic predisposition for men and for people from the Indian subcontinent to develop coronary heart disease, but such predispositions are not fixed and interrelate with social circumstances to translate into risk. The finding that migrants between countries come to take on the risk characteristics of the country to which they migrate suggests that the role of genetic factors is only minor (Marmot *et al.*, 1975).

Finally, there has been much recent research into the role of psychosocial factors in influencing variations in health and these are reviewed in some detail below.

The Whitehall studies

Two major epidemiological studies have been undertaken which examine the lifestyles, social and economic circumstances, and health status of people working within the British Civil Service in Whitehall, London. Twenty years separate the two studies, but both Whitehall I and Whitehall II (Marmot *et al.*, 1991) showed that large socioeconomic differences in health persist. Using Civil Service grades as the basis of the analysis, they found grade differences in a number of health behaviours. For example, smoking is more common in the lower grades and is associated with a number of specific causes of death. However, when smoking as a factor is controlled for, there remains a steep gradient of mortality for diseases not related to smoking, even among non-smokers (Marmot *et al.*, 1984). Whitehall II found different attitudes to health between the grades; more people in the lower grades believed that they could not take preventive measures to reduce their risk of heart attack (Marmot *et al.*, 1991).

Elements of the work environment seem to play an important part in these grade differences. Low grade workers reported less control, less variety in the work and less use of their skills. The link between these aspects of work and health has been explored earlier (see Chapter 11). No differences were perceived between the grades in Type A behaviour pattern, but hostility was found to be higher in the lower grades. Job security also seems to be important; Ferrie *et al.* (1995) reported that increasing levels of job insecurity were associated with increasing deterioration in health status, and loss of employment is associated with higher morbidity and mortality (Morris *et al.*, 1994).

The amount of disposable income available to a person is another measure that may contribute to an explanation of social class differences. Davey-Smith *et al.* (1990) examined car ownership as part of the Whitehall study and found that both occupational status and car ownership were independently related to mortality. Of course this does not mean that owning a car protects a person against health threats, but indicates that possessing a reasonable level of disposable income (sufficient to purchase a car) is positively related to longevity.

The Whitehall studies were carried out among men, but the pattern of findings is not restricted to men. Similar social class differences have been found amongst women too. For example, the General Household Survey (OPCS, 1986) found that women in social class I reported an average of eighteen days per year where activity was restricted, compared to forty-three days per year for women in social class V (OPCS, 1986).

What the Whitehall studies suggest is that differences in social grading are important as a *psychological variable* as a predictor of life circumstances. Both Whitehall I and Whitehall II showed that men in the lower grades were more likely to report financial difficulties, inadequate social support and stressful life events (Marmot *et al.*, 1991). This idea that social differences may in fact have a psychological basis has been developed by the work of Richard Wilkinson which makes comparisons between income distribution and health in different countries (Wilkinson, 1996).

Differences between countries

Wilkinson's work has charted the differences in health that exist within and between countries examining the relationship between income distribution and life expectancy (the absolute measure of health!). Bringing together a number of strands of evidence, he concludes that the scale of income differences within societies underlie the different life expectancies found in different countries. In Britain during the Second World War, people were healthier and there was an increase in life expectancy of 7 per cent. Wilkinson suggests that this is linked to the narrowing of income differentials and the shared burden of the 'war effort'. Looking at current evidence, he suggests that health, and in particular, mortality, is more responsive to changes in income amongst the least well-off. He contrasts the situations in Britain and Japan: in 1970 these two countries had similar income distributions and similar life expectancies. By 1992, Japan had the highest life expectancy in the world, whilst Britain's had hardly changed. In explaining this shift, Wilkinson points out that Japan has the most egalitarian distribution of income of any country whilst in Britain since the mid-1980s, income distribution has widened and during this period mortality amongst men and women aged between 15 and 44 years has actually increased. In terms of class effects, mortality has fallen most rapidly amongst the higher social classes in Britain and amongst the lower social classes in Japan.

A further thread of evidence comes from the fate of Hungary. During the Soviet occupation of Hungary, its people had one of the highest life expectancies in the world. Since independence, life expectancy has actually fallen and the death rate has risen from eleven per thousand to fourteen per thousand. Wilkinson argues that the strong social cohesion which was a feature of the country during its occupation has been replaced by individualistic goals that have become entrenched as income distribution has widened within the new market economy.

Thus, Wilkinson concludes that health is determined less by people's absolute standard of living than by their standard *relative* to others in their society. He summarises thus:

> National average death rates are so strongly influenced by the size of the gap between rich and poor in each society that differences seem to be

the most important explanation of why average life expectancy differs from one developed country to another.

(Wilkinson, 1996, p. 25)

The relationship between equality of income distribution and health has been examined in two recent studies in the United States. Kaplan *et al.* (1996) found a significant correlation between the proportion of well-off households and variations in death rates. Income inequality was also associated with a large number of other health outcomes including the proportion of live births, the proportion of sedentary people, of smokers and of disability. In another study Kennedy *et al.* (1996) used the aptly named Robin Hood Index to determine the degree of inequality in income distribution in each US state. They also found that there was a positive correlation between the score of a state on the index and several causes of mortality, independent of poverty and of smoking. In other words it was the *size of the gap* between rich and poor, as distinct from the absolute standard of living experienced by the poor that was related to mortality.

The significance of these findings upon income distribution for the psychology of health should be apparent. People need the basics to survive, but they have other needs to flourish. Psychology can identify these other needs but they include dimensions of social support, and perhaps feelings of belonging and being valued within a society.

Regional inequalities in health

A further factor influencing health in England and Wales is the region in which a person lives. Not only is it the case that there are variations between different parts of the country, with the South having lower mortality than the North, but it is also true that the extent of inequalities between social classes I and V are greater in the North than in the South. The differential between the North and the South also exists in terms of morbidity for many illnesses, acute and chronic, including heart disease, bronchitis and rheumatism (Cox *et al.*, 1987; and see Figure 16.2). Moreover, health differences can exist within relatively small geographical regions. For example, in the London boroughs of Camden and Islington, eight of the forty-six borough wards have mortality rates below the national average. You will not be surprised that these wards are the most affluent and include Hampstead, Belsize Park and Swiss Cottage. The more economically deprived wards of Kings Cross and Bloomsbury suffer significantly higher rates of mortality. Thus mortality as a measure of well-being shows variations that reflect local, national and international conditions.

Women's health

It might be asked: Why focus on women's health and not on men's? We will show in this section that women not only have particular needs, they have also suffered neglect in health research and in health psychology. Recent books on

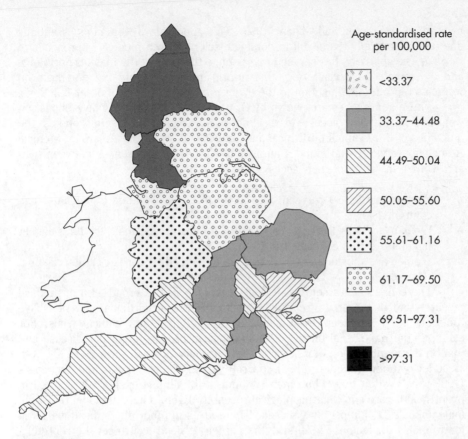

Age-standardised rate
per 100,000

<33.37

33.37–44.48

44.49–50.04

50.05–55.60

55.61–61.16

61.17–69.50

69.51–97.31

>97.31

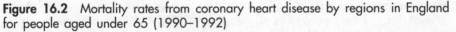

Figure 16.2 Mortality rates from coronary heart disease by regions in England for people aged under 65 (1990–1992)

Source: *Public Health Common Data Set* (1993)

women's health have argued that women's health is a socially constructed phenomenon. Travis (1988) has demonstrated this by drawing upon historical evidence to show that the examination of women's health reflects prevailing sociocultural standards. Lawrence and Bendixon (1992) examined historical approaches to conceptualising women's anatomy and identified two approaches: hierarchical and differential. The hierarchical approach, which they place historically as being dominant from the classical Greeks to the mid-seventeenth century, assumes that men and women share the same biological structures, except that the 'female is, as it were, a mutilated male' (Aristotle, quoted by Lawrence and Bendixon). Gradually though, there became a need to express the differences between men and women, partly to explain and justify women's subordinate position in society. The primacy of women's role as reproducers of the species became increasingly emphasised, most memorably in a statement from the eighteenth century where a woman is described as 'a pair of ovaries with a human being attached, whereas a man is a human being furnished with a pair of testes' (quoted by Stanton, in Stanton and Gallant, 1995). This approach to woman as essentially different biologically tends still to dominate scientific and medical approaches to women. The approach has served to perpetuate the view of the male as normative and the female as deviant from that norm, and to promote the emphasis on women's reproductive function to the exclusion or diminution of other functions.

These approaches are shown by Stanton to have had a negative impact on women's health and access to treatment. For example, Stanton quotes the outcomes of the Council on Ethical and Judicial Affairs of the American Medical Association (1991), who found a number of significant differences between men and women in terms of their access to medical procedures:

- Women are 25–30 per cent less likely to receive kidney transplants (age controlled for);
- Women are less likely to be referred for diagnostic tests for lung cancer (smoking status controlled for);
- Women are substantially less likely to be referred for cardiac catheterisation.

There has been a serious neglect of women in the broad area of medical research and in the area of coronary health disease in particular. Women have routinely been excluded from major epidemiological and clinical trials. For example, the major trial on the effects of aspirin on cardiovascular disease and that on the identification of risk factors for coronary heart disease (MRFIT) both excluded women (Stanton, 1995). Carroll (1992) quotes Rodin and Ickovics's (1990) observation that 'white men continue to be almost exclusively studied in major health care and pharmacological research. Even in animal-model research, male animals are almost always used.' There are a number of justifications given for women's exclusion. The first is the perceived need to protect the reproductive capacities of women and to protect their foetuses; once again the emphasis is upon women as reproducers above all else. It is not clear why men's reproductive capacities can be ignored in such cavalier fashion! Further, since it is sometimes difficult to ascertain whether a woman is pregnant there is an approach that assumes every woman within a specific age group to be pregnant unless there is evidence to the contrary. Women are often characterised as 'more complicated' than men; their hormonal variations add unwanted 'noise' to measures. Finally, in terms of research into coronary heart disease it has been argued that women are at less immediate risk of CHD than men. Other justifications given are that there are higher costs involved in trials that include women, particularly if the end-point is mortality since women live longer, thus extending a study by slowing down the gathering of end-point data.

There has recently been a move in the United States to remedy this long-term neglect of women by researchers. The Women's Health Initiative is a national, long-term study over fifteen years, which focuses on the prevention of heart disease, breast and colorectal cancers, and osteoporosis – all of which are diseases which affect women greatly, especially in their older years. The initiative has three components: a set of randomised clinical trials involving more than 64,500 women between the ages of 50 and 79 years, an observational study of 100,000 women looking at the determinants of chronic disease, and a community prevention study. The clinical trials will examine the protective effect for women of a low fat diet, of calcium and vitamin D supplementation and of hormone replacement therapy (Matthews *et al.*, 1997).

There remains, however, the gender paradox. On many self-report measures of symptoms and distress women score higher than men (Verbrugge, 1980). Women also make far greater use of health services, visiting their general practitioners more frequently than men throughout their lives. Nevertheless, women live longer than men, by about six to seven years on average. Women are apparently unhealthy but long lived, whereas men are healthy but die young.

Why do women live longer than men? Taylor (1995) has reviewed a number of different possibilities. A biological approach argues that women are biologically fitter for survival. This is supported by the evidence that shows that although more males are conceived, more males are miscarried or stillborn. This higher death rate for males persists throughout infancy such that though more males than females are born, by the age of 20 there are more female survivors than males. This argument poses a deeper question: What is it that makes women 'fitter' for survival? Taylor points out that some factors may be genetic and others hormonal: certainly women's buffered X-chromosome may protect against certain disorders and oestrogen seems to offer protection against heart disease (Holden, 1987). Women may have stronger immune systems, although again this is not so much an explanation as another question about why this should be so. Alternative non-biological explanations focus on the different lifestyles of men and women. Men are argued to be more likely to engage in dangerous occupations and lifestyles; they have greater access to dangerous equipment including guns; they have higher accident rates for driving cars and motorcycles. Until recently, men were more likely than women to smoke, to drink alcohol and to consume illegal drugs. Finally, there is evidence of different coping styles and strategies between women and men. Women in particular seem to derive support from others and social support has been shown consistently to help maintain good health and deal effectively with health problems (Wingard, 1982). These gender-related differences in behaviour are changing rapidly. It remains to be seen whether the overall gender differences described here will diminish as differences in behaviour and lifestyles also diminish.

The other aspect of the paradox is that women suffer greater morbidity than men across a range of illnesses including physical and mental disorders (Verbrugge, 1985). Why should this be so? It has been suggested that the reasons are psychological; for example, women are more likely than men to report symptoms and take on a 'sick-role'. As Graham points out this type of explanation merely explains away women's health problems as an artefact of their gender (Graham, 1993). Feminist theorists have taken issue with such 'explanations' and instead have sought explanations gained from women's own understanding of their health and the social conditions that affect it (e.g. Wilkinson and Kitzinger, 1994). They argue that what is needed is an understanding in terms of women's research on health rather than the conventional health research (often by men) upon women.

Racial and ethnic differences in health

International and national research has documented differences between the health status of different ethnic groups. Wide disparities continue to exist in morbidity and mortality between, for example, white Americans and black or Hispanic Americans. Especially disturbing is recent evidence which suggests that these disparities, far from decreasing are in fact increasing (e.g. Lillie-Blanton *et al.*, 1996). Current disparities could, however, be the result of socioeconomic differences between the different ethnic groups since it is equally well documented that white Americans enjoy better economic circumstance and higher standards of education and social services than other Americans. Lillie-Blanton *et al.* further suggest that much of the published research on race/ethnicity and health reinforces beliefs that health status is fundamentally a characteristic inherent within the individual and his or her ethnic group, with the attached assumption that there is little that can be done to develop effective interventions.

Racial differences in infant mortality are perhaps the most widely studied racial disparity. Many studies have shown that black Americans are more likely than white to give birth to premature and low birth weight babies. Different researchers have come to different conclusions about the cause of these well-established differences. Lieberman *et al.* (1987) found no difference in rate of prematurity between black and white American mothers when their economic status was controlled for. In contrast, Schoendorf *et al.* (1992) found a significantly higher incidence of low birth weight in black babies after controlling for sociodemographic factors. Similarly, Singh and Yu (1995) examined long-term trends in infant mortality from 1950 to 1991 and found that infant mortality rates were significantly higher amongst black than white babies at all levels of maternal income.

There are also perceived differences between different racial and ethnic groups in terms of vulnerability to particular disorders. Essential hypertension has been found to be higher in black than white Americans. Once again studies have found that there is a confounding of social class and ethnic variation in blood pressure level. However, a study of black and white American women in Massachusetts found that the risk of hypertension for black women was twice that for white and that differences persisted even after controlling for socioeconomic status (Adams-Campbell *et al.*, 1993). Similar differences between black and white men have been reported in the UK too. Lillie-Blanton *et al.* (1996, p. 430) concluded their review of racial differences in health by commenting: 'The development of knowledge on the effects of race and social class has been hampered by the limited pool of researchers interested in the area and the under development of the methodological tools for research in this area.'

In the UK there continue to exist inequalities between different ethnic groups in relation to social factors such as housing and employment and in relation to income. It is therefore no surprise to find there are marked ethnic differences too in relation to health (Ahmed, 1993). People whose ethnic origins are in South Asia (Indians, Pakistanis, Bangladeshis and Sri Lankans) and who are now living in the UK have especially high rates of coronary heart disease. A study of mortality from ischaemic heart disease between 1979 and 1983 found that mortality from coronary heart disease was 36 per cent higher in men and 46 per cent higher in women aged 20 to 69 years who had been born in South Asia, than for the rates for England and Wales as a whole (Balarajan, 1991). Similarly, there is higher mortality from strokes and other circulatory diseases among both men and women living in the UK but who were born in Africa or in the Caribbean (Marmot *et al.*, 1984).

The reasons for such differences are likely to be complex and multi-factorial; genetic differences will be compounded by socioeconomic and lifestyle differences. We do know, however, that health care services are, in general, under-used by people from ethnic minority groups and this may further affect adversely the relative health of minority groups.

Reasons why health services may be under-used by ethnic minority groups include the language communication problems, lack of knowledge about the availability of services and cultural problems. An effective way of overcoming these problems is through the use of bilingual health workers: advocates, interpreters and link workers. In this respect health service provision should reflect the needs of the communities served (White *et al.*, 1996).

Psychosocial influences

From the discussions above it will be clear that morbidity and mortality are not equally distributed within a population. There are inequalities in health that are related to socioeconomic status, gender and ethnicity. Of course, it is likely that these factors will interact in their effects upon illness and health.

The differences that exist between social classes, between men and women, and between ethnic groups are well documented. Can they be explained? Or, more importantly, can they be explained in terms of processes that will allow interventions to be planned which will eliminate the inequalities that exist? In the UK the government's Health of the Nation programme (DHSS, 1992) made only brief reference to the problem that in reaching its targets for improvements in the nation's health, *variations* in relation to its targeted areas – coronary heart disease and stroke, cancer, sexual health including HIV/AIDS, mental illness and accidents – would have to be overcome. To achieve this, the mechanisms by which social variations occur must be identified and there is increasing attention being paid to the role of psychological factors in social inequalities in health. However, the Health of the Nation approach has been criticised (e.g. Marks, 1994) for ignoring the psychological and social factors that influence individuals' choices about health-related behaviours, assuming them to be decisions made by rational decision makers operating 'in a sociocultural, political and economic vacuum' (p. 20).

Stress process is one psychological aspect that might have importance for understanding the link between health outcomes and social class and ethnicity. Psychosocial stress impacts on autonomic, neuroendocrine and immunologic processes and is related to a wide range of physical and psychological illnesses influencing morbidity and mortality (see Chapter 3). It may be supposed that psychosocial stressors are not distributed equally between different social classes,

325

nor between different ethnic groups within a society, and perhaps not between women and men, in which case they might have a differential impact upon the health of these various groups.

Carroll and his colleagues (Carroll *et al.*, 1993, 1994) have considered and rejected four possible explanations put forward to account for the health differentials between social classes. These are: measurement artefact, social selection, lifestyle factors, and social causation. Instead they favour explanations based upon psychological factors such as stressful life events and lack of social support.

A new public health strategy

A new health strategy to break the cycle of ill health due to poverty and deprivation has been announced by the recently appointed Minister for Public Health (*BMJ*, 12 July 1997). This will commit the Labour government to a major change in policy. It was introduced as 'being tough on the causes of ill health'. The Minister for Public Health, Tessa Jowell, cited current inequalities such as those in parts of Birmingham and Coventry where male life expectancy is below retirement age; and that a baby born today into a family in social class I or II can expect to live five years longer than a baby born into social class IV or V. It remains to be seen whether this new commitment to change will result in fewer inequalities in health. If change is to occur, the significance of psychological factors must not be ignored. Health psychology research should be an important component of these new strategies.

Key point summary

- We are not all equally healthy. Many variations in health are associated with demographic variables such as race, gender and social class. It is likely that these differences in health status are the outcome of genetic, psychological and social factors. However, psychologists have tended to disregard the important role that social factors can play in determining health status.
- Social class differences in health are well established. Two major studies of civil servants in Whitehall have shown that these differences cannot be attributed to differences in lifestyle behaviours. Psychological factors such as perceived control have been shown to be important.
- The work of Richard Wilkinson has offered insights into health variations between countries. It seems likely again that psychosocial variables, in particular the equality of income distribution in a society, will impact on health.
- Women's health has been neglected by many researchers. There is now a new research initiative in the United States which will seek to redress this imbalance and focus attention on disorders of health particularly associated with older women.
- Health differences between different ethnic groups are likely to be the outcome of genetic predispositions and triggering environmental factors.

The health of migrants has proved a useful way to disentangle the predictive elements.

● Psychosocial factors underpin many of the variations outlined in this chapter. A new public health policy will seek to irradicate the major effects of poverty and deprivation upon health.

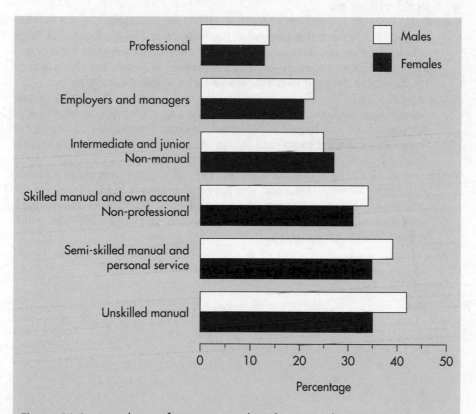

Figure 16.3 Prevalence of cigarette smoking by sex and socioeconomic group for adults in Great Britain, 1992

Source: *OPCS General Household Survey*

Figure 16.3 shows gender and class variations in smoking. The data indicate that different social classes show different smoking patterns by gender.

● What does this mean in terms of individual responsibility for health?
● Could it be argued that the lower social classes are responsible for their higher mortality rates? What alternative explanations can you give?
● What do you understand by 'good health'? What do you think determines it?

Further reading

Ahmad, W. I. U. (ed.) (1993) *'Race' and Health in Contemporary Britain*. Buckingham: Open University Press. This edited collection covers the significant aspects of race/ethnicity in relation to all aspects of health in the UK including current health issues, health policy, politics and equality, and health promotion.

Carroll, D., Bennett, P. and Davey-Smith, G. (1993) Socioeconomic health inequalities: their origins and implications. *Psychology and Health*, 8, 295–316. This article gives an excellent insight into why health psychologists have begun to become interested in the topic of inequalities in health and the role they might play in devising interventions to tackle those inequalities.

Macintyre, S. (1997) The Black Report and beyond: what are the issues? *Social Science and Medicine*, 44(6), 723–745. This paper provides an overview of the precursors and impact of the Black Report. It considers the variety of explanations offered to account for variations in health and the underlying mechanisms of these variations and inequalities.

Wilkinson, R. G. (1996) *Unhealthy Societies: The Afflictions of Inequality*. London: Routledge. Richard Wilkinson has provided a unique commentary on the relationship between material success and good health over many years. This book will have significant influence upon health researchers and policy makers in the coming years.

Glossary

abortion A miscarriage of birth, especially when deliberately induced to terminate a pregnancy.

abstinence Abstaining from the intake of a desired substance such as a food or drug.

Acquired Immune Deficiency Syndrome (AIDS) A deficiency of the immune system caused by a viral infection (HIV) which results in vulnerability to diseases caused by bacterial and viral infections, and malignant (cancerous) disease.

acute pain Short-term pain resulting from damage to the body's tissues.

addiction Dependence (psychological and/or pharmacological) upon a drug resulting from chronic use.

adherence Following the advice or recommended treatment of a health professional.

adrenal glands Endocrine glands located on the top of each kidney: the outer cortex secretes glucocorticoid hormones and the inner medulla adrenaline and noradrenaline.

adrenalin A hormone manufactured by the adrenal medulla and also a sympathetic synaptic transmitter.

adrenococorticotrophic hormone (ACTH) A hormone released by the pituitary gland that stimulates the adrenal cortex to release glucocorticoid hormones that influence glucose metabolism and reactions to stress (cortisol).

aerobic exercise Exercise that increases oxygen consumption over a prolonged period, for example, by running, swimming or cycling.

aetiology The causes or factors related to the development of a disorder.

allostasis The principle of maintaining physiological stability by varying internal responses to match changing environmental demands.

329

angina pectoris A cardiovascular disorder where restricted blood supply to the myocardium results in breathlessness and chest pains.

angiography A technique for viewing cardiovascular damage by the use of X-rays after a dye has been injected into the circulation.

anorexia nervosa An eating disorder characterised by self-induced weight loss and fear of fatness accompanied by disturbance of body image causing self-perception of fatness even after weight loss.

antidepressants A general term for drugs that affect neurotransmitters in the brain and alleviate the symptoms of depression.

antipsychotics A general term for drugs that are used to alleviate the symptoms of psychosis.

appraisal Cognitive processes by which sensory experiences are evaluated in terms of their personal significance and the availability of coping strategies.

atherosclerosis A disease process involving the formation of fatty plaques in the arteries. Where plaques form in the coronary arteries they restrict blood flow (and thus oxygen supply) to the heart causing angina (chest pain) and myocardial infarction (heart attack).

autonomic nervous system A subdivision of the nervous system that regulates the functions of internal glands and organs. It is divided into the sympathetic (promotes functions under challenging conditions including stress) and parasympathetic (promotes functions under relaxation conditions) divisions.

AZT Azidothymidine, the drug developed as the first treatment against infection with HIV.

behavioural intention An individual's commitment to carry out a particular action or behaviour in the future.

biofeedback Training procedures where feedback about a physiological system or response is provided to develop learned regulation of the specified system/response.

biopsychosocial model A model of health and illness that examines the relationships between biological, psychological and social factors.

Bortner rating scale A self-report scale of fourteen bipolar descriptors used to measure Type A behaviour.

breast self-examination (BSE) A health-protective habit for women of self-examining their breasts to detect any abnormality.

buffering The process where factors alleviate potentially harmful effects of stressors upon a person's health.

bulimia nervosa An eating disorder characterised by recurrent episodes of binge eating followed by self-induced vomiting or laxative abuse accompanied by a fear of fatness.

caffeinism A state of high nervousness and muscle tremor caused by excessive consumption of caffeine.

cancer A condition where malignant tumours develop from uncontrolled growth of tissue.

carcinogen A substance in the external or internal environment that causes development of cancer.

central nervous system The collection of neurones that together comprise the brain and spinal cord.

cerebrovascular accident (CVA) Sudden impairment of the supply of blood to the brain, often as a result of blockage to a blood vessel, causing a stroke.

cholesterol A fat found in many foods and an essential nutrient. High serum levels are a risk factor for coronary heart disease.

chronic pain Persistent pain for more than three months, often without evidence of organic aetiology.

clinical trial A design where one treatment is compared against another to see which is more effective.

cohort trial A study where a group of people are recruited and followed through an experience of treatment to see how their condition changes over time.

compliance A term used interchangeably with adherence (see above).

compulsive eating A dysfunctional pattern of eating where habitual consumption replaces eating to meet nutritional requirements.

condom   A contraceptive sheath worn on the penis (male) or inside the vagina (female) during sexual intercourse.

contraception   A means of preventing pregnancy.

controllability   A construct used to explain the impact of environmental and psychosocial variables on the physical and mental health of individuals and populations.

conversion hysteria   A psychodynamic term that refers to the situation where psychic conflict becomes translated into somatic symptoms.

coping   The cognitive and behavioural efforts an individual makes to manage stressful demands.

coronary heart disease (CHD)   A group of diseases that includes angina (chest pain), myocardial infarction (heart attack) and sudden cardiac death.

cortisol   A type of glucocorticoid hormone that regulates carbohydrate metabolism and provides defence against inflammation.

cross-sectional study   An experimental design involving measurement at a particular moment in time of groups of individuals and comparing them on some outcome measure(s).

dependent variable   A variable whose value can be observed to change as a consequence of changes in the value of a manipulated independent variable.

depression   A psychiatric disorder consisting of dejected mood, insomnia and weight loss often accompanied by feelings of guilt and/or worthlessness.

detoxification   Treatment to eliminate a drug from the body and end dependence upon it.

diabetes mellitus   A disorder caused by insulin deficiency.

diagnosis   The identification of illness or disease based on a patient's symptoms and signs.

dizygotic twins   Non-identical twins arising from fertilisation of two eggs by separate sperms.

dopamine   A catecholamine neurotransmitter in the brain.

eating disorder   Any serious and chronic disturbance of eating that gives rise to unhealthy consequences.

endocrine system   A body system that transfers information between cells in different parts of the body by way of chemical messengers (hormones) released into the circulation.

epidemiology   The study of the distribution and determinants of health-related states in specified populations for the control of disease and illness.

essential hypertension   A condition of elevated blood pressure where there is no apparent physical cause.

fear-avoidance model of pain   A model of the pain process that draws upon fear of pain as a primary determinant of responses to the pain experience.

fibrinogen   A soluble protein in the blood involved in coagulation. When the body is injured it is converted into insoluble fibrin which is an important constituent of atherosclerosis plaques.

focus group   A qualitative technique developed by social and market researchers in which a small group of individuals interactively give their views and impressions upon a specified topic. These are used to evaluate attitudes towards the topic.

foetal alcohol syndrome   The pattern of psychological and physical symptoms found in infants whose mothers had high alcohol intakes during pregnancy.

Framingham Type A Scale   A ten-item self-report measure of Type A behaviour derived from the large-scale Framingham Heart Study conducted in the USA.

gate-control theory of pain   (Melzack and Wall) A theory of pain which argues that structures in the spinal cord act as a gate for the sensory input that is experienced as pain.

General Adaption Syndrome   A three-stage model of the reactions to stress developed by Selye. The stages comprise an alarm reaction during which the body is made ready to respond to threat, followed by a stage of resistance where the organism attempts to overcome that threat, and finally a state of exhaustion when there is a depletion of physiological resources.

hassles   Daily events which require an adaptation or adjustment compelling a mobilisation of resources, i.e. coping (e.g. having a row at work).

health action process approach   A theoretical approach to the adoption of health behaviours developed by Schwarzer which identifies stages in the process – planning, action, maintenance.

health behaviours Any behaviour that is part of maintaining well-being and avoiding illness and disease.

health belief model (HBM) Originally devised to predict preventive health behaviours, it has undergone revisions but retains its core of predicting health behaviours through individuals' beliefs.

health habit A health behaviour that is well established and carried out semi-automatically (for example, teeth cleaning).

health psychology The field of psychology that is concerned with applied and theoretical aspects of health enhancement, disease prevention, illness treatment and rehabilitation.

helplessness A condition that occurs when an individual's attempts at control are unsuccessful and the situation remains unaltered.

high density lipoprotein A type of lipoprotein that confers some protection against coronary heart disease.

hormone A chemical substance released into the bloodstream that affects the activity/ function of other parts (organs) of the body.

Human Immunodeficiency Virus (HIV) The virus that attacks the body's immune system, reducing its ability to protect against the opportunistic infections or attack by cancerous agents that are symptomatic of AIDS.

hypertension Elevation of blood pressure above normal levels.

hypnosis An altered state of awareness brought about by techniques that induce deep relaxation and increased susceptibility to suggestions.

hypoglycaemia The fall in blood glucose level that occurs when glucose leaves the bloodstream faster than it is replaced. This is common in patients with insulin-treated diabetes and results in hunger, weakness, light-headedness and mental confusion. Untreated, it can lead to death.

immune system A bodily system that neutralises and eliminates the factors that cause disease.

immunoglobulin A class of proteins that have antibody activity; it includes IgA, IgD, IgE, IgG, IgM.

immunoglobulin A (IgA) A type of immunoglobulin with antibody activity found in seromucous secretions including saliva and milk.

independent variable A variable that is manipulated by an experimenter to determine its effect upon another variable (the dependent variable).

insulin A hormone released from the pancreas which is responsible for regulating the blood glucose level.

insulin-dependent diabetes (also called Type I diabetes) A severe form of diabetes where the cells that should produce insulin have died. It requires continuing treatment with insulin.

Jenkins Activity Survey A simple paper and pencil instrument to measure Type A behaviour through self-report.

Korsakoff's psychosis A condition caused by alcoholism that gives rise to thiamine deficiency which in turn results in irreversible brain lesions leading to mental confusion and loss of memory.

life events Events (environmental stressors) that bring about changes in an individual's life demanding adaptation.

liver cirrhosis Damage to the liver caused by excess alcohol consumption resulting in the production of non-functional scar tissue.

locus of control A scale measuring a person's belief in their control over the environment measured from internal (events under own control) to external (fatalistic belief that events are due to chance or 'luck').

longitudinal study A study involving a research design where the same group of subjects are observed/tested repeatedly over an extended period of time – sometimes several years.

low density lipoprotein (LDL) A type of lipoprotein that is linked as a risk factor for coronary heart disease.

lymphocytes A class of white blood cells found in lymph which are involved in the immune function.

mammography A method of screening women for breast cancer by X-ray (currently available in the UK for women between the ages 50 to 64 years).

melanoma A cancer of the skin.

metastasis The spread of cancerous cells from the original site to other parts of the body.

monozygotic twins Twins formed when a single sperm has fertilised a single egg that splits into twins who share identical genes.

morbidity A measure of the incidence and/or prevalence of illness and disease in a population at a particular time.

mortality rate A calculation by epidemiologists of the population death rate which can also be used to determine expectation of life in different populations.

myocardial infarction (heart attack) The result of severe obstruction to the flow of blood to the heart with consequent restriction of supply of oxygen which causes damage to the heart muscle tissue (myocardium).

natural killer (NK) cells A type of lymphocyte of the immune system, which acts in a non-specific way to invading cells.

neuroticism A personality factor ranging from one extreme of nervousness, anxiety and temperamental instability to the other extreme of emotional stability.

neurotransmitter A chemical released by a neurone that affects the electrical activity of (an)other neurones.

nicotine A stimulant drug that is the psychoactive ingredient of tobacco.

nociception The process of receiving sensory information from pain receptors.

non-compliance Failure to follow the advice or recommended treatment of a physician/health provider.

non-insulin-dependent diabetes mellitus (NIDDM) The most common form of diabetes (also known as Type II) caused by glucose intolerance usually developed in middle age. It can be treated by modification of lifestyle factors.

noradrenaline A major transmitter substance in the autonomic nervous system.

obesity The condition of having excess body fat as compared to population norms.

operant conditioning The process by which the frequency of occurrence of a behaviour is modified by the consequences (positive or negative) of that behaviour.

parenting style Patterns of parental behaviour towards their children that may influence child health. Four styles were identified by Baumrind: authoritative, indulgent, authoritarian, and neglecting.

passive smoking Exposure of non-smokers to tobacco smoke in their environment.

pathogenesis The mode of development of a disease.

peripheral nervous system The collection of nerves from the CNS to the periphery and from the periphery to the CNS.

placebo A treatment that gives rise to a clinically significant response independent of its physiological actions as a result of the patient's belief in its efficacy.

planned behaviour theory A sociocognitive model of voluntary behaviour where intentions formed through the combined effects of attitudes, subjective norms and perceived control are the most immediate determinant of behaviour.

polygraph An electronic device (multiple pen writer) for recording simultaneously several physiological responses such as muscle activity, respiration, cardiovascular responses and electrical properties of the skin.

preventive health behaviours Actions taken by a person to reduce their risk of developing illness or disease or worsening an existing condition.

primary prevention Actions or behaviours to help disease-free individuals avoid illness or disease.

primiparous woman A woman bearing a child for the first time.

prospective study/design A longitudinal study that follows disease-free individuals and tracks their development of disease.

protection motivation theory A theory of the adoption of health behaviours originated by Rogers which builds upon the health beliefs model by incorporating motivational elements.

psychogenic (non-specific) pain Pain that has no apparent organic aetiology.

psychoneuroimmunology The field of study that examines the effects of psychological factors and neural systems on the immune system.

psychophysiological disorder A category of disorders characterised by physical symptoms and dysfunctions that are related to psychological processes.

psychophysiology A subdiscipline of psychology that studies the relationships between psychological processes and physiological systems.

quality of life Health is defined in broad terms and quality of life is an attempted index of the sum total of measures that contribute to health.

reactivity A term used in relation to the response of a physiological system (for example, heart rate) to a challenge. High reactivity is implicated in the development of cardiovascular diseases.

relaxation training Forms of training such as yoga, meditation, progressive muscle relaxation, etc. that allow a person to achieve a state of parasympathetic dominance characterised by decreases in muscle tension, heart rate, blood pressure and respiration.

resilience The quality that allows a person to deal effectively with challenging or stressful experiences without experiencing debilitating effects.

retrospective study A study that looks back at the occurrence of illness or disease in a particular sample of population.

risk factor A characteristic that is associated at greater frequency with people with a disease than with people without that disease.

sarcoma A cancer of the body's connective tissue.

self-efficacy Belief that a person can behave effectively in a particular situation to produce desired outcomes.

self-esteem A generalised evaluative attitude towards the self that influences moods and behaviour.

self-regulation model A theory of the adoption of health behaviours developed by Leventhal based upon problem solving and planning to achieve a desired state.

serotonin (5-HT) A central nervous system transmitter.

serum cholesterol The level of cholesterol found in the serum of the blood. High levels of serum cholesterol are associated with increased risk of cardiovascular disease.

serum triglycerides One of the components of serum lipids that are linked to the development of atherosclerotic plaques.

social learning theory A learning theory developed by Bandura and Mischel which stresses the importance of observation and imitation of the behaviour of others.

social readjustment rating scale (Holmes and Rahe) A scale of the differences in magnitude of various life events measured as life change units, used to measure the amount of stress an individual is experiencing.

social support The support a person receives from relationships with other people defined in terms of number of social contacts or satisfaction with contacts.

socioeconomic status Measures of the inequalities in societies based upon objective measures including income and occupation used to stratify the population into groups.

stress An umbrella term that may refer to the strains felt within an individual facing a difficult challenge or the demands within the environment that individuals must adapt to.

stress-diathesis model A model that proposes that psychopathology is the result of an interaction between an individual's predisposition (genetics, past history, development) and the exposure to particular stressors.

stressor Any stimulus that requires an organism to make an adaptation or adjustment.

structured interview (SI) A method of assessing Type A behaviour based upon observation of the interviewee's style of responding rather than self-report questionnaire answers.

sub-acute pain Pain that has lasted between one and three months.

subjective expected utility model A model developed by Luker that argues that performance of a particular behaviour depends upon a person's expectation of a specific desired outcome.

sudden infant death syndrome (cot death)   Death of an infant in its sleep within its first year with no forewarning or predicting signs.

survey   A method of collecting data/information in a fixed format from a large number of people.

symptoms   The signs and sensations that are interpreted as indicators of illness or disease.

testicular self-examination (TSE)   A health-protective habit for men of self-examining the testicles for signs of abnormality.

thalassaemia   An inherited disorder of haemoglobin production which can cause death in childhood.

tolerance   The process where increasing intake of a drug is required to maintain a constant level of physiological/psychological effect.

trans-theoretical model of health   Developed by Prochaska and DiClemente, this is a model of behaviour change describing, at each stage of change, different processes of change needed to modify current behaviour and then maintain the new behaviour.

Type A behaviour pattern   A behaviour pattern first identified by Rosenman that is characterised by ambition and competitive, compulsive, urgent behaviour that is linked to the risk of coronary heart disease.

unrealistic optimism   A bias in judgement that results in over-confidence in a person's capacities and underestimation of the risk associated with particular behaviours.

uplifts   Positive daily events that give satisfaction or pleasure and which may buffer the effects of stressors (cf. hassles), e.g. gaining a high grade for an essay.

withdrawal   An adverse physiological and/or psychological reaction caused by reducing/eliminating ingestion of a drug after tolerance to that drug has been established.

Bibliography

Abdulrahim, D., White, D. G., Phillips, K. C. and Boyd, G. (1996) *HIV Infection Control: Drug Use and Health Care for Women in a Multi-Ethnic Setting*. Report to North Thames Regional Health Authority.

Abdulrahim, D., White, D. G., Phillips, K. C., Boyd, G., Nicholson, J. and Elliott, J. (1994) *Ethnicity and Drug Use. Towards the Design of Community Interventions*. London: North East Thames Regional Health Authority.

Abraham, C. S. and Sheeran, P. (1993) Inferring cognitions, predicting behaviour: two challenges for social cognition models. *Health Psychology Update*, 14, 18–23.

Abraham, C. S., Sheeran, P., Abrams, D. and Spears, R. (1994) Exploring teenagers' adaptive and maladaptive thinking in relation to the threat of HIV infection. *Psychology and Health*, 9, 253–272.

Abrams, M. (1985) Birth control use by teenagers: One and two years post abortion. *Journal of Adolescent Health Care*, 6, 196–200.

Acton, T. (1989) In your hands: a psychological view of the immuno-deficiency virus (HIV). *Royal Society of Medicine. The AIDS Letter*, 12 (April–May): 1–3.

Adam, E. and Golding, J. (1996) Maternal smoking and drinking during pregnancy. In: J. Golding (ed.) *Pregnancy in the 90s. The European Longitudinal Study of Pregnancy and Childhood*. Bristol: Sansom and Company.

Adams, I. B. and Martin B. R. (1996) Cannabis: pharmacology and toxicology in animal and humans. *Addiction*, 91, 1585–1614.

Adams-Campbell, L. L., Brambilla, D. J. and McKinley, S. M. (1993) Correlates of prevalence of self-reported hypertension among African-American and white women. *Ethnic Diseases*, 3, 119–125.

Ader, R. (ed.) (1981) *Psychoneuroimmunology*. New York: Academic Press.

337

Adler, N. (1982) The abortion experience: social and psychological influences and after effects. In H. S. Friedman and M. S. DiMatteo (eds) *Interpersonal Issues in Health Care*. New York: Academic Press.

Adler, N., David, H. P., Major, B. N., Roth, S. H., Russo, N. F. and Wyatt, G. E. (1992) Psychological factors in abortion: a review. *American Psychologist*, 47, 1194–1204.

Aggleton, P., Hart, G. and Davies, P. (1989) *AIDS: Social Representations and Social Practice*. Lewes: Falmer Press.

Aggleton, P., Homans, H., Mojsa, J., Watson, S. and Watney, S. (1989) *AIDS: Scientific and Social Issues. A Resource for Health Educators*. Edinburgh: Churchill Livingstone.

Agras, W. S., Horne, M. and Taylor, C. B. (1982) Expectation and the blood pressure lowering effects of relaxation. *Psychosomatic Medicine*, 44, 389–395.

Agras, W. S., Southam, M. A. and Taylor, C. B. (1983) Long term persistence of relaxation induced blood pressure lowering during the working day. *Journal of Consulting and Clinical Psychology*, 51, 792–794.

Agras, W. S., Taylor, C. B., Kraemer, H. C., Southam, M. A. and Schneider, J. A. (1987) Relaxation training for essential hypertension at the workplace: II The poorly controlled hypertensive. *Psychosomatic Medicine*, 49, 264–273.

Ahmed, W. I. U. (1993) *'Race' and Health in Contemporary Britain*. Buckingham: Open University Press.

Aitkens, J. D., Wallander, J. K., Bell, D. S. H. and Cole, J. A. (1992) Daily stress variability, learned resourcefulness, regimen adherence and metabolic control in type 1 diabetes mellitus: evaluation of a path model. *Journal of Consulting and Clinical Psychology*, 60, 113–118.

Ajzen, I. (1985) From intentions to actions: a theory of planned behavior. In: J. Kuhl and J. Beckmann (eds) *Action-Control: From Cognition to Behavior*. Heidelberg: Springer.

Ajzen, I. and Fishbein, M. (1980) *Understanding Attitudes and Predicting Social Behavior*. Englewood Cliffs, NJ: Prentice-Hall.

Ajzen, I. and Madden, T. J. (1986) Prediction of goal directed behavior: attitudes, intentions and perceived behavioral control. *Journal of Experimental Social Psychology*, 22, 453–474.

Alexander, A. B. (1975) An experimental test of the assumptions relating to the use of electromyographic biofeedback as a general relaxation technique. *Psychophysiology*, 12, 656–662.

Alexander, F. (1939) Emotional factors in essential hypertension. *Psychosomatic Medicine*, 1, 175–179.

Alexander, F. (1950) *Psychosomatic Medicine: Its Principles and Applications*. New York: Norton.

Alexander, G. R. and Korenbrot, C. C. (1995) The role of prenatal care in preventing low birth weight. *Future Child*, 5 (1), 103–120.

Alexander, M. A. and Sherman, J. B. (1991) Factors associated with obesity in school children. *Journal of School Nursing*, 7, 6–10.

Allan, D. and Armstrong, D. (1984) Patient attitudes towards radiographic examinations involving contrast media. *Clinical Radiology*, 35, 457–459.

Allcock, N. (1996) Factors affecting the assessment of postoperative pain: a literature review. *Journal of Advanced Nursing*, 24, 1144–1151.

Allen, I. (1981) *Family Planning, Sterilisation and Abortion Services*. London: The Policy Studies Institute No. 595.

Alogna, M. (1980) Perception of severity of disease and health locus of control in compliant and non-compliant diabetic patients. *Diabetes Care*, 3, 533–534.

Alterman, T., Shekelle, R. B., Vernon, S. W. and Burau, K. D. (1994) Decision latitude, psychologic demand, job strain, and coronary heart disease in the western electric study. *American Journal of Epidemiology*, 139(6), 620–627.

American Psychiatric Association (1994) *Diagnostic and Statistical Manual of Mental Disorders – 4th Edition*. Washington, DC: APA.

American Psychological Association Interdivisional Committee on Adolescent Abortion (1987) Adolescent abortion: psychological and legal issues. *American Psychologist*, 42, 73–78.

American Public Health Association (1991) *Healthy Communities 2000 Model Standards*. Washington, DC: APHA.

Amir, D. (1987) Preventive behaviour and health status among the elderly. *Psychology and Health*, 1, 353–378.

Anderson, B. J., Brackett, J., Ho, J. and Laffel, L. (1996) *Developmental Issues and Family Involvement in the Care of Adolescents with IDDM*. Paper presented at 10th European Health Psychology Conference (4–6 September), Dublin.

Anderson, B. J., Miller, J. P., Auslander, W. F. and Santiago, J. V. (1981) Family characteristics of diabetic adolescents: relationship to metabolic control. *Diabetes Care*, 4, 586–594.

Anderson, N. B. (1989) Racial differences in stress induced cardiovascular reactivity and hypertension: current status and substantive issues. *Psychological Bulletin*, 105, 89–105.

Andersson, S. O., Mattsson, B. and Lynøe, N. (1995) Patients frequently consulting general practitioners at a primary health care centre in Sweden – a comparative study. *Scandinavian Journal of Social Medicine*, 23 (4), 251–257.

Andrasik, F. and Holroyd, K. A. (1983) Specific and non-specific effects in the biofeedback treatment of tension headache: three year follow up. *Journal of Consulting and Clinical Psychology*, 51, 634–636.

Andrasik, F., Blanchard, E. B., Areana, J. G., Saunders, N. L. and Barron, K. D. (1982) Psychophysiology of recurrent headaches: methodological issues and new empirical findings. *Behaviour Therapy*, 13, 407–429.

Andreassi, J. L. (1980) *Psychophysiology: Human Behavior and Physiological Response*. Oxford: Oxford University Press.

Appel, M. (1986) Hypertension. In: K. A. Holroyd and T. L. Creer (eds) *Self-Management of Chronic Disease*. New York: Academic Press.

Arber, S. and Sawyer, L. (1985) The role of the receptionist in general practice: 'A dragon behind the desk'? *Social Science and Medicine*, 20, 911–921.

Arena, J. G., Bruno, G. M., Hannah, S. L. and Meador, K. J. (1995) A comparison of frontal electromyographic biofeedback training, trapezius electromyographic biofeedback training, and progressive muscle-relaxation therapy in the treatment of tension headache. *Headache*, 35, 411–419.

Arnet, J. W. and Zahler, L. P. (1993) Dietary intake and health habits of healthy, retired, elderly men. *Journal of Nutrition for the Elderly*, 12(3), 43–58.

Arnetz, B. B., Brenner, S.-O. and Levi, L. (1991) Neuroendocrine and immunologic effects of unemployment and job insecurity. *Psychotherapy and Psychosomatics*, 55, 76–80.

Ashton, H. (1987) (ed.) *Brain Systems, Disorders, and Psychotropic Drugs*. Oxford: Oxford University Press.

Atwell, J. R., Flanagan, R. C., Bennett, R. L., Allan, D. C., Lucas, B. A. and McRoberts, J. W. (1984) The efficacy of patient-controlled analgesia in patients recovering from flank incisions. *Journal of Urology*, 132, 701–703.

Auerbach, D., Carter, H. W., Garfinkel, L. and Hammond, E. C. (1976) Cigarette smoking and coronary heart disease, a macroscopic and microscopic study. *Chest*, 70, 697–705.

Austoker, J. (1990) *Breast Cancer Screening: A Practical Guide for Primary Care Teams*. Oxford: National Breast Screening Programme.

Austoker, J. (1994a) Screening for cervical cancer. *British Medical Journal*, 309, 241–248.

Austoker, J. (1994b) Screening for ovarian, prostate and testicular cancers. *British Medical Journal*, 309, 315–320.

Austoker, J. (1995) *Cancer Prevention in Primary Care*. London: BMJ Publishing Group.

Averill, J. R., O'Brien, L. and De Witt, G. W. (1977) The influence of response effectiveness on the preference for warning and on psychophysiological stress reactions. *Journal of Personality*, 45, 395–418.

Babor, T. F., Edwards, G. and Stockwell, T. (1996) Science and the drinks industry: cause for concern. *Addiction*, 91, 5–9.

Bailey, B. J. and Kahn, A. (1993) Apportioning illness management authority: how diabetic individuals respond to help. *Qualitative Health Research*, 3, 55–73.

Baker, G. H. B. (1987) Invited review: psychological factors and immunity. *Journal of Psychosomatic Research*, 31, 1–10.

Balarajan, R. (1991) Ethnic differences in mortality from ischaemic heart disease and cere-brovascular disease in England and Wales. *British Medical Journal*, 302, 560–564.

Baldwin, J. D. and Baldwin, J. I. (1988) Factors affecting AIDS-related sexual risk taking behavior among college students. *Journal of Sex Research*, 25: 181–196.

Ballard, J. E., Koepsell, T. D. and Rivara, F. (1992) Association of smoking and alcohol drinking with residential fire injuries. *American Journal of Epidemiology*, 135, 26–34.

Bandura, A. (1977) *Social Learning Theory*. Englewood Cliffs, NJ: Prentice-Hall.

Bandura, A. (1984) Recycling misconceptions of perceived self-efficacy. *Cognitive Therapy and Research*, 8, 231–255.

Bandura, A. (1986) *Social Foundations of Thought and Action: A Social Cognitive Theory*. Englewood Cliffs, NJ: Prentice-Hall.

Banion, C. R., Miles, M. S. and Carter, M. C. (1983) Problems of mothers in management of children with diabetes. *Diabetes Care*, 6, 548–551.

Barefoot, J. C., Dahlstrom, W. G. and Williams, R. B. (1983) Hostility, CHD incidence, and total mortality: a 25 year follow up study of 255 physicians. *Psychosomatic Medicine*, 45, 59–63.

Barker, D. J. P. (1995) *Mothers, Babies and Diseases in Later Life*. London: BMJ Publishing Group.

Barker, G. and Rich, S. (1992) Influences on adolescent sexuality in Nigeria and Kenya: find-ings from recent focus group discussion. *Studies in Family Planning*, 23, 199–210.

Barlow, J., Bishop, P. and Pennington, D. (1996) How are written patient-education materials used in out-patient clinics? Insight from rheumatology. *Health Education Journal*, 55, 275–284.

Barnes, J., Stein, A., Smith, T., Pollock, J. and the ALSPAC Study Team (1997) Extreme attitudes to body shape, social and psychological factors and a reluctance to breast feed. *Journal of the Royal Society of Medicine*, 90, 551–559.

Barr, M., Pennebaker, J.W. and Watson, D. (1988) Improving blood pressure estimation through internal and environmental feedback. *Psychosomatic Medicine*, 50, 37–45.

Bartrop, R. W., Luckhurst, E., Lazarus, L., Kihlo, L. G. and Penny, R. (1977) *Lancet*, i, 834–836.

Basch, C., Dicicco, I. and Malfetti, J. (1989) A focus group study on decision processes of young drivers: reasons that may support a decision to drink and drive. *Health Education Quarterly*, 16, 389–396.

Bates, M. S. and Rankinhill, L. (1994) Control, culture and chronic pain. *Social Science and Medicine*, 39, 629–645.

Baumrind, D. (1967) Child care practices anteceding 3 patterns of preschool behavior. *Genetic Psychology Monographs*, 75, 43–88.

Baumrind, D. (1990) Parenting styles and adolescent development. In: J. Brooks-Gunn, R. Lerner and A. C. Petersen (eds) *The Encyclopedia on Adolescence*. New York: Garland.

Beard, R. W., Belsey, E. M., Lal, S., Lewis, S. and Greer, H. S. (1974) Contraceptive practice before and after out-patient termination of pregnancy, Kings Termination Study II. *British Medical Journal*, i, 418–421.

Beard, T. C. (1990) Hypertension after INTERSALT: prospectives for prevention. *Journal of Cardiovascular Pharmacology*, 16 (Suppl. 7), 31–38.

Beardow, R., Oerton, J. and Victor, C. (1989) Evaluation of the cervical cytology screening programme in an inner city health district. *British Medical Journal*, 299, 98–100.

Beardslee, W. R. (1989) The role of self-understanding in resilient individuals: the development of a perspective. *American Journal of Orthopsychiatry*, 59, 266–278.

Beardslee, W. R., Hoke, L., Wheelock, I., Clarke Rothberg, P., Van de Velde, P. and Swatling, S. (1992) Initial findings on preventive intervention for families with parental affective disorders. *The American Journal of Psychiatry*, 149, 1335–1340.

Beardslee, W. R., Keller, M. B., Lavori, P. W., Klerman, G. L., Dorer, D. J. and Samuelson, H. (1988) Psychiatric disorder in adolescent offspring of parents with affective disorder in a non-referred sample. *Journal of Affective Disorders*, 15, 313–322.

Beardslee, W. R., Keller, M. B., Lavori, P. W., Stanley, J. and Sacks, N. (1993) The impact of parental affective disorder on depression in offspring: a longitudinal follow-up in a non-referred sample. *Journal of American Academy of Child Adolescent Psychology*, 32, 723–730.

Beck, A. T., Ward, C. H., Medelson, M., Mock, J. and Erbaugh, J. (1961) An inventory for measuring depression. *Archives of General Psychiatry*, 4, 561–571.

Beck, J. G. and Davies, D. K. (1987) Teen contraception: a review of perspectives on compliance. *Archives of Sexual Behaviour*, 16, 337–369.

Becker, M. E. (1974) The health belief model and personal health behaviour. *Health Education Monographs*, 2, 324–508.

Becker, M. H. and Joseph, J. G. (1988) AIDS and behavior change to reduce risk: a review. *American Journal of Public Health*, 78, 462–467.

Becker, M. H. and Maiman, L. A. (1975) Sociobehavioral determinants of compliance with health and medical care recommendations. *Medical Care*, 13, 10–24.

Becker, M. H. and Maiman, L. A. (1976) Sociobehavioral determinants of compliance. In D. L. Sackett and R. B. Haynes (eds) *Compliance with Therapeutic Regimens*. Baltimore: Johns Hopkins University Press.

Becker, M. H. and Rosenstock, I. M. (1984) Compliance with medical advice. In: A. Steptoe and A. Mathews (eds) *Health Care and Human Behaviour*. London: Academic Press.

Beecher, H. K. (1959) *Measurement of Subjective Responses: Quantitative Effects of Drugs*. New York: Oxford University Press.

Belloc, N. B. and Breslow, L. (1972) Relationship between physical health status and health practices. *Preventive Medicine*, 1, 409–421.

Belsky, J., Fish, M. and Isabella, R. (1991) Continuity and discontinuity in infant negative and positive emotionality: family antecedents and attachment consequences. *Developmental Psychology*, 27, 421–431.

Ben Nation, S., Yirmiya, R., Liebeskind, J. C., Taylor, A. N. and Gale, R. P. (1991) Stress increases metastatic spread of a mammary tumor in rats: evidence for mediation by the immune system. *Brain Behaviour and Immunity*, 5, 193–205.

Bendelow, G. (1993) Pain perceptions, emotions and gender. *Sociology of Health and Illness*, 15, 273–294.

Bennett, B. (1996) How nurses in a stroke rehabilitation unit attempt to meet the psychological needs of patients who become depressed following a stroke. *Journal of Advanced Nursing*, 23, 314–321.

Bennett, P. (1994) Should we intervene to modify Type A Behaviour Pattern in patients with manifest heart disease? *Behavioral and Cognitive Psychotherapy*, 22, 125–145.

Bennett, P. and Carroll, D. (1994) Cognitive-behavioural interventions in cardiac rehabilitation. *Journal of Psychosomatic Research*, 38(3), 169–182.

Benoit, D., Parker, K. C. H. and Zeanah, C. H. (1997) Mothers' representations of their infants assessed prenatally: stability and association with infants' attachment classification. *Journal of Child Psychology and Psychiatry*, 38, 307–313.

Bensing, J., Schreurs, K. and Derijk, A. (1996) The role of the general practitioner's affective behaviour in medical encounters. *Psychology and Health*, 11 (6), 825–838.

Berenson, G. S. (ed.) (1986) *Causation of Cardiovascular Risk Factors in Children: Perspectives on Cardiovascular Risk in Early Life*. New York: Raven Press.

Beresford, J. M. and Gervaize, P. A. (1986) The emotional impact of abnormal pap smears on patients referred for colposcopy. *Colposcopy, Gynecology, and Lasar Surgery*, 2, 83–87.

Berg, R. L. (1976) The high cost of self deception. *Preventive Medicine*, 5, 483–495.

Bergman, J. and Dews, P. B. (1987) Dietary caffeine and its toxicity. *Nutritional Toxicology*, 2, 199–221.

Bergner, M., Bobbitt, R. A., Carter, W. B. and Gilson, D. (1981) The sickness impact profile: development and final revision of a health status measure. *Medical Care*, 19, 787–805.

Bertolli, J., St. Louis, M. E., Simonds, R. J., Nieburg, P., Kamenga, M., Brown, C., Tarande, M., Quinn, T. and Ou, C. Y. (1996) Estimating the timing of mother-to-child transmission of human immunodeficiency virus in a breast feeding population in Kinshasa, Zaire. *Journal of Infectious Diseases*, 174, 722–726.

Betschart, J. (1988) Parents' understanding of and guilt over their children's blood glucose control. *The Diabetes Educator*, 13, 398–401.

Bijur, P., Kurzon, M., Hamelsky, V. and Power, C. (1991) Parent-adolescent conflict and adolescent injuries. *Journal of Developmental and Behavioral Pediatrics*, 12, 92–97.

Bingley, P. J. and Gale, E. A. M. (1989) Rising incidence of IDDM in Europe. *Diabetes Care*, 12, 289–295.

Bishop, G. H. (1946) Neural mechanisms of cuteaneous sense. *Physiological Review*, 26, 77–102.

Bitti, P., Gremigni, P., Bertolotti, G. and Zotti, A. M. (1995) Dimensions of anger and hostility in cardiac patients, hypertensive patients, and controls. *Psychotherapy and Psychosomatics*, 64, 3–4, 162–172.

Black Report (1980) *Inequalities In Health: Report Of A Research Working Group.* London: HMSO.

Blanchard, C. G., Labrecque, M. S., Ruckdeschel, J. C. and Blanchard, E. B. (1988) Information and decision-making preferences of hospitalised adult cancer patients. *Social Science and Medicine*, 27, 1139.

Blanchard, E. B. (1979) Biofeedback and the modification of cardiovascular dysfunctions. In: R. J. Gatchel and K. P. Price (eds) *Clinical Applications of Biofeedback: Appraisal and Status.* New York: Pergamon Press.

Blanchard, E. B. and Andrasik, F. (1985) *Management of Chronic Headaches: A Psychological Approach.* New York: Pergamon.

Blanchard, E. B. and Young, L. D. (1974) Clinical applications of biofeedback training: a review of evidence. *Archives of General Psychiatry*, 30, 573–589.

Blanchard, E. B., McCoy, G. C., Musso, A., Gerardi, M. A., Pallmeyer, T. P., Gerardi, R. J., Cotch, P. A., Siracusa, A. and Andrasik, F. (1986) A controlled comparison of thermal biofeedback and relaxation training in the treatment of essential hypertension: I Short-term and long-term outcome. *Behaviour Therapy*, 17, 563–579.

Blankenhorn, D. H., Nessim, S. A., Johnson, R. L., Sanmarco, M. E., Azen, S. P. and Cashin-Hempill, L. (1987) Beneficial effects of combined colestipol-niacin therapy on coronary atherosclerosis and coronary venous bypass grafts. *Journal of the American Medical Association*, 257, 3233–3240.

Blaxter, M. (1983) The causes of disease: women talking. *Social Science and Medicine*, 17, 59–69.

Blaxter, M. (1987) Evidence on inequality in health from a national survey. *Lancet*, ii, 30–33.

Bloom-Cerkoney, K. A. and Hart, L. K. (1980) The relationship between the health belief model and compliance of persons with diabetes mellitus. *Diabetes Care*, 3, 594–598.

Blount, R., Sturges, J. and Powers, S. (1990) Analysis of child and adult behavioral variations by phase of medical procedure. *Behavior Therapy*, 21, 33–48.

Blumberg, J. (1994) Nutrient requirements of the healthy elderly – should there be specific RDAs? *Nutrition Reviews*, 52(8), 515–518.

Blumenthal, J. A. (1985) Relaxation therapy, biofeedback and behavioral medicine. *Psychotherapy*, 22, 516–530.

Bodansky, J. (1994) *Diabetes.* 2nd edn. London: Wolfe.

Bondy, S. J . (1996) Overview of studies on drinking patterns and consequences. *Addiction*, 91, 1663–1674.

Bongaarts, J. (1976) Intermediate fertility variables and marital fertility rates. *Population Studies*, 30, 227–241.

Booth-Kewley, S. and Friedman, H. S. (1987) Psychological predictors of heart disease: a quantitative review. *Psychological Bulletin*, 101, 343–362.

Botting, B. and Crawley, R. (1995) Trends and patterns in childhood mortality and morbidity. In: B. Botting (ed.) *The Health Of Our Children.* Decennial Supplement. Office of Population Censuses and Surveys. Series DS no. 11. London: HMSO, pp. 61–81.

Boyle, C. M. (1970) Differences between patients' and doctors' interpretations of some common medical terms. *British Medical Journal*, 2, 286–289.

Boyle, M. (1992) The abortion debates: an analysis of psychological assumptions underlying legislation and professional decision-making. In J. Ussher and P. Nicolson (eds) *The Psychology of Women's Health and Health Care.* London: Macmillan.

Boyle, M. (1997) *Re-thinking Abortion: Psychology, Gender, Power and the Law.* London: Routledge.

Bradley, C. (1979) Life events and the control of diabetes mellitus. *Journal of Psychosomatic Research,* 23, 159–162.

Bradley, C. (1994) The well-being questionnaire. In C. Bradley (ed.) *Handbook of Psychology and Diabetes.* London: Harwood Academic.

Bradley, C. and Lewis, K. S. (1990) Measures of psychological well-being and treatment satisfaction developed from the responses of people with tablet-treated diabetes. *Diabetic Medicine,* 7, 445–451.

Bradley, C., Brewin, C., Gamsu, D. and Moses, J. (1984) Development of scales to measure perceived control of diabetes mellitus and diabetes related health beliefs. *Diabetic Medicine,* 1, 213–218.

Bradley, C., Lewis, K., Jennings, A. and Ward, S. (1990) Scales to measure perceived control developed specifically for people with tablet treated diabetes. *Diabetic Medicine,* 7, 685–694.

Bradley, L. A., Young, L. D., Anderson, K. O., Turner, R. A., Agudelo, C. A., McDaniel, L. K., Pisko, E. J., Semble, E. L. and Morgan, E. M. (1987) Effects of psychological therapy on pain behaviour of rheumatoid arthritis patients. *Arthritis and Rheumatism* 30, 1105–1114.

Brady, J. V. (1958) Ulcers in 'executive' monkeys. *Scientific American,* 199, 95–100.

Braken, M. B., Klerman, L. V. and Braken, M. (1978) Abortion, adoption or motherhood: an empirical study of decision making during pregnancy. *American Journal of Obstetrics and Gynecology,* 130, 251–262.

Brehm, J. (1966) *A Theory of Psychological Reactance.* New York: Academic Press.

Brener, J. M. (1981) Control of internal activities. *British Medical Bulletin,* 37, 169–174.

Breslow, L. and Enstrom, J. E. (1980) Persistence of health habits and their relationship to mortality. *Preventive Medicine,* 9, 469–483.

Breuer, J. and Freud, S. (1893) *Studies in Hysteria.* London: Hogarth Press.

Brezinka, V. (1992) Conservative treatment of childhood and adolescent obesity. In: S. Maes, H. Leventhal and M. Johnston (eds) *International Review of Health Psychology, Vol. 1.* Chichester: Wiley.

Bristol, J. B., Emmett, P. M., Heaton, K. W. and Williamson, R. C. N. (1985) Sugar, fat and risk of colorectal cancer. *British Medical Journal,* 291, 1467–1470.

Bristow, M., Hucklebridge, F., Clow, A. and Evans, P. D. (1997) Modulation of secretory Immunoglobulin A in saliva in relation to an acute episode of stress and arousal. *Journal of Psychophysiology,* 11.

British Diabetic Association (1996) *Diabetes in the United Kingdom: A Report .* London: British Medical Association Publication.

British Medical Association (1995) *Alcohol: Guidelines on Sensible Drinking.* London: British Medical Association Publication.

Broadhead, R., Heckathorn, D., Grund, J., Stern, S. and Anthony, L. (1995) Drug users versus outreach workers in combating AIDS: preliminary results of a peer-driven intervention. *The Journal of Drug Issues,* 25, 531–564.

Bronfenbrenner, U. (1979) *The Ecology Of Human Development.* Cambridge, MA: Harvard University Press.

Brooke, O. G., Anderson, H. R., Bland, J. M., Peacock, J. L. and Stewart, C. M. (1989) Effects on birth weight of smoking, alcohol, caffeine, socioeconomic factors, and psychosocial stress. *British Medical Journal,* 298, 795–801.

Brorsson, B. and Herlitz, C. (1988) The AIDS epidemic in Sweden: changes in awareness, attitudes and behaviour. *Scandinavian Journal of Social Medicine,* 16, 2129–2135.

Brown, G. W. (1993) Life events and affective disorders: replications and limitations. *Psychomatic Medicine,* 55, 248–259.

Brown, G. W. and Harris, T. O. (1978) *Social Origins of Depression. A Study of Psychiatric Disorder in Women.* London: Tavistock.

Brown, G. W. and Harris, T. O. (1986) Establishing causal links: the Bedford College studies of depression. In: H. Katschnig (ed.) *Life Events and Psychiatric Disorders.* Cambridge, Cambridge University Press.

Brown, R. T., Doepke, K. J. and Kaslow, N. J. (1993) Risk-resistance-adaptation model for pediatric chronic illness: sickle cell syndrome as an example. *Clinical Psychology Review*, 13, 119–132.

Brownell, K. D. and Cohen, L. R. (1995) Adherence to dietary regimens 1: an overview of research. *Behavioral Medicine*, 20(4), 149–154.

Brubaker, R. and Fowler, C. (1990) Encouraging college males to perform testicular self examination: evaluation of a persuasive message based on the revised theory of reasoned action. *Journal of Applied Social Psychology*, 20, 1411–1422.

Brubaker, R. and Wickersham, D. (1990) Encouraging the practice of testicular self examination: a field application of the theory of reasoned action. *Health Psychology*, 9(2), 154–163.

Bruce, M. S. and Lader, M. H. (1986) Caffeine: clinical and experimental effects in humans. *Human Psychopharmacology*, 1, 63–82.

Bruch, M. A. and Haynes, M. J. (1987) Heterosocial anxiety and contraceptive behaviour. *Journal of Research in Personality*, 21, 343–360.

Brunson, B. I. and Matthews, K. A. (1981) The Type A coronary prone behaviour pattern and reactions to uncontrollable stress. An analysis of performance strategies, affect and attributions during failure. *Journal of Personality and Social Psychology*, 40, 906–918.

Buetow, S. A. (1995) What do general practitioners and their patients want from general practice and are they receiving it? – A framework. *Social Science and Medicine*, 40(2), 213–221.

Buller, M. K. and Buller, D. B. (1987) Physicians' communication style and patient satisfaction. *Journal of Health and Social Behaviour*, 28, 375–388.

Burr, M. L. (1995) Explaining the French paradox. *Journal of the Royal Society for Health*, 115(4), 217–219.

Burton, A. K. and Tillotson, M. (1991) Does leisure sports activity influence lumbar mobility or the risk of low back trouble? *Journal of Spinal Disorders*, 4, 329–336.

Burton, A. K., Tillotson, K. M., Main, C. J. and Hollis, S. (1995) Psychosocial predictors of outcome in acute and sub-chronic low-back trouble. *Spine*, 20, 722–728.

Burton, A. K., Waddell, G., Burtt, R. and Blair, S. (1996) Patient educational material in the management of low back pain in primary care. *Bulletin Hospital for Joint Diseases*, 55, 138–141.

Burton, M. V., Parker, R. W., Farrell, A., Bailey, D., Conneely, J., Booth, S. and Elcombe, S. (1995) A randomized controlled trial of preoperative psychological preparation for mastectomy. *Psycho-Oncology*, 4(1), 1–19.

Bush, J. P., Melamed, B., Sheras, P. and Greenbaum, P. (1986) Mother–child patterns of coping with anticipatory medical stress. *Health Psychology*, 5, 137–157.

Bussing, R. and Johnson, S. (1992) Psychosocial issues in hemophilia before and after the AIDS crises: a review of current research. *General Hospital Psychiatry*, 14, 387–403.

Byers, E. S. and Lewis, K. (1988) Dating couples' disagreements over the desired level of sexual intimacy. *Journal of Sex Research*, 24, 15–29.

Byers, R. E., Graham, S., Haughey, B. P., Marshall, J. R. and Swanson, M. K. (1987) Diet and lung cancer risk: findings from the Western New York Diet Study. *American Journal of Epidemiology*, 125, 351–363.

Byrne, D., Rosenman, R. H., Schiller, E. and Chesney, M. A. (1985) Consistency and variation among instruments purporting to measure the Type A behaviour pattern. *Psychosomatic Medicine*, 47, 242–261.

Byrne, D., Napier, A. and Cuschieri, A. (1988) How informed is signed consent? *British Medical Journal*, 296, 839–840.

Caceres, C. F., Rosasco, A. M., Mandel, J. S. and Hearst, N. (1994) Evaluating a school-based intervention for STD/AIDS prevention in Peru. *Journal of Adolescent Health*, 15(7), 582–591.

Cadman, D., Boyle, M., Szatmari, P. and Offord, D. R. (1987) Chronic illness, disability, and mental and social well-being: findings of the Ontario Child Health Study. *Pediatrics*, 79, 805–812.

Cairns, D. and Pasino, J. A. (1977) Comparison of verbal reinforcement and feedback in the operant treatment of disability due to chronic low back pain. *Behaviour Therapy* 8, 621–630.

Calabrese, L. H. (1990) Exercise, immunity, cancer and infection. In: C. Bouchard, R.J. Shephard, T. Stephens, J. R. Sutton and B. D. McPherson (eds), *Exercise Fitness and Health: A Consensus of Current Knowledge*. Champaign, Ill: Human Kinetics Books.

Calman, K. C. (1984) Quality of life in cancer patients – an hypothesis. *Journal of Medical Ethics*, 10, 124–127.

Calvillo, E. and Flaskerud, J. (1993) Evaluation of pain response by Mexican American and Anglo-American women and their nurses. *Journal of Advanced Nursing*, 18(3), 451–459.

Caplan, H., Cogill, S., Alexandra, H., Robson, K. M., Katz, R. and Kumar, R. (1989) Maternal depression and the emotional development of the child. *British Journal of Psychiatry*, 154, 818–822.

Carlson, J. G., Basilio, C. A. and Heaukulani, J. D. (1983) Transfer of EMG training: another look at the general relaxation issue. *Psychophysiology*, 20, 530–536.

Carmel, S., Shani, E. and Rosenberg, L. (1994) The role of age and an expanded health belief model in predicting skin cancer protective behavior. *Health Education Research*, 9(4), 433–447.

Caron, H. S. and Roth, H. P. (1968) Patients' cooperation with a medical regimen. *Journal of the American Medical Association*, 203, 922–926.

Carroll, D. (1992) *Health Psychology: Stress Behaviour and Health*. London: Falmer Press.

Carroll, D., Bennett, P. and Smith, G. D. (1993) Socio-economic health inequalities – their origins and implications. *Psychology and Health*, 8(5), 295–316.

Carroll, D., Davey Smith, G. and Bennett, P. (1994) Health and socio-economic status. *The Psychologist*, 7, 122–125.

Carroll, D., Hewitt, J. K., Last, K. A., Turner, J. R. and Sims, J. (1985) A twin study of cardiac reactivity and its relationship to parental blood pressure. *Physiology and Behaviour*, 34, 103–106.

Carroll, D., Ring, C., Shrimpton, J., Evans, P., Willemsen, G.H. and Hucklebridge, F. (1996) Secretory immunoglobulin A and cardiovascular response to acute psychological challenge. *International Journal of Behavioral Medicine*, 3, 266–279.

Cassel, J. (1975) Studies of hypertension in migrants. In: O. Paul (ed.) *Epidemiology and Control of Hypertension*. New York: Stratton.

Cassileth, B. R. (1996) Stress and the development of breast cancer – persistent and popular link despite contrary evidence. *Cancer*, 77, 1015–1016.

Cassileth, B. R., Lusk, E. J., Miller, D. S., Brown, L. L. and Miller, C. (1985) Psychosocial correlates of survival in advanced malignant diseases. *New England Journal of Medicine*, 312, 1551–1555.

Cassileth, B. R., Zupkis, R. V., Suton-Smith, K. and March, V. (1980) Information and participation preferences among cancer patients. *Annals of Internal Medicine*, 92, 832–836.

Casswell, S. (1996) Drinking guidelines offer little over and above the much needed public health policies. *Addiction*, 91, 26–29.

Cataldo, M. F., Dershewitz, R. A., Wilson, M., Christophersen, E. R., Finney, J. W., Fawcett, S. B. and Seekins, T. (1986) Childhood injury control. In: N. A. Krasegor, J. D. Arasteh and M. F. Cataldo (eds) *Child Health Behavior. A Behavioral Pediatrics Perspective*. New York: John Wiley.

Caterson, I. D. (1990) Management strategies for weight control. Eating, exercise and behaviour. *Drugs*, 39 (Suppl. 3), 20–32.

Cavanagh, S. (1983) The prevalence of emotional and cognitive dysfunction in a general medical population: using the MMSE, GHQ and BDI. *General Hospital Psychiatry*, 5, 15–24.

Cella, D. F. and Holland, J. C. (1988) Methodological considerations in studying the stress-illness connection in women with breast cancer. In: C. L. Cooper (ed.) *Stress and Breast Cancer*. Chichester: John Wiley.

Center for Disease Control (CDC) (1981) Kaposi's sarcoma and pneumocystis pneumonia among homosexual men – New York City and California. *Morbidity and Mortality Weekly Reports*, 30, 305–308.

CDC (1982) Unexplained immunodeficiency and opportunistic infections in children – New York, New Jersey, California. *Morbidity and Mortality Weekly Reports*, 31, 665–667.

CDC (1985) *Education and Foster Care of Children Infected with Human T-lymphotropic Virus Type 3/lymphadenopathy Associated Virus*. Atlanta, Georgia: CDC.

CDC (1987) Classification system for human immunodeficiency virus (HIV) infection in children under 13 years of age. *Morbidity and Mortality Weekly Reports*, 36, 225–230, 235–236.

Chadwick, E. (1842) *Report of an Enquiry into the Sanitary Conditions of the Labouring Population of Great Britain*. London: Poor Law Commission.

Chaitchik, S., Kreitler, S., Shaked, S., Schwartz, I. and Rosin, R. (1992) Doctor–patient communication in a cancer ward. *Journal of Cancer Education*, 7, 41.

Chalmers, B. E. (1982) Stressful life events: their past and present status. *Current Psychological Reviews*, 2, 123–138.

Chapman, C. R. and Turner, J. A. (1986) Psychological control of acute pain in medical settings. *Journal of Pain Symptom Management*, 1, 9–20.

Chapman, C. R., Casey, K. L., Dubner, R., Foley, K. M., Gracely, R. H. and Reading, A. E. (1985) Pain measurement: an overview. *Pain*, 22, 1–31.

Chapman, S. and Hodgson, J. (1988) Showers in raincoats: attitudinal barriers to condom use in high risk heterosexuals. *Community Health Studies*, 12, 97–105.

Chapman, S., Wong, W. L. and Smith, W. (1993) Self exempting beliefs about smoking and health: differences between smokers and ex-smokers. *American Journal of Public Health*, 83(2), 215–219.

Chapman, S. L. (1991) Chronic pain: psychological assessment and treatment. In: J. J. Sweet, R. H. Rozensky and S. M. Toavian (eds) *Handbook of Clinical Psychology in Medical Settings*. New York: Plenum.

Cherkin, D. C., Deyo, R. A., Street, J. H., Hunt, M. and Barlow, W. (1996) Pitfalls of patient education: limited success of a program for back pain in primary care. *Spine*, 21, 345–355.

Chesney, M. A., Black, G. W., Swan, G. E. and Ward, M. M. (1987) Relaxation training for essential hypertension at the worksite: I. The untreated mild hypertensive. *Psychosomatic Medicine*, 49, 250–263.

Chick, J., Lloyd, G. and Crombie, E. (1985) Counselling problem drinkers in medical wards: a controlled study. *British Medical Journal*, 290, 965–967.

Chilman, C. S. (1985) Feminist issues in teenage parenting. *Child Welfare*, 64, 225–234.

Christie, M. J. and Woodman, D. D. (1980) Biochemical methods. In: I. Martin and P. H. Venables (eds) *Techniques in Psychophysiology*. Chichester: John Wiley and Sons.

Christopher, E. (1991) Family planning and reproductive decisions. *Journal of Reproductive and Infant Psychology*, 9, 217–226.

Chrousos, G. P. and Gold, P. W. (1996) Stress, endocrine manifestations, and disease. In: C. Cooper (ed.) *Handbook of Stress, Medicine and Health*. London: CRC Press.

Clare, A. W. and Tyrrell, J. (1994) Psychiatric aspects of abortion. *Irish Journal of Psychological Medicine*, 11, 92–98.

Cleary, P. D. (1987) Why people take precautions against health risks. In: N. D. Weinstein (ed.) *Taking Care: Understanding and Encouraging Self-Protective Behaviours*. Cambridge: Cambridge University Pres.

CSAG (Clinical Standards Advisory Group) (1994) *Management Guidelines for Back Pain*. London: HMSO.

Clow, A., Hucklebridge, F. and Evans, P. (1997) The role and regulation of monoamines in stress. In: E. R. De Kloet, D. Ben Nathan, E. Grauer and A. Levy (eds) *New Frontiers in Stress Research. Modulation of Brain Function*. New York: Harwood Academic.

Coates, T. J. (1982) Hypertension in adolescents. In: A. Baum and J. E. Singer (eds) *Handbook of Psychology and Health, Volume II: Issues in Child Health and Adolescent Health*. Hillsdale, NJ: LEA.

Cobliner, W. G., Schulman, H. and Smith, V. (1975) Patterns of contraceptive failures: the role of motivation reexamined. *Journal of Biosocial Science*, 7, 307–318.

Cody, R. and Lee, C. (1990) Behaviors, beliefs and intentions in skin cancer prevention. *Journal of Behavioral Medicine*, 13(4), 373–389.

Cohen, J. B., Hauser, L. B. and Wofsy, C. B. (1989) Women and IV drugs: parenteral and hetero-sexual transmission of human immunodeficiency virus. *Journal of Drug Issues*, 19, 39–56.

Cohen, M. J., Heinrich, R. L., Collins, G. A. and Bonnebakker, A. D. (1980) Group outpatient physical or behavioural therapy for chronic low back pain. Paper presented at the Annual Meeting of the American Pain Society, New York, September.

Cohen, S. and Lichtenstein, E. (1990) Perceived stress, quitting smoking, and smoking relapse. *Health Psychology*, 9, 466–478.

Cohen, S., Tyrrell, D. A. J. and Smith, A. P. (1993) Negative life events, perceived stress, negative affect, and susceptibility to the common cold. *Journal of Personality and Social Psychology*, 64, 131–140.

Cohn, J. F., Campbell, S. B., Matias, R. and Hopkins, J. (1990) Face-to-face interactions of post-partum depressed and nondepressed mother–infant pairs at 2 months. *Developmental Psychology*, 26, 15–23.

Colditz, G. A. (1993) Epidemiology of breast cancer. Findings from the nurses' health study. *Cancer*, 15 February, 71, (Suppl. 4), 1480–1489.

Coles, C. (1990) Diabetes education: letting the patient into the picture. *Practical Diabetes*, 7, 110–112.

Comitas, L. (1976) Cannabis and work in Jamaica: a refutation of the amotivational syndrome. *Annals of the New York Academy of Science*, 24–32.

Communicable Disease Reports (1995) 5, 97–98.

Conklin, M. (1983) Men's knowledge and beliefs about the testicle self-exam. *American Journal of Nursing*, 83, 200–205.

Connell, C., Kubisch, A., Schorr, L. and Weiss, C. (1995) *New Approaches To Evaluating Community Initiatives*. Washington, DC: The Aspen Institute.

Connor, W.H. (1974) Effects of brief relaxation training on autonomic response to anxiety-provoking stimuli. *Psychophysiology*, 11, 591–599.

Conor, P. M., Kirby, M., Coen, R., Coakley, D., Lawlor, B. A. and O'Neil, D. (1996) Family members' attitudes toward telling the patient with Alzheimer's disease their diagnosis. *British Medical Journal*, 313, 529–530.

Contento, I. R., Basch, C., Shea, S., Gutin, B., Zybert, P., Michela, J. L. and Rips, J. (1993) Relationship of mothers' food choice criteria to food intake of preschool children: identi-fication of family subgroups. *Health Education Quarterly*, 20(2), 243–259.

Conviser, R. and Rutledge, J. H. (1989) Can public policies limit the spread of HIV among IV drug users? *Journal of Drug Issues*, 19, 113–128.

Cooper, C., Cooper, R. D. and Faragher, E. B. (1986) Psychosocial stress as a precursor to breast cancer: a review. *Current Psychological Research and Reviews*, 5(3), 268–280.

Cooper, E. T. (1984) A pilot study on the effects of the diagnosis of lung cancer on family rela-tionships. *Cancer Nursing*, 7, 301–308.

Coste, J., Paalaggi, J. B. and Spira, A. (1992) Classification of non-specific low back pain. Part 1. Psychological involvement in low back pain. *Spine*, 17, 1028–1037.

Council on Ethical and Judicial Affairs (1991) Gender disparities in clinical decision making. *Journal of the American Medical Association*, 266, 559–562.

Cowell, J. M., Montgomery, A. C. and Talashek, M. L. (1989) Cardiovascular risk assessment in school-age children: partnership in health promotion. *Public Health Nursing*, 6, 67–73.

Cox, A. D. (1988) Maternal depression and impact on children's development. *Archives of Disease in Childhood*, 63, 90–95.

Cox, D. J. and Gonder-Frederick, L. (1992) Major developments in behavioural diabetes research. *Journal of Consulting and Clinical Psychology*, 60, 28–38.

Cox, D. J., Gonder-Frederick, L. and Saunders, J. T. (1991) Diabetes: clinical issues and manage-ment. In: J. J. Sweet, R. H. Razensky and S. M. Tovain (eds) *Handbook of Clinical Psychology in Medical Settings*. New York: Plenum.

Cox, D. J., Taylor, A. B., Nowacek, B., Holley-Wilcox, P., Pohl, S. and Guthrow, E. (1984) The relationship between psychological stress and insulin-dependent diabetic blood glucose control: preliminary investigations. *Health Psychology*, 3, 63–75.

Cox, N., Blaxter, M., Buckle, A. *et al.* (1987) *The Health and Lifestyle Survey: Preliminary Report*. Cambridge: The Health Promotion Research Trust.

Cox, T. (1988) Psychological factors in stress and health: In: S. Fisher and J. Reason (eds) *Handbook of Life Stress, Cognition and Health*. Chichester: John Wiley & Sons.

Cox, T. and Mackay, C. (1982) Psychosocial factors and psychophysiological mechanisms in the aetiology and development of cancers. *Social Science and Medicine*, 16, 381–396.

CRC (1995) *Annual Report 1994/95*. Thorpe, PA: University of New England.

Crisson, J. E. and Keefe, F. J. (1988) The relationship of locus of control to pain coping strategies and psychological distress in chronic pain patients. *Pain*, 35, 147–154.

Crombie, I. K. (1996) *A Pocket Guide to Critical Appraisal*. London: BMJ Publishing Group.

Cumming, D. C. (1990) Discussion: reproduction: exercise related adaptations and the health of men and women. In: C. Bouchard, R. J. Shephard, T. Stephens, J. R. Sutton and B. D. McPherson (eds) *Exercise Fitness and Health: A Consensus of Current Knowledge*. Champaign, Ill: Human Kinetics Books.

Cunningham-Burley, S. and Irvine, S. (1987) 'And have you done anything so far?' An examination of lay treatment of children's symptoms. *British Medical Journal*, 295, 700–702.

Cvetkovich, G. and Grote, B. (1981) Psychosocial maturity and teenage contraceptive use: an investigation of decision-making and communication skills. *Population and Environment*, 4, 211–226.

Cvetkovich, G. and Grote, B. (1983) Adolescent development and teenage fertility. In: D. Byrne and W. A. Fisher (eds) *Adolescents, Sex and Contraception*. Hillsdale, NJ: Lawrence Erlbaum.

D'Angelo, L. J., Brown, R., English, A. and Hein, K. (1994) HIV infection and AIDS in adolescents: a position paper for the Society of Adolescent Medicine. *Journal of Adolescent Health*, 15, 427–434.

D'Atri, D. A. and Ostfield, A. M. (1975) Crowding: its effects on the elevation of blood pressure in a prison setting. *Preventive Medicine*, 4, 550–566.

Dahl, L. K. (1961) Possible role of excess salt consumption in the pathogenesis of essential hypertension. *American Journal of Cardiology*, 8, 571–575.

Dahl, L. K. and Love, R. A. (1957) Etiological role of sodium chloride intake in essential hypertension in humans. *Journal of the American Medical Association*, 164, 397–400.

Dahlstrom, W. G. and Welsh, G. S. (1960) *An MMPI Handbook*. Minneapolis: University of Minnesota Press.

Dantzer, R. (1989) Neuroendocrine correlates of control and coping. In: A. Steptoe and A. Appels (eds) *Stress, Personal Control and Health*. Chichester: John Wiley & Sons.

Davey, B. (1989) *Immunology: A Foundation Text*. Chichester: John Wiley & Sons.

Davey-Smith, G., Shipley, M. J. and Rose, G. (1990) Magnitude and causes of socio-economic differentials in mortality; further evidence from the Whitehall study. *Journal of Epidemiology and Community Health*, 44, 265–270.

Davis, H. and Fallowfield, L. (1996) Evaluating the effects of counselling and communication. In: H. Davis and L. Fallowfield (eds) *Counselling and Communication in Health Care*. Chichester: John Wiley & Sons.

Davis, M. S. (1966) Variations in patients' compliance with doctors' orders: analysis of congruence between survey responses and results of empirical investigations. *Journal of Medical Education*, 41, 1037–1048.

Davis, W. K., Hess, G. E. and Hiss, R. G. (1988) Psychosocial correlates of survival in diabetes. *Diabetes Care*, 11, 538–545.

Davison, D. and Parrott, A. C. (1997) Ecstasy (MDMA) in recreational users: self-reported psychological and physiological effects. *Human Psychopharmacology*, 12, 221–226.

Davitz, J. and Davitz, L. (1981) *Inferences of Patients' Pain and Psychological Distress*. New York: Springer Publishing.

Day Report (1993) The incidence and prevalence of AIDS:HIV disease in England and Wales for 1992–1997. Report of a Working Group (Chair: N. Day). *Communicable Disease Report (CDR)*, 3, S1–S17.

DCCT Research Group (1988) Reliability and validity of a diabetes quality of life measure for the diabetes control and complications trial (DCCT). *Diabetes Care*, 725–732.

DCCT Research Group (1993) The effect of intensive treatment of diabetes on the development and progression of long-term complications in insulin-dependent diabetes mellitus. *New England Journal of Medicine,* 329, 977–986.

De Freitas, B. and Schwartz, G. (1979) Effects of caffeine on chronic psychiatric patients. *American Journal of Psychiatry,* 136, 1337–1338.

Deburgh, S. (1996) The preventive paradox disarmed. *Drug and Alcohol Review,* 15(1), 18–20.

Delahanty, D. L., Dougall, A. L., Schmitz, J. B., Harken, L., Trakowski, J. H., Jenkins, F. J. and Baum, A. (1996) Time course of natural killer cell activity and lymphocyte proliferation in response to two acute stressors in healthy men. *Health Psychology,* 155, 48–55.

Dembroski, T. M., MacDougall, J. M., Williams, R. B., Haney, T. L. and Blumenthal, J. A. (1985) Components of Type A, hostility, and anger-in: relationship to angiographic findings. *Psychosomatic Medicine,* 47, 219–233.

Derogatis, L. R., Abeloff, M. D. and McBeth, C. D. (1976) Cancer patients and their physicians in the perception of psychological symptoms. *Psychosomatics,* 17, 197–201.

Devine, E. C. and Cook, T. D. (1983) A meta-analysis of psychoeducational interventions on length of postsurgical hospital stay. *Nursing Research,* 32, 267–274.

Devine, E. C. and Cook, T. D. (1986) Clinical and cost-saving effects of psychoeducational interventions with surgical patients: a meta-analysis. *Research in Nursing and Health,* 9, 89–105.

deWeerdt, I., Visser, A. and van der Veen, E. (1989) Attitude behaviour and theories in diabetes education programmes. *Patient Education and Counselling,* 14, 3–19.

DHSS (1980) *Inequalities in Health: Report of a Working Group Chaired by Sir Douglas Black.* London: Department of Health and Social Security.

DHSS (1992) *The Health of the Nation. A Strategy for Health in England.* London: HMSO.

DHSS (1995) *Department of Health: Variations in Health: What can the Department of Health and NHS Do?* London: HMSO.

DHSS and Welsh Office (1987) *AIDS: Monitoring Responses to the Public Education Campaign February 1986–February 1987.* London: HMSO.

DiBlasio, F. A. and Belcher, J. R. (1995) Gender differences among homeless persons – special services for women. *American Journal of Orthopsychiatry,* 65(1), 131–137.

DiClemente, R. J. (1993) Preventing HIV/AIDS amongst adolescents: schools as agents of behavioural change. *Journal of the American Medical Association,* 270, 760–762.

DiClemente, R. J. and Temoshok, L. (1985) Psychological adjustment to having cutaneous malignant melanoma as a predictor of follow-up clinical states. *Psychosomatic Medicine,* 47, 87–89.

Diener, E. (1984) Subjective well-being. *Psychological Bulletin,* 95, 542–575.

Dimatteo, M. R. and DiNicola, D. D. (1982) *Achieving Patient Compliance.* New York: Pergamon Press.

Dimatteo, M. R., Reiter, R. C. and Gambone, J. C. (1994) Enhancing medication adherence through communication and informed collaborative choice. *Health Communications,* 6(4), 253–265.

Dimatteo, M. R., Sherbourne, C. D., Hays, R. D., Ordway, L., Kravitz, R. L., Mcglynn, E. A., Kaplan, S. and Rogers, W. H. (1993) Physicians' characteristics influence patients' adherence to medical treatment – results from the medical outcomes study. *Health Psychology,* 12 (2), 93–102.

Dodd, M. J. (1987) Efficacy of proactive information on self-care in radiation therapy patients. *Heart and Lung,* 16, 538–544.

Dohery, Y. A. and Hall, D. A. (1996) *Change Counselling in Diabetes Project: The Results of a Needs Assessment.* Paper presented at the BPS Special Group in Health Psychology Annual Conference (3–5 July), York.

Dohrenwend, B. S. and Dohrenwend, B. P. (1974) *Stressful Life Events: Their Nature and Effects.* New York: John Wiley & Sons.

Doleys, D. M., Crocker, M. and Patton, D. (1982) Response of patients with chronic pain to exercise quotas. *Physical Therapy,* 62, 1111–1114.

Doll, R. and Peto, R. (1976) Mortality in relation to smoking: 20 years' observations on male British doctors. *British Medical Journal*, ii, 1525–1536.

Dornbusch, S. M., Ritter, P. L., Liederman, P. H., Roberts, D. F. and Fraleigh, M. J. (1987) The relation of parenting style to adolescent school performance. *Child Development*, 58, 1244–1257.

Douds, A. C. and Maxwell, J. D. (1994) Alcohol and the heart – good and bad news. *Addiction*, 89(3), 259–261.

Dowling, J. (1983) Autonomic measures and behavioural indices of pain sensitivity. *Pain*, 16, 193–200.

Downey, G. and Coyne, J. C. (1990) Children of depressed parents: an integrative review. *Psychological Bulletin*, 108, 50–76.

Doyle, A., Pang, F. Y., Bristow, M., Hucklebridge, F., Evans, P. and Clow, A. (1996) Urinary cortisol and endogenous monoamine oxidose inhibitors, but not isatin, are raised in anticipation of stress and/or arousal in normal individuals. *Stress Medicine*, 12, 43–49.

Drapkin, R. G., Wing, R. R. and Shiffman, S. (1995) Responses to hypothetical risk situations: do they predict weight loss in a behavioural treatment program or the context of dietary lapses? *Health Psychology*, 14, 427–434.

Dunbar, F. (1943) *Psychosomatic Diagnosis*. New York: Harper & Row.

Dunbar, M. (1989) *The Effects of Psychological and Educational Interventions on the Recovery of Surgical Patients: A Meta-analysis*. Unpublished dissertation submitted in completion of B.Sc. Psychology, Polytechnic of East London.

Duncan, G., Harper, C., Ashwell, E., Mant, D., Buchan, H. and Jones, L. (1990) Termination of pregnancy: lessons for prevention. *British Journal of Family Planning*, 15, 112–117.

Dworkin, B. (1988) Hypertension as a learned response: the baroreceptor reinforcement. In: T. Elbert, W. Langosch, A. Steptoe and D. Vaitl (eds) *Behavioural Medicine in Cardiovascular Disorders*. Chichester: John Wiley & Sons.

Economides, D. and Braithwaite, J. (1994) Smoking, pregnancy and the fetus. *Journal of the Royal Society of Health*, 114, 198–201.

Eddy, D. M. and Clanton, C. H. (1982) The art of diagnosis: solving the clinicopathological exercise. *The New England Journal of Medicine*, 306, 1263–1268.

Edell, B. H., Edington, S., Herd, B., O'Brien, R. M. and Witkin, G. (1987) Self efficacy and self motivation as predictors of weight loss. *Addictive Behaviors*, 12, 63–66.

Edelstein, J. and Linn, M. W. (1985) The influence of the family on control of diabetes. *Social Science and Medicine*, 21, 545–551.

Edmundson, E., Parcel, G. S., Perry, C. L., Feldman, H. A., Smyth, M., Johnson, C. C., Layman, A., Bachman, K., Perkins, T., Smith, K. and Stone, E. (1996) The effects of the child and adolescent trial for cardiovascular health intervention on psychosocial determinants of cardiovascular disease risk behavior among third-grade students. *American Journal of Health Promotion*, 10(3), 217–225.

Edwards, G., Anderson, P. and Babor, T. F. (1994) *Alcohol Policy and the Public Good*. Oxford: Oxford University Press.

Effective Health Care (1996) *The Management of Primary Breast Cancer*, 2, No. 6. NHS Centre for Reviews and Dissemination.

Eiser, C. (1993) *Growing Up With A Chronic Disease. The Impact On Children And Their Families*. London: Kingsley Publishers.

Eiser, C., Havermans, G., Parkyn, T. and McNinch, A. (1994) When a child has cancer: parents' experiences around the diagnosis. *Psycho-Oncology*, 4, 197–203.

Eiser, J. R., Eiser, C. and Pauwels, P. (1993) Skin cancer – assessing perceived risk and behavioural attitudes. *Psychology and Health*, 8(6), 393–404.

Elias, M. F., Robbins, M. A., Rice, A. and Edgecombe, J. L. (1982) A behavioral study of middle-aged chest pain patients: physical symptom reporting, anxiety and depression. *Experimental Aging Research*, 8, 45–51.

Ellermeier, W. and Westphal, W. (1995) Gender differences in pain ratings and pupil reactions to painful pressure stimuli. *Pain*, 61: 435–439.

Ellerton, M. L. and Merriam, C. (1994) Preparing children and families psychologically for day surgery – an evaluation. *Journal of Advanced Nursing*, 19(6), 1057–1062.

Ellis, A. (1962) *Reason and Emotion in Psychotherapy*. New York: Lyle Stuart.

Ellis, A. (1984) Rational emotive therapy. In: R. J. Corsini (ed.) *Current Psychotherapies, 3rd edn*. Itasca, Ill: Peacock Press.

Elson, B. D., Hauri, P. and Cunis, D. (1977) Physiological changes in yoga meditation. *Psychophysiology*, 14, 52–57.

Engel, G. L. (1959) Psychogenic pain and the pain prone patient. *American Journal of Medicine*, 26, 899–918.

Engel, G. L. (1977) The need for a new medical model: a challenge for biomedicine. *Science*, 196, 129–135.

Engs, R. C. (1996) Women, alcohol, and health: a drink a day keeps the heart attack away? *Current Opinion in Psychiatry*, 9(3), 217–220.

Engstroem, I. (1991) Parental distress and social interaction in families with children with inflammatory bowel disease. *Journal of the American Academy of Child and Adolescent Psychiatry*, 30, 904–912.

Epstein, L. H., Wing, R. R., Valoski, A. and DeVos, D. (1988) Long term relationship between weight and aerobic fitness change in children. *Health Psychology*, 7, 47–53.

Epstein, M. and Oster, J. R. (1984) *Hypertension: A Practical Approach*. Philadelphia: Saunders.

Eriksen, W. (1994) The role of social support in the pathogenesis of coronary heart disease. *Family Practice*, 11(2), 201–209.

Evans, P. D. (1989) *Motivation and Emotion*. London: Routledge.

Evans, P. D. and Edgerton, N. (1991) Life events and mood as predictors of the common cold. *British Journal of Medical Psychology*, 64, 35–44.

Evans, P. D. and Edgerton, N. (1992) Mood states and minor illness. *British Journal of Medical Psychology*, 65, 177–186.

Evans, P. D. and Fearn, J. M. (1985) Type A behaviour pattern, choice of active coping strategy and cardiovascular activity in relation to threat of shock. *British Journal of Medical Psychology*, 58, 95–99.

Evans, P. D. and Moran, P. (1987a) The Framingham Type A scale, vigilant coping and heart rate reactivity. *Journal of Behavioural Medicine*, 10, 311–321.

Evans, P. D. and Moran, P. (1987b) Cardiovascular unwinding, Type A behaviour pattern and locus of control. *British Journal of Medical Psychology*, 60, 261–265.

Evans, P. D., Phillips, K. C. and Fearn, J. M. (1984) On choosing to make aversive events predictable or unprecitable: some behavioural and psychophysiological findings. *British Journal of Psychology*, 75, 377–391.

Evans, P. D., Pitts, M. K. and Smith, K. (1988) Minor infection, minor life events and the four day desirability dip. *Journal of Psychosomatic Research*, 32, 533–539.

Evans, P. D., Bristow, M., Hucklebridge, F., Clow, A. and Walters, N. (1993) The relationship between secretory immunity, mood and life events. *British Journal of Clinical Psychology*, 33, 227–236.

Evans, P. D., Bristow, M., Hucklebridge, F., Clow, A. and Pang, F.-Y. (1994) Stress, arousal, cortisol and secretory immunoglobulin A in students undergoing assessment. *British Journal of Clinical Psychology*, 33, 575–576.

Evans, P. D., Doyle, A., Hucklebridge, F. and Clow, A. (1996) Positive but not negative life events predict vulnerability to upper respiratory tract illness. *British Journal of Health Psychology*, 1, 339–348.

Evans, P. D., Hucklebridge, F., Clow, A. and Doyle, A. (1995) Secretory immunoglobulin A as a convenient biomarker in health survey work. In: J. Rodriques-Marin (ed.) *Health Psychology and Quality of Life Research. Volume 2*. Alicante, University Press.

Eysenck, H. J. (1985) Personality, cancer and cardiovascular disease: a causal analysis. *Personality and Individual Differences*, 6, 535–556.

Eysenck, H. J. (1990) The prediction of death from cancer by means of personality stress questionnaire – too good to be true. *Perceptual and Motor Skills*, 71, 216–218.

Eysenck, H. J. and Fulkner, D. W. (1983) The components of Type A behaviour and its genetic determinants. *Personality and Individual Differences*, 4, 499–505.

Faber, M. M. (1986) A review of efforts to protect children from injury in car crashes. *Family and Community Health*, 9, 25–41.

Faller, H., Schilling, S. and Lang, H. (1995) Causal attribution and adaptation among lung cancer patients. *Journal of Psychosomatic Research*, 39(5), 619–627.

Fallowfield, L., Ford, S. and Lewis, S. (1995) No news is not good news: information preferences of patients with cancer. *Psycho-Oncol*, 4(3), 197–202.

Fallowfield, L., Rodway, A. and Baum, A. (1990) What are the psychological factors influencing attendance, non-attendance and re-attendance at a breast screening centre? *Journal of the Royal Society of Medicine*, 83, 547–551.

Fallowfield, L., Hall, A., Maguire, P., Baum, M. and A'Hern, R. P. (1994a) Psychological effects of being offered choice of surgery for breast cancer. *British Medical Journal*, 309, 448.

Fallowfield, L., Hall, A., Maguire, P., Baum, M. and A'Hern, R. P. (1994b) A question of choice: results of a prospective 3-year follow-up study of women with breast cancer. *The Breast*, 3, 202–208.

Family Heart Study Group (1994) Randomised controlled trial evaluating cardiovascular screening and intervention in general practice: principal results of British family heart study. *British Medical Journal*, 308, 313–319.

Fant, R. V., Schuh, K. J. and Stitzer, M. L. (1995) Response to smoking as a function of prior amounts. *Psychopharmacology*, 119, 385–390.

Farkas, A. J., Pierce, J. P., Zhu, S. H., Rosbrook, B., Berry, C., Gilpin, E. A. and Kaplan, R. M. (1996) Addiction versus stages of change models in predicting smoking cessation. *Addiction*, 91, 1271–1280.

Fava, G., Pilowsky, I., Pierfederici, A., Bernardi, M. and Pathak, D. (1982) Depression and illness behavior in a general hospital: a prevalence study. *Psychotherapy and Psychosomatics*, 38, 141–153.

Favaro, A. and Santonastaso, P. (1995) Effects of parents' psychological characteristics and eating behaviour on childhood obesity and dietary compliance. *Journal of Psychosomatic Research*, 39(2), 145–151.

Feldman, E., Mayou, R., Hawton, K., Ardern, M. and Smith, E. B. O. (1987) Psychiatric disorder in medical inpatients. *Quarterly Journal of Medicine*, 63, 405–412.

Fendrich, W. and Weissman, M. M. (1990) Family risk factors, parent depression and psychopathology in offspring. *Developmental Psychology*, 26, 40–50.

Fergusson, D. M., Lynskey, M. T. and Horwood, J. L. (1995) The role of peer affiliations, social, family and individual factors in continuities in cigarette smoking between childhood and adolescence. *Addiction*, 90, 647–659.

Fernandez, E. (1982) A classification system of cognitive coping strategies of pain. *Pain*, 35, 147–154.

Ferrie, J. E., Shipley, M. J., Marmot, M. G., Stansfield, S. and Smith, G. D. (1995) Health effects of anticipation of job change and non-employment: longitudinal data from the Whitehall II study. *British Medical Journal*, 311(7015), 1264–1269.

Feuerstein, M. and Gainer, J. (1982) Chronic headache: etiology and management. In: D. M. Doleys, R. L. Meredith and A. R Ciminero (eds) *Behavioural Medicine: Assessment and Treatment Strategies*. New York: Plenum.

Field, T., Alpert, B., Vega-Lahr, N., Goldstein, S. and Perry, S. (1988) Hospitalisation stress in children: sensitizer and repressor coping styles. *Health Psychology*, 7, 433–445.

Field, T., Healy, B., Goldstein, S. and Guthertz, M. (1990) Behavior-state matching and synchrony in mother–infant interactions of nondepressed versus depressed dyads. *Developmental Psychology*, 26, 7–14.

Fillingim, R. B. and Maixner, W. (1996) The influence of resting blood-pressure and gender on pain responses. *Psychosomatic Medicine*, 58, 326–332.

Fishbein, M. (1972) Towards an understanding of family planning behaviors. *Journal of Applied Social Psychology*, 2, 214–227.

Fishbein, M. and Ajzen, I. (1975) *Belief, Attitude, Intention and Behavior: An Introduction to Theory and Research*. Reading, MA: Addison-Wesley.

Fisher, A. A. (1977) The health belief model and contraceptive behaviour: limits to the application of a conceptual framework. *Health Education Monograph*, 5, 244–250.

Fisher, S. (1986) *Stress and Strategy*. London: Lawrence Erlbaum Associates.

Fisher, S. (1996) Life stress, personal control and the risk of disease. In: C. Cooper (ed.) *Handbook of Stress, Medicine and Health*. London: CRC Press.

Fishman, B., Cooke, E., Hammock, S., Gregory, B. and Thomas, J. (1989) Familial transmission of fear: effects of maternal anxiety and presence on children's response to dental treatment. Paper presented at the Florida Conference on Child Health Psychology, Gainesville, FL.

Fletcher, B.C. (1988) The epidemiology of occupational stress. In: C. L. Cooper and R. Payne (eds) *Causes, Coping and Consequences of Stress at Work*. Chichester: John Wiley & Sons.

Fletcher, S., Morgan, T., O'Malley, M., Earp, J. A. and Degnan, D. (1989) Is breast self examination predicted by knowledge, attitudes, beliefs or sociodemographic characteristics. *American Journal of Preventive Medicine*, 5(4), 207–215.

Flor, H., Haag, G., Turk, D. C. and Koehler, H. (1983) Efficacy of EMG biofeedback, psychotherapy, and conventional medical treatment for chronic back pain. *Pain*, 17, 21–31.

Folsom, A. R., Kaye, S. A., Sellers, T. A., Hong, C.-P., Cerhan, J. R., Potter, J. D. and Prineas, R. J. (1993) Body fat distribution and 5-year risk of death in older women. *Journal of the American Medical Association*, 269, 483–487.

Folstein, S. E., Franz, M. L., Jensen, B. A., Chase, G. A. and Folstein, M. F. (1983) Conduct disorder and affective disorder among the offspring of patients with Huntington's Disease. *Psychological Medicine*, 13, 45–52.

Fonagy, P., Steele, H. and Steele, M. (1991) Maternal representations of attachment during pregnancy predict the organization of infant–mother attachment at one year of age. *Child Development*, 62, 891–905.

Fonagy, P., Steele, M., Steele, H., Higgitt, A. and Target, M. (1994) The Emanuel Miller Memorial Lecture, 1992. The theory and practice of resilience. *Journal of Child Psychology and Psychiatry*, 35, 231–257.

Ford, N. (1994) Cultural and developmental factors underlying the global pattern of the transmission of HIV/AIDS. In: D.R. Phillips and Y. Verhasselt (eds) *Health and Development*. London: Routledge.

Ford, S., Fallowfield, L. and Lewis, S. (1996) Doctor–patient interactions in oncology. *Social Science and Medicine*, 42(11), 1511–1519.

Fordyce, W. E., Fowler, R. S., Lehmann, J. F., DeLateur, B., Sand, P. L. and Trieschmann, R. B. (1973) Operant conditioning in the treatment of chronic pain. *Archives of Physical Rehabilitation Medicine*, 54, 399–408.

Fordyce, W. E., McMahon, R., Rainwater, G., Jackins, S., Questad, K., Murphy, T. and DeLateur, B. (1981) Pain complaint–exercise performance relationship in chronic pain. *Pain*, 10, 311–321.

Fordyce, W. E., Roberts, A. H. and Sternbach, R. A. (1985) The behavioural management of chronic pain: a response to critics. *Pain*, 22, 113–125.

Fordyce, W. E., Shelton, J. L. and Dundore, D. E. (1982) The modification of avoidance learning and pain behaviours. *Journal of Behavioural Medicine*, 5, 405–414.

Fox, B. H. (1981) Psychosocial factors and the immune system in human cancer. In: R. Ader (ed.) *Psychoneuroimmunology*. New York: Academic Press.

Frank, A. (1993) Low back pain. *British Medical Journal*, 306, 901–909.

Frankish, C. J. and Linden, W. (1996) Spouse-pair risk-factors and cardiovascular reactivity. *Journal of Psychosomatic Research*, 40(1), 37–51.

Frazier, L. M., Carey, T. S., Lyles, M. F. and McGaghe, W. C. (1991) Lengthy bed-rest prescribed for acute low back pain. *Southern Medical Journal*, 84, 603–606.

Frederikson, L. G. and Bull, P. E. (1995) Evaluation of a patient education leaflet designed to improve communication in medical consultations. *Patient Education and Counselling*, 25(1), 51–57.

Freedman, R. and Ianni, P. (1985) Effects of general and thematically relevant stressors in Raynaud's diseae. *Journal of Psychosomatic Research*, 29, 275–280.

Freeman, E. W., Rickels, K., Huggins, G. R., Mudd, E. H., Garcia, C. R. and Dickens, H. O. (1980) Adolescent contraceptive use: comparisons of male and female attitudes and information. *American Journal of Public Health*, 70, 790–797.

Friedman, H. S. and Booth-Kewley, S. (1988) Validity of the Type A construct: a reprise. *Psychological Bulletin*, 104, 381–384.

Friedman, M., Thoresen, C. E., Gill, J.J., Ulmer, D., Powell, L. H., Price, V. A., Brown, B., Thompson, L., Rabin, D., Breall, W. S., Bourg, E., Levy, R. and Dixon, T. (1986) Alteration of Type A behavior and its effect on cardiac recurrences in post-myocardial infarction patients: summary of the Recurrent Coronary Prevention Project. *American Heart Journal*, 112, 653–665.

Friedman, S., Southern, J. L., Abdul-Quadar, A., Primm, D. C., Des Jarlais, D., Kleinman, P., Mauge, C., Goldsmith, D. S., El-Sadr, E. and Maslansky, R. (1987) The AIDS epidemic amongst blacks and hispanics. *Milbank Quarterly*, 65, Supplement 2.

Furnham, A. and Linfoot, J. (1987) The Type A behaviour pattern and the need to prove oneself: a correlated study. *Current Psychological Reviews and Research*, 6, 125–135.

Furnham, A. and Steele, H. (1993) Measuring locus of control: a critique of general, children's, health- and work-related locus of control questionnaires. *British Journal of Psychology*, 84(4), 443–480.

Galatzer, A., Amir, S., Gil, R., Karp, M. and Laron, A. (1982) Crisis intervention program in newly diagnosed diabetic children. *Diabetic Care*, 5, 414–419.

Galsworthy, T.D. (1994) Osteoporosis: statistics, intervention and prevention. *Annals of the New York Academy of Sciences*, 736, 158–164.

Garbarino, J. (1982) Sociocultural risk: dangers to competence. In: C. Kopp and J. Krakow (eds) *Child Development in a Social Context*, Reading, MA: Addison-Wesley.

Garmezy, N. and Rutter, M. (1983) *Stress, Coping And Development In Children*. New York: McGraw-Hill.

Garn, S. and Clark, D. (1976) Trends in fatness and the origins of obesity. *Pediatrics*, 57, 443–456.

Garne, J., Aspegren, K., Balldin, G. and Ranstam, J. (1997) Increasing incidence of and declining mortality from breast cancer. *Cancer*, 79(1), 69–74.

Garrison, W.T. and McQuiston, S. (1989) *Chronic Illness During Childhood And Adolescence: Psychological Aspects*. Newbury Park, CA: Sage.

Gatchel, R., Korman, M., Weiss, C., Smith, D. and Clarke, L. (1978) A multiple response evaluation of EMG biofeedback performance during training and stress-induction conditions. *Psychophysiology*, 15, 253–258.

Gawler, I. (1986) *You Can Conquer Cancer*. Wellingborough: Thorsons.

Geersten, H. R., Gray, R. M. and Ward, J. R. (1973) Patient non-compliance within the context of seeking medical care for arthritis. *Journal of Chronic Diseases*, 26, 689–698.

Gentry, W. D., Foster, S. and Haney, T. (1972) Denial as a determinant of anxiety and perceived health status in the coronary care unit. *Psychosomatic Medicine*, 34, 39–45.

Gentry, W. D., Chesney, A. P., Hall, R. P. and Harburg, E. (1981) Effect of habitual anger-coping pattern on blood pressure in black/white, high/low stress area respondents. *Psychosomatic Medicine*, 43, 88–93.

George, C., Kaplan, N. and Main, M. (1985) The Adult Attachment Interview (AAI). Unpublished manuscript, University of California at Berkeley, Department of Psychology.

Geyer, S. (1993) Life events, chronic difficulties and vulnerability factors preceding breast cancer. *Social Science and Medicine*, 37(12), 1545–1555.

Ghodsian, M., Zajicek, E. and Wolkind, S. (1984) A longitudinal study of maternal depression and child behaviour problems. *Journal of Child Psychology and Psychiatry*, 25, 91–109.

Gil, K. M., Williams, D. A., Thompson, R. J. Jr and Kinney, T. R. (1991) Sickle cell disease in children and adolescents: the relation of child and parent pain coping strategies to adjustment. *Journal of Pediatric Psychology*, 16, 643–663.

Gil, K. M., Keefe, F. J., Sampson, H. A., McCaskill, C. C., Rodin, J. and Crisson, J. E. (1987)

The relation of stress and family environment to atopic dermatitis symptoms in children. *Journal of Psychosomatic Research*, 31, 673–684.

Gill, J. J., Price, V. A., Friedman, M., Thoresen, C. E., Powell, L. H., Ulmer, D., Brown, B. and Drews, F. R. (1985) Reduction of Type A behavior in healthy middle-aged American military officers. *American Heart Journal*, 110, 503–514.

Glanz, K., Kristal, A. R., Sorenson, G., Palombo, R., Heimendinger, J. and Probert, C. (1993) Development and validation of measures of psychosocial factors influencing fat- and fibre-related dietary behaviour. *Preventive Medicine*, 22, 373–387.

Glasgow, M. S., Engel, B. T. and D'Lugoff, B. (1989) A controlled study of a standardised behavioral stepped treatment for hypertension. *Psychosomatic Medicine*, 51, 10–26.

Glasgow, R. E. (1991) Compliance to diabetes regimens. In: J. A. Cramer and B. Spiker (eds) *Patient Compliance in Clinical Trials*. New York: Raven Press.

Glasgow, R. E., Toobert, D. J., Hampson, S. E. and Wilson, W. (1995) Behavioural research at the Oregon Research Institute. *Annals of Behavioural Medicine*, 17, 32–40.

Glass, D. C. (1977) *Behaviour Patterns, Stress and Coronary Disease*. Hillsdale, NJ: Erlbaum.

Glassman, A. H. (1993) Cigarette smoking: implications for psychiatric illness. *American Journal of Psychiatry*, 150, 546–553.

Gleaves, D. H., Williamson, D. A., Eberenz, K. P., Sebastian, S. B. and Barker, S. E. (1995) Clarifying body-image disturbance: analysis of a multidimensional model using structural modeling. *Journal of Personality Assessment*, 64, 478–493.

Goffman, E. (1961) *Asylums*. Garden City, NY: Doubleday.

Goldberg, G. R. and Prentice, A. M. (1994) Maternal and fetal determinants of adult diseases. *Nutrition Reviews*, 52(6), 191–200.

Goldberg, S., Morris, P., Simmons, R. J., Fowler, R. S. and Levinson, H. (1990) Chronic illness in infants and parenting stress: a comparison of three groups of parents. *Journal of Pediatric Psychology*, 15, 347–358.

Goldenring, J. M. and Purtell, E. (1984) Knowledge of testicular cancer risk and need for self-examination in college students: a call for equal time for men in teaching early cancer detection techniques. *Pediatrics*, 74, 1093–1096.

Goldsmith, S., Gabrielson, M., Gabrielson, I., Matthews, V. and Potts, L. (1972) Teenagers, sex and contraception. *Family Planning Perspectives*, 4, 32–38.

Goldstein, I. B., Shapiro, D., Thananopavarn, C. and Sambhi, M. P. (1982) Comparison of drug and behavioral treatments of essential hypertension. *Health Psychology*, 1, 7–26.

Goodinson, S. M. and Singleton, J. (1989) Quality of life – a critical review of current concepts, measurements and their clinical application. *International Journal of Nursing Studies*, 26, 359–369.

Goodman, S. H. and Brumley, H. E. (1990) Schizophrenic and depressed mothers: relational deficits in parenting. *Developmental Psychology*, 26, 31–39.

Gordon, D. J., Burge, D., Hammen, C., Adrian, C., Jaenicke, C. and Hiroto, D. (1988) Observations of interactions of depressed women with their children. Unpublished manuscript, Department of Psychology, University of California.

Gordon, D. J., Probstfield, J. L., Garrison, R. J., Neaton, J. D., Castelli, W. P., Knoke, J. D., Jacobs, D. R., Bangdiwala, S. and Tyroler, H. A. (1989) High density lipoprotein cholesterol and cardiovascular disease: four prospective American studies. *Circulation*, 79, 8–15.

Gore, C. J., Owen, N., Pederson, D. and Clarke, A. (1996) Educational and environmental interventions for cardiovascular health promotion in socially disadvantaged primary schools. *Australian and New Zealand Journal of Public Health*, 20(2), 188–194.

Gottlieb, B. H. (1992) Quandries in translating support concepts to intervention. In: B. H. Gottlieb (ed.) *Marshalling Social Support: Formats, Processes and Effects*. San Francisco: CA: Sage.

Gottlieb, H., Stritte, C., Koller, R., Madorsky, A., Hockersmith, V., Kleeman, M. and Wagner, J. (1977) Comprehensive rehabilitation of patients having chronic low back pain. *Archives of Physical Medicine and Rehabilitation*, 58, 101–108.

Gould-Martin, K., Paganini-Hill, A., Casagrande, C., Mack, T. and Ross, R. K. (1982) Behavioral and biological determinants of surgical stage of breast cancer. *Preventive Medicine*, 11, 429–440.

Gowers, S., Norton, K., Halek, C. and Crisp, A. H. (1994) Outcome of outpatient psychotherapy in a random allocation treatment study of anorexia nervosa. *International Journal of Eating Disorders*, 15, 165–177.

Gracey, D., Stanley, N., Burke, V., Corti, B. and Beilin, L. J. (1996) Nutritional knowledge, beliefs and behaviours in teenage school students. *Health Education Research*, 11(2), 187–204.

Graham, H. (1993a) Women's smoking: government targets and social trends. *Health Visitor*, 66, 80–82.

Graham, H. (1993b) Research literature on women and health. *Health Psychology Update*, 12, 4–7.

Graham, P., Rutter, M., Yule, W. and Pless, I. (1967) Childhood asthma: a psychosomatic disorder? Clinical and epidemiological considerations. *British Journal of Preventive Social Medicine*, 21, 78–85.

Green, M. (1983) Coming of age in developmental pediatrics. *Pediatrics*, 72, 275–282.

Green, M. (1986) Developmental psychobiologic implications for pediatrics. In: N. A. Krasnegor, J. D. Arasteh and M. F. Cataldo (eds) *Child Health Behavior. A Behavioral Pediatrics Perspective*. New York: John Wiley & Sons.

Greenstadt, L., Shapiro, D. A. and Whitehead, R. (1986) Blood pressure discrimination. *Psychophysiology*, 23, 500–509.

Greer, H. S. and Morris, T. (1975) Psychological attributes of women who develop breast cancer: a controlled study. *Journal of Psychosomatic Research*, 19, 147–153.

Greer, H. S., Morris, T. and Pettingale, K. W. (1979) Psychological response to breast cancer: effect on outcome. *Lancet*, ii, 785–787.

Griffith, L. S., Field, B. J. and Lustman, P. J. (1990) Life stress and social support in diabetes: association with glycaemic control. *International Journal of Psychiatry in Medicine*, 20, 365–372.

Griffith, R. R. and Woodson, P. P. (1988) Caffeine physical dependence: a review of human and laboratory animal studies. *Psychopharmacology*, 94, 437–451.

Griffiths, M. (1990) Contraceptive practices and contraceptive failures among women requesting termination of pregnancy. *British Journal of Family Planning*, 16, 16–18.

Groome, L. J., Swiber, M. J., Bentz, L. S., Holland, S. B. and Atterbury, J. L. (1995) Maternal anxiety during pregnancy: effect on fetal behavior at 38 to 40 weeks gestation. *Journal of Developmental and Behavioural Pediatrics*, 16, 391–396.

Gross, C., Kangas, J. R., Lemieux, A. M. and Zehrer, C. L. (1995) One-year change in quality of life profiles in patients receiving pancreas and kidney transplants. *Transplantation Proceedings*, 27, 3067–3068.

Gunn, W., Pinsky, P., Sacks, J. and Schonberger, L. (1991) Injuries and poisonings in out-of-home child care and home care. *American Journal of Diseases in Childhood*, 145, 779–781.

Guyton, A. C. (1977) Personal views on mechanisms of hypertension. In: J. Genest, E. Koiw and O. Kuchel (eds) *Hypertension: Physiopathology and Treatment*. New York: McGraw-Hill.

Guyton, A. C., Coleman, T. G., Bower, J. D. and Grainger, H. J. (1970) Circulatory control in hypertension. *Circulation Research*, 27 (Supplement II), 135–147.

Hackett, T. P. and Cassem, N. H. (1975) Psychological intervention in myocardial infarction. In: W. Gentry and R. Williams (eds) *Psychological Aspects of Myocardial Infarction and Coronary Care*. St Louis: Mosby.

Hadley, S. A. and Saarmann, L. (1991) Lipid physiology and nutritional considerations in coronary heart disease. *Critical Care Nurse*, 11(10), 28–39.

Hadlow, J. and Pitts, M. K. (1991) The understanding of common health terms by doctors, nurses and patients. *Social Science and Medicine*, 32(2), 193–196.

Hahn, S. R., Thompson, K. S. and Wills, T. A. (1994) The difficult doctor–patient relationship: somatization, personality and psychopathology. *Journal of Clinical Epidemiology*, 47, 637–657.

Halford, W. K., Cuddihy, S. and Mortimer, R. H. (1990) Psychological stress and blood glucose regulation in Type I diabetic patients. *Health Psychology*, 6, 1–14.

Hall, J. A., Epstein, A. M., Deciantis, M. L. and Mcneil, B. J. (1993) Physicians' liking for their patients – more evidence for the role of affect in medical care. *Health Psychology*, 12 (2), 140–146.

Hall, W., Solowij, N. and Leon, J. (1996) Summary of the Australian National Strategy Monograph No.25 'The Health and Psychological Consequences of Cannabis Use'. *Addiction*, 91, 759–773, (with commentaries by other authors).

Hamill, E. and Ingram, I. M. (1974) Psychiatric factors in the abortion decision. *British Medical Journal*, i, 229–232.

Hammen, C., Adrian, C., Gordon, D., Burge, D., Jaenicke, C. and Hiroto, D. (1987) Children of depressed mothers: maternal strain and symptom predictors of dysfunction. *Journal of Abnormal Psychology*, 96, 190–198.

Hampson, S. E., Glasgow, R. E. and Toobert, D. J. (1990) Personal models of diabetes and their relations to self-care activities. *Health Psychology*, 9, 632–646.

Hannay, D. R. (1980) The illness iceberg and trivial consultations. *Journal of the Royal College of General Practitioners*, 30, 551–554.

Hansteen, R. W., Miller, R. D., Lonero, L., Reid, L. D. and Jones, B. (1976) Effects of alcohol and cannabis on closed course car driving. *Annals of the New York Academy of Sciences*, 282, 240–246.

Hapidou, E. G. and De Catanzaro, D. (1992) Responsiveness to laboratory pain in women as a function of age and childbirth pain experience. *Pain*, 48, 177–181.

Harburg, E., Blakelock, E. H. and Roper, P. J. (1979) Resentful and reflective coping with arbitrary authority and blood pressure: Detroit. *Psychosomatic Medicine*, 41, 189–202.

Harder, D. W. and Greenwald, D. S. (1992) Parent and family interaction and child predictors of outcome among sons at psychiatric risk. *Journal of Clinical Psychology*, 48, 151–164.

Hardman, A., Maguire, P. and Crowther, D. (1989) The recognition of psychiatric morbidity on a medical oncology ward. *Journal of Psychological Research*, 33, 235–239.

Harkins, S. W. and Chapman, C. R. (1977) Age and sex differences in pain perception. In: D. J. Anderson and B. Matthews (eds) *Pain in the Trigeminal Region*, Amsterdam: Elsevier.

Harris, D. M. and Guten, S. (1979) Health protective behaviour: an exploratory study. *Journal of Health and Social Behavior*, 20, 17–29.

Harris, R. and Linn, M. W. (1985) Health beliefs, compliance and control of diabetes mellitus. *Southern Medical Journal*, 78, 162–166.

Harris, T., Brown, G. and Bifulco, T. (1986) Loss of parent in childhood and adult psychiatric disorder: the role of lack of adequate parental care. *Psychological Medicine*, 16, 641–659.

Harrison, J. A., Mullen, P. D. and Green, L. (1992) A meta-analysis of studies of the health belief model with adults. *Health Education Research*, 7, 107–116.

Hart, G. (1989) AIDS, homosexual men and behavioural change. In: C. J. Martin and D. V. McQueen (eds) *Readings for a New Public Health*. Edinburgh: Edinburgh University Press.

Hart, G., Boulton, M., Fitzpatrick, R., McClean, J. and Dawson, J. (1992) 'Relapse' to unsafe behaviour amongst gay men: a critique of recent behavioural HIV/AIDS research. *Sociology of Health and Illness*, 14, 216–232.

Hart, J. T. (1987) *Hypertension. Community Control of High Blood Pressure* (2nd edn). Edinburgh: Churchill Livingstone.

Hassett, J. (1978) *A Primer of Psychophysiology*. New York: W. H. Freeman & Co.

Hastings, T. and Kern, J. M. (1994) Relationship between bulimia, childhood sexual abuse and family environment. *International Journal of Eating Disorders*, 15, 103–111.

Hathaway, D. (1986) Effect of pre-operative intervention on post-operative outcomes: a meta-analysis. *Nursing Research*, 35, 269–275.

Hatton, D. L., Canam, C., Thorne, S. and Hughes, A. M. (1995) Perceptions of caring for an infant or toddler with diabetes. *Journal of Advanced Nursing*, 22, 569–577.

Haug, M. R. (1993) *The Role of Patient Education in Doctor–Patient Relationships*. Kentucky, Lexington, KY: University Press of Kentucky.

Hausenstein, E. J. (1990) The experience of distress in parents of chronically ill children. Potential or likely outcome. *Journal of Clinical Child Psychology*, 19, 347–358.

Hauser, S. T., Jacobson, A. M., Wertlieb, D., Brink, S. and Wentworth, S. (1985) The contribution of family environment to perceived competence and illness adjustment in diabetic and acutely ill adolescents. *Family Relations*, 34, 99–108.

Hauser, S. T., Jacobsen, A. M., Wertlieb, D., Weiss-Parry, B., Follansbee, D., Wolfsdorf, J. I., Herskowitz, R. D., Houlihan, T. and Rajpart, D. C. (1986) Children with recently diagnosed diabetes: interactions with their families. *Health Psychology*, 5, 273–296.

Hawkes, C. (1974) Communicating with the patient – an example drawn from neurology. *British Journal of Medical Education*, 8, 57–63.

Haynes, R. B. (1979) Strategies to improve compliance with referrals, appointments and prescribed medical regimens. In: R. B. Haynes, D. W. Taylor and D. L. Sackett (eds) *Compliance in Health Care*. Baltimore: Johns Hopkins University Press.

Haynes, R. B. (1987) Patient compliance, then and now. Guest Editorial. *Patient Education and Counseling*, 10, 103–105.

Haynes, R. B., Taylor, D. W. and Sackett, D. L. (1979) *Compliance in Health Care*. Baltimore, MD: Johns Hopkins University Press.

Haynes, R. B., Taylor, D. W., Sackett, D. L., Gibson, E. S., Bernholz, C. D. and Mukherjee, J. (1980) Can simple clinical measurements detect non-compliance? *Hypertension*, 2, 757–764.

Haynes, S. G., Feinleib, M. and Kannel, W. B. (1980) The relationship of psychosocial factors to coronary heart disease in the Framingham study III. Eight year incidence of coronary heart disease. *American Journal of Epidemiology*, 111, 37–58.

Haynes, S. G., Levine, S and Scotch, N. (1978) The relationship of psychosocial factors to coronary heart disease in the Framingham Study: I. Methods and risk factors. *American Journal of Epidemiology*, 107, 362–381.

Heather, N. and Robertson, I. (1981) *Controlled Drinking*. London: Methuen.

Heinicke, C. M., Diskin, S. D., Ramsey-Klee, D. M. and Given, K. (1983) Pre-birth characteristics and family development in the first year of life. *Child Development*, 54, 194–208.

Heltz, J. W. and Templeton, B. (1990) Evidence of the role of psychosocial factors in diabetes mellitus: a review. *American Journal of Psychiatry*, 147, 1275–1282.

Henley, S. and Furnham, A. (1989) The Type A behaviour pattern and self-evaluation. *British Journal of Medical Psychology*, 62, 51–59.

Hennig, P. and Knowles, A. (1990) Factors influencing women over 40 years to take precautions against cervical cancer. *Journal of Applied Social Psychology*, 20(19), 1612–1621.

Hennrikus, D., Girgia, A., Redman, S. and Sanson-Fisher, R. W. (1991) A community study of delay in presenting to medical practitioners with signs of melanoma. *Archives of Dermatology*, 127, 356–361.

Henry, J. P. and Stephens, P. M. (1967) *Stress, Health and the Social Environment*. New York: Springer-Verlag.

Herbert, T. B. and Cohen, S. (1993a) Depression and immunity: a meta-analytic review. *Psychological Bulletin*, 113(3), 472–486.

Herbert, T. B. and Cohen, S. (1993b) Stress and immunity in humans: a meta-analytic review. *Psychosomatic Medicine*, 55, 364–379.

Herbert, T. B., Cohen, S., Marsland, A. L., Bachen, E. A., Rabin, B. S., Muldoon, M. F. and Manuck, S. B. (1994) Cardiovascular reactivity and the course of immune response to an acute psychological stressor. *Psychosomatic Medicine*, 56, 337–344.

Herold, E. S. (1981) Contraceptive embarrassment and contraceptive behaviour among young single women. *Journal of Youth and Adolescence*, 10, 233–243.

Herold, E. S. (1983) The Health Belief Model: can it help us to understand contraceptive use amongst adolescents? *Journal of School Health*, 53, 19–21.

Hersh, E. M. and Peterson, E. A. (1988) Editorial: The AIDS epidemic – AIDS research in the life sciences. *Life Sciences*, 42, i–iv.

Hilgard, E. R. (1975) The alleviation of pain by hypnosis. *Pain*, 1, 213–231.

Hilgard, E. R. (1978) Hypnosis and pain. In: R. A. Sternbach (ed.) *The Psychology of Pain*. New York: Raven.

Hilgard, E. R. and Hilgard, J. R. (1975) *Hypnosis in the Relief of Pain*. Los Altos, CA: Kaufmann.

Hill, D., Gardner, G. and Rassaby, J. (1985) Factors predisposing women to take precautions against breast and cervix cancer. *Journal of Applied Social Psychology*, 15(1), 59–79.

Hill, J. O., Sparling, P. B., Shields, T. W. and Heller, P. A. (1987) Effects of exercise and food restriction on body composition and metabolic rate in obese women. *American Journal of Clinical Nutrition*, 46, 622–630.

Hill, R. D. (1987) *Diabetes Health Care*. Cambridge: Chapman and Hall Medical.

Hirayama, T. (1981) Non smoking wives of heavy smokers have a higher risk of lung cancer: a study from Japan. *British Medical Journal*, 282, 183–185.

Hirsch, B. and Moos, R. (1985) Psychosocial adjustment of adolescent children of a depressed, arthritic, or normal patient. *Journal of Abnormal Psychology*, 94, 154–164.

Hirsch, I., Matthews, M., Rawlings, S., Broughton, J., Breyfogle, R., Simonds, J., Kossey, K., England, J., Weidmeyer, H., Little, R. and Goldstein, D. (1983) Home capillary blood glucose monitoring (HBGM) for diabetic youths: a one-year follow-up of 98 patients. *Diabetes*, 32, 164.

Hixenbaugh, P. and Warren, L. (1994) Psychological well-being and adherence in diabetic patients. *Abstracts of the XXVI International Congress of Psychology*. Montreal, Canada, 16–21 August, 157.

Hixenbaugh, P. and Warren, L. (1996) *Diabetes Mellitus: The Role of Knowledge and Health Professional Support in Adaptation and Adherence*. Paper presented at the 10th Conference of the European Health Psychology Society. Dublin, Ireland, September.

Hobbs, P., Haran, D., Pendleton, L. L., Jones, B. E. and Posner, T. (1984) Public attitudes and cancer education. *International Review of Applied Psychology*, 33, 565–586.

Hochstadt, N. J. and Trybula, J. (1980) Reducing missed appointments in a community health centre. *Journal of Community Psychology*, 8, 261–265.

Hoelscher, T. J., Lichstein, K. L., Fischer, S. and Hegarty, T. B. (1987) Relaxation treatment of hypertension: do home relaxation tapes enhance treatment outcome? *Behavior Therapy*, 18, 33–37.

Holden, C. (1987) Is alcoholism treatment effective? *Science*, 236, 20–22.

Holland, J., Ramazanoglu, C., Scott, S., Sharpe, S. and Thompson, T. (1990) *Don't Die of Ignorance . . . I Nearly Died of Embarrassment*, WRAP Paper 2. London: The Tufnell Press.

Holland, J. C. and Rowland, J. H. (eds) (1990) *Handbook of Psychosocial Oncology*. New York: Oxford University Press.

Holland, J., Ramazanoglu, C., Scott, S., Sharpe, S. and Thompson, T. (1991) *Pressure, Resistance and Empowerment: Young Women and the Negotiation of Safer Sex*, WRAP Paper 6. London: The Tufnell Press.

Holmes, T. H. and Rahe, R. H. (1967) The social readjustment rating scale. *Journal of Psychosomatic Research*, 11, 213–218.

Holmgren, K. (1994) Repeat abortion and contraceptive use. Report from an interview study in Stockholm. *Gynaecological and Obstetric Investigations*, 37, 254–259.

Homedes, N. (1991) Do we know how to influence patients' behaviour? *Family Practice*, 8(4), 412–423.

Horwood, L. J., Fergusson, D. M. and Shannon, F. T. (1985) Social and familial factors in the development of early childhood asthma. *Pediatrics*, 75, 859–868.

Houston, K. B. (1983) Psychophysiological responsivity and the Type A behaviour pattern. *Journal of Research in Personality*, 17, 22–39.

Howes, M. J., Hoke, L., Winterbottom, M. and Delafield, D. (1994) Psychosocial effects of breast cancer on the patient's children. *Journal of Psychosocial Oncology*, 12, 1–21.

Hubley, J. H. (1988) Aids in Africa: a challenge to health education. *Health Education Research*, 3, 41–47.

Huffman, S. L. and Martin, L. (1994) Child nutrition, birth spacing, and child mortality. *Annals of the New York Academy of Science*, 709, 236–248.

Hughes, J. R. (1996) The future of smoking cessation therapy in the United States. *Addiction*, 91, 1797–1802.

Hunt, S. M. and MacLeod, M. (1987) Health and behavioural change: some lay perspectives. *Community Medicine*, 9, 68–76.

Hussey, L. C. and Giliand, K. (1989) Compliance, low literacy and locus of control. *Nursing Clinics of North America*, 24(3), 605–611.

Ingelhammer, E., Moller, A., Svanberg, B., Tornbom, M., Lija, H. and Hamberger, L. (1994) The use of contraceptive methods among women seeking a legal abortion. *Contraception*, 50, 143–152.

Ingham, J. G. and Miller, P. M. (1986) Self referral to primary care: symptoms and social factors. *Journal of Psychosomatic Research*, 30, 49–56.

Ingham, R. (1988) Behaviour change and safe sex: a social psychology approach. *Proceedings of the First Conference of the Health Psychology Section*, Leicester: British Psychological Society.

Irvine, M. J., Johnston, D. W., Jenner, D. A. and Marie, G. V. (1986) Relaxation and stress management in the treatment of essential hypertension. *Journal of Psychosomatic Research*, 30, 437–450.

Israel, A. C., Solotar, L. C. and Zimand, E. (1990) An investigation of two parental involvement roles in the treatment of obese children. *International Journal of Eating Disorders*, 9, 557–564.

Jaccard, J. J. and Davidson, A. R. (1972) Towards an understanding of family planning behaviours: an initial investigation. *Journal of Applied Social Psychology*, 2, 228–235.

Jacobsen, P. B., Manne, S. L., Gorfinkle, K., Schorr, O., Rapkin, B. and Redd, W. H. (1990) Analysis of child and parent behavior during painful medical procedures. *Journal of Clinical Child Psychology*, 17, 194–202.

Jacobson, A. M. and Leibovich, F. B. (1984) Psychological issues in diabetes mellitus. *Psychosomatics*, 25, 7–15.

Jacobson, A. M., Adler, A. G., Derby, L., Anderson, B. J. and Wolsdorf, J. I. (1991) Clinic attendance and glycaemic control. *Diabetes Care*, 14, 599–601.

Jahanshahi, M. and Marsden, C. D. (1989) Motor disorders. In: G. Turpin (ed.) *Handbook of Clinical Psychophysiology*. Chichester: Wiley.

James, P. T., Dohery, Y. A. and Hall, D. A. (1996) *Be Realistic when Teaching Change Counselling Skills in Diabetes*. Paper presented at the BPS Special Group in Health Psychology Annual Conference (3–5 July), York.

Janis, I. L. (1958) *Psychological Stress – Psychoanalytic and Behavioural Studies of Surgical Patients*. New York: John Wiley.

Janis, I. L. (1969) *Stress and Frustration*. New York: Harcourt Brace & Janovich.

Janis, I. L. and Mann, I. (1977) *Decision Making: A Psychological Analysis of Conflict, Choice and Commitment*. New York: Free Press.

Janz, N. K. and Becker, M. H. (1984) The health belief model: a decade later. *Health Education Quarterly*, 11, 1–47.

Jary, J. (1996) The concerns of breast cancer patients following surgery. *Journal of Cancer Care*, 5, 31–37.

Jeffery, R. W. (1992) Is obesity a risk factor for cardiovascular disease? *Annals of Behavioral Medicine*, 14, 109–112.

Jemmot, J. B. and Magloire, K. (1988) Academic stress, social support and secretory immunoglobulin A. *Journal of Personality and Social Psychology*, 55, 803–810.

Jencks, C. and Mayer, S. (1990) The social consequences of growing up in a poor neighborhood. In: L. E. Lynn and M. G. H. McGeary (eds), *Inner City Poverty in the United States*. Washington, DC: National Academy Press.

Jenkins, C. D. (1971) Psychologic and social precursors of coronary heart disease. *New England Journal of Medicine*, 284, 244–255, 307–317.

Jenkins, C. D. (1976) Recent evidence supporting psychologic and social risk factors for coronary heart disease. *New England Journal of Medicine*, 294, 987–994, 1033–1038.

Jennings, G., Nelson, L., Nestel, P., Esler, M., Korner, P., Burton, D. and Bazem, M. (1986) The effects of changes in physical activity on major cardiovascular risk factors, haemodynamics, sympathetic function and glucose utilisation in man: a controlled study of four levels of activity. *Circulation*, 73, 30–40.

Johnson, A. M., Wadsworth, J., Wellings, K. and Field, J. (1994) *Sexual Attitudes and Lifestyles.* Oxford: Blackwell Scientific Publications.

Johnson, J. E. and Leventhal, H. (1974) Effects of accurate expectations and behavioural instructions on reactions during a noxious medical examination. *Journal of Personality and Social Psychology,* 29, 710–718.

Johnson, J. E., Leventhal, H. and Dabbs, J. H. (1971) Contribution of emotional and instrumental response processes in adaptation to surgery. *Journal of Personality and Social Psychology,* 20, 55–64.

Johnson, J. E., Rice, V. H., Fuller, S. S. and Endress, M. P. (1978) Sensory information, instruction in coping strategy and recovery from surgery. *Research in Nursing and Health,* 1, 4–17.

Johnson, S. B. (1980) Psychosocial factors in juvenile diabetes: a review. *Journal of Behavioural Medicine,* 3, 95–115.

Johnssen, A. and Hanssen, L. (1977) Prolonged exposure to a stressful stimulus (noise) as a cause of raised blood pressure in man. *Lancet,* 1, 86–87.

Johnston, D. W. (1984) Biofeedback, relaxation and related procedures in the treatment of psychophysiological disorders. In: A. Steptoe and A. Matthews (eds) *Health Care and Human Behaviour.* London: Academic Press.

Johnston, D. W. (1987) The behavioural control of high blood pressure. *Current Psychological Research and Reviews,* 6, 99–114.

Johnston, D. W. (1989) Will stress management prevent coronary heart disease? *The Psychologist: Bulletin of the British Psychological Society,* 2, 275–278.

Johnston, D. W., Anastasiades, P. and Wood, C. (1990) The relationship between cardiovascular responses in the laboratory and in the field. *Psychophysiology,* 27, 34–44.

Johnston, M. (1980) Anxiety in surgical patients. *Psychological Medicine,* 10, 145–152.

Johnston, M. (1982) Recognition of patients' worries by nurses and by other patients. *British Journal of Clinical Psychology,* 21, 255–261.

Johnston, M. (1987) Emotional and cognitive aspects of anxiety in surgical patients. *Communication and Cognition,* 20, 261–276.

Johnston, M. (1988a) Health psychology: an integrated discipline? *Health Psychology Update No. 1. (Newsletter of the Health Section of the British Psychological Society).*

Johnston, M. (1988b) Impending surgery. In: S. Fisher and J. Reason (eds), *Handbook of Life Stress, Cognition and Health.* Chichester: John Wiley & Sons.

Johnston, M. and Carpenter, L. (1980) Relationship between pre-operative anxiety and post-operative state. *Psychological Medicine.* 10, 361–367.

Johnston, M. and Vögele, C. (1993) Benefits of psychological preparation for surgery: a meta-analysis. *Annals of Behavioural Medicine,* 15, 245–256.

Johnston, M., Bromley, I., Boothroyd-Brooks, M., Dobbs, W., Ilson, A. and Ridout, K. (1987) Behavioural assessments of physically disabled patients: agreement between rehabilitation therapists and nurses. *International Journal of Rehabilitation,* 10(4), 205–213.

Jones, D. R., Goldblatt, P. O. and Leon, D. A. (1984) Bereavement and cancer: some data on deaths of spouses from the longitudinal office of population censuses and surveys. *British Medical Journal,* 3, 461–464.

Jones, M. and Parrott, A. C. (1997) Stress and arousal rhythms in smokers and nonsmokers working day and night shifts. *Stress Medicine,* 13, 91–97.

Jorenby, D. E., Keehn, D. S. and Fiore, M. C. (1995) Comparative efficacy and tolerability of nicotine replacement therapies. *CNS Drugs,* 3, 227–236.

Julius, S., Jamerson, K., Mejia, A., Krause, I., Schork, N. and Jones, K. (1990) The association of borderline hypertension with target organ changes and higher coronary risk. Tecumseh Blood Pressure Study. *Journal of the American Medical Association,* 264, 354–358.

Justice, A. (1985) Review of the effects of stress on cancer in laboratory animals: importance of time of stress application and type of tumour. *Psychological Bulletin,* 98, 108–138.

Kantner, J. and Zelnick, M. (1972) Sexual experiences of young unmarried women in the U.S. *Family Planning Perspectives,* 4, 9–18.

Kanto, J., Laine, M., Vuorisalo, A. and Salonen, M. (1990) Pre-operative preparation. *Nursing Times*, 86(20), 39–41.

Kaplan, G. A., Pamuk, E. R., Lynch, J. W., Cohen, R. D. and Balfour, J. L. (1996) Inequality in income and mortality in the United States: analysis of mortality and potential pathways. *British Medical Journal*, 312(7037), 999–1003.

Kaplan, J. R., Adams, M. R., Clarkson, T. B., Manuck, S. B., Shively, C. A. and Williams, J. K. (1996) Psychosocial factors, sex differences, and atherosclerosis. *Psychosomatic Medicine*, 58, 6, 598–611.

Kaplan, N. M. (1982) *Clinical Hypertension* (3rd edn). Baltimore, ML: Williams & Wilkins.

Karmel, M. (1972) Total institutions and models of adaptation. *Journal of Clinical Psychology*, 28, 574–576.

Katz, R. C., Meyers, K. and Walls, J. (1995) Cancer awareness and self-examination practices in young men and women. *Journal of Behavioral Medicine*, 18(4), 377–384.

Kavanagh, D. J., Gooley, S. and Wilson, P. (1993) Prediction of adherence and control in diabetes. *Journal of Behavioural Medicine*, 16, 509–522.

Kazak, A. E. and Meadows, A. T. (1989) Families of young adolescents who have survived cancer: social-emotional adjustment, adaptability, and social support. *Journal of Pediatric Psychology*, 14, 175–191.

Kearns, R. D., Turk, D. C. and Rudy, T. E. (1985) The West Haven–Yale Multidimensional Pain Inventory. *Pain*, 23, 345–356.

Keesling, B. and Friedman, H. S. (1995) Interventions to prevent skin cancer: experimental evaluation of informational and fear appeals. *Psychology and Health*, 10(6), 477–490.

Kegeles, S. M., Allen, N. E. and Irwin, C. E. (1988) Sexually active adolescents and condoms: changes over one year in knowledge, attitudes and use. *American Journal of Public Health*, 78, 460–461.

Kelder, S. H., Perry, C. L., Klepp, K. I. and Lytle, L. L. (1994) Longitudinal tracking of adolescent smoking, physical activity and food choice behaviours. *American Journal of Public Health*, 84, 1121–1126.

Kelleher, D. (1994) Self-help groups and their relationship to medicine. In: J. Gabe (ed.) *Challenging Medicine*. London: Routledge.

Keller, M. B., Beardslee, W. R., Dorer, D. J., Lavori, P. W., Samuelson, H. and Klerman, G. R. (1986) Impact of severity and chronicity of parental affective illness on adaptive functioning and psychopathology in children. *Archives of General Psychiatry*, 43, 930–937.

Kelley, A. J. (1979) A media role for public health compliance? In: R. B. Haynes, D. W. Taylor and D. L. Sackett (eds) *Compliance in Health Care*. Baltimore, ML: Johns Hopkins University Press.

Kellmer Pringle, M. (1980) *A Fairer Future for Children*. London: Macmillan Press.

Kemeny, M. E., Cohen, F., Zegans, L. S. and Conant, M. A. (1989) Psychological and immunological predictors of genital herpes recurrence. *Psychosomatic Medicine*, 51, 195–208.

Kemm, J. R. (1987) Eating patterns in childhood and adult health. *Nutrition* 4(4), 205–215.

Kempner, W. (1948) Treatment of hypertensive vascular disease with rice diet. *American Journal of Medicine*, 4, 545–577.

Kendrick, D. (1994) Children's safety in the home: parents' possession and perceptions of the importance of safety equipment. *Public Health*, 108, 21–25.

Kennedy, B. P., Kawachi, I. and Prothrow-Smith, D. (1996) Income distribution and mortality: cross sectional ecological study of the Robin Hood index in the United States. *British Medical Journal*, 312(7037), 1004–1007.

Kern, J. M. and Hastings, T. (1995) Differential family environments of bulimics and victims of childhood sexual abuse: achievement orientation. *Journal of Clinical Psychology*, 51(4), 499–506.

Kiecolt-Glaser, J. K. and Glaser, R. (1986) Psychological influences on immunity. *Psychosomatics*, 27, 621–624.

Kiecolt-Glaser, J. K., Glaser, R., Williger, D., Stout, J., Messick, G., Sheppard, S., Ricker, D., Romisher, S. C., Briner, W. and Bonnel, G. (1985) Psychosocial enhancement of immunocompetence in a geriatric population. *Health Psychology*, 4, 25–41.

Killion, C. M. (1995) Special health care needs of homeless pregnant women. *Advances in Nursing Science*, 18(2), 44–56.

Kincey, J. and Saltmore, S. (1990) Stress and surgical treatments. In: M. Johnston and L. Wallace (eds), *Stress and Medical Procedures*. Oxford: Oxford University Press.

Kincey, J., Stratham, S. and McFarlane, T. (1991) Women undergoing colposcopy: their satisfaction with communication, health knowledge and level of anxiety. *Health Educational Journal*, 50, 70–72.

King's Fund Policy Institute Report (1996) *Counting the Cost: The Real Impact of Non Insulin Dependent Diabetes*. Commissioned by the British Diabetic Association.

Kirscht, J. P., Kirscht, J. L. and Rosenstock, I. M. (1981) A test of interventions to increase adherence to hypertension regimens. *Health Education Quarterly*, 8, 261–272.

Kitzinger, J. (1994) The methodology of focus groups – the importance of interaction between research participants. *Sociology of Health and Illness*, 16(1), 103–121.

Klenerman, L., Slade, P. D., Stanley, I. M., Pennie, B., Reilly, J. P., Atchinson, L. E., Troup, J. D. G. and Troup, M. J. (1995) The prediction of chronicity in patients with an acute attack of low back pain in a general practise setting. *Spine*, 20, 478–484.

Klesges, R. C., Stein, R. J., Eck, L. H., Isbell, T. R. and Kiesges, L. M. (1991) Parental influence on food selection in young children and its relationships to childhood obesity. *American Journal of Clinical Nutrition*, 55, 859–864,

Knekt, P. (1991) Role of vitamin E in the prophylaxis of cancer. *Annals of Medicine*, 23, 3–12.

Knowler, W. C., Pettitt, D. J. and Saad, M. F. (1991) Obesity in the Pima Indians: its magnitude and relationship with diabetes. *American Journal of Clinical Nutrition*, 53, 15435–15515.

Knutsen, S. F. and Knutsen, R. (1991) The Tromso survey: the family intervention study – the effect of intervention on some coronary risk factors and dietary habits, a 6-year follow-up. *Preventive Medicine*, 20, 197–212.

Kobasa, S. C., Maddi, S. R. and Kahn, S. (1982) Hardiness and health: a prospective study. *Journal of Personality and Social Psychology*, 42, 168–177.

Kochanska, G., Radke-Yarrow, M., Kuczynski, L. and Friedman, S. L. (1987) Normal and affectively ill mothers' beliefs about their children. *American Journal of Orthopsychiatry*, 57, 345–350.

Kodiath, M. F. and Kodiath, A. (1995) A comparative study of patients who experience chronic malignant pain in India and the United States. *Cancer Nursing*, 18, 189–196.

Koester, S. and Hoffer, L. (1994) Indirect sharing: additional HIV risks associated with drug injection. *AIDS and Public Policy Journal*, 9, 100–105.

Koolhaas, J. and Bohus, B. (1989) Social control in relation to neuroendocrine and immunological responses. In: A. Steptoe and A. Appels (eds) *Stress, Personal Control and Health*. Chichester: John Wiley & Sons.

Koppe, J. G. (1995) Nutrition and breast-feeding. *European Journal of Obstetrics, Gynecology and Reproductive Biology*, 61(1), 73–78.

Korsch, B. M., Gozzi, E. K. and Francis, V. (1968) Gaps in doctor–patient communication. *Pediatrics*, 42, 855–871.

Koski, M. L. and Kumento, A. (1977) The interrelationship between diabetic control and family life. *Paediatric and Adolescent Endocrinology*, 3, 41–45.

Krantz, D. S. and Manuck, S. B. (1984) Acute psychophysiological reactivity and risk of cardiovascular disease: a review and methodological critique. *Psychological Bulletin*, 96, 435–464.

Krisst, D. A. and Engel, B. T. (1975) Learned control of blood pressure in patients with high blood pressure. *Circulation*, 51, 370–378.

Krystal, J. H., Price, L. H., Opsahl, C., Ricaurte, G. A. and Heninger, G. R. (1992) Chronic 3.4-methylenedioxymethamphetamine (MDMA) use: effects on mood and neuropsychological function? *American Journal of Drug and Alcohol Abuse*, 18, 331–341.

Kulik, J. A. and Mahler, H. I. M. (1993) Emotional support as a moderator of adjustment and compliance after coronary artery bypass surgery: a longitudinal study. *Journal of Behavioural Medicine*, 16, 45–64.

Kulik, J. A., Moore, P. J. and Mahler, H. I. M. (1993) Stress and affiliation: hospital room-mate effects on preoperative anxiety and social interaction. *Health Psychology*, 12, 118–124.

La Greca, A. M., Follensbee, D. J. and Skyler, J. S. (1990) Developmental and behavioural aspects of diabetes management in children and adolescents. *Children's Health Care*, 19, 132–139.

Landrey, M. J. and Smith, D. E. (1988) AIDS and chemical dependency: an overview. *Journal of Psychoactive Drugs*, 20, 141–147.

Lanting, C. I., Fidler, V., Huisman, M., Towen, B. C. L. and Boersma, E. R. (1994) Neurological differences between 9-year-old children fed breast milk or formula milk as babies. *Lancet*, 344, 1319–1322.

Laragh, J. H. and Pecker, M. S. (1983) Dietary sodium and essential hypertension: some myths, hopes and truths. *Annals of Internal Medicine*, 98, 735–743.

Laron, Z., Galatzer, A., Amir, S., Gill, R., Karp, M. and Mimoumi, M. (1979) A multidisciplinary comprehensive ambulatory treatment scheme for diabetes mellitus in children. *Diabetes Care*, 2, 342–348.

Lask, B. (1975) Short-term psychiatric sequelae to therapeutic termination of pregnancy. *British Journal of Psychiatry*, 128, 173–177.

Last, J. (1963) The iceberg: completing the clinical picture in general practice. *Lancet*, ii, 28–31.

Lau, R. R. and Hartman, K. A. (1983) Common sense representations of common illness. *Health Psychology*, 2, 167–185.

Lauer, R. M., Burns, T. L., Clarke, W. R. and Mahoney, L. T. (1991) Childhood predictors of future blood pressure. *Hypertension*, 18, 74–81.

Lavallee, Y. J., Lamontagne, Y., Pinard, G., Annable, L. and Tetreault, L. (1977) Effects of EMG feedback, diazepam, and their combination on chronic anxiety. *Journal of Psychosomatic Research*, 21, 65–71.

Law, C. M., Barker, D. J., Richardson, W. W., Sheill, A. W., Grime, L. P., Armand-Smith, N. G. and Cruddas, A. M. (1993) Thinness at birth in a northern industrial town. *Journal of Epidemiology and Community Health*, 47, 255–259.

Lawrence, S. C. and Bendixon, K. (1992) His and hers: male and female anatomy in anatomy texts for US medical students, 1890–1989. *Social Science and Medicine*, 35, 925–934.

Lazarus, A. (1985) Psychiatric sequelae of legalised elective first trimester abortion. *Journal of Psychosomatic Obstetrics and Gynaecology*, 4, 141–150.

Lazarus, R. S. (1974) Psychological stress and coping in adaptation and illness. *International Journal of Psychiatry in Medicine*, 5, 321–333.

Lazarus, R. S. and Folkman, S. (1984) *Stress, Appraisal and Coping*. New York: Springer.

Lefebvre, R. C. and Flora, J. A. (1988) Social marketing and public health intervention. *Health Education Quarterly*, 15, 299–315.

Leifman, H., Kuhlhorn, E., Allebeck, P., Andreasson, S. and Romelsjo, A. (1995) Antecedents and covariates of a sober lifestyle and its consequences. *Social Science and Medicine*, 41, 113–121.

Leighton, R. F. (1990) Management of the patient with a low HDL-cholesterol. *Clinical Cardiology*, 13(8), 521–532.

Leonard, B. E. (1989) Animal models in psychopharmacology. In: I. Hindmarch and P. D. Stonier (eds) *Human Psychopharmacology: Methods and Measures, Vol. 2*. Chichester: Wiley.

Letham, J., Slade, P. D., Troup, J. D. G. and Bentley, G. (1983) Outline of a fear-avoidance model of exaggerated pain perception. Part 1. *Behavioural Research Therapy*, 21, 401–408.

Leventhal, H. and Cameron, L. (1987) Behavioral theories and the problem of compliance. *Patient Education and Counselling*, 10, 117–138.

Leventhal, H. and Nerenz, D. (1982) Representations of threat and the control of stress. In: M. D. Jaremko and M. Jaremko (eds) *Stress Management and Prevention: A Cognitive-Behavioral Approach*. New York: Plenum Press.

Leventhal, H., Meyer, P. and Nerenz, D. (1980) The common sense representation of illness danger. In: S. Rachman (ed.) *Medical Psychology*. New York: Pergamon Press.

Levesque, L. and Charlesbois, M. (1977) Anxiety, locus of control and the effect of pre-operative teaching on patients' physical and emotional state. *Nursing Papers*, 8, 11–26.

Lewis, F. M. (1990) Strengthening family supports: cancer and the family. *Cancer*, 65, 752–759.

Lewis, K. S. and Bradley, C. (1994) Measures of diabetes specific health beliefs. In: C. Bradley (ed.) *Handbook of Psychology and Diabetes*. London: Harwood Academic.

Lewis, R., Ellison, E. and Woods, J. (1985) The impact of breast cancer on the family. *Seminars in Oncological Nursing*, 1, 206–213.

Ley, P. (1972) Complaints made by hospital staff and patients: a review of the literature. *Bulletin of the British Psychological Society*, 25, 115–120.

Ley, P. (1988) *Communicating with Patients: Improving Communication, Satisfaction and Compliance*. London: Croom Helm.

Ley, P. and Spelman, M. S. (1965) Communications in an outpatient setting. *British Journal of Social and Clinical Psychology*, 4, 114–116.

Ley, P. and Spelman, M. S. (1967) *Communicating with the Patient*. London: Staples Press.

Licata, A. A. (1994) Prevention and osteoporosis management. *Cleveland Clinical Journal of Medicine*, 61(6), 451–460.

Lichtman, R. R., Taylor, S. E., Wood, J. V., Bluming, A. Z., Dosik, G. M. and Leibowitz, R. L. (1984) Relations with children after breast cancer. The mother–daughter relationship at risk. *Journal of Psychosocial Oncology*, 2, 1–19.

Lieberman, E., Ryan, K. J., Monson, R. R. and Schoenbaum, S. C. (1987) Risk factors accounting for racial differences in the rate of premature birth. *New England Journal of Medicine*, 317, 743–748.

Light, K. and Girdler, S. S. (1993) Cardiovascular health and disease in women. In: C. Niven and D. Carroll (eds), *The Health Psychology Of Women*. London: Harwood Academic.

Light, K. C. and Obrist, P. A. (1983) Task difficulty, heart rate reactivity and cardiovascular response to an appetitive reaction time task. *Psychophysiology*, 20, 301–312.

Lillie-Blanton, M. and Laveist, T. (1996) Race/ethnicity, the social environment, and health. *Social Science and Medicine*, 43(1), 83–91.

Lillie-Blanton, M., Parsons, P. E., Gayle, H. and Dievler, A. (1996) Racial differences in health: not just black and white, but shades of gray. *Annual Review of Public Health*, 17, 411–448.

Lin, E. H., Katon, W., Von Korff, M. *et al.* (1991) Frustrating patients: physician and patient perspectives among distressed high users of medical services. *Journal of General and Internal Medicine*, 6, 241–246.

Linn, B. S., Linn, M. W. and Klimas, N. G. (1988) Effects of psychophysical stress on surgical outcome. *Psychosomatic Medicine*, 50, 230–244.

Linton, S. L. (1985) The relationship between activity and chronic back pain. *Pain*, 21, 289–294.

Livingston, W. K. (1953) What is pain? *Scientific American*, 196, 59–66.

Llewelyn, S. P. (1989) Caring: the cost to nurses and relatives. In: A. K. Broome (ed.) *Health Psychology: Processes and Applications*. London: Chapman and Hall.

Lloyd, C. E., Robinson, N. and Fuller, J. H. (1992) Education and employment experiences in young adults with Type I diabetes mellitus. *Diabetic Medicine*, 9, 661–666.

Locker, D. (1981) *Symptoms and Illness: The Cognitive Organization of Disorder*. London: Tavistock Publications.

Longnecker, M. P. and MacMahon, B. (1988) A meta-analysis of alcohol consumption in relation to risk of breast cancer. *Journal of the American Medical Association*, 260, 652–656.

Lowe, G. (1984) Alcohol and alcoholism. In: D. J. Sanger and D. E. Blackman (eds) *Aspects of Psychopharmacology*. London: Methuen.

Lucas, A., Morley, R., Cole, T. J., Lister, G. and Leeson-Payne, C. (1992) Breast milk and subsequent intelligence quotient in children born pre-term. *Lancet*, 339, 261–264.

Luker, K. (1975) *Taking Chances: Abortion and the Decision not to Contracept*, Berkeley: University of California Press.

Luker, K. (1977) Contraceptive risk-taking and abortion: results and implications of a San Francisco Bay study. *Studies in Family Planning*, 8, 190–196.

Lumley, M. A., Melamed, B. G. and Abeles, L. A. (1993) Predicting children's presurgical anxiety and subsequent behaviour changes. *Journal of Pediatric Psychology*, 18, 481–497.

Lustman, P. J. and Clouse, R. E. (1990) Relationship of psychiatric illness to impotence in men with diabetes. *Diabetes Care*, 4(6), 640–647.

Lustman, P. J., Amado, H. and Wetzel, R. D. (1983) Depression in diabetics: a critical appraisal. *Comprehensive Psychiatry*, 24, 1, 65–74.

Lustman, P. J., Griffith, L. S. and Clouse, R. E. (1988) Depression in adults with diabetes: results of a 5-yr follow-up study. *Diabetes Care*, 11, 605–612.

Luthar, S. S. and Zigler, E. (1991) Vulnerability and resilience: a study of high risk adolescents. *Child Development*, 62, 600–616.

Lyons, J. S., Perrotta, P. and Hancher-Kvam, S. (1988) Perceived social support from family and friends: measurement across disparate samples. *Journal of Personality Assessment*, 52, 42–47.

McAnarney, E. R., Lawrence, R. A., Ricciuti, H. N., Polley, J. and Szilagyi, M. (1986) Interactions of adolescent mothers and their 1-year-old children. *Pediatrics*, 78, 585–590.

McArdle, J. M. C., George, W. D., McArdle, C. S., Smith, D. C., Moodie, A. R., Hughson, A. V. M. and Murray, G. D. (1996) Psychological support for patients undergoing breast cancer surgery: a randomised study. *British Medical Journal*, 312, 813–817.

McCarthy, W. H. and Shaw, H. M. (1989) Skin cancer in Australia. *The Medical Journal of Australia*, 150, 469–470.

McCaul, K. D., Glasgow, R. E. and Schafer, L. C. (1987) Diabetes regimen behaviours: predicting behaviour. *Medical Care*, 25, 868–881.

McCaul, K. D., Reid, P. A., Rathage, R. W. and Martinson, B. (1996) Does concern about breast cancer inhibit or promote breast cancer screening? *Basic and Applied Social Psychology*, 18(2), 183–194.

McCaul, K. D., Sandgren, A. K., O'Neill, H. K. and Hinsz, V. B. (1993) The value of the theory of planned behavior, perceived control, and self efficacy expectations for predicting health-protective behaviors. *Basic and Applied Social Psychology*, 14(2), 231–252.

McClung, H. J., Boyne, L. and Heitlinger, L. (1995) Constipation and dietary fiber intake in children. *Pediatrics*, 96(5 Pt 2), 999–1000.

Maccoby, E. E. and Martin, J. A. (1983) Socialization in the context of the family: parent–child interaction. In: P. H. Mussen (ed.) *Handbook of Child Psychology*, Volume IV. New York: John Wiley & Sons.

McCool, W. F., Dorn, L. D. and Susman, E. J. (1994) The relation of cortisol reactivity and anxiety to perinatal outcome in primiparous adolescents. *Research in Nursing and Health*, 17, 411–420.

McGee, H. M., O'Boyle, C. A., Hickey, A., O'Malley, K. and Joyce, C. R. B. (1991) Assessing the quality of life of the individual: the SEIQoL with a healthy and a gastroenterology unit population. *Psychological Medicine*, 21, 749–759.

McGee, R., Williams, S. and Elwood, M. (1994) Depression and the development of cancer – a meta-analysis. *Social Science and Medicine*, 38(1), 187–192.

McGee, R., Williams, S. and Elwood, M. (1996) Are life events related to the onset of breast cancer? *Psychological Medicine*, 26(3), 441–447.

McHugh, P., Lewis, S., Ford, S., Newland, E., Rustin, G., Coombes, C., Smith, D., O'Reilly, S. and Fallowfield, L. (1995) The efficacy of audiotapes in promoting psychological well-being in cancer patients: a randomised control trial. *British Journal of Cancer*, 74, 388–392.

Macintyre, S. (1997) The Black Report and beyond: what are the issues? *Social Science and Medicine*, 44(6), 723–745.

McKie, L. (1993) Women's views of the cervical smear test: implications for nursing practice – women who have not had a smear test. *Journal of Advanced Nursing*, 18, 972–979.

McKie, L. (1995) The art of surveillance or reasonable prevention? The case of cervical screening. *Sociology of Health and Illness*, 17(4), 441–457.

McKim, W. A. (1991) *Drugs and Human Behaviour* (2nd edn). Englewood Cliffs, NJ: Prentice-Hall.

MacMahon, S., Cutler, J., Britaain, E. and Higgins, M. (1987) Obesity and hypertension: epidemiological and clinical issues. *European Heart Journal*, 8, 57–70.

McManus, F. (1996) Clinical uses of biofeedback. *Journal of Psychophysiology*, 10, 78–79.

McNeill, B. J., Pauker, S. G., Sox, H. C. and Tversky, A. (1982) On the elicitation of preferences for alternative therapies. *New England Journal of Medicine*, 306, 1259–1262.

McPherson, K., Steel, C. M. and Dixon, J. M. (1995) Breast cancer-epidemiology, risk factors and genetics. In: J. Dixon (ed.) *ABC of Breast Disease*. London: BMJ Publishing Group.

Maeland, J. G. and Havik, O. E. (1987) Psychological predictors for return to work after a myocardial infarction. *Journal of Psychosomatic Research*, 31, 471–481.

Maguire, P. (1994) ABC of breast diseases – psychological aspects. *British Medical Journal*, 30, 1649–1652

Main, C. J. (1983) The modified somatic perception questionnaire. *Journal of Psychometric Research*, 27, 503–514.

Main, C. J. and Waddell, G. (1991) A comparison of cognitive measures in low back pain: statistical structure and clinical validity at initial assessment. *Pain*, 46, 287–298.

Main, C. J., Wood, P. L., Hollis, S., Spanswick, C. C. and Waddell, G. (1992) The distress and risk assessment method (D.R.A.M.): a simple patient classification to identify distress and evaluate the risk of poor outcome. *Spine*, 17, 40–52.

Maixner, W. and Humphrey, C. (1993) Gender differences in pain and cardiovascular responses to forearm ischemia. *Clinical Journal of Pain*, 9, 16–25.

Malpass, D., Treiber, F., Turner, J. R., Davies, H., Thompson, W., Levy, M. and Strong, W. B. (1997) Relationships between children's cardiovascular stress response and resting cardiovascular functioning one year later. *Journal of Psychophysiology*, 25, 139–144.

Mangan, G. L. and Golding, J. F. (1984) *The Psychopharmacology of Smoking*. Cambridge: Cambridge University Press.

Mann, A. H. (1977) Psychiatric morbidity and hostility in hypertension. *Psychological Medicine*, 7, 653–659.

Mann, A. H. (1986) The psychological aspects of hypertension. *Journal of Psychosomatic Research*, 30, 527–541.

Mann, A. H. and Brennan, P. J. (1987) Type A behaviour score and the incidence of cardiovascular disease: a failure to replicate the claimed associations. *Journal of Psychosomatic Research*, 31, 685–692.

Mann, N. P. and Johnston, D. I. (1982) Total glycosylated haemoglobin (HbA$_1$) levels in diabetic children. *Archives of Disease in Childhood*, 57, 434–437.

Manuck, S. B. (1994) Cardiovascular reactivity in cardiovascular disease: 'Once more unto the breach'. *International Journal of Behavioral Medicine*, 1, 4–31.

Manuck, S. B. and Proietti, J. M. (1982) Parental hypertension and cardiovascular response to cognitive and isometric challenge. *Psychophysiology*, 19, 481–489.

Markova, I. and Wilkie, P. (1988) Representations, concepts and social change: the phenomenon of AIDS. *Journal for the Theory of Social Behaviour*, 17, 389–409.

Marks, D. (1994) Psychology's role in the Health of the Nation. *The Psychologist*, 7, 119–121.

Marks, D. F. (1995) Mortality and alcohol consumption. The dose–response relation is probably linear. *British Medical Journal*, 310, 325–326.

Marmot, M. G. (1984) Geography of blood pressure and hypertension. *British Medical Bulletin*, 40, 380–386.

Marmot, M. G. and Brunner, E. (1991) Alcohol and cardiovascular disease – the status of the U-shaped curve. *British Medical Journal*, 303(6802), 565–568.

Marmot, M. G., Adelstein, A. and Balusu, L. (1984) *Immigrant Mortality in England and Wales, 1970–78*. London: HMSO.

Marmot, M. G., Shipley, M. J. and Rose, G. (1984) Inequalities in death: specific explanations of a general pattern. *Lancet*, i (8384), 1003–1006.

Marmot, M. G., Davey Smith, G., Stansfield, S., Patel, C., North, F. and Head, J. (1991) Health inequalities amongst British civil servants: The Whitehall II Study. *Lancet*, 337, 1387–1393.

Marmot, M. G., Rose, G., Shipley, M. and Hamilton, P. J. S. (1978) Employment grade and coronary heart disease in British civil servants. *Journal of Epidemiology and Community Health*, 3, 244–249.

Marmot, M. G., Syme, S. L., Kagan, H., Kato, J. B. and Belsky, J. (1975) Epidemiological studies of coronary heart disease and stroke in Japanese men living in Japan, Hawaii and California. *American Journal of Epidemiology*, 102, 514–525.

Marsland, A. L., Manuck, S. B., Fazzari, T. V., Stewart, C. J. and Rabin, B. S. (1995) Stability of individual differences in cellular immune responses to acute psychological stress. *Psychosomatic Medicine*, 57, 295–298.

Marteau, T. M. and Johnston, M. (1987) Health psychology: the danger of neglecting psychological models. *Bulletin of the British Psychological Society*, 40, 82–85.

Marteau, T. M., Kidd, J., Michie, S., Cook, R., Johnston, M. and Shaw, R. W. (1993) Anxiety, knowledge and satisfaction in women receiving false positive results on routine prenatal screening: a randomized controlled trial. *Journal of Psychosomatic Obstetrics and Gynaecology*, 14, 185–196.

Martin, I. and Venables, P.H. (eds) (1980) *Techniques in Psychophysiology*. Chichester: John Wiley & Sons.

Matarazzo, J. D. (1980) Behavioral health and behavioral medicine. Frontiers for a new health psychology. *American Scientist*, 35, 807–817.

Matarazzo, J. D. (1983) Behavioural immunogens and pathogens in health and illness. In: B. L. Hammonds and C. J. Scheirer (eds) *Psychology and Health. The Master Lecture Series, Volume 3*. Washington, DC: American Psychological Association.

Mathews, A. and Ridgeway, V. (1981) Personality and surgical recovery: a review. *British Journal of Clinical Psychology*, 20, 243–260.

Mathews, A. and Ridgeway, V. (1984) Psychological preparation for surgery. In: A. Steptoe and A. Mathews (eds) *Health Care and Human Behaviour*. London: Academic Press.

Matthews, K. A. (1982) Psychological perspectives on the Type A behaviour pattern. *Psychological Bulletin*, 91, 293–323.

Matthews, K. A. (1988) Coronary heart disease and Type A behaviours: update on and alternative to the Booth-Kewley and Friedman (1987) quantitative review. *Psychological Bulletin*, 104, 373–380.

Matthews, K. A., Glass, D. C., Rosenman, R. H. and Bortner, R. W. (1977) Competitive drive, pattern A, and coronary heart disease: a further analysis of some data from the Western Collaborative Group Study. *Journal of Chronic Diseases*, 30, 489–498.

Matthews, K. A., Shumaker, S. A., Bowen, D. J., Langer, R. D., Hunt, J. R., Kaplan, R. M., Klesges, R. C. and Ritenbaugh, C. (1997) Women's health initiative: Why now? What is it? What's new? *American Psychologist*, 52(2), 101–116.

Mattsson, A. (1972) Long-term physical illness in childhood: a challenge to psychosocial adaptation. *Pediatrics*, 50, 801–811.

Maxwell, C. and Boyle, M. (1995) Risky heterosexual practices amongst women over 30: gender, power and long-term relationships, *AIDS Care*, 7, 277–293.

Maxwell, D. L., Polkey, M. I. and Henry, J. A. (1994) Hyponatraemia and catatonic stupor after taking 'ecstasy'. *British Medical Journal*, 307, 1399.

May, B. (1991) Diabetes. In: M. Pitts and K. Phillips (eds) *The Psychology of Health: An Introduction*. London: Routledge.

Mayer, T. J. and Mark, M. M. (1995) Effects of psychosocial interventions with adult cancer patients: a meta-analysis of randomised experiments. *Health Psychology*, 14, 101–108.

Mayes, B. T., Sime, W. E. and Ganster, D. C. (1984) Convergent validity of Type A behaviour pattern scales and their ability to predict physiological responsiveness in a sample of female public employees. *Journal of Behavioural Medicine*, 7, 83–108.

Mayou, R. and Hawton, K. E. (1986) Psychiatric disorder in the general hospital. *British Journal of Psychiatry*, 149, 172–190.

Mayou, R. and Sharpe, M. (1995) Patients whom doctors find difficult to help – an important and neglected problem. *Psychosomatics*, 36(4), 323–325.

Meade, T. W. (1988) The epidemiology of haemostatic and other variables in coronary artery disease. *European Heart Journal*, 9, 836–849.

Meadows, P. (1987) Study of the women overdue for a smear test in a general practice cervical screening programme. *Journal of the Royal College of General Practitioners*, 37, 500–503.

Mechanic, D. (1978) *Medical Sociology* (2nd edn). New York: Free Press.

Medical Research Council (MRC) (1985) MRC Trial of Treatment of mild hypertension: principal results. *British Medical Journal*, 291, 97–104.

Medical Research Council Working Party (1981) Adverse reactions to benedrofluazide and propranolol for the treatment of mild hypertension. *Lancet*, ii, 539–543.

Meichenbaum, D. and Jaremko, M. E. (eds) (1983) *Stress Reduction and Prevention*. New York: Plenum Press.

Meichenbaum, D. and Turk, D. C. (1987) *Facilitating Treatment Adherence: A Practitioner's Guidebook*. New York: Plenum Press.

Melamed, B. G. (1974) *Ethan has an Operation* (Film). In Cleveland, OH: Western Reserve University, Health Sciences Communication Center.

Melamed, B. G. (1984) Health intervention: collaboration for health and science. In: B. L. Hammonds and C. J. Scheier (eds) *Psychology and Health, Master Lecture Series, Volume 3*. Washington, DC: American Psychological Association.

Melamed, B. G. (1988) Section overview: current approaches to hospital preparation. In: B. G. Melamed, K. A. Matthews, D. K. Routh, B. Stabler and N. Schneiderman (eds) *Child Health Psychology*. Hillsdale, NJ: Lawrence Erlbaum.

Melamed, B. G. and Siegal, L. J. (1975) Reduction of anxiety in children facing hospitalisation and surgery by use of filmed modelling. *Journal of Consulting and Clinical Psychology*, 43, 511–521.

Melamed, B. G., Dearborn, M. and Hermecz, D. A. (1983) Necessary considerations for surgery preparation: age and previous experience. *Psychosomatic Medicine*, 45, 517–525.

Melamed, B. G., Yurcheson, R., Fleece, L., Hutcherson, S. and Hawes, R. (1978) Effects of film modelling on the reduction of anxiety-related behaviours in individuals varying in level of previous experience in the stress situation. *Journal of Consulting and Clinical Psychology*, 46, 1357–1367.

Melzack, R. (1975) The McGill Pain Questionnaire: major properties and scoring methods. *Pain*, 1, 277–299.

Melzack, R. and Wall, P. D. (1965) *Pain Mechanisms: A New Theory. Science*, 150, 971–979.

Melzack, R. and Wall, P. D. (1991) *The Challenge of Pain*. Harmondsworth: Penguin.

Mendes De Leon, C. F., Powell, L. H. and Kaplan, B. H. (1991) Change in coronary prone behaviors in the Recurrent Coronary Prevention Project. *Psychosomatic Medicine*, 53(4), 407–419.

Metson, D. (1988) Lessons from an audit of unplanned pregnancies. *British Medical Journal*, 297, 8 October, 904–906.

Meyer, D., Leventhal, H. and Guttman, M. (1985) Common-sense models of illness: the example of hypertension. *Health Psychology*, 4, 115–135.

Miller, N. E. (1969) Learning of visceral and glandular response. *Science*, 153, 434–445.

Miller, N. E. and Dworkin, B. R. (1977) Critical issues in therapeutic applications of biofeedback. In: G. E. Scwartz and J. Beatty (eds) *Biofeedback: Theory and Research*. New York: Academic Press.

Miller, S. M. and Mangan, C. E. (1983) Interacting effects of information and coping style in adapting to gynecologic stress: should the doctor tell all? *Journal of Personality and Social Psychology*, 45, 223–236.

Mills, D. E. and Ward, R. P. (1986) Attenuation of stress-induced hypertension by exercise independent of training effects: an animal model. *Journal of Behavioral Medicine*, 9, 599–605.

Mills, M., Puckering, C., Pound, A. and Cox, A. (1985) What is it about depressed mothers that influences their child's functioning? In: J. E. Stevenson (ed.) *Recent Research in Developmental Psychopathology*. Oxford: Pergamon Press.

Mills, S., Campbell, M. J. and Waters, W. E. (1986) Public knowledge of AIDS and the DHSS advertisement campaign. *British Medical Journal*, 293, 1089–1090.

Mirowsky, J. and Ross, C. E. (1983) Patient satisfaction and visiting the doctor: a self-regulating system. *Social Science and Medicine*, 17, 1353–1361.

Mischel, W. (1974) Processes in delay of gratification. In: L. Berkowitz (ed.) *Advances in Experimental Social Psychology*, 7. New York: Academic Press.

Moatti, J. P., Manesse, L., Le Gales, C., Pages, J. P. and Fagnani, F. (1988) Social perception of AIDS in the general public: a French study. *Health Policy*, 9, 1–8.

Modan, M. and Kalkin, H. (1991) Hyperinsulinemia or increased sympathetic drive as links for obesity and hypertension. *Diabetes Care*, 14, 470–487.

Moffic, H. S. and Paykel, E. S. (1975) Depression in medical inpatients. *British Journal of Psychiatry*, 126, 346–353.

Mok, J. (1988) Children born to women with HIV infection. *Royal Society of Medicine. The AIDS Letter*, 7(June/July), 1–2.

Morisky, D. E., Green, L. W. and Levine, D. M. (1986) Concurrent and predictive validity of a self-reported measure of medication adherence. *Medical Care*, 24, 67–74.

Morrell, D. C. and Wade, C. J. (1976) Symptoms perceived and recorded by patients. *Journal of the Royal College of General Practitioners*, 26, 398–403.

Morris, J. and Elwood, M. (1996) Sun exposure modification programmes and their evaluation: a review of the literature. *Health Promotion International*, 11(4), 321–332.

Morris, J. K., Cook, D. G. and Shaper, A. G. (1994) Loss of employment and mortality. *British Medical Journal*, 308, 1135–1139.

Morrison, D. M. (1985) Adolescent contraceptive behavior: a review. *Psychological Bulletin*, 98, 538–568.

Mrazek, D. A., Klinnert, M. D., Mrazek, P. and Macey, T. (1991) Early asthma onset: consideration of parenting issues. *Journal of the American Academy of Child and Adolescent Psychiatry*, 30, 277–282.

Mulleady, G. (1987) A review of drug abuse and HIV infection. *Psychology and Health*, 1, 149–163.

Mulleady, G. and Sher, L. (1989) Lifestyle factors for drug users in relation to risks for HIV. *AIDS Care*, 1, 45–50.

Mulleady, G., Phillips, K. C. and White, D. G. (1989) Issues in sexual counselling for HIV positive drug users. Paper presented to International Conference on Health Psychology, Cardiff.

Mulleady, G., White, D. G., Phillips, K. C. and Cupitt, C. (1990) Reducing sexual transmission of HIV: the challenge for counselling. *Counselling Psychology Quarterly*, 3, 325–341.

Mumford, E., Schlesinger, H. J. and Glass, G. V. (1982) The effects of psychological intervention on recovery from surgery and heart attacks. An analysis of the literature. *American Journal of Health*, 72, 141–151.

Murray, L., Kempton, C., Woolgar, M. and Hooper, R. (1993) Depressed mothers' speech to their infants and its relation to infant gender and cognitive development. *Journal of Child Psychology and Psychiatry*, 34, 1083–1102.

Muscat, A. T., Harris, R. E., Haley, N. J. and Wynder, E. L. (1991) Cigarette smoking and plasma cholesterol. *American Heart Journal*, 121, 141–147.

Najman, J. M., Klein, D. and Munro, C. (1982) Patient characteristics negatively stereotyped by doctors. *Social Science and Medicine*, 16, 1781–1789.

Naliboff, B. D., Benton, D., Soloman, G. F., Morley, J. E., Fahey, J. L., Bloom, E. T., Makinodan, T. and Gilmore, S. L. (1991) Immunological changes in young and old adults during brief laboratory stress. *Psychosomatic Medicine*, 53, 121–132.

Naliboff, B. D., Soloman, G. F., Gilmore, S. L., Fahey, G. L., Benton, D. and Pine, J. (1995) Rapid changes in cellular immunity following a confrontational role-play stressor. *Brain, Behaviour and Immunity*, 9, 207–219.

Nathan, D. M., Fogel, H., Norman, D., Russell, P. S., Tolkoff-Rubin, N., Delmonico, F. L., Auchinloss, H., Camuso, J. and Cosimi, A. B. (1991) Long-term metabolic and quality of life results with pancreatic/renal transplantation in insulin-dependent diabetes mellitus. *Transplantation*, 52, 85–91.

Nathoo, V. (1988) Investigation of non-responders at a cervical screening clinic in Manchester. *British Medical Journal*, 296, 1041–1042.

National Institute of Health (1993) *Respiratory Health Effects of Passive Smoking*. Report by the National Institute for Health, and US Environmental Protection Agency, Maryland.

Neef, N., Scutchfield, D., Elder, J. and Bender, S. (1991) Testicular self examination by young men: an analysis of characteristics associated with practice. *Journal of American College Health*, 39(4), 187–190.

Nelson, E., Sloper, P., Charlton, A. and While, D. (1994) Children who have a parent with cancer. A pilot study. *Journal of Cancer Education*, 9, 30–36.

Newburgh, L. H. and Conn, J. W. (1979) A new interpretation of hyperglycaemia in obese middle-aged persons. *Journal of the American Medical Association*, 112, 7–11.

Newcombe, M. D. and Bentler, P. M. (1989) Substance use and abuse amongst children and teenagers. *American Psychologist*, 44, 242–248.

Newell, M. L., Dunn, D. T., Peckham, C. S. *et al.* (63 other authors) (1996) Vertical transmission of HIV-1: maternal immune status and obstetric factors. *AIDS*, 10, 1675–1681.

NHS Centre for Reviews and Dissemination (1995) Benign prostatic hyperplasia. *Effective Health Care*, 2(2).

Nichols, K. A. (1981) Psychological care in general hospitals. *Bulletin of the British Psychological Society*, 34, 90–94.

Nichols, K. A. (1984) The nurse and the psychologist. *Nursing Times*, 80, 22–24.

Nichols, K. A. (1993) *Psychological Care in Physical Illness*. London: Chapman and Hall.

Northouse, L. (1988) Family issues in cancer care. *Advances in Psychosomatic Medicine*, 18, 82–101.

NRC (1989) *National Research Council Report of the Committee on AIDS Research and the Behavioral, Social and Statistical Sciences*. Washington, DC: National Academy Press.

O'Connor, N. J., Manson, J. E., O'Connor, G. T. and Buring, J. E. (1995) Psychosocial risk factors and non-fatal myocardial infarction. *Circulation*, 92(6), 1458–1464.

O'Dowd, T. C. (1988) Five years of heartsink patients in general practice. *British Medical Journal*, 297, 528–530.

O'Halloran, C. M. and Altmaier, E. M. (1995) The efficacy of preparation for surgery and invasive medical procedures. *Patient Education and Counselling*, 25(1), 9–16.

Obrist, P. A. (1981) *Cardiovascular Psychophysiology. A Perspective*. New York: Plenum Press.

Office for National Statistics (1996a) *Series Abortion No. 21*. London: HMSO.

Office for National Statistics (1996b) *Monitor: Population and Health AB*, 96/7(21), November. London: HMSO.

Offord, D. R., Boyle, M. H. and Racine, Y. A. (1989) Ontario child health study: correlates of disorder. *Journal of the American Academy of Child and Adolescent Psychiatry*, 28, 856–860.

Oldenburg, B., Perkins, R. J. and Andrews, G. (1985) Controlled trial of psychological intervention in myocardial infarction. *Journal of Consulting and Clinical Psychology*, 53, 852–859.

Ong, L. M. L., Dehaes, J. C. J. M., Hoos, A. M. and Lammes, F. B. (1995) Doctor–patient communication: a review of the literature. *Social Science and Medicine*, 40(7), 903–918.

OPCS (1986) *General Household Survey for 1984*. London: HMSO.

Orbell, S. and Sheeran, P. (1993) Health psychology and uptake of preventive health services – a review of 30 years' research on cervical screening. *Psychology and Health*, 8(6), 417–433.

Orr, D. P., Golden, M. P., Myers, G. and Marrero, D. G. (1983) Characteristics of adolescents with poorly controlled diabetes referred to a tertiary care centre. *Diabetes Care*, 6, 170–175.

Orvaschel, H., Walsh-Allis, G. and Ye, W. (1988) Psychopathology in children of parents with recurrent depression. *Journal of Abnormal Child Psychology*, 16, 17–28.

Otero-Sabogal, R., Sabogal, F., Perez-Stable, E. J. and Hiatt, R. A. (1995) Dietary practices, alcohol consumption, and smoking behavior: ethnic, sex, and acculturation differences. *Journal of National Cancer Institute Monograph*, 18, 73–82.

Paffenbarger, R. S., Hyde, R. T., Wing, A. L. and Hsieh, C. (1986) Physical activity, all-cause mortality of college alumni. *New England Journal of Medicine*, 314, 605–613.

Pagel, M. D. and Davidson, A. R. (1984) A comparison of three social–psychological models of attitude and behavioral plan: prediction of contraceptive behavior. *Journal of Personality and Social Psychology*, 47, 517–533.

Panaccione, V. F. and Wahler, R. G. (1986) Child behaviour, maternal depression, and social coercion as factors in the quality of child-care. *Journal of Abnormal Child Psychology*, 14, 263–278.

Parkerson, G. R., Broadhead, W. E. and Tse, C.-K. J. (1990) The Duke health profile, a 17 item measure of health and dysfunction. *Medical Care*, 28, 1052.

Parkerson, G. R., Connis, R. T., Broadhead, W. E., Patrick, D. L., Taylor, T. R. and Tse, C.-K. J. (1993) Disease-specific versus generic measurement of health-related quality of life in insulin-dependent diabetic patients. *Medical Care*, 31, 629–639.

Parrott, A. C. (1994) Individual differences in stress and arousal during cigarette smoking. *Psychopharmacology*, 115, 389–396.

Parrott, A. C. (1995a) Stress modulation over the day in cigarette smokers. *Addiction*, 90, 233–244.

Parrott, A. C. (1995b) Smoking cessation leads to reduced stress; but why? *International Journal of the Addictions*, 30, 1509–1516.

Parrott, A. C. (1996) Smoking cessation counselling: the stages of change model. In: R. Bayne, I. Horton and J. Bimrose (eds) *New Directions in Counselling*. London: Routledge.

Parrott, A. C. (1997) The psychobiology of MDMA (ecstasy): symposium report. *Journal of Psychopharmacology* (in press).

Parrott, A.C. and Craig, D. (1995) Psychological functions served by nicotine chewing gum. *Addictive Behaviors*, 20, 271–278.

Parrott, A. C. and Garnham, N. J. (unpublished) Comparative mood states and cognitive skills of cigarette smokers, deprived smokers, and nonsmokers (submitted).

Parrott, A. C. and Grimwood, D. (1996) *Cigarette Smoking and Mood Control in Psychiatric Patients*. Regional meeting of the World Federation of Societies of Biological Psychiatry. Cairns, Australia (June).

Parrott, A. C., Lees, A., Garnham, N. J., Jones, M. and Wesnes, K. (1998, in press) Cognitive task performance impairments in regular MDMA users. *Journal of Psychopharmacology*.

Patel, C. (1994) Identifying psychosocial and other risk factors in Whitehall-II study. *Homeostasis in Health and Disease*, 35(1–2), 71–83.

Patel, C. and North, W. (1975) Randomised controlled trial of yoga and biofeedback in the management of hypertension. *Lancet*, ii, 93–95.

Patel, C., Marmot, M. G. and Terry, D. J. (1981) Controlled trial of biofeedback-aided behavioural methods in reducing mild hypertension. *British Medical Journal*, 282, 2005–2008.

Patel, C., Marmot, M. G., Terry, D. J., Carruthers, M., Hunt, B. and Patel, M. (1985) Trial of relaxation in reducing coronary risk: four year follow up. *British Medical Journal*, 290, 1103–1106.

Patrick, D. L. and Deyo, R. A. (1989) Generic and disease-specific measures in assessing health status and quality of life. *Medical Care*, 27 (Suppl 3), S217.

Patterson, J. M. (1991) Family resilience to the challenge of a child's disability. *Pediatric Annals*, 20, 491–499.

Patterson, J. M. (1995) Promoting resilience in families experiencing stress. *Pediatric Clinics of North America*, 42(1), 47–63.

Patterson, J. M. and Leonard, B. J (1994) Caregiving and children. In: E. Kahana, D. Biegel and M. Wykel (eds) *Family Caregiving across the Lifespan*. Newbury Park, CA: Sage.

Patterson, J. M., Budd, J., Goetz, D. and Warwick, W. J. (1993) Family correlates of a ten-year pulmonary health trend in cystic fibrosis. *Pediatrics*, 91, 383–389.

Payne, S. (1990) Lay representations of breast cancer. *Psychology and Health*, 5, 1–11.

Peacock, J. L., Bland, J. M. and Anderson, H. R. (1995) Preterm delivery: effects of socioeconomic factors, psychological stress, smoking, alcohol, and caffeine. *British Medical Journal*, 311, 531–535.

Pearce, K. A. and Furberg, C. D. (1994) The primary prevention of hypertension. *Cardiovascular Risk Factors*, 4, 147–153.

Pearl, R. (1939) *Natural History of Population*. Oxford: Oxford University Press.

Pearlin, L. I. and Turner, H. A. (1987) The family as a context of the stress process. In: S. V. Kasl and C. L. Cooper (eds), *Stress and Health: Issues in Research Methodology*. London: Wiley.

Pelletier, D. L. (1994) The potentiating effects of malnutrition on child mortality: epidemiologic evidence and policy implications. *Nutrition Reviews*, 52(12), 409–415.

Pendleton, D., Schofield, T., Tate, P. and Havelock, P. (1993) *The Consultation: An Approach to Learning and Teaching*. Oxford: Oxford University Press, p. 32.

Pennebaker, J. W. (1982) *The Psychology of Physical Symptoms*. New York: Springer.

Pennebaker, J. W. and Watson, D. (1988) Blood pressure estimation and beliefs among normotensives and hypertensives. *Health Psychology*, 7, 309–328.

Perelson, A. S., Essunger, P., Cao, Y., Vesanen, M., Hurley, A., Saksela, K. and Markowitz, M. (1997) Decay characteristics of HIV-I infected compartments during combination therapy. *Nature*, 387, 188–191.

Perkins, K. A., Dubbert, P. M., Martin, J. E., Faulstich, M. E. and Harris, J. K. (1986) Cardiovascular reactivity to psychological stress in aerobically trained versus untrained mild hypertensives and normotensives. *Health Psychology*, 5, 407–421.

Perry, C. L., Crockett, S. J. and Pirie, P. (1987) Influencing parental health behaviors: implications for community assessments. *Health Education*, 18, 68–77.

Peters, L. and Esses, L. (1985) Family environment as perceived by children with a chronically ill parent. *Journal of Chronic Diseases*, 38, 301–308.

Peters, R. K., Moraye, B., Bear, M. S. and Thomas, D. (1989) Barriers to screening for cancer of the cervix. *Preventive Medicine*, 18, 133–146.

Peterson, J. L. and Bakeman, R. (1989) AIDS and iv drug use among ethnic minorities. *Journal of Drug Issues*, 19, 27–37.

Peto, R., Lopez, A. D., Boreham, J., Thun, M. and Heath, C. (1994) *Mortality from Smoking in Developed Countries*. World Health Organization Report. Oxford: Oxford University Press.

Petridou, E., Kouri, N., Trichopoulos, D., Revinthi, K., Skalkdis, Y. and Tong, D. (1994) School injuries in Athens: socioeconomic and family risk factors. *British Medical Journal*, 490–491.

Peyrot, M. and McMurry, J. (1985) Psychosocial factors in diabetes control: adjustment of insulin treated adults. *Psychosomatic Medicine*, 47, 542–557.

Philips, H. C. and Jahanshahi, M. (1986) The components of pain behaviour report. *Behavioural Research Therapy*, 24, 117–125.

Phillips, K. C. (1979) Biofeedback as an aid to autogenic training. In: B. A. Stoll (ed.) *Mind and Cancer Prognosis*. Chichester: Wiley.

Phillips, K. C. (1987) Psychophysiology: a discipline in search of its paradigm? *Journal of Psychophysiology*, 1, 101–104.

Phillips, K. C. (1988) Strategies against AIDS. *The Psychologist: Bulletin of the British Psychological Society*, 1, 46–47.

Phillips, K. C. (1989a) The psychology of AIDS. In: A. Colman and J. G. Beaumont (eds) *Psychology Survey No. 7*. Leicester: British Psychological Society.

Phillips, K. C. (1989b) Psychophysiological consequences of behavioural choice in aversive situations. In: A. Steptoe and A. Appels (eds) *Stress, Personal Control and Health*. Chichester: Wiley.

Pickard, B. M. (1986) Feeding children: in the beginning – nutrition and pregnancy. *Nutrition and Health*, 4(3), 155–166.

Pickering, T. G. and Miller, N. E. (1977) Learned voluntary control of heart rate and rhythm in two subjects with premature ventricular contractions. *British Heart Journal*, 39, 152–159.

Pickett, C. and Clum, G. A. (1982) Comparative treatment strategies and their interaction with locus of control in the reduction of post-surgical pain and anxiety. *Journal of Consulting and Clinical Psychology*, 50, 439–441.

Pierce, P. F. (1993) Deciding on breast cancer treatment: a description of decision behavior. *Nursing Research*, 42(1), 23–27.

Pill, R. and Stott, N. (1986) Looking after themselves: health protective behaviour among British working class women. *Health Education Research*, 1, 111–119.

Pilowsky, I. and Spence, N. D. (1975) Patterns of illness behaviour in patients with intractable pain. *Journal of Psychosomatic Research*, 19, 279–287.

Piot, P., Plummer, F., Mhalu, F., Lamboray, J.-L., Chin, J. and Mann, J. M. (1988) AIDS: an international perspective. *Science*, 239, 573–579.

Pittner, M. S. and Houston, B. K. (1980) Response to stress, cognitive coping strategies, and the Type A behaviour pattern. *Journal of Personality and Social Psychology*, 39, 147–157.

Pitts, M. K. (1996) *The Psychology of Preventive Health*. London: Routledge.

Pitts, M. K. and Healey, S. (1989) Factors influencing the inferences of pain made by three health professions. *Physiotherapy Practice*, 5, 65–68.

Pitts, M. K. and Jackson, H. (1989) AIDS and the press: an analysis of the coverage of AIDS by Zimbabwe newspapers. *AIDS Care*, 1, 77–83.

Pitts, M. K., McMaster, J. and Wilson, P. (1991) An investigation of preconditions necessary for the introduction of a campaign to promote breast self examination amongst Zimbabwean women. *Journal of Applied and Community Psychology*, 1(1), 33–42.

Pleck, J. H., Sonenstein, F. L. and Ku, L. C. (1990) Contraceptive attitudes and intention to use condoms in sexually experienced and inexperienced adolescent males. *Journal of Family Issues: Special Issue: Adolescent Sexuality, Contraception and Childbearing*, 11, 294–312.

Pless, I. B., Peckham, C. S. and Power, C. (1989) Predicting traffic injuries in childhood: a cohort analysis. *Journal of Pediatrics*, 115, 932–938.

Polatin, P. E., Kinney, R. K., Gatchel, R. J., Lillo, E. and Mayer, T. G. (1993) Psychiatric illness and chronic low back pain. The mind and the spine – which goes first? *Spine*, 18, 66–71.

Pollock, J. I. (1994) Long-term associations with infant feeding in a clinically advantaged population of babies. *Developmental Medicine and Child Neurology*, 36, 429–440.

Poole, K. (1996) The evolving role of the clinical nurse specialist within the comprehensive breast cancer centre. *Journal of Clinical Nursing*, 5(6), 341–349.

Poskitt, E. M. E. (1993) Which children are at risk of obesity? *Nutrition Research*, 13, S83–S93.

Potter, J. F. and Beavers, D. G. (1984) Pressor effects of alcohol in hypertension. *Lancet*, i, 119–122.

Potter, R. (1963) Additional measures of use effectiveness. *Millbank Memorial Fund Quarterly*, 41, 400.

Potts, M. (1977) *Abortion*. Cambridge: Cambridge University Press.

Power, C. (1992) A review of child health in the 1958 birth cohort: National Child Development Study. *Pediatric and Perinatal Epidemiology*, 6, 81–110.

Power, C. (1995) Children's physical development. In: B. Botting (ed.) *The Health of our Children*. Decennial Supplement. Office of Population Censuses and Surveys. Series DS no. 11. London: HMSO.

Power, R., Hunter, G. M., Jones, S. G. and Donaghue, M. (1994) The sharing of injecting paraphernalia among illicit drug users. *AIDS*, 8, 1509–1511.

Prazar, G. and Felice, M. (1975) The psychological and social effects of juvenile diabetes. *Paediatric Annals*, 4, 351–358.

Price, V. (1982) *Type A Behavior Pattern: A Model for Research and Practice*. New York: Academic Press.

Prineas, E. J. (1991) Clinical interaction of salt and weight change on blood pressure levels. *Hypertension*, 17, 143–149.

Prochaska, J. O. and DiClemente, C. C. (1982) Transtheoretical therapy: towards a more integrative model of change. *Psychotherapy: Theory, Research and Practice*, 20, 161–173.

Prochaska, J. O. and DiClemente, C. C. (1983) Stages and processes of self-change of smoking: toward an integrative model of change. *Journal of Consulting and Clinical Psychology*, 51, 390–395.

Prochaska, J. O. and DiClemente, C. C. (1992) Stages of change in the modification of problem behaviors. In: M. Hersen, R. M. Eisler and P. M. Miller (eds) *Progress in Behavior Modification*. Newbury Park, CA: Sage.

Prochaska, J. O., DiClemente, C. C. and Norcross, J. C. (1992) In search of how people change. *American Psychologist*, 47, 1102–1114.

Prochaska, J. O., Redding, C. A., Harlow, L. L., Rossi, J. S. and Velicer, W. F. (1994a) The transtheoretical model of change and HIV prevention – a review. *Health Education Quarterly*, 21(4), 471–486.

Prochaska, J. O., Velicer, W. F., Rossi, J. S., Goldstein, M. G., Marcus, B. H. and Rakowski, W. (1994b) Stages of change and decisional balance for 12 problem behaviors. *Health Psychology*, 13(1), 39–46.

Prout, A. (1996) *Families, Cultural Bias and Health Promotion*. London: Health Education Authority.

Pruyn, J., van der Borne, H., de Reuver, R., de Boer, M., Ter Pelkwijk, M. and de Jong, P. (1988) The locus of control scale for cancer patients. *Tijdscrift vour Sociale Gezondherdszong*, 66, 404–408.

Puente, A. E. and Beiman, I. (1980) The effects of behavior therapy, self-relaxation, and tran-scendental meditation on cardiovascular stress response. *Journal of Clinical Psychology*, 36, 291–295.

Quadrel, M. J., Fischoff, B. and Davis, W. (1993) Adolescent (in)vulnerability. *American Psychologist*, 48(2), 102–116.

Radcliffe Richards, J. (1982) *The Sceptical Feminist*. Harmondsworth: Penguin.

Radke-Yarrow, M. and Zahn-Waxler, C. (1990) Research on children of affectively ill parents: some considerations for theory and research on normal development. *Development and Psychopathology*, 2, 349–366.

Ragland, D. R. and Brand, R. J. (1988) Type A behaviour and mortality from coronary heart disease. *New England Journal of Medicine*, 318, 65–69.

Rahe, R. H. and Lind, E. (1971) Psychosocial factors and sudden cardiac death: a pilot study. *Journal of Psychosomatic Research*, 15, 19–24.

Rainville, J., Ahern, D. K., Phalen, L., Childs, L. A. and Sutherland, R. (1992) The association of pain with physical activities in chronic low back pain. *Spine*, 17, 1060–1064.

Rakowski, W., Dube, C. E., Marcus, B. H., Prochaska, J. O., Velicer, W. F. and Abrams, D. B. (1992) Assessing elements of women's decisions about mammography. *Health Psychology*, 11(2), 111–118.

Rasmussen, H. (1974) Organisation and control of endocrine systems. In: R. H. Williams (ed.) *Textbook of Endocrinology* (5th edn). Philadelphia: Saunders.

Rassaby, J., Larcombe, I., Hill, D. and Wake, F. R. (1983) Slip, Slop, Slap: health education about skin cancer. *Cancer Forum*, 7, 63–69.

Ratip, S. and Modell, B. (1996) Psychosocial and sociological aspects of the Thalassemias. *Seminars in Hematology*, 33, 53–65.

Ratip, S., Skuse, D., Porter, J., Wonke, B., Yardumian, A. and Modell, B. (1995) Psychosocial and clinical burden of thalassaemia intermedia and its implications for prenatal diagnosis. *Archives of Disease in Childhood*, 72, 402–412.

Reading, A. E., Cox, D. N. and Sledmere, C. M. (1982) Issues arising from the development of new male contraceptives. *Bulletin of the British Psychological Society*, 35, 369–371.

Reiss, D., Gonzales, S. and Kramer, N. (1986) Family process, chronic illness and death. *Archives of General Psychiatry*, 43, 795–804.

Rhodes, T. and Hartnoll, I. (eds) (1996) *AIDS, Drugs and Prevention: Perspectives on Individual and Community Action*. London: Routledge.

Ricaurte, G. A. and McCann, U. D. (1992) Neurotoxic amphetamine analogues: effects in monkeys and implications for humans. *Annals of the New York Academy of Sciences*, 648, 371–382.

Rice, K., Warner, N., Tye, T. and Bayer, A. (1997) Telling the diagnosis to patients with Alzheimer's disease: geriatricians' and psychiatrists' practices differ. *British Medical Journal*, 314, 376.

Richman, N., Stevenson, J. and Graham, P. (1982) *Preschool To School: A Behavioural Study*. London: Academic Press.

Ridgeway, V. and Mathews, A. (1982) Psychological preparation for surgery: a comparison of methods. *British Journal of Clinical Psychology*, 21, 243–260.

Rigotti, N.A. (1989) Cigarette smoking and body weight. *New England Journal of Medicine*, 320, 931–933.

Rime, B., Ucros, C. G., Bestgen, Y. and Jeanjean, M. (1989) Type A behaviour pattern: specific coronary risk factor or general disease-prone condition? *British Journal of Medical Psychology*, 62, 229–240.

375

Rivara, F., DiGuiseppi, C., Thompson, R. and Calonge, N. (1989) Risk of injury to children less than 5 years of age in day care versus home care settings. *Pediatrics*, 84, 1011–1016.

Roberts, I. (1996) Out-of-home day care and health. *Archives of Disease in Childhood*, 74, 73–76.

Roberts, I. and Pless, B. (1995) Social policy as a cause of childhood accidents: the children of lone mothers. *British Medical Journal*, 311, 925–928.

Roberts, I. and Power, C. (1996) Does the decline in child injury mortality vary by social class? A comparison of class specific mortality in 1981 and 1991. *British Medical Journal*, 313, 784–786.

Roberts, I., Norton, R. and Taua, B. (1996) Child pedestrian injury rates: the importance of exposure to risk relating to socioeconomic and ethnic differences, in Auckland, New Zealand. *Journal of Epidemiological Community Health*, 50, 162–165.

Roberts, R., Brunner, E. and Marmot, M. (1995) Psychological factors in the relationship between alcohol and cardiovascular morbidity. *Social Science and Medicine*, 41(11), 1513–1516.

Robertson, D. and Curatolo, P. W. (1984) The cardiovascular effects of caffeine. In: P. B. Dews (ed.) *Caffeine. Perspectives from Recent Research*. Berlin: Springer-Verlag.

Robertson, J. R., Bucknall, A., Welsby, P., Inglis, J., Peutherer, J. and Brettle, R. (1986) Epidemic of AIDS related virus (HTLV III/LAV) infection among intravenous drug users. *British Medical Journal*, 292, 527–529.

Robin, A. L., Siegel, P. T., Koepke, T., Moye, A. W. and Tice, S. (1994) Family therapy versus individual therapy for adolescent females with anorexia nervosa. *Journal of Developmental and Behavioral Pediatrics*, 15, 111–116.

Robinson, J. O. (1964) A possible effect of selection on the test scores of a group of hypertensives. *Journal of Psychosomatic Research*, 8, 239–243.

Robinson, J. O. and Granfield, A. J. (1986) The frequent consulter in primary medical care. *Journal of Psychosomatic Research*, 30, 589–600.

Rodin, G. M. (1990) Quality of life in adults with insulin-dependent diabetes mellitus. *Psychotherapy and Psychosomatics*, 54, 132–139.

Rodin, G. M., Johnson, L. E., Garfinkle, P. E., Daneman, D. and Kenshole, A. B. (1986) Eating disorders in female adolescents with insulin-dependent diabetes mellitus. *International Journal of Psychiatry Medicine*, 16, 49–57.

Rodin, J. and Ickovitcs, J. R. (1990) Women's health: review and research agenda as we approach 21st century. *American Psychologist*, 45, 1018–1034.

Rogers, E. M. (1987) The diffusions of innovations perspective. In: N. D. Weinstein (ed.) *Taking Care: Understanding and Encouraging Self-Protective Behaviour*. Cambridge: Cambridge University Press.

Rogers, R. W. (1983) Cognitive and physiological processes in fear appeals and attitude change: a revised Theory of Protection Motivation. In: J. Cacioppo and R. Petty (eds) *Social Psychophysiology*. New York: Guilford Press.

Rogers, W. (1984) Changing health related attitudes and behavior: the role of preventive health psychology. In: J. H. Harvey, E. Maddux, R. P. McGlynn and C. D. Stoltenberg (eds) *Social Perception in Clinical and Counselling Psychology*. Lubbock, TX: Texas Technical University Press.

Roland, M. and Dixon, M. (1989) Randomised controlled trial of an educational booklet for patients presenting with back pain in general practice. *Journal of the Royal College of General Practitioners*, 39, 244–246.

Rose, G. and Marmot, M. G. (1981) Social class and coronary heart disease. *British Heart Journal*, 45, 13–19.

Rose, J. E. and Mountcastle, V. B. (1959) Touch and kinesthesis. *Handbook of Physiology*, 1, 387–429.

Rose, M. J., Klenerman, L., Atchinson, L. and Slade, P. D. (1992) An application of the fear-avoidance model to three chronic pain problems. *Behaviour Research Therapy*, 30, 359–365.

Rosenberg, S. J., Peterson, R. A., Hayes, J. R., Hatcher, J. and Headen, S. (1988) Depression in medical in-patients. *British Journal of Medical Psychology*, 61, 245–254.

Rosenfeld, A. and Caplan, G. (1983) Adaptation of children of parents suffering from cancer: a preliminary study of a new field for primary prevention research. *Journal of Primary Prevention*, 3, 244–250.

Rosenfeld, J. and Shohat, J. (1983) Obesity and hypertension. In: F. Gross and T. Strasser (eds) *Mild Hypertension: Recent Advances*. New York: Raven Press.

Rosenheim, E. and Reicher, R. (1985) Informing children about parent's terminal illness. *Journal of Child Psychology and Psychiatry*, 26 (6), 995–998.

Rosenman, R. H., Brand, R. J., Jenkins, C. D., Friedman, M., Straus, R. and Wurm, M. (1975) Coronary heart disease in the Western Collaborative Group Study: final follow-up experience of eight and a half years. *Journal of American Medical Association*, 233, 872–877.

Rosensteil, A. K. and Keefe, F. J. (1983) The use of coping strategies in chronic low back pain patients: relationship to patient characteristics and current adjustments. *Pain*, 17, 33–34.

Rosenstock, I. M. (1966) Why people use health services. *Millbank Memorial Fund Quarterly*, 44, 94.

Rosenstock, I. M. (1974) Historical origins of the health belief model. *Health Education Monograph*, 2, 409–419.

Roter, D. L. and Hall, J. A. (1992) *Doctors Talking with Patients, Patients Talking with Doctors*. Westport, CT: Auburn House.

Roth, H. P. (1987) The measurement of compliance. *Patient Education and Counseling*, 10, 107–116.

Rotter, J. B. (1954) *Social Learning and Clinical Psychology*. New York: Prentice-Hall.

Rotter, J. B. (1966) Generalised expectancies for internal versus external control of reinforcement. *Psychological Monographs*, 80, 1–28.

Rovinsky, J. J. (1972) Abortion recidivism. *Journal of Obstetrics and Gynaecology*, 39, 649–659.

Rowland, N., Maynard, A., Beveridge, A., Kennedy, P., Wintersgill, W. and Stone, W. (1987) Doctors have no time for alcohol screening. *British Medical Journal*, 295, 95–96.

Royal College of Physicians (1983) *Health or Smoking: Follow up Report*. London: Pitman.

Royal College of Physicians and Royal College of Psychiatrists (1995) *The Psychological Care of Medical Patients*. Royal College of Physicians and Royal College of Psychiatrists.

Royal College of Psychiatrists (1986) *Alcohol: Our Favourite Drug*. London: Tavistock Publications.

Rubin, R. R. and Peyrot, M. (1992) Psychological problems in diabetes: a review of the literature. *Diabetes Care*, 15, 1640–1657.

Rudolph, K. D., Dennig, M. D. and Weisz, J. R. (1995) Determinants and consequences of children's coping in the medical setting: conceptualization, review, and critique. *Psychological Bulletin*, 118, 328–357.

Ruesch, S. (1948) The infantile personality – the core problem of psychosomatic medicine. *Psychomatic Medicine*, 10, 134–149.

Russell, G. F. M., Szmukler, G. I., Dare, C. and Eisler, I. (1987) An evaluation of family therapy in anorexia nervosa and bulimia nervosa. *Archives of General Psychiatry*, 44, 1047–1056.

Russell, M. A. H. (1989) Subjective and behavioural effects of nicotine in humans: some sources of individual variation. *Progress in Brain Research*, 79, 289–302.

Rutter, M. (1987) Psychosocial resilience and protective mechanisms. *American Journal of Orthopsychiatry*, 57, 316–331.

Rutter, M. (1989) Psychiatric disorder in parents as a risk factor for children. In: D. Schaffer, I. Phillips and N. B. Enger (eds) *Prevention of Mental Disorder, Alcohol and Other Drug Use in Children and Adolescents*. Rockville, MD: Office for Substance Abuse, USDHHS.

Rutter, M. and Quinton, D. (1984) Parental psychiatric disorder: effects on children. *Psychological Medicine*, 14, 853–880.

Rutter, M., Tizard, J. and Whitmore, K. (1970) *Education, Health and Behaviour*. London: Longmans, Green & Co.

Ryan, G. M. and Sweeney, P. J. (1980) Attitudes of adolescents toward pregnancy and contraception. *American Journal of Obstetrics and Gynecology*, 137, 358–366.

Ryder Richardson, C. (1995) *Mind over Cancer*. London: W. Foulsham and Co Ltd.

Sackett, D. L. and Snow, J. C. (1979) The magnitude of compliance and non-compliance. In: D. W Taylor and D. L. Sackett (eds) *Compliance in Health Care*. Baltimore, MD: Johns Hopkins University Press.

Salmon, P., Woloshynowych, M. and Valori, R. (1996) The measurement of beliefs about physical symptoms in English general practice patients. *Social Science and Medicine*, 42(11), 1561–1567.

Samora, J., Saunders, L. and Larson, M. (1961) Medical vocabulary knowledge among hospital patients. *Journal of Health and Human Behaviour*, 2, 83–89.

Sansom, D., Wakefield, J. and Yule, R. (1970) Cervical cytology in the Manchester region: changing patterns of response. *The Medical Officer* (June), 357–359.

Sarafino, E. P. (1994) *Health Psychology: Biopsychosocial Interactions*. New York: John Wiley & Sons.

Satterthwaite, D., Hart, R., Levy, C., Mitlin, D., Ross, D., Smit, J. and Stephens, C. (1997) *The Environment for Children: Understanding and Acting on the Environmental Hazards that Threaten Children and their Parents*. Earthscan.

Saunders, N. (1995) *Ecstasy and the Dance Culture*. London: Neal's Yard Desktop Publishing.

Scambler, G. and Scambler, A. (1984) The illness iceberg and aspects of consulting behaviour. In: J. H. R. Fitzpatrick, S. Newman, G. Scambler and J. Thompson (ed.) *The Experience of Illness*. London: Tavistock Publications.

Schafer, L. C., McCaul, K. D. and Glasgow, R. E. (1986) Supportive and non-supportive family behaviours: relationship to adherence and metabolic control in persons with type 1 diabetes. *Diabetes Care*, 9, 179–185.

Scheier, M. F. and Carver, C. S. (1985) Optimism, coping and health: assessment and implications of generalised outcome expectancies. *Health Psychology*, 4, 219–247.

Scheier, M. F. and Carver, C. S. (1992) Effects of optimism on psychological and physical well-being: the influence of generalised outcome expectancies on health. *Journal of Personality*, 55, 169–210.

Schinke, S. P. (1984) Preventing teenage pregnancy. In: M. Hersen, R. M. Eisler and R. M. Miller (eds) *Progress in Behavior Modification*, 16. New York: Academic Press.

Schleifer, S. J., Keller, S. E., Camerino, M., Thornton, J. C. and Stein, M. (1983) Suppression of lymphocyte stimulation following bereavement. *Journal of the American Medical Association*, 250, 374–377.

Schneider, N. G., Olmstead, R., Nilsson, F., Mody, F., Franzon, M. and Doan, K. (1996) Efficacy of a nicotine inhaler in smoking cessation: a double-blind placebo controlled study. *Addiction*, 91, 1293–1306.

Schoebinger, R., Florin, I., Reichbauer, M., Lindemann, H. and Zimmer, C. (1993) Childhood asthma: mothers' affective attitude, mother–child interaction and children's compliance with medical requirements. *Journal of Psychosomatic Research*, 37, 697–707.

Schoebinger, R., Florin, I., Zimmer, C., Lindemann, H. and Winter, H. (1992) Childhood asthma: paternal critical attitude and father–child interaction. *Journal of Psychosomatic Research*, 8, 743–750.

Schoenborn, C. A. (1993) The Alameda Study – 25 years on. In: S. Maes, H. Leventhal and M. Johnston (eds) *International Review of Health Psychology*. Chichester: Wiley.

Schoendorf, K. C., Hogue, C. J. R., Kleinman, J. C. and Rowley, D. (1992) Mortality among infants of black as compared with white college-educated parents. *New England Journal of Medicine*, 326, 1522–1526.

Schor, E. L. (1995) The influence of families on child health. *Pediatric Clinics of North America*, 42(1), 89–102.

Schorr, L. (1988) *Within Our Reach: Breaking the Cycle of Disadvantage*. New York: Anchor.

Schrire, S. (1986) Frequent attenders – a review. *Family Practice*, 3, 272–275.

Schwab, J. J., Bialow, M. R., Brown, J. and Holzer, C. F. (1967) Diagnosing depression in medical inpatients. *Annals of Internal Medicine*, 67, 695–707.

Schwarzer, R. and Fuchs, R. (1996) Self efficacy and health behaviours. In: M. Conner and P. Norman (eds) *Predicting Health Behaviour*. Milton Keynes: Open University Press.

Schwarzer, R., Bassler, J., Kwiatek, P., Schroder, K. and Zhang, J. X. (1997) The assessment of optimistic self-beliefs: comparison of the German, Spanish and Chinese versions of the general self-efficacy scale. *Applied Psychology: An International Review*, 46(1), 69–88.

Sciacca, J. P., Phipps, B. L., Dube, D. A. and Ratliff, M. I. (1995) Influences on breast-feeding by lower-income women: an incentive-based, partner-supported educational program. *Journal of American Dietetic Association*, 95(3), 323–328.

Scott, A., Shiell, A. and King, M. (1996) Is general practitioner decision making associated with patient socio-economic status? *Social Science and Medicine*, 42(1), 35–46.

Scott, S., Deary, I. and Pelosi, A. J. (1995) General practitioners' attitudes to patients with a self diagnosis of myalgic encephalomyletis. *British Medical Journal*, 310, 508.

Seers, K. (1987) *Pain Anxiety and Recovery in Patients Undergoing Surgery*. University of London.

Sein, E., Eastham, E. J. and Kolvin, I. (1988) The psychology of chronic childhood illnesses. In: K. Granville-Grossman (ed.) *Recent Advances in Clinical Psychiatry*. Edinburgh: Churchill Livingstone.

Selam, J. L., Micossi, P., Dunn, F. L. and Nathan, D. M. (1992) Clinical trial of programmable implantable insulin pump for Type I diabetes. *Diabetes Care*, 15, 877–884.

Seligman, M. E .P. (1975) *Helplessness: On Depression, Development and Death*. San Francisco: W. H. Freeman.

Selye, H. (1956) *The Stress of Life*. New York: McGraw-Hill.

Series, H., Boeles, S., Dorkins, E. and Peveler, R. (1994) Psychiatric complications of 'Ecstasy' use. *Journal of Psychopharmacology*, 8, 60–61.

Sexton, M., Bross, D., Hebel, J. R., Schumann, B. C., Gerace, T. A., Lasser, N. and Wright, N. (1987) Risk-factor changes in wives with husbands at high risk of coronary heart disease (CHD): the spin-off effect. *Journal of Behavioral Medicine*, 10(3), 251–261.

Shapiro, D. and Goldstein, I. B. (1982) Biobehavioral perspectives on hypertension. *Journal of Consulting and Clinical Psychology*, 50, 841–858.

Shapiro, D., Schwartz, G. and Tursky, B. (1972) Control of diastolic blood pressure in man by feedback and reinforcement. *Psychophysiology*, 9, 296–304.

Shapiro, S., Venet, W., Strax, P., Venet, L. and Roeser, R. (1985) Selection, follow up and analysis in the Health Insurance Plan study: a randomized trial with breast cancer screening. *National Cancer Institute Monographs*, 67, 65–74.

Sharpe, J. N., Brown, R. T., Thompson, N. J. and Eckman, J. (1994) Predictors of coping with pain in mothers and their children with sickle cell syndrome. *Journal of the American Academy of Child and Adolescent Psychiatry*, 33, 1246–1255.

Sharpe, M., Mayou, R., Seagroatt, V., Surawy, C., Warwick, H., Bulstrode, C., Dawber, R. and Lane, D. (1994) Why do doctors find some patients difficult to help? *Quarterly Journal of Medicine*, 87, 187–193.

Shedivy, D. I. and Kleinman, K. M. (1977) Lack of correlation between frontalis EMG and either neck EMG or verbal ratings of tension. *Psychophysiology*, 14, 182–186.

Sheeran, P. and Orbell, S. (1996) How confidently can we infer health beliefs from question-naire responses? *Psychology and Health*, 11(2), 273–290.

Shekelle, R. B., Gale, M., Ostfeld, A. M. and Paul, O. (1983) Hostility, risk of coronary heart disease and mortality. *Psychosomatic Medicine*, 45, 109–114.

Shekelle, R. B., Raynor, W. J., Ostfeld, A. M., Garron, D. C., Bieliauskas, L. A., Liu, S. C., Maliza, C. and Paul, O. (1981) Psychological depression and 17 year risk and death from cancer. *Psychosomatic Medicine*, 43, 117–125.

Sher, L. (1987) An evaluation of the UK government health education campaign on AIDS. *Psychology and Health*, 1, 61–72.

Sherman, J. B., Alexander, M. A., Clark, L., Dean, A. and Webster, L. (1992) Instruments measuring maternal factors in obese preschool children. *Western Journal of Nursing Research*, 14, 555–575.

Shillitoe, R. W. (1988) *Psychology and Diabetes: Psychological Factors in Management and Control*. London: Chapman and Hall.

Shillitoe, R. W. and Miles, D. W. (1989) Diabetes mellitus. In: A. Broome (ed.) *Health Psychology: Processes and Applications*. New York: Chapman and Hall.

Shu, X. O., Hatch, M. C., Mills, J., Clemens, J. and Susser, M. (1995) Maternal smoking, alcohol drinking, caffeine consumption, and fetal growth: results from a prospective study. *Epidemiology*, 6, 115–120.

Siegel, K., Karus, D. and Raveis, V. H. (1996) Adjustment of children facing the death of a parent due to cancer. *Journal of the American Academy of Child and Adolescent Psychiatry*, 35, 442–450.

Siegel, L. (1988) AIDS: perceptions versus realities. *Journal of Psychoactive Drugs*, 20, 149–152.

Siegel, L. and Smith, K. E. (1989) Children's strategies for coping with pain. *Pediatrician*, 16, 110–118.

Silver, B. V. and Blanchard, E. (1978) Biofeedback and relaxation training in the treatment of psychophysiological disorders: or are the machines really necessary? *Journal of Behavioural Medicine*, 1, 217–239.

Silverman, P. R. and Worden, J. W. (1992) Children's reactions in the early months after the death of a parent. *American Journal of Orthopsychiatry*, 62, 93–104.

Siminoff, L. A. and Fetting, J. H. (1991) Factors affecting treatment decisions for a life threatening illness: the case of medical treatment of breast cancer. *Social Science and Medicine*, 32, 813.

Siminoff, L. A., Fetting, J. H. and Abeloff, M. D. (1989) Doctor–patient communication about breast cancer adjuvant therapy. *Journal of Clinical Oncology*, 7(9), 1192–1200.

Simonds, J. R., Goldstein, P., Walker, B. and Rawlings, S. S. (1981) The relationship between psychological factors and blood glucose regulation in insulin-dependent diabetic adolescents. *Diabetes Care*, 4, 610–615.

Simonton, O. C., Simonton, S. M. and Creighton, J. L. (1980) *Getting Well Again*. London: Bantam Books.

Simpson, M. A. (1982) Therapeutic uses of truth. In: E. Wilkes (ed.) *The Dying Patient*. Lancaster: MTP Press.

Singer, E., Rogers, T. F. and Corcoran, M. (1987) The polls. A report – AIDS. *Public Opinion Quarterly*, 51, 580–595.

Singh, G. K. and Yu, S. M. (1995) Infant mortality in the United States: trends, differentials and projections, 1950 through 2010. *American Journal of Public Health*, 85, 957–964.

Singh, V. N. and Gaby, S. K. (1991) Premalignant lesions: role of antioxidant vitamins and beta-carotene in risk reduction and prevention of malignant transformation. *American Journal of Clinical Nutrition*, 53 (1 Suppl), 386S–390S.

Sirota, A. D., Schwartz, G. E. and Shapiro, D. (1976) Voluntary control of human heart rate: effect on reaction to aversive stimulation. A replication and extension. *Journal of Abnormal Psychology*, 85, 473–476.

Siscovick, D. S. (1990) Risks of exercising: sudden cardiac death and injuries. In: C. Bouchard, R. J. Shephard, T. Stephens, J. R. Sutton and B. D. McPherson (eds) *Exercise Fitness and Health: A Consensus of Current Knowledge*. Champaign, Ill: Human Kinetics Books,

Skelly, A. H., Marshall, J. R., Haughey, B. P., Davis, P. J. and Dunford, R. G. (1995) Self-efficacy and confidence in outcomes as determinants of self-care practices in inner-city, African-American women with non-insulin dependent diabetes. *The Diabetes Educator*, 21, 38–46.

Skevington, S. M. (1995) *Psychology of Pain*. Chichester: Wiley.

Skinner, B. F. (1971) *Beyond Freedom and Dignity*. New York: Knopf.

Skog, O. J. (1996) Public health consequences of the J-curve hypothesis of alcohol problems. *Addiction*, 91, 325–337.

Slade, P. D., Troup, J. D. G., Letham, J. and Bentley, G. (1983) The fear-avoidance model of exaggerated pain perception. Part II: Preliminary studies of coping strategies for pain. *Behavioural Research Therapy*, 21, 409–416.

Smetana, J. G. and Adler, N. E. (1979) Decision-making regarding abortion: a value X expectancy analysis. *Journal of Population*, 2, 338–357.

Smith, A. (1976) Should the doctor tell the truth when the patient has cancer? *The Times*, May.

Smith, P., Weinman, M. and Nenny, S. W. (1984) Desired pregnancy during adolescence. *Psychological Reports*, 54, 227–231.

Smith, P. B. and Pedersen, D. R. (1988) Maternal sensitivity and patterns of infant–mother attachment. *Child Development*, 59, 1097–1101.

Smith, T. W., Houston, B. K. and Zurawski, R. M. (1985) The Framingham Type A scale: cardiovascular and cognitive-behavioural responses to interpersonal challenge. *Motivation and Emotion*, 9, 123–134.

Solowij, N., Hall, W. and Lee, N. (1992) Recreational MDMA use in Sydney: a profile of ecstasy users and their experience with the drug. *British Journal of Addiction*, 87, 1161–1172.

Sontag, S. (1983) *Illness as Metaphor*. Harmondsworth: Penguin.

Sorensen, G., Lewis, B. and Bishop, R. (1996) Gender, job factors, and coronary heart disease risk. *American Journal of Health Behavior*, 20(1), 3–13.

Sorensen, R. C. (1973) *Adolescent Sexuality in Contemporary America*. New York: World.

Sorensen, T. I. A., Hoist, C. and Stunkard, A. J. (1992) Childhood body mass index – genetic and familial environmental influences assessed in a longitudinal adoption study. *International Journal of Obesity*, 16, 705–714.

Southam, M. A., Agras, W. S., Taylor, C. B. and Kraemer, H. C. (1982) Relaxation training: blood pressure lowering during the working day. *Archives of General Psychiatry*, 39, 715–717.

Spilker, B. (1990) *Quality of Life Assessments in Clinical Trials*. New York: Raven Press.

Spitzer, W. O., LeBlanc, F. E. and Dupuis, M. (1987) Scientific approach to the assessment and management of activity-related spinal disorders: a monograph for clinicians. *Spine*, 12S, S1–S59.

Sroufe, L. A. and Rutter, M. (1984) The domain of developmental psychopathology. *Child Development*, 55, 17–29.

Staessen, J., Fagard, R. and Amery, A. (1988) Obesity and hypertension. *Acta Cardiologica*, 23, 37–44.

Stall, R., McKusick, L., Wiley, J., Coates, T. J. and Ostrow, D. G. (1986) Alcohol and drug use during sexual activity and compliance with safe sex guidelines for AIDS: the AIDS Behavioral Research Project. *Health Education Quarterly*, 13, 359–371.

Stamler, J., Stamler, R. and Neaton, J. D. (1993) Blood pressure, systolic and diastolic, and cardiovascular risks: US population data. *Archives of Internal Medicine*, 153, 598–615.

Stamler, J., Rose, G., Stamler, R., Elliott, P., Dyer, A. and Marmot, M. (1989) INTERSALT study findings: public health and medical care implications. *Hypertension*, 89, 570–577.

Stamler, R. (1991) Implications of the INTERSALT study. *Hypertension*, 17 (Suppl 1), 1017–1020.

Stanton, A. (1987) Determinance of adherence to medical regimens by hypertensive patients. *Journal of Behavioral Medicine*, 10, 377–394.

Stanton, A. L. (1995) Psychology of women's health: barriers and pathways to knowledge. In: A. L. Stanton and S. J. Gallant (eds) *The Psychology of Women's Health*. Washington, DC: American Psychological Association.

Stanton, A. L. and Gallant, S. J. (1995) *The Psychology of Women's Health*. Washington, DC: American Psychological Association.

Staples, B. and Pharoah, P. O. D. (1994) Child health statistical review. *Archives of Disease in Childhood*, 71, 548–554.

Stapleton, J. A., Russell, M. A. H., Feyerabend, C., Wiseman, S. M., Gustavsson, G., Sawe, U. and Wiseman, D. (1995) Dose effects and predictors of outcome in a randomised trial of transdermal nicotine patches in general practice. *Addiction*, 90, 31–42.

Steel, J. M., Young, R. J., Lloyd, G. G. and Macintyre, C. C. A. (1989) Abnormal eating attitudes in young insulin-dependent diabetics. *British Journal of Psychiatry*, 155, 515–521.

Steffen, V. (1990) Men's motivation to perform the testicle self exam: effects of prior knowledge and an educational brochure. *Journal of Applied Social Psychology*, 20(8), 681–702.

Stein, A., Murray, L., Cooper, P. and Fairburn, C. G. (1996) Infant growth in the context of maternal eating disorders and maternal depression: a comparative study. *Psychological Medicine*, 26, 569–574.

Stein, A., Woolley, H., Cooper, S. D. and Fairburn, C. G. (1994) An observational study of mothers with eating disorders and their infants. *Journal of Child Psychology and Psychiatry*, 35, 733–748.

Steptoe, A. (1981) *Psychological Factors in Cardiovascular Disease*. London: Academic Press.

Steptoe, A. (1983) Stress, helplessness and control: the implications of laboratory studies. *Journal of Psychosomatic Research*, 27, 361–367.

Steptoe, A. (1989) Psychophysiological interventions in behavioural medicine. In: G. Turpin (ed.) *Handbook of Clinical Psychophysiology*. Chichester: Wiley.

Steptoe, A. and Swada, Y. (1989) Assessment of baroreceptor reflex function during mental stress and relaxation. *Psychophysiology*, 26, 140–147.

Steptoe, A., Patel, C., Marmot, M. G. and Hunt, B. (1987) Frequency of relaxation practice, blood pressure reduction, and the general effects of relaxation following a controlled trial of behaviour modification for reducing coronary risks. *Stress Medicine*, 3, 101–107.

Sterling, P. and Eyer, J. (1988) Allostasis: a new paradigm to explain arousal pathology. In: S. Fisher and J. Reason (eds) *Handbook of Life Stress, Cognition and Health*. Chichester: Wiley.

Stimson, G. (1995) AIDS and drug injecting in the United Kingdom 1987 to 1993: the policy response and the prevention of the epidemic. *Social Science and Medicine*, 41, 699–716.

Stimson, G. and Donaghue, M. (1996) Health promotion and the facilitation of individual change. The case of syringe distribution and exchange. In: T. Rhodes and R. Hartnoll (eds) *AIDS, Drugs and Prevention. Perspectives on Individual and Community Action*. London: Routledge.

Stimson, G. V. and Webb, B. (1975) *Going to See the Doctor: The Consultation Process in General Practice*. London: Routledge & Kegan Paul.

Stockwell, T., Hawks, D., Lang, E. and Rydon, P. (1996) Unravelling the preventive paradox for acute alcohol problems. *Drug and Alcohol Review*, 15(1), 7–15.

Stoll, B. A. (1988) Neuroendocrine and psychoendocrine influences of breast cancer growth. In: C. L. Cooper (ed.) *Stress and Breast Cancer*. Chichester: Wiley.

Stone, A. A., Bruce, R. and Neale, J. M. (1988) Changes in daily event frequency precede episodes of physical symptoms. *Journal of Human Stress*, 13, 70–74.

Stone, E. J., Perry, C. L. and Luepker, R. V. (1989) Synthesis of cardiovascular behavioural research for youth health promotion. *Health Education Quarterly*, 16, 155–169.

Stoyva, J. and Budzynski, T. (1974) Cultivated low arousal – and anti-stress response? In: L.V. DiCara (ed.) *Recent Advances in Limbic and Autonomic Nervous System Research*. New York: Plenum.

Strasser, T. (1992) Equal blood pressure levels carry different risks in different risk factor combinations. *Journal of Human Hypertension*, 6, 261–264.

Stroebel, C. F. and Glueck, B. C. (1973) Biofeedback treatment in medicine and psychiatry: an ultimate placebo? *Seminars in Psychiatry*, 5, 379–393.

Stylianos, S. and Eichelberger, M. R. (1993) Pediatric trauma. Prevention strategies. *Pediatric Clinics of North America*, 40(6), 1359–1367.

Sullivan, J. M. (1991) Salt sensitivity: definition, conception, methodology and long-term issues. *Hypertension*, 17, 61–68.

Surgeon General (1988) *Nicotine Addiction: The Health Consequences of Smoking*. Washington, DC: US Government Printing Office.

Surridge, D. H. C., Williams-Erdahl, D. L., Lawson, J. S., Donald, M. W., Monga, T. N., Bird, C. E. and Letemendia, F. J. J. (1984) Psychiatric aspects of diabetes mellitus. *British Journal of Psychiatry*, 145, 269–276.

Surwit, R. S. and Feinglos, M. N. (1988) Stress and autonomic nervous system in Type II diabetes: a hypothesis. *Diabetes Care*, 11, 83–85.

Sutton, J. R., Farrell, P. A. and Harber, V. J. (1990) Hormonal adaptation to physical activity. In: C. Bouchard, R. J. Shephard, T. Stephens, J. R. Sutton and B. D. McPherson (eds) *Exercise Fitness and Health: A Consensus of Current Knowledge*. Champaign, Ill: Human Kinetics Books.

Symonds, T. L., Burton, A. K., Tillotson, K. M. and Main, C. J. (1995) Absence due to low back trouble can be reduced by psychosocial intervention at the workplace. *Spine*, 20, 2738–2745.

Symonds, T. L., Tillotson, K. M., Burton, A. K. and Main, C. J. (1996) Absence from low back trouble: the role of attitudes and beliefs. *Journal of Occupational Medicine*, 46, 25–32.

Tamura, M., Hirano, H., Ohmori, O., Higashi, K. and Matsuoka, S. (1995) Induction of salivary IgA by stress and its suppression by smoking. *Neurosciences (Japan)*, 21 (S2), 85–88.

Taras, H. L. and Gage, M. (1995) Advertised foods on children's television. *Archives of Pediatrics and Adolescent Medicine*, 149(6), 649–652.

Tate, P. (1994) *The Doctor's Communication Handbook*. Oxford: Radcliffe Medical Press.

Tattersall, R. B. and Jackson, J. G. (1982) Social and emotional complications of diabetes. In: R. Jarrett and H. Keen (eds) *Complications of Diabetes* (2nd edn). London: Arnold.

Tattersall, R. B. and Lowe, J. (1981) Diabetes in adolescence. *Diabetologia*, 26, 517–523.

Taylor, C .B., Sheikh, J., Agras, W. S., Roth, W. T., Margraf, J., Ehlers, A., Maddock, R. J. and Gossard, D. (1986) Ambulatory heart rate changes in patients with panic attacks. *American Journal of Psychiatry*, 143, 478–482.

Taylor, N., Hall, G. M. and Salmon, P. (1996) Is patient-controlled analgesia controlled by the patient? *Social Science and Medicine*, 43(7), 1137–1143.

Taylor, S. E. (1979) Hospital patient behaviour: reactance, helplessness or control? *Journal of Social Issues*, 35, 156–184.

Taylor, S. E. (1983) Adjustment to threatening events: a theory of cognitive adaptation. *American Psychologist*, 38, 1161–1173.

Taylor, S. E. (1995) *Health Psychology*. New York: McGraw-Hill.

Taylor, S. E. and Armor, D. A. (1996) Positive illusions and coping with adversity. *Journal of Personality*, 64(4), 873–898.

Taylor, S. E., Lichtman, R. R. and Wood, J. V. (1984) Attributions, beliefs about control, and adjustment to breast cancer. *Journal of Personality and Social Psychology*, 46(3), 489–502.

Taylor, S. E., Kemeney, M. E., Reed, G. M. and Skokan, L. A. (1991) Self generated feelings of control and adjustment to physical illness. *Journal of Social Issues*, 47, 91–109.

Teagarden, D. and Weaver, C. M. (1994) Calcium supplementation increases bone density in adolescent girls. *Nutrition Reviews*, 52(5), 171–173.

Tessler, R. C., Mechanic, D. and Diamond, M. (1976) The effect of psychological distress on physician utilization: a prospective study. *Journal of Health and Social Behaviour*, 17, 353.

Theorell, T. (1976) Selected illnesses and somatic factors in relation to two psychosocial stress indices – a prospective study on middle-aged construction building workers. *Journal of Psychosomatic Research*, 20, 7–20.

Theorell, T. (1982) Review of research on life events and cardiovascular illness. *Advances in Cardiology*, 29, 140–147.

Theorell, T. (1989) Personal control at work and health: a review of epidemiological studies in Sweden. In: A. Steptoe and A. Appels (eds) *Stress, Personal Control and Health*. Chichester: Wiley.

Theorell, T. (1996) Critical life changes and cardiovascular disease. In: C. Cooper (ed.) *Handbook of Stress, Medicine, and Health*. London: CRC Press.

Theorell, T. and Emlund, N. (1993) On physiological effects of positive and negative life changes – a longitudinal study. *Journal of Psychosomatic Research*, 37, 653–659.

Thompson, D., Webster, R. and Sutton, T. W. (1994) Coronary care unit patients' and nurses' ratings of intensity of ischaemic chest pain. *Intensive and Critical Care Nursing*, 10, 83–88.

Thompson, R. J., Zeman, J. L., Fanurik, D. and Sirotkin-Roses, M. (1992) The role of parent stress and coping and family functioning in parent and child adjustment to Duchenne Muscular Dystrophy. *Journal of Clinical Psychology*, 48, 11–19.

Thompson, S. C. (1981) Will it hurt less if I can control it? A complex answer to a simple question. *Psychological Bulletin*, 90, 89–101.

Thoresen, C. E. and Kirmil-Gray, K. (1983) Self-management psychology and the treatment of childhood asthma. *Journal of Allergy and Clinical Immunology*, 72, 596–606.

383

Thurman, C. W. (1985a) Effectiveness of cognitive behavioral treatments in reducing Type A behavior among university faculty. *Journal of Counselling Psychology*, 32, 74–83.

Thurman, C. W. (1985b) Effectiveness of cognitive behavioral treatments in reducing Type A behavior among university faculty: one year later. *Journal of Counselling Psychology*, 32, 445–448.

Titmuss, R. M. (1943) *Birth, Poverty and Wealth*. London: Hamish Hamilton Medical Books.

Toubas, P. L., Duke, J. C., McCaffree, M. A., Mattice, C. D., Bendell, D. and Orr, W. C. (1986) Effects of maternal smoking and caffeine habits on infantile apnea: a retrospective study. *Pediatrics*, 78, 159–163.

Townsend, P., Davidson, N. and Whitehead, M. (1992) *Inequalities in Health: The Black Report and the Health Divide*. Harmondsworth: Penguin.

Travis, C. B. (1988) *Women and Health Psychology: Biomedical Issues*. Hillsdale, NJ: Erlbaum.

Troup, J. G. D. (1988) The perception of musculoskeletal pain and incapacity for work: prevention and early treatment. *Physiotherapy*, 74, 435–439.

Tsuang, M. T. and Faraone, S. V. (1990) *Genetics of Mood Disorders*. Baltimore, MD: Johns Hopkins University Press.

Turk, D. C. and Flor, H. (1984) Aetiological theories and treatments for chronic back pain. II. Psychological models and interventions. *Pain*, 19, 209–233.

Turk, D. C. and Meichenbaum, D. H. (1989) A cognitive-behavioural approach to pain. In: P. D. Wall and R. Melzack (eds) *Textbook of Pain*. London: Churchill Livingstone.

Turk, D. C. and Rudy, T. E. (1987) Towards a comprehensive assessment of chronic pain patients. *Behaviour Research Therapy*, 25, 237–249.

Turk, D. C., Meichenbaum, D. and Genest, M. (1983) *Pain and Behavioural Medicine*. London: Guilford Press.

Turner, C., Anderson, P., Fitzpatrick, R., Fowler, G. and Mayon-White, R. (1988) Sexual behaviour, contraceptive practice and knowledge of AIDS of Oxford University students. *Journal of Biosocial Science*, 20, 445–451.

Turpin, G. (1985) Ambulatory psychophysiological monitoring: techniques and applications. In: D. Papakostopoulos, S. Butler and I. Martin (eds) *Clinical and Experimental Neuropsychophysiology*. London: Croom Helm.

Tversky, A. and Kahnemann, D. (1974) Judgement under uncertainty: heuristics and biases. *Science*, 185, 1124–1131.

United Kingdom Prospective Diabetes Study Group (UKPDSG) (1991) UK Prospective Diabetes Study (UKPDS) 6. Complications in newly diagnosed Type II diabetic patients and their association with different clinical and biochemical risk factors. *Diabetes Research*, 13, 1–11.

USA Department of Health (1994) *Preventing Tobacco Use among Young People*. Washington, DC: US Department of Health and Human Services,

Uvin, P. (1994) The state of world hunger. *Nutrition Reviews*, 52(5), 151–161.

Vaile, M. S. B., Calnan, M., Rutter, D. R. and Wall, B. (1993) Breast cancer screening services in three areas: uptake and satisfaction. *Journal of Public Health Medicine*, 15(1), 37–45.

van den Boom, D.C. (1991) The influence of infant irritability on the development of the mother–infant relationship in the first six months of life. In: J. K. Nugent, B. M. Lester and T. B. Brazelton (eds) *The Cultural Context of Infancy* (Vol. 2). Norwood, NJ: Ablex.

van den Boom, D.C. (1994) The influence of temperament and mothering on attachment and exploration: an experimental manipulation of sensitive responsiveness among lower-class mothers with irritable infants. *Child Development*, 65, 1457–1477.

Van den Broucke, S., Vandereycken, W. and Vertommen, H. (1995a) Marital communication in eating disorder patients: a controlled observational study. *International Journal of Eating Disorders*, 17(1), 1–21.

Van den Broucke, S., Vandereycken, W. and Vertommen, H. (1995b) Conflict management in married eating disorder patients: a controlled observational study. *Journal of Social and Personal Relationships*, 12(1), 27–48.

Van der Ploeg, H. M. (1988) Stressful medical events: a survey of patients' perceptions. In: S. Maes, C. D. Spielberger, P. B. Defares, and I. G. Sarason (eds) *Topics in Health Psychology*. New York: John Wiley & Sons.

Vaughn, C. E. and Leff, J. P. (1976) The measurement of expressed emotion in the families of psychiatric patients. *British Journal of Social and Clinical Psychology*, 15, 157–165.

Verbrugge, L. M. (1980) Sex differences in complaints and diagnoses. *Journal of Behavioral Medicine*, 3, 327–356.

Verbrugge, L. M. (1985) Gender and health: an update on hypotheses and evidence. *Journal of Health and Social Behavior*, 26, 156–182.

Victor, R., Mainardi, J. A. and Shapiro, D. (1978) Effects of biofeedback and voluntary control procedures on heart rate and perception of pain during the cold pressor test. *Psychosomatic Medicine*, 40, 216–225.

Viney, L. L., Benjamin, Y. N., Clarke, A. M. and Bunn, T. A. (1985) Sex differences in the psychological reactions of medical and surgical patients to crisis intervention counselling: sauce for the goose may not be sauce for the gander. *Social Science and Medicine*, 20, 1199–1205.

Visitainer, M. A. and Wolfer, J. A. (1975) Psychological preparation for surgical pediatric patients. *Pediatrics*, 56, 187–202.

Viswesvaran, C. and Schmidt, F. L. (1992) A meta-analytic comparison of the effectiveness of smoking cessation methods. *Journal of Applied Psychology*, 77, 554–561.

Vobecky, J. S. (1986) Nutritional aspects of preconceptional period as related to pregnancy and early infancy. *Progress in Food and Nutrition Science*, 10 (1–2), 205–236.

Volicier, B. J. and Bohannon, M. W. (1975) A hospital rating scale. *Nursing Research*, 24, 352–359.

Von Dras, D. D. and Lichty, W. (1990) Correlates of depression in diabetic adults. *Behaviour Health and Ageing*, 1(2), 79–84.

Vostanis, P., Cumella, S., Briscoe, J. and Oyebode, F. (1996) A survey of psychosocial characteristics of homeless families. *European Journal of Psychiatry*, 10(2), 108–117.

Waal-Manning, H. J., Knight, R. G., Spears, G. F. and Paulin, J. M. (1986) The relationship between blood pressure and personality in a large unselected adult sample. *Journal of Psychosomatic Research*, 30, 361–368.

Wadden, T. A. (1984) Relaxation therapy for essential hypertension: specific or non-specific effects. *Journal of Psychosomatic Research*, 28, 53–61.

Wadhwa, P. D., Sandman, C. A., Porto, M., Dunkel-Schetter, C. and Garite, T. J. (1993) The association between prenatal stress and infant birth weight and gestational age at birth: a prospective investigation. *American Journal of Obstetrics and Gynecology*, 169, 858–865.

Wadsworth, J., Taylor, B., Osborn, A. and Butler, N. R. (1984) Teenage mothering: child development at five years. *Journal of Child Psychology and Psychiatry*, 25, 305–314.

Wallace, L. M. (1984) Psychological preparation as a method of reducing the stress of surgery. *Journal of Human Stress*, 10, 62–77.

Wallander, J. L, Varni, J. W., Babani, L., Tweedle-Banis, H. T. and Wilcox, K. T. (1989) Family resources for psychological maladjustment in chronically ill and handicapped children. *Journal of Pediatric Psychology*, 14, 157–173.

Wallander, J. L., Varni, J. W., Babani, L., Banis, H. T. and Wilcox, K. T. (1988) Children with chronic physical disorders: maternal reports of their psychological adjustment. *Journal of Pediatric Psychology*, 13, 197–212.

Wallerstein, N. and Bernstein, E. (1994) Introduction to community empowerment, participatory education, and health. *Health Education Quarterly*, 21, 141–148.

Wallston, B. S. and Wallston, K. A. (1984) Social psychological models of health behavior. An examination and integration. In: A. Baum, S. E. Taylor and J. E. Singer (eds) *Handbook of Psychology and Health: Volume 4. Social Psychological Aspects of Health*. Hillsdale, NJ: Lawrence Erlbaum.

Wallston, B. S., Wallston, K. A., Kaplan, G. D. and Naides, S. A. (1976) Development and evaluation of the health locus of control scale (HLC). *Journal of Consulting and Clinical Psychology*, 44, 580–585.

Wallston, K. A. (1994) Cautious optimism versus cockeyed optimism. *Psychology and Health*, 9(3), 201–203.

Wallston, K. A., Wallston, B. S. and DeVellis, R. (1978) Development of the multidimensional health locus of control (MHLC) scales. *Health Education Monographs*, 6, 161–170.

Wallston, T. S. (1978) *Three Biases in the Cognitive Processing of Diagnostic Information*. Psychometric Laboratory, University of North Carolina, Chapel Hill.

Warburton, D. M. (1992) Smoking within reason. *Journal of Smoking-related Disorders*, 3, 55–59.

Warburton, D. M., Revell, A. D. and Thompson, D. H. (1991) Smokers of the future. *British Journal of Addiction*, 86, 621–625.

Wardle, J., Pernet, A. and Stephens, D. (1995) Psychological consequences of positive results in cervical cancer screening. *Psychology and Health*, 10(3), 185–194.

Wardle, J., Pernet, A., Collins, W. and Bourne, T. (1994) False positive results in ovarian cancer screening – one year follow-up of psychological status. *Psychology and Health*, 10(1), 33–40.

Ware, J. E. Jr, Davies-Avery, A. and Donald, C. A. (1978) Conceptualization and measurement of health for adults in the health insurance study: Vol. V. *General Health Perception*. California: the RAND Corporation. Publication No. R-1987/5 – HEW.

Warren, L. and Hixenbaugh, P. (1995) Psychosocial needs and experiences of adults with diabetes: their relationship to regimen adherence from the patients' perspective. Paper presented at the Annual Conference of the BPS Special Group in Health Psychology (6–8 September), Bristol.

Warren, L. and Hixenbaugh, P. (1996) *The Role of Health Beliefs and Locus of Control on Regimen Adherence from a Life-Span Perspective*. Paper presented at the BPS Special Group in Health Psychology Annual Conference (3–5 July), York.

Warren, L. and Hixenbaugh, P. (In press) Adherence and diabetes. In: L. M. Myers and K. Midence (eds) *Adherence to Treatment: A Medical and Psychological Approach*. London: Harwood Academic.

Washington, A. C., Rosser, P. L. and Cox, E. P. (1983) Contraceptive practices of teenage mothers. *Journal of the National Medical Association*, 75, 1059–1063.

Wason, P. C. and Johnson-Laird, P. N. (1972) *Thinking and Reasoning*. Harmondsworth: Penguin.

Watson, M., Denston, S., Baum, M. and Greer, S. (1988) Counselling breast cancer patients: a specialist nurse service. *Counselling Psychology Quarterly*, 1(1), 25–34.

Watters, J. K. (1988) Meaning and context: the social facts of intravenous drug use and HIV transmission in the inner city. *Journal of Psychoactive Drugs*, 20, 173–177.

Watters, J. K. (1989) Observations on the importance of social context in HIV transmission among intravenous drug users. *Journal of Drug Issues*, 19, 9–26.

Watters, W. W. (1980) Mental health consequences of abortion and refused abortion. *Canadian Journal of Psychiatry*, 25, 68–73.

Weinman, J. (1981) *An Outline of Psychology as Applied to Medicine*. Bristol: John Wright & Sons Ltd.

Weinman, J. and Johnston, M. (1988) Stressful medical procedures: an analysis of the effects of psychological interventions and of the stressfulness of the procedures. In: S. Maes, C. D. Spielberger, P. B. Defares, and I. G. Sarason (eds) *Topics in Health Psychology*. New York: John Wiley & Sons.

Weinstein, N. D. (1987) Unrealistic optimism about susceptibility to health problems: conclusions from a community wide sample. *Journal of Behavioral Medicine*, 10, 481–500.

Weinstein, N. D. (1988) The precaution adoption process. *Health Psychology*, 7, 355–386.

Weiss, J. M. (1977) Psychological and behavioural influences on gastrointestinal lesions in animal models. In: J. D. Maser and M. E. P. Seligman (eds) *Psychopathology: Animal Models*. San Francisco, LA: Freeman.

Wellings, K. (1988) Perceptions of risk: media treatments of AIDS. In: P. Aggleton and H. Homans (eds) *Social Aspects of AIDS*. London: Falmer Press.

Wells, K. B., Golding, J. and Burnam, M. (1988) Psychiatric disorder in a sample of the general population with and without chronic medical conditions. *American Journal of Psychiatry*, 145, 976–981.

Wertlieb, D. (1993) Towards a family centred pediatric psychology: challenge and opportunity in the international year of the family (special edition editorial). *Journal of Pediatric Psychology*, 18, 541–547.

West, R. J. (1992) The nicotine replacement paradox in smoking cessation: how does nicotine gum really work? *British Journal of Addiction*, 87, 165–167.

Westhead, J. N. (1985) Frequent attenders in general practice: medical, psychological and social characteristics. *Journal of the Royal College of General Practitioners*, 35, 337–340.

White, A., Freeth, S. and O'Brien, M. (1990) *Infant Feeding 1990.* London: Office of Population Censuses and Surveys, HMSO.

White, D. G. (1997) Variation in family circumstances: implications for children and their parents. In: C. A. Niven and A. Walker (eds) *The Psychology of Reproduction. 3. Current Issues in Infancy and Parenthood.* London: Butterworth Heinemann.

White, D. G., Phillips, K. C., Minns, A. and Sims, J. (1996) *Ethnic Minority Communities' Knowledge of and Needs for Health Advocacy Services in East London.* Report to the Department of Health.

White, D. G., Phillips, K. C., Mulleady, M. and Cupitt, C. (1993) Sexual issues and condom use among injecting drug users. *AIDS Care*, 5, 427–437.

White, D. G., Phillips, K. C., Clifford, B., Davies, M., Elliott, J. R. and Pitts, M. K. (1989) AIDS and intimate relationships: adolescents' knowledge and attitudes. *Current Psychology: Research and Reviews*, 8, 130–143.

White, D. G., Phillips, K. C., Pitts, M. K., Clifford, B., Elliott, J. R. and Davies, M., (1988) Adolescents' perceptions of AIDS. *Health Education Journal*, 47, 117–119.

White, K. L. (1988) *The Task of Medicine.* Menlo Park, CA: The Henri Kaiser Family Foundation.

Whitehouse, C. R. (1991) Teaching of skills in United Kingdom medical schools. *Medical Education*, 25, 311–318.

Wikby, A., Hornquist, J. O., Stenstrum, U. and Anderson, P. O. (1993) Background factors, long-term complications, quality of life and metabolic control in insulin dependent diabetes. *Quality of Life Research*, 2, 281–286.

Wilcox, A. J. (1993) Birth weight and perinatal mortality: the effect of maternal smoking. *American Journal of Epidemiology*, 137, 1098–1104.

Wilkinson, R. G. (1996) *Unhealthy Societies. The Afflictions of Inequality.* London: Routledge.

Wilkinson, S. (1991) Factors which influence how nurses communicate with cancer patients. *Journal of Advanced Nursing*, 16, 677–688.

Wilkinson, S. and Kitzinger, C. (1994) *Women and Health: Feminist Perspectives.* London: Falmer Press.

Williams, R. B. (1978) Psychophysiological processes. The coronary prone behaviour pattern and coronary heart disease. In: T. M. Dembroski, S. M. Weiss, J. L. Shields, S. G. Haynes and M. Feinleib (eds) *Coronary Prone Behaviour.* New York: Springer-Verlag.

Williams, R. B. (1989) *The Trusting Heart: Great News about Type A Behavior.* New York: Random House.

Wills, T. A. and Shiffman, S. (1985) Coping behaviour and its relation to substance use: a conceptual framework. In: S. Shiffman and T. A. Wills (eds) *Coping and Substance Use.* New York: Academic Press.

Wilson, J. F. (1981) Behavioural preparation for surgery: benefit or harm? *Journal of Behavioural Medicine*, 4, 79–102.

Wilson, R. G., Hart, A. and Dawes, P. J. (1988) Mastectomy or conservation: the patients' choice. *British Medical Journal*, 297, 1167–1169.

Wilson, W. J. (1987) *The Truly Disadvantaged: The Inner City, the Underclass, and Public Policy.* Chicago: University of Chicago Press.

Wilson-Barnett, J. (1976) Patients' emotional reactions to hospitalisation. *Journal of Advanced Nursing*, 1, 351–358.

Wilson-Barnett, J. (1992) Psychological reactions to medical procedures. *Psychotherapy and Psychosomatics*, 57, 118–127.

Wilson-Barnett, J. (1994) Preparing patients for invasive medical and surgical procedures. Policy implications for implementing specific psychological interventions. *Behavioral Medicine*, 20(1), 23–26.

Wilton, T. and Aggleton, P. (1991) Condoms, coercion and control: heterosexuality and the limits to HIV/AIDS education. In: P. Aggleton, G. Hart and P. Davies (eds) *AIDS: Responses, Interventions and Care*. London: The Falmer Press.

Wingard, D. L. (1982) The sex differential in mortality rates: demographic and behavioral factors. *American Journal of Epidemiology*, 115, 205–216.

Winkelstein, W., Samuel, M., Padian, N. S. and Wiley, J. A. (1987) The San Francisco men's health study III: reduction in human immunodeficiency virus transmission among homosexual/bisexual men, 1982–1986. *American Journal of Public Health*, 76, 685–689.

Wise, P. (1994) *Depression and Diabetes*. Paper Presented at the Joint Meeting of the Royal College of Psychiatrists' Liaison Group and the BDA (November). Bristol.

Wise, T. and Rosenthal, J. (1982) Depression, illness beliefs, and severity of illness. *Journal of Psychosomatic Research*, 26, 247–253.

Wold, D. A. (1968) The adjustment of siblings to childhood leukaemia. Unpublished medical thesis, University of Washington, Seattle.

Wolf, M. W., Putnam, S. M., James, S. A. and Stiles, W. B. (1978) The medical interview satisfaction scale: development of a scale to measure patient perceptions of physician behaviour. *Journal of Behavioural Medicine*, 1, 391–401.

Wolf, S. L., Nacht, M. and Kelly, J. L. (1982) EMG feedback training during dynamic movement for low back pain patients. *Behaviour Therapy*, 13, 395–406.

Woodcock, A., Spiegal, N. and Kinmouth, A. L. (1996) *The Diabetes Care From Diagnosis Project: Training Nurses in an Empowerment Approach to Care for People with Non-insulin Dependent Diabetes (NIDDM) in General Practice*. Paper presented at the BPS Special Group in Health Psychology Annual Conference (3–5 July), York.

Woodrow, R. M., Friedman, G. D., Siegelaub, A. B. and Collen, M. F. (1972) Pain tolerance: differences according to age, sex and race. *Psychosomatic Medicine*, 34, 548–556.

Woods, P. J. and Burns, J. (1984) Type A behaviour and illness in general. *Journal of Behavioural Medicine*, 7, 411–415.

Woodside, D. B., Shekterwolfson, L., Garfinkel, P. E., Olmsted, M. P., Kaplan, A. S. and Maddocks, S. E. (1995) Family interactions in bulimia nervosa. Study design, comparisons to established population norms, and changes over the course of an intensive day hospital treatment program. *International Journal of Eating Disorders*, 17(2), 105–115.

World Health Organization (1946) *Constitution*. Geneva: WHO.

World Health Organization (1978) Technical Report Series. *Induced Abortion*, 623. Geneva: WHO.

World Health Organization (1983) *Primary Prevention of Essential Hypertension*. Report of WHO Scientific Group, Report Series 686. Geneva: WHO.

World Health Organization (1992) *Current and Future Dimensions of the HIV/AIDS Pandemic: A Capsule Summary*. Geneva: WHO.

World Health Organization (1995) *Weekly Epidemiological Record*, 70, 5–8.

World Health Organization (1996a) *Hypertension Control*. WHO Technical Report Series 862. Geneva: WHO.

World Health Organization (1996b) *Measuring Quality of Life*. Geneva: Division of Mental Health, WHO.

Wright, L. (1979) Health care psychology. Prospects for the well-being of children. *American Psychologist*, 34, 1001–1006.

Wulfert, E. and Wan, C. (1993) Condom use: a self-efficacy model. *Health Psychology*, 12(5), 346–353.

Yates, A. (1980) *Biofeedback and the Modification of Behavior*. New York: Plenum Press.

Zabin, L. S. and Clark, S. D. Jr (1983) Institutional factors affecting teenagers' choice and reasons for delay in attending a family planning clinic, *Family Planning Perspectives*, 15, 25–29.

Zborowski, M. (1952) Cultural components in responses to pain. *Journal of Society Issues*, 8, 16–30.

Zeanah, C. H., Keener, M. A., Anders, T. F. and Vieira-Baker, C. C. (1987) Adolescent mothers' perceptions of their infants before and after birth. *American Journal of Orthopsychiatry*, 57, 351–360.

Zeier, H., Brauchli, P. and Joller-Jemelka, H. I. (1996) Effects of work demands on immunoglobulin A and cortisol in air-traffic controllers. *Biological Psychology*, 42, 413–423.

Zelnick, M. and Kantner, J. F. (1977) Sexual and contraceptive experience of young unmarried women in the United States, 1976 and 1971. *Family Planning Perspectives*, 9, 55–71.

Zelnick, M. and Shah, F. K. (1983) First intercourse among young Americans. *Family Planning Perspectives*, 15, 64–70.

Zieglar, J. B., Cooper, D. A., Johnson, R. O. and Gold, J. (1985) Postnatal transmission of AIDS – associated retro-virus from mother to infant. *Lancet*, i, 896–898.

Zigmond, A. S. and Snaith, R. P. (1983) The hospital anxiety and depression scale. *Acta Psychiatric Scandinavian*, 67, 361–370.

Zung, W. W. K. (1965) A self-rating depression scale. *Archives of General Psychiatry*, 12, 63–70.

Zuravin, S. J. (1988) Severity of maternal depression and three types of mother-to-child aggression. *American Journal of Orthopsychiatry*, 59, 377–389.

Author index

Subject index